£28.00

THE SCOTLAND ACT 1998

AUSTRALIA
LBC Information Services
Sydney

CANADA and USA
Carswell
Toronto

NEW ZEALAND
Brooker's
Auckland

SINGAPORE and MALAYSIA
Sweet and Maxwell Asia
Singapore and Kuala Lumpur

THE SCOTLAND ACT 1998

Second Edition

by

C.M.G. Himsworth, B.A., LL.B.
Solicitor and Professor of Administrative Law,
University of Edinburgh

and

C.R. Munro, B.A., LL.B.
Professor of Constitutional Law, University of Edinburgh

EDINBURGH
W. GREEN/Sweet & Maxwell
2000

First published 1999
Second Edition 2000

Published in 2000 by W. Green & Son Ltd
21 Alva Street
Edinburgh EH2 4PS

Typeset by LBJ Typesetting Ltd of Kingsclere

Printed and bound in Great Britain by
MPG Books Ltd, Bodmin, Cornwall

No natural forests were destroyed to make this product;
only farmed timber was used and replanted

A CIP catalogue record for this book is available from the British Library

ISBN 0414 01394 8

PREFACE

The rueful reflection that "a week is a long time in politics" has been shown to have force in a Scottish, as well as in a British, context. The Scottish Parliament may have been in operation for only a little over a year but much has happened in that time, both in politics and the law. As a result, the first edition of this book has been overtaken by events and the publication of this second edition has been called for more quickly than we should have imagined.

The text of the Scotland Act has been updated to incorporate amendments as necessary, and the annotations have been revised and, in many cases, rewritten to take account of the substantial amount of subordinate legislation, Acts of the Scottish Parliament, decided cases and other developments since the first edition.

The Introduction has been extended and the full text of the Standing Orders adopted by the Scottish Parliament has been appended.

We should like to record our thanks to Ben Kemp for the valuable contribution made to this edition by his research assistance.

C.M.G. Himsworth
C.R. Munro
Edinburgh
July 2000

INTRODUCTION

Scotland Before and After the Union

Claims to nationhood, which may have a resonance in constitutional debates, may be based on various criteria, but a period of statehood may be relevant, and is favourable rather than otherwise to the issue.

In this connection, it is worth remembering that Scotland had a long history of statehood. In the ninth century Kenneth MacAlpin, the King of the Scots in Dalriada, became King of the Picts too. In 1018 one of his successors, Malcolm II, conquered Lothian when he defeated the Angles at the battle of Carham, and in the same year succeeded to the Kingdom of the Britons in Strathclyde. He and his grandson Duncan I, who followed him, thus became kings of all Scotland. From that date onwards, Scotland was a recognisable country with, two or three interregnal periods apart, a continuous line of succession to the throne.

Unlike Wales and Ireland, Scotland was able to maintain its independence. The overlordship of Edward I of England was briefly acknowledged when he was invited to adjudge upon rival claims to the Scottish throne in 1292. But within two years his chosen man, John Balliol, and his counsellors were rebelling. Edward defeated the Scots at Dunbar, but if he thought that he had subdued them, was soon disabused of that notion by the patriot William Wallace. Wallace routed the English army at Stirling Bridge (1297), was defeated at Falkirk (1298), but continued to harry the English forces until his betrayal and death. Robert Bruce, who was crowned king in 1306, carried on where Wallace left off, and his campaigns culminated in a brilliant victory over Edward II at Bannockburn in 1314. Liberation of the country was complete, although the Scottish barons' insecurity led them to send an address to the Pope (the Declaration of Arbroath) in 1320, asserting the rightfulness of King Robert's claim to the throne and soliciting recognition and support. England's King Edward III acknowledged Scotland's independence in the Treaty of Northampton (1328).

There were intermittent hostilities between Scotland and England in the sixteenth century, but the conversion of Scotland to Protestantism began to bring the people of the two countries closer. Then in 1603, when Elizabeth 1 died, James VI of Scotland became King James I of England too. He was the son of Mary, Queen of Scots, and the great-great-grandson of Henry VII of England.

What occurred in 1603 was merely a personal union of the Crowns, contingent on the different laws of succession to the throne in Scotland and in England. Following the personal union some trade restrictions between the two countries were abolished, and a common citizenship was introduced. But there was no union of the countries or their laws, and the English Parliament could no more make laws for Scotland than could the Scottish Parliament or Estates (as it was more commonly known) legislate for England. In fact, the circumstance of personal union was not very popular in Scotland, because the seat of royal government had been removed to London. When discontents arose during the reign of Charles I they were felt all the more keenly in Scotland. The Scottish Presbyterian force of Covenanters took up arms against the King before the English parliamentary forces, and, for the rest of the seventeenth century, events were to follow a broadly similar pattern in both countries. Successful rebellion was followed by the constitutional experiments of the Commonwealth and the Protectorate; with the Restoration, following Cromwell's death, separate Parliaments met again, and there was a return to earlier practice: with the flight of the unpopular James VII of Scotland and II of England, there was a bloodless revolution, and a limited monarchy was arranged, under the terms embodied in the Bill of Rights enacted by the English Parliament and the Claim of Right in Scotland.

In the 17 years that followed, the Scottish Parliament displayed a greater authority than it had ever before evinced. The greater assertiveness of the body, and the enhanced importance of both Parliaments as against the Crown, were amongst the causes of the progress to a more complete union. There were other underlying trends conducive to harmony, and perhaps unity, such as the geographical factor of sharing an island off the continent of Europe, common dynastic and religious influences, and economic interests.[1]

There had in fact been several earlier attempts to bring about union. Commissioners representing the Scottish and English Parliaments had been appointed in 1604 and again in 1670 in order to negotiate on the matter, but on these as on other occasions the efforts did not bear fruit.

However, after 1688, when it became clearer that the monarchy was to be a limited monarchy, constitutionally responsible to a Parliament, it was not easy to see how the monarchy could be responsible at one and the same time to two Parliaments each pursuing its own policies. These contradictions were exposed, and perhaps exploited, when in the midst of war against Louis XIV the Scottish Parliament passed an Act (the Act anent Peace and War of 1703) to the effect that no future Sovereign should have power to make war or peace without its consent. There were other causes of friction between the countries, such as the disastrous failure of the Darien scheme, and feelings were running high. When a Scottish ship was seized on the Thames, and an English ship captured in the Firth of Forth, the two countries seemed to be on the brink of war.

Perhaps it was that which brought them to their senses. The two Parliaments asked the Queen to appoint Commissioners on their behalf, with a view to negotiating a treaty of union. The Commissioners met in Whitehall and reached early agreement on the three main points: an incorporating union, guarantees by the English of complete freedom of trade, and acceptance by the Scots of the descent of the Crown according to the Act of Settlement. With a compromise on Scottish representation in the new Parliament, the new endeavour was completed in nine weeks.

The Commissioners on both sides made concessions, and the provisions of the union legislation which resulted are not such as to suggest a shotgun marriage. The position of Scotland's established church had, for example, been kept outside the Commissioners' remit as being non-negotiable. The English Commissioners were obliged not only to concede freedom of trade and navigation, but to grant tax exemptions and payments in compensation. The Scottish Commissioners had to agree to the Hanoverian succession.

The Scottish Commissioners also had to settle for an "incorporating" union, by which was meant that both countries merged their legislatures and identity. Such an arrangement was naturally seen by the statesmen of the time as offering the most suitable form of Government. Some of the Scottish Commissioners, notably Andrew Fletcher of Saltoun, were attracted to a more "federal" conception of union. What they seem to have had in mind was rather what we should call a confederation, a league of states without a supreme, central legislature on the model of the Dutch United Provinces. But an arrangement like that would have been open to the same dangers as the status quo. A truly federal solution would have been a different matter but that was scarcely in the Commissioners' contemplation, as there was not, until the American example in 1787, an obvious model for such a form.

Therefore what was established was a full political and economic union. The union legislation consisted of a principal Act composed of 25 articles,

---

[1] See R. H. Campbell, "A Historical Perspective on the Union" and J. Morrill, "The English, the Scots and the British" in *Scotland and the Union* (P. S. Hodge, ed., 1994).

and three associated Acts which provided for the continuance of the different established churches in Scotland and England and the precise manner of electing the Scottish representatives to the House of Commons and the House of Lords. These Acts of Union were separately enacted first by the Scottish Parliament, then by the English, which were legislating for their own demise, to be succeeded by the Parliament of Great Britain. The legislation is in Scotland often referred to as "the Treaty".

Some lawyers in Scotland have argued that (in the law of Scotland, if not in English law) the union legislation enjoys a special legal status, so that the United Kingdom Parliament is unable to alter it or at least unable to alter some of its more important terms.[2] The argument was encouraged. if not inspired, by some *obiter dicta* in *MacCormick v. Lord Advocate,*[3] when a challenge to the Queen's chosen designation as "Elizabeth II" was dismissed, not entirely unsympathetically. However, the argument is difficult to sustain since numerous alterations have in fact occurred and the courts, if they are not powerless to intervene to prevent them, have never actually done so.[4] The evolution of society since 1707 has been reflected in the evolution of the union, notwithstanding the precise terms of the provisions as they were enacted then, which can evidently be repealed expressly or by implication. The creation of a devolved Scottish Parliament under the Scotland Act 1998 does not as such, it may be noticed, involve any alteration or breach of the articles of the union legislation (which provided for representation in the new Parliament of Great Britain, but did not in terms abolish the Scottish Parliament or the English). By contrast, it is easy to conceive that the Scottish Parliament, in exercise of its powers under the Act of 1998, might legislate inconsistently with provisions of the union legislation, or at least might be argued to have done so. So arguments of legal impediment to change might have been expected to be raised, even if we would expect them to be defeated. The prospect induced the draftsmen to insert a provision in the hope of precluding the advancement of such arguments, and section 37 provides that the union legislation shall "have effect subject to this Act". If the union legislation were really unalterable, this provision would be ineffective, whereas its being given effect should go far to settle the argument.

In the years immediately following 1707, the union was not popular on either side of the border. However by the later eighteenth century, the benefits of the union were becoming more generally appreciated. Home and colonial markets had been opened to Scottish traders and venturers as well as English, and the advances brought by the agrarian and industrial revolutions were enabling the people of northern and southern Britain to take full advantage of them. The industrial success of Scotland, first within the customs union of Great Britain and then increasingly in an international free trade economy in the nineteenth century. in which Glasgow became "the second city of the Empire", could hardly be gainsaid. Economically, socially and culturally, the Scottish people had in many respects become more like their southern neighbours, with whom commercial interchange and social intercourse had become commonplace.

Moreover, as historians have argued persuasively, there were powerful forces combining to form and shape a British political identity in the eighteenth and early nineteenth centuries, in particular Protestantism, the external threat posed by France, and the commercial opportunities of

---

[2] T. B. Smith, "The Union of 1707 as Fundamental Law" [1957] P.L. 99, J.D.B. Mitchell, *Constitutional Law* (2nd ed., 1968).

[3] 1953 S.C. 396.

[4] For a fuller discussion, see C. R. Munro, "The Union of 1707 and the British Constitution" in *Scotland and Union* (P. S. Hodge, ed., 1994).

Empire.[5] However, the same historians observe that by the later nineteenth century those factors which had been propitious were altering or waning, and a consequent decline in the success of the branding of Britain was beginning to set in, even if the common experience of embroilment in the two World Wars may have helped to obscure and even to delay the process.

The Evolution of Devolution

The union had not, in fact, been designed to effect a complete assimilation. As one historian observed: "The men who negotiated the Treaty had no interest in creating a united British nation and therefore enabled the Scots to preserve their own national identity within the Union."[6] Most obviously, the preservation of different identities was reflected in the continuance of separate legal systems, a characteristic also of the union of Great Britain and Ireland in 1800. This feature, unusual in a state which was not federal, contributed to the proposal formulated by political scientists that the United Kingdom was perhaps better regarded as a union, rather than a unitary, state[7].

After the union of 1707, there was no reason of principle why special arrangements should be made for Scotland in the matter of executive government. However, perhaps because distance lent bewilderment, there were always differences. In the eighteenth century, political management made of Scotland virtually a separate satrapy, as in the long period from the 1760s to the start of the nineteenth century when the influence of Henry Dundas (later Viscount Melville) was paramount. In the nineteenth century government functions were often carried out separately in Scotland through agencies and boards such as the Board of Supervision (concerned with relief of the poor) and the Fishery Board or, like schools and policing, were essentially organised at local level. In aspects of civil society such as religion and education, distinctive traditions had been preserved and different practices developed from those south of the border.

Against this background, the decision to differentiate the handling of Scottish affairs more clearly within central government did not represent a sharp break from the past. The policy, initially formulated by Gladstone's Liberal Government, was actually implemented by its Conservative successor, in 1885, when a Scottish Office was created as a department of government, whose minister, the Secretary for Scotland, was to be responsible for law and order, education, and a few other matters. From 1892 onwards, it became the practice to allocate a place in the cabinet to that person, and in 1926 the holder's office was raised in status to that of Secretary of State. From 1939, the principal base of the Scottish Office was in Edinburgh, first at St Andrew's House on Calton Hill and later in more modern, often less pleasing, buildings.

These moves, from 1885 onwards, represented an arrangement which may be called administrative devolution, where the central government, without creating legislatures and executive governments derived from them in different parts of the state, arranges for aspects of its work to be conducted by a department which is defined *territorially* rather than *functionally*. What was devised in this fashion for Scotland was later to be followed (more slowly, and in a rather more limited way) for Wales, and (in rather different circumstances) for Northern Ireland at some periods.

---

[5] See L. Colley, *Britons: Forging the Nation 1707–1837* (1992); K. Robbins, *Great Britain: Identities, Institutions* and *the Idea of Britishness* (1998).
[6] B.P. Levack, *The Formation of the British State (1987)*, p.212.
[7] S. Rokkan and D. Unwin (eds.), *The Politics of Territorial Identity* (1982).

Over the years, the functions and importance of the Scottish Office significantly, if gradually, increased.[8] By the end of 1998, the Secretary of State for Scotland with six junior ministers and a Scottish Office organised in five main departments, had responsibility for most functions of the United Kingdom government in Scotland, with the major exceptions of defence, foreign policy, taxation and social security.

Through administrative devolution and in some other ways, it may be said that the nationhood of Scotland was afforded some recognition in constitutional arrangements. However, there was arguably a weakness or flaw at the heart of the system of administrative devolution, in as much as the exercise of extensive executive and administrative powers was not properly matched by a territorial legislature or an adequate political base. Besides, it might be argued that the Scottish legal system had been poorly served by a United Kingdom Parliament which failed to find sufficient time for the enactment of distinctive legislation for Scotland and had sometimes been insensitive to its different legal traditions.

Political pressures for constitutional reform led the Government in 1969 to set up a Royal Commission on the Constitution, chaired in its later stages by Lord Kilbrandon. Its report, published in 1973, rejected the case for independence for Scotland and Wales, and dismissed the possibility of federalism.[9] Beyond that, the commissioners found it difficult to agree, but a majority favoured a scheme of devolving legislative powers to an elected assembly in Scotland and a smaller number supported legislative devolution for Wales.

These proposals, although far from unanimous, were influential a few years later when a Labour Government was induced to bring forward legislation. Their first attempt, the Scotland and Wales Bill 1976, did not complete its passage. Following a parliamentary pact with the Liberals, a second attempt succeeded, and after protracted proceedings in both Houses, the Scotland Act 1978 (c.51) and the Wales Act 1978 (c.52) became law.[10] These would have given directly elected assemblies to Scotland and Wales, the Scottish one having legislative powers and the Welsh only executive powers. However, amongst the amendments made to the Bills, there was one which proved fatal. Referendums were planned for Scotland and Wales, so as to give electors an opportunity to say whether they wanted the proposals to come into effect. A backbench M.P. successfully proposed that if fewer than 40 per cent of those entitled to vote were to vote "Yes", then orders for the repeal of the legislation would have to be laid before Parliament. At the polls on March 1, 1979, only 11.9 per cent of the electorate in Wales voted "'Yes". In Scotland, a majority of those who voted were in favour of the Scotland Act 1978 proposals, because 32.9 per cent of the electorate said "Yes" and only 30.8 per cent said "No". However, 36.3 per cent of the electorate did not vote, and so the threshold requirement was not satisfied. The results led indirectly to a change of government, after defeat on a vote of confidence, and repealing orders were laid before Parliament and approved in the early weeks of the new Conservative Government in 1979.

The Labour Party could not be entirely absolved from the suspicion that its actions in government from 1974 to 1979 had been driven by political

---

[8] A.G. Donaldson, "Administrative and Legislative Devolution" in *Independence and Devolution: The Legal Implications for Scotland* (J. P. Grant, ed., 1976); A. Midwinter, M. Keating and J. Mitchell, *Politics and Public Policy in Scotland* (1991).

[9] Cmnd. 5460–1 (1973). For discussion, see T. C. Daintith, "The Kilbrandon Report: Some Comments", and other essays in *Devolution* (H. Calvert, ed., 1975).

[10] See A. W. Bradley and D. J. Christie, *The Scotland Act* 1978 (1979); D. Foulkes, J. B. Jones and R. A. Witford (eds.), *The Welsh Veto: The Wales Act 1978 and the Referendum* (1983).

expediency as much as clear principle. However, in its years in opposition, the party became more sympathetic to greater decentralisation of power. Besides, for a party which held (after the 1987 general election) 50 seats in Scotland, there were obvious electoral advantages to be garnered from espousing the cause of a Scottish Parliament, if it were popular, and losses to be risked if it did not. Moreover, especially after Mr John Smith became the party's leader in 1992, there could be no doubt over the party's commitment to the cause. For John Smith, who had piloted the Scotland Act 1978 through the Commons, the project of Scottish home rule was, quite simply, "unfinished business".

Political parties' policies were important, because only a party (or coalition of parties) in government could deliver constitutional reforms. It was also significant that some pressure groups were formed in the wake of the 1979 referendum or later, which were influential in keeping the issue of reform in front of the public and the parties during the long period of Conservative governments. One such group was the Campaign for a Scottish Assembly, a gathering of notables which through a committee in 1988 produced a report entitled A *Claim of Right for Scotland*, which asserted the right of the people of Scotland to decide on their own constitution. The report also recommended that a convention should be brought into being to draw up a scheme for a Scottish assembly or parliamentary body.

Accordingly, a body calling itself the Scottish Constitutional Convention was set up and held its first meeting in March 1989. The Conservatives refused to join the body, and the Scottish National Party withdrew before meetings began, having formed the view that the option of independence was not likely to be seriously pursued under the *modus operandi* of proceeding by consensus. The Labour Party and the Liberal Democrats participated in the Convention, however, along with the Greens and a few other minor parties, and representatives or delegates of local authorities, trade unions, churches and some other organisations. Although it had no official status, the body did contain 59 of the 72 MPs and six Scottish MEPs. The joint chairs of the Convention were drawn from Labour (Lord Ewing of Kirkford) and the Liberal Democrats (Sir David Steel, the former leader of the party), and its Executive was chaired by Canon Kenyon Wright. In November 1990 the Convention published a report, *Towards Scotland's Parliament*, with the central proposal of a directly elected Scottish Parliament which would have a defined range of powers and responsibilities, including exclusive responsibility on many matters,

Through collaboration in the Convention, Labour and the Liberal Democrats entered the 1992 general election with a broad measure of agreement on Scottish constitutional reform, although there were some matters, including the method of election of the Parliament and the method of funding Scottish government, on which agreement had not been secured or there were differences between the parties. After the 1992 election, the Convention appointed a commission to tackle some of the outstanding disagreements and problems, and its work was incorporated in the Convention's final report, *Scotland's Parliament. Scotland's Right*, which was presented on St Andrew's Day, 1995. The report was notable for its thoroughness and attention to detail as well as principle. The proposals were for a Parliament of 129 members, elected under an additional member system; a power to increase or decrease the basic rate of income tax by a maximum of 3p in the pound to be given to the Scottish Parliament, but with funding chiefly through an assigned budget from central government; and substantial devolution of legislative and executive functions to a Scottish Parliament and an Executive formed from it.

The Scottish Constitutional Convention must be counted as an effective pressure group. Its work over a period of years in progressively developing a scheme for constitutional reform meant that a sympathetic government could import the proposals more or less wholesale. With other proposals on more technical matters that could be added as appropriate, a government could avail itself of a reform package which was "off the peg" to the extent that it was willing to do so.

The Labour Party entered the general election in 1997 with a commitment to legislate for a Scottish Parliament within a year of taking office, assuming affirmative referendum results (in a change of policy in 1996, it had also committed itself to test the Scottish electorate's view on the two questions of their support for a Scottish Parliament and on the principle of its possessing tax-varying powers, in advance of legislating).

When the general election brought Labour to power (with a huge overall majority of 179), the new Government acted quickly on constitutional reforms, as it had promised, and published White Papers regarding proposals for Scottish and Welsh devolution in July 1997. The White Paper on Scottish devolution[11] was a best seller in the shops. Preparations were taken forward under the Referendums (Scotland and Wales) Act 1997 (c.61), and in September 1997 electors in Scotland and Wales were able to vote in pre-legislative referendums, in the knowledge of the White Paper proposals.[12] In the Scottish voting, on September 11, on the first question, 1,775,045 electors (or 74.3 per cent of those voting) agreed "that there should be a Scottish Parliament", while 614,400 (or 25.7 per cent) disagreed. The turnout figure was 60 per cent. On the second question, the voting was 63.5 per cent for, and 36.5per cent against, the proposition that the "Scottish Parliament should have tax-varying powers".

By these results, the Government had secured a specific mandate for the constitutional reform which would extend devolution by establishing a Scottish Parliament with wide-ranging competence. On December 18, 1997 it published the Scotland Bill, to put its proposals in legislative form.[13] There is a constitutional convention to the effect that Bills of first class constitutional importance should have all their stages on the floor of the House of Commons and, notwithstanding some apprehensions to the contrary, it was adhered to for the Scotland Bill.

The Scotland Bill in Parliament

The circumstances under which the Scotland Bill was introduced into Parliament did much to determine the conditions of its progress through the two Houses. The combination of the Labour Government's manifesto commitment to devolution; the size of the Government's majority and the lack of Scottish Conservative representation in the House of Commons; and the publication of the White Paper and its approval by referendum all produced a relatively controlled response to a Bill of such high constitutional significance and with a pre-history of great political contention. The Bill could not be described as having been bitterly fought and debates were, in the main, subdued. It is true that the Bill, like others of "first class constitutional importance" remained on the floor of the House at committee stage in the House of Commons. Those proceedings were, however, made the subject of a time-table motion[14] and this had a clear impact on the extent and quality of debate in that House. It is also true that the Bill joined others in going right to the wire at the end of a very long parliamentary session. Because of a very large number of Lords amendments, there was a need for a two-day "consideration" stage in the Commons followed, because of the rejection of some of the amendments, by a further stage in the Lords. But all these were the signs of a need for quite technical adjustments to a complex

---

[11] *Scotland's Parliament,* Cm. 3658.
[12] See C. R. Munro, "Power to the People" [1997] P.L. 579.
[13] See C. M. G. Himsworth and C. R. Munro, *Devolution and the Scotland Bill* (1998).
[14] *Hansard,* H.C. Vol. 304, col. 254.

Bill in a parliamentary session burdened with the other devolutionary measures, further special provision for Northern Ireland and the Human Rights Act. They were not signs of a sustained campaign of political opposition or of a significant conflict between the Houses. Michael Ancram M.P. in the Commons and the Lords Mackay of Ardbrecknish and of Drumadoon in the Upper House adopted, for the most part, a restrained, probing and technical style of official opposition. More colourful opposition came from the SNP, on certain issues from the Liberal Democrats, and, from the Labour benches, Tam Dalyell M.P.

Turning briefly to the content of the parliamentary proceedings, it may be useful to divide the business into that which was productive of change in the text of the Bill and, on the other hand, those, mainly more substantial, debates which produced no such textual change.

The overall dimensions of the Bill did not change greatly during its parliamentary passage. In crude terms it gained 16 further clauses and a new Schedule[15]. Most of the changes made did not have a high constitutional or political profile and were made on the Government's initiative. Some amendments were made to improve the "interlinkage" with the Government of Wales Bill and the Northern Ireland Bill as they too progressed through Parliament and provision needed to be made in parallel[16]. Similarly, there were changes made to improve links with the Human Rights Bill, also in the interests of compatibility between the two statutory schemes.[17] More substantial were the changes made to restructure the core provisions defining the competences of the Scottish Parliament and Scottish Executive. The provision which is now section 29 was quite radically recast and Schedule 4 expanded to enable a greater reliance upon the "entrenchment" of named statutes and to adjust the handling of the interface between "Scots private law" (and "Scots criminal law") and reserved matters[18]. What is now section 101 was redesigned and relocated[19]. The main provisions on executive competence were restyled[20] and there were consequential amendments to Schedule 6 (devolution issues). These alterations were defended as not producing substantive change, as too were the changes to the scheme for the making of subordinate legislation now contained in sections 112 to 115 and Schedule 7[21] and the more sporadic amendments to Schedule 8.

On the other hand, the introduction of the rule in section 44(3) (making, the holding of "Ministerial office" incompatible with membership of the Scottish Executive)[22]; the redefinition of the function of the Presiding Officer in relation to the legislative competence of a Bill in the Scottish Parliament[23]; and the tightening of the audit provisions and the requirement of an Auditor General for Scotland[24] were points of substantive change where the Government was compelled to make some response to the pressure of parliamentarians. Probably most notable in this category was the progressive remodelling of section 95 (appointment and removal of judges), in response, in particular, to strong pressure from judicial members of the House of Lords[25]. Certain of the alterations to Schedule 5 (reserved matters) may also

---

[15] Sched. 7 on procedure for subordinate legislation.

[16] See, *e.g.* s.106.

[17] See ss.57,100.

[18] *Hansard,* H.C. Vol. 312. cols 254–262; H.L. Vol. 592, cols 816–843.

[19] See the note on that section.

[20] See ss.53, 54.

[21] See note on s.112.

[22] *Hansard,* H.C. Vol. 319, col. 434.

[23] Finally resolved at *Hansard,* H.L Vol. 594, cols 1171–1175.

[24] ss.69,70.

[25] *See Hansard,* H.C. Vol. 312, col. 775; H.L. Vol. 593, col. 398 and Vol. 594, cols 17, 586. 1175.

be interpreted as Government rethinking under some pressure[26], although other changes of substance were more the product of the evolution of policy in problematic fields such as fisheries[27] and industrial development[28] and there was quite substantial technical[29] and presentational[30] amendment.

If there is a rule of parliamentary procedure on Bills that there will always be an inverse relationship between the proportion of time spent in debate and the amendments actually made to a Bill, it is a rule that was very satisfactorily observed in the debates on the Scotland Bill. At a general level, there had to be the opportunity (especially in the second reading debates) for the Government to restate its case for the scheme of devolution it was proposing[31] for the SNP to present the case for independence or for a much more substantially devolved form of government on the road to independence[32]; for the Liberal Democrats, whilst generally supportive, to argue for a federal United Kingdom[33] and, within the scheme proposed, for maintaining the size of the Scottish Parliament against proposals for the reduction of the number of MSPs in line with the future reduction in Scottish representation at Westminster.[34] There was also the opportunity for Mr Dalyell to sustain his attack on what he saw as "the paving Bill for the dissolution of the United Kingdom".[35] In addition to the second reading debate itself, the Bill's opponents in the House of Commons took the further opportunity of a setpiece debate at report stage on a new clause, which would have required a review of the role of Scottish members of the House of Commons, to discuss the "English dimension".[36]

Another major element in the debates in both Houses was the attention given to the legislative competence of the Scottish Parliament and, in particular, the listing of the reserved matters in Schedule 5. These provided the opportunity for restating the case for a more powerful Parliament and, on the other hand, the dangers to the union; for testing the logic and coherence of the Government's overall scheme; for exploring quite technical aspects of the probable operation in practice of the division of responsibilities[37]; for the exposure of issues of national sensitivity[38] and of local concern[39]; and for important debates on broadcasting[40], abortion,[41] euthanasia[42] and equal opportunities[43].

---

[26] See the removal from the list of reserved matters of certain provisions of the Theatres Act 1968 and the Hypnotism Act 1952: *Hansard,* H.C. Vol. 309, col. 979.

[27] See note on s.30(3).

[28] *Hansard*, H.L. Vol. 592, col. 1126.

[29] Pts I, III of Sched. 5.

[30] Introducing the numbered "Sections" in Pt II of Sched. 5.

[31] *Hansard,* H.C. Vol. 304. col. 19 (Donald Dewar M.P.): H.L. Vol. 590, col. 1567 *et.seq.*(Lord Sewel).

[32] *e.g. at Hansard,* H.C. Vol. 304, col. 57 (Alex Salmond M.P.).

[33] *e.g. at Hansard,* H.C. Vol. 304, col. 47 (James Wallace M.P.).

[34] *Hansard,* H.L. Vol. 594, col. 1181.

[35] *Hansard,* H.C. Vol. 304, col. 85.

[36] *Hansard,* H.C. Vol. 311, cols 734–836.

[37] One recurring theme was the power to control guns and drug abuse *(Hansard* H.C. Vol. 309. col. 958; H.L. Vol. 592. col. 1060); and another, plant breeders' rights *(Hansard,* H.C. Vol. 309, col. 984; H.L. Vol. 592. col. 1097).

[38] *e.g.* the issue of Scottish banknotes *(Hansard,* H.C. Vol. 309. col. 954; H.L. Vol. 592. col. 1056); agreements on inward investment *(Hansard,* H.C. Vol. 309, col. 984).

[39] Relating, for instance, to the functions of the Crown Estate Commissioners *(Hansard,H.C.* Vol. 309, col. 906); the treatment of islands areas *(Hansard,* H.C. Vol. 309, col. 939); and shipping services *(Hansard,* H.C. Vol. 309.col. 1064).

[40] *Hansard,* H.C. Vol. 304, col. 185; H.L. Vol. 592, col. 1308 and Vol. 594, col. 234.

[41] *Hansard,* H.C. Vol. 309, cols 1093–1113; H.L. Vol. 592, cols 1284–1308 and Vol. 594, cols 202–214.

[42] *Hansard,* H.C. Vol. 594, cols 202–216.

[43] *Hansard,* H.C. Vol. 309, cols 1114–1132.

Another recurring theme was that of future relationships between the United Kingdom and Scottish governments. Provisions in the Bill itself provided the main focus for such debates, notably those containing the Secretary of State's powers of intervention (now sections 35 and 58) raising for some the spectre of Secretary of State as Governor-General[44] but, for others, the uncertain future of the office once the devolved arrangements were in place.[45] Similar opportunities were taken to question the quality of intergovernmental relations when the financial provisions of the Bill were discussed. Much attention focused on the tax-varying power, principally the more technical aspects relating to the administration of collection and the details of liability,[46] but also on the dangers of what Mr Dalyell called "girning" in Scotland when, inevitably, the annual financial settlements were not as generous as some would wish them to be.[47] There might also be "girning" south of the border if financial allocations to Scotland were perceived to be *too* generous.

The subject of intergovernmental relations also took the debate into areas where the matter of concern was not so much a problem on the face of the Bill but rather that the Bill was silent on important issues which should be included. Three such issues were prominent in debate; relationships between the Scottish and U.K. Ministers: representation of the United Kingdom in E.C. institutions; and relations between the Scottish Executive and local government. The prospect that Edinburgh-London relationships would be conducted on the basis of a series of concordats and joint committees had been trailed in the White Paper and attracted further comment from Ministers in debate.[48] Opposition attention, especially from the SNP, focused on the risk of jumping the gun and having the content of these concordats settled before the Scottish Executive even came into existence[49] and, rather separately, that there would be merit in having the status of concordats made more formal by requiring explicit provision for them in the Scotland Act, by requiring concordats not only to be agreed by relevant ministers but also to be endorsed by the two Parliaments, and by providing for a "register" of concordats to be maintained.[50] Concordats were likely to be used to regulate, among other things, the handling of relations with E.C. institutions. On this there were strong calls for the Government's assurances of Scottish representation in U.K. delegations to be specifically provided for.[51] Comparisons were drawn, in particular, with the constitutional guarantees given to the *Länder* in the Federal Republic of Germany.[52] On local government, concerns were expressed about future relations with the Scottish Parliament and Executive but the role of the (McIntosh) Commission on Local Government and the Scottish Parliament was acknowledged.[53]

Finally, in this list of topics on which there were important debates but ultimately without impact on the text of the Act itself, there should be mentioned two proposals related to the discussion of the provisions on the judges and on the new functions under the Scotland Act of courts in general and the Judicial Committee of the Privy Council in particular.[54] One was the

---

[44] *Hansard,* H.C. Vol. 312, col. 262.
[45] *ibid.* col. 270—"a poor creature after May 1999 whose job will soon evaporate" (Mr Dalyell).
[46] See note on s.75.
[47] *Hansard.* H.C. Vol. 306, col. 615.
[48] *Hansard,* H.C. Vol. 309, col. 1158 and Vol. 312, col. 192; H.L. Vol. 592, col. 1487.
[49] *Hansard,* H. C. Vol. 309. col. 1155
[50] *Hansard,* H.C. Vol. 309, col. 1149 and Vol. 312, col. 185.
[51] *Hansard,* H.C. Vol. 309, col. 914; H,L. Vol. 592, col. 1630.
[52] Hansard, H.C. Vol. 309, col. 930.
[53] *ibid.* col. 949.
[54] See note on s. 103.

proposal that there be established a Judicial Services Commission to assume some responsibilities for judicial appointments in Scotland.[55] More significantly there were amendments put down seeking to substitute for the Judicial Committee a fully-fledged constitutional court which would have ultimate jurisdiction in relation to devolution issues arising in all parts of the United Kingdom.[56]

Constitutional Implications of the Scotland Act

As we have noticed, the process of devolution has been evolutionary, and the Act marks a further stage in this process, albeit an important one. It is salutary to be reminded of this, because in recent years the term "devolution", at least in Scottish political discourse, has come to be identified almost exclusively with the provision of a Scottish Parliament. Another reason to keep the history in mind is so as not to be deceived about the extent of change. The areas devolved under the Act are largely coterminous with the responsibilities of the Scottish Office as they were in 1998 and, because the legal system has always remained separate, Scots law was already different from English law in fields such as land law, family law and criminal law, either because the common law differed or because the United Kingdom Parliament had legislated separately and divergently for the two jurisdictions.

What does of course alter is that there is a directly elected Parliament for Scotland, from which a Scottish Executive (headed by a First Minister) is formed. So far as the enactment of new law is concerned, the existence of a dedicated legislature should eliminate complaints along the lines that the Westminster Parliament legislated insufficiently often (as well as insufficiently sensitively) for the needs of Scots law. So far as executive Government is concerned, the exercise of power will be in the hands of those politicians whose parties succeed in a Scottish, instead of in a United Kingdom, election. Previously, when the majority in the House of Commons and the majority of Scottish M.P.s came from different parties (as they did between 1959 and 1964, between 1970 and 1974, and from 1979 to 1997) then the Secretary of State had perhaps something of the appearance of being a colonial governor.

Some of these cures could conceivably cause other ills, however. At the time of writing, the prospects for reform of the electoral system used for elections to the House of Commons are uncertain (although a referendum on an alternative system[57] has been promised) and the future composition of the second chamber at Westminster, even after the passing of the House of Lords Act 1999 (c.34) and the report of a Royal Commission[58], remains unsettled. What is certain is that the Scottish Parliament is composed from an additional member system of proportional representation. One probable consequence of that choice, in the light of voting patterns, is that the Scottish Executive will normally be formed from a coalition of parties. Another likely consequence is that, with different electoral arrangements and timetables, the Scottish Parliament and Executive in years to come will bear a quite different political complexion from the Houses of Parliament and Her Majesty's Government in London. So far as the two Parliaments are concerned, a different complexion is certain, because the Scottish National Party enjoys substantial electoral support, which will be reflected in the composition of the Scottish Parliament. As a party which seeks Scottish independence, the SNP might not appear to be a natural partner in a coalition with a party which

---

[55] *Hansard,* H.C. Vol. 307, cols 1150–1152.

[56] *Hansard,* H.C. Vol. 312, cols 202–215; H.L. Vol. 593, cols. 1963–1986.

[57] As to which there was published in October 1998 the Report of the Independent Commission on the Voting System, Cm. 4090–I (1998).

[58] The Commission, chaired by Lord Wakeham, published its report in January 2000: A House for the Future, Cm.4534 (2000).

aims to sustain or even strengthen the union, but that is not to say that it may never happen. Since the Liberal Democrats are more inclined to favour a federal arrangement and the Conservative Party has had to overcome earlier scepticism about the reform, none of the other main parties has quite the same attitude as Labour to the constitutional issues.

The Labour Government was hoping to satisfy what seemed to be the most preferred constitutional option amongst Scottish electors, and was doing so under a calculation that maintaining the status quo, when it failed to please, was more destabilising and threatening, while the provision of a new constitutional settlement could help to secure the union. Back in 1973, the Royal Commission on the Constitution[59] considered that a scheme of legislative devolution was not incompatible with stability, but on that the jury is still out and it would not be unfair to characterise the policy as a calculated gamble. The Select Committee on Scottish Affairs, in a report published a few days after the Scotland Act became law, was critical of the piecemeal nature of the Government's approach to constitutional reforms, and pointed to areas of possible conflict which had the potential to encourage movement towards independence.[60]

The problem which is foreseeable is not exactly gridlock, as it might be in a constitution with interlocking checks and balances. It is plain in point of form that the scheme of the Scotland Act 1998 is devolutionary, not federal. The Scottish Parliament is not a co-ordinate institution, but a subordinate one, restricted to legislating within its conferred powers, and it has no exclusive sphere of competence. The continuing competence of the United Kingdom Parliament to legislate for Scotland, not merely on reserved matters but on any matter, is explicitly restated in section 28(7) of the Act. Legally, the restatement is otiose, as judicial office-holders who sit in the Lords and others observed during the parliamentary debates.[61] The provision nonetheless serves as a symbolic reminder that devolution should not be mistaken for federalism, let alone independence.

Legally, therefore, there is no reason why the Scottish Parliament could not be abolished by a later Act of the United Kingdom Parliament. However, the reality is that abolition is not foreseeable, politically, albeit that it is possible, legally. Moreover, as regards devolved matters the expectation is that Westminster will not normally legislate for Scots law in these areas without the consent of the Scottish Parliament. The Government's assurances on this point during the parliamentary debates arguably created a constitutional convention on the spot[62] and, designated as "the Sewel convention", it has been referred to quite often since.

In the result, it may not go too far to suggest that the relation between Scotland and the United Kingdom becomes semi-federal. Westminster and Whitehall have legal powers to intervene, but will be loath to impose them on unbiddable Scottish institutions, which may appear (and may claim) to be more representative of the popular will in Scotland.

Disagreements will be apt to engender disenchantment in Scotland, and are liable to be exploited for political ends. As we have seen, a few sources of friction, such as the reservation to Westminster of broadcasting and abortion law, were raised in the parliamentary debates. Others, perhaps less easily foreseeable, are likely to emerge. The Scottish Parliament's legislative competence is not inconsiderable, but it is (by section 29 of the Act) limited not only by the extent of matters reserved to Westminster, but by Community

---

[59] Cmnd. 5460–I (1973).
[60] Select Committee on Scottish Affairs, *The Operation of Multi-Layer Democracy*, H.C. 460–1(1997–98).
[61] See note on s.28(7) following.
[62] *ibid.*

law and the European Convention on Human Rights as imported via the Human Rights Act 1998. The Scotland Act itself is not (except in a few respects, under Schedule 4, paragraph 4) amendable by the Scottish Parliament. which therefore cannot extend its own competence without Westminster's concurrence. Section 30 of the Act, which enables the extent of competence to be altered by Order in Council subject to the approval of the Houses of Parliament and the Scottish Parliament, may present the appearance of being an invitation to treat, and may turn out to be a hostage to fortune. Certainly, the Scottish Parliament will in any event be able to discuss and debate and pass resolutions on matters (such as independence) which it lacks the power to legislate on. Whether this will defuse or engender frustration must be questionable.

The decision to include a second question in the referendum may owe something to the Conservative Party's pre-election gibes about a "tartan tax" as may the careful limitation of the power to vary the basic rate of income tax for Scottish taxpayers in Part IV of the Act. With threats and warnings being uttered by business interests, some of the political parties at least may be reluctant to use even that limited power of variation which is conferred, and so the arrangement smacks of tokenism. Certainly, its significance is dwarfed by the larger issue of the amount of block funding to be assigned each year from the United Kingdom Government, as to which section 64 of the Act merely provides that the Secretary of State may pay "such amounts as he may determine".

Political battles on budgetary questions of that sort are not new, but will assume different dimensions when they take place not merely within the United Kingdom Government, but between the United Kingdom Parliament and Government and other representative institutions. With the nearly simultaneous enactment of the Government of Wales Act 1998 (c.38) and the Northern Ireland Act 1998 (c.47) there are many inter-relationships to be developed alongside other and further constitutional reforms which are taking place. Aspects of the relationships between the United Kingdom institutions and the Scottish Parliament and Executive which, as has been noted already, are only partly provided for in the Act, remain unclear in various ways.

Even the consequences for the United Kingdom Parliament and Government have still to receive full and proper consideration. The conundrum which has come to be known as the "West Lothian question"[63] was, predictably, raised again by Mr Dalyell and others, but answer came there none. Section 86 of the Act should have the consequence of a reduction in the number of Scottish seats in the Commons, although not immediately but some years hence. However, such an adjustment does not address the question in principle, but merely mitigates its effects. Other ways of responding to the problem will require consideration, although they all have their difficulties. Some questions of scrutiny and accountability also demand attention: for example, how far members at Westminster are precluded from asking questions about matters within devolved competence is not entirely certain.[64] Nor are the means and extent of accountability of the Secretary of State for Scotland entirely clear, if indeed the position survives in its altered form. Practices of British government are liable to be affected in other, subtler ways. The prominence of Scottish M.P.s in Mr Blair's Cabinet may be unrepeatable, for example, and matters such as political party organisation and party leadership contests could be influenced.

In the light of the measures for Wales and Northern Ireland, it would be wrong to regard the Scotland Act 1998 as merely unilateral, but it would not

---

[63] See C. M. G. Himsworth and C. R. Munro, *Devolution and the Scotland Bill* (1998), pp.32–34.
[64] But see Devolution Guidance Note No.1, paras. 4.6–4.8.

be wrong to depict the constitutional reforms of which it forms part as asymmetrical, not only because of the different relationships which obtain between London and Edinburgh, Cardiff and Belfast, but also because of the missing part of the equation that is England. The question of devolving power to the English regions may have been "a dog which has not barked in the night",[65] but there are already signs that its canine slumbers are becoming uneasy. The scraps which have been thrown so far, in the Regional Development Agencies Act 1998 (c.45) and the elected mayor and strategic authority for London, may not satisfy for long, and to an extent may even seem to aggravate the imbalances and anomalies.

We are no doubt apt to exaggerate the need for symmetry which, indeed, did not altogether obtain before 1998. Perhaps, like Catalonia in the asymmetrical Spanish scheme or Bavaria in the regularly formed German federation, Scotland will be a more contented nation under the new constitutional dispensation which, in that event, will earn praise from many quarters. Some of its denizens, of course, will be satisfied by nothing less than Scottish independence, albeit "independence in Europe". From any perspective, what is already evident is that the enactment of the Scotland Act 1998 does not only affect Scotland, but has profound implications for Westminster politics and brings a new dynamic to the British constitution.

Early Days

What precisely the constitutional implications are will only become clearer in the short to medium term, and it would be foolhardy to rush to judgment on the consequences. The most that can sensibly be done, some eighteen months after the Scotland Act was passed and some twelve months after the Scottish Parliament began sitting, is to reflect on the tendencies shown in these early days.

Preparation for the establishment of the Parliament and the Executive might have, and arguably should have, been more leisurely, but the United Kingdom Government was anxious to keep up the impetus of reform. Arrangements were therefore made for voting to elect members of the Scottish Parliament at a general election on May 6, 1999, a day on which local government elections were already scheduled. Along with an unfamiliar electoral system, the election involved some other novelties, either by law or on a voluntary basis, such as national limits on party spending and a monitoring Election Commission.[66]

The turnout for the general election, at 58.8 per cent, was respectable, if perhaps slightly disappointing. In the constituency contests, Labour candidates were successful in 53 seats out of the 73. Their disproportionate success in that respect meant that regional seats were very largely allocated to other parties: in the overall result, Labour's total was 56 seats, the Scottish National Party won 35, the Conservatives 18 and the Liberal Democrats 17 seats.[67] A Scottish Socialist Party candidate won a regional seat in Glasgow and a Green candidate in the Lothians. There was an interesting contest in Falkirk West where the MP for the same constituency at Westminster, Mr Dennis Canavan, stood as an Independent after failing to gain selection as a Labour candidate for the Scottish Parliament, and won with a majority of more than

---

[65] D. Marquand, "Regional Devolution" in *The Changing Constitution* (J. Jowell and D. Oliver eds., 2nd ed., 1989), p.386.

[66] J. McFadden, "Elections to the Scottish Parliament: A Guide to the Law" 1999 *Scottish Law and Practice Quarterly* 123.

[67] See W. L. Miller, "Modified Rapture All Around: The First Elections to the Scottish Parliament" 34 (1999) *Government and Opposition* 299; D. Denver and I. MacAllister, "The Scottish Parliament Elections 1999: An Analysis of the Results" 28 (1999) *Scottish Affairs* 10.

12,000 votes. One possible interpretation was that a centralising or "control freak" tendency which some commentators had identified in the party calling itself New Labour had, on this occasion, backfired. However, it is fair to remember that it was that party, with a huge majority in the Commons, which willingly legislated to put in place an electoral system for the Scottish Parliament which was always likely to deny them an overall majority.

Perhaps attitudes to electoral systems and to some other matters will be influenced by Scottish experience. In the different setting of the National Assembly for Wales, Labour decided to form a minority administration following the corresponding general election, but the resignation of Mr Alun Michael as First Secretary in February 2000 was symptomatic of difficulties within the administration as well as relationships with outside. In Scotland, Labour chose otherwise. Mr Donald Dewar, approved as the Parliament's nominee for First Minister on May 13, 1999, wasted little time before entering into negotiations with another party in the hopes of securing a coalition agreement which would enable the formation of an executive with an overall majority in the Parliament. The choice of the Liberal Democrats as prospective partner surprised nobody, given the parties' successful collaboration in the Scottish Constitutional Convention and relative closeness in policies.

A partnership agreement was concluded within a matter of days, which provided for the Leader of the Scottish Liberal Democrats (Mr Jim Wallace MSP) to be nominated as Deputy First Minister and for the allocation of ministerial portfolios to be discussed between the partners. Four Liberal Democrats were thus to be found in a ministerial team which (with the Lord Advocate and the Solicitor General for Scotland) numbered 21. With a share of power came responsibility: all the business of the Executive was to engage the collective responsibility of all Ministers[68], and the two parliamentary parties were each to make their own "business management arrangements, including measures to ensure effective Party support for the Executive."[69] On the whole, these arrangements seem to have operated effectively to date, although party management has not always been easy. One or two backbench Liberal Democrats, more independent or perhaps less enthusiastic about the party's liaison with Labour than their colleagues, have tended to chafe at the bit. Labour's backbenchers have been generally loyal, but in May 2000 displayed assertiveness to a sufficient extent to induce the withdrawal of an Executive amendment aimed at weakening, if not wrecking, the Abolition of Poindings and Warrant Sales Bill which had been introduced by the Scottish Socialist Party MSP, Tommy Sheridan. The occasion was hailed as the first significant public defeat of the Executive by the Parliament, although as yet it is unclear whether Mr Sheridan may have won merely a battle, and not the war.

The thorny issue of student fees provided a matter of substance for the coalition partners to overcome, as the other parties had campaigned with promises to abolish fees for home students in Scottish universities, while Labour had favoured their retention in the financing of higher education. The issue was kicked into touch by an agreement to refer it to an independent committee of inquiry. The subsequent report of that committee, chaired by Mr Andrew Cubie, offered a way forward with the abolition of up-front fees and their replacement by a graduate tax. The Executive felt able to accept the scheme suggested, with modifications, and the coalition therefore survived what had been predicted to be its toughest test. When there are

---

[68] On which, see the Executive Secretariat's guide, *The Scottish Executive: A Guide to Collective Decision-Making.*
[69] Part III of the Scottish Coalition Agreement. See P. Goldenberg, "The Scottish Coalition Agreement" 20 (1999) *Amicus Curiae* 4.

different regimes in force for students in Scotland and English universities, the situation may on one view appear untidy and anomalous, but on another view the outcome may be seen as a vindication of coalition politics and a successful example of devolved government in action.

The Scottish Parliament's legislative activity was steady, rather than spectacular, in the first year. By the end of June 2000, six Acts had received the royal assent and three Bills were awaiting it. The very first Act to be passed, the Mental Health (Public Safety and Appeals) (Scotland) Act 1999, followed an outcry over the release of a convicted killer from a mental hospital, and was introduced as emergency legislation so as to be passed with accelerated progress under provisions in Standing Orders for that purpose[70]. After this somewhat inauspicious start, there were two financial measures of a necessary kind, there was a short Act to enable a question about religion to be included in Scotland in the census, and there were substantial law reforms in the Adults with Incapacity (Scotland) Act 2000 and the Abolition of Feudal Tenure etc. (Scotland) Act 2000. The latter had been heralded as flagship legislation and was a product of Scottish Law Commission efforts followed by processes of consultation and deliberations. It could be presented as a systematic and overdue reform of Scots law of a kind which the United Kingdom Government might have struggled to find space for in its programme of Bills at Westminster.

It did not take long for a question of the Parliament's competence to be tested in the courts as a "devolution issue". There were doubts about the compliance of the Mental Health (Public Safety and Appeals) (Scotland) Act 1999 with "Convention rights" in the terms of the Human Rights Act 1998: by its decision in *Anderson v The Scottish Ministers*[71] the Inner House of the Court of Session may have assuaged them. Challenges to acts or failures to act by the Scottish Executive as being incompatible with Convention rights were especially prominent, through cases such as *Starrs v. Ruxton*[72] and *Brown v. Stott*.[73] However, there has as yet been no litigation concerning the Parliament's observance of the line between reserved and devolved matters.

Questions of members' standards were raised by the so called "Lobbygate" affair which blew up in October 1999, but it was shown to be rather overblown when a Standards Committee investigation concluded that there was no evidence of any MSP's misconduct.[74] An arguable breach of a rule banning paid advocacy formed the basis of the complaint in *Whaley v. Lord Watson of Invergowrie*,[75] in which the Inner House judges emphasised the subordinate nature of the Parliament but stepped back from interdicting a member from proceeding with a Bill at the behest of a member of the public opposed to the Bill. The Standards Committee spent some months considering what method and procedures should be employed in the investigation of complaints, and it is anticipated that there will be legislation to allow for the appointment of an independent commissioner to assist the Committee in the future.

Reactions to the first year of the Parliament's operation have been distinctly mixed. The escalating costs of the project for a new building in the Holyrood area were controversial, if not scandalous, and there were other decisions, such as choosing to debate members' allowances and expenses at almost the earliest opportunity, which could be regarded as public relations errors. The news media have been ready to criticise and indeed, for some

---

[70] See the Standing Orders, Rule 9.21.
[71] The Scottish Courts Website (decision of June 16, 2000).
[72] 2000 S.L.T. 42.
[73] 2000 S.C.C.R. 314.
[74] Standards Committee, 1st Report, SP Paper 27 (1999).
[75] 2000 S.L.T. 475.

tastes, perhaps too ready: the Prime Minister, Mr Blair, who visited and addressed the Parliament in March 2000, admonished the media with the aphorism that "scepticism is healthy, cynicism is corrosive." Further controversy was courted when the Executive persisted in its aim of repealing the provision which banned the promotion of homosexuality by local authorities[76]. The Scottish businessman, Mr Brian Souter, was provoked to organise and fund a "Keep the Clause" campaign and to arrange an unofficial referendum on the issue, in which more than a million voters apparently favoured retention of the provision. The accompaniment of the repeal with guidance as to the values which should influence the teaching of sex education in schools, in the finally agreed terms of the Ethical Standards in Public Life etc. (Scotland) Bill was a compromise of sorts. It is not obvious that anything should be inferred from the events or their outcome, other than that some social issues are divisive. Perhaps also any lingering notions that Holyrood politics would involve a more consensual style of "new politics" have been undermined as this and other causes of contention emerged. The old politics is not so easily extinguished. That said, in its use of first names and its avoidance of archaisms and flummery, Holyrood is apt to provide an attractive contrast with Westminster in certain respects at least, and the early signs are encouraging for some innovations such as the use of functional committees for legislative as well as other purposes.

The media and others have not always been careful to distinguish between the Parliament and the Executive in criticism and comments, but it is a distinction which needs to be kept in mind. If the public have not been enamoured of everything done in their name by the new institutions, that is not to say that reversal of the process of devolution is any more conceivable than it was at the time of the passing of the Scotland Act 1998. Indeed, reversal has if anything become less conceivable, as the Conservative Party has gradually come to acknowledge that the existence of a Scottish Parliament was demanded by *vox populi* and their representatives at Holyrood have assumed the traditional opposition politicians' roles. There was even a Conservative by-election victory in Ayr in March 2000, after the Labour member resigned from his seat.

With Labour being the dominant partner in the Scottish Executive and also forming the United Kingdom Government at the same time, it might be expected that harmonious relations would obtain between the two administrations. On the whole, that expectation has been borne out, although tensions have surfaced from time to time. A source of friction and embarrassment was the turmoil caused by the inadvertent supply of genetically modified seed to Scottish farmers, when it became apparent that information on the seed provided by the manufacturer to the United Kingdom Government ministry had not been passed on to the Minister of Agriculture in the Scottish Executive.

Such occurrences test the efficiency and resilience of the regime of concordats established between the United Kingdom Government and the devolved administrations in Edinburgh and Cardiff. The Memorandum of Understanding[77] and four overarching concordats on EU business, international relations, financial assistance to industry, and statistics were published on October 1, 1999. These establish a general framework within which business between the United Kingdom Government and the devolved administrations is to be concluded. They are intended to facilitate good relations and, although explicitly stated to be not legally binding, there is an expectation that they should be observed by all parties (moreover, they are

---

[76] Local Government Act 1986, s.2A (generally known as "section 28", having been inserted by the Local Government Act 1988, s.28).
[77] Cm. 4444 (1999); SE/99/36.

supposed to hold good equally when different parties are in office in Edinburgh and in London). One product of the Memorandum of Understanding is the Joint Ministerial Committee, a consultative forum of ministers able to meet in a variety of formats to discuss matters of common concern. JMC Action Committees have been set up to promote discussion of common issues in the fields of poverty, the knowledge economy and the National Health Service. A further product of the Memorandum of Understanding has been the conclusion of 17 bilateral concordats agreed between the Scottish Executive and individual United Kingdom Departments to set frameworks for dealings between them.

Even with generally harmonious intergovernmental relations, predictably there have been occasions when the reservation of matters to Westminster has been a source of friction or dissatisfaction at Holyrood. The Scottish Parliament made most of the running in raising the issue of the Roman Catholic disability as regards succession to the Crown, and there was a sense of frustration when the United Kingdom Government declined to take it up. In May 2000 the Home Secretary's decision to allow entry to the United Kingdom of the boxer Mike Tyson (a convicted rapist), for a fight in Glasgow, attracted condemnation in the Scottish Parliament, on grounds of substance as well as the manner in which it had been taken. However, when some SNP members tried to persuade the Parliament to call on the Executive to petition for judicial review of the Home Secretary's decision, Labour members recoiled, perhaps belatedly perceiving a risk that disagreement was being exploited for political ends.

Within Scotland, other interrelationships are being worked out against the background of the Scotland Act, as the Parliament and the Executive turn their attention to the position of local authorities.[78] Within the United Kingdom, the prospects for regional government in England remain unclear, although the election of a Mayor and London Assembly took place in London in May 2000. There was a reminder that the "West Lothian question" had not disappeared in the following month, when the respected Labour backbencher, Mr Frank Field, introduced a Private Member's Bill in the House of Commons which sought to confine to English MPs the right to vote on purely English affairs. The constitutional reforms of 1998 may turn out to involve "unfinished business" in more ways than one.

---

[78] See the Report of the (McIntosh) Commission on Local Government and the Scottish Parliament (June 1999) and the Scottish Executive's Response (September 1999).

SCOTLAND ACT 1998

(1998 c. 46)

ARRANGEMENT OF SECTIONS

PART I

THE SCOTTISH PARLIAMENT

The Scottish Parliament

PART II

THE SCOTTISH ADMINISTRATION

Ministers and their staff

Ministerial functions

Property and liabilities

Transfer of additional functions

PART III

FINANCIAL PROVISIONS

PART IV

THE TAX-VARYING POWER

An Act to provide for the establishment of a Scottish Parliament and
Administration and other changes in the government of Scotland; to
provide for changes in the constitution and functions of certain public
authorities; to provide for the variation of the basic rate of income tax in
relation to income of Scottish taxpayers in accordance with a resolution of
the Scottish Parliament; to amend the law about parliamentary constituencies in Scotland; and for connected purposes.   [19th November 1998]

PARLIAMENTARY DEBATES
  Hansard, HC Vol. 303, col. 329 (1R), Vol. 304, col. 19 (MfA, 2R), 149 (M), Vol. 305, cols. 356
(Rep.), 357, 529 (Comm.), Vol. 306, cols. 160, 568 (Comm.), Vol. 307, cols. 40, 1079 (Comm.),
Vol. 309, cols. 902, 1052 (Comm.), Vol 311, col. 734 (AC), Vol. 312, cols. 171 (AC), 743 (3R),
Vol. 319, cols. 377 (AC), 641 (AC). HL Vol. 589, col. 1648 (1R), Vol. 590, cols. 1153 (MfA),
1567, 1599, 1687, 1709 (2R), Vol. 591, cols. 671 (MfA), 1234, 1277, 1323 (Comm.), Vol. 592, cols.
151, 188, 439, 458, 768, 816, 1040, 1121, 1262 (MfA), 1277, 1348, 1428, 1620, 1697 (Comm.), Vol.
593, cols. 261, 337, 409, 578 (Comm.), 1117 (MfA), 1567, 1640, 1917, 1926, 2003, Vol. 594, cols.
10, 41, 92, 142, 185, 234 (Rep.), Vol. 594, cols. 509, 531 (3R), 1170 (CCA).

INTRODUCTION
  In a sense, the background to the Scotland Act 1998 (c.46) may be traced back to 1707. The
union of Scotland with England and Wales to form the United Kingdom of Great Britain,

achieved by means of legislation enacted by the two Parliaments in Edinburgh and London, established a common Parliament and executive, whilst leaving in place separate courts and legal systems. Since that date, there has not existed a Scottish Parliament (nor, for that matter, an English Parliament).

However, as has been suggested, the U.K. is more happily regarded as a union, rather than a unitary state. There was never a complete assimilation of the nations composing the union state. When demands for Irish home rule were prominent in the later nineteenth century, it was decided to differentiate the handling of Scottish affairs more clearly by the creation, in 1885, of a Scottish Office as a department of government. From 1892 the Scottish Minister was, by practice, allocated a place in the cabinet, and in 1926 the holder's office was raised in status to that of a Secretary of State. Since 1939, the principal base of the Scottish Office has been in Edinburgh and over the years the role and importance of the Scottish Office has gradually increased, so that many matters such as education, health, or prisons, which in England fell within the remit of Ministers whose office was functionally defined, were in Scotland placed under the responsibility of the Secretary of State for Scotland, whose office was territorially defined. The system has been termed "administrative devolution" and what was devised in this fashion for Scotland was later to be followed (more slowly and in a rather more limited way) for Wales and (in rather different circumstances) for Northern Ireland.

Through administrative devolution and in some other ways, it may be said that the nationhood of Scotland was afforded some recognition in constitutional arrangements. However, there was arguably a weakness or flaw at the heart of the system of administrative devolution, in as much as the exercise of extensive executive and administrative powers was not properly matched by a territorial legislature or an adequate political base. Besides, it might be argued that the Scottish legal system had been poorly served by a U.K. Parliament which failed to find sufficient time for the enactment of distinctive legislation for Scotland and had sometimes been insensitive to its different legal traditions.

Political pressures for constitutional reform led the Government in 1969 to set up a Royal Commission on the Constitution, chaired in its later stages by Lord Kilbrandon. Its report (Cmnd. 5460-1), published in 1973, rejected the case for independence for Scotland and Wales and dismissed the possibility of federalism. Beyond that, the Commissioners found it difficult to agree, but a majority favoured a scheme of devolving legislative powers to an elected assembly in Scotland and a smaller number supported legislative devolution for Wales.

These proposals, although far from unanimous, were influential a few years later when a Labour Government was induced to bring forward legislation. Their first attempt, the Scotland and Wales Bill 1976, did not complete its passage. Following a parliamentary pact with the Liberals, a second attempt succeeded and after protracted proceedings in both Houses, the Scotland Act 1978 (c.51) and the Wales Act 1978 (c.52) became law. These would have given directly elected assemblies to Scotland and Wales with the Scottish assembly having legislative powers and the Welsh only executive powers. However, of the amendments made to the Bills, one proved to be fatal. Referendums were planned for Scotland and Wales, so as to give electors an opportunity to say whether they wanted the proposals to come into effect. A backbench Labour MP successfully proposed that if less than 40 per cent of those entitled to vote were to vote "Yes", then orders for the repeal of the legislation would have to be laid before Parliament. At the polls on March 1, 1979, only 11.9 per cent of the electorate in Wales voted "Yes". In Scotland, a majority of those who voted were in favour of the Scotland Act 1978 proposals, because 32.9 per cent of the electorate said "Yes" and only 30.8 per cent said "No". However, 36.3 per cent of the electorate did not vote and so the threshold requirement was not satisfied. The results led indirectly to a change of government, after defeat on a vote of confidence, and repealing orders were laid before Parliament and approved in the early weeks of the new Conservative Government in 1979.

The Labour Party could not be entirely absolved from the suspicion that its actions in government from 1974 to 1979 had been driven by political expediency as much as clear principle. However, in its years in opposition, the party became more sympathetic to greater decentralisation of power. Besides, for a party which held (after the 1987 general election) 50 seats in Scotland, there were obvious electoral advantages to be garnered from espousing the cause of a Scottish Parliament, if it were popular, and losses to be risked if it did not. Moreover, especially after Mr John Smith became the party's leader in 1992, there could be no doubt over the party's commitment to the cause. For John Smith, who had piloted the Scotland Act 1978 through the Commons, the project of Scottish home rule was, quite simply, "unfinished business".

The political parties' policies were important, because only a party (or coalition of parties) in government could deliver constitutional reforms. It was also significant that some pressure groups were formed in the wake of the 1979 referendum, or later, which were to be influential in keeping the issue of reform in front of the public and the parties during the long period of Conservative governments. One such group was the Campaign for a Scottish Assembly, a gathering of notables which through a committee in 1988 produced a report entitled A Claim of Right for Scotland, that asserted the right of the people of Scotland to decide on their own constitution. The report also recommended that a convention should be brought into being to draw up a scheme for a Scottish assembly or parliamentary body.

Accordingly, a body calling itself the Scottish Constitutional Convention was set up and held its first meeting in March 1989. The Conservatives refused to join the body and the SNP withdrew before meetings began, having formed the view that the option of independence was not likely to be seriously pursued under the modus operandi of proceeding by consensus. The

Labour Party and the Liberal Democrats participated in the Convention, however, along with the Green Party and a few other minor parties as did representatives or delegates of local authorities, trade unions, churches etc. and other organisations. Although it had no official status, the body did contain 59 of the 72 MPs and six Scottish MEPs. The joint chairs of the Convention were drawn from Labour (Lord Ewing of Kirkford) and the Liberal Democrats (Sir David Steel, the former leader of the party) and its Executive was chaired by Canon Kenyon Wright. In November 1990 the Convention published a report, *Towards Scotland's Parliament*, with the central proposal of a directly elected Scottish Parliament which would have a defined range of powers and responsibilities, including exclusive responsibility on many matters.

Through collaboration in the Convention, Labour and the Liberal Democrats entered the 1992 general election with a broad measure of agreement on Scottish constitutional reform, although there were some matters, including the method of election of the Scottish Parliament and the method of funding Scottish government, on which agreement had not been secured or there were differences between the parties. After the 1992 election, the Convention appointed a commission to tackle some of the outstanding disagreements and problems and its work was incorporated in the Convention's final report, *Scotland's Parliament. Scotland's Right*, presented on St. Andrew's Day, 1995. The report was notable for its thoroughness and attention to detail as well as principle. The proposals were for a Parliament of 129 members to be elected under an additional member system; a power to increase or decrease the basic rate of income tax by a maximum of three pence in the pound to be given to the Scottish Parliament, but with funding chiefly through an assigned budget from central government; and a substantial devolution of legislative and executive functions to a Scottish Parliament and an executive formed from it.

The Scottish Constitutional Convention must be counted as an effective pressure group. Its work over a period of years in progressively developing a scheme for constitutional reform meant that a sympathetic government could import the proposals more or less wholesale. With other proposals on more technical matters that could be added as appropriate, a government could avail itself of a reform package which was "off the peg" to the extent that it was willing to do so.

The Labour Party entered the general election in 1997 with a commitment to legislate for a Scottish Parliament within a year of taking office, assuming affirmative referendum results (in a change of policy in 1996, it had also committed itself to test the Scottish electorate's view on the two questions of their support for, a Scottish Parliament and on the principle of its possessing tax-varying powers, in advance of legislating).

When the general election brought Labour to power, with a majority of 179, the new Government acted quickly on constitutional reforms, as it had promised, and published White Papers regarding proposals for Scottish and Welsh devolution in July 1997. *Scotland's Parliament*, Cm. 3658 (1997) ("The White Paper") on Scottish devolution, was a best seller in the shops. Preparations were taken forward under the Referendums (Scotland and Wales) Act 1997 (c.61) and on September 11, 1997 electors in Scotland and Wales were able to vote in pre-legislative referendums, in the knowledge of the White Paper proposals. In the Scottish referendum, on the first question, 1,775,045 electors (or 74.3 per cent of those voting) agreed "that there should be a Scottish Parliament", while 614,400 (or 25.7 per cent) disagreed. The turnout figure was 60 per cent. On the second question, the voting was 63.5 per cent for and 36.5 per cent against, the proposition that the "Scottish Parliament should have tax-varying powers".

By these results, the Government had secured a specific mandate for the constitutional reform that would extend devolution by establishing a Scottish Parliament with wide-ranging competence. On December 18, 1997 the Government published the Scotland Bill. There is a constitutional convention to the effect that Bills of first class constitutional importance should have all their stages on the floor of the House of Commons and, notwithstanding some apprehensions to the contrary, it was adhered to for the Scotland Bill. After a relatively untroubled parliamentary passage, the Bill received Royal Assent on November 19, 1998.

The Act in Outline

Part I of this Act provides for the establishment, composition and powers of the Scottish Parliament ("the Parliament"). The first general election for membership of the Scottish Parliament will be held on a day appointed by the Secretary of State (expected to be May 6, 1999). The Scottish Parliament will have a fixed term of four years, although there is provision for an extraordinary general election in limited circumstances. The franchise for elections corresponds to that which applies for local government elections, so that persons registered in constituencies in Scotland for that purpose will form the electorate. The disqualifications from membership of the House of Commons, with a few exceptions, correspond to the disqualifications which will apply to membership of the Scottish Parliament. However, an unfamiliar electoral system applies. A mixed system will mean that the Scottish Parliament has two categories of members, some elected as single members representing constituencies under the "first past the post" system and some produced by the operation of a list system, on a regional basis, designed so that the composite representation from the region approximates to, or at least approaches, proportionality.

The Parliament will elect a Presiding Officer and deputies, to preside over the proceedings and perform other assigned functions. An appointed Clerk of the Scottish Parliament heads the administration and a parliamentary corporation is established to hold property, provide facilities for the Scottish Parliament and act in legal proceedings. Some minimum requirements are imposed with regard to the conduct of the Parliament's proceedings, beyond which the Scottish Parliament will be able to make further provision by means of standing orders. There are also some basic requirements concerning rules to be made on members' interests, including a ban on paid advocacy and provision for the registration and declaration of financial interests. Some counterparts to the parliamentary privileges enjoyed by Westminster are statutorily created for the Scottish Parliament, including some protection of proceedings from the laws of defamation and contempt of court, the preservation of validity of Acts made by the Scottish Parliament notwithstanding any invalidity in proceedings leading to enactment, and powers to call for witnesses and documents on devolved matters.

The Parliament is a subordinate legislature and its competence is restricted in effect to Scots law. Its legislation must be compatible with European Community law and "the Convention rights" within the meaning of the Human Rights Act 1998 (c.42). Besides, there are some enactments which the Scottish Parliament may not modify, including (with limited exceptions) the provisions of the Scotland Act 1998, and there are reserved matters specified which are outside its competence, although there is provision for Her Majesty by Order in Council to alter the boundaries of these restrictions. The U.K. Parliament's competence to legislate for Scotland is affirmed. There is provision for pre-enactment scrutiny of Bills in the Scottish Parliament on the question of whether they are competent, for a reference by a Law Officer to the Judicial Committee of the Privy Council for its adjudication on competence, and for the Secretary of State to intervene to prohibit submission of a Bill for Royal Assent on certain other grounds, such as the interests of national security.

Part II of this Act deals with the executive powers of government within the devolution scheme, which will be exercised by the Scottish Administration, consisting of ministers and civil servants. At the top, there is the Scottish Executive or "the Scottish Ministers", consisting of the First Minister, other ministers and the Scottish Law Officers. The First Minister is to be appointed by Her Majesty the Queen from among the members of the Parliament, on the nomination of the Parliament, normally within 28 days of a general election or a vacancy's arising for another reason. Other ministers, to be drawn from members of the Parliament, are appointed by the First Minister subject to the agreement of the Parliament. Separate provision is made for the appointment of the Lord Advocate and the Solicitor General for Scotland as the Scottish Law Officers, with appointment to these offices recommended to Her Majesty the Queen by the First Minister, subject to the agreement of the Parliament. To assist the Scottish Executive, there may additionally be junior Scottish Ministers, appointed by the First Minister from among the members of the Scottish Parliament and subject to its agreement. Civil servants appointed to the staff of the Scottish Administration will form part of the Home Civil Service.

Provision is made for legislation (including Acts of Parliament) to confer statutory functions on the Scottish Ministers, but there is also a general transfer of powers and functions of U.K. Ministers of the Crown, whether derived from prerogative or statutory sources, to the Scottish Ministers, "so far as they are exercisable within devolved competence". The latter is subject to some specified instances of shared powers, where U.K. Ministers will also be able to exercise functions, and the Secretary of State also has powers to prevent or require actions of the Scottish Executive to secure compatibility with international obligations and to revoke subordinate legislation which is otherwise within the competence of the Scottish Executive on that and certain other grounds. There is also provision for the transfer of additional functions to be exercisable by the Scottish Ministers, through Orders in Council so providing.

Part III makes financial provisions. There is established a Scottish Consolidated Fund, into which payments will be made out of money provided by the U.K. Parliament, of such amounts as the Secretary of State may determine. Payments out of the Fund may be made as authorised under this Act or other legislation, including Acts of the Parliament. There are limited borrowing powers reposed in the Scottish Ministers and corresponding lending powers conferred on the Secretary of State. There are provisions for financial control, accounts and audit, and an office of Auditor General for Scotland is established for the independent scrutiny of accounts and for the examination of the economy, efficiency and effectiveness with which resources have been used.

Part IV concerns the tax-varying power. The Scottish Parliament is empowered to pass a resolution with the effect of varying the basic rate of income tax percentage by up to three points (upwards or downwards) for a year of assessment. Such a variation, if resolved upon, would affect income tax payers who are treated as resident in the United Kingdom, if they are persons whose "closest connection", as defined, is with Scotland in the relevant year of assessment. The accounting provision necessary for the transfer into or out of the Scottish Consolidated Fund consequential upon a decision either to increase or reduce the rate of tax for Scottish taxpayers is allowed for, and the Scottish Ministers are empowered to reimburse central government for the additional administrative expenses. There is provision for the Treasury to propose appropriate amendments to the Parliament's tax-varying powers in order to maintain their having broadly the same "practical extent", if changes to the income tax structure in the U.K. are in contemplation which would significantly affect the Parliament's incidental power. There is further provision for the Treasury to make statutory amendments consequential upon the introduction of the tax-varying power.

Part V is concerned with miscellaneous and general matters. There is provision for the remuneration of members of the Scottish Parliament and members of the Scottish Executive and junior Scottish Ministers, for the exemption of these persons from jury service and for their being obliged to take oaths on assumption of office. An amendment of the Parliamentary Constituencies Act 1986 (c.56) will affect the process of electoral area apportionment for Scottish constituencies at the U.K. Parliament (which in turn will later affect the composition of the Parliament, which is related). A new Law Officer post is created in the U.K. Government, of an Advocate General for Scotland. For bodies designated by Order in Council as "cross-border public authorities," with functions extending to devolved areas, there are provisions to require consultation of the Scottish Ministers and tabling of reports before the Scottish Parliament, and enabling adaptations and transfers of responsibilities and property.

Further provision is made for adjudication on those issues of competence and vires which are termed "devolution issues", when they arise in the courts of Scotland, England and Wales or Northern Ireland, as the case may be. Provisions enable references to higher courts and in some circumstances, appeals. The decisions of the Judicial Committee of the Privy Council, to which there may be references or appeals from courts of each of the three jurisdictions for this purpose, are binding in all legal proceedings. An interpretation section instructs that Parliament legislation and Scottish Executive subordinate legislation should be read "as narrowly as is required for it to be within competence, if such a reading is possible". When a court or tribunal decides that provisions enacted or made are ultra vires, it is empowered to remove or limit any retrospective effect of the decision, or to suspend its effect for a period to allow correction of the defect.

Amongst the miscellaneous provisions, there is a duty on the Scottish Parliament to provide for the investigation of complaints of executive maladministration; there are provisions concerning the processes of appointment and removal of the judges of the Court of Session; and there is provision for financial assistance for the parliamentary work of the opposition parties in the Parliament. There are widely expressed supplementary powers to make subordinate legislation to make provisions consequential on the Act, or on Acts made by the Parliament, or on subordinate legislation made by a member of the Scottish Executive.

Part VI contains supplementary provisions. Powers to make subordinate legislation under this Act, unless a contrary intention is stated, may be exercised either by Order in Council or by a Minister of the Crown by Order. There are general provisions for the scope of these law-making powers generally, and exceptionally powers for the modification of provisions in or made under this Act and for retrospective law-making in a few specified instances. Procedures are specified as required in relation to law-making powers conferred by the Act. Additionally, there is a power for transitional provisions to be made as necessary or expedient. There are consequential modifications of enactments and arrangements made, which flow from the establishment of the Parliament, the Scottish Executive, the Scottish Consolidated Fund and the office of the Auditor General for Scotland.

COMMENCEMENT
The following provisions came into force on November 19, 1998 by s.130(1): ss.1–18, 112–116, 125 (part), 126–132, Scheds 1, 7, 8, paras 10, 11, 19, 23(1), 23(6). The remaining provisions will be brought into effect by order, with different days being appointed for different purposes.

The following provisions will be brought into force by the Scotland Act 1998 (Commencement) Order 1998 (S.I. 1998 No. 3178 (C.79)) on the following dates: January 25, 1999: ss.21(8) (part), 37, 38(3), 51(4) (part), 51(7) (part), 56(2) (part), 60 (part), 62 (part), 71(6) (part), 88 (part), 97 (part), 103(3) (part), 105, 106, Sched. 2, paras 2(2)–(4) (part), 7 (part); April 1, 1999: s.64(1), (2) and (8); May 6, 1999: ss.19–22, 23 (part), 24–26, 30, 38(1), (2), (4)–(6), 40–43, 44 (except 44(1)(c)), 45–47, 48(1) (part), 49–51, 52 (part), 57(2), 58, 59–60, 61(4) (part), 69, 73–80, 81–85, 89 (part), 92, 93 (part), 96, 97, 98–100, 103, 108–111, 123 (part), 125 (part), Scheds 2, 3, 5, 6, 8 paras 13, 14, 18, 24, 25, 26, 28, 30, 31, 33; May 20, 1999: ss.27, 44(1)(c), 48, 52, 57(3), 61(1)–(3), 62, 87, 123, 125 (part), Sched. 8, paras 2, 7, 32, Sched. 9 (part); July 1, 1999 ("the principal appointed day"): all remaining provisions except those to be brought into force on April 1, 2000: ss.120, 125 (rem.), Sched. 8, para. 20.

ABBREVIATIONS
"the Parliament": the Scottish Parliament, established by s.1 of this Act
"the White Paper": *Scotland's Parliament* Cm. 3658 (1997)

PART I

THE SCOTTISH PARLIAMENT

The Scottish Parliament

The Scottish Parliament

1.—(1) There shall be a Scottish Parliament.

(2) One member of the Parliament shall be returned for each constituency (under the simple majority system) at an election held in the constituency.

(3) Members of the Parliament for each region shall be returned at a general election under the additional member system of proportional representation provided for in this Part and vacancies among such members shall be filled in accordance with this Part.

(4) The validity of any proceedings of the Parliament is not affected by any vacancy in its membership.

(5) Schedule 1 (which makes provision for the constituencies and regions for the purposes of this Act and the number of regional members) shall have effect.

DEFINITIONS
"constituency": s.126(1).
"the Parliament": s.126(1).
"proceedings": s.126(1).
"region": s.126(1).
"regional members": s.126(1).

GENERAL NOTE
This section establishes a unicameral Scottish Parliament and (in conjunction with the following sections and Sched.1) provides for its composition. The composition is the product of a mixed electoral system. One part is composed of members singly representing constituencies, while another part consists of additional members elected on a regional basis under a proportional representation system, as set out in what follows.

Subs. (1)
Its plain terms and placing at the head of this Act may be thought to symbolise a clear and settled will. Whereas, by s.1 of the Government of Wales Act 1998 (c.38), the National Assembly for Wales is a body corporate, the Scottish Parliament is an unincorporated association created by statute.

Subs. (2)
This provides for the first element of the composition: single members are returned for each constituency under the simple majority or "first past the post" system which is familiar through its use for elections to the House of Commons. Such members are returned either at general elections (as provided for in ss.2 and 3) or at by-elections to fill vacancies (as provided for in s.9).

Subs. (3)
This provides for the second element of the composition: the additional members forming part of the Parliament's membership are "regional members", returned under the proportional representation system specified in subsequent provisions of the Act, either at general elections or under the provision for filling vacancies among such members (in s.10).

Subs. (4)
This provides for the validity of the Parliament's proceedings to be unaffected by a vacancy in any seat. The provision is arguably unnecessary, but has been inserted out of caution.

Subs.(5)
This gives effect to Sched. 1, which makes further provision for the constituencies and regions and numbers to be elected for the composition of the Parliament. The constituencies for the purpose of subs. (2) currently number 73, being the same as the constituencies for elections to the House of Commons, except that Orkney and Shetland are for this purpose two separate constituencies. The regions for the purpose of subs. (3) number eight, which return seven members each, so that there are 56 regional members and the membership of the Scottish Parliament numbers 129. However, s.86 amends the rules with regard to apportionment of Scottish constituencies for the U.K. Parliament and Sched. 1 makes provisions for the Boundary Commission for Scotland to carry out electoral area reviews, so that the numbers will presumptively be altered (downwards) in future. Section 86 and Sched. 1 are annotated below.

General elections

Ordinary general elections
2.—(1) The day on which the poll at the first ordinary general election for membership of the Parliament shall be held, and the day, time and place for the meeting of the Parliament following that poll, shall be appointed by order made by the Secretary of State.
(2) The poll at subsequent ordinary general elections shall be held on the first Thursday in May in the fourth calendar year following that in which the previous ordinary general election was held, unless the day of the poll is determined by a proclamation under subsection (5).
(3) If the poll is to be held on the first Thursday in May, the Parliament—
(a) is dissolved by virtue of this section at the beginning of the minimum period which ends with that day, and

(b) shall meet within the period of seven days beginning immediately after the day of the poll.

(4) In subsection (3), "the minimum period" means the period determined in accordance with an order under section 12(1).

(5) If the Presiding Officer proposes a day for the holding of the poll which is not more than one month earlier, nor more than one month later, than the first Thursday in May, Her Majesty may by proclamation under the Scottish Seal—

(a) dissolve the Parliament,

(b) require the poll at the election to be held on the day proposed, and

(c) require the Parliament to meet within the period of seven days beginning immediately after the day of the poll.

(6) In this Act "the Scottish Seal" means Her Majesty's Seal appointed by the Treaty of Union to be kept and used in Scotland in place of the Great Seal of Scotland.

DEFINITIONS

"by virtue of": s.126(11).
"the Parliament": s.126(1).
"Presiding Officer": s.19.
"the Scottish Seal": subs. (6).

GENERAL NOTE

Whereas the term of the U.K. Parliament is, within the five year maximum specified by the Parliament Act 1911 (c.13), indefinite and subject to the royal prerogative of dissolution, the Parliament, on the other hand, will have a fixed term of four years, normally, and its meeting and dissolution are determined by statute. This section provides for ordinary general elections, while the succeeding section provides for extraordinary general elections. Ordinary general elections will be held on the first Thursday in May every four years, subject to variations of the date being allowed for within prescribed limits. This section also provides for the dissolution of the Scottish Parliament prior to an election and the meeting of the Scottish Parliament following an election.

Subs. (1)

An Order made under this provision specified that polling for the first ordinary general election was on May 6, 1999 and that the first meeting of the Parliament was on May 12, 1999 at the Church of Scotland Assembly Hall in Edinburgh: The Scottish Parliament (First Ordinary General Election and First Meeting) Order 1999 (S.I. 1999 No. 788).

Subs. (2)

Subsequent ordinary general elections are held on the first Thursday in May four calendar years after the previous such election, unless there is an alternative date selected under subs. (5) below. The second general election should take place on May 1, 2003.

Subss. (3), (4)

These provide for the dissolution of the Scottish Parliament before an ordinary general election held on the first Thursday in May, to occur at the beginning of "the minimum period" ending with that day. The minimum period will be as specified in accordance with an order made by the Secretary of State under s.12 (which enables provision to be made for the conduct of the election).

In order to prevent any appreciable hiatus between the election and the first meeting, the Scottish Parliament is also required to meet within seven days following the poll (as calculated under the rule in s.4, excluding certain non-working days). Note also that, under s.46, the Scottish Parliament must nominate one of its members for appointment as First Minister within 28 days of the poll.

Subs. (5)

A limited measure of flexibility over the date of an ordinary general election is provided by this, in case the first Thursday in May should for some reason be unsuitable. The Presiding Officer may propose to Her Majesty an alternative day for the election, not more than one month earlier or one month later than the first Thursday in May. Her Majesty may then, by proclamation under the Scottish Seal, dissolve the Parliament, require the poll to be held on the proposed day, and require the Scottish Parliament to meet within seven working days. The flexibility over the date is limited, so that there should be little or no risk of it being altered for political as opposed to purely practical reasons. It is also significant, in this respect, that it is for the Presiding Officer, not the Secretary of State or the First Minister, to make such a proposal.

Provisions as to the making of the proclamation, the prescribed form of words, and requirements as to publication, are contained in the Scottish Parliament (Letters Patent and Proclamations) Order 1999 (S.I. 1999 No. 737).

Subs. (6)
This makes provision about the Scottish Seal. It should be read in conjunction with s.38, which is annotated below.

Extraordinary general elections

3.—(1) The Presiding Officer shall propose a day for the holding of a poll if—

   (a) the Parliament resolves that it should be dissolved and, if the resolution is passed on a division, the number of members voting in favour of it is not less than two—thirds of the total number of seats for members of the Parliament, or

   (b) any period during which the Parliament is required under section 46 to nominate one of its members for appointment as First Minister ends without such a nomination being made.

(2) If the Presiding Officer makes such a proposal, Her Majesty may by proclamation under the Scottish Seal—

   (a) dissolve the Parliament and require an extraordinary general election to be held,

   (b) require the poll at the election to be held on the day proposed, and

   (c) require the Parliament to meet within the period of seven days beginning immediately after the day of the poll.

(3) If a poll is held under this section within the period of six months ending with the day on which the poll at the next ordinary general election would be held (disregarding section 2(5)), that ordinary general election shall not be held.

(4) Subsection (3) does not affect the year in which the subsequent ordinary general election is to be held.

DEFINITIONS
"the Parliament": s.126(1).
"Presiding Officer": s.19.
"the Scottish Seal": s.2(6).

GENERAL NOTE
When parliamentary bodies have a fixed term, normally, it is necessary or desirable to build in a safety valve. For that reason, there is provision here for "extraordinary general elections" to be held in exceptional circumstances. Such elections must be proposed by the Parliament's Presiding Officer, in order to be sanctioned by Her Majesty, in two different situations. First, if no nomination of a First Minister has been made within the period prescribed under s.46 (normally 28 days) for the Scottish Parliament to make one. Secondly, when the Scottish Parliament resolves that it should be dissolved. If the resolution is passed on a division, it requires the support of at least "two thirds of the total number of seats" to be effective for this purpose and would therefore require the votes of 86 or more members in a Parliament of 129. The necessity of something more than a simple majority of those present and voting is designed to ensure that premature dissolution takes place only in exceptional circumstances. The sort of situation for which these provisions cater is, for example, where the Executive loses the support of most of the Scottish Parliament (perhaps because a coalition between parties has foundered) and no new administration can be formed from the existing composition that would enjoy sufficient support. The good intention behind the adoption of a qualified majority has been to separate the timing of elections from the control of the Executive, so that the timing of dissolutions is not manipulated for party advantage.

Subs. (2)
Provisions as to the making of the proclamation, the prescribed form of words, and requirements as to publication, are contained in the Scottish Parliament (Letters Patent and Proclamations) Order 1999 (S.I. 1999 No. 737).

Subss. (3), (4)
These provide for the relation between ordinary and extraordinary general elections. If an extraordinary general election is held within six months before an ordinary general election would be due, it replaces the ordinary general election. Otherwise, however, it does not affect the normal quadrennial cycle. So if, for example, an ordinary general election is due to be held in May 2003 and there were an extraordinary general election in December 2002, the next ordinary general election would take place in May 2007; but, if there were an extraordinary general election in September 2002, the Scottish Parliament elected would only be of seven or eight months' duration, because the ordinary general election would take place as due in May 2003.

Calculating time for meeting of the Parliament

4. In calculating any period of days for the purposes of section 2(3)(b) or (5)(c) or section 3(2)(c), Saturday, Sunday, Christmas Eve, Christmas Day, Good Friday, a bank holiday in Scotland or a day appointed for public thanksgiving or mourning shall be disregarded.

DEFINITIONS
"Scotland": s.126(1) and (2).

GENERAL NOTE
This section is related to ss.2 and 3. When general elections are held under the provisions of s.2(3) or (5), or s.3(2), there are requirements for the Scottish Parliament to meet within a period of seven days beginning on the day immediately after polling day. However, by this section, Saturdays, Sundays and certain special days or holidays as specified must be disregarded in making the calculation.

Candidates

5.—(1) At a general election, the candidates may stand for return as constituency members or regional members.

(2) A person may not be a candidate to be a constituency member for more than one constituency.

(3) The candidates to be regional members shall be those included in a list submitted under subsection (4) or individual candidates.

(4) Any registered political party may submit to the regional returning officer a list of candidates to be regional members for a particular region (referred to in this Act, in relation to the region, as the party's "regional list").

(5) A registered political party's regional list has effect in relation to the general election and any vacancy occurring among the regional members after that election and before the next general election.

(6) Not more than twelve persons may be included in the list (but the list may include only one person).

(7) A registered political party's regional list must not include a person—
  (a) who is included in any other list submitted under subsection (4) for the region or any list submitted under that subsection for another region,
  (b) who is an individual candidate to be a regional member for the region or another region,
  (c) who is a candidate to be a constituency member for a constituency not included in the region, or
  (d) who is a candidate to be a constituency member for a constituency included in the region but is not a candidate of that party.

(8) A person may not be an individual candidate to be a regional member for a particular region if he is—
  (a) included in a list submitted under subsection (4) for the region or another region,
  (b) an individual candidate to be a regional member for another region,
  (c) a candidate to be a constituency member for a constituency not included in the region, or
  (d) a candidate of any registered political party to be a constituency member for a constituency included in the region.

(9) In this Act, "registered political party" means a party registered under the Registration of Political Parties Act 1998.

DEFINITIONS
"constituency": s.126(1).
"constituency member": s.126(1).
"region": s.126(1).
"regional list": subs. (4).
"regional member": s.126(1).
"regional returning officer": s.12(6).
"registered political party": subs. (9).

GENERAL NOTE

This section is predicated upon there being constituency members as well as members returned for regional seats, and so has to be read in conjunction with the earlier provisions for composition of the Scottish Parliament and elections as well as ss.6–8 on the proportional representation system (while ss.15–18 deal with disqualifications affecting membership). Note that this section concerns candidature at a general election, methods of filling casual vacancies in seats being dealt with in ss.9 and 10. The chief purpose of the section is to bar various forms of double candidature, although a candidate may stand as a regional member and also as a constituency member for a constituency in the same region.

Subss. (1), (3)

Persons may stand for election as constituency members, whether as candidates representing a political party or independently as "individual candidates". Persons may stand for election as regional members, either as individual candidates or as persons included in a political party's list submitted under the provisions of this section. Persons may stand for both a constituency and a regional seat, subject to the combinations which are excluded by subss. (7) and (8), but could only be returned for one of them.

Subss. (2), (7), (8)

A person may not be a candidate for the constituency election in more than one constituency. It is of interest to notice that there is no corresponding rule for elections to the House of Commons, and a small number of candidates (usually "fringe" candidates) have stood in several constituencies at general elections.

A political party's list for a region may not include persons who are standing for another party or as an individual candidate or in another region (whether as a constituency candidate or as a list candidate). A person may not be an individual candidate to be a regional member for a region if he or she is standing for a party or in another region (whether as a constituency candidate or as a list candidate).

Subss. (4), (5), (6), (9)

Political parties have to be registered under legislation in order to submit a list of candidates under this section. The Registration of Political Parties Act 1998 (c.48) was enacted, at least in part, to meet the need created by these provisions and the corresponding ones in the Government of Wales Act 1998 (c.38).

A registered political party may then submit to the person designated by the Secretary of State as regional returning officer its list of candidates for the Scottish Parliament for the region in question. The list is operative not only for the general election for which it is submitted but for the period until the next, so that it is to be used for filling casual vacancies when appropriate, under s.10.

Lists submitted by parties may have from one to twelve persons on them. Although a party cannot win more than seven regional seats in the region, it is sensible to have a larger number on the list, because some candidates may be returned as constituency members and so effectively drop out and also because of the use of the list to fill casual vacancies later. The names on the list (either explicitly or implicitly) have to be ranked in order, since the operation of processes provided for under ss.8 and 10 assumes a ranking for those purposes. Because the ranking is done by the party, this is called a "closed list" system. An alternative system could involve an "open list", in which electors select their choices from amongst the party's candidates or may change the order of candidates presented by the party. The Government resisted amendments which would have introduced an "open list" on grounds of principle (on the argument that the party is the fundamental organising principle in our democratic process) and practicality (*Hansard*, H.L. Vol. 592, cols. 191–193). At around the same period, the European Parliamentary Elections Bill of session 1997–1998 failed to complete its passage in the session when it was introduced, when the House of Lords insisted on amendments to introduce an "open list" for the proportional representation system proposed in that Bill (it later became law as the European Parliamentary Elections Act 1999 (c.1), without the consent of the House of Lords).

The Political Parties, Elections and Referendums Bill, which is before the UK Parliament at the time of writing, will if enacted replace the main provisions of the Registration of Political Parties Act 1998 and will involve a consequential amendment to subs. (9).

Poll for regional members

6.—(1) This section and sections 7 and 8 are about the return of regional members at a general election.

(2) In each of the constituencies for the Parliament, a poll shall be held at which each person entitled to vote as elector may give a vote (referred to in this Act as a "regional vote") for—

(a) a registered political party which has submitted a regional list, or

(b) an individual candidate to be a regional member for the region.

(3) The right conferred on a person by subsection (2) is in addition to any right the person may have to vote in any poll for the return of a constituency member.

DEFINITIONS
"constituencies": s.126(1).
"constituency member": s.126(1).
"the Parliament": s.126(1).
"region": s.126(1).
"regional list": s.5(4).
"regional member": s.126(1).
"registered political party": s.5(9).

GENERAL NOTE
 This section is the first of three concerned with the election of the regional members to the Parliament, as subs. (1) rather prosaically explains. Its effect is to entitle voters in each constituency, on top of their right to vote for a constituency member, to exercise a vote which will be counted towards the election of the regional members for the region of which the constituency forms part. Electors are thus entitled, but not obliged, to cast two votes. The second vote, as we might naturally think of it, may be cast either for an individual candidate standing as a regional member (if there are any) or for a registered political party which has submitted a list of candidates for return as regional members in the relevant region. Such votes are used to determine which persons will become the regional members of the Scottish Parliament after a general election under the provisions of ss.7 and 8.

Calculation of regional figures

[1]**7.**—(1) The persons who are to be returned as constituency members for constituencies included in the region must be determined before the persons who are to be returned as the regional members for the region.

(2) For each registered political party which has submitted a regional list, the regional figure for the purposes of section 8 is—

(a) the total number of regional votes given for the party in all the constituencies included in the region, divided by

(b) the aggregate of one plus the number of candidates of the party returned as constituency members for any of those constituencies.

(3) Each time a seat is allocated to the party under section 8, that figure shall be recalculated by increasing (or further increasing) the aggregate in subsection (2)(b) by one.

(4) For each individual candidate to be a regional member for the region, the regional figure for the purposes of section 8 is the total number of regional votes given for him in all the constituencies included in the region.

NOTE
 [1] Modified by S.I. 1999 No. 787, Sched. 2, r.70(3). Effective March 11, 1999. This requires subs. (1) to be modified accordingly when a constituency poll is countermanded or abandoned because of the death of a candidate.

DEFINITIONS
"constituencies": s.126(1).
"constituency member": s.126(1).
"region": s.126(1).
"regional list": s.5(4).
"regional members": s.126(1).
"regional vote": s.6(2).
"registered political party": s.5(9).

GENERAL NOTE
 This is part of the set of sections concerned with candidates (s.5) and the election of regional members (ss.6–8). Determination of the victorious constituency candidates is to be carried out first, by subs. (1), before calculations of the regional votes. One practical reason for this lies in the fact that a person may be a constituency candidate as well as a regional candidate. If elected as a constituency member, such a person will effectively be deleted from a party's regional list, if appearing on one (s.8(5)), or will be disregarded in the calculations for allocations of regional seats if he or she was an "individual" regional candidate, not on a party's list (s.8(3)).
 More generally, however, a reason to determine first which persons are to become constituency members, lies in the objective of using the regional votes correctively. That is to say that the results for parties of the constituency contests are taken account of in the allocation of regional seats, with adjustments accordingly. The aim behind the electoral system chosen is to seek to ensure that if a party's candidates in the constituencies have won disproportionately few seats, considering its level of support as evidenced in the regional voting, then the party will be compensated by being allocated more or "additional" seats from the party lists of candidates, as

against parties gaining a disproportionately high number of constituency seats. By this means, the overall representation should approximate to party proportionality. The approximation to proportionality would be likely to be higher if the system were applied nationally rather than on a regionally divided basis, but something would arguably be lost in so far as the regional members may be expected to have a territorial link with their electors, albeit a weaker link than constituency members should have.

Subss. (2), (3), (4)
See the General Note to s.8 below.

Allocation of seats to regional members

8.—(1) The first regional member seat shall be allocated to the registered political party or individual candidate with the highest regional figure.

(2) The second and subsequent regional member seats shall be allocated to the registered political party or individual candidate with the highest regional figure, after any recalculation required by section 7(3) has been carried out.

(3) An individual candidate already returned as a constituency or regional member shall be disregarded.

(4) Seats for the region which are allocated to a registered political party shall be filled by the persons in the party's regional list in the order in which they appear in the list.

(5) For the purposes of this section and section 10, a person in a registered political party's regional list who is returned as a member of the Parliament shall be treated as ceasing to be in the list (even if his return is void).

(6) Once a party's regional list has been exhausted (by the return of persons included in it as constituency members or by the previous application of subsection (1) or (2)) the party shall be disregarded.

[1](7) If (on the application of subsection (1) or any application of subsection (2)) the highest regional figure is the regional figure of two or more parties or individual candidates—

the subsection in question shall apply to each of them; or

(b) if paragraph (a) would result in more than the correct number of seats for the region being allocated, the subsection in question shall apply as if the regional figure for each of those parties or candidates had been adjusted in accordance with subsection (8).

[2](8) The regional figure for a party or candidate is adjusted in accordance with this subsection by—

(a) adding one vote to the total number of regional votes given for the party or candidate in all the constituencies included in the region; and

(b) (in the case of a party) recalculating the regional figure accordingly.

[2](9) If, on the application of the subsection in question in accordance with subsection (7)(b), seats would be allocated to two or more parties or individual candidates and that would result in more than the correct number of seats for the region being allocated, the regional returning officer shall decide between them by lot.

NOTES
[1] As amended by S.I. 1999 No. 787, Sched. 2, r.63. Effective March 11, 1999.
[2] Inserted by S.I. 1999 No. 787, Sched. 2, r.63. Effective March 11, 1999.

DEFINITIONS
"constituency member": s.126(1).
"the Parliament": s.126(1).
"region": s.126(1).
"regional figure": s.7(2).
"regional list": s.5(4).
"regional member": s.126(1).
"regional returning officer": s.12(6).
"registered political party": s.5(9).

GENERAL NOTE
This section provides the rules for determining the allocation of seats to regional members. The key determinant is the "regional figure". For an "individual" or independent candidate in a

region, that figure is simply the total number of regional votes given for him or her in the region (s.7(4)). For a political party which has submitted a list of candidates, the regional figure is obtained by adding together the number of regional votes for the party in all the constituencies of the region and dividing the sum by one plus the number of constituency seats gained by the party (which may be none), by s.7(2). Then the first regional seat goes to the party or the individual candidate with the highest regional figure (s.8(1)). Whenever a party gains a regional member seat, the party's regional figure is then recalculated by adding one more to the divisor (s.7(3)). The second and subsequent regional member seats are then allocated to the party or the individual candidate with the highest regional figure each time, following any necessary recalculations (s.8(2)).

This method of allocation employs what is known as the "d'Hondt formula" or the largest average rule. The object is to secure that, when all the seats have been allotted, the average number of votes required to win one seat shall be, as nearly as possible, the same for each party. There are other possible methods which could have been adopted, such as the largest remainder method or the "Sainte-Laguë formula" (which is more exactly proportional and fairer to the smaller parties) and members of the Houses of Parliament indulged in some discussion of these arcane matters, but the Government defended its choice as being "simpler to understand, more logical to apply, easier to explain to the public at large and to those operating it, is consistent with the approach adopted for the European Parliament and the Welsh Assembly and it is the system explained in the White Paper" (*Hansard*, H.L. Vol. 592, col. 208).

Subss. (3) to (6)
In allocating the seats to persons following the calculations, persons already returned are disregarded. Subsection (5) provides for their removal from the list in order to preclude any argument that, when a Member loses his or her seat through failure to take the oath or by disqualification, the presence of their name on the list would entitle them to be returned to the Scottish Parliament again. Subject to disregarding those already returned, persons from a party's regional list are selected according to the order in which they appeared in the list. If a party's list is exhausted, its success up to that point brings the penalty of its being disregarded from that point, so presumably parties will ensure that their lists are long enough for the possibility not to arise.

Subss. (7) to (9)
These provide for the situation arising, in the course of calculations, of two or more parties or individual candidates having the same regional figure. In that situation, a seat should be allocated to each, except where that process would result in the return of too many candidates, in which event subs. (8) provides for an adjustment to the calculations to be used as a tie-breaker, with recourse to the drawing of lots if there is still deadlock, according to subs. (9). These provisions were added or amended by Sched. 2 of the Scottish Parliament (Elections etc.) Order 1999 (S.I. 1999 No. 787), made under s.12 of this Act.

Vacancies

Constituency vacancies

9.—(1) Where the seat of a constituency member is vacant, an election shall be held to fill the vacancy (subject to subsection (4)).

(2) The date of the poll shall be fixed by the Presiding Officer.

(3) The date shall fall within the period of three months—

(a) beginning with the occurrence of the vacancy, or

(b) if the vacancy does not come to the notice of the Presiding Officer within the period of one month beginning with its occurrence, beginning when it does come to his notice.

(4) The election shall not be held if the latest date for holding the poll would fall within the period of three months ending with the day on which the poll at the next ordinary general election would be held (disregarding section 2(5)).

(5) For the purposes of this section, the date on which a vacancy is to be treated as occurring shall be determined under standing orders.

(6) A person may not be a candidate at such an election if he is a member of the Parliament or a candidate in another election to fill a vacancy.

DEFINITIONS
"constituency": s.126(1).
"the Parliament": s.126(1).
"Presiding Officer": s.19.
"standing orders": s.126(1).

GENERAL NOTE
This section is related to the other sections dealing with elections and, along with the next, provides for the filling of vacancies in the membership of the Parliament. This section applies to vacancies in the constituency member element.

Vacancies may arise through the death of a member, or through resignation (see s.14) or disqualification (see ss.15–18). If, during the lifetime of a Parliament, a vacancy occurs in its constituency membership, a by-election must be held to fill that vacancy unless the latest date for holding the by-election (calculated in accordance with subs. (3)) would fall within the three month period preceding the next ordinary general election (see s.2).

The date of the poll in the by-election is to be fixed by the Presiding Officer and is to be within three months of the vacancy occurring (as determined by standing orders) or (if this is more than a month later than its occurrence) of its coming to the notice of the Presiding Officer. By contrast, there is no equivalent time-limit for the holding of by-elections to fill vacancies in the House of Commons (although the Recess Elections Act 1975 (c.66) provides a means by which the issue of a writ could be required during a recess). The difference may be attributed to the fixed-term duration of the Scottish Parliament and its much smaller membership than the Commons.

When by-elections are held under this section, the simple majority electoral system will apply (s.1(2)); the franchise will be as defined in s.11; and other rules concerning the conduct of the elections (which may be varied for the purpose of by-elections) will be as provided for in s.12.

Subs. (2)

The fact that it is the Presiding Officer who is under a duty to fix the date of the by-election will, along with subs. (3), prevent the timing of by-elections being influenced by considerations of party political advantage. By contrast, when a vacancy arises in the House of Commons while it is in session, although it is the Speaker who authorises the issue of a writ for the by-election, the warrant for its issue is made on the order of the House, and by convention the necessary motion is moved by the Chief Whip of the party which held the seat before the vacancy occurred. It appears that under subs. (2), the Presiding Officer may fix the date for the by-election whether the Scottish Parliament is in session or not.

Subs. (3)

It might be assumed that, normally, vacancies would come immediately to the Presiding Officer's attention. However, special provision is made here in case, exceptionally, they do not. Perhaps a vacancy arising might not come to notice immediately in a recess, or conceivably a member (for example, on a climbing or waterborne activity) might disappear, without its being known for some time whether he or she is dead.

Subs. (4)

For the limited period involved, it is thought justifiable to leave constituents unrepresented by any constituency member, rather than have the cost and trouble of an election, for the sake of filling a seat for a short term, given that a general election is imminent.

Subs.(5)

For the provision made currently, see the Standing Orders, Rule 1.5.

Subs. (6)

Existing members of the Parliament, however returned, may not stand in a by-election under this provision. Nor may persons who are candidates for another vacancy (which replicates the rule for general elections in s.5(2)).

Regional vacancies

10.—(1) This section applies where the seat of a regional member is vacant.

(2) If the regional member was returned as an individual candidate, or the vacancy is not filled in accordance with the following provisions, the seat shall remain vacant until the next general election.

(3) If the regional member was returned (under section 8 or this section) from a registered political party's regional list, the regional returning officer shall notify the Presiding Officer of the name of the person who is to fill the vacancy.

[1](4) The regional returning officer shall ascertain from that party's regional list the name and address of the person whose name appears highest on that list ("the first choice") and shall take such steps as appear to him to be reasonable to contact the first choice to ask whether he will—

(a) state in writing that he is willing and able to serve as a regional member for that region; and

(b) deliver a certificate signed by or on behalf of the nominating officer of the registered party which submitted that regional list stating that he may be returned as a regional member from that list.

[2](4A) Where—

within such period as the regional returning officer considers reasonable—

    (i) he decides that the steps he has taken to contact the first choice have been unsuccessful; or

    (ii) he has not received from that person the statement and certificate referred to in subsection (4) above; or

(b) that person has—

    (i) stated in writing that he is not willing to serve as a regional member for that region; or

    (ii) failed to deliver the certificate referred to in subsection (4)(b) above,

the regional returning officer shall repeat the procedure required by subsection (4) above in respect of the person (if any) whose name and address appears next in that list ("the second choice") or, where sub-paragraph (a) or (b) of this subsection applies in respect of that person, in respect of the person (if any) whose name and address appear next highest after the second choice in that list and the regional returning officer shall continue to repeat the procedure until the regional returning officer has notified the Presiding Officer of the name of the person who is to fill the vacancy or the names in the list are exhausted.

[1](5) Where a person whose name appears on that list provides the statement and certificate referred to in subsection (4) above, the regional returning officer shall notify to the Presiding Officer the name of that person.

[2](5A) Where—

(a) under subsection (4A) above, the regional returning officer has asked a second or other subsequent choice the questions referred to in subsection (4) above; and

(b) the person who was asked those questions on an earlier occasion then provides the statement and certificate referred to in that subsection,

that statement and certificate shall have no effect unless and until the circumstances described in sub-paragraph (a) or (b) of subsection (4A) apply in respect of the second or other subsequent choice.

(6) Where a person's name has been notified under subsection (3), this Act shall apply as if he had been declared to be returned as a regional member for the region on the day on which notification of his name was received by the Presiding Officer.

(7) For the purposes of this section, the date on which a vacancy is to be treated as occurring shall be determined under standing orders.

NOTES

  [1] Substituted by S.I. 1999 No. 787, art. 88. Effective March 11, 1999.

  [2] Inserted by S.I. 1999 No. 787, art. 88. Effective March 11, 1999.

DEFINITIONS

"Presiding Officer": s.19.

"region": s.126(1).

"regional list": s.5(4).

"regional member": s.126(1).

"regional returning officer": s.12(6).

"registered political party": s.5(9).

"standing orders": s.126(1).

GENERAL NOTE

  This is the second section dealing with the filling of vacancies in the membership of the Parliament, this one catering for vacancies in the regional member element. It has to be understood in the context of the earlier provisions for the proportional representation system and regional members and seats, in ss.1(3), 5, 6, 7 and 8.

  This section provides that, when a regional seat is vacated by a member who had been allocated from a registered political party's list, the vacancy should in principle be filled by the next person on the list. The continuing currency of the list for this purpose is ensured by the earlier provision to that effect, s. 5 (5). The regional returning officer has the duty of notifying the appropriate name of the person to fill the vacancy to the Presiding Officer. A problem belatedly recognised was the possibility of persons on a party's list having become turncoats in the interim. Therefore, subss. (4) (4A) (5) and (5A) were inserted in substitution for the previous provisions by article 88 of the Scottish Parliament (Elections etc.) Order 1999 (S.I. 1999 No. 787) to provide a procedure for the regional returning officer to be satisfied, within a period considered reasonable, that the next highest person (or "first choice") is not only still willing and able to serve but also still acceptable to the party, which failing the same criteria of entitlement would be applied to the second choice and further down the list as necessary. However, where the vacancy cannot be filled in this way (for example, because the list is exhausted), the seat will remain vacant until the next general election. Also, when a regional seat is vacated by a member who was returned as an "individual" or independent candidate, the seat remains vacant until the following general election.

These provisions provide a pragmatic solution to a problem or deficiency of list systems as electoral systems. By-elections, at least as normally understood, are impractical or inappropriate means to fill casual vacancies arising under the system. Persons who are notified under these provisions and then deemed to be returned under subs. (6) have not been successful in an election as such, but the logic of the system (in which electors voted for the nominee's party in sufficient numbers) entitles them to replace the former member with almost equivalent justification.

Subs. (7)

For the provision made currently, see the Standing Orders, Rule. 1.5.

Franchise and conduct of elections

Electors

11.—(1) The persons entitled to vote as electors at an election for membership of the Parliament held in any constituency are those who on the day of the poll—

(a) would be entitled to vote as electors at a local government election in an electoral area falling wholly or partly within the constituency, and

(b) are registered in the register of local government electors at an address within the constituency.

(2) A person is not entitled to vote as elector in any constituency—

(a) more than once at a poll for the return of a constituency member, or

(b) more than once at a poll for the return of regional members,

or to vote as elector in more than one constituency at a general election.

DEFINITIONS
"constituency": s.126(1).
"constituency member": s.126(1).
"the Parliament": s.126(1).
"regional member": s.126(1).

GENERAL NOTE
This section provides for the franchise for Scottish Parliament elections. Following the proposal of the White Paper (para. 8.3), the franchise is defined so as to correspond to the franchise for voting in local authority elections. Under these rules, in the Representation of the People Act 1983 (c. 2) as amended, the key determinant of entitlement to vote is residency and electoral registers are complied on a local basis according to that criterion. The inclusion of a person's name on the register for a constituency is a condition precedent for voting, so that persons who are qualified to vote may vote in a constituency provided that their names appear on the register. If, however, their names are not included on the register, they will be unable to vote, even if they should otherwise be entitled to.

The appearance of a person's name on the electoral register is conclusive evidence as to whether the person is resident in the constituency on the qualifying date. The concept of residence may, however, cause difficulties for Electoral Registration Officers, from whose determinations there can be an appeal to the Registration Appeal Court. In case law, the courts have taken a broad, matter-of-fact approach to the concept. It is recognised that a person may have more than one residence and students in university accommodation for part of the year, away from their normal home, provide an example: *Fox v. Stirk* [1970] 2 Q.B. 463. It has also been recognised that the quality of accommodation is irrelevant, so that somebody sleeping in a tent is just as entitled to be registered as someone inhabiting a mansion: *Hipperson v. Electoral Registration Officer for Newbury* [1985] Q.B. 1060.

There are liable to be difficulties when persons have more than one home. By s.5 of the Representation of the People Act 1983, the purpose and circumstances of presence at an address may be taken into account. In one Scottish case, a family's use of a holiday cottage for three and a half months of each year was held to be insufficient to qualify as "residence": *Scott v. Phillips*,1974 S.L.T. 32. In another, use of a property at weekends by a prospective parliamentary candidate in a constituency was held sufficient: *Dumble v. Electoral Registration Officer for Borders*,1980 S.L.T. (Sh. Ct.) 60. In any event, since residence is the key criterion, the rules will have the effect of disqualifying most expatriate Scots, while allowing most non-Scots who live in Scotland to vote.

Since the franchise is defined as it is for local government elections, it means that two categories of persons who may not vote in elections for the House of Commons are included: first, peers eligible to sit in the House of Lords, who are residents; and second, nationals of other European Community states resident in Scotland. Commonwealth citizens and citizens of the Republic of Ireland, if they are residents, will be able to vote, as they are in House of Commons elections. One category of persons enabled to vote in Westminster elections will not be able to vote in elections to the Parliament, however: by the Representation of the People Act 1985 (c. 50) as amended, the normal rule of residence is waived for some expatriate U.K. citizens, but for elections to the Parliament, this category is not being accorded the same generosity.

Further provision about the franchise and its exercise and other electoral matters was made in the Scottish Parliament (Elections etc.) Order 1999 (S.I. 1999 No. 787), under the power given in s.12.

Subs. (2)
Under the foregoing sections, electors have the right to vote in a constituency once for the return of a constituency member and once for the return of a regional member, if there are polls for both. Otherwise, this subsection disentitles electors from plural voting.

Power to make provision about elections

12.—(1) The Secretary of State may by order make provision as to—
(a) the conduct of elections for membership of the Parliament,
(b) the questioning of such an election and the consequences of irregularities, and
(c) the return of members of the Parliament otherwise than at an election.
(2) The provision that may be made under subsection (1)(a) includes, in particular, provision—
(a) about the registration of electors,
(b) for disregarding alterations in a register of electors,
(c) about the limitation of the election expenses of candidates and registered political parties,
(d) for the combination of polls at elections for membership of the Parliament with polls at other elections,
(e) for modifying the application of section 7(1) where the poll at an election for the return of a constituency member is abandoned (or notice of it is countermanded), and
(f) for modifying section 8(7) to ensure the allocation of the correct number of seats for the region.
(3) The provision that may be made under subsection (1)(c) includes, in particular, provision modifying section 10(4) and (5).
(4) An order under subsection (1) may—
(a) apply, with or without modifications or exceptions, any provision made by or under the Representation of the People Acts or the European Parliamentary Elections Act 1978 or by any other enactment relating to parliamentary elections, European Parliamentary elections or local government elections,
(b) modify any form contained in, or in regulations or rules made under, the Representation of the People Acts so far as may be necessary to enable it to be used both for the original purpose and in relation to elections for membership of the Parliament, and
(c) so far as may be necessary in consequence of any provision made by this Act or an order under subsection (1), modify any provision made by any enactment relating to the registration of parliamentary electors or local government electors.
(5) The return of a member of the Parliament at an election may be questioned only under Part III of the Representation of the People Act 1983 as applied by an order under subsection (1).
(6) For the purposes of this Act, the regional returning officer for any region is the person designated as such in accordance with an order made by the Secretary of State under this subsection.

DEFINITIONS
"constituency member": s.126(1).
"enactment": ss.113(6) and 126(1).
"modify": s.126(1).
"the Parliament": s.126(1).
"parliamentary": s.126(1).
"region": s.126(1).
"regional returning officer": s.12(6).
"registered political party": s.5(9).

GENERAL NOTE
This section provides for the conduct of elections to the Scottish Parliament and election campaigns, but does so by enabling provisions rather than through substantive rules. There is an intricate body of rules about the conduct of U.K. parliamentary elections (and what is permitted or not in election campaigns) in the Representation of the People Act 1983 (c.2), as amended. With due modifications, many of the same rules have been applied to other elections such as European Parliament elections. This section allows the adoption or the adaptation of the rules applicable to Westminster, European Parliament or local government elections, within the discretion of the Secretary of State in framing rules for elections to the Parliament.

Under this section, detailed arrangements have been made by the Scottish Parliament (Elections etc.) Order 1999 (S.I. 1999 No. 787).

Subs. (1)
This provides for the scope of the ministerial power to make provisions, on the conduct of elections, on dealing with any election irregularities, and on the return of members as a result of a regional vacancy (as to which the substantive rules are found in s.10). By virtue of s.115 and Sched. 7, any ministerial order under this section will be subject to affirmative resolution procedure in both the House of Commons and the House of Lords. The provisions of this Act on elections are protected from modification by virtue of s.29 and Sched. 4.

Subs. (2)
This further explains the scope of the power, by way of examples, which are not exhaustive. Subsection (2)(c) envisages limitations on election expenditure by candidates and notably allows for the imposition of limits on parties' spending too (as to the latter it seems likely, at the time of writing, to be superseded, if the provisions of the Political Parties, Elections and Referendums Bill become law as expected and effect a consequential repeal). By instance subs.(2)(e), special provision can be made to enable the return of regional members where a poll at a constituency election is abandoned (or notice of it countermanded), notwithstanding s.7(1). By subs. (2)(f), the ministerial orders may make provision to deal with ties in the regional figures, perhaps modifying s.8(7), in order to ensure that the correct number of seats is allocated.

Subs. (3)
The competence to make provisions on the return of members as a result of a regional vacancy, already expressed, extends to the possible modification of s.10 and has been used for that purpose, as noticed above: see General Note to s.10.

Subs. (4)
This supplements the provisions on the scope of the ministerial powers, by confirming that existing statutory rules and procedures for elections of other kinds may be adopted, with or without modification.

Subs. (5)
This provides that the return of a member at an election may be questioned only under an election petition procedure as under the Representation of the People Act 1983 when applied by order to these elections, and so to that extent constrains the ministerial discretion.

Subs. (6)
An order such as mentioned here will not be subject to any approval of the Houses of Parliament or the Scottish Parliament. The Scottish Parliament (Regional Returning Officers) (Scotland) (No.2) Order 1999 (S.I. 1999 No. 829) was made under this provision to designate officials.

Duration of membership

Term of office of members

13. The term of office of a member of the Parliament begins on the day on which the member is declared to be returned and ends with the dissolution of the Parliament.

DEFINITIONS
"the Parliament": s.126(1).

GENERAL NOTE
This section provides precisely for the duration of the term of office of members of the Parliament. The term of office begins on the day that the member is declared to be returned, either as a result of an election or (in the case of regional members returned to fill a vacancy) because the day on which notification is received by the Presiding Officer is to be treated as such, by s.10(6). The term of office ends, normally, when the Scottish Parliament is dissolved under s.2(5) or s.3(2). A person's term might also be ended by death, resignation under s.14, or cessation of membership through disqualification (s.17) or as a consequence of failure to take the required oath (s.84(3)).

Resignation of members

14. A member of the Parliament may at any time resign his seat by giving notice in writing to the Presiding Officer.

DEFINITIONS
"the Parliament": s.126(1).
"Presiding Officer": s.19.

GENERAL NOTE
Here is provided a straightforward method by which members of the Scottish Parliament may resign. The procedure may be contrasted with the situation in the House of Commons, where there is no means to resign as such and the traditional device employed is the appointment of an MP to a disqualifying office, with a few Crown sinecures (such as Bailiff and Steward of the Chiltern Hundreds) maintained for that purpose (see s.4 of the House of Commons Disqualification Act 1975 (c. 24)). When resignation causes a vacancy, the provisions of s.9 (if the member was a constituency member) or of s.10 (if the member was a regional member) come into play.

Disqualification

Disqualification from membership of the Parliament

15.—(1) A person is disqualified from being a member of the Parliament (subject to section 16) if—
  (a) he is disqualified from being a member of the House of Commons under paragraphs (a) to (e) of section 1(1) of the House of Commons Disqualification Act 1975 (judges, civil servants, members of the armed forces, members of police forces and members of foreign legislatures),
  (b) he is disqualified otherwise than under that Act (either generally or in relation to a particular parliamentary constituency) from being a member of the House of Commons or from sitting and voting in it,
  (c) he is a Lord of Appeal in Ordinary, or
  (d) he is an office-holder of a description specified in an Order in Council made by Her Majesty under this subsection.
  (2) An office-holder of a description specified in an Order in Council made by Her Majesty under this subsection is disqualified from being a member of the Parliament for any constituency or region of a description specified in the Order in relation to the office-holder.
  (3) In this section "office-holder" includes employee or other post-holder.

DEFINITIONS
"the Parliament": s.126(1).

GENERAL NOTE
This is the first of four sections dealing with disqualifications from membership of the Parliament. This section establishes that, with a few differences, the grounds on which a person is disqualified from membership of the Scottish Parliament correspond broadly to those applicable to membership of the House of Commons. The section must be read in conjunction with s.16, which sets out some of the differences and provides exceptions and relief from disqualification.
The House of Commons Disqualification Act 1975 (c. 24) disqualifies categories of persons from membership of the House of Commons because they hold offices or employments which are deemed to be incompatible with membership of the House on constitutional grounds. Five categories which are specified in the 1975 Act (judges, civil servants, members of the armed forces, members of police forces and members of foreign legislatures) are equally applicable as disqualifications from membership of the Scottish Parliament (subs. (1)(a)). The judges who are Lords of Appeal in Ordinary (whose inclusion in the House of Commons Disqualification Act 1975 was unnecessary because they were already disqualified as members of the House of Lords)

are specifically disqualified from membership of the Scottish Parliament by subs. (1)(c) above. The House of Commons Disqualification Act 1975 (as amended) also specifies offices and posts which, while they are held, disqualify the holder from the House of Commons (such as Director General of Fair Trading, Governor of the British Broadcasting Corporation, or Procurator Fiscal). The Order in Council power provided in subs. (1)(d) enables Her Majesty in Council to legislate along similar lines for disqualifying offices in connection with the Parliament, and the Scottish Parliament (Disqualification) Order 1999 (S.I. 1999 No.680) did so. By the power provided in subs. (2), Part II of the Order disqualified Her Majesty's Lord-Lieutenants and Lieutenants for associated constituencies and regions only.

The structure of s.15 is such that anyone not disqualified by reference to its provisions is qualified. It is clear, therefore, that there is no residential qualification for membership of the Parliament.

It is also evident that various forms of dual mandate are not prohibited. Section 15 does not prohibit a member of the Scottish Parliament from being a member of the House of Commons or of the European Parliament, or a member of the National Assembly of Wales or of a local authority. Fifteen of the MSPs elected in 1999 were also MPs at the time, and one was a MEP. It is arguable that dual membership is advantageous, for cross fertilisation. However, given the extremely heavy workload involved in a dual mandate and perhaps also given public expectations of their representatives, it is not likely to be a common phenomenon beyond the first term of the Parliament, except perhaps where Scottish Parliament membership and local authority membership are combined. Political parties, in the absence of legislative prohibition, may themselves seek to exclude or discourage dual mandates.

Subs. (1)(b)
Disqualified otherwise than under that Act. There are several other disqualifications which are imported by these words. In outline, they are as follows:
Aliens are disqualified from membership at common law and by the Act of Settlement 1700, s.3, as amended by Sched. 7 of the British Nationality Act 1981 (c. 61). Under the latter provision, citizens of the Republic of Ireland and Commonwealth citizens as defined are not classified as aliens for this purpose. Section 16(2) below also excepts from the definition of aliens for the present purposes citizens of the European Union, provided that they are resident in the U.K.
Persons under 21 years of age are disqualified from membership by the Parliamentary Elections Act 1695, s.7 (applied to Scotland by the Acts of Union in 1707).
Mental illness is a disqualification at common law. There is also a procedure for notification and for vacation of the seat under s.141 of the Mental Health Act 1983 (c. 20), which s.17(4) and Sched. 8 below apply to membership of the Scottish Parliament.
Undischarged bankrupts, by s.427 of the Insolvency Act 1986 (c. 45), the provisions of which are also attracted under s.17(4) below to membership of the Scottish Parliament.
Convicted prisoners serving a sentence of more than one year's detention (or an indefinite sentence) in the U.K. or Ireland are disqualified by the Representation of the People Act 1981 (c. 34).
Persons guilty of corrupt or illegal election practices under the Representation of the People Act 1983 (c. 2) as amended may in consequence be disqualified from being elected for a period, either generally or for a particular constituency.
Senior local government officials who hold "politically restricted" posts are disqualified and barred from being candidates under the authority of the Local Government and Housing Act 1989 (c.42). The restrictions were extended to the Scottish Parliament in respect of Scottish local authorities by the Local Government Officers (Political Restrictions) Amendment Regulations 1998 (S.I. 1998 No. 3116 (S.188)) and in respect of English by the Local Government Officers (Political Restrictions) (Amendment) Regulations 1999 (S.I. 1999 No. 715).

Exceptions and relief from disqualification

16.—(1) A person is not disqualified from being a member of the Parliament merely because—

(a) he is a peer (whether of the United Kingdom, Great Britain, England or Scotland), or

(b) he has been ordained or is a minister of any religious denomination.

(2) A citizen of the European Union who is resident in the United Kingdom is not disqualified from being a member of the Parliament merely because of section 3 of the Act of Settlement (disqualification of persons born outside the United Kingdom other than Commonwealth citizens and citizens of the Republic of Ireland).

(3) Subsection (4) applies where a person was, or is alleged to have been, disqualified from being a member of the Parliament (either generally or in relation to a particular constituency or region) on any ground other than one falling within section 15(1)(b).

(4) The Parliament may resolve to disregard any disqualification incurred by that person on the ground in question if it considers that—

(a) the ground has been removed, and

(b) it is proper to disregard any disqualification so incurred.

(5) A resolution under this section shall not—

(a) affect any proceedings under Part III of the Representation of the People Act 1983 as applied by an order under section 12, or

(b) enable the Parliament to disregard any disqualification which has been established in such proceedings or in proceedings under section 18.

DEFINITIONS
"constituency": s.126(1).
"the Parliament": s.126(1).
"region": s.126(1).

GENERAL NOTE
This is the second of the four sections dealing with disqualifications from membership of the Parliament. It provides that certain persons are not disqualified and it also provides in certain circumstances for the Scottish Parliament to disregard a disqualification in relation to a particular person.

Subs. (1)
This provision enables two categories of persons who are barred from membership of the House of Commons to be eligible for membership of the Parliament. First, peers and peeresses who may sit in the House of Lords, since they are already members of Parliament, may not sit in the House of Commons. However, apart from the Lords of Appeal in Ordinary, who are excluded by s.15(1) above, they are not to be disqualified from membership of the Parliament. Such persons, if elected, would simply be ordinary members of the unicameral Parliament.

Secondly, some (but not all) priests and clergy are disqualified from the House of Commons by the House of Commons (Clergy Disqualification) Act 1801 or the Roman Catholic Relief Act 1829. These anachronistic and discriminatory exclusions are not applied to membership of the Scottish Parliament.

Has been ordained. This is designed to cover priests in the Roman Catholic Church, to whom s.9 of the Roman Catholic Relief Act 1829 applied; and to cover clergy of the Church of England and the Church of Ireland, to whom the words of s.1 of the House of Commons (Clergy Disqualification) Act 1801 have been held to apply.

Ministers of any religious denomination. This is designed to cover Church of Scotland Ministers, who were specifically included in the disqualifications in s.1 of the House of Commons (Clergy Disqualification) Act 1801. However, the breadth of the phrase used should be adequate to remove any doubts concerning clergy possibly caught by the words of the House of Commons (Clergy Disqualification) Act 1801, the interpretation of which has been problematic.

Subs. (2)
For the House of Commons, U.K. citizenship, citizenship of the Republic of Ireland, or citizenship of a Commonwealth country listed for this purpose is required. Any of these will satisfy for membership of the Parliament. So too will citizenship of another E.C. state, but only when the person concerned is resident in the U.K.

Subss. (3), (4), (5)
These provisions are the counterpart of s.6(2)(3) of the House of Commons Disqualification Act 1975 (c. 24), which permits the House of Commons to direct, by order, that a disqualification or alleged disqualification may be disregarded. Only disqualifications on the ground of incompatible office or employment, falling within s.15(1)(a), (c), or (d) or s.15(2), can be so treated. Like the Commons, the Scottish Parliament may resolve to disregard a disqualification only if the two separate conditions in subs. (4) are satisfied: the Scottish Parliament might, for example, doubt whether the second condition is satisfied and refuse relief except in cases where the disqualification arose merely from inadvertence. Even if the ground for disqualification is removed, a member will by s.17 lose his or her seat if the Scottish Parliament does not grant relief. Under subs. (5), decisions of an Election Court (if and as applied under s.12) or of the Court of Session in proceedings under s.18, will prevail over any resolution of the Scottish Parliament made under this section.

Effect of disqualification

17.—(1) If a person who is disqualified from being a member of the Parliament or from being a member for a particular constituency or region is returned as a member of the Parliament or (as the case may be) as a member for the constituency or region, his return shall be void and his seat vacant.

(2) If a member of the Parliament becomes disqualified from being a member of the Parliament or from being a member for the particular

constituency or region for which he is sitting, he shall cease to be a member of the Parliament (so that his seat is vacant).

(3) Subsections (1) and (2) have effect subject to any resolution of the Parliament under section 16.

(4) Subsection (2) also has effect subject to section 141 of the Mental Health Act 1983 (mental illness) and section 427 of the Insolvency Act 1986 (sequestration etc); and where, in consequence of either of those sections, the seat of a disqualified member of the Parliament is not vacant he shall not cease to be a member of the Parliament until his seat becomes vacant but—

(a) he shall not participate in any proceedings of the Parliament, and

(b) any of his other rights and privileges as a member of the Parliament may be withdrawn by a resolution of the Parliament.

(5) The validity of any proceedings of the Parliament is not affected by the disqualification of any person from being a member of the Parliament or from being a member for the constituency or region for which he purports to sit.

DEFINITIONS
"constituency": s.126(1).
"the Parliament": s.126(1).
"proceedings": s.126(1).
"region": s.126(1).

GENERAL NOTE
This section provides in subs. (1) that where a person disqualified under s.15 is elected to the Parliament, his or her election is void and the seat is vacant; similarly, by subs. (2), if a person becomes disqualified after being elected, he or she ceases to be a member and the seat is vacated by process of law. In either case, these results are subject to there having been no relief from them under s.16. In the cases of disqualification for mental illness or for bankruptcy, these results are also subject to the particular provisions for disqualification and vacation of seats which apply to members of the House of Commons under s.141 of the Mental Health Act 1983 (c. 20) and s.427 of the Insolvency Act 1986 (c. 45) and which are extended to members of the Scottish Parliament by subs. (4). Subsection (4) also provides that, in cases where those provisions apply, disqualification will result in the member's being unable to take part in proceedings for the duration of the disqualification (and may result in withdrawal of other rights and privileges, depending on resolution of the Parliament), but that the seat will not be vacated immediately. Subsection (5) provides that even if a disqualified person has participated in proceedings of the Parliament, their validity may not be questioned for that reason.

Judicial proceedings as to disqualification

18.—(1) Any person who claims that a person purporting to be a member of the Parliament is disqualified or has been disqualified at any time since being returned may apply to the Court of Session for a declarator to that effect.

(2) An application in respect of any person may be made whether the grounds on which it is made are alleged to have subsisted when the person was returned or to have arisen subsequently.

(3) No declarator shall be made—

(a) on grounds which subsisted when the person was returned, if an election petition is pending or has been tried in which the disqualification on those grounds of the person concerned is or was in issue, or

(b) on any ground, if a resolution under section 16 requires that any disqualification incurred on that ground by the person concerned is to be disregarded.

(4) The person in respect of whom an application is made shall be the defender.

(5) The applicant shall give such caution for the expenses of the proceedings as the Court of Session may direct; but any such caution shall not exceed £5,000 or such other sum as the Scottish Ministers may by order specify.

(6) The decision of the court on an application under this section shall be final.

(7) In this section "disqualified" means disqualified from being a member of the Parliament or from being a member for the constituency or region for which the person concerned purports to sit.

DEFINITIONS
"constituency": s.126(1).
"disqualified": subs. (7).
"the Parliament": s.126(1).
"region": s.126(1).
"Scottish Ministers": s.44(2).

GENERAL NOTE
This section is a counterpart to s.7 of the House of Commons Disqualification Act 1975 (c. 24), which gives jurisdiction to the Judicial Committee of the Privy Council to decide questions of disqualification arising under that Act. The Judicial Committee has no jurisdiction to make a declaration on disqualification which arises otherwise than under the House of Commons Disqualification Act 1975 (c. 24), however, whereas there is no comparable limitation under s.18 on the jurisdiction of the Court of Session. Section 7 of the House of Commons Disqualification Act 1975 is otherwise followed in several important respects. Like the Judicial Committee, the Court of Session has jurisdiction whether the grounds of disqualification are alleged to have existed at the time of the election or to have arisen subsequently, subject to the two provisos (contained in subs. (3)) that no declarator may be made where an election petition involving the same ground is pending or has already been tried or where the Scottish Parliament has under s.16 resolved that the disqualification or alleged disqualification should be disregarded.
The section seems to provide a simple alternative to the procedure by election petition under Pt III of the Representation of the People Act 1983 (c. 2), as applied to the Scottish Parliament elections by virtue of the Scottish Parliament (Elections etc.) Order 1999 (S.I. 1999 No. 787) made under s.12, but some differences should be noted. First, election petitions must be presented within 21 days of the return of the election, while under s.18 there is no time limit on the making of applications. Secondly, an election petition must be brought by a registered elector for the constituency in question, by an unsuccessful candidate, or by any person claiming to have been validly nominated as a candidate; while, under s.18, there are no such restrictions (although it is interesting to consider whether the formulation here may still leave room for the imposition of a locus standi requirement by the court). There are, therefore, some significant differences to justify the alternative procedure.

Subs. (3)
The purpose of these provisos is to avoid potential conflicts of jurisdiction.

Subs. (4)
This provides for the person in respect of whom the challenge is raised to defend the application, rather than some other person such as the returning officer.

Subs. (5)
Provision for caution (security) of up to £5000 to be required for the expenses of the application should deter frivolous or vexatious applications, and the maximum amount may be varied by order of the Scottish Ministers. The present maximum sum is the same as an election court may currently order in relation to an election petition.

Subs.(6)
This rules out the possibility of appeal to the House of Lords.

Presiding Officer and administration

Presiding Officer
19.—(1) The Parliament shall, at its first meeting following a general election, elect from among its members a Presiding Officer and two deputies.
(2) A person elected Presiding Officer or deputy shall hold office until the conclusion of the next election for Presiding Officer under subsection (1) unless he previously resigns, ceases to be a member of the Parliament otherwise than by virtue of a dissolution or is removed from office by resolution of the Parliament.
(3) If the Presiding Officer or a deputy ceases to hold office before the Parliament is dissolved, the Parliament shall elect another from among its members to fill his place.
(4) The Presiding Officer's functions may be exercised by a deputy if the office of Presiding Officer is vacant or the Presiding Officer is for any reason unable to act.

(5) The Presiding Officer may (subject to standing orders) authorise any deputy to exercise functions on his behalf.

(6) Standing orders may include provision as to the participation (including voting) of the Presiding Officer and deputies in the proceedings of the Parliament.

(7) The validity of any act of the Presiding Officer or a deputy is not affected by any defect in his election.

DEFINITIONS
"by virtue of": s.126(11).
"functions": s.126(1).
"the Parliament": s.126(1).
"proceedings": s.126(1).
"standing orders": s.126(1).

GENERAL NOTE
Section 19 provides for the election of a Presiding Officer and two deputies by the Parliament from its members and prescribes their term of office; allows the exercise of the Presiding Officer's functions by a deputy when the Presiding Officer is unable to act or that office is vacant; authorises the Presiding Officer to delegate functions to a deputy, subject to standing orders; and envisages that standing orders may provide rules on the participation and voting of these three officers in the proceedings of the Parliament.

According to the White Paper, the intention was that the Presiding Officer "will ensure the efficient conduct and administration of Scottish parliamentary business and chair sessions of that Parliament" (para. 9.5). In some respects, therefore, the Presiding Officer's role is comparable to that of the Speaker in the House of Commons. However, in other respects their duties and powers contrast. There are statutory functions conferred on the Presiding Officer by ss.2, 3 and 9 (in connection with the dates for holding general elections and by-elections), s.10 (receiving notification of the filling of a vacancy in a regional seat), s.14 (receiving notice of a member's resignation), s.21 (membership of the Scottish Parliamentary Corporate Body), s.26 (administering oaths to witnesses before the Parliament), ss.31–35 (in connection with the scrutiny of Bills and the submissions of Bills for the Royal Assent) and ss.45 and 46 (recommending the Parliament's choice of First Minister to Her Majesty and designating another person to exercise the First Minister's functions in certain circumstances). Other functions are assigned under Standing Orders.

Constitutional conventions may be expected to develop concerning the Presiding Officer, but on one matter it was felt safer to legislate. By a Government amendment to Sched. 3, it has to be ensured through Standing Orders that the three persons who hold the office of Presiding Officer or deputy do not all represent the same party.

Subss. (1), (7)
The Parliament is required to elect from its membership a Presiding Officer and two deputies at its first meeting following a general election. As members cannot take part in any proceedings until they have taken the oath of allegiance (s.84(2)), the election has to be subsequent to their discharge of that duty. A defect in the election will not, however, invalidate actions of a Presiding Officer or deputy.

Subss. (2), (3)
The three persons elected under subs. (1) will normally hold their offices until the next such election (at which they might be re-elected if they remain members of the Parliament, or might be replaced), since the dissolution of the Scottish Parliament does not terminate their tenure. Otherwise, a person will cease to hold the office if he or she resigns from it, is removed from it by resolution of the Parliament, or ceases to be a member of the Scottish Parliament otherwise than through a dissolution. On the occurrence of a vacancy before the Scottish Parliament is dissolved, the Scottish Parliament is required to elect a replacement.

Subss.(4), (5)
If the office of Presiding Officer is vacant or the office-holder is for any reason unable to act, the deputies may exercise the Presiding Officer's functions. Besides, a deputy may be authorised by the Presiding Officer to exercise the Presiding Officer's functions, subject to any limitation or restriction on such delegation which might be contained in standing orders. For the provision made currently, see the Standing Orders, Rule. 3.1.

Subs. (6)
The three office-holders are also members of the Parliament. While it is probable that conventional understandings will develop as to their behaviour when acting in the offices of Presiding Officer or deputy, this subsection enables provision to be made in standing orders to regulate their participation in parliamentary business. For the provision made currently, see the Standing Orders, Rules 3.1. and 11.5.

Clerk of the Parliament

[1]**20.**—(1) There shall be a Clerk of the Parliament.

(2) The Clerk shall be appointed by the Scottish Parliamentary Corporate Body (established under section 21).

(3) The Clerk's functions may be exercised by any Assistant Clerk if the office of Clerk is vacant or the Clerk is for any reason unable to act.

(4) The Clerk may authorise any Assistant Clerk or other member of the staff of the Parliament to exercise functions on his behalf.

NOTE
[1] Modified by S.I. 1999 No. 441, art. 2(2). Effective May 6, 1999.

DEFINITIONS
"functions": s.126(1).
"the Parliament": s.126(1).
"staff of the Parliament": Sched. 2, para. 3.

GENERAL NOTE
This section should be read in conjunction with s.21 and Sched. 2. The section provides for the appointment of an official as Clerk of the Scottish Parliament by the Scottish Parliamentary Corporate Body (which is established under s.21). The person appointed becomes a member of the staff of the Parliament, whose terms and conditions of appointment are determined by the Scottish Parliamentary Corporate Body (Sched. 2, para. 3). It is also provided that the Clerk may delegate functions to an Assistant Clerk or other member of the staff of the Scottish Parliament (subs. (4)) and that an Assistant Clerk may exercise the Clerk's functions in the event of a vacancy in the office or the Clerk's being for any reason unable to act (subs. (3)). Specific mention is made of the Clerk, because the Clerk is the senior official and performs an important role in the functioning of the Parliament. The Clerk has statutory functions under s.24 (summoning of witnesses and documents) and s.28 (adding the date of royal assent to Acts) and other functions are assigned under Standing Orders.

Scottish Parliamentary Corporate Body

[1]**21.**—(1) There shall be a body corporate to be known as "The Scottish Parliamentary Corporate Body" (referred to in this Act as the Parliamentary corporation) to perform the functions conferred on the corporation by virtue of this Act or any other enactment.

(2) The members of the corporation shall be—
(a) the Presiding Officer, and
(b) four members of the Parliament appointed in accordance with standing orders.

(3) The corporation shall provide the Parliament, or ensure that the Parliament is provided, with the property, staff and services required for the Parliament's purposes.

(4) The Parliament may give special or general directions to the corporation for the purpose of or in connection with the exercise of the corporation's functions.

(5) Any property or liabilities acquired or incurred in relation to matters within the general responsibility of the corporation to which (apart from this subsection) the Parliament would be entitled or subject shall be treated for all purposes as property or (as the case may be) liabilities of the corporation.

(6) Any expenses of the corporation shall be payable out of the Scottish Consolidated Fund.

(7) Any sums received by the corporation shall be paid into that Fund, subject to any provision made by or under an Act of the Scottish Parliament for the disposal of or accounting for such sums.

(8) Schedule 2 (which makes further provision about the corporation) shall have effect.

NOTE
[1] Modified by S.I. 1999 No. 441, art. 6. Effective May 6, 1999.

DEFINITIONS
"by virtue of": s.126(11).

"enactment": ss.113(6) and 126(1).
"functions": s.126(1).
"the Parliament": s.126(1).
"Presiding Officer": s.19.
"property": s.19.
"standing orders": s.126(1).

GENERAL NOTE
This section is linked to the previous two in making arrangements for the administration of the Scottish Parliament and to Sched. 2 which makes more detailed provision. Section 21 provides for the establishment, members and functions of the Scottish Parliamentary Corporate Body. As the Scottish Parliament itself is not a body corporate, it is convenient for there to be created a body with legal powers to hold property, make contracts and handle money, and bring or defend legal proceedings by or against the Scottish Parliament (as to which, see s.40). The thinking behind these provisions has been influenced by similar arrangements made in respect of the U.K. Parliament. The House of Commons (Administration) Act 1978 (c. 36) established the House of Commons Commission as a corporate body for the purpose of appointment of staff. The Parliamentary Corporate Bodies Act 1992 (c. 27) established Corporate Officers for each House at Westminster, with powers to hold property and to enter into contracts.

Subs. (1)
This establishes the Scottish Parliamentary Corporate Body (which may also be referred to as "the Parliamentary corporation") and provides that it is to perform the functions conferred on it under this Act or any other enactment.

Subs. (2)
This provides for the membership of the Scottish Parliamentary Corporate Body, in a way intended to ensure that the Scottish Parliament is closely involved. For the provision made currently, see the Standing Orders, Rules 3.6-3.10.

Subs. (3)
This sets out the Scottish Parliamentary Corporate Body's main functions. For greater detail, see Sched. 2.

Subs. (4)
This enables the Scottish Parliament to give directions to the Scottish Parliamentary Corporate Body.

Subs. (5)
This provides for property (including contractual rights) and liabilities of the Scottish Parliament which relate to matters within the general responsibility of the Scottish Parliamentary Corporate Body to be treated as property or liabilities of the Scottish Parliamentary Corporate Body. Modification of subs. (5) by the Scottish Parliament is permitted under Sched. 4.

Subss.(6), (7)
These link the financial arrangements for the Scottish Parliamentary Corporate Body to the provisions for the Scottish Consolidated Fund in Pt III of the Act, expenses being payable out of the Fund and receipts being payable into it, subject to any provision for the disposal of, or accounting for, such money being made by an Act of the Scottish Parliament.

Subs. (8)
This gives effect to the further provisions in Sched. 2. See the General Note to Sched. 2 below.

Proceedings etc.

Standing orders

22.—(1) The proceedings of the Parliament shall be regulated by standing orders.

(2) Schedule 3 (which makes provision as to how certain matters are to be dealt with by standing orders) shall have effect.

DEFINITIONS
"proceedings": s.126(1).
"the Parliament": s.126(1).
"standing orders": s.126(1).

GENERAL NOTE
In the White Paper, the Government said that it would "provide a framework for the Scottish Parliament, but it will be left open to that Parliament itself to develop procedures which best

meet its purposes" (para. 9.11). In accordance with those intentions, this Act provides for certain matters only, although perhaps in total they number more than might have been expected.

First, it may be noticed that some matters are mandatory. Some minimum or necessary requirements regarding the content of standing orders are insisted on. Five such matters are mentioned in Sched. 3 (the preservation of order; the holding of proceedings in public; the reporting and publishing of proceedings; the composition of committees; and procedure on Bills involving Crown interests). But there are several other provisions which mandate the content of standing orders, such as those in ss.9(5), 10(7), 21(2), 31(3), 36(1), 36(4), 36(5), 70(3) and 74(5).

Secondly, this Act mentions other matters about which standing orders may make provision. Again, some of these are mentioned in Sched. 3 (exclusion from proceedings, and withdrawal of rights and privileges, of members; conditions of attendance of members of the public at proceedings; appointment of sub-committees; and exclusion of non-members from the proceedings of committees and sub-committees). Besides, there are several other provisions which allow for standing orders to be made discretionarily, such as those in ss.19(5), 19(6), 23(8), 26(1), 26(4), 27(1), 31(3) and 36(3).

Beyond these cases, what this provision does is to give the Scottish Parliament authority to regulate its proceedings by standing orders as it chooses and important matters such as the dates and times of sitting, the general disposition of functions and the committee structure, are at its discretion.

The Secretary of State for Scotland established, before this Act was passed, a Consultative Steering Group, on which the four main political parties in Scotland were all represented, under the chairmanship of the Minister of State, Mr. Henry McLeish. It was charged with considering the operational needs, working and procedures of the Scottish Parliament and reporting with proposals to inform the preparation of draft standing orders for possible adoption by the Parliament. Its work was of considerable assistance, and the Parliament was able to adopt Standing Orders in December 1999. For the provisions which are current, see the Standing Orders. See also the General Note to Sched. 3 below.

Power to call for witnesses and documents

23.—(1) The Parliament may require any person—

(a) to attend its proceedings for the purpose of giving evidence, or

(b) to produce documents in his custody or under his control,

concerning any subject for which any member of the Scottish Executive has general responsibility.

(2) Subject to subsection (3), the Parliament may impose such a requirement on a person outside Scotland only in connection with the discharge by him of—

(a) functions of the Scottish Administration, or

(b) functions of a Scottish public authority or cross-border public authority, or Border rivers functions (within the meaning of section 111(4)), which concern a subject for which any member of the Scottish Executive has general responsibility.

(3) In relation to the exercise of functions of a Minister of the Crown, the Parliament may not impose such a requirement on—

(a) him (whether or not he continues to be a Minister of the Crown), or

(b) a person who is or has been in Crown employment, within the meaning of section 191(3) of the Employment Rights Act 1996,

unless the exercise concerns a subject for which any member of the Scottish Executive has general responsibility.

(4) But the Parliament may not impose such a requirement in pursuance of subsection (3) in connection with the exercise of functions which are exercisable—

(a) by the Scottish Ministers as well as by a Minister of the Crown, or

(b) by a Minister of the Crown only with the agreement of, or after consultation with, the Scottish Ministers.

(5) Subsection (4)(b) does not prevent the Parliament imposing such a requirement in connection with the exercise of functions which do not relate to reserved matters.

(6) Where all the functions of a body relate to reserved matters, the Parliament may not impose such a requirement on any person in connection with the discharge by him of those functions.

(7) The Parliament may not impose such a requirement on—

(a) a judge of any court, or

(b) a member of any tribunal in connection with the discharge by him of his functions as such.

(8) Such a requirement may be imposed by a committee or sub-committee of the Parliament only if the committee or sub-committee is expressly authorised to do so (whether by standing orders or otherwise).

(9) A person is not obliged under this section to answer any question or produce any document which he would be entitled to refuse to answer or produce in proceedings in a court in Scotland.

(10) A procurator fiscal is not obliged under this section to answer any question or produce any document concerning the operation of the system of criminal prosecution in any particular case if the Lord Advocate—

(a) considers that answering the question or producing the document might prejudice criminal proceedings in that case or would otherwise be contrary to the public interest, and

(b) has authorised the procurator fiscal to decline to answer the question or produce the document on that ground.

DEFINITIONS
"body": s.126(1).
"cross-border public authority": s.88(5).
"document": s.126(1).
"functions": s.126(1).
"member of the Scottish Executive": s.44(1).
"Minister of the Crown": s.126(1).
"the Parliament": s.126(1).
"proceedings": s.126(1).
"reserved matters": Sched. 5.
"Scotland": s.126(1)(2).
"Scottish Administration": s.126(6).
"Scottish Ministers": s.44(2).
"Scottish public authority": s.126(1).
"standing orders": s.126(1).
"tribunal": s.126(1).

GENERAL NOTE
This is the first of four consecutive sections concerning the Parliament's power to call for witnesses and documents. At Westminster, the Houses of Parliament, as the High Court of Parliament, have similar powers to ordinary courts of law and have an inherent jurisdiction to deal with breaches of privilege or any offences to their authority, dignity or functioning which they classify as contempt of Parliament, whether committed by members or outside persons. How far the Scottish Parliament could competently assert similar powers within its authority to make procedural rules is doubtful and the safer course is found in reliance on explicit statutory provision. Here there are specific provisions for summoning witnesses: the Scottish Parliament is given power to require persons to attend to give evidence or produce documents in their custody or control, in defined circumstances. There are procedural requirements in s.24 and ancillary powers in ss.25 and 26. These powers are appropriate on constitutional grounds, given the expectation that the Scottish Parliament and its committees should have the ability to investigate, question and scrutinise the work of the Scottish Executive and other bodies and to hold the Scottish Executive to account for its actions. The provisions here are liable to be supplemented by standing orders and constitutional conventions are likely to develop concerning accountability. While s.23 defines the circumstances in which persons may be required to give evidence, it will of course be perfectly possible for persons to give evidence on invitation when not required, if they agree to do so.

Subs. (1)
This and the following provisions may appear slightly obscure, but represent an attempt to state in ordinary language what it is that the Scottish Parliament may require somebody to give evidence about. The key determinant is set out here in (perhaps deceptively) simple words, so that the question turns on whether the evidence concerns a "subject for which any member of the Scottish Executive has general responsibility". The formulation will obviously cover functions conferred on Scottish Ministers under or by virtue of other provisions in the Act, such as ss.53, 63, 89 and 111, the retained functions of the Lord Advocate and the functions of the First Minister. However, the formulation is also intended to cover areas which fall within the responsibility of the Scottish administration because they are devolved. The Lord Advocate, explaining the provision, gave this example:

"For example, in the field of health there are large areas of activity where Ministers' specific functions, as such, are limited, as matters stand, to making appointments to the bodies which exercise direct responsibility for the delivery of services. We would not want there to be any room to argue that the Parliament's power to hold inquiries into health issues was limited to the narrow 'functions' of making appointments. It should be able to investigate such issues, without facing artificial constraints. Similar issues could arise in areas where local authorities are responsible for the actual delivery of services". (*Hansard*, H.L. Vol. 593, cols. 1918–1919).

Subs. (2)
For those outside Scotland, the Scottish Parliament can only impose a requirement in connection with a person's discharge of functions of the Scottish Administration, or functions of a Scottish public authority or cross-border public authority, or Borders rivers functions, where those functions concern a subject for which any member of the Scottish Executive has general responsibility. So, for example, a representative of a cross-border public authority can be summoned only in connection with the functions of that body relating to devolved matters, because only those functions concern a subject for which a member of the Scottish Executive has general responsibility.

Subss. (3), (4), (5), (6)
The Parliament will have very limited powers to impose a requirement to give evidence on Ministers of the Crown and their civil servants. In relation to the exercise of ministerial functions, a Minister of the Crown or civil servant may only be called to answer for the exercise of such a function in so far as it concerns a subject for which a member of the Scottish Executive has general responsibility. So far a devolved subject where a UK Minister exercises functions with the agreement of or after consultation with the Scottish Ministers, then a requirement to attend may be imposed. The particular purpose behind the protection given is to avoid the problem of "double accountability", so that individuals do not find themselves answerable to two different parliamentary bodies at once. The protection is extended to former Ministers and civil servants. In effect, the Scottish Parliament cannot impose requirements on a former Minister of the Crown or civil servant in relation to the exercise of ministerial functions, if it cannot impose such a requirement on the current Minister or his civil servants. By subs. (6), persons discharging functions of bodies, all the functions of which relate to reserved matters, may not be required to give evidence in relation to those functions.

Subs. (7)
The Parliament's powers in this matter do not extend to judges of any court (including the European Court of Justice or the European Court of Human Rights), or to members of tribunals which adjudicate in legal proceedings as regards the tribunal functions.

Subs. (8)
For the power to make standing orders, see s.22. For provision regarding committees made currently, see the Standing Orders, Rule 12.4.

Subs. (9)
The Scottish courts recognise various privileges such as the privilege against self incrimination and privileges in connection with litigation, and witnesses in the Parliament are entitled to the same privileges.

Subs. (10)
The independence of the Lord Advocate in decision-making is carefully preserved in this Act (see s.48) and there are restrictions on the accountability of the Lord Advocate and the Solicitor General for Scotland to the Scottish Parliament (see s.27(3)). This provision empowers the Lord Advocate effectively to extend a privilege to a procurator fiscal in relation to withholding evidence concerning the prosecution system in any particular case where he or she considers that its disclosure would be contrary to the public interest.

Witnesses and documents: notice

24.—(1) A requirement under section 23 shall be imposed by the Clerk giving the person in question notice in writing specifying—
  (a) the time and place at which the person is to attend and the particular subjects concerning which he is required to give evidence, or
  (b) the documents, or types of documents, which he is to produce, the date by which he is to produce them and the particular subjects concerning which they are required.
(2) Such notice shall be given—
  (a) in the case of an individual, by sending it, by registered post or the recorded delivery service, addressed to him at his usual or last known address or, where he has given an address for service, at that address,
  (b) in any other case, by sending it, by registered post or the recorded delivery service, addressed to the person at the person's registered or principal office.

DEFINITIONS
"Clerk": s.20 and Sched. 2, para. 3.
"documents": s.126(1).

GENERAL NOTE
   This sets out the arrangements for the Clerk of the Parliament to give written notice when the Scottish Parliament exercises its power to call for witnesses and documents under s.23, and sets out requirements in relation to service of notices. See further the Standing Orders, Rule 12.4.

Subs. (1)
   The wording of (b) is clumsy, not to say ungrammatical. The intention behind it is presumably to allow specification of documents by reference to subject matter as an alternative to, or in addition to, specification of particular documents.

Witnesses and documents: offences

   25.—(1) Any person to whom a notice under section 24(1) has been given who—
   (a) refuses or fails to attend proceedings as required by the notice,
   (b) refuses or fails, when attending proceedings as required by the notice, to answer any question concerning the subjects specified in the notice,
   (c) deliberately alters, suppresses, conceals or destroys any document which he is required to produce by the notice, or
   (d) refuses or fails to produce any such document,
      is guilty of an offence.
   (2) Subsection (1) is subject to sections 23(9) and (10) and 27(3).
   (3) It is a defence for a person charged with an offence under subsection (1)(a), (b) or (d) to prove that he had a reasonable excuse for the refusal or failure.
   (4) A person guilty of an offence under this section is liable on summary conviction to a fine not exceeding level 5 on the standard scale or to imprisonment for a period not exceeding three months.
   (5) Where an offence under this section which has been committed by a body corporate is proved to have been committed with the consent or connivance of, or to be attributable to any neglect on the part of—
   (a) a director, manager, secretary or other similar officer of the body corporate, or
   (b) any person who was purporting to act in any such capacity,
      he, as well as the body corporate, is guilty of that offence and liable to be proceeded against accordingly.

DEFINITIONS
"proceedings": s.126(1).

GENERAL NOTE
   This is the third of four sections concerning the power to call for witnesses and documents. Persons competently summoned commit a summary offence (for which they may be fined or imprisoned for up to three months) if they refuse or fail without statutory justification (by s.23(9) or (10) or s.27(3) or reasonable excuse to attend or co-operate as required. Subsection (5) makes provision for the commission of the offence by a body corporate.
   The creation of offences dealt with in the ordinary courts would tend to suggest that the Scottish Parliament (even if it has the power, which is doubtful) is not intended to ape the Houses of Parliament in exercising an independent penal jurisdiction where outside persons are concerned.

Witnesses and documents: general

   26.—(1) The Presiding Officer or such other person as may be authorised by standing orders may—
   (a) administer an oath to any person giving evidence in proceedings of the Parliament, and
   (b) require him to take the oath.
   (2) Any person who refuses to take an oath when required to do so under subsection (1)(b) is guilty of an offence.

(3) Subsection (4) of section 25 applies to an offence under subsection (2) as it applies to an offence under that section.

(4) Standing orders may provide for the payment of allowances and expenses to persons—

(a) attending proceedings of the Parliament to give evidence, or

(b) producing documents which they have been required or requested to produce,

whether or not in pursuance of a notice under section 24(1).

(5) For the purposes of sections 23 to 25 and this section, a person shall be taken to comply with a requirement to produce a document if he produces a copy of, or an extract of the relevant part of, the document.

DEFINITIONS
"document": s.126(1).
"the Parliament": s.126(1).
"Presiding Officer": s.19.
"proceedings": s.126(1).
"standing orders": s.126(1).

GENERAL NOTE
This is the fourth section on witnesses and documents and has ancillary provisions. Persons giving evidence in proceedings of the Scottish Parliament may be required to take an oath and refusal constitutes a summary offence. Allowances and expenses may be payable to persons giving evidence or producing documents, subject to provision in standing orders. For provisions made currently in the Standing Orders, see Rules 2.6 and 12.4.

Subs. (1)
Note that the requirement to take the oath may be applied to persons attending by invitation to give evidence as well as those required to attend by a notice issued under s.24. Affirmation will be an alternative to taking an oath: as this is provided for by the Oaths Act 1978 (c. 19), it does not have to be expressly stated.

Subss. (2), (3)
Refusal to take an oath when required is made an offence, under the same terms as the offence created by s.25.

Subs. (4)
This allows for standing orders to provide for the payment of expenses and allowances to persons giving evidence or producing documents and again not only to persons required to do so under s.23. See Standing Orders, Rules 2.6 and 12.4.

Subs. (5)
This provides that production of a copy of a document suffices for compliance.

Participation of the Scottish Law Officers

27.—(1) If the Lord Advocate or the Solicitor General for Scotland is not a member of the Parliament—

(a) he may participate in the proceedings of the Parliament to the extent permitted by standing orders, but may not vote, and

(b) standing orders may in other respects provide that they are to apply to him as if he were such a member.

(2) Subsection (1) is without prejudice to section 39.

(3) The Lord Advocate or the Solicitor General for Scotland may, in any proceedings of the Parliament, decline to answer any question or produce any document relating to the operation of the system of criminal prosecution in any particular case if he considers that answering the question or producing the document—

(a) might prejudice criminal proceedings in that case, or

(b) would otherwise be contrary to the public interest.

DEFINITIONS
"document": s.126(1).
"the Parliament": s.126(1).
"proceedings": s.126(1).

Scotland Act 1998

"standing orders": s.126(1).

GENERAL NOTE

This section is part of the set dealing with the proceedings of the Scottish Parliament and concerns the roles of the Lord Advocate and the Solicitor General for Scotland in that body. It should be read in conjunction with other provisions on membership of the Parliament and on offices and some which refer specifically to these office holders, as noted below.

Subss.(1), (2)

The Lord Advocate and the Solicitor General for Scotland are appointed under s.48, effectively being selected by the First Minister, who must make recommendations to Her Majesty for appointments and dismissals, with the agreement in either case of the Parliament. Persons appointed to these offices may be, but need not be, elected members of the Parliament. Section 39(8) provides that, for the purpose of the rules on members' interests, the holders of these offices will be subject to the same rules as members, even if they are not members. In other respects, if an appointee is a member of the Parliament, the normal rules apply; whereas, if an appointee is not a member, he or she may not vote in the Parliament, but may however participate in proceedings and in other respects be treated as if a member, in both cases as permitted by standing orders. For the provision made currently, see the Standing Orders, Rule 4.5.

Subs. (3)

The Lord Advocate and the Solicitor General for Scotland have various functions. An important capacity of the Lord Advocate is to act as head of the systems of criminal prosecution and investigation of deaths in Scotland. Section 48(5) ensures that decisions in this capacity will continue to be taken independently and s.29(2)(e) makes it out with the competence of the Scottish Parliament to legislate to remove the Lord Advocate from this capacity. How far the principle of independence in decision-making need or does imply a diminution of accountability to others for decisions is, in the abstract, more debatable, but this subsection is one of a number of provisions which are liable to limit questioning and scrutiny of decisions. Subsection (3) allows the Lord Advocate or the Solicitor General for Scotland to decline to answer or provide information to the Scottish Parliament about prosecutions in particular cases when they consider that it might be prejudicial to the proceedings to do so or would otherwise be contrary to the public interest. Section 23(10) allows the Lord Advocate to embargo a procurator fiscal's evidence to the Scottish Parliament on similar grounds. Besides, s.23(9) enables the withholding of evidence from the Parliament which might be withheld from a court, for example on grounds of public interest immunity, and Sched. 3 requires that standing orders should include a provision to prevent conduct which would constitute a contempt of court.

Legislation

Acts of the Scottish Parliament

28.—(1) Subject to section 29, the Parliament may make laws, to be known as Acts of the Scottish Parliament.

(2) Proposed Acts of the Scottish Parliament shall be known as Bills; and a Bill shall become an Act of the Scottish Parliament when it has been passed by the Parliament and has received Royal Assent.

(3) A Bill receives Royal Assent at the beginning of the day on which Letters Patent under the Scottish Seal signed with Her Majesty's own hand signifying Her Assent are recorded in the Register of the Great Seal.

(4) The date of Royal Assent shall be written on the Act of the Scottish Parliament by the Clerk, and shall form part of the Act.

(5) The validity of an Act of the Scottish Parliament is not affected by any invalidity in the proceedings of the Parliament leading to its enactment.

(6) Every Act of the Scottish Parliament shall be judicially noticed.

(7) This section does not affect the power of the Parliament of the United Kingdom to make laws for Scotland.

DEFINITIONS

"Clerk": s.20 and Sched. 2, para. 3.
"the Parliament": s.126(1).
"proceedings": s.126(1).
"Scotland": s.126(1), (2).
"Scottish Seal": s.2(6).

GENERAL NOTE

Lawmaking by legislation constitutes one of the chief functions of the Scottish Parliament, although it does not exhaust its functions. This is the first of a set of sections concerning aspects

35

of the legislative role, especially as regards the Parliament's powers (and limits and controls over them) and, to an extent, its procedures. The general provisions in this section vary from the uncontentious and formal to the controversial and highly significant.

Subs. (1)
Here the general power to legislate is conferred on the Parliament, with the important proviso that it is subject to provisions in the following section, which delimits its legislative competence. Here too it is provided that laws made by the Scottish Parliament are to be known as Acts of the Scottish Parliament. Pending any replacement by the Scottish Parliament, provision has been made for the numbering, citation and interpretation of Acts of the Scottish Parliament by the Scotland Act 1998 (Transitory and Transitional Provisions) (Publication and Interpretation etc. of Acts of the Scottish Parliament) Order 1999 (S.I. 1999 No. 1379).

Subs. (2)
There is also laid down an official terminology for proposed Acts which, as at the U.K. Parliament, are to be known as Bills. Bills will become law as Acts of the Scottish Parliament when they are passed by the Scottish Parliament (which may include reconsideration after the initial passing, and possibly amendment before final approval, under s.36) and receive the Royal Assent. Since Her Majesty is part of the Parliament of the U.K. (or the Queen in Parliament) but will not be part of the Scottish Parliament, the function of Royal Assent is arguably even more formal in this situation. Certainly, the expectation implied is that the Sovereign is subject to a constitutional convention in this regard (presumably involving advice of the First Minister, although one wonders about the potential for conflicting advice to be offered).

Subss. (3), (4)
These provide for the method of signifying Royal Assent: for Letters Patent under the Scottish Seal, see s.38 and note thereto, and the Scottish Parliament (Letters Patent and Proclamations) Order 1999 (S.I. 1999 No.737). The beginning of the day on which it is signified is treated as marking the receipt of Royal Assent (which is equivalent to the rule for Acts of the U.K. Parliament, under s.4 of the Interpretation Act 1978 (c. 30)). The Clerk of the Scottish Parliament is responsible for adding the date of Royal Assent to Acts.

Subs. (5)
This provision may be viewed alongside several others which create statutorily for the Scottish Parliament some elements of parliamentary privilege comparable to, if less extensive than, the privileges enjoyed by the Houses at Westminster. Consider also ss.22, 23–26, 39, 41, 42 and 85, and the restrictions on proceedings against the Parliament in s.40.
This provision may also be compared to several others which seek to protect actions against legal challenges notwithstanding claims of disqualification or invalidity or defects in procedures. See ss.1(4), 17(5), 19(7), 50, 69(3).
Along with s.22 and other provisions, this carries the clear implication that the Scottish Parliament will be the master of its own procedures. Beyond that, as explained by Lord Sewel for the Government: "The intention is that that provision should have the effect that an Act of the Scottish Parliament may not be challenged on any procedural grounds. In that respect, it is intended to make the position of an Act of the Scottish Parliament similar to that of an Act of the U.K. Parliament . . . [and] in a different position from subordinate legislation which can be challenged on the basis that the procedure prescribed for making the subordinate legislation has not been complied with." (*Hansard*, H.L. Vol. 593, col. 1946).
In so far as it is effective, therefore, the provision should result in something equivalent to the "enrolled Act rule" applicable to Acts of the U.K. Parliament, as shown in cases such as *Pickin v. British Railways Board* [1974] A.C. 765. The provision seems apt to preclude challenges on the basis that standing orders or procedural rules of the Scottish Parliament have not been followed. However, the effect of the provision in certain instances may be more doubtful. For example, what if the "invalidity in the proceedings" related to a matter on which this Act imposes requirements (such as with regard to stages of Bills, by s.36, or as to consent when there are Crown interests involved, by Sched.3)? The courts necessarily retain the power to identify what is or is not an "Act of the Scottish Parliament", and it may be argued on analogy with *Anisminic Ltd v. Foreign Compensation Commission* [1969] 2 A.C. 147 that the ouster clause would lose effect if the product in question is not an "Act" at all.

Subs. (6)
This provision ensures that the Parliament's legislation is treated as within the knowledge of courts in the United Kingdom, without evidence being given of it. The equivalent rule for Acts of the U.K. Parliament is in the Interpretation Act 1978, s.3.

Subs. (7)
The White Paper stated that "the U.K. Parliament is, and will remain sovereign in all matters" and "Westminster will be choosing to exercise that sovereignty by devolving legislative responsibilities to a Scottish Parliament without in any way diminishing its own powers. The Government recognise that no U.K. Parliament can bind its successors" (para. 4.2). This provision translates that orthodox theory of the legislative supremacy of the U.K. Parliament into statutory expression.

The provision has been inserted partly for the avoidance of doubt, because legally it is otiose. As Lord Hope of Craighead, a former Lord President of the Court of Session, noted, "it simply states the obvious", since the basic principle as he understood it was that "the Parliament at Westminster cannot abandon its own sovereignty" (*Hansard*, H.L. Vol. 592, col. 796).

However, the subsection was also insisted on for its symbolic and defining characteristics. As was explained for the Government, "in making such an arrangement it is important to capture in the Bill the essence of devolution as opposed to some other model such as, perhaps, federalism" (*Hansard*, H.L. Vol. 593, col. 1950). For that reason, the Government resisted amendments which would have narrowed the scope of the affirmation to reserved matters, against the view expressed by Lord Steel of Aikwood that: "As worded at present, it is provocative and, indeed, positively offensive because it almost invites this Parliament to meddle in the future in the law-making of Scotland on those matters which this Bill devolves to Scotland" (*Hansard*, H.L. Vol. 593, col. 1947). In the White Paper, it had been noticed that: "There may be instances (for example, international obligations which touch on devolved as well as reserved matters) where it will be more convenient for legislation to be passed by the U.K. Parliament" (para. 4.4). The Government mentioned that reservation more than once in debates, while attempting to pacify critics with the understanding that, in the words of Lord Sewel, ". . . as happened in Northern Ireland earlier in the century, we would expect a convention to be established that Westminster would not normally legislate with regard to devolved matters in Scotland without the consent of the Scottish Parliament" (*Hansard*, H.L. Vol. 592, col. 791). The "Sewel convention" has since entered the language of Scottish constitutional practice and, when Bills are introduced at Westminster which touch upon matters within the legislative competence of the Scottish Parliament, that Parliament is invited to indicate its consent by approval of a "Sewel motion" to that effect.

Examples so far have been motions in respect of the Representation of the People Bill (SPOR 13 January 2000, col. 187), the Sexual Offences Bill (SPOR 19 January 2000, col.219) the Political Parties, Elections and Referendums Bill (SPOR 9 March 2000, col.647) and the Regulation of Investigatory Powers Bill (SPOR 6 April 2000, col. 1464). The UK Government's commitment to the Sewel convention is now contained in the Memorandum of Understanding (Cm. 4444; SE/99/36 para.13) and developed in Devolution Guidance Note (DGN) 1 "Common Working Arrangements (see also the Scottish Executive's "Guidance Note on Common Working Arrangements"); DGN 10 "Post Devolution Primary Legislation affecting Scotland"; and DGN 13 "Handling of Parliamentary Business in the House of Lords". The UK Government has undertaken to extend the restraint of the Westminster Parliament to Private Members' Bills. For further discussion of the background to these arrangements, see the 4th Report of the H.C. Procedure Committee "The Procedural Consequences of Devolution" (1998-99, H.C. 185).

Special arrangements had to apply to Bills already proceeding through the Westminster Parliament at the time of the Scottish Parliament was established. The Scottish Parliament was invited to consent to the Bills which became the Pollution Prevention and Control Act 1999 (c.24) and the Food Standards Act 1999 (c.28). (See SPOR 9 June 1999, col. 358 where the First Minister made a general statement about Bills in the UK Parliament.)

At Westminster the passing of the Mental Health (Amendment) (Scotland) Act 1999 (c.32) was celebrated as a historic landmark, being potentially the last piece of exclusively Scottish legislation within the competence of the Scottish Parliament to be handled at Westminster (*Hansard*, H.L. 22 October 1999, col. 1380).

Legislative competence

29.—(1) An Act of the Scottish Parliament is not law so far as any provision of the Act is outside the legislative competence of the Parliament.

(2) A provision is outside that competence so far as any of the following paragraphs apply—

(a) it would form part of the law of a country or territory other than Scotland, or confer or remove functions exercisable otherwise than in or as regards Scotland,

(b) it relates to reserved matters,

(c) it is in breach of the restrictions in Schedule 4,

(d) it is incompatible with any of the Convention rights or with Community law,

(e) it would remove the Lord Advocate from his position as head of the systems of criminal prosecution and investigation of deaths in Scotland.

(3) For the purposes of this section, the question whether a provision of an Act of the Scottish Parliament relates to a reserved matter is to be determined, subject to subsection (4), by reference to the purpose of the provision, having regard (among other things) to its effect in all the circumstances.

(4) A provision which—

(a) would otherwise not relate to reserved matters, but

(b) makes modifications of Scots private law, or Scots criminal law, as it
    applies to reserved matters,
is to be treated as relating to reserved matters unless the purpose of the
provision is to make the law in question apply consistently to reserved
matters and otherwise.

DEFINITIONS
"Act of the Scottish Parliament": s.28(1).
"Community law": s.126(9).
"confer": s.126(1)
"the Convention rights": s.126(1).
"enactment": ss. 113 (6), 126(1).
"functions": s.126(1).
"modify": s.126(1).
"the Parliament": s.126(1).
"reserved matters": Sched. 5.
"Scotland": s.126(1), (2).
"Scots criminal law": s.126(5).
"Scots private law": s.126(4).

GENERAL NOTE
Although the law-making powers of the Scottish Parliament are conferred by s.28, it is s.29
which defines the limits of the legislative competence of the Parliament and, therefore, becomes
a provision central to the whole devolutionary scheme. Section 29 is, however, only the first of a
group of provisions and it must be read with Sched. 4 and then with s.30 and Sched.5 to obtain a
full view of the Parliament's powers and the statutory limits imposed upon them. The definition
given by this group of provisions of the "legislative competence" of the Parliament is, in turn,
essential to an understanding of the rules contained in s.31 (Scrutiny of Bills before introduction), s.32 (Submission of Bills for Royal Assent), s.33 (Scrutiny of Bills by the Judicial
Committee), s.35 (Power of the Secretary of State to intervene) and s.98 and Sched. 6 which
provide for the resolution of "devolution issues". Although ss.29, 30 and Scheds 4, 5 are
concerned only with the legislative competence of the Parliament, that definition is then used in
s.54 as the basis of what is there defined as the "devolved competence" of the Scottish Ministers.
For an understanding, therefore, of the executive powers of the Scottish Ministers which are
dealt with in ss.52–58, reference must be made to s. 29 and its dependent provisions.
    The provisions contained in s.29 (and Sched. 4) were quite heavily amended during their
parliamentary passage, but they remain broadly faithful to the scheme of devolution of legislative
power heralded in the White Paper. Paragraph 4.3 recalled that the way in which the Scotland
Act 1978 conferred legislative and executive power was by transferring specifically defined
competences to the new Scottish bodies, whilst leaving all other powers to continue to be
exercised by the Westminster Parliament and U.K. Ministers. The scheme was very complex as it
involved long lists of areas of competence allocated to groups, further refined by reference to
additional lists of existing Westminster statutes. The conclusion drawn in the White Paper was
that this was an inappropriate method for use in the new scheme. The 1978 scheme "would have
required frequent updating and might have given rise to regular legal arguments about whether
particular matters were or were not devolved". That approach, the Government said, was
incompatible with their objective of "ensuring maximum clarity and stability". In this respect they
had reached the same conclusion as the Constitution Unit in *Scotland's Parliament: Fundamentals for a New Scotland Act* (1996), Chaps. 3 and 4.
    It was, therefore, proposed that, following the approach of the Northern Ireland Constitution
Act 1973, there would be a listing of matters reserved to the U.K. Parliament rather than
specifying devolved matters and that is indeed the basis of the scheme now introduced by s.29
and its satellite provisions. It is the "reserved matters" that are listed in Sched. 5 rather than the
powers specifically transferred to the Scottish Parliament. Whether the "clarity and stability"
sought by the Government have been achieved is, however, a matter for debate and will be
resolved only as the devolved system operates in practice. Sceptics have already pointed out that
Sched. 5 has become quite a long and complicated listing of "reserved matters" and the
operation of the rules now contained in Sched. 4 will not be without its own difficulties. Much
will depend upon the emerging relationship between Holyrood and Westminster; the extent to
which the powers of the new Parliament are challenged in the courts; and, when that occurs, the
courts' interpretation of the power-conferring provisions, taking into account the interpretative
aids offered within those provisions themselves and, very importantly, by s.101. That section
invites the narrowest reading possible of any provision of an Act of the Scottish Parliament
which could be read as outside competence. Some of the difficulties raised are discussed in the
General Note to s.101.

Subs. (1)
    This subsection establishes the whole structure of the Act's definition of "legislative
competence". It draws the line by reference not to what the Parliament may do but to what it
may not do. Although amendments were proposed to make this point even clearer (for instance,
by substituting "only to the extent that" for "so far as"), the intention seems clear enough to

enable certain provisions or aspects of provisions to be held to be outside the Parliament's competence while other provisions in the same Act are saved (*c.f.* s.6(1) of the Northern Ireland Act 1998 (c.47) which states: A provision of an Act is not law if it is outside the legislative competence of the Assembly).

Subs. (2)(a)
This paragraph prevents the Parliament from enacting a provision purporting to form part of the law of somewhere other than Scotland or regulating functions exercisable other than "in or as regards Scotland". It should be read with the definition of "Scotland" in s.126(1), *i.e.*, including internal waters and territorial sea; s.126(2) which enables boundaries of internal waters and territorial sea to be determined by Order in Council; and s.30(3) which permits the specification of functions "as being, or as not being, functions which are exercisable in or as regards Scotland".
See the notes on those sections.

Subs. (2)(b)
At the heart of the devolution settlement is the definition of "reserved matters". These are the matters excluded from the legislative competence of the Scottish Parliament and "reserved" instead to the Westminster Parliament.
They also, in consequence, define the limits of the executive power of the Scottish Ministers since, as explained above, their "devolved competence" is defined by reference to the legislative competence of the Scottish Parliament (see s.52, 53 but see also s.63). The concept of "reserved matters" is also very important for the treatment the Scotland Act gives to public authorities in the devolution settlement and, in particular, those which combine responsibilities for reserved and "non-reserved" matters. (See General Note to s.88 which serves as a general introduction to the treatment of public bodies and see also Pt. III of Sched.5). Although the terminology "devolved matters" was used in earlier versions of the Bill, it was deleted at report stage in the House of Lords (*Hansard*, H.L. Vol. 593, col. 1959.)
The points at which "reserved matters" are dealt with are distributed at different points in the Act. In this section, there is subs. (2)(b), (c) and then subss. (3), (4). Important in the interpretation of these provisions are the definitions of "Scots private law" and "Scots criminal law" in s.126(4), (5). Subsections (2)(b) and (c) require reference to Sched. 4 (on the "law on reserved matters", para. 2) and Sched. 5. Then s.30(2) authorises the amendment of Scheds. 4 and 5; and the special interpretation section (s.101) is also important.
Although this note does not attempt to discuss the detailed contents of Sched. 5, it is intended to provide a combined comment on all these closely-related provisions. The starting point is subs. (2)(b) which states, simply enough, that a provision of an Act of the Scottish Parliament is outside the Parliament's legislative competence if "it relates to reserved matters". The term "reserved matters" is not, as such, further defined by the Act. Instead, one turns to Sched. 5 where a list of reserved matters is provided. In Pt. I of Sched. 5, there are "General Reservations" dealt with under the headings: The Constitution, Political Parties, Foreign Affairs, Public Service, Defence and Treason. Then Pt. II contains a much longer list of "Specific Reservations". It is prefaced by three preliminary paragraphs to assist understanding of the structure of the "Sections" of reserved matters and their interpretation. The Sections in Pt. II are grouped under eleven heads:
A. Financial and Economic Matters
B. Home Affairs
C. Trade and Industry
D. Energy
E. Transport
F. Social Security
G. Regulation of the Professions
H. Employment
I. Health and Medicines
J. Media and Culture
K. Miscellaneous
Part III of Sched. 5 also contains five paragraphs of "General Provisions" which deal mainly with the reservation of public bodies. Taking Sched. 5 as a whole, it is intended to give clear guidance, in its definition of reserved matters, to the Parliament, the Presiding Officer, members of the Scottish Executive and, perhaps above all, to the courts who may have to rule on any challenges which arise as to the limits of the legislative competence of the Parliament. The Act does, however, recognise that total clarity of meaning is elusive and it offers certain interpretative guides. The question, when a provision of an Act of the Scottish Parliament is under examination, is whether "it relates to reserved matters". What does "relate to" mean? How is a court to interpret a provision which appears to have both a reserved and a non-reserved aspect to it?
These are questions to which the Act seeks to give a specific answer in terms of s.29(3). There it is stated that the question of whether a provision "relates to a reserved matter is to be determined, subject to subs. (4), by reference to the purpose of the provision, having regard (among other things) to its effect in all the circumstances".
Before commenting on that specific provision, it is important to remember that s.101 may also be relevant. That section (on which see the separate note) requires that a provision which might,

on any ground, be read as outside competence must be "read as narrowly as is required for it to be within competence, if such a reading is possible and is to have effect accordingly." This may serve to save many border-line provisions.

Returning, however, to s.29(3), this lays down a primary test of purpose, having regard to the effect of the provision in all the circumstances. When this test was introduced at committee stage in the House of Lords (*Hansard*, H.L. Vol. 592, col. 818 *et seq.*), the Minister (Lord Sewel) said that it reflected the "respection doctrine" which the courts had developed in dealing with cases arising from Commonwealth constitutions and the Government of Ireland Act 1920. He quoted from Lord Atkin in the Northern Ireland case of *Gallagher v. Lynn* [1937] A.C. 863:

> "It is well established that you are to look at the 'true nature and character of the legislation' . . . the 'pith and substance of the legislation'. If, on the view of the statute as a whole, you find the substance of the legislation is within the express powers, then it is not invalidated if incidentally it affects matters which are outside the authorised field" (at p.870).

Thus, it was intended that any question of whether a provision "relates to" a reserved matter should be determined by reference to its "pith and substance" or its purpose and if its purpose was a devolved one then it would not be outside legislative competence merely because it incidentally affected a reserved matter. A degree of trespass into reserved areas was inevitable because reserved and other areas were not divided into neat watertight compartments.

The Minister went on to explain that a clause which saved provisions which incidentally affected reserved matters (such a clause had been included in earlier versions of the Bill) might not be sufficient. It was necessary instead to insist on the application of a "purpose" test. He took, as an example of an overlapping provision, one which dealt in general with pollution control (an area intended to be devolved) but which, in particular, contained provisions about water pollution from coal-mines or dust from open cast mining. These would affect the reserved matter of coal mining. If the courts were to take the view that the provisions related to a reserved matter, however, it would make a nonsense of the devolution of pollution control. Instead, subs. (3) is intended to help the courts take the view that a provision is for a permitted purpose even though it also affects reserved matters. This could be the case even if the ancillary effects on reserved matters were significant and not merely minor. The Minister mentioned examples in relation to local authorities and the reorganisation of local government by the Parliament. A reorganisation would have ancillary effects on the administration of local authority functions concerning weights and measures, health and safety at work, data protection or housing benefit. These effects, whilst purely ancillary, might be significant. As long as the substantive rules of entitlement to benefit, etc., are not changed, the Scottish Parliament should be free to enact the reorganisation Act for the *purpose* of reorganisation.

It may be commented that, although the difficulties mentioned by the Minister are real and the devices used in the Act may be a useful response, other interpretative difficulties may be generated. The relationship between tests of "pith and substance", "true nature and character" and the "respection doctrine" is a fraught one. (See especially H. Calvert *Constitutional Law in Northern Ireland* (1968) Ch. 11. Calvert appears to have created the terminology of "respection" upon which the Minister relied. See too *R (Hume) v. Londonderry Justices* [1972] NILR 91 and B. Hadfield *The Constitution of Northern Ireland* (1989)) The relationship between those tests and doctrines and the "purpose" test in subs. (3) is also uncertain. The assessment of "purpose" having regard to "effect in all the circumstances" (*c.f.* s.126(3) which refers to "likely effects") may also be not without difficulties. The interpretation of legislation bridging the reserved and devolved areas will certainly be problematic.

There is, however, a special category of overlap between effects on reserved and non-reserved matters which gets special recognition by the Act—in the first instance, by subs. (4). The special case is where a provision of a Scottish Act makes modifications of "Scots private law" or "Scots criminal law". These are two categories defined in s.126(4), (5) and the definitions are not themselves without difficulty. There is, for instance the curiosity of the inclusion of the "judicial review of administrative action" in the "private law" of Scotland. More broadly, the definitions give recognition to some of the major categories of the law (much of it, but not all, "common law" rather than statutory) as they are conventionally recognised by lawyers.

These branches of the law have a special significance in the process of devolution because one of the main points of the exercise is to provide the Scottish legal system with a legislature capable of making changes to the law without recourse to the Westminster Parliament. The White Paper made it clear that, in broad terms, the civil and criminal law of Scotland would be devolved. In terms of the structure of the Scotland Act, they would not be reserved.

However, this is also the cause of difficulty. The division between reserved and non-reserved is largely drawn along lines which recognise different types of governmental responsibility that may be allocated (not necessarily without controversy but ultimately in an intelligible way) on one side or other of the "reserved" line. That is what Sched. 5 does in its listing of reserved matters, although, as already noted, the categorisation may easily produce legal provisions which have a dual aspect and that is what the "purpose" test of subs. (3) is designed to address.

With civil and criminal law the problem is potentially more severe because these are quite different categories which do not, at all, respect the policy-based classification of governmental responsibilities. Criminal law and procedure may be an essential element in the regulation of both reserved and non-reserved matters; the civil law, perhaps above all the law of contract, even more so. If broad changes, perhaps by way of a statutory restatement or codification, of the law were to be made, it is almost inevitable that the boundary between reserved and non-reserved would be crossed.

The response to this dilemma in subs. (4) is to adhere to a purpose test. A provision which would not otherwise be treated as relating to reserved matters but does so as it makes modifications of Scots private law or Scots criminal law will *prima facie* be treated as relating to reserved matters. If, however, the purpose is to make the law apply "consistently" to reserved matters and otherwise, then presumably (but this is not made absolutely clear) it should be treated as not relating to reserved matters. Clearly the primary target is a general enactment making new private law or criminal law rules across the board and the aim is that such an enactment should not be held to be outside the competence of the Parliament. There may, however, be difficulties in the interpretation of "consistently" in this context and there may also be difficulties with the "purpose" of a provision being consistency. Presumably, those promoting a Bill in the Scottish Parliament (see s.31(1)) will go to some trouble to state their purpose in terms of such consistency?

There is, however, a further contribution to the interpretation of "reserved matters" in Sched. 4 to the Act. The general purpose of that Schedule and its increasing size and significance as the Scotland Bill progressed through Parliament are explained in the General Note to Sched. 4 itself. Applied by subs. (2)(c), the Sched. 4 serves to "entrench" against modification by the Scottish Parliament many provisions of the Scotland Act itself and also a list of further "particular enactments". Paragraph 2 of Sched. 4, however, seeks to extend a similar form of protection to the "law on reserved matters". "An Act of the Scottish Parliament cannot modify, or confer power by subordinate legislation to modify, the law on reserved matters" (para. 2(1)). The paragraph defines "the law on reserved matters" to mean "(a) any enactment the subject-matter of which is a reserved matter and which is comprised in an Act of Parliament or subordinate legislation under an Act of Parliament and (b) any rule of law which is not contained in an enactment and the subject-matter of which is a reserved matter". In this context, "Act of Parliament" does not include the Scotland Act itself (para. 2(2)).

The use of Sched. 4 to protect from modification the law on reserved matters may, at first sight, seem strange—stranger even than the use of the Schedule to protect the other enumerated enactments? Reserved matters are already excluded from the Parliament's competence by Sched. 5 and many of the reservations are expressed by reference to the "subject-matter" of particular statutory provisions. That Schedule might be thought sufficient to achieve the restriction of competence that is sought? (See, *e.g.* Lord Clyde at *Hansard*, H.L. Vol. 592, col. 824)

The answer seems to be that the prohibition contained in para. 2(1) has been imposed simply in order to enable the exceptions permitted by para. 2(3), (4) and para. 3, to have effect. (See also the provision made in Pt. III of the Schedule which is dependent upon the terms of Pt. I). Paragraph 2(3) extends the provision made by s.29(4) for the modification of Scots private law or Scots criminal law. Here the purpose is to recognise, as explained by the Minister that it is "important to ensure that the Scottish Parliament can legislate on the general rules of Scots private law and criminal law across the board and without fragmenting the general principles which distinguish Scots law as a separate system of law. The new test in Sched. 4 applies generally. In the case of Scots private and criminal law, however, it applies only to certain specified aspects of private law and to the rules of Scots private and criminal law which are special to reserved matters-those which result in a distinct and separate treatment of a reserved matter" (*Ibid.* col. 821).

Three examples of rules "special to a reserved matter" were suggested:
1. Section 90 of the Copyright, Design and Patents Act 1988 which provides for assignation of copyright.
2. The rule that gaming contracts cannot be enforced as they are *sponsiones ludicrae*.
3. The Proceeds of Crime (Scotland) Act 1995 which provides for confiscation of proceeds of drug trafficking.

On the other hand, an example of rules lacking such a "special" character were those defining how a person may sign a document under Scots law, which may apply to both reserved and devolved areas. The dividing line between the "special" and the "non-special" may not, however, always be easy to discern.

The "specified aspects of private law" are those referred to in para. 2(3)(a), (b), (c), (d), (e) and (4) (interest on sums due in respect of taxes, etc., and obligations of trustees or managers in relation to pension schemes).

Paragraph 3 of Sched. 4, by another limitation on the application of para. 2, states that the bar on modification of the law on reserved matters does not apply to modifications which are incidental to, or consequential on, provision made ... which does not relate to "reserved matters". As explained by the Minister, this could save a provision even if it appears to deal entirely with a reserved matter. This could arise "if there is an Act of the Scottish Parliament about a devolved matter which omits to make a necessary consequential amendment to a reserved matter. It would be possible for an Act of the Scottish Parliament simply to make that "missed consequential". By itself, it would appear to relate to a reserved matter but, when read in the context of the prior Act of the Scottish Parliament, it can be seen to be for the devolved purpose" (*Ibid.* col. 820). That possibility of a later provision being saved by its association with an earlier provision is enacted by the parenthetic phrase in para. 3(1)(a). However, the effect on reserved matters must be not greater than is "necessary to give effect to the purpose of the provision" (para. 3(1)(b). This reasserts a "purpose" test but, at this point, it is qualified by subpara. (2) which requires that the question of what is "necessary" to give effect to the purpose of the original provision must be judged by the extent of the law-making powers of the Scottish Parliament itself and not, for instance, by taking account of the possibility of using the powers of the Westminster Parliament or a Minister of the Crown. "Clearly it is sensible to allow the Scottish Parliament to complete its legislative task" (*Ibid.* col. 822).

Finally, on Sched. 4 in so far as it relates to reserved matters, the rules in Pt. II, para. 7, should be noted. Within the limitations of Pt. I of the Schedule, the restatement of the law is permitted. However, such a restatement will then be treated, where appropriate, as "law on reserved matters" and will, therefore, continue to be subject to the restrictions imposed on the modification of such law.

One last cause of concern may yet be the connections to be drawn between, on the one hand, these and other restrictions in Sched. 4 and, on the other, the more broadly cast restrictions imposed by Sched. 5. It should be remembered that even what is apparently permitted in relation to the "law on reserved matters" by Sched. 4 must also clear the hurdles of the "reserved matters" in Sched. 5 and the "purpose" test in s.29(3).

Subs. (2)(c)

For discussion of the "restrictions in Schedule 4" see, on "the law on reserved matters", the General Note to subs. (2)(b) and, on the remainder, the General Note to the Schedule itself.

Subs. (2)(d)

This paragraph prohibits the Parliament from legislating in a manner which is incompatible with "the Convention rights" or with Community law.

As to Convention rights, it reinforces the position to be established when the Human Rights Act 1998 (c.42) is brought fully into effect. See also ss.57, 100 and 129(2) of this Act and Sched. 4, paras. 1(2)(f), 13(1)(b); Sched. 5 para. 7(2) and Sched, 6 para. 1. The "Convention rights" have the same definition as in the Human Rights Act 1998 (see s.126(1)). The Human Rights Act 1998 defines Acts of the Scottish Parliament as "subordinate legislation" (s.21(1)) and they may be invalidated under that Act if incompatible with the Convention rights. For the handling of "devolution issues" and involvement of the Judicial Committee under the Scotland Act, see Sched. 6.

It should be noted that the restriction in subs. 2(d) does not place the whole field of human rights beyond the competence of the Scottish Parliament. Subject to the restrictions in Sched. 4 (and also in Sched. 5, Head L2.), the Parliament is free to legislate on human rights matters, *e.g.* to establish a human rights commission. Note too that, in the event of a declaration of "incompatibility" of a U.K. Act in an area now within the competence of the Scottish Parliament, it would be for the relevant member of the Scottish Executive to decide whether to make a remedial order (subject to approval in draft by the Scottish Parliament) under s.10 (and Sched. 2) of the Human Rights Act 1998.

As to Community Law, the paragraph reconfirms the overall subordination of domestic law to Community law as defined in s.126(9). Any provision which is incompatible with Community Law is *ultra vires*. Account should also be taken of ss.57, 106 (both in relation to executive functions) and para. 7(2) of Sched. 5 which excepts from the general reservation of foreign affairs "observing and implementing . . . obligations under Community law".

Subs. (2)(e)

This imposes a special form of reservation in relation to the position of the Lord Advocate. See the General Note to s.48.

Subss. (3),(4)

See the General Note to s.29(2)(b) for discussion of these subsections.

Legislative competence: supplementary

30.—(1) Schedule 5 (which defines reserved matters) shall have effect.

(2) Her Majesty may by Order in Council make any modifications of Schedule 4 or 5 which She considers necessary or expedient.

(3) Her Majesty may by Order in Council specify functions which are to be treated, for such purposes of this Act as may be specified, as being, or as not being, functions which are exercisable in or as regards Scotland.

(4) An Order in Council under this section may also make such modifications of—

(a) any enactment or prerogative instrument (including any enactment comprised in or made under this Act), or

(b) any other instrument or document,

as Her Majesty considers necessary or expedient in connection with other provision made by the Order.

DEFINITIONS
"document": s.126(1).
"enactment": ss.113(6), 126(1).
"functions": s.126(1).
"modify": s.126(1).

"prerogative instrument": s.126(1).
"reserved matters": Sched. 5.
"Scotland": s.126(1), (2).

GENERAL NOTE
The significance of "reserved matters" (*i.e.* reserved to Westminster and, therefore, excluded from the legislative competence of the Scottish Parliament) is discussed in the General Note to s.29. Further provision is made by para. 2 of Sched. 4. The list of reserved matters is, however, set out in Sched. 5 and it is this section which gives effect to the Schedule and provides for the amendment of both Sched. 4 and Sched. 5. There is also an important power enabling the specification of functions "exercisable in or as regards Scotland".

Subs. (1)
This subsection provides simply for Sched. 5 to have effect.

Subs. (2)
The White Paper (para. 4.4) made it clear that the boundary between reserved and devolved matters would need "to be adjusted as appropriate". Such an adjustment might be in either direction. The mechanism for this would be an Order in Council approved by both the Westminster and Scottish Parliaments.
This subsection makes the provision necessary to modify Sched. 4 or Sched. 5 for this purpose. By virtue of Sched. 7 the Order in Council must be made using the Type A procedure, *i.e.* requiring the prior approval of a draft of the Order by resolution of both Houses at Westminster and of the Scottish Parliament. See also subs. (4) (authorising the modification of other provisions in this Act and other enactments.)
Although s.113(5) makes provision for the general use of subordinate legislation to modify enactments other than the Scotland Act and s.114(1) provides for the amendment of the Scotland Act 1998 itself (*other than* Scheds. 4 and 5), it was considered important that the power to amend those two Schedules, the "heart of the devolution settlement", should be separately provided. Section 114(3) provides that an Order in Council under this section may have retrospective effect.
The Scotland Act 1998 (Modifications of Schedules 4 and 5) Order 1999 (S.I. 1999 No. 1749) has been made. With effect from July 1, 1999, it adjusted the terms of both Sched. 4 and Sched. 5 to modify the provisions made for financial assistance for political parties (art.2) (see note on s.97); and it made further modifications to Sched. 5 in respect of functions of the Export Credits Guarantee Department (art.3), the interception of communications (art.4), access to information (art.5), and health and safety at work (art.6). See also the Scotland Act 1998 (Modifications of Schedule 4) Order 2000 (S.I. 2000 No. 1831).

Subs. (3)
In terms of s.29(2)(a), it is outside the legislative competence of the Scottish Parliament (and then, by ss.53, 54, outside the devolved competence of the Scottish Ministers) if a provision in an Act of the Parliament "would form part of the law of a country or territory other than Scotland, or confer or remove functions exercisable otherwise than in or as regards Scotland". "Scotland" is defined to include "so much of the internal waters and territorial sea of the United Kingdom as are adjacent to Scotland" (s.126(1)) and power is conferred to determine, by Order in Council "any boundary between waters which are to be treated as internal waters or territorial sea of the United Kingdom, or sea within British fishing limits, adjacent to Scotland and those which are not" (s.126(2)).
However, at a late stage in the progress of the Scotland Bill, the Government announced that, following "careful thought", further flexibility was required in relation to the devolution arrangements for sea-fisheries (*Hansard*, H.L., Vol. 592, col. 835 *et seq.*). This subsection was introduced at that stage. Also introduced were amendments to s.126(1), (2) referred to above and Section C6 (Sea Fishing) in Pt. II of Sched. 5 which makes a specific reservation of the "regulation of sea fishing outside the Scottish zone (except in relation to Scottish fishing boats)". "Scottish fishing boat" is defined to mean "a fishing vessel which is registered in the register maintained under section 8 of the Merchant Shipping Act 1995 and whose entry in the register specifies a port in Scotland as the port to which the vessel is to be treated as belonging". By s.126(1), "the Scottish zone" means the sea within British fishery limits (that is, the limits set by or under section 1 of the Fishery Limits Act 1976) which is adjacent to Scotland".
As explained (*ibid.* col. 838), the intention was to use the division of legal competences to produce greater certainty about the fishing management responsibilities of the respective fisheries Ministers within the U.K. The Scottish Ministers would be responsible for managing fisheries within the Scottish zone and for managing Scottish boats and Ministers of the Ministry of Agriculture Fisheries and Food would be responsible for managing fisheries within the English zone and for managing English boats. Similar combined responsibilities were to apply to Wales and Northern Ireland.
It was acknowledged that the overlapping responsibilities, which this need to regulate both by sea area and by fishing boats produces would open up a possibility that U.K. fishing boats might in future be required to operate under separate licences issued by the fisheries administrations of the different parts of the U.K. The hope was, however, expressed that arrangements on the basis of a single licence would continue to operate.

A related concern (*ibid.*, col. 837) was that of ensuring U.K. compliance with the EC common fisheries policy and the strengthening of s.56 (undertaken at House of Lords report stage), was anticipated—see s.56(2), (3).

Within this strategy of divided overall competencies but the need for the Scottish Parliament and the Scottish Ministers to take responsibility for fisheries in the Scottish zone and for Scottish fishing boats, s.30(3) is designed to ensure that, where necessary, an Order in Council could be used to specify functions (and purposes) which are "exercisable in or as regards Scotland" and thus remove doubt in the interpretation of s.29(2)(a), if that were left unqualified by this order-making power. The use of s.30(3) was intended to make quite clear which functions would be transferred to the Scottish Ministers under s.53 and thus avoid the risk of both Scottish and U.K. Ministers seeking to exercise identical functions. It was anticipated that, although the power would be used principally for fisheries functions, it would have other uses, for example in relation to protection of the marine environment. In addition to clarifying the basis of distribution of existing functions, s.30(3) would also clarify for the future the power of the Scottish Parliament to confer new functions on the Scottish Ministers (*ibid.*, cols. 836–7).

By Sched. 7, an Order in Council under this section attracts the Type A procedure, requiring prior approval as a draft by both Houses at Westminster and by the Scottish Parliament. Subsection (4) enables an Order to amend enactments (including this Act) and s.114(3) permits retrospective effect.

The Scotland Act 1998 (Functions Exercisable in or as Regards Scotland) Order 1999 (S.I. 1999 No. 1748) made extensive provision under s.30 (3), with effect from 30 June 1999. By art. 3 and Sched. 1, functions under 23 listed enactments are specified as being or, as the case may be, not being functions exercisable in or as regards Scotland. Articles 4 and 8 and Sched. 2 make provision in respect of certain functions relating to prisoners. Articles 5, 6, 7 provide for functions (including functions under Community Law) in relation to fisheries, aquaculture, agriculture and marine dredging. The Order should be read with the Scotland Act 1998 (Modification of Functions) Order 1999 (S.I. 1999 No. 1756) made under s. 106.

Subs. (4)

See notes on subss. (2), (3). This permits an Order in Council under those subsections to modify enactments including this Act.

Scrutiny of Bills before introduction

31.—(1) A member of the Scottish Executive in charge of a Bill shall, on or before introduction of the Bill in the Parliament, state that in his view the provisions of the Bill would be within the legislative competence of the Parliament.

(2) The Presiding Officer shall, on or before the introduction of a Bill in the Parliament, decide whether or not in his view the provisions of the Bill would be within the legislative competence of the Parliament and state his decision.

(3) The form of any statement, and the manner in which it is to be made, shall be determined under standing orders, and standing orders may provide for any statement to be published.

DEFINITIONS
"Act of the Scottish Parliament": s.28(1).
"legislative competence": s.29.
"member of the Scottish Executive": s.44(1).
"the Parliament": s.126(1).
"Presiding Officer": s.19.
"standing orders": s.126(1).

GENERAL NOTE

This section adopts into the Scotland Act 1998 a mechanism similar to that deployed in the Human Rights Act 1998 (c.42) where s.19 provides that a Minister "in charge of a Bill" in the Westminster Parliament must make a written statement that the provisions of the Bill are (or, within the scheme of that Act, are not) compatible with the "Convention rights". By the terms of this section in the Scotland Act, the relevant member of the Scottish Executive must state that a Bill would be within the legislative competence of the Scottish Parliament (on which see ss.29–30). The requirement of the formal statement is one of a group of devices intended to ensure that the limits of legislative competence are not breached. See also ss.32–36 and ss.98–103 and Sched. 6.

The section also requires a statement from the Presiding Officer as to whether the provisions of a Bill are within the competence of the Parliament.

Subs. (1)

The requirement of a statement is imposed only on a member of the Scottish Executive and thus applies only to "Executive" Bills and not, *e.g.* to a Member's Bill or a Private Bill in the

Parliament. The concept of a Minister being "in charge of a Bill" is not one which is further explained either in this Act or in the Human Rights Act 1998 but will presumably not be problematic?

For the form of required statement, see subs. (3).

Subs. (2)

This requirement of a decision and statement from the Presiding Officer is in a form not settled until the final stage of the Bill—Consideration of Commons Amendments by the House of Lords (*Hansard*, H.L. Vol. 594, cols. 1171–1175). Originally there had been a requirement of a statement which was expressly stated to be subject to overruling by the Parliament. The House of Lords sought to remove the Parliament's overruling power but, arguing that this might produce an abrupt and anomalous block on the progress of a Bill without recourse to the Judicial Committee, the Government reinstated the more limited role for the Presiding Officer. A negative statement from the Presiding Officer would be a warning to the Parliament but could not block a Bill.

Subs. (3)

Standing orders are required to determine the manner and form of statements under this section and, provision has been made: see the Standing Orders, Rule 9.3. In addition, the Rule requires that a Bill be accompanied by a financial memorandum and also, in the case of an Executive Bill, by explanatory notes and a policy memorandum (in accordance with the recommendations of the Consultative Steering Group).

Submission of Bills for Royal Assent

32.—(1) It is for the Presiding Officer to submit Bills for Royal Assent.

(2) The Presiding Officer shall not submit a Bill for Royal Assent at any time when—

  (a) the Advocate General, the Lord Advocate or the Attorney General is entitled to make a reference in relation to the Bill under section 33,

  (b) any such reference has been made but has not been decided or otherwise disposed of by the Judicial Committee, or

  (c) an order may be made in relation to the Bill under section 35.

(3) The Presiding Officer shall not submit a Bill in its unamended form for Royal Assent if—

  (a) the Judicial Committee have decided that the Bill or any provision of it would not be within the legislative competence of the Parliament, or

  (b) a reference made in relation to the Bill under section 33 has been withdrawn following a request for withdrawal of the reference under section 34(2)(b).

(4) In this Act—

"Advocate General" means the Advocate General for Scotland,

"Judicial Committee" means the Judicial Committee of the Privy Council.

DEFINITIONS
"Advocate General": subs. (4).
"Judicial Committee": subs. (4).
"legislative competence": s.29.
"the Parliament": s.126(1).
"Presiding Officer": s.19.

GENERAL NOTE

This section is one of group intended to ensure that the limits of the legislative competence of the Scottish Parliament laid down in ss.29, 30 and Scheds. 4, 5 are not breached. See also s.31 (Scrutiny of Bills before introduction), ss.33, 34 (Scrutiny by Judicial Committee and ECJ), s.35 (Secretary of State's power to intervene), s.36 (Stages of Bills) and ss.98–103 and Sched. 6 (Devolution issues).

This section provides both that it is the Presiding Officer's responsibility to submit all Bills for Royal Assent and that the Presiding Officer must not submit a Bill for Royal Assent if it may be subject to the scrutiny of the Judicial Committee or the Secretary of State in procedures laid down in ss.33–35.

Subs. (1)

This provides simply for the duty of the Presiding Officer to submit Bills for Royal Assent, on which see also s.28(2)–(4).

Subs. (2)

Section 33 (and also s.34) provides for pre-Assent scrutiny of a Bill by the Judicial Committee (of the Privy Council) and s.35 provides for the Secretary of State to intervene to prohibit the enactment of a Bill in certain circumstances. Those sections lay down timetables according to which their procedures must be triggered and it is the purpose of this subsection to ensure that the Presiding Officer is prevented from 'jumping the gun' by submitting a Bill for Assent before the time limits for possible recourse to and decisions under, ss.33 or 35 have expired. The standard period required to elapse between the 'passing' of a Bill (see ss.28(2), 36(1)) and its submission for Royal Assent is 4 weeks (see ss.33(2), 35(3)) but this period may be shortened if notice is given to the Presiding Officer of an intention not to invoke the procedures under ss.33, 35 by the relevant authorities (see ss.33(3), 35(4), (5)).

It may, however, *be lengthened* if the procedure to refer to the Judicial Committee under s.33 is invoked and their decision is awaited. Subsection (2)(b) requires that submission for Royal Assent be prevented until the reference has been decided or 'otherwise disposed of. It is not stated what other forms of disposal there might be, but presumably one possibility might be disposal following the withdrawal of the reference by the relevant law officer or intimation not to proceed?

Subs. (3)

Paragraph (a) is a necessary adjunct to subs. (2). The intention is to prohibit submission of the Bill for Royal Assent at a time when action might be taken (or is being taken) under ss.33, 35. That is achieved by subs. (2). The Act's scheme is also to prohibit Royal Assent for a Bill in respect of which a 'negative' decision has been made. In the case of an order by the Secretary of State under s.35, that prohibition (subject to the possibility of amendment of the Bill under s.36(4), (5)) is contained in s.35(1) itself.

In the case of a reference to the Judicial Committee under s.33, however, the prohibition is contained in this paragraph. If a Bill or a provision of a Bill is held by the Judicial Committee to be outwith the legislative competence of the Parliament, it cannot be submitted for Royal Assent without amendment. Provision for the amendment of a Bill in these circumstances is made by s.36(4), (5).

Thus the effect of the paragraph is to permit a Bill whose competence is not successfully challenged at this stage in the Judicial Committee to proceed to Royal Assent and to the statute book. It does not, however, prevent the possibility of post-enactment challenge under Sched. 6, but see also s.103(1).

Paragraph (b) is required because of the possibility of an Art. 234 reference from the Judicial Committee to the ECJ. See the General Note to s.34.

Subs. (4)

For the Advocate General, see s.87.

For further discussion of the composition and role of the Judicial Committee; see s.103.

Scrutiny of Bills by the Judicial Committee

33.—(1) The Advocate General, the Lord Advocate or the Attorney General may refer the question of whether a Bill or any provision of a Bill would be within the legislative competence of the Parliament to the Judicial Committee for decision.

(2) Subject to subsection (3), he may make a reference in relation to a Bill at any time during—

(a) the period of four weeks beginning with the passing of the Bill, and

(b) any period of four weeks beginning with any subsequent approval of the Bill in accordance with standing orders made by virtue of section 36(5).

(3) He shall not make a reference in relation to a Bill if he has notified the Presiding Officer that he does not intend to make a reference in relation to the Bill, unless the Bill has been approved as mentioned in subsection (2)(b) since the notification.

DEFINITIONS

"Advocate General": s.32(4).

"by virtue of": s.126(11).

"Judicial Committee": s.32(4).

"legislative competence": s.29.

"the Parliament": s.126(1).

"Presiding Officer": s.19.

"standing orders": s.126(1).

GENERAL NOTE

This is one of a group of sections whose general purpose is to ensure that the Scottish Parliament enacts only legislation which is within its "legislative competence" as defined by ss.29, 30 and Scheds. 4, 5 and to resolve any disputes which may arise about the extent of that competence. Other provisions are s.31 (Scrutiny of Bills before introduction), s.32 (Submission of Bills for Royal Assent), s.35 (Power of Secretary of State to intervene) and ss.98–103 and Sched. 6 (Devolution issues, etc.,).

Questions about the legislative competence of a Bill or Act of the Scottish Parliament may arise in a number of different circumstances. They may, for instance, be raised by ordinary citizens adversely affected by the provisions of an Act of the Parliament once they are brought into operation and these may be dealt with as "devolution issues" under Sched. 6. There is no provision in the Scotland Act for any pre-enactment challenge to a Scottish Bill made by a member of the public.

In s.33, however, the Act does make provision for the pre-enactment testing of the legislative competence of a Bill in the Scottish Parliament on the initiative of one (or more) of the three named law officers. This takes the form of a reference to the Judicial Committee of the Privy Council at the stage after the passing of a Bill by the Parliament itself but before it receives Royal Assent. (For this purpose the submission of a Bill for Assent is required to be delayed, if necessary: see s.32.)

The reference of a Bill may be made by the law officer of the Scottish Executive, the Lord Advocate. A reference by the Lord Advocate is, however, unlikely to arise in relation to one of the Scottish Executive's own Bills although such a reference would be conceivable, *e.g.* to clarify a legal uncertainty, in order perhaps to attempt to forestall a challenge to the Bill in the future, or in consequence of an undertaking made in the course of debate on the Bill. Another possibility for intervention by the Lord Advocate might be in respect of a non-Executive Bill which has succeeded in being passed by the Parliament.

More likely, however, would be a reference by one of the U.K. Government's law officers, the Advocate General or the Attorney General. Much will no doubt depend upon the developing political relationships between the Scottish Executive and the U.K. Government, but conflict between the two as to the legislative competence of the Scottish Parliament has to be a possibility. This was acknowledged in the White Paper which referred to the need for a short delay between the passing of a Scottish Bill and Royal Assent "to ensure that the U.K. Government is content as to *vires*. In the event of a dispute between the Scottish Executive and the U.K. Government about *vires* remaining unresolved, there will be provision for it to be referred to the Judicial Committee of the Privy Council" (para. 4.17). The White Paper also referred to the opportunity for U.K. departments to discuss any concerns they might have about the *vires* of a Bill (and any proposed amendments) with the Scottish Executive at any stage of its passage through the Parliament (para. 4.16) - a position subsequently reinforced by the Memorandum of Understanding and Devolution Guidance Note No.1 on "Common Working Arrangements".

It should also be borne in mind that the U.K. Government may have concerns not just about the *vires* of a Bill but also about the possibility of the need to take action under s.35 (on grounds, *e.g.* of incompatibility with international obligations).

If the Judicial Committee decides that a Bill (or a provision of a Bill) would not be within the Parliament's legislative competence, the Bill must not be submitted for Royal Assent in its unamended form (see s.32(3)). For the procedure for approval in amended form, see s.36(4), (5).

Subs. (1)

This confers the power to refer on the three law officers. For the Judicial Committee itself and the rules regulating its procedures (the Judicial Committee (Devolution Issues) Rules Order 1999 (S.I. 1999 No. 665)), see s.103.

Subss. (2), (3)

These regulate the timing of a reference and provide for a standard period of four weeks from the passing of a Bill (and see s.32). That time limit is again triggered in the event of an "approval" of a Bill under s.36(4), (5). A law officer may intimate to the Presiding Officer an intention *not* to refer a Bill. Such intimation does not, of course, bind other law officers but, if all three (and the Secretary of State under s.35(4)) do notify the Presiding Officer, the Bill could more rapidly proceed to Royal Assent - as was the case, for instance, with the first Bill passed by the Parliament. The Mental Health (Public Safety and Appeals) (Scotland) Act 1999 (asp 1) was passed by the Parliament on 8 September 1999 and received Royal Assent on September 13, 1999. The effect of notification of the Presiding Officer is cancelled if a Bill is approved in amended form under s.36(4), (5).

ECJ references

34.—(1) This section applies where—

(a) a reference has been made in relation to a Bill under section 33,

(b) a reference for a preliminary ruling has been made by the Judicial Committee in connection with that reference, and

(c) neither of those references has been decided or otherwise disposed of.

(2) If the Parliament resolves that it wishes to reconsider the Bill—

(a) the Presiding Officer shall notify the Advocate General, the Lord Advocate and the Attorney General of that fact, and

(b) the person who made the reference in relation to the Bill under section 33 shall request the withdrawal of the reference.

(3) In this section "a reference for a preliminary ruling" means a reference of a question to the European Court under Article 177 of the Treaty establishing the European Community, Article 41 of the Treaty establishing the European Coal and Steel Community or Article 150 of the Treaty establishing the European Atomic Energy Community.

DEFINITIONS
"Advocate General": s.34(4).
"Judicial Committee": s.32(4).
"the Parliament": s.126(1).
"Presiding Officer": s.19.
"reference for a preliminary ruling": subs. (3).

GENERAL NOTE
    This section, which was added to the Bill at report stage in the House of Lords, takes account of the possibility that a reference to the Judicial Committee of the Privy Council under s.33 may lead to a reference by the Judicial Committee for a preliminary ruling under Art.234 (previously Art. 177) of the Treaty Establishing the European Community. This could lead, in turn, to the prospect of a very substantial delay in reaching a decision on the legislative competence of a provision in a Scottish Bill and, therefore, progress towards its enactment.
    The answer provided by this section is that, if the Parliament itself resolves that it wishes to reconsider the Bill, the person who referred it to the Privy Council (whether Advocate General, the Lord Advocate, or Attorney General) must, on notification from the Presiding Officer request the withdrawal of the reference from the ECJ. This then triggers a "reconsideration" stage under s.36(4)(b), (5). See also s.32(3)(b) which prohibits the Presiding Officer from submitting for Royal Assent a Bill which has been withdrawn from an Art. 234 reference under this section and remains unamended.
    Even if such a Bill *is* amended on reconsideration prior to approval, it would remain susceptible to a further reference to the Judicial Committee (see s.33(2)(b)).
    Procedural provision for a reference to the ECJ is made by rule 5.49 in the Schedule to the Judicial Committee (Devolution Issues) Rules Order 1999 (S.I. 1999 No. 665) (see s.103).

Power to intervene in certain cases

35.—(1) If a Bill contains provisions—
(a) which the Secretary of State has reasonable grounds to believe would be incompatible with any international obligations or the interests of defence or national security, or
(b) which make modifications of the law as it applies to reserved matters and which the Secretary of State has reasonable grounds to believe would have an adverse effect on the operation of the law as it applies to reserved matters,
he may make an order prohibiting the Presiding Officer from submitting the Bill for Royal Assent.

(2) The order must identify the Bill and the provisions in question and state the reasons for making the order.

(3) The order may be made at any time during—
(a) the period of four weeks beginning with the passing of the Bill,
(b) any period of four weeks beginning with any subsequent approval of the Bill in accordance with standing orders made by virtue of section 36(5),
(c) if a reference is made in relation to the Bill under section 33, the period of four weeks beginning with the reference being decided or otherwise disposed of by the Judicial Committee.

(4) The Secretary of State shall not make an order in relation to a Bill if he has notified the Presiding Officer that he does not intend to do so, unless the Bill has been approved as mentioned in subsection (3)(b) since the notification.

(5) An order in force under this section at a time when such approval is given shall cease to have effect.

DEFINITIONS
"by virtue of": s.126(11).

"enactment": ss.113(6), 126(1).
"international obligations": s.126(10).
"Judicial Committee": s.32(4).
"legislative competence": s.29.
"the Parliament": s.126(1).
"Presiding Officer": s.19.
"reserved matters": Sched. 5.
"standing orders": s.126(1).

GENERAL NOTE
This section is probably one of the politically most controversial provisions in the Act. It received much attention in the parliamentary debates on the Bill and was amended significantly at Committee stage in both Houses.

The scheme for the devolution of legislative authority to the Scottish Parliament is set out in ss.28–30 and Scheds. 4, 5. The Parliament has the power to legislate for Scotland subject to the restrictions imposed on its legislative competence (s.29) and, in particular, the reservation to the Westminster Parliament of those matters listed in Sched. 5. The Act then provides a number of mechanisms designed to ensure that the Scottish Parliament confines itself to legislating within the defined areas of competence. These are to be found in s.31 (Scrutiny of Bills before introduction), s.32 (Submission of Bills for Royal Assent), s.33, 34 (Scrutiny of Bills by the Judicial Committee and ECJ references) and ss.98–103 and Sched. 6 (Judicial scrutiny including the handling of "devolution issues"). The principle underpinning these mechanisms is that questions of what the Parliament can and cannot do (*i.e.* questions of its legislative competence) are questions ultimately requiring a decision by a court. Such questions may arise in circumstances of political conflict, in particular disagreement between the Scottish Executive or Scottish Parliament on the one hand and the U.K. Government on the other as to the extent of the Parliament's powers. The questions are, however, to be resolved by courts, in particular by judicial review in the Court of Session and will turn on the interpretation by courts of the terms of the Act. Special provision is made for pre-Assent review by the Judicial Committee of the Privy Council and that court is also the court for the final determination of post-Assent "devolution issues" under Sched. 6.

One clear consequence of this scheme of reliance upon courts for the determination of questions of legislative competence is that Ministers of the U.K. Government have no general power to override the legislative power of the Scottish Parliament. U.K. ministers may seek to negotiate with the Scottish Executive and to persuade them not to proceed with Bills of doubtful legislative competence. The U.K. Government's law officers have the power to trigger a pre-Assent reference to the Privy Council and to ensure the determination of a post-Assent devolution issue: but U.K. Ministers have no general power to intervene on political grounds. This general position does, however, have to be qualified in a number of ways:

1. If only as a matter of last resort, it is within the formal competence of the Westminster Parliament (on the initiative of the U.K. Government) to legislate directly for Scotland on any matter, whether by amendment of the Scotland Act itself or otherwise. This is a position reconfirmed by s.28(7).
2. The Act does itself also contain provisions enabling U.K. Ministers to use subordinate legislation to affect the operation of an Act of the Scottish Parliament or to respond to Acts which are, or may be, outside legislative competence and to the "purported" exercise of functions by a member of the Scottish Executive. See ss.104, 107.
3. And, of course, the whole scheme of devolution operates against the background of a relationship between the Scottish and U.K. Governments and Parliaments which may enable the U.K. Ministers to impose some pressure upon the Scottish Parliament not to legislate in ways "unacceptable" to the U.K. Government. The financial dependency of the Scottish Executive (see Pt. III of the Act) may be a factor in this.

What makes s.35 controversial in this context is that it does contain specific powers available to the Secretary of State by which the U.K. Government could prevent the enactment of legislation by the Scottish Parliament in certain circumstances. It is the section which evokes in its critics the spectre of the Secretary of State as Governor General—an image retained from the time of the debates leading to the Scotland Act 1978. A parallel provision enabling the Secretary of State to intervene in relation to the exercise of executive power is contained in s.58.

Section 35 enables the Secretary of State to prohibit the Presiding Officer of the Parliament from submitting a Bill for Royal Assent in the circumstances referred to in subs. (1), *i.e.* where provisions in the Bill would in his belief be "incompatible with any international obligations or the interests of defence or national security", or would have "an adverse effect on the operation of the law as it applies to reserved matters".

Subss. (1), (2)
These contain the power of the Secretary of State referred to. It is, of course, exercisable by *any* Secretary of State and is not, therefore, confined to use by the Secretary of State for Scotland or dependent upon the continued existence of that office. The order to be made attracts Type I procedure under Sched. 7, *i.e.* subject to annulment by resolution of either House of the Westminster U.K. Parliament.

Paragraph (a) of subs. (1) authorises a response in the interests of "defence or national security". These are, in terms of Sched. 5, reserved matters (see Pt. I, para. 9 and Pt. II, Section B8) but that position is reinforced by this additional protection.

The Scottish Parliament is not expressly forbidden to legislate in a manner incompatible with U.K. international obligations (a term which excludes obligations to observe and implement Community law or the Convention rights) and the Government resisted attempts to build in such obligations as a matter of legislative competence. This might have required the courts to decide issues not of domestic law but in the unfamiliar territory of broader international obligations. It should, in passing, be noted that the operation of s.35 is not (unlike s.58) subject to an equivalent modification of effect created by s.106.

Paragraph (b) should be read against the background of the rules regulating the legislative competence of the Scottish Parliament in relation to reserved matters. (See the General Note to s.29.) Despite a general prohibition of legislation in relation to reserved matters, the Scottish Parliament *is* given the power to affect these, if only in an ancillary way. Action in the courts would be uncertain or unavailable to prevent what the Secretary of State is now empowered to believe is "an adverse effect" on the operation of the law as it applies to reserved matters.

Both paragraphs require a statement of reasons (subs. (2)) for the exercise of the power and, in appropriate cases, an order by the Secretary of State could no doubt be made the subject of judicial review, *e.g.* on grounds of irrationality.

Subss. (3)–(5)

These subsections contain provisions equivalent to those made in s.33(2), (3) as to the timing (normally within four weeks of passing of the Bill, but taking account of any reference to the Judicial Committee/approval under s.36(5)) of the Secretary of State's intervention and intimation of intention not to do so. Presumably notification to the Presiding Officer by one Secretary of State binds all—a consideration which may either prompt substantial co-ordination in Whitehall or, on the other hand, routinely result in the delay of Royal Assent to Scottish Bills!

Stages of Bills

36.—(1) Standing orders shall include provision—

(a) for general debate on a Bill with an opportunity for members to vote on its general principles,

(b) for the consideration of, and an opportunity for members to vote on, the details of a Bill, and

(c) for a final stage at which a Bill can be passed or rejected.

(2) Subsection (1) does not prevent standing orders making provision to enable the Parliament to expedite proceedings in relation to a particular Bill.

(3) Standing orders may make provision different from that required by subsection (1) for the procedure applicable to Bills of any of the following kinds—

(a) Bills which restate the law,

(b) Bills which repeal spent enactments,

(c) private Bills.

(4) Standing orders shall provide for an opportunity for the reconsideration of a Bill after its passing if (and only if)—

(a) the Judicial Committee decide that the Bill or any provision of it would not be within the legislative competence of the Parliament,

(b) a reference made in relation to the Bill under section 33 is withdrawn following a request for withdrawal of the reference under section 34(2)(b), or

(c) an order is made in relation to the Bill under section 35.

(5) Standing orders shall, in particular, ensure that any Bill amended on reconsideration is subject to a final stage at which it can be approved or rejected.

(6) References in subsection (4), sections 28(2) and 38(1)(a) and paragraph 7 of Schedule 3 to the passing of a Bill shall, in the case of a Bill which has been amended on reconsideration, be read as references to the approval of the Bill.

DEFINITIONS
"enactment": ss.113(6), 126(1).
"Judicial Committee": s.32(4).
"legislative competence": s.29.
"modify": s.126(1).
"the Parliament": s.126(1).
"standing orders": s.126(1).

GENERAL NOTE
This section serves two main purposes. On the one hand, it lays down (in subss. (1)–(3)) some general rules about the provision to be made in the standing orders of the Scottish Parliament

for the handling of its legislative business. This general part of the section might have been more appropriately located elsewhere in the Act. However, subss. (4)–(6) then make more specific procedural provision directly consequential upon the provisions in ss.31–35 for the scrutiny of Bills, the reference of Bills to the Judicial Committee of the Privy Council (and ECJ) and the Secretary of State's power to intervene.

Subs. (1)

The general power of the Scottish Parliament to make laws, as Acts of the Scottish Parliament, is contained in s.28. That section also provides for proposed Acts to be known as Bills and for a Bill to become an Act when it has been passed by the Parliament and received Royal Assent.

Section 22 and Sched. 3 provide for the Parliament to make standing orders for the regulation of its proceedings. Subsection (1) requires that standing orders must provide for the stages of Bills to include the equivalent of a "second reading" debate at Westminster (*i.e.* on general principles), a "committee stage" for consideration of detail; and a final "third reading" stage at which a Bill may be passed or rejected.

In the Standing Orders made by the Parliament, Chapter 9 contains provisions on Bill Procedures. In particular, Rules 9.5 -9.8 provide for the three stages of Bills required by subs. (1).

Subs. (2)

This is intended to ensure that the Parliament may, if it wishes, depart from the standard procedures laid down in accordance with subs. (1) and adopt an expedited procedure on a particular Bill.

In the Parliament's Standing Orders, Rule 9.21 "Emergency Bills" provides for the expedited procedure which may be proposed for an Executive Bill. The procedure was invoked in respect of the Mental Health (Public Safety and Appeals) (Scotland) Act 1999 (asp 1) and the Census (Amendment) (Scotland) Act 2000 (asp 3).

Subs. (3)

This subsection permits different procedural provision for the three types of Bill mentioned:
  (a) Restating the law—presumably a power extending beyond mere statutory consolidation into "restatement" of the common law. See also Sched. 4, para. 7.
  (b) Repealing spent enactments. See again Sched. 4, para. 7.
  (c) Private Bills.
In the Parliament's Standing Orders, Rule 9.18 makes provision for Consolidation Bills. Where appropriate, a Consolidation Bill may be referred to as a Codification Bill. Rules 9.19 and 9.20 provide for Statute Law Repeals Bills and Statute Law Revision Bills respectively. Rule 9.17 provides for Private Bills and, at the time of writing, includes the provision drawn, perhaps inappropriately, from the Westminster provisional order procedure under the Private Legislation Procedure (Scotland) Act 1936 (c.52), by which Private Bills may be introduced only on March 27 and November 27 in each year. It is to be expected that this rule will soon be replaced.

Subs. (4)

Subsection (4) requires that standing orders provide for the consequences of the use of the three named procedures by the creation of a "reconsideration" stage of a Bill:
  (a) Under s.33(1) (and see also s.32(2)) a reference may be made to the Judicial Committee on the *vires* of a Bill. Such a reference must normally be made within four weeks of the passing of the Bill and subs. (4) now provides for a reconsideration stage if the Bill, or any provision, is held to be outside the legislative competence of the Parliament.
  (b) Under s.34, a reference to the Judicial Committee may be sent on a preliminary reference to the ECJ but subsequently withdrawn by the appropriate Law Officer. Such a withdrawal is to be done on the basis of a resolution by the Parliament to reconsider the Bill for which provision is now made.
  (c) Under s.35, by which the Secretary of State may make an order prohibiting the Presiding Officer from submitting a Bill for Royal Assent in its existing form. Again, standing order provision for reconsideration is required. In the Parliament's Standing Orders, Rule 9.9 makes the required provision for the reconsideration of Bills passed by the Parliament.

Subs. (5)

This reconfirms the necessity, following reconsideration in any (or a combination) of the circumstances in subs. (4), for a "final" stage for approval or rejection of a Bill. It may, of course, not actually be final because a further reference to the Judicial Committee (see s.33(2)(b)) or a further order made by the Secretary of State (s.35(3)(b)) may follow.

Paragraph 5 of Rule 9.9 provides: "After amendments have been disposed of, the Parliament shall consider and decide the question whether to approve the Bill".

Subs. (6)

This is a subsection designed to ensure that references to the "passing" of a Bill in subs. (4) and also in s.28 (Acts of the Scottish Parliament), s.38 (Letters Patent and proclamations) and para. 7 of Sched. 3 (Standing orders in respect of Crown interests) are interpreted to include reference to the "approval" of a Bill following reconsideration under subs. (5).

Acts of Union

37. The Union with Scotland Act 1706 and the Union with England Act 1707 have effect subject to this Act.

GENERAL NOTE

This provision is designed to ensure that neither the Scotland Act 1998 nor legislation or actions authorised under its terms should be vulnerable to challenge on the ground of their inconsistency with the Acts of Union in 1706–07.

The Acts passed by the Scottish Parliament and the English Parliament at that time brought about the union of Scotland with England and Wales and provided for a Parliament of Great Britain. Since then, there have been many repeals and amendments of the provisions in the union legislation. Nonetheless, it is still argued by some that the position in Scots law is that there are a few Articles in the Acts of Union which have a "fundamental" status and are not freely alterable by the U.K. Parliament, a view which was encouraged, if not inspired, by some *obiter dicta* in *MacCormick v. Lord Advocate*,1953 S.C. 396. Accordingly, it has sometimes been argued in litigation in modern times that statutory provisions were incompetent or invalid, as being inconsistent with Articles of the union legislation which (on this argument) has been entrenched against ordinary amendment or repeal. *Gibson v. Lord Advocate*,1975 S.L.T. 134 and *Murray v. Rogers*,1992 S.L.T. 221 provide examples. The courts, however, have not struck down or set aside any provisions on such a ground in any of these cases, and recently Lords of Appeal in the Committee of Privileges of the House of Lords found that the provisions which were to be enacted in the House of Lords Act 1999 (c.34) were not incompetent as being in breach of fundamental law in the union legislation or the agreement on which it was based: *Lord Gray's Motion* 2000 S.C. (H.L) 46.

The creation of a devolved Scottish Parliament does not as such involve any "breach" of the union legislation of 1706–07, which provided for the composition of the new Parliament of Great Britain, but did not, in terms, abolish the Scottish or the English Parliament. However, it is easy to conceive that the Scottish Parliament, in exercise of its powers under the Act, might legislate inconsistently with provisions of the union legislation, or at least might be argued to have done so. So arguments of legal impediment to change might have been expected to be raised, even if we would expect them to be defeated. The prospect induced the insertion of this section, in the hope of precluding the advancement of such arguments. If the union legislation were really unalterable, this provision would be ineffective, whereas its being given effect should go far to settle the argument.

A few provisions of the union legislation are unamendable by the Scottish Parliament (and in subordinate legislation authorised by it), not because they are "fundamental", but by virtue of the limitations on competence in this Act. Thus, under Sched. 4 the provisions in Arts. 4 and 6 of the Union with Scotland Act 1706 and of the Union with England Act 1707, so far as they relate to freedom of trade, are protected from modification and under Sched. 5 aspects of the constitution, including the union of the Kingdoms of Scotland and England, are reserved matters.

Letters Patent and proclamations

38.—(1) The Keeper of the Registers of Scotland shall record in the Register of the Great Seal—

(a) all Letters Patent signed with Her Majesty's own hand signifying Her Assent to a Bill passed by the Parliament, and

(b) all royal proclamations under sections 2(5) and 3(2),

which have passed under the Scottish Seal.

(2) On recording such Letters Patent he shall intimate the date of recording to the Clerk.

(3) Her Majesty may by Order in Council make provision as to—

(a) the form and manner of preparation, and

(b) the publication,

of such Letters Patent and proclamations.

(4) If the First Minister so directs, impressions with the same device as the Scottish Seal shall be taken in such manner, of such size and on such material as is specified in the direction.

(5) Each such impression—

(a) shall be known as a Wafer Scottish Seal, and

(b) shall be kept in accordance with directions of the First Minister.

(6) If a Wafer Scottish Seal has been applied to Letters Patent or a proclamation mentioned in subsection (1), the document has the same validity as if it had passed under the Scottish Seal.

DEFINITIONS

"Clerk": s.20 and Sched. 2, para. 3.
"document": s.126(1).
"the Parliament": s.126(1).
"Scottish Seal": s.2(6).

GENERAL NOTE
This section is consequential upon the provisions for Letters Patent to signify Royal Assent to Bills of the Scottish Parliament (s.28(3)) and for royal proclamations to dissolve the Parliament and require that elections be held (ss.2(5), 3(2)). Instead of such Letters Patent and proclamations passing under the Great Seal of the U.K., it has been considered symbolically appropriate that the Scottish Seal (as defined in s.2(6)) should be employed.

Subs. (1)
This requires that the documents passed under the Scottish Seal in accordance with s.28(3) or s.2(5) or s.3(2) should be recorded in the Register of the Great Seal by the Keeper of the Registers of Scotland.

Subs. (2)
This requires the Keeper to intimate the date of the recording of Letters Patent to the Clerk of the Scottish Parliament. Note that the date of recording in the Register is the date of Royal Assent (s.28(3)) and that the Clerk is required to endorse the date of the Act on the Act of the Parliament in question.

Subs. (3)
This provides that more detailed provision as to the preparation and publication of the relevant Letters Patent and proclamations may be made by Order in Council. The Scottish Parliament (Letters Patent and Proclamations) Order 1999 (S.I. 1999 No.737) made such provision.

Subss. (4), (5), (6)
By these provisions, the First Minister, who is Keeper of the Scottish Seal (s.45(7)), may direct that impressions of the Scottish Seal may be made in a specified manner and kept in accordance with his or her directions. The Wafer Scottish Seal Directions 1999 (S.S.I. 1999 No.130) were made under these powers. The impressions, known as Wafer Scottish Seals, may be used on any Letters Patent signifying Royal Assent to Bills of the Scottish Parliament or any royal proclamations to dissolve the Parliament with the same validity as if it had passed under the Scottish Seal. Without provision for a wafer seal (which is done by embossment with a die), the Scottish Seal would have to be affixed as wax pendant attached by a ribbon, which would be inconvenient and expensive. The provision made is similar to that made by the Great Seal Act 1884 (c.30) for a Wafer Great Seal (of the U.K.).

Members' interests

39.—(1) Provision shall be made for a register of interests of members of the Parliament and for the register to be published and made available for public inspection.

(2) Provision shall be made—

(a) requiring members of the Parliament to register in that register financial interests (including benefits in kind), as defined for the purposes of this paragraph,

(b) requiring that any member of the Parliament who has a financial interest (including benefits in kind), as defined for the purposes of this paragraph, in any matter declares that interest before taking part in any proceedings of the Parliament relating to that matter.

(3) Provision made in pursuance of subsection (2) shall include any provision which the Parliament considers appropriate for preventing or restricting the participation in proceedings of the Parliament of a member with an interest defined for the purposes of subsection (2)(a) or (b) in a matter to which the proceedings relate.

(4) Provision shall be made prohibiting a member of the Parliament from—

(a) advocating or initiating any cause or matter on behalf of any person, by any means specified in the provision, in consideration of any payment or benefit in kind of a description so specified, or

(b) urging, in consideration of any such payment or benefit in kind, any other member of the Parliament to advocate or initiate any cause or matter on behalf of any person by any such means.

(5) Provision made in pursuance of subsections (2) to (4) shall include any provision which the Parliament considers appropriate for excluding from proceedings of the Parliament any member who fails to comply with, or contravenes, any provision made in pursuance of those subsections.

(6) Any member of the Parliament who—

(a) takes part in any proceedings of the Parliament without having complied with, or in contravention of, any provision made in pursuance of subsection (2) or (3), or

(b) contravenes any provision made in pursuance of subsection (4), is guilty of an offence.

(7) A person guilty of an offence under subsection (6) is liable on summary conviction to a fine not exceeding level 5 on the standard scale.

(8) In this section—

(a) "provision" means provision made by or under an Act of the Scottish Parliament,

(b) references to members of the Parliament include references to the Lord Advocate and the Solicitor General for Scotland, whether or not they are such members.

DEFINITIONS

"the Parliament": s.126(1).
"proceedings": s.126(1).
"provision": subs. (8).

GENERAL NOTE

This supplements the rules on the Scottish Parliament's procedures and operation, by obliging the making of detailed provisions so that members of the Parliament work within a regulated framework of rules on members' interests, to ensure propriety in the conduct of business by the Parliament. The Lord Advocate and the Solicitor General for Scotland are counted as members for the purpose of this section (subs. (8)).

The problems of distinguishing between proper and improper influences or pressures and of dealing with the improper were prominent in the House of Commons in the 1990s. When these problems seemed to be at their height, Mr. Major's Government established (in 1994) a Committee on Standards in Public Life, chaired until 1997 by Lord Nolan, to undertake a series of inquiries and recommend reforms. A priority for the Nolan Committee was to make recommendations concerning the enforcement of standards in the House of Commons and the recommendations in the First Report of the Committee on Standards in Public Life, Cm. 2850 (1995) were largely accepted by and implemented in the House.

The Nolan Committee's approach and recommendations undoubtedly helped to shape these provisions on members' interests for the Scottish Parliament. The fact that there are statutory provisions is in itself significant, because it remains open to question whether (in the case of the House of Commons) a system of self-regulation can command sufficient public confidence and respect.

Some requirements are here statutorily imposed on the Scottish Parliament and have to be satisfied by the enactment of legislation, either in Acts of the Scottish Parliament or in subordinate legislation made under them, because of the stipulation in subs. (8)(a). There is nothing to prevent some other, perhaps more procedural, matters being elaborated in standing orders.

Provisions were made initially by the Secretary of State in the form of the Scotland Act 1998 (Transitory and Transitional Provisions) (Members' Interests) Order 1999 (S.I. 1999 No.1350), and it was an alleged breach of a provision there which formed the basis of the unsuccessful petition for interdict in *Whaley v. Lord Watson of Invergowrie*, 2000 S.L.T. 475. As was observed by the Lord President there, section 39 was not the source of that Order, and legislation had not then been enacted to comply with section 39 (which remains the position at time of writing). In due course the Parliament should bring forward its own legislation to replace and develop the existing statutory provisions. The Lord President and Lord Morison emphasised in the case referred to that Standing Orders, adopted by resolution of the Parliament, are not to be counted as legislation. See the Standing Orders, for some further rules regarding members. Rule 1.6 envisages a Code of Conduct to be agreed by the Parliament on the motion from the Standards Committee, and a Code of Conduct for Members was agreed in February 2000 (SP Paper 64).

Subs. (1)

This requires the establishment of a register of members' interests, which must be published and available for public inspection. The definition of financial interests which are required to be registered has to be by legislation (subs. (2)).

Subs. (2)

This also requires legislation to ensure the declaration of financial interests by members of the Parliament before their participation in any proceedings relating to the matter.

Subs. (3)

This enables legislation to prevent or restrict the participation of members in proceedings of the Parliament when they have interests as defined for subs. (2).

Subs. (4)
Another duty is to legislate for a ban on paid advocacy as specified, whether direct or through another member.

Subs. (5)
As provided for in legislation, there may also be provision effectively to suspend members from participation in proceedings (which might extend also to the facilities and privileges afforded to members) as a penalty for contraventions or failure to comply with the requirements imposed under subss. (2) to (4).

Subss. (6), (7)
Alternatively or additionally, contraventions or failure to comply may be treated as an ordinary criminal offence, punishable by fine. Presumably the gravity of the offence will be a factor in determining whether an internal sanction or a criminal charge is more appropriate, or whether a form of double jeopardy is justified. Notice that s.43, annotated below, deals with criminal liability for corruption offences.

Legal issues

Proceedings by or against the Parliament etc

40.—(1) Proceedings by or against the Parliament shall be instituted by or (as the case may be) against the Parliamentary corporation on behalf of the Parliament.
(2) Proceedings by or against—
(a) the Presiding Officer or a deputy, or
(b) any member of the staff of the Parliament,
shall be instituted by or (as the case may be) against the corporation on his behalf.
(3) In any proceedings against the Parliament, the court shall not make an order for suspension, interdict, reduction or specific performance (or other like order) but may instead make a declarator.
(4) In any proceedings against—
(a) any member of the Parliament,
(b) the Presiding Officer or a deputy,
(c) any member of the staff of the Parliament, or
(d) the Parliamentary corporation,
the court shall not make an order for suspension, interdict, reduction or specific performance (or other like order) if the effect of doing so would be to give any relief against the Parliament which could not have been given in proceedings against the Parliament.
(5) References in this section to an order include an interim order.

DEFINITIONS
"the Parliament": s.126(1).
"the Parliamentary corporation": s.21(1).
"Presiding Officer": s.19.
"staff of the Parliament": Sched. 2, para. 3.

GENERAL NOTE
The Scottish Parliament is an unincorporated association, whereas the Parliamentary corporation established under s.21 is a corporate body. The Parliamentary corporation is to be the body which represents the Parliament in all legal proceedings by, or against, the Parliament, by subs. (1) and provisions here are also aimed at preventing action being pursued by the back door, against individuals associated with the Parliament, when in connection with the Parliament.
The general purpose behind subss. (3) to (5) is to provide a broad protection against attempts to interfere with the business of the Parliament through the use of court proceedings. To that end, there is a restriction of the remedies which may be granted, with orders for suspension, interdict, reduction or specific performance (or other like order), including interim orders, being made unavailable, while the option of a declarator is left open. Unlike the U.K. Parliament with its customary privileges, the Scottish Parliament is a statutory body and the availability of declarator means that it is not entirely above the law. However by affording it a measure of protection akin to privilege, the hope is that it will generally be able to go about its business without undue interruption from legal proceedings.
In the interesting and instructive case of *Whaley v. Lord Watson of Invergowrie*, 2000 S.L.T. 475, a majority in the Inner House of the Court of Session refused the petitioners, who were

seeking interim interdict to prevent an MSP (whom they alleged was in breach of statutory provisions on members' interests) from proceeding with a Bill which he was introducing. The court emphasised that the Scottish Parliament was merely a creation of statute, and so had to work within the scope of its powers, although the Lord President and Lord Prosser concluded that the provisions had not been intended to enable members of the public to bring proceedings for interdict to prevent a threatened breach, assuming that there was one. Whereas the Lord Ordinary in the Outer House had dismissed the petition amongst other grounds on the basis of subss. (3) and (4), the Lord President and Lord Morison considered that on the facts of this case an interdict against the first respondent (the MSP, Lord Watson of Invergowrie) could not have the effect of interdicting any wrong by the Parliament, which (as represented by the Parliamentary corporation) was the second respondent. Lord Prosser did not dissent from that analysis on the particular facts, but had some misgivings about it and regarded the scope of subs. (4) as unclear.

The consequences of a court's making a declarator are not entirely clear. According to the Government's spokesman: "It will, of course, be for the Parliament itself to decide how it should react to any such declaration. The Parliament would not be liable for contempt of court if it merely decided to take no action . . ." (*Hansard*, H.L. Vol. 593, col. 2019).

Defamatory statements

41.—(1) For the purposes of the law of defamation—

(a) any statement made in proceedings of the Parliament, and

(b) the publication under the authority of the Parliament of any statement,

shall be absolutely privileged.

(2) In subsection (1), "statement" has the same meaning as in the Defamation Act 1996.

DEFINITIONS
"the Parliament": s.126(1).
"proceedings": s.126(1).
"statement": subs. (2), referring to the Defamation Act 1996 (c.31).

GENERAL NOTE
The privilege of freedom of speech is part of the law and custom of the Westminster Parliament, which was put on a statutory foundation by Art. 9 of the Bill of Rights in 1688. The privilege affords members of the Houses an immunity from being prosecuted or sued in legal proceedings in respect of their participation in the business of the Houses. In the absence of privilege at common law, legislative provision must necessarily be made for the Scottish Parliament to the extent that it is thought appropriate to provide "privileges" of a similar kind. This section and the next may be considered as conferring a form of the privilege of freedom of speech on the Parliament which is, however, more restricted that the Westminster Houses enjoy, being limited to defences against two particular legal wrongs in certain circumstances. The justification of these provisions is found in the belief that it is in the public interest for members of the Parliament to be able to discuss and debate matters freely without fear of legal penalties.

Section 41 is concerned with the law of defamation. The law on defamation in Scotland is broadly similar to the equivalent English law, although there are certain differences (for example, criminal libel no longer exists in Scots law). The provision on extent (s.131) means that this section will have effect in all jurisdictions in the United Kingdom. What it does is to provide a complete defence (absolute privilege) against proceedings for defamation for any statements made in the "proceedings of the Parliament" and for publications of statements made under the Parliament's authority. Its application turns on words and phrases which are more problematical than they first appear, as noted below.

Statement. By s.17 of the Defamation Act 1996 (c. 31) this "means words, pictures, visual images, gestures or any other method of signifying meaning". Thus widely defined, this term seems apt to cover oral and written contributions, printed papers and more besides, which are in "proceedings". The word "publication" is undefined here, but may be widely interpreted, so that "publication . . . of any statement" seems apt to extend also to radio or television broadcasts, for example.

Proceedings of the Parliament. The definition section (s.126) provides only limited guidance. The phrase "proceedings in Parliament" is used in s.13 of the Defamation Act 1996 (c.31), where some instances are given of activities which are to be construed as falling within it for the purpose of that section, although the phrase is not exhaustively defined. The phrase "proceedings in Parliament" is also found in Art. 9 of the Bill of Rights and its employment there to delineate the scope of the privilege of freedom of speech has caused difficulties of interpretation and application. The use of a similar phrase in connection with the Scottish Parliament should not engender difficulties in clear cases such as oral statements in debate or committee or rulings by the Presiding Officer. However, other matters, such as informal conversations and notes or correspondence to or from members, are far from clear for equivalent purposes in the Westminster Parliament. Notwithstanding these uncertainties, the Government's spokesman seemed to imply that the extent of privilege at Westminster was well established and expressed the intention that "the same broad construction" should be placed on the phrase used in this Act

(*Hansard*, H.L. Vol. 592, cols. 1447–1448). Interestingly, however, a different approach was adopted in s.77 of the Government of Wales Act 1998 (c.38), which instances several categories of qualifying communications.

Under the authority of the Parliament. The Scottish Parliament is required to provide for the reporting of proceedings and for the publication of the reports (Sched. 3) and so presumably the official reports which result fall within this phrase, as well as the Parliament's official papers. Broadcasts which are transmitted under and within the authority of the Parliament should also be covered. More widely, the Parliament's Standing Orders also profess that "any statement which is required or authorised to be published in pursuance of these Rules is published under the authority of the Parliament": see the Standing Orders, Rule 14.4. However, again the phrase is liable to give rise to more difficulties than might appear. The passing of the Parliamentary Papers Act 1840 (which includes a similar phrase) was only necessary because of a protracted conflict between the House of Commons and the courts on the extent of privilege in connection with a report ordered by the House, following the decision in *Stockdale v. Hansard* (1839) 9 Ad. & E.1.

Certainly, unofficial reports of the proceedings of the Scottish Parliament or its papers, such as may be provided by newspapers or broadcasters, for example, will not be published "under the authority of the Parliament" and therefore they will be subject to the ordinary law. However, by s.15 and Sched. 1 of the Defamation Act 1996, qualified privilege attaches to a "fair and accurate report of proceedings in public of a legislature anywhere in the world".

Again, as part of the general law, members of the Parliament, when unable to benefit from the defence of absolute privilege here, may not be left defenceless. The defence of qualified privilege should avail for anything done by members in carrying out their duties, provided there is an absence of malice, analogously to *Beach v. Freeson* [1972] 1 Q.B. 14, involving a member of the House of Commons.

Contempt of court

42.—(1) The strict liability rule shall not apply in relation to any publication—

(a) made in proceedings of the Parliament in relation to a Bill or subordinate legislation, or

(b) to the extent that it consists of a fair and accurate report of such proceedings made in good faith.

(2) In subsection (1), "the strict liability rule" and "publication" have the same meanings as in the Contempt of Court Act 1981.

DEFINITIONS
"the Parliament": s.126(1).
"publication": subs. (2), referring to the Contempt of Court Act 1981 (c. 49).
"statement": subs. (2), referring to the Contempt of Court Act 1981 (c. 49).
"subordinate legislation": s.126(1).

GENERAL NOTE
Like s.41, this section may be seen as giving the Scottish Parliament a modified version of the wider immunity which attaches to the U.K. Parliament by virtue of the law of parliamentary privilege, in this instance to afford some exemption from the law of contempt of court.

The exemption is limited to some kinds of business in the Scottish Parliament (and extends secondarily to the fair and accurate reporting of these kinds) and does not apply to others, which will therefore be fully subject to the law of contempt of court. Thus it appears that if there were potentially prejudicial comment on legal proceedings which were sub judice in the course of a debate on a Bill, this provision would probably apply to shield the speaker (and reporters thereof), whereas if the same comment were made in the course of a general debate or in questions to ministers, there would be no protection. However, beyond clear cases, there may sometimes be difficulty in interpreting the scope of the exemption. It is debatable whether, for example, a pre-legislative committee is engaged in "proceedings . . . in relation to a Bill" or whether questions to ministers about their actions under delegated powers are "proceedings . . . in relation to subordinate legislation".

The immunity is also limited in so far as it is only the strict liability form of contempt from which there is exemption. The strict liability form of contempt is defined in the Contempt of Court Act 1981 (c. 49), but as the provisions of the 1981 Act were untidily grafted on to the common law (which was not entirely superseded), disapplication of the offence is less than total, even for the restricted category of parliamentary business to which it is intended to apply.

As the Parliament is required in standing orders to provide for "preventing conduct which would constitute . . . contempt of court" and to provide for "a sub judice rule" (Sched. 3, para. 1), the hope must be that instances of contemptuous conduct (or conduct which would be contemptuous but for the exemption) will be infrequent anyway.

Corrupt practices

43. The Parliament shall be a public body for the purposes of the Prevention of Corruption Acts 1889 to 1916.

DEFINITIONS
"the Parliament": s.126(1).

GENERAL NOTE
This section makes the members and staff of the Scottish Parliament subject to liability for the criminal offences in the Public Bodies Corrupt Practices Act 1889 (c. 69), the Prevention of Corruption Act 1906 (c. 34) and the Prevention of Corruption Act 1916 (c. 64), which are together known as the Prevention of Corruption Acts 1889 to 1916, by ensuring that the Parliament is a public body for their purpose. Those Acts penalise the corrupt making or accepting of payments, in money or kind, for activity (or forbearance) in connection with a public body's business. This section might be considered in conjunction with the more precise rules concerning members' interests and associated prohibitions and offences in s. 39.

The reform and modernisation of the offences contained in the Prevention of Corruption Acts 1889 to 1916 is under active consideration and was the subject of a report by the Law Commission: *Legislating the Criminal Code: Corruption* (1998), Law Commission No. 248, H.C. 254. The application of the present law to members of the Houses of Parliament at Westminster is unclear. In the meantime, even if the formulations of offences in the above Acts are not entirely satisfactory, this provision ensures that the offences are applicable to the Scottish Parliament in principle.

PART II

THE SCOTTISH ADMINISTRATION

GENERAL NOTE
Part II of this Act makes provision for establishing the executive branch of government and confers powers upon it. In line with the proposals made in the White Paper, the essential elements are; (1) the Scottish Executive, headed by the First Minister and otherwise consisting of Ministers drawn from the Parliament and the Law Officers; (2) a number of junior Ministers, also drawn from the Parliament; (3) non-ministerial office-holders; and (4) staff who are members of the Home Civil Service. Together these constitute the Scottish Administration and, although not all the rules are specified in the legislation and there is scope for innovation, the assumption is that the system broadly replicates the "Westminster model" of government. Although it was a document which focused primarily on the way the Parliament would operate, the report of the Consultative Steering Group on the Scottish Parliament "Shaping Scotland's Parliament" (Scottish Office, December 1998) contained many recommendations relating to the procedures for the appointment of members of the Executive and for their accountability to the Parliament and its Committees which have been influential.

Ministers and their staff

The Scottish Executive

44.—(1) There shall be a Scottish Executive, whose members shall be—
(a) the First Minister,
(b) such Ministers as the First Minister may appoint under section 47, and
(c) the Lord Advocate and the Solicitor General for Scotland.
(2) The members of the Scottish Executive are referred to collectively as the Scottish Ministers.
(3) A person who holds a Ministerial office may not be appointed a member of the Scottish Executive; and if a member of the Scottish Executive is appointed to a Ministerial office he shall cease to hold office as a member of the Scottish Executive.
(4) In subsection (3), references to a member of the Scottish Executive include a junior Scottish Minister and "Ministerial office" has the same meaning as in section 2 of the House of Commons Disqualification Act 1975.

DEFINITIONS
"members of the Scottish Executive": subss. (1), (4).
"Ministerial office": subs. (4).

GENERAL NOTE

Subs. (1)
As anticipated in para. 2.6 of the White Paper, the Scottish Executive comprises the First Minister (for whom further provision is made by ss.45, 46), Ministers appointed by the First Minister (s.47) and the two Scottish Law Officers (s.48). Junior Scottish Ministers appointed

under s.49 are not treated as "members of the Scottish Executive" except where special provision is made to that effect. (See subs. (4) and s.81(5).). In practice, those appointed as junior ministers have been given the title "deputy minister".

An important early development has been the emergence of the Scottish Cabinet as a product of the initial coalition. Membership of the Cabinet extends to all members of the Scottish Executive, with the exception of the Solicitor General. (See the Scottish Executive: A Guide to Collective Decision Making (August 1999); and the Scottish Ministerial Code (August 1999).)

The inclusion of the Law Officers in the membership of the Scottish Executive was not uncontroversial in debate - see, *e.g. Hansard*, H.C. Vol. 306, col. 161 *et seq.* It was argued that their independence might be put at risk. This is a matter which has remained controversial. See, *e.g.* the debates in the Parliament referred to in the note on s.48(1).

Subs. (2)

The collective term "the Scottish Ministers" is used to denote the body on whom statutory functions are conferred (s.52) and especially as the body to whom functions formerly exercised by Ministers of the Crown are transferred (ss.53, 63). Any member of the Scottish Executive, including the Law Officers, may exercise functions conferred on the Scottish Ministers (ss.52(3), 59(4)), except that functions vested in the First Minister, or in the Law Officers alone ("retained functions" of the Lord Advocate) may be exercised by those persons only.

Subss. (3), (4)

In response to concerns expressed earlier, these subsections were inserted at third reading in the House of Lords (*Hansard*, H.L. Vol. 594, cols. 539–541). The Government conceded that it would be inappropriate for the same person to hold office both as a U.K. Minister and a member of the Scottish Executive—although a similar argument had not been accepted in relation to Wales. Section 2 of the House of Commons Disqualification Act 1975 (c.24) defines "Ministerial office" by reference to the list of offices set out in Sched. 2 to that Act.

The First Minister

45.—(1) The First Minister shall be appointed by Her Majesty from among the members of the Parliament and shall hold office at Her Majesty's pleasure.

(2) The First Minister may at any time tender his resignation to Her Majesty and shall do so if the Parliament resolves that the Scottish Executive no longer enjoys the confidence of the Parliament.

(3) The First Minister shall cease to hold office if a person is appointed in his place.

(4) If the office of First Minister is vacant or he is for any reason unable to act, the functions exercisable by him shall be exercisable by a person designated by the Presiding Officer.

(5) A person shall be so designated only if—

(a) he is a member of the Parliament, or

(b) if the Parliament has been dissolved, he is a person who ceased to be a member by virtue of the dissolution.

(6) Functions exercisable by a person by virtue of subsection (5)(a) shall continue to be exercisable by him even if the Parliament is dissolved.

(7) The First Minister shall be the Keeper of the Scottish Seal.

DEFINITIONS
"by virtue of": s.126(11).
"functions": s.126(1).
"the Parliament": s.126(1).
"Presiding Officer": s.19.
"Scottish Seal": s.2(6).

GENERAL NOTE

This section makes provision for the First Minister; whose pre-eminence in the Scottish Executive is assured by powers to appoint Ministers (s.47), to recommend the Law Officers (s.48) and to appoint junior Scottish Ministers (s.49). Functions may be conferred on the First Minister directly (s.52(2), (5)) and the Scotland Act itself confers some important powers, *e.g.* in relation to the appointment and removal of judges (s.95).

In many respects, the position of First Minister is designed to replicate for Scottish government the position of Prime Minister, secured largely by conventional rather than statutory rules, for U.K. government. A major difference is that the First Minister lacks the control enjoyed by the Prime Minister over the length of a parliamentary term. The First Minister cannot request a dissolution of the Scottish Parliament.

Although some of the rules which have a conventional character in relation to the U.K. Prime Minister are cast in statutory form in relation to the First Minister, much still depends upon the non-statutory background of the party system—although, in turn, the adoption for the Scottish Parliament of proportional representation clearly produces some differences. With more rules reduced to statutory form, one issue of interest is the extent to which they may be treated as justiciable by the courts, *e.g.* s.45(2).

Subs. (1)

The First Minister is appointed by the Queen and, in formal terms, holds office thereafter at the Queen's pleasure. As a system of "parliamentary government", the Act requires the First Minister (as well as all the Ministers and junior Ministers, but not the Law Officers) to be MSPs.

For the circumstances and machinery of appointment of a First Minister, see s.46. Conventional rules will no doubt develop to ensure that the First Minister's tenure is not in practice "at Her Majesty's pleasure".

Subss. (2), (3)

These provide that a First Minister's tenure in office comes to an end if (1) his or her resignation is tendered; or (2) he or she is required to resign following a vote in the Parliament of no confidence in the Scottish Executive; or (3) a successor is appointed (pursuant to the procedures in s.46). It appears that the tendering of resignation creates an immediate vacancy (see s.46(2)(b)), although the Standing Orders of the Parliament provide for the Presiding Officer to notify the Parliament "if the resignation is accepted by Her Majesty", which implies that some prior indication of the acceptance of the resignation is required.

The Standing Orders also make provision for motions of no confidence, whether in respect of the Scottish Executive, a member of the Executive, or of a junior Minister, (Rule 8.12).

Subss. (4), (5), (6)

These subsections provide for the functions of the First Minister to be exercisable by a person (effectively an Acting Prime Minister) designated by the Presiding Officer in the event that the office of First Minister is vacant or the First Minister "is for any reason unable to act". The person designated must be a member of the Scottish Parliament (or have ceased to be an MSP on a dissolution) but his or her functions (like those of a First Minister or other Minister) may continue beyond the dissolution of the Parliament.

Provision has been made in the Parliament's Standing Orders for the Presiding Officer to notify the Parliament of a designation under s.45(4) (Rule 4.2).

The power to designate a replacement was not invoked when the First Minister, Donald Dewar M.S.P., entered hospital for heart surgery in May 2000 (see SPOR, W.A. S1W-6565, 8 May 2000).

Subs. (7)

For the Scottish Seal, see s.38.

Choice of the First Minister

46.—(1) If one of the following events occurs, the Parliament shall within the period allowed nominate one of its members for appointment as First Minister.

(2) The events are—

(a) the holding of a poll at a general election,

(b) the First Minister tendering his resignation to Her Majesty,

(c) the office of First Minister becoming vacant (otherwise than in consequence of his so tendering his resignation),

(d) the First Minister ceasing to be a member of the Parliament otherwise than by virtue of a dissolution.

(3) The period allowed is the period of 28 days which begins with the day on which the event in question occurs; but—

(a) if another of those events occurs within the period allowed, that period shall be extended (subject to paragraph (b)) so that it ends with the period of 28 days beginning with the day on which that other event occurred, and

(b) the period shall end if the Parliament passes a resolution under section 3(1)(a) or when Her Majesty appoints a person as First Minister.

(4) The Presiding Officer shall recommend to Her Majesty the appointment of any member of the Parliament who is nominated by the Parliament under this section.

DEFINITIONS

"by virtue of": s.126(11).

"the Parliament": s.126(1).
"Presiding Officer": s.19.

GENERAL NOTE

Section 45(1) provides that the First Minister is to be appointed by the Queen. Section 46 now makes provision for the events which lead to an appointment and the procedure according to which an appointment is to be made.

The Standing Orders of the Parliament make provision for the procedures for the nomination of the First Minister (Rule 4.1).

Subss. (1), (4)

Subsection (1) provides that it is for the Scottish Parliament to nominate (within the period allowed by subs. (3)) one of its own members if any of the four events specified in subs. (2) occurs. By subs. (4), the Presiding Officer must recommend for appointment by the Queen the person nominated by the Parliament. Although the Act nowhere states that the Presiding Officer's recommendation must be accepted, there is no doubt that an understanding that this will occur does underpin the arrangements made. It is assumed that the Queen should take no further advice—above all, not from her U.K. Ministers—but simply proceed to the appointment.

The direct involvement of the Parliament in the nomination process, producing a formal process of prior nomination of possible candidates and of voting, provides the opportunity for a quite different approach to the appointment of the First Minister in Scotland from that adopted for the Prime Minister in the Westminster system. The operation of (normally) fixed-term Parliaments and the different system for the election of MSPs also produce change and make the procedure for nomination by the Parliament after an open process of voting more of a reality. Nothing in the section, however, prevents the very rapid nomination of a single candidate for appointment as First Minister, following private negotiation, if the party balance and political conditions in general permit this.

For the nomination procedure and the system of voting to be adopted, see the Parliament's Standing Orders, Rule 4.1 and 11.10. Mr Donald Dewar MSP was selected for nomination as First Minister on May 13, 1999 (SPOR cols. 13–26).

On the avoidance of challenge to the validity of actions based on a defect in the nomination procedure, see s.50.

Subs. (2)

The "events", specified in subs. (2), in which a nomination must be made are:

(a) *the holding of a poll at a general election.* In the Westminster system, a Prime Minister who is sufficiently successful in a general election simply continues in office without interruption. Under the rule in subs. (1), however, the Scottish Parliament must presumably renominate even though the same person is to remain in office. If this occurs, the consequences for the obligation of the Presiding Officer to recommend and the Queen to appoint to an office which has not been vacated are unclear.

On the occasion of the first general election, however, the need for nomination of the First Minister was evident. The same is true in the event that an incumbent First Minister clearly "loses" a general election or continuation in office is problematic in a "hung" Parliament. Under s.45(3), the appointment of a new First Minister brings to an end the term of office of his or her predecessor.

(b) *the First Minister tenders his or her resignation.* Section 45(2) does not make completely clear the effect of the tendering of resignation but it does trigger the need for the nomination by the Scottish Parliament of a person for appointment as First Minister. See s.45(4), (5), (6).

(c) the office becomes vacant (other than by resignation). See s.45(4), (5), (6).

(d) *the First Minister ceases to be an MSP, otherwise than by dissolution.* This reconfirms the need for the First Minister (as with all other Ministers and junior Ministers) to be MSPs. If he or she ceases to be an MSP, *e.g.* by resignation under s.14 or by disqualification under s.15, the nomination procedure is triggered. That does not apply where membership of the Parliament has ceased simply by virtue of dissolution of the Parliament itself. In that event, the First Minister continues in office until the holding of the general election requires a new nomination to be made.

Subs. (3)

The nomination by the Parliament under subs. (1) must be made within a specified period of 28 days beginning on the day of the event (subs. (2)) which triggers the nomination. That period may, however, be extended if another "event" occurs, in which case the period of 28 days then runs from the date of that second event. Perhaps the most likely combination of events would be a general election followed a little later by the resignation of the First Minister?

On the other hand, the period allowed for nomination is stated to end if the Parliament resolves to dissolve itself under s.3(1)(a), in which case, resignation apart, the holding of an extraordinary general election under s.3(2) would trigger the need for a new nomination.

It is also provided that the period allowed for nomination is brought to an end when the Queen "appoints a person as First Minister", although it seems unclear how that appointment could have been made other than on the nomination of the Parliament (and otherwise the final clause seems otiose).

If the period allowed for nomination ends without a nomination being made, the Presiding Officer must propose a day for the holding of a poll at an extraordinary general election (s.3(1)(b)).

Ministers

47.—(1) The First Minister may, with the approval of Her Majesty, appoint Ministers from among the members of the Parliament.

(2) The First Minister shall not seek Her Majesty's approval for any appointment under this section without the agreement of the Parliament.

(3) A Minister appointed under this section—
(a) shall hold office at Her Majesty's pleasure,
(b) may be removed from office by the First Minister,
(c) may at any time resign and shall do so if the Parliament resolves that the Scottish Executive no longer enjoys the confidence of the Parliament,
(d) if he resigns, shall cease to hold office immediately, and
(e) shall cease to hold office if he ceases to be a member of the Parliament otherwise than by virtue of a dissolution.

DEFINITIONS
"by virtue of": s.126(11).
"the Parliament": s.126(1).

GENERAL NOTE
Once appointed under ss.45, 46, it is for the First Minister to appoint the other members of the Scottish Executive and the junior Scottish Ministers (s.48).

Subss. (1), (2)
As with the First Minister, all other Ministers must, when appointed, also be MSPs. The appointments must have "the agreement of the Parliament", which adds a requirement not imposed at Westminster although nothing is said about how the "agreement" has to be intimated. The arrangements for obtaining the agreement of the Parliament have, however, been spelled out in the Standing Orders. Rule 4.6 provides that the First Minister must seek agreement by a motion in respect of an individual MSP or by a motion in respect of a group of two or more MSPs. For proceedings on the Ministers initially appointed to the Scottish Executive, see SPOR 19 May 1999 cols. 57–102.
In addition to the agreement of the Parliament, the (formal) approval of the Queen is required. On the avoidance of challenge to actions based on any defect in the agreement procedure, see s.50.

Subs. (3)
The rules of tenure of office of Ministers are set out. In a formal sense, a Minister's tenure may be ended by the Queen (para. (a)) but, much more importantly, a Minister may be dismissed by the First Minister, with no requirement of parliamentary agreement (para. (b)). Resignation (to take effect immediately) is open to a Minister at any time (see Standing Orders, Rule 4.8) but all Ministers are required to resign if there is a vote of no confidence by the Parliament (paras. (c), (d)). For motions of no confidence, see the note on s.45(2). As with the First Minister, a Minister loses office if he or she ceases to be an MSP—unless by dissolution (para. (e)).
Although s.46 appears to require that, following a general election, the Parliament must nominate a First Minister (even if only the existing First Minister), there is no express obligation that other Ministers be reappointed if the First Minister chooses not to dismiss them but continue them in office. It is perhaps to be implied, however, that subs. (1) imposes a continuing obligation that all Ministers be drawn from members of the Parliament. If not, a question which is left open by s.47(3)(e) is whether, if a Minister ceases to be an MSP "by virtue of a dissolution" of the Parliament and then fails to be re-elected, that Minister could be retained in office, even if only briefly?

The Scottish Law Officers

48.—(1) It is for the First Minister to recommend to Her Majesty the appointment or removal of a person as Lord Advocate or Solicitor General for Scotland; but he shall not do so without the agreement of the Parliament.

(2) The Lord Advocate and the Solicitor General for Scotland may at any time resign and shall do so if the Parliament resolves that the Scottish Executive no longer enjoys the confidence of the Parliament.

(3) Where the Lord Advocate resigns in consequence of such a resolution, he shall be deemed to continue in office until the warrant of appointment of the person succeeding to the office of Lord Advocate is granted, but only for the purpose of exercising his retained functions.

(4) Subsection (3) is without prejudice to section 287 of the Criminal Procedure (Scotland) Act 1995 (demission of office by Lord Advocate).

(5) Any decision of the Lord Advocate in his capacity as head of the systems of criminal prosecution and investigation of deaths in Scotland shall continue to be taken by him independently of any other person.

(6) In Schedule 2 to the House of Commons Disqualification Act 1975 (Ministerial offices) and Part III of Schedule 1 to the Ministerial and other Salaries Act 1975 (salaries of the Law Officers), the entries for the Lord Advocate and the Solicitor General for Scotland are omitted.

DEFINITIONS
"the Parliament": s.126(1).
"Scotland": s.126(1), (2).

GENERAL NOTE
The starting point for the discussion of the position of the Scottish Law Officers (the Lord Advocate and the Solicitor General for Scotland) under the new arrangements for devolved government in Scotland is the proposal made in the White Paper to include criminal law and procedure, civil law, the criminal justice and prosecution systems and the civil and criminal courts among the matters devolved to the Scottish Parliament (para. 2.4). Since these matters included most of the responsibilities of the Lord Advocate, it followed that it was "appropriate that the Law Officers of the Scottish Executive should be the Lord Advocate and the Solicitor General for Scotland" (para. 4.8).

These proposals are carried forward into the Scotland Act. With the reservation of limited and specific aspects of criminal law in Sched. 5, legislative power over such matters is devolved to the Parliament and s.44 ensures the inclusion of the Law Officers within the Scottish Executive.

A consequence of the Lord Advocate and the Solicitor General becoming the Law Officers to the Scottish Executive was the need for a new Scottish Law Officer to the U.K. Government (White Paper, para. 4.9) and that is met by the creation of the Advocate General for Scotland (s.87). Certain of the former functions of the Lord Advocate had to be transferred to the Advocate General. See the Transfer of Functions (Lord Advocate and Advocate General for Scotland) Order 1999 (S.I. 1999 No.679).

Another important proposal made in the White Paper, however, was that the "traditional independence" of the Lord Advocate as public prosecutor would be maintained (para. 4.8) and this is a principle carried forward into the Act. It was clearly seen as a matter of importance not only for the devolved government in Scotland but also for the U.K. Government. The Lord Advocate has responsibilities for the prosecution of offences in all those areas of the criminal law which are devolved but also for the prosecution of offences within the scope of the reserved matters—such as treason but also, more routinely, in relation to the misuse of drugs, firearms offences, consumer protection and many others. There is no separate U.K. prosecution authority for these offences but there is a clear U.K. interest in independent and efficient prosecutions.

To establish the Lord Advocate's independence, the Act contains a number of related provisions. Most importantly, s.29(2)(e) restricts the legislative competence of the Scottish Parliament by prohibiting a provision if "it would remove the Lord Advocate from his position as head of the systems of criminal prosecution and investigation of deaths in Scotland". Then s.52(3)–(6) define the "retained functions" of the Lord Advocate and prevent them from being discharged by members of the Scottish Executive at large. See also ss.27(3), 53(2), 61, 62.

It is, however, this section (s.48) which makes the core provision for the appointment of the Law Officers and for related matters. In taking account of the changes made by s.48 and the related provisions, it should be borne in mind that, subject to adjustments made by Sched. 8 (see paras. 2, 4, 7, 31) and Sched. 9, existing statutory provisions relating to the office of the Lord Advocate/Solicitor General continue to apply. For discussion, see *The Laws of Scotland: Stair Memorial Encyclopaedia*, Vol. 5, para. 535 *et seq.* In particular, the Law Officers Act 1944, s.2(1) provides the Solicitor General with the power to perform "functions authorised or required, by any enactment or otherwise, to be discharged by the Lord Advocate".

For the removal of "non-Law Officer" functions from the Lord Advocate (by the Transfer of Functions (Lord Advocate and Secretary of State) Order 1999 (S.I. 1999 No.678)) prior to their transfer under ss.53, 63, see the General Note to those sections.

Subs. (1)
This follows the pattern of appointment of other members of the Scottish Executive in that appointments are initiated by the First Minister. In the case of the Law Officers, however, there is the formal difference that the First Minister "recommends"; more importantly, the appointees do not require to be members of the Parliament (but see s.27); and the Law Officers are given what may be added security of tenure in that they cannot be removed without "the agreement of the Parliament".

The Standing Orders of the Parliament make provision for the appointment of the Law Officers (Rule 4.3) and for their removal (Rule 4.4). For the proceedings on the appointment of the initial Law Officers, see SPOR 18 May 1999, cols. 29–35; and for the appointment of their replacements (on the elevation of Lord Hardie to the bench) SPOR 17 February 2000, cols. 1230–1259.

Subss. (2), (3), (4)

Subsection (2) makes provision equivalent to that in ss.45(2), 47(3)(c) and 49(4)(c). Subsection (3) makes necessary provision for the continuity of discharge of "retained functions". It applies only to the Lord Advocate, whose office is continued for those functions only and does not extend to functions as an "ordinary" member of the Scottish Executive. Section 287 of the 1995 Act makes specific provision for the continued effectiveness of indictments if a Lord Advocate dies or demits office. For motions of no confidence, see the note on s.45(2).

Subs. (5)

For discussion of the Lord Advocate's existing role as "head of the systems of criminal prosecution and investigation of deaths in Scotland" and the independence he or she is expected to maintain see *S.M.E.*, Vol. 5, para. 535 *et seq.* Section 29(2)(e) assists in securing this position and so too does the provision made for the separation of "retained functions". One consequence of "entrenching" the Lord Advocate's position in relation to criminal prosecutions must be to deny to the Scottish Parliament the opportunity to confer powers of prosecution upon other public bodies, if it wished to do so.

Subs. (6)

As they cease to be U.K. Ministers, the entries for the Lord Advocate and Solicitor General for Scotland are deleted from the lists in the two Acts of 1975.

Junior Scottish Ministers

49.—(1) The First Minister may, with the approval of Her Majesty, appoint persons from among the members of the Parliament to assist the Scottish Ministers in the exercise of their functions.

(2) They shall be known as junior Scottish Ministers.

(3) The First Minister shall not seek Her Majesty's approval for any appointment under this section without the agreement of the Parliament.

(4) A junior Scottish Minister—

(a) shall hold office at Her Majesty's pleasure,

(b) may be removed from office by the First Minister,

(c) may at any time resign and shall do so if the Parliament resolves that the Scottish Executive no longer enjoys the confidence of the Parliament,

(d) if he resigns, shall cease to hold office immediately, and

(e) shall cease to hold office if he ceases to be a member of the Parliament otherwise than by virtue of a dissolution.

DEFINITIONS

"by virtue of": s.126(11).
"functions": s.126(1).
"the Parliament": s.126(1).
"Scottish Ministers": s.44(6).

GENERAL NOTE

In addition to those Ministers appointed under s.47 and becoming members of the Scottish Executive under s.44, the First Minister may appoint other Ministers known as "junior Scottish Ministers". The rules governing their appointment and tenure are the same as for Ministers appointed under s.47 (see the notes on that section). See the Parliament's Standing Orders, Rules 4.6–4.8. For proceedings on the appointment of the initial junior (deputy) ministers, see SPOR 19 May 1999 cols. 103–130.

Junior Ministers are appointed "to assist the Scottish Ministers in the exercise of their functions", a formula which presumably enables junior Ministers to discharge functions formally exercisable by the Scottish Ministers. For motions of no confidence, see the note on s.45(2).

Validity of acts of Scottish Ministers etc

50. The validity of any act of a member of the Scottish Executive or junior Scottish Minister is not affected by any defect in his nomination by the Parliament or (as the case may be) in the Parliament's agreement to his appointment.

DEFINITIONS

"member of the Scottish Executive": s.44(1).
"the Parliament": s.126(1).

GENERAL NOTE

As part of a group of similar provisions—see also s.19(7) (Presiding Officer), s.28 (5) (Acts of the Scottish Parliament), s.69(3) (Auditor General for Scotland)—this section was added at report stage in the House of Lords to protect the acts of any member of the Scottish Executive from invalidity on grounds of defect in nomination by or agreement to his or her appointment by the Parliament. The point is to prevent undue interference with the Parliament's business. See *Hansard*, H.L. Vol. 593, cols. 1676 and 2037.

The Civil Service

51.—(1) The Scottish Ministers may appoint persons to be members of the staff of the Scottish Administration.

(2) Service as—

(a) the holder of any office in the Scottish Administration which is not a ministerial office, or

(b) a member of the staff of the Scottish Administration,

shall be service in the Home Civil Service.

(3) Subsection (1) and the other enactments conferring power to appoint such persons shall have effect subject to any provision made in relation to the Home Civil Service by or under any Order in Council.

(4) Any Civil Service management function shall be exercisable by the Minister for the Civil Service in relation to the persons mentioned in subsection (2) as it is exercisable in relation to other members of the Home Civil Service; and, accordingly, section 1 of the Civil Service (Management Functions) Act 1992 (delegation of functions by Ministers) shall apply to any such function as extended by this section.

(5) Any salary or allowances payable to or in respect of the persons mentioned in subsection (2) (including contributions to any pension scheme) shall be payable out of the Scottish Consolidated Fund.

(6) Section 1(2) and (3) of the Superannuation Act 1972 (delegation of functions relating to civil service superannuation schemes etc.) shall have effect as if references to a Minister of the Crown (other than the Minister for the Civil Service) included the Scottish Ministers.

(7) The Scottish Ministers shall make payments to the Minister for the Civil Service, at such times as he may determine, of such amounts as he may determine in respect of—

(a) the provision of pensions, allowances or gratuities by virtue of section 1 of the Superannuation Act 1972 to or in respect of persons who are or have been in such service as is mentioned in subsection (2), and

(b) any expenses to be incurred in administering those pensions, allowances or gratuities.

(8) Amounts required for payments under subsection (7) shall be charged on the Scottish Consolidated Fund.

(9) In this section—

"Civil Service management function" means any function to which section 1 of the Civil Service (Management Functions) Act 1992 applies and which is vested in the Minister for the Civil Service,

"the Home Civil Service" means Her Majesty's Home Civil Service.

DEFINITIONS
"by virtue of": s.126(11).
"Civil Service management function": subs. (9).
"enactment": ss.113(6), 126(1).
"function": s.126(1).
"holder of any office in the Scottish Administration": s.126(7).
"the Home Civil Service": subs. (9).
"member of the staff of the Scottish Administration": s.126(7).
"Minister of the Crown": s.126(1).
"Scottish Ministers": s.44(2).

GENERAL NOTE
This section makes provision for the staffing of devolved government in Scotland. In the White Paper, it was stated that the "Government intend that staffing arrangements for supporting the Scottish Parliament and the Scottish Executive should reflect the highest standards of public service: integrity, political impartiality, objectivity, accountability, recruitment on basis of fair and open competition and promotion on merit" (para. 10.8).

It was further explained that it was likely that staff would in practice be drawn from the existing staff of the Scottish Office and its Agencies. Staff would remain members of the Home Civil Service and, therefore, continue to hold office under the Crown on terms and conditions of service determined in accordance with the provisions of the Civil Service Management Code (para. 10.11).

Under the Scotland Act itself, the Civil Service of the State (with the exception of the subject-matter of Part I of the Sheriff Courts and Legal Officers (Scotland) Act 1927 (appointments of sheriff clerks and procurators fiscal etc.) and Pt III of the Administration of Justice (Scotland) Act 1933 (officers of the High Court of Justiciary and of the Court of Session) is a reserved matter (Sched. 5, Pt I, para. 8). But see notes on subss. (1) and (4) below.

Subs. (1)

Despite the general reservation referred to, it is for the Scottish Ministers to appoint members of the staff of the Scottish Administration.

The term "Scottish Administration" is not directly defined in the Act but references to it are to be interpreted as references to (a) the office-holders in the Scottish Administration and (b) the members of the staff of the Scottish Administration (s.126(6)). Then the "office-holders" are defined to be (a) the members of the Scottish Executive and junior Scottish Ministers and, on the other hand, (b) the "holders of offices in the Scottish Administration which are not ministerial offices"—the non-ministerial offices being the Registrar General of Births, Deaths and Marriages for Scotland, the Keeper of the Registers and the Keeper of the Records of Scotland (and any others specified by Order in Council) (s.126(7)(a), (8)). Finally, the "members of the staff of the Scottish Administration" (*i.e.* those referred to in this subsection) are defined as the staff of *both* the holders of ministerial *and* non-ministerial offices (s.126(7)(b)).

It should be noted that this section does not, therefore, extend to the staff of the Scottish Parliament (see Sched. 2, para. 3).

Subs. (2)

As mentioned in the White Paper (see above), all the members of staff of the Scottish Administration (together with the non-ministerial office-holders) are civil servants, in the Home Civil Service.

Subs. (3)

Although appointments are made by the Scottish Ministers, the power to appoint is made subject to provision made by or under any (prerogative) Order in Council in relation to the Home Civil Service. Currently the relevant Order in Council is the Civil Service Order in Council 1995 and that serves to extend to the Scottish Administration the Civil Service Management Code (but see subs. (4)), including the Civil Service Commissioners' Code (with principles of fair and open competition for appointments) and the Civil Service Code of Conduct.

Subs. (4)

The integration of the staff of the Scottish Administration into the Home Civil Service is a process to be read subject to the provision already made in recent years to enable a very considerable diversity of practice to develop between departments and agencies as to the terms and conditions applicable to staff in their sectors. The principal mechanism for the achievement of this diversity has been s.1 of the Civil Service (Management Functions) Act 1992 (c.61) which enables the Minister for the Civil Service (the Prime Minister) to delegate to ministers the "management functions" there referred to. It is this flexibility of approach to the determination of terms and conditions which is extended to the staff of the Scottish Administration by this subsection.

Subss. (5)–(8)

These provide for the payment of salaries, allowances and pensions to staff of the Scottish Administration (payable out of the Scottish Consolidated Fund, on which see s.64); payments to the Minister for the Civil Service (subs. (7)); and making these payments a charge on the Scottish Consolidated Fund (see s.65(1)).

Ministerial functions

Exercise of functions

52.—(1) Statutory functions may be conferred on the Scottish Ministers by that name.

(2) Statutory functions of the Scottish Ministers, the First Minister or the Lord Advocate shall be exercisable on behalf of Her Majesty.

(3) Statutory functions of the Scottish Ministers shall be exercisable by any member of the Scottish Executive.

(4) Any act or omission of, or in relation to, any member of the Scottish Executive shall be treated as an act or omission of, or in relation to, each of

them; and any property acquired, or liability incurred, by any member of the Scottish Executive shall be treated accordingly.

(5) Subsection (4) does not apply in relation to the exercise of—

(a) functions conferred on the First Minister alone, or

(b) retained functions of the Lord Advocate.

(6) In this Act, "retained functions" in relation to the Lord Advocate means—

(a) any functions exercisable by him immediately before he ceases to be a Minister of the Crown, and

(b) other statutory functions conferred on him alone after he ceases to be a Minister of the Crown.

(7) In this section, "statutory functions" means functions conferred by virtue of any enactment.

DEFINITIONS
"conferred": s.126(1).
"enactment": ss.113(6), 126(1).
"functions": s.126(1).
"member of the Scottish Executive": s.44(1).
"Minister of the Crown": s.126(1).
"property": s.126(1).
"retained functions": subs. (6).
"Scottish Ministers": s.44(2).
"statutory functions": subs. (7).

GENERAL NOTE

This section is the first of a group of provisions that deal with the way in which functions are conferred on the Scottish Executive established by s.44. Section 52 paves the way for those that follow by providing that functions, as well as being conferred separately on the First Minister or Lord Advocate, may be conferred on the Scottish Executive in their collective title of the Scottish Ministers. Thereafter, ss.53, 54 are (with s.63) the crucial sections in the devolution of executive power. Later provisions include s.58, which contains the Secretary of State's power to prevent or require executive action.

It may be useful to note at this point that one of the principal functions exercisable by the Scottish Ministers is the making of delegated legislation. Powers will increasingly be conferred by Acts of the Scottish Parliament and many have already been conferred by transfer under ss.53, 54 and 63. Procedurally, that is a process assisted by the "translation" provisions of s.118. No doubt the Scottish Parliament will in due course make general provision, equivalent to the Statutory Instruments Act 1946, for the handling of delegated legislation. In the meantime, however, transitional provision has been made by the Scotland Act 1998 (Transitory and Transitional Provisions) (Statutory Instruments) Order 1999 (S.I. 1999 No. 1096). The Order creates the "Scottish Statutory Instrument" and applies to S.S.I.s rules substituted for those in the 1946 Act. Significantly, the informal "21 day rule" applicable to instruments subject to annulment at Westminster is adopted into the Order (art.10(2)) and, in the rules referring to the reckoning of days, no account is to be taken of any time during which the Parliament is dissolved or in recess for more than four days (art.13(1)).

Subs. (1)

This subsection enables statutory functions to be conferred on the Scottish Ministers. Acts of the Scottish Parliament will in due course confer most of these functions, although initially the powers vested in the Scottish Ministers have been those transferred by ss.53, 54 and 63 (which include powers deriving from the prerogative). Section 117 provides for a general modification of pre-commencement enactments to convert references to a Minister of the Crown to references to the Scottish Ministers (see also ss.118–124).

Subs. (2)

This reinforces the approach taken in ss.45, 47, 48 and 49 where ministerial appointments are made either by the Queen or with her approval. Functions are formally exercisable on behalf of the Queen.

Subss. (3), (5)

This is an important provision which ensures that, although statutory functions are vested in the Scottish Ministers collectively, they are exercisable by any member of the Scottish Executive. This does not extend to functions conferred individually on the First Minister or to the "retained functions" of the Lord Advocate, as confirmed by subs. (5). Thus, although the Lord Advocate could, as a member of the Scottish Executive, exercise planning powers (however improbably), other Ministers could not exercise any of the Lord Advocate's retained functions.

See also s.59(4) which provides that a document may be executed on behalf of the Scottish Ministers by any member of the Scottish Executive.

Subs. (4)

This subsection reinforces the collective character of the Scottish Executive. Acts, omissions, property or liabilities of any member of the Executive are to be treated as the act, omission etc. of each of them.

As with subs. (3), this collective approach does not apply to functions conferred on the First Minister alone or to retained functions of the Lord Advocate (see subs. (5)).

Subs. (6)

This subsection, as it applies to subs. (5), is one of several provisions in the Act which are designed to protect the autonomy of the Scottish Law Officers. Section 29(2)(e) restricts the legislative competence of the Parliament in that it may not "remove the Lord Advocate from his position as head of the systems of criminal prosecution and investigation of deaths". Section 48 (especially s.48(5)) also seeks to protect the independence of the office of Lord Advocate and further specific provision is made in ss.27, 53, 57, 61, 62.

By the device of the "retained functions", the Act ensures that functions conferred specifically on the Lord Advocate are exercisable only by the Lord Advocate (or Solicitor General). The term applies both to future functions conferred and to functions exercisable by the Lord Advocate "immediately before he ceases to be a Minister of the Crown". Many of the (non-Law Officer) functions previously conferred on the Lord Advocate by name did not continue to be exercisable by him but were instead transferred by order to another Minister of the Crown (see the Transfer of Functions (Lord Advocate and Secretary of State) Order 1999 (S.I. 1999 No.678). Some of these functions were then transferred to the Scottish Ministers, in a second stage of transfer, under s.53 or s.63.

General transfer of functions

53.—(1) The functions mentioned in subsection (2) shall, so far as they are exercisable within devolved competence, be exercisable by the Scottish Ministers instead of by a Minister of the Crown.

(2) Those functions are—

(a) those of Her Majesty's prerogative and other executive functions which are exercisable on behalf of Her Majesty by a Minister of the Crown,

(b) other functions conferred on a Minister of the Crown by a prerogative instrument, and

(c) functions conferred on a Minister of the Crown by any pre-commencement enactment,

but do not include any retained functions of the Lord Advocate.

(3) In this Act, "pre-commencement enactment" means—

(a) an Act passed before or in the same session as this Act and any other enactment made before the passing of this Act,

(b) an enactment made, before the commencement of this section, under such an Act or such other enactment,

(c) subordinate legislation under section 106, to the extent that the legislation states that it is to be treated as a pre-commencement enactment.

(4) This section and section 54 are modified by Part III of Schedule 4.

DEFINITIONS
"devolved competence": s.54.
"enactment": ss.113(6), 126(1).
"functions": s.126(1).
"Minister of the Crown": s.126(1).
"pre-commencement enactment": subs. (3).
"prerogative instrument": s.126(1).
"retained functions": s.52(6).
"Scottish Ministers": s.44(2).
"subordinate legislation": s.126(1).

GENERAL NOTE

Although s.52 makes general provision for the exercise of powers by the Scottish Ministers, the most important powers they currently enjoy are those which were previously exercised by U.K. Ministers of the Crown but which have been transferred to the Scottish Ministers by this Act. It is s.53 (with definitional and interpretative support from s.54) which provides for that transfer. All those powers, whether deriving from the royal prerogative or from statute, which were vested in Ministers of the Crown prior to "Devolution Day" on July 1, 1999, were transferred on that day to the Scottish Ministers in so far as they are exercisable within the devolved fields of government, *i.e.* within what is defined in s.54 as "devolved competence".

There are some exceptions from and qualifications to this general rule. An important exception made by the section itself is the "retained functions of the Lord Advocate" (see subs. (2)). See also s.55 (Functions exercisable with agreement); s.56 (Shared powers); s.57 (Community law and Convention rights); ss.59–62 (Property and liabilities); s.63 (Power to transfer, functions) and, as to commencement and transitional provision, ss.129, 130. Also important is s.58 which enables the Secretary of State, in defined circumstances, to intervene to prevent or require action by a member of the Scottish Executive.

Making provision supplementary to s.53, are ss.117–124. Neither s.53 nor those supplementary provisions applies in relation to "cross-border public authorities" (see s.88).

For the transfer of functions in the opposite direction (*i.e.* from members of the Scottish Executive to Ministers of the Crown), see s.108.

Subss. (1), (2)
See above.

Subs. (3)
The concept of the "pre-commencement enactment" is important in the identification of functions to be transferred under this section and also in the supplementary provisions in ss.117–122. It may include subordinate legislation made under s.106, an important section which has been used to adapt functions prior to their transfer under this section or s.63. The Scotland Act 1998 (Modification of Functions) Order 1999 (S.I. 1999 No.1756) has been made under s.106 and art.1(3) of the Order states that it is to be treated as a pre-commencement enactment.

In addition a number of Acts of the UK Parliament, passed since the Scotland Act 1998, have stated that they too are to be treated as pre-commencement enactments, thus ensuring the devolution of executive functions for which they provide. See the Adoption (Intercountry Aspects) Act 1999 (c.18) s.16 (2); the Access to Justice Act 1999 (c.22) s.109(7); the Pollution Prevention and Control Act 1999 (c.24) s.5(3); and the Water Industry Act 1999 (c.9) s.14(3). On the other hand, the Breeding and Sale of Dogs (Welfare) Act 1999 (c.11) was not stated to be a pre-commencement enactment and an order to transfer functions under s.63 was required in that case.

Subs. (4)
For the impact on this section and s.54 of Pt. III of Sched. 4, see the General Note to that Schedule.

Devolved competence

54.—(1) References in this Act to the exercise of a function being within or outside devolved competence are to be read in accordance with this section.

(2) It is outside devolved competence—

(a) to make any provision by subordinate legislation which would be outside the legislative competence of the Parliament if it were included in an Act of the Scottish Parliament, or

(b) to confirm or approve any subordinate legislation containing such provision.

(3) In the case of any function other than a function of making, confirming or approving subordinate legislation, it is outside devolved competence to exercise the function (or exercise it in any way) so far as a provision of an Act of the Scottish Parliament conferring the function (or, as the case may be, conferring it so as to be exercisable in that way) would be outside the legislative competence of the Parliament.

DEFINITIONS
"Act of the Scottish Parliament": s.28(1).
"by virtue of": s.126(11).
"conferring": s.126(1).
"function": s.126(1).
"legislative competence": s.29.
"the Parliament": s.126(1).
"subordinate legislation": s.126(1).

GENERAL NOTE
Just as it is necessary in ss.29, 30 and Scheds. 4, 5 to define the "legislative competence" of the Scottish Parliament, so too it is necessary to define the limits of the executive competence of the Scottish Ministers. The Act does this in a number of different ways and it is important to note s.52 (which enables statutory functions to be conferred on the Scottish Ministers in so far as that is done by the Scottish Parliament within the area of its legislative competence); s.56 (Shared

powers); s.57 (Community law and Convention rights); and s.63 (Power to transfer additional functions). Also affecting the exercise of powers by the Scottish Ministers is s.58 which gives the Secretary of State the power, in defined circumstances, to intervene to prevent or require action.

However, the main powers to be exercised by the Scottish Ministers are those formerly exercised by Ministers of the Crown but transferred to the Scottish Ministers by s.53. There had to be a test for distinguishing the powers conferred by existing statutes (or deriving from the prerogative) which were to be transferred to the Scottish Ministers from those to be retained by Ministers of the Crown. Some were appropriate for transfer under the scheme for devolution and some were not. That test is provided by s.54. It defines "devolved competence"—(the term used in s.53)—and does so by equating the "devolved competence" of Ministers to the "legislative competence" of the Scottish Parliament. In the first instance, the areas on which it is competent for the Parliament to legislate—(in particular, that is, devolved matters but not reserved matters)—are the areas within which the Scottish Ministers can exercise their powers, including the making of delegated legislation.

This provides an attractive initial simplicity and symmetry of approach. It is, however, a situation which was complicated when the powers under s.63 were exercised to confer additional powers on the Scottish Ministers but not on the Scottish Parliament. It is also a situation which is just as likely to attract legal disputes about the limits of the competence conferred as in the case of the powers of the Parliament. For this reason the special provision made for the determination of "devolution issues" (ss.98–103 and Sched. 6) are extended to action taken (or not taken) by members of the Scottish Executive.

Subs. (1)
The expression used in s.53 is "within devolved competence". As with the definition of the powers of the Parliament under s.29, however, this section identifies the boundary line by defining functions "outside devolved competence".
Note the application to this section (and s.53) of Pt III of Sched. 4. See s.53(4).

Subs. (2)
For the rules on "legislative competence" adopted into this section, see ss.29, 30 and Scheds. 4, 5. See also s.101 which is intended to assist the process of interpretation in relation to subordinate legislation (as well as Acts of the Scottish Parliament).

Subs. (3)
This extends to functions other than making, confirming or approving subordinate legislation the same test of competence deriving from the legislative competence of the Parliament.

Functions exercisable with agreement

55.—(1) A statutory provision, or any provision not contained in an enactment, which provides for a Minister of the Crown to exercise a function with the agreement of, or after consultation with, any other Minister of the Crown shall cease to have effect in relation to the exercise of the function by a member of the Scottish Executive by virtue of section 53.

(2) In subsection (1) "statutory provision" means any provision in a pre-commencement enactment other than paragraph 5 or 15 of Schedule 32 to the Local Government, Planning and Land Act 1980 (designation of enterprise zones).

DEFINITIONS
"by virtue of": s.126(11).
"enactment": ss.113(6), 126(1).
"function": s.126(1).
"member of the Scottish Executive": s.44(1).
"Minister of the Crown": s.126(1).
"pre-commencement enactment": s.53(3).
"statutory provision": subs. (2).

GENERAL NOTE
Many statutory powers conferred on a Minister of the Crown are stated to be exercisable by that Minister only with the agreement of, or following consultation with, another Minister. Typically a power is exercisable by "the Secretary of State" with the agreement of the Treasury (included within the definition of "Minister of the Crown" in this Act).
In the case of powers transferred from a Minister of the Crown to the Scottish Ministers under s.53, this section ensures that a power becomes exercisable by a member of the Scottish Executive free from the obligation to obtain the agreement of the specified U.K. Minister. It would clearly be contrary to the general purposes of executive devolution to leave members of the Scottish Executive subject to the control of a U.K. Minister or the Treasury in that way. Similar provision has been made by Order in Council under s.63 when that section has been used

to transfer to the Scottish Ministers functions additional to those transferred under s.53. See also the provision made in s.108 in relation to powers transferred from a member of the Scottish Executive. It would, of course, be competent for the Scottish Parliament to impose its own requirements of agreement or of consultation when it confers functions on the Scottish Ministers.

The one exception to the rule that statutory obligations to obtain the agreement of U.K. Ministers are ended when functions are transferred to the Scottish Ministers is that identified in subs. (2). Paragraphs 5 and 15 of Sched. 32 to the Local Government, Planning and Land Act 1980 (c.65) authorise the Secretary of State to make an order designating (and then modifying) an enterprise zone—in both cases with the consent of the Treasury. Uniquely, that opportunity for Treasury control over a function within the devolved competence of the Scottish Ministers is to be retained, on the grounds that continued Treasury oversight of tax privileges conferred by the grant of enterprise zone status should be retained. (See also Sched. 4, para. 1(2)(d).)

It should be noted that, although s.55 has the effect of removing the requirement of agreement or consultation with another Minister of the Crown in respect of a function now exercisable by a member of the Scottish Executive (with the assistance in some cases of modification under s.106), the section did not remove such requirements in respect of the same functions exercisable on a continuing basis by Ministers of the Crown in relation to England. Formally, the requirement to involve the Secretary of State for Scotland continued! These requirements appear to have been largely removed by a series of transfer of functions orders under the Ministers of the Crown Act 1975 (c.26). (See S.I.s 1999 Nos. 3141, 3142 and 3143.)

Shared powers

56.—(1) Despite the transfer by virtue of section 53 of any function under—

(a) section 17(1) of the Ministry of Transport Act 1919 (power to make advances for certain purposes),

(b) any Order in Council under section 1 of the United Nations Act 1946 (measures to give effect to Security Council decisions),

(c) section 9 of the Industrial Organisation and Development Act 1947 (levies for scientific research, promotion of exports, etc.),

(d) section 5 of the Science and Technology Act 1965 (funding of scientific research),

(e) section 1 of the Mineral Exploration and Investment Grants Act 1972 (contributions in respect of mineral exploration),

(f) sections 10 to 12 of the Industry Act 1972 (credits and grants for construction of ships and offshore installations),

(g) sections 2, 11(3) and 12(4) of the Employment and Training Act 1973 (power to make arrangements for employment and training etc. and to make certain payments),

(h) sections 7 to 9 and 11 to 13 of the Industrial Development Act 1982 (financial and other assistance for industry), and

(i) sections 39 and 40 of the Road Traffic Act 1988 (road safety information and training),

the function shall be exercisable by a Minister of the Crown as well as by the Scottish Ministers.

(2) Despite the transfer of any other function by virtue of section 53, the function shall, if subordinate legislation so provides, be exercisable (or be exercisable so far as the legislation provides) by a Minister of the Crown as well as by the Scottish Ministers.

(3) Subordinate legislation under subsection (2) may not be made so as to come into force at any time after the function in question has become exercisable by the Scottish Ministers.

(4) Any power referred to in section 53(2)(a) to establish, maintain or abolish a body, office or office-holder having functions which include both—

(a) functions which are exercisable in or as regards Scotland and do not relate to reserved matters, and

(b) other functions,

shall, despite that section, be exercisable jointly by the Minister of the Crown and the Scottish Ministers.

(5) In subsection (4), "office-holder" includes employee or other post-holder.

DEFINITIONS
"by virtue of": s.126(11).
"function": s.126(1).
"Minister of the Crown": s.126(1).
"office-holder": subs. (5).
"reserved matters": Sched. 5.
"Scotland": s.126(1), (2).
"the Scottish Ministers": s.44(2).
"subordinate legislation": s.126(1).

GENERAL NOTE
General provision for the transfer of functions from U.K. Ministers of the Crown to the Scottish Ministers is made by s.53. Provided that the functions are exercisable within "devolved competence" (as defined by s.54) they are exercisable by the Scottish Ministers to the exclusion of Ministers of the Crown. That principle of transfer, on an exclusive basis, is carried forward by s.55, which, with one exception, removes any secondary control by a U.K. Minister over the exercise of a function. (That is the formal position, although it is one which is subject to adjustment in the practical operation of devolution in terms of the guidance provided by the concordats agreed between U.K. Ministers and the Scottish Executive—see "Introduction").

However, by s.56 and then s.57, some measure of joint exercise of power by a U.K. Minister is retained. In this section, three separate forms of provision are made. Subsection (1) provides for the joint exercise of specific functions (most involving the contribution of funding) enumerated in the subsection itself. Subsections (2), (3) (added at report stage in the House of Lords) allow that list of jointly-exercisable functions to be extended by subordinate legislation. Separately, subss. (4), (5) (also added at report stage in the House of Lords) provide for certain powers exercisable in relation to bodies, with mixed functions combining "devolved" and "reserved" matters, to be exercisable jointly. It is important to observe that the arrangements made in this section for the sharing of powers cannot be disturbed by an Act of the Scottish Parliament, even though the subject matter of the functions involved is not reserved. See Sched. 4, para. 6.

Subs. (1)
The functions listed under the nine heads in this subsection remain exercisable by the appropriate Minister of the Crown, as well as by the Scottish Ministers to whom the functions are transferred by s.53:

(a) Since they are not reserved under Pt. II, Head E of Sched. 5, the powers under the 1919 Act to make grants and loans for the construction of railways, harbours, canals etc are transferred by s.53 but remain jointly exercisable.

(b) United Nations Security Council resolutions (including the application of sanctions) are jointly enforceable.

(c) Although the Research Councils are reserved under Pt. II, Section C12, Sched. 5, the powers under the 1947 Act to impose levies on industry are not, but become jointly exercisable.

(d) Section 5 of the 1965 Act is reserved (Pt. II, Section C12, Sched. 5) so far as relating to Research Councils and their funding. Funding of other scientific research under the section is to be shared.

(e) Section 1 of the 1972 Act permits contributions towards expenditure on exploration for mineral deposits. That becomes a shared function. Under Pt. II, Section D2, of Sched. 5, the exploration for oil and natural gas is reserved.

(f) Powers to guarantee loans (and make grants for the payment of loan interest) for the construction of ships and off-shore installations becomes shared. (See Pt. II, Section D2, Sched. 5)

(g) Assistance for arrangements for employment and training is shared.

(h) Powers to assist industry under the specified sections of the 1982 Act are shared. The designation of assisted areas under s.1 of the Act is reserved—Pt. II, Section C13, of Sched. 5.

(i) Powers to promote road safety under ss.39, 40 of the 1988 Act are shared. They are excepted from the general reservation of the 1988 Act under Pt. II, Section E1, of Sched. 5.

Subss. (2), (3)
These subsections enable subordinate legislation to be made extending the list of functions which, though transferred to the Scottish Ministers by s.53, are exercisable by a Minister of the Crown as well. By s.104 this power to make subordinate legislation is an "open power" and, by virtue of Sched. 7, requires a Type G procedure, *i.e.* subject to negative resolution of either House of the U.K. Westminster Parliament.

If left unqualified, the power in subs. (2) would permit substantial inroads into the powers of the Scottish Ministers. However, subs. (3) provides that the subordinate legislation may not be made to come into force after the transfer of a function to the Scottish Ministers. As mentioned in the General Note to s.30(3), the principal anticipated use of the power was in relation to sea fisheries regulation and such provision was duly made by the Scotland Act 1998 (Concurrent Functions) Order 1999 (S.I. 1999 No.1592). Statutory powers of the Scottish Ministers (*e.g.* under the Sea Fish (Conservation) Act 1967 (c.84)) so far as exercisable in relation to British (but not

Scottish) fishing boats within the Scottish zone and in relation to Scottish boats outside the Scottish zone are concurrently exercisable by the Secretary of State. Provision is also made *inter alia* in respect of powers under the Animal Health Act 1981 (c.22).

It should be noted that under s.63 additional functions have been transferred to the Scottish Ministers, some of which are exercisable concurrently with a Minister of the Crown.

Subss. (4), (5)

Described as complementing the provision made in ss.88–90 for cross-border public authorities (*Hansard*, H.L. Vol. 593, col. 2040), these subsections enable the Scottish Ministers and U.K. Ministers of the Crown to act jointly to establish, maintain or abolish a body combining devolved functions and others.

Community law and Convention rights

57.—(1) Despite the transfer to the Scottish Ministers by virtue of section 53 of functions in relation to observing and implementing obligations under Community law, any function of a Minister of the Crown in relation to any matter shall continue to be exercisable by him as regards Scotland for the purposes specified in section 2(2) of the European Communities Act 1972.

(2) A member of the Scottish Executive has no power to make any subordinate legislation, or to do any other act, so far as the legislation or act is incompatible with any of the Convention rights or with Community law.

(3) Subsection (2) does not apply to an act of the Lord Advocate—

(a) in prosecuting any offence, or

(b) in his capacity as head of the systems of criminal prosecution and investigation of deaths in Scotland,

which, because of subsection (2) of section 6 of the Human Rights Act 1998, is not unlawful under subsection (1) of that section.

DEFINITIONS

"by virtue of": s.126(11).
"Community law": s.126(9).
"the Convention rights": s.126(1).
"function": s.126(1).
"member of the Scottish Executive": s.44(1).
"Minister of the Crown": s.126(1).
"Scotland": s.126(1), (2).
"Scottish Ministers": s.44(2).
"subordinate legislation": s.126(1).

GENERAL NOTE

Section 57 serves three different purposes. It is, in the first place, to be seen as one of the group of sections distributing executive power between Ministers of the Crown and Scottish Ministers. Section 53 provides for the general transfer of functions to the Scottish Ministers. Under s.63 additional functions may be transferred or made exercisable by both a Minister of the Crown and the Scottish Ministers and s.56 provides for certain (shared) powers, whilst transferred to the Scottish Ministers under s.53, to be exercisable also by Ministers of the Crown. Now, s.57(1) in effect extends that list of powers by providing that, where the Scottish Ministers are empowered to use s.2(2) of the European Communities Act 1972 (c.28) to implement obligations under Community law, a Minister of the Crown also retains the power to use s.2(2) for the same purpose. It is another "shared" power, most similar perhaps to that referred to in s.56(1)(b) which also relates to a power retained by a Minister of the Crown to give effect to an "international" obligation.

But because it is concerned with Community law, s.57(1) joins a wider group on that subject. Schedule 5 (Pt. I, para. 7) "reserves" foreign affairs including relations with the European Communities (and their institutions) but excepts from reservation "observing and implementing . . . obligations under Community law" and assisting Ministers of the Crown in that regard. In addition, s.29(2)(d) prohibits the Scottish Parliament from legislating in a manner incompatible with Community law and Sched. 4 para. 1 prevents modification of the principal terms of the European Communities Act 1972 (some of which are themselves amended by Sched. 8 para. 15 of this Act). In so far as s.57(2) prohibits any member of the Scottish Executive from doing anything incompatible with Community law, it duplicates (and perhaps also reinforces) the prohibition in s.29(2)(d) read with ss.53, 54, but it also ensures that the prohibition extends to executive acts done by the Scottish Ministers under powers conferred by s.63 and to the functions of the Lord Advocate. See also Sched. 6 para. 1(e), (Devolution issues).

Although not all of its content is directly reflected in the terms of the Scotland Act 1998, Chapter 8 of the White Paper was devoted to "Relations with the European Union". The Government set out a guiding principle of the closest possible working relationships and involvement of the Scottish Executive in EU matters. The Scottish Executive would be involved in process of policy formation and negotiation, in the scrutiny and implementation of EU legislation and in links with European institutions. Specifically in relation to implementation of Community obligations, it was stated that the Scottish Executive would itself be held liable for any failures for which it was responsible. In the light of the power of Ministers of the Crown to intervene under s.57(1), however, it seems that in many circumstances such a responsibility for failure would be shared.

The third purpose of the section is (again in a process of duplication and reinforcement) to restrain the Scottish Executive from doing anything incompatible with the "Convention rights". Section 29(2)(d) prohibits the Scottish Parliament from enacting legislation contrary to the Convention rights and this restriction is extended to the Scottish Executive as an aspect of "devolved competence" (ss.53, 54). Section 57(2) reinforces that position but also extends to powers conferred on the Scottish Ministers by s.63 and to the functions of the Lord Advocate. On the prosecutorial role of the Lord Advocate see *Starrs v. Ruxton* 2000 J.C. 208; 2000 S.L.T. 42; *H.M.Advocate v. Montgomery* 2000 J.C. 111, *McNab v. H.M.Advocate* 2000 J.C. 80; *H.M.Advocate v. Robb* 2000 JC 127; *Paton v. Ritchie* 2000 S.L.T. 239. On the Scottish Ministers (in relation to the maintenance of an impartial judiciary), see *Clancy v. Caird* 2000 S.L.T. 546. Sched. 4 para. 1(2)(e) protects the Human Rights Act 1998 (c.42) from modification by the Parliament. See also s.100 which extends to the operation of the Scotland Act certain of the restrictions contained in the Human Rights Act 1998; s.129(2) (Transitional) and Sched. 6 para. 1(e) (Devolution issues). For discussion of *Clancy v. Caird* 2000 S.L.T. 546 and the question of whether an omission or failure to act under s.57(2) is a "devolution issue" under Sched.6, see the note on para. 1 of that Schedule.

Subsection (3) was added at report stage in the House of Lords (*Hansard*, H.L. Vol. 593, cols. 2040–42). Section 6(1) of the Human Rights Act 1998 makes it unlawful for a public authority (which could include the Lord Advocate and other prosecution authorities in the U.K.) to "act in a way which is incompatible with a Convention Right". However, s.6(2) provides that s.6(1) does not apply if (a), as a result of provisions in primary legislation, the public authority could not have acted differently or (b) in the case of provisions in or under primary legislation which cannot be read as compatible with Convention rights, the authority was acting to give effect to or enforce those provisions. It was explained that subs. (2) gave protection to any prosecution authority which sought to prosecute a statutory offence which was itself contrary to Convention rights. It was important, however, to ensure that, where such protection was afforded, it should remain fully available to all U.K. prosecution authorities and it was necessary to insert s.57(3) to ensure that, in circumstances where, for example, the Crown Prosecution Service was able to prosecute an offence in England, the Lord Advocate was not precluded from bringing a prosecution under the same legislation in Scotland because of the application to him or her of s.57(2).

In the *Starrs v. Ruxton* 2000 J.C. 208; 2000 S.L.T. 42 the effect of subs. (3) was considered but the court rejected arguments that the procurator fiscal could invoke its protection. No primary legislation had compelled her to proceed with the prosecution. (See 2000 J.C. at 231, S.L.T. at 58 (Lord Cullen) and 2000 J.C. at 255, 256, S.L.T. at 72, 73 (Lord Reed).)

Power to prevent or require action

58.—(1) If the Secretary of State has reasonable grounds to believe that any action proposed to be taken by a member of the Scottish Executive would be incompatible with any international obligations, he may by order direct that the proposed action shall not be taken.

(2) If the Secretary of State has reasonable grounds to believe that any action capable of being taken by a member of the Scottish Executive is required for the purpose of giving effect to any such obligations, he may by order direct that the action shall be taken.

(3) In subsections (1) and (2), "action" includes making, confirming or approving subordinate legislation and, in subsection (2), includes introducing a Bill in the Parliament.

(4) If any subordinate legislation made or which could be revoked by a member of the Scottish Executive contains provisions—

(a) which the Secretary of State has reasonable grounds to believe to be incompatible with any international obligations or the interests of defence or national security, or

(b) which make modifications of the law as it applies to reserved matters and which the Secretary of State has reasonable grounds to believe to have an adverse effect on the operation of the law as it applies to reserved matters,

the Secretary of State may by order revoke the legislation.

(5) An order under this section must state the reasons for making the order.

DEFINITIONS
"action": subs. (3).
"enactment": s.126(1).
"international obligations": s.126(10).
"modifications": s.126(1).
"legislative competence": s.29.
"member of the Scottish Executive": s.44(1).
"the Parliament": s.126(1).
"reserved matters": Sched. 5.
"subordinate legislation": s.126(1).

GENERAL NOTE
This section operates in parallel with s.35 and the General Note to that section explains much of the background. Section 35 makes provision for the Secretary of State to intervene to prevent a Bill in the Scottish Parliament from becoming law, not on the ground that the Bill would be outwith the Parliament's legislative competence but on the grounds that, in his or her view, the Bill's provisions (1) would be incompatible with any international obligations or the interests of defence or national security; or (2) make modifications of the law as it applies to reserved matters with an "adverse effect" on the operation of that law.

Now, s.58 (which was heavily amended at the House of Lords committee stage) makes somewhat equivalent provision in relation to action taken or proposed to be taken not by the Parliament but by a member of the Scottish Executive. Subsection (4) gives similar powers to the Secretary of State in respect of subordinate legislation within the competence of a member of the Scottish Executive as s.35 in respect of Bills in the Parliament. The differences are that the powers are targeted on subordinate legislation already made rather than on measures prior to enactment and, secondly, the Secretary of State is given the power directly to revoke the legislation.

In addition to that power in subs. (4), subss. (1)–(3) give the Secretary of State further powers aimed solely at compliance with international obligations. These apply to categories of "action" including but extending beyond the making of subordinate legislation and are discussed further in the notes below. However, the effect of restricting these powers to ensuring compliance with international obligations does mean that the Secretary of State is left without powers to intervene under this section in the interests of "defence or national security".

Subss. (1)–(3), (5)
These provide the Secretary of State (any Secretary of State) with the powers to intervene to order that action should not be taken or, on the other hand, that it should be taken. An order, which in the case of subs. (2) may be an order to introduce a Bill in the Scottish Parliament to give effect to the international obligations, must state the reasons for making it. Such an order to introduce a Bill might not ensure its enactment, in which case an Act of the Westminster Parliament may be required.

The Secretary of State's powers have to be read subject to s.106 which, *inter alia*, enables the modification of functions of the Scottish Ministers requiring them to implement an international obligation by reference to quantifiable results. Any enforcement is restricted to the level of obligation imposed.

An order made under subss. (1), (2) attracts type I procedure under Sched. 7, *i.e.* subject to annulment by either House of Parliament. Any such order would be judicially reviewable.

Notice too the power under s.107 to make subordinate legislation in respect of, *inter alia*, failure by a member of the Scottish Executive to exercise a function or to exercise it properly.

Subss. (4), (5)
Subsection (4) contains the power by order (again subject to Type I procedure as above) to revoke subordinate legislation of a member of the Scottish Executive—or subordinate legislation which such a member could revoke, *i.e.* including legislation made, pre-devolution, by a Minister of the Crown.

Property and liabilities

Property and liabilities of the Scottish Ministers

59.—(1) Property may be held by the Scottish Ministers by that name.

(2) Property acquired by or transferred to the Scottish Ministers shall belong to, and liabilities incurred by the Scottish Ministers shall be liabilities of, the Scottish Ministers for the time being.

(3) In relation to property to be acquired by or transferred to, or belonging to, the Scottish Ministers or liabilities incurred by the Scottish Ministers, references to the Scottish Ministers—

(a) in any title recorded in the Register of Sasines or registered in the Land Register of Scotland, or

(b) in any other document,

shall be read in accordance with subsection (2).

(4) A document shall be validly executed by the Scottish Ministers if it is executed by any member of the Scottish Executive.

DEFINITIONS
"document": s.126(1).
"member of the Scottish Executive": s.44(1).
"property": s.126(1).
"Scottish Ministers": s.44(2).

GENERAL NOTE
This section is the first of four which deal with the property and liabilities of the Scottish Ministers, including the Lord Advocate and the First Minister. They operate in parallel with earlier sections which confer powers on the Scottish Ministers; enable further functions to be conferred; and transfer functions from Ministers of the Crown—see, in particular, s.52 (Exercise of functions) which provides for functions to be exercised by the Scottish Ministers and, separately, by the First Minister alone and, as "retained functions", by the Lord Advocate; and ss.53, 54 (General transfer of functions and Devolved competence) which transfer functions within devolved competence (other than retained functions of the Lord Advocate).

This group of sections (ss.59–62) recognises that associated with the exercise of functions (whether transferred from Ministers of the Crown or newly conferred) are "property and liabilities" for which provision must also be made. ("Property" is defined in s.126(1) to include "rights and interests of any description"). Thus ss.59(1) and 61(1) provide for property to be held by the Scottish Ministers and the Lord Advocate respectively. There is no directly equivalent provision in respect of the First Minister.

Then s.59(2) provides for property acquired by or transferred to the Scottish Ministers and liabilities incurred by them to be the property and liabilities of the Scottish Ministers for the time being, with specific provision made in s.59(3) for references to such property and liabilities in the Register of Sasines, the Land Register or in any other document to be interpreted accordingly. Equivalent provision is made in respect of the Lord Advocate in s.61(2), (3). Similar provision is also made in respect of the First Minister in s.61(4), although it seems to have been thought unnecessary to include a rule equivalent to that in ss.59(3) and 61(3).

See also, in relation to *transfers* of property made by subordinate legislation, s.60 (Scottish Ministers), s.62 (Lord Advocate), s.90 (Transfers of property of cross-border public authorities), s. 109 (Agreed redistribution of property and liabilities), s.116 (Supplementary provision concerning transfer of property) and para. 2 of Sched. 2 (Transfer of property of the Scottish Parliamentary Corporate Body).

In addition, s.104 enables provision to be made which is consequential upon any Act of the Scottish Parliament. Article 6 of the Public Finance and Accountability (Scotland) Act 2000 (Transfer of NAO Staff etc.) Order 2000 (S.I. 2000 No.935) transferred property from the Comptroller and Auditor General to Audit Scotland.

Subss. (1)–(3)
See above.

Subs. (4)
Section 44(2) provides that members of the Scottish Executive are to be referred to collectively as the "Scottish Ministers" and it is in that name that functions are conferred or transferred by ss.52, 53. Section 52(3) provides, however, that functions of the Scottish Ministers are exercisable by any member of the Scottish Executive and this subsection confirms that a document may be validly executed by any member of the Scottish Executive.

Transfers to the Scottish Ministers

60.—(1) Subordinate legislation may provide—
(a) for the transfer to the Scottish Ministers of any property belonging to a Minister of the Crown or government department, or
(b) for the Scottish Ministers to have such rights or interests in relation to any property belonging to a Minister of the Crown or government department as the person making the legislation considers appropriate (whether in connection with a transfer or otherwise).

(2) Subordinate legislation may provide for the transfer to the Scottish Ministers of any liabilities to which a Minister of the Crown or government department is subject.

(3) Subordinate legislation under this section may only be made in connection with any transfer or sharing of functions of a Minister of the Crown by virtue of section 53, 63 or 89 or in any other circumstances in

which the person making the legislation considers it appropriate to do so for the purposes of this Act.

DEFINITIONS
"devolved competence": s.54.
"devolved functions": subs. (4).
"functions": s.126(1).
"government department": s.126(1).
"Minister of the Crown": s.126(1).
"property": s.126(1).
"retained functions": s.52(6).
"Scottish Ministers": s.44(2).
"subordinate legislation": s.126(1).

GENERAL NOTE
For an introduction to this group of sections (ss.59–62), see the General Note to s.59. That section (in relation to the Scottish Ministers) and s.61 (in relation to the Lord Advocate and the First Minister) make general provision in respect of property held and liabilities incurred.

Now this section (in respect of the Scottish Ministers) and s.62 (in respect of the Lord Advocate) make more specific provision for the transfer by subordinate legislation of any property belonging to a Minister of the Crown (or Government department) together with such rights or interests in relation to any such property (though not necessarily property transferred) considered to be appropriate. Similar provision is made for the transfer of liabilities (subs. (2)). By virtue of s.112, the power to make subordinate legislation under this section is an "open power" subject to the "extensions" under s.113. By Sched. 7, the relevant subordinate legislation (as type G) is subject to the negative procedure in both Houses of the Westminster Parliament. See also s.116 (Transfer of property: supplementary). For other powers to transfer property, see ss.62, 90, 109 and para. 2 of Sched. 2.

Under the Transfer of Property etc. (Scottish Ministers) Order 1999 (S.I. 1999 No. 1104) general provision is made for the transfer of rights and interests in land and corporeal moveable property (other than certain excepted property) used wholly or mainly for or in connection with a transferred function (art.2). A transferred function is any function of a Minister of the Crown transferred to the Scottish Ministers by virtue of s.53, 63 or 89 so as to be exercisable by the Scottish Ministers instead of by a Minister of the Crown (art 1(2)). Special provision is made for Bute House (transferred) (art.3); forestry land and premises (art.4); the transfer of other rights and interests and liabilities (Art.5); property with mixed use (art.6); Dover House (excepted) (art.7); St. James' House (New St. Andrew's House) (excepted) (art.8); the Seal of the Secretary of State for Scotland (excepted) (art.9); departmental records (excepted) (art.10); radioactive incidents and tide gauge equipment (excepted) (art.11); and the determination of disputes (by the Secretary of State or an arbiter appointed by the Lord President) (art.12).

Subss. (1), (2)
See above.

Subs. (3)
In earlier versions of s.60, other mechanisms were used to identify the actual property which might be transferred under the section by reference to its former use in relation to functions now to be transferred to the Scottish Ministers. This subsection is less specific but enables the use of the power in connection with the three named sections under which functions may be transferred (*i.e.* ss.53, 63, 89) as well as in other "appropriate" circumstances.

Property and liabilities of the Lord Advocate and the First Minister

61.—(1) Property may be held by the Lord Advocate by that name.

(2) Property acquired by or transferred to the Lord Advocate shall belong to, and liabilities incurred by the Lord Advocate shall be liabilities of, the Lord Advocate for the time being.

(3) In relation to property to be acquired by or transferred to, or belonging to, the Lord Advocate or liabilities incurred by the Lord Advocate, references to the Lord Advocate—

(a) in any title recorded in the Register of Sasines or registered in the Land Register of Scotland, or

(b) in any other document,

shall be read in accordance with subsection (2).

(4) Any rights and liabilities acquired or incurred by the First Minister shall be rights or (as the case may be) liabilities of the First Minister for the time being.

DEFINITIONS
"document": s.126(1).

"property": s.126(1).

Transfers to the Lord Advocate

62.—(1) Subordinate legislation may provide—
    (a) for the transfer to the Lord Advocate of any property belonging to a
        Minister of the Crown or government department, or
    (b) for the Lord Advocate to have such rights or interests in relation to any
        property belonging to a Minister of the Crown or government depart-
        ment as the person making the legislation considers appropriate
        (whether in connection with a transfer or otherwise).

    (2) Subordinate legislation may provide for the transfer to the Lord
Advocate of any liabilities to which a Minister of the Crown or government
department is subject.

    (3) Subordinate legislation under this section may only be made in
connection with the Lord Advocate becoming a member of the Scottish
Executive or having any retained functions or in any other circumstances in
which the person making the legislation considers it appropriate to do so for
the purposes of this Act.

DEFINITIONS
"function": s.126(1).
"government department": s.126(1).
"Minister of the Crown": s.126(1).
"property": s.126(1).
"retained functions": s.52(6).
"subordinate legislation": s.126(1).

GENERAL NOTE
    For an introduction to this group of sections (ss.59–62) see the General Note to s.59.
    The powers under this section have been used to make the Transfer of Property etc. (Lord
Advocate) Order 1999 (S.I. 1999 No.1105). The Order made provision for the transfer to the
Lord Advocate of all rights and interests belonging to a Minister of the Crown or government
department in any land and corporeal moveable property (other than excepted property) which
was used wholly or mainly for or in connection with a relevant function (art.2). Relevant
functions are the retained functions of the Lord Advocate (s. 52(6)(a)) and functions of any
procurator fiscal or depute procurator fiscal (art.1(2)). Provision is also made for the transfer of
other rights and interests and liabilities (art.3); property with mixed use (art.4); Carlton Gardens
(excepted) (art.5); and the determination of disputes (by the Secretary of State or arbiter
appointed by the Lord President) (art.6).

Subss. (1), (2)
    These make provision (in relation to property of the Lord Advocate) equivalent to that made
in relation to the Scottish Ministers by s.60(1), (2). As with s.60, the power to make subordinate
legislation is an "open power" to be exercised according to the (Type G) negative procedure at
Westminster.

Subs. (3)
    There is a flexibility built into the use of the power in this section which reflects the complexity
of the Lord Advocate's functions, as a member of the Scottish Executive but also with separate
"retained functions". See ss.52, 53 and 63.

Transfer of additional functions

Power to transfer functions

63.—(1) Her Majesty may by Order in Council provide for any functions,
so far as they are exercisable by a Minister of the Crown in or as regards
Scotland, to be exercisable—
    (a) by the Scottish Ministers instead of by the Minister of the Crown,
    (b) by the Scottish Ministers concurrently with the Minister of the Crown,
        or

(c) by the Minister of the Crown only with the agreement of, or after consultation with, the Scottish Ministers.

(2) Where an Order is made under subsection (1)(a) or (b) in relation to a function of a Minister of the Crown which is exercisable only with the agreement of, or after consultation with, another Minister of the Crown, the function shall, unless the Order provides otherwise, be exercisable by the Scottish Ministers free from any such requirement.

(3) An Order under this section may, in particular, provide for any function exercisable by the Scottish Ministers by virtue of an Order under subsection (1)(a) or (b) to be exercisable subject to a requirement for the function to be exercised with the agreement of, or after consultation with, a Minister of the Crown or other person.

DEFINITIONS
"functions": s.126(1).
"Minister of the Crown": s.126(1).
"Scottish Ministers": s.44(2).

GENERAL NOTE
This is a very important section in the construction of the overall scheme for the devolution of power to the Scottish Parliament and Executive. The powers are conferred separately on each, but the starting point is to confer the same range of powers. Thus the "legislative competence" conferred on the Parliament by ss.29, 30 and Scheds. 4, 5, is used as the basis of the definition of the executive competence conferred on the Scottish Ministers by ss.53, 54.

It was, however, always made clear (see White Paper, para. 2.7) that the Government would use powers under the Scotland Act 1998 to confer on the Scottish Ministers an additional range of functions. Some matters reserved by Sched. 5 to the Westminster Parliament were to be transferred on an executive basis to the Scottish Ministers and this was to be done using the order-making power in this section. By Order in Council, functions of a Minister of the Crown may be transferred to become exercisable (in or as regards Scotland) (a) by the Scottish Ministers or (b) by the Scottish Ministers concurrently with the Minister of the Crown or (c) by the Minister of the Crown, but only with the agreement of the Scottish Ministers or after consultation with them. In the case of (a) or (b), the transfer is subject to the conditions in subss. (2) and (3).

Account should be taken of certain important related provisions:
1. Section 106 provides for subordinate legislation to make provision considered "appropriate for the purpose of enabling or otherwise facilitating the transfer of a function to the Scottish Ministers by virtue of section 53 or 63". That power takes account of the fact that in its original form, a statutory power may not be immediately divisible into a power exercisable by the Scottish Ministers and, on the other hand, the Minister of the Crown. Similarly s.30(3) enables provision to be made for certain functions to be treated either as being or as not being functions in or as regards Scotland.
2. Section 60 enables an appropriate transfer of property and liabilities to the Scottish Ministers, consequent upon a transfer of functions under ss.53, 63, or 89.
3. Section 108 (see also s.109) makes provision for the transfer of functions in the opposite direction. Presumably a second Order in Council under s.63 could be used to adjust or revoke the terms of an earlier Order made under the same section but an Order in Council under s.108 could transfer functions to a Minister of the Crown, whether originally transferred to the Scottish Ministers by s.53 or s.63 or indeed directly conferred by the Scottish Parliament under s.52.
4. Section 93 enables arrangements to be made for the performance of specified functions of the Scottish Ministers to be discharged by a UK Minister (or vice versa) on an agency basis. Those specified functions may (and do in practice) include functions initially transferred to the Scottish Ministers under s.63.
5. Section 115 and Sched. 7 make general provision for the parliamentary procedures to be adopted in the making of subordinate legislation. Orders in Council under s. 63 require, in the terminology of Sched. 7, Type A procedure, *i.e.* before the making of the Order in Council a draft must first be approved by a resolution of both Houses at Westminster and of the Scottish Parliament.
6. Section 124 (2) enables the effect of ss.94 and 117–122 to be modified in relation to the exercise of other powers to make subordinate legislation. That subsection can be used to extend the scope of those provisions where they originally apply to a "pre-commencement enactment" to apply instead to other "enactments". The provisions themselves deal with the necessary modification of such "pre-commencement enactments" to accommodate the exercise of powers (including powers to make subordinate legislation) by the Scottish Ministers instead of Ministers of the Crown; to adjust accounting, audit and reporting requirements; and to adjust references originally made to the Consolidated Fund. As they stand, those sections do appropriately refer to "pre-commencement enactments" and modify references accordingly. However, in the case of

an Order in Council under s. 63, made after the passing of this Act and therefore perhaps transferring functions under later legislation, it might be necessary for certain "post-commencement enactments" to be read subject to the same modifications.

7. Schedule 6, para. 1 defines "devolution issues" for the purpose of the procedures laid down in that Schedule. Included among the categories of "devolution issue" are questions of whether a function is "a function of the Scottish Ministers" which clearly might turn on the exercise of the power in s.63.

It should be noted that, in the case of some of the powers proposed to be transferred by the Order in Council to the Scottish Ministers from the Secretary of State, the Lord Chancellor or Treasury, they were not currently exercisable by those Ministers/Departments. They were exercisable by the Lord Advocate in his capacity as a (U.K.) Scottish Law Officer. To make them available for transfer to the Scottish Ministers under s.63, they were first transferred by an ordinary inter-ministerial order from the Lord Advocate to the Secretary of State, the Lord Chancellor or Treasury as appropriate. (See the Transfer of Functions (Lord Advocate and Secretary of State) Order 1999 (S.I. 1999 No.678)).

As to the probable actual use of the powers s.63, an indication of this was given during the parliamentary passage of the Scotland Bill when a draft of an Order in Council was published. This showed an intention (subject, of course, to the consent of both Parliaments) to transfer extensive executive powers to the Scottish Ministers in relation to matters including: betting, gaming and lotteries, police, funding for Gaelic television and radio, tribunals (procedural rules), energy, transport, public sector pensions and health. It was indicated too that the power to require *consultation* with the Scottish Ministers would be used in relation to matters including: designation of areas of sea for offshore oil development, powers in relation to nuclear installations, appointments to the Independent Television Commission, Radio Authority, Broadcasting Standards Commission, to the Equal Opportunities Commission and the Commission for Racial Equality.

Effect was given to these intentions by the Scotland Act 1998 (Transfer of Functions to the Scottish Ministers, etc.) Order 1999 (S.I. 1999 No. 1750). The Order contains a substantial list of functions transferred, or to be exercised concurrently, or to be exercised subject to consultation. They are noted (as "Executive Devolution") in the annotations to Sched.5.

A further order under s.63 is the Scotland Act 1998 (Transfer of Functions to the Scottish Ministers etc.) (No.2) Order 1999 (S.I. 1999 No.3321). This was a consequence of the passing of the Breeding and Sale of Dogs (Welfare) Act 1999 and transfers relevant functions to the Scottish Ministers. That Act did not itself provide for it to be treated as a "pre-commencement enactment" for the purpose of the Scotland Act.

See also the Scotland Act 1998 (Transfer of Functions to the Scottish Ministers etc.) Order 2000 (S.I. 2000 No. 1563).

Subs. (1)
For general discussion, see above. Note, in addition, that the power under this section is to transfer to "the Scottish Ministers" and not, *e.g.* to the Lord Advocate alone. The standard form of transfer is simply to the Scottish Ministers but with the other options of concurrency (para. (b)) or merely requiring agreement or consultation with the Scottish Ministers (para. (c)).

The powers in the subsection, insofar as they are used to transfer functions under (a) or (b), must be read subject to subss. (2), (3).

Subs. (2)
This subsection contains provision equivalent to that in s.55(1) and normally removes the need for involvement of any other Ministers in the exercise of the transferred function. As with the exception contained in s.55(2), however, such a requirement may be retained.

Subs. (3)
As a complement to subs. (2), this subsection enables new requirements of agreement or consultation to be imposed.

Part III

Financial Provisions

General Note
In any system of decentralised government, from fully-fledged federalism to democratic local self-government, financial arrangements are of the highest importance. It may be that the provisions devoted to finance in the Scotland Act 1998 itself are themselves rather brief but this belies their significance for the scheme of devolution as a whole. As the Constitution Unit said: "The heart of the devolution settlement will be the arrangements for financing the Scottish Executive's actions" (*Scotland's Parliament: Fundamentals for a New Scotland Act* (1996), para. 202). Their report laid down criteria that the new financial arrangements should satisfy.

Similar criteria appeared in the Government's White Paper as the objectives to underpin the financing of developed government:
"The financial arrangements for the Scottish Parliament will be designed to ensure that:
  • Scotland will continue to benefit from its appropriate share of U.K. public expenditure;

- The Scottish Parliament's assigned budget is determined by a method which is objective, transparent and widely accepted;
- The Scottish Parliament has the maximum freedom to determine its own expenditure priorities;
- The Scottish Parliament has a defined and limited power to vary central government taxation in Scotland and alter its overall spending accordingly;
- The U.K. Government can maintain proper control over public expenditure and public borrowing at the U.K. level;
- There are clear lines of accountability for local government spending and taxation; and
- U.K. taxpayers as a whole will be insulated from the effects of local decisions which add to Exchequer-funded expenditure in Scotland." (Para. 7.2.).

Overall, the arrangements to be made should "provide a structure for funding the Scottish Parliament that will establish that Parliament on a sound financial basis both on its own terms and in terms of its relationship with the U.K. The system will provide an important element of continuity and the stability necessary for sensible long-term planning. It crucially will introduce direct accountability for spending priorities in Scotland. The proposals provide new opportunities. They will support the establishment of a powerful and effective Scottish Parliament capable of serving fully Scotland's interests and, at the same time, they recognise and acknowledge the continuing and legitimate interests of the U.K. as a whole." (Para. 7.28)

The arrangements to be made to implement these objectives are only partially reflected in the Scotland Act itself. On some central aspects the Act is silent, leaving much to be worked out as the practice of devolution proceeds. This is especially true of the working out of the arrangements for the revenue funding of Scottish government. Only outline statutory provision is made—principally in s.64(2).

The most important groups of provisions relating to finance are:

1. Schedule 5, Head A (Financial and Economic Matters), Section A1 (Fiscal, Economic and Monetary Policy). Read with ss.29, 30, this reserves to Westminster "Fiscal, economic and monetary policy, including the issue and circulation of money, taxes and excise duties. . ." Excepted from reservation are "Local taxes to fund local authority expenditure".

It is this reservation that places taxation in general beyond the competence of the Parliament and Executive.

2. Part IV—The Tax-Varying Power. By virtue of ss.73–80 the Scottish Parliament is given the specific tax-varying power contained in those sections.

3. Part III—Financial Provisions. Otherwise, all important provision is made in this Part of the Act. It establishes the Scottish Consolidated Fund (ss.64–65); it provides for lending and borrowing powers (ss.66–68 and ss.71–72); and it makes important provision for financial control (ss.69, 70).

Developments which have occurred since the passing of the Scotland Act—especially the financial arrangements now established by the Scottish Parliament itself—are referred to in the notes on the sections which follow. One document of general importance, however, has been the Report of the Financial Issues Advisory Group (FIAG) which was established by the Secretary of State for Scotland in February 1998, in parallel with the Consultative Steering Group, to advise on financial proceedings in the Scottish Parliament. The FIAG Report, published in 1999, contained a series of recommendations on budgetary procedures and accounting and audit arrangements (making comparative reference to arrangements at Westminster where relevant) which formed the basis for the provision now made by the Scottish Parliament in the Public Finance and Accountability (Scotland) Act 2000 (asp 1) and in its Standing Orders.

Scottish Consolidated Fund

64.—(1) There shall be a Scottish Consolidated Fund.

(2) The Secretary of State shall from time to time make payments into the Fund out of money provided by Parliament of such amounts as he may determine.

(3) Sums received by an office-holder in the Scottish Administration shall be paid into the Fund.

(4) Subsection (3) is subject to any provision made by or under an Act of the Scottish Parliament for the disposal of or accounting for such sums.

(5) The Treasury may, after consulting with the Scottish Ministers, by order designate receipts of any description specified in the order which are payable into the Fund (or would be but for any provision made by or under an Act of the Scottish Parliament).

(6) The Scottish Ministers shall make payments to the Secretary of State, at such times and by such methods as the Treasury may from time to time determine, of sums equal to the total amount outstanding in respect of designated receipts.

(7) Amounts required for the payment of sums under subsection (6) shall be charged on the Fund.

(8) The Fund shall be held with the Paymaster General.

DEFINITIONS
"Act of the Scottish Parliament": s.28(1).
"office-holder in the Scottish Administration": s.126(7).
"Scottish Ministers": s.44(2).

GENERAL NOTE
This is the first of three sections dealing with the creation and operation of the Scottish Consolidated Fund. They contain provisions (largely technical in nature) which are broadly parallel to those made (by the Consolidated Fund Act 1816 and Exchequer and Audit Departments Act 1866) in respect of the U.K. Consolidated Fund.

Other related provisions of importance, in addition to the other sections in Pt. III, include s.119 (Consolidated Fund etc.) which makes necessary adaptations to pre-commencement enactments dealing with, inter alia, payments out of and charges on the Consolidated Fund so far as they are concerned with "Scottish functions" and paras. 4(3), (4) and (5) of Sched. 4 which determine the extent to which provisions of the Scotland Act 1998 relating to the Scottish Consolidated Fund may be modified by the Scottish Parliament. See also Sched. 8, para.9 (remuneration of members of the Lands Tribunal for Scotland).

Subs. (1)
This subsection simply establishes the Fund. Paragraph 4 of Sched. 4 "entrenches" this provision, although modifications of some other aspects of Pt.III are permitted and provision for a Scottish Loans Fund could be made.

Subs. (2)
Far from being merely technical, this subsection is one of the most important provisions in the whole Act. Although it is cryptic in style, it provides the statutory basis for the transfer of funds from the U.K. Government to finance the operation of the Scottish Parliament and Administration.

In the White Paper, the Government's proposal for meeting their overall funding objectives was that there would be a continuation in relation to the Scottish Parliament of the arrangements then used for the funding of most Scottish Office expenditure. This was done by means of what was called the "block and formula" system, according to which, a "block" from overall U.K. resources was made available annually to the Secretary of State. (Chap. 5 and Annex B.) Each year the size of the block was calculated by reference to the previous year's figure adjusted by increases in line with a formula, "the Barnett formula", which ensured that, in relation to each spending programme within the block, any increase (or decrease) is in line with equivalent changes in expenditure south of the border. The formula, named after Joel (now Lord) Barnett, Chief Secretary to the Treasury at the time, was first deployed at the time when the Scotland Act 1978 was passed and provided that, for each £85 of planned expenditure on equivalent services in England, Scotland would received £10—a position adjusted in 1992 to take account of different population distributions.

In broad terms, the Government's proposal was that the Scottish Parliament should have an overall assigned budget and that resources currently made available under this block and formula system to the Scottish Office would be made available on the authority of the Westminster Parliament by grant to the Scottish Parliament under the new block arrangements. The Scottish Executive (subject to the consent of the Parliament) would then have the same sort of freedom previously enjoyed by the Scottish Office to allocate funds within the assigned budget to Scottish spending programmes.

These intentions have to be read subject to two main qualifications:

1. The position described is one which has been complicated by some, largely technical, adjustments to the block arrangements which have, for instance, brought into the block system some budgets (including some Agriculture, Fisheries and Food expenditure and the Crown Office) which were previously excluded. (White Paper, Annex B.) A full statement of the funding proposals (incorporating such adjustments) was published by the Treasury on March 31, 1999—see Funding the Scottish Parliament, National Assembly for Wales and Northern Ireland Assembly: A Statement of Funding Policy.

2. Another complicating factor is that the whole block system and the assumptions about the fair distribution of funding between Scotland and the rest of the United Kingdom on the U.K. on which it is based have become a matter of intense scrutiny and debate. The question of whether the original "needs-based" funding calculation made prior to 1978 which gave an apparent advantage to Scottish spending has, in fact, given Scotland higher levels of public expenditure and, if so, whether this is justified, is hotly contested. Leading the assault have been politicians and business people from England. Their concerns were reflected in evidence given to the Treasury Select Committee of the House of Commons which held a brief inquiry into the formula towards the end of 1997. The report of the Committee was brief and did not contain detailed recommendations for the future. The Committee did urge, however, that the needs assessment, on which the future use of the

Barnett Formula (or a successor formula) would be based, should be brought up to date. (The Barnett Formula (1997–98) H.C. 341, para. 12.)

Turning to the Act itself, one finds very little of the detail of these arrangements spelled out. The means of ensuring the revenue funding for Scottish government is by establishing the Scottish Consolidated Fund and then providing that "[t]he Secretary of State shall from time to time make payments into the Fund out of money provided by Parliament of such amounts as he may determine" (s.64(2)). Nothing further is specified as to the level at which the Secretary of State may fix the funding to be provided nor the procedures to be followed, although procedures for consultation between treasury Ministers, the Secretary of State an the Scottish Executive—together with procedures for dispute resolution—are set out in the Statement of Funding Policy (March 1999) above.

The White Paper made no commitment, however, to setting up an independent body (such as a commission politically independent of either government) to make recommendations in the light of an objective economic assessment. The need for such a body in order to reduce the number of disputes based merely upon subjective and politically-generated assessments of the relative deserts of Scotland and the rest of the United Kingdom had been stressed by some commentators. (See especially the Constitution Unit's *Scotland's Parliament: Fundamentals for a New Scotland Act* (1996), Chap. 5.)

Subs. (3), (4)

Joining the payments received from the Secretary of State are sums received by members of the Scottish Executive and other office-holders in the Scottish Administration which must be paid into the Scottish Consolidated Fund, subject to any alternative arrangements made by or under an Act of the Scottish Parliament. This would permit the retention of receipts by any office-holder in the Scottish Administration to set against expenditure and it would enable the Scottish Parliament to make arrangements equivalent to those applicable to the U.K. Consolidated Fund by which the U.K. Parliament provides for sums to be appropriated in aid of the sum voted. It permits the net accounting of receipts.

The power to vary the effect of subs. (3) by legislation under subs. (4) has been exercised, with effect from April 1, 2000, by s.9 of the Public Finance and Accountability (Scotland) Act 2000 (asp 1) in respect of the Keeper of the Registers of Scotland. (Transitional provision had earlier been made by the Scotland Act 1998 (Transitory and Transitional Provisions) (Finance) Order 1999 (S.I. 1999 No. 441), art.22.) For additional special provision in respect of the accounts of the Keeper, see the note on s.71 (5), (6).

Subss. (5), (6), (7)

These subsections enable the designation by the Treasury of certain receipts otherwise payable into the Scottish Consolidated Fund for the purpose of making them payable instead to the Secretary of State. This mechanism is intended to be used to ensure that receipts such as interest payments or fines should continue to be paid into the U.K. Consolidated Fund. Subsection (7) provides direct authority for the payments, *i.e.* without the need for the additional approval of the Scottish Parliament.

An order under subs. (5) attracts Type K procedure under Sched. 7, *i.e.* an instrument subject to annulment by the House of Commons.

The Scotland Act (Designation and Receipts) Order 2000 (S.I. 2000 No.687) designated, with effect from April 1, 2000, certain receipts for the purposes of subss. (5)–(7): fines, forfeitures and fixed penalties; certain dividends and interest; and sums received from the European Social Fund in respect of training expenditure incurred by Scottish Enterprise and Highlands and Islands Enterprise. (Transitional provision had earlier been made by the Scotland Act 1998 (Transitory and Transitional Provisions) (Finance) Order 1999 (S.I. 1999 No. 441), art.8.)

Subs. (8)

As with other public funds, the Scottish Consolidated Fund is formally held with the Paymaster General.

Payments out of the Fund

65.—(1) A sum may only be paid out of the Scottish Consolidated Fund if—

(a) it has been charged on the Fund by any enactment,

(b) it is payable out of the Fund without further approval by virtue of this Act, or

[1](c) it is paid out for or in connection with any of the purposes mentioned in subsection (2) in accordance with rules made by or under an Act of the Scottish Parliament.

(2) Those purposes are—

(a) meeting expenditure of the Scottish Administration,

(b) meeting expenditure payable out of the Fund under any enactment.

(3) A sum paid out of the Fund shall not be applied for any purpose other than that for which it was charged or (as the case may be) paid out.

NOTE
[1] Modified by S.I. 1999 No. 441, art. 10. Effective July 1, 1999 until April 1, 2000.

DEFINITIONS
"Act of the Scottish Parliament": s.28(1).
"by virtue of": s.126(11).
"enactment": s.126(1).
"Scottish Administration": s.126(6).

GENERAL NOTE
This is the second of three sections dealing with the Scottish Consolidated Fund. It specifies the circumstances in which payments may be made out of the Fund and, in the case of authorisation by the Scottish Parliament, the purposes for which such payments may be made. It also restricts the purposes for which sums paid out of the Fund may be applied.
See also s.119 (Consolidated Fund, etc.) which modifies pre-commencement enactments to take account of the Scottish Consolidated Fund; and paras. 4, 5 of Sched. 4.

Subs. (1)
Payments out of the Scottish Consolidated Fund may be made in only three circumstances. It may be expected that, in practice, most payments will be made under the authority of para. (c), *i.e.* in accordance with rules made by or under an Act of the Scottish Parliament (see below). Otherwise payments must be either (a) statutorily charged on the Fund or (b) made payable without further approval by virtue of provisions in this Act.
Category (a) includes payments deriving from all charges imposed by enactment, *i.e.* including an Act of the U.K. Parliament (including this Act—see, *e.g.* the amendment made to the Lands Tribunal Act 1949, by Sched. 8, para.9 and the enactments amended by s.119) and, in due course, Acts of the Scottish Parliament. The charging procedure is used for judicial salaries (as with members of the Lands Tribunal for Scotland but also the salaries of judges in the ordinary courts, on which see Sched. 4, para. 5) and also payments to the Secretary of State in respect of "designated receipts" (see s.64(6), (7)) and loans (see ss.66(2) and 71(7)).
Category (b) covers other payments authorised for direct payment, without the further approval of the Scottish Parliament. (See, *e.g.* ss.89, 119).
As to category (c), general provision for the authorisation of expenditure from the Scottish Consolidated Fund has now been made by the Public Finance and Accountability (Scotland) Act 2000 (asp 1). For the year to March 31, 2000, however, transitional provision had to be made and this was done by the Scotland Act 1998 (Transitory and Transitional Provisions) (Appropriations) Order 1999 (S.I. 1999 No.674) (as subsequently amended by S.S.I.s 2000 Nos. 69 and 175). The year to March 31, 2001 is another transitional year. Sections 1–3, 4 (2)–(5) and 7 of the 2000 Act do not take effect until April 1, 2001 (Public Finance and Accountability (Scotland) Act 2000 (Commencement) Order 2000 (S.S.I. 2000 No.10)) and transitional provision has been made (Public Finance and Accountability (Scotland) Act 2000 (Transitional, Transitory and Saving Provisions) (No.2) Order 2000 (S.S.I. 2000 No.46), art.2). With effect from 2001–2002, the Public Finance and Accountability (Scotland) Act 2000 restricts the use of resources for any purpose in any financial year to amounts authorised by a Budget Act (s.1) and, apart from special arrangements for emergencies (s.2) and contingencies (s.3), payments may be made out of the Scottish Consolidated Fund only in accordance with such authorisation (s.4). No sum may be paid out, except in accordance with a credit granted on the Fund by the Auditor General for Scotland (s.5 and see also the Scotland Act ss.69, 70).
To make provision for 2000–2001, the Scottish Parliament has (in terms of S.S.I. 2000 No. 46, art.2(2)) passed the Budget (Scotland) Act 2000 (asp 2). At the time of its introduction as a Bill, there were also published the Scottish Executive's "Scotland's Budget Documents 2000–01" which included an explanation of the relationship between the UK Government's and the Scottish Executive's public expenditure plans.
In place of the general provision in ss.2, 3 of the Public Finance and Accountability (Scotland) Act 2000 (which do not come into effect until April 2001), the Budget (Scotland) Act 2000 contains special provision for contingency and emergency funding during 2000–2001 (ss.3,5).
An important feature of the Budget (Scotland) Act 2000, which will be continued in future Budget Acts, is the provision made in s.6 for budget revisions. Following discussion initiated in the FIAG Report (see General Note on Part III above) and followed up in the Scottish Executive's Consultation Paper on a Financial Framework for the Scottish Parliament (July 1999) and the Policy Memorandum which accompanied the Public Finance and Accountability (Scotland) Bill, provision is made for the amendment of amounts of expenditure authorised by the Budget Act by means of an order made by the Scottish Ministers, subject to prior approval in draft by resolution of the Parliament. Unlike the position at Westminster, there is no need for further primary legislation to authorise the modifications proposed. Provision for the handling of Budget Bills in the Parliament has been made in the Standing Orders at Rule 9.16 (as substituted on January 20, 2000).

Subs. (2)
This defines the purposes for which the Scottish Parliament may approve payments out of the Fund.

Subs. (3)
This confines the use of sums paid out of the Fund to the purposes for which they were charged or for which payment was authorised.

Borrowing by the Scottish Ministers etc

66.—(1) The Scottish Ministers may borrow from the Secretary of State any sums required by them for the purpose of—

(a) meeting a temporary excess of sums paid out of the Scottish Consolidated Fund over sums paid into that Fund, or

(b) providing a working balance in the Fund.

(2) Amounts required for the repayment of, or the payment of interest on, sums borrowed under this section shall be charged on the Fund.

(3) Sums borrowed under this section shall be repaid to the Secretary of State at such times and by such methods, and interest on them shall be paid to him at such rates and at such times, as the Treasury may from time to time determine.

(4) A member of the Scottish Executive may borrow money only under this section or under any power conferred by any other Act of Parliament.

DEFINITIONS
"member of the Scottish Executive": s.44(1).
"Scottish Ministers": s.44(2).

GENERAL NOTE
The Scottish Ministers do not have a general power to borrow. However, this section does, as the third in a group of sections dealing with the Scottish Consolidated Fund, permit the Scottish Ministers to borrow from the Secretary of State for the very limited purposes of meeting a temporary shortfall, or providing a working balance, in the Fund. Amounts borrowed are themselves a charge on the Fund and are to be repaid in accordance with rules laid down by the Treasury (see subs. (3)), *i.e.* without the need for further authority from the Scottish Parliament (see s.65). Any other power to borrow would require separate authority in a U.K. Act (subs. (4)).

See also s.67 (Lending by the Secretary of State), s.71 (Existing debt) and s.72 (Accounts of loans to the Scottish Ministers).

Lending by the Secretary of State

67.—(1) The Treasury may issue to the Secretary of State out of the National Loans Fund such sums as are required by him for making loans under section 66.

(2) The aggregate at any time outstanding in respect of the principal of sums borrowed under that section shall not exceed £500 million.

(3) The Secretary of State may by order made with the consent of the Treasury substitute for the amount (or substituted amount) specified in subsection (2) such increased amount as may be specified in the order.

(4) Sums received by the Secretary of State under section 66(3) shall be paid into the National Loans Fund.

GENERAL NOTE
This section is consequential upon the power conferred on the Secretary of State (by s.66) to lend sums to the Scottish Ministers for limited purposes in relation to the Scottish Consolidated Fund. It authorises the Treasury to issue the necessary sums from the National Loans Fund (subs. (1)) and requires repayment of sums (received back under s.66(3)) into that Fund. The maximum (principal) amount to be borrowed is fixed at £500m (subs. (2))-subject to increase by order (subs. (3)). Such an order would be subject, under Sched. 7, to Type E procedure, *i.e.* requiring approval in draft by resolution of the House of Commons.

See also s.71 (Existing debt) and s.72 (Accounts of loans to the Scottish Ministers).

Borrowing by statutory bodies

68.—(1) If a member of the Scottish Executive lends money to a body established under any enactment, the rate of interest on the loan shall not be less than the lowest rate determined by the Treasury under section 5 of the National Loans Act 1968 in respect of similar loans made out of the National Loans Fund on the day the loan is made.

(2) A body established under any enactment shall not, in pursuance of a power conferred by virtue of an Act of the Scottish Parliament, borrow money in a currency other than sterling except with the consent of the Scottish Ministers given with the approval of the Treasury.

DEFINITIONS
"Act of the Scottish Parliament": s.28(1).
"body": s.126(1).
"by virtue of": s.126(11).
"enactment": ss.113(6), 126(1).
"member of the Scottish Executive": s.44(1).
"Scottish Ministers": s.44(2).

GENERAL NOTE
This section puts in place two important reservations of Treasury control in relation to lending by members of the Scottish Executive to public bodies.
Subsection (1) requires that the rate of interest on any such loans must not be less than that determined by the Treasury in respect of "similar loans" from the National Loans Fund.
Subsection (2) imposes on borrowing by public bodies under an Act of the Scottish Parliament a requirement, widely imposed by Acts of the U.K. Parliament, that, where borrowing is done in a currency other than sterling, Treasury approval must be given.

The Auditor General for Scotland

69.—(1) There shall be an Auditor General for Scotland who shall be an individual appointed by Her Majesty on the nomination of the Parliament.

(2) A recommendation shall not be made to Her Majesty for the removal from office of the Auditor General for Scotland unless the Parliament so resolves and, if the resolution is passed on a division, the number of members voting in favour is not less than two—thirds of the total number of seats for members of the Parliament.

(3) The validity of any act of the Auditor General for Scotland is not affected by any defect in his nomination by the Parliament.

(4) The Auditor General for Scotland shall not, in the exercise of any of his functions, be subject to the direction or control of any member of the Scottish Executive or of the Parliament.

(5) Subsection (4) does not apply in relation to any function conferred on him of preparing accounts.

DEFINITIONS
"functions": s.126(1).
"member of the Scottish Executive": s.44(1).
"the Parliament": s.126(1).

GENERAL NOTE
This section was created in its present form at House of Lords committee stage when its provisions were extracted from what is now s.70 (*Hansard*, H.L. Vol. 592, col. 1721). Those provisions had been inserted into the Bill at House of Commons report stage (*Hansard*, H.C. Vol. 312, col. 764) when the mechanisms for financial control of the Scottish Ministers were strengthened in response to the expression of concern about weaknesses in arrangements previously made, especially the fears of the Chairman of the Public Accounts Committee, Mr. David Davis M.P.. Instead of leaving the issue of audit and its independence for the Scottish Parliament to arrange, this section makes express provision for the appointment of an Auditor General for Scotland. The functions of the Auditor General are conferred by legislation made under s.70.
Additional provision has been made concerning the office and functions of the Auditor General for Scotland by the Public Finance and Accountability (Scotland) Act 2000 (asp 1). For further discussion of that Act and the new institutional and procedural provision it makes for the audit of Scottish public authorities, see s.70. Section 13 of the 2000 Act provides for the salary of the Auditor General, the terms and conditions of office, and vacancies in the office.

Subs. (1)
The Auditor General for Scotland is to be a person appointed by Her Majesty the Queen on the Parliament's nomination.
The Standing Orders of the Parliament have made provision for the nomination of the Auditor General for Scotland, a procedure which involves the appointment of a selection panel (Rule 3.11).

Subs. (2)
Security of tenure is sought by the requirement of a two-thirds vote for removal in the Scottish Parliament.
Standing Orders provide that a motion for a resolution to recommend removal may be proposed by any MSP (Rule 3.12).

Subs. (3)
This is a provision parallel to that made by s.50 in respect of the appointment of members of the Scottish Executive.

Subss. (4), (5)
Subsection (4) is intended to provide a further measure of protection for the independence of the Auditor General. For a parallel provision, see s.70(5). Section 69(5) does, however, permit the regulation of the preparation of the Auditor General's own accounts and their audit. See the Public Finance and Accountability (Scotland) Act 2000 ss.19(8), 25.

Financial control, accounts and audit

70.—(1) Scottish legislation shall provide—

(a) for proper accounts to be prepared by the Scottish Ministers, by the Lord Advocate and by other persons to whom sums are paid out of the Scottish Consolidated Fund, of their expenditure and receipts,

(b) for the Scottish Ministers to prepare an account of payments into and out of the Fund,

(c) for the Auditor General for Scotland to exercise, or ensure the exercise by other persons of, the functions mentioned in subsection (2),

(d) for access by persons exercising those functions to such documents as they may reasonably require,

(e) for members of the staff of the Scottish Administration designated for the purpose to be answerable to the Parliament in respect of the expenditure and receipts of each part of the Scottish Administration, and

(f) for the publication of parliamentary accounts and of reports on such accounts and for the laying of such accounts and reports before the Parliament.

(2) The functions referred to in subsection (1)(c) are—

(a) issuing credits for the payment of sums out of the Fund,

(b) examining parliamentary accounts (which includes determining whether sums paid out of the Fund have been paid out and applied in accordance with section 65), and certifying and reporting on them,

(c) carrying out examinations into the economy, efficiency and effectiveness with which the Scottish Ministers and the Lord Advocate have used their resources in discharging their functions, and

(d) carrying out examinations into the economy, efficiency and effectiveness with which other persons determined under Scottish legislation to whom sums are paid out of the Fund have used those sums in discharging their functions.

(3) Standing orders shall provide for the consideration by the Parliament of accounts and reports laid before it in pursuance of subsection (1)(f).

(4) Scottish legislation may make further provision for the purpose of ensuring that persons who receive sums derived from the Fund are accountable including, in particular, provision for any person to whom subsection (1)(a) does not apply to be accountable for his expenditure and receipts in respect of functions for which he receives sums derived from the Fund.

(5) Persons (other than the Auditor General for Scotland) charged with the exercise of any function mentioned in subsection (2) or other like function conferred by Scottish legislation shall not, in the exercise of that or any ancillary function, be subject to the direction or control of any member of the Scottish Executive or of the Parliament.

(6) Scottish legislation may not require any cross-border public authority to prepare accounts if any other legislation requires—

(a) the authority to prepare accounts of its expenditure and receipts, and

(b) the accounts to be examined, certified and reported on by the Auditor General for Scotland, the Comptroller and Auditor General or a person appointed by either of them.

(7) Subsection (2)(b) does not apply to accounts prepared by the Auditor General for Scotland.

(8) This section does not require Scottish legislation to impose any requirement which is imposed by any other legislation.

(9) In this section—

"parliamentary accounts" means—

(a) any accounts prepared in pursuance of subsection (1)(a) or (b), and

(b) any accounts referred to in subsection (6) which are required to be examined, certified and reported on by the Auditor General for Scotland or any person appointed by him,

"Scottish legislation" means provision made by or under an Act of the Scottish Parliament and "other legislation" means provision made by any other enactment.

DEFINITIONS
"Act of the Scottish Parliament": s.28(1).
"Auditor General for Scotland": s.69.
"cross-border public authority": s.88(5).
"document": s.126(1).
"enactment": ss.113(6), 126(1).
"functions": s.126(1).
"members of the Scottish Executive": s.44(1).
"members of the staff of the Scottish Administration": s.126(7).
"other legislation": subs. (9).
"the Parliament": s.126(1).
"parliamentary accounts": subs. (9).
"Scottish Administration": s.126(6).
"Scottish legislation": subs. (9).
"Scottish Ministers": s.44(2).
"standing orders": s.126(1).

GENERAL NOTE
Paragraph 7.27 of the White Paper stated:
"The detailed arrangements which the Scottish Parliament makes to control and scrutinise the spending of the Scottish Executive will be a matter for the Scottish Parliament and its committees, but the Scotland Bill will lay a general obligation on the Scottish Parliament to establish effective scrutiny and audit arrangements".

As already noted, however, in relation to s.69, the arrangements to be made by the Scotland Act itself were strengthened, in particular by establishing the office of Auditor General for Scotland in that section. Another specific addition was the requirement to designate "accounting officers" on the staff of the Scottish Administration (see s.70(1)(e)).

A further requirement proposed by the White Paper itself was that suitable audit machinery would have to be agreed before the Scottish Parliament became fully operational in order to ensure that the actions of the Scottish Executive could be called to account as soon as it assumed its responsibilities (para. 7.27). The Financial Issues Advisory Group (FIAG) was established in February 1998 to consider these matters and a prominent issue in the Group's deliberations and recommendation was the relationship between the new office of the Auditor General for Scotland and the arrangements then operating for the audit of local authority and health service accounts by the Accounts Commission.

At the point that the Scottish Parliament and Executive were established, temporary provision was made by the Scotland Act 1998 (Transitory and Transitional Provisions) (Finance) Order 1999 (S.I. 1999 No.441). This has, however, been replaced by the provision now made, with effect from April 1, 2000, by Part 2 of the Public Finance and Accountability (Scotland) Act 2000 (asp 1) (See the Public Finance and Accountability (Scotland) Act 2000 (Commencement) Order 2000 (S.S.I 2000 No.10).)

The Act creates two new bodies. One is called Audit Scotland and consists of the Auditor General for Scotland, the Chairman of the Accounts Commission (the body where responsibilities under the Local Government (Scotland) Act 1973 relate primarily to the audit of local authority accounts) and three other members appointed jointly by the Auditor General and the Chairman (s.10(1), (2)). The principal duty of Audit Scotland is to provide assistance and support to both the Auditor General and to the Accounts Commission (s.10(3)). (For further provision on Audit Scotland, see Sched. 2 to the Act and see also the Public Finance and Accountability (Scotland) Act 2000 (Transfer of NAO Staff etc.) Order 2000 (S.I. 2000 No.935) made under s.104 of the Scotland Act 1998.) The composition and the responsibilities of the Accounts Commission have been amended (to transfer the audit of Scottish health authorities to the Auditor General) and the Controller of Audit has become a member of the staff of Audit Scotland (Sched. 4).

The other new body created by the 2000 Act is the Scottish Commission for Public Audit (s.12 and Sched. 3). This is a parliamentary body consisting of the convener of the Audit Committee of the Scottish Parliament and four other MSPs appointed by the Parliament. The Commission has a supervisory role on behalf of the Parliament and can require the supply of information by Audit Scotland (s.13 (3)), in respect of which it also has audit responsibilities (ss.19(8) and 25).

Subs. (1)
One technical amendment made in the House of Commons, along with the substantive changes referred to above, was to introduce (uniquely) into this section the concept of "Scottish legislation" as the device for the implementation of most of the section's requirements.

Scottish legislation must provide for the preparation of accounts (paras. (a), (b)); the functions of the Auditor General for Scotland (see s.69) and "other independent persons" (see subss. (2), (5)) (para. (c)); the right of access of the Auditor General and independent persons to documents reasonably required by them (para. (d)); the designation of staff of the Scottish Administration to be answerable to the Parliament (para. (e)); and, finally, for the publication and laying before the Parliament of accounts and reports (para. (f)).

Following the temporary provision made by the Scotland Act 1998 (Transitory and Transitional Provisions) (Finance)Order 1999 (S.I. 1999 No. 441) the Scottish Parliament has made provision for these matters, with effect from April 1, 2000, in Part 2 of the Public Finance and Accountability (Scotland) Act 2000. The principal institutional changes have been referred to in the General Note. Other provisions of the Act (listed in the order of subject matter set out in s.70 (1)) include:

Sections 19,30 (duty to prepare accounts and consolidated public accounts)
Sections 21,22 (audit of accounts)
Sections 23 (economy, efficiency and effectiveness examinations)
Section 24 (access to documents and information)
Section 14,15 (principal accountable officer for the Scottish Administration and accountable officers). The terminology of "accountable officer" has been adopted instead of "accounting officer", as used in Whitehall. Sections 16, 17 and 18 of the Act make provision for accountable officers for the Parliamentary corporation and Audit Scotland.
Section 22 (5) (publication and laying of accounts and reports)

Subs. (2)
This specifies the functions of the Auditor General for Scotland. They are broadly the same as those defined for the Comptroller and Auditor General under the National Audit Act 1983 (c.44) (and see Sched. 8, para. 20).

For the provision now made by the Public Finance and Accountability (Scotland) Act 2000, see the note on subs. (1). See also subs. (7) below.

Subs. (3)
Section 22 and Sched. 3 make general provision for the making of standing orders by the Parliament. The Parliament's Standing Orders provide for the laying of reports and other documents before the Parliament (Rule 14.1); and the remit of the Audit Committee (Rule 6.7) which includes considering and reporting on accounts and reports laid before the Parliament by the Auditor General for Scotland.

Subs. (4)
This enables the extension of the obligations imposed by subs. (1) to other persons receiving sums from the Scottish Consolidated Fund.

Section 19 (3) of the Public Finance and Accountability (Scotland) Act 2000 extends the obligation to prepare accounts to non-ministerial holders of offices in the Scottish Administration, when this is required by the Scottish Ministers.

Subs. (5)
This attaches to the "persons" referred to in subs. (1)(c), (d) the same requirement of independence as is attached to the Auditor General by s.69(4).

Subs. (6)
For "cross-border public authorities" see ss. 88–90. The point of this subsection (*Hansard*, H.L. Vol. 592, col. 1718) is to avoid dual accounting and dual auditing for those CBPAs which receive part of their income directly from the Scottish Consolidated Fund. The Forestry Commission and the Food Standards Agency were mentioned by the Minister. The subsection prevents the Scottish Parliament from imposing accounting and audit requirements where these are already imposed by other legislation. See also subs. (8).

Subs. (7)
This subsection relieves the Auditor General for Scotland from the obligation to examine his or her own accounts.

Provision has been made by the Public Finance and Accountability (Scotland) Act 2000 for accounts to be prepared by Audit Scotland (not, in terms, the Auditor General for Scotland) and for their audit on behalf of the Scottish Commission for Public Audit (ss.19(8) and 25).

Subs. (8)
There is no need for new Scottish legislation to impose requirements under this section which are imposed by some other enactment. See also subs. (6).

Existing debt

71.—(1) Subsections (2) to (4) apply where—

(a) power to lend money under a provision of a pre-commencement enactment was exercised by the Secretary of State,

(b) the sums required by him for the exercise of the power were issued by the Treasury out of the National Loans Fund, and

(c) the power is exercisable by the Scottish Ministers by virtue of section 53, or would have been so exercisable but for the repeal of the pre-commencement enactment.

(2) Any amount payable by way of repayment of or interest on the loan shall be paid to the Scottish Ministers and into the Scottish Consolidated Fund (instead of to the Secretary of State and into the National Loans Fund).

(3) Amounts equal to those which are to be received by the Scottish Ministers in repayment of principal shall be treated as being amounts of advances made on the commencement of this section to the Scottish Ministers by the Secretary of State.

(4) Such advances shall be repaid to the Secretary of State at such times and by such methods, and interest on them shall be paid to him at such rates and at such times, as the Treasury may from time to time determine.

(5) Subsection (6) applies to any amount outstanding immediately before the commencement of this subsection in respect of the principal of the sum treated by virtue of section 2(3) of the Government Trading Funds Act 1973 as issued to the Registers of Scotland Executive Agency Trading Fund on the day on which the order establishing that fund came into force ("the issue date").

(6) The Secretary of State may, with the agreement of the Treasury, by order provide—

(a) for the amount to be treated as an advance made by him to the Scottish Ministers on the issue date, and

(b) for the advance to be repaid to him at such times and by such methods, and for interest on the advance to be paid to him at such rates and at such times, as were determined by the Treasury under section 2B(3) of that Act in respect of the sum referred to in subsection (5).

(7) Sums required to be paid under subsection (4) or (6) shall be charged on the Scottish Consolidated Fund.

(8) Sums received under subsection (4) or (6) shall be paid into the National Loans Fund.

DEFINITIONS
"by virtue of": s.126(11).
"issue date": subs. (5).
"pre-commencement enactment": s.53(3).
"Scottish Ministers": s.44(2).

GENERAL NOTE
This section makes provision closely related to that in ss.66, 67. Whereas those sections deal with the making of new loans by the Secretary of State to the Scottish Ministers for limited purposes, this section provides (a) that certain existing debts owed to the Secretary of State instead became repayable (with the interest due) to the Scottish Ministers but also (b) that they were in turn to be treated as advances by the Secretary of State; as a charge on the Scottish Consolidated Fund; and repayable on terms determined by the Treasury. There is no need for the Scottish Parliament to give further approval for the payments (see s.65(1)), which are to the National Loans Fund.

The arrangements apply only to the types of loan specified in subs. (1): where the power to lend (by the Secretary of State) was under a pre-commencement enactment; the sums were issued from the National Loans Fund (*i.e.* not where provided by parliamentary vote); and the original power is now exercisable by the Scottish Ministers (or would be but for its repeal). This limits the scope of the section to sums lent to public bodies in relation to devolved matters.

Special provision is made by subss. (5), (6) in respect of the amount outstanding under s.2 of the Government Trading Funds Act 1973 (c.63), as issued to the Registers of Scotland Executive Agency Trading Fund. Under the power conferred by subs. (6), the Scotland Act 1998 (Transfer of Borrowing of the Registers of Scotland Executive Agency Trading Fund) Order 1999 (S.I. 1999 No.1596) has provided that the amount outstanding under that statute should be treated as an advance to the Scottish Ministers and that it should be repaid as previously determined. (See also the special arrangements in respect of the Registers of Scotland Executive Agency Trading Fund referred to in the note on s.64 (3), (4).)

Accounts of loans to the Scottish Ministers

72. The Secretary of State shall, for each financial year—

(a) prepare, in such form and manner as the Treasury may direct, an account of sums paid and received by him under sections 66, 67 and 71, and

(b) send the account to the Comptroller and Auditor General not later than the end of November in the following financial year,

and the Comptroller and Auditor General shall examine, certify and report on the account and shall lay copies of it and of his report before each House of Parliament.

DEFINITIONS
"financial year": s.126(1).

GENERAL NOTE
Section 72 lays down the accounting and auditing requirements in respect of sums paid and received by the Secretary of State under ss.66, 67 and 71.

PART IV

THE TAX-VARYING POWER

GENERAL NOTE
One of the most distinctive and best known proposals of the Scottish Constitutional Convention was that the Scottish Parliament should have an independent power to vary levels of income tax in Scotland. They said:

"In the Western democracies all principal levels of national and local government have powers over taxation. While the Parliament's income will be principally based on totals of expenditure set at U.K. level, the power to vary the rate of tax is vital if the Parliament is to be properly accountable. Critics of the proposal to establish a Parliament in Scotland repeatedly state that such a power is essential for an effective Parliament.

Scotland's Parliament will have the power to increase or cut the basic rate of income tax for Scottish taxpayers by a maximum of 3p in the pound. This will give it a greater degree of independence." *Scotland's Parliament: Scotland's Right* (1995) p. 27.

Such a power to vary income tax in Scotland was not included in the 1978 Act and the total dependence of the proposed Assembly on funding decisions made by the U.K. Government had, as the Convention said, been criticised. Their tax-varying proposal was taken forward in the White Paper which announced that, subject to the outcome of the referendum, the Scottish Parliament should have such a power. (Para. 7.11.). It was not, however, made clear whether the necessary statutory scheme would be included in this Act or whether separate provision would be made. In the event, this Act has itself made provision for the tax-varying powers in Pt. IV.

In the White Paper, the Government did outline the main provisions of the scheme. They remained committed, in the first instance, to providing a tax-varying power by way of a power to vary income tax rather than any other tax. Income tax, they claimed, was broadly based and easy to administer, relatively simple and easy to understand and free of the difficulties associated with the other major tax bases such as VAT, corporation tax, or National Insurance. They also ruled out the use of the council tax or non-domestic rates for this purpose as liable to "over-burden the local government finance system and undermine the accountability of local government to its electorate". (para. 7.12.).

Thus the Scottish Parliament would have the power to increase or decrease the basic rate of income tax set by the U.K. Parliament by a maximum of 3pence which would currently be the equivalent of a power to raise or forgo £450m in a year. The White Paper recognised, however, that attaching the tax-varying power to the basic rate of income tax made it vulnerable to changes in the U.K. income tax structure and so an undertaking was given to preserve the Scottish Parliament's ability to vary its income through the tax structure by up to £450m, index-linked to maintain its value. Changes in the mechanism for protecting that tax take would be the subject of joint discussion between the Scottish Executive and U.K. Government (paras. 7.13–7.14.).

Beyond the commitment to the principle of the tax-varying power, the White Paper did not go into much more detail. It was, however, made clear that the savings and dividend income of individuals would not be subject to the tax-varying powers. (Para. 7.15.). One consequence of this would be to simplify somewhat the identification of those people subject to any variation ordered by the Scottish Parliament. The test of liability would be "residence"— a concept described by the White Paper as well established in tax law: "A Scottish resident will be an individual who is resident in the U.K. for income tax purposes and who in any tax year spends at least half of his time in Scotland (when in the U.K.) or whose principal home is in Scotland. These concepts will be set out in legislation." (para. 7.16.).

Tax collection would be done by the Inland Revenue, with employees paying as usual by PAYE. (Para. 7.17.). The White Paper estimated the costs to the Government of establishing the mechanisms for tax variation at £10m, with running costs at about £8 per annum. The Scottish Parliament would be required to meet the administration costs incurred by the Inland Revenue but there would also be additional costs in setting up PAYE collection which would be borne by employers. (paras 7.18–7.19).

In the Act itself, the key provisions are: those in Sched. 5, which reserve matters including "taxes and excise duties" to the Westminster Parliament; those in Pt. III, which contains general Financial Provisions in relation to the Scottish Parliament and Executive; and those in Pt. IV. See also s.110 (Scottish taxpayers for social security purposes).

Despite the importance attached to the inclusion of the tax-varying power in the Scotland Act, it should be observed that the Partnership Agreement concluded between the political parties which constituted the initial governing coalition contains a commitment not to use the power in the course of the first Parliament.

Power to fix basic rate for Scottish taxpayers

73.—(1) Subject to section 74, this section applies for any year of assessment for which income tax is charged if—

(a) the Parliament has passed a resolution providing for the percentage determined to be the basic rate for that year to be increased or reduced for Scottish taxpayers in accordance with the resolution,

(b) the increase or reduction provided for is confined to an increase or reduction by a number not exceeding three which is specified in the resolution and is either a whole number or half of a whole number, and

(c) the resolution has not been cancelled by a subsequent resolution of the Parliament.

(2) Where this section applies for any year of assessment the Income Tax Acts (excluding this Part) shall have effect in relation to the income of Scottish taxpayers as if any rate determined by the Parliament of the United Kingdom to be the basic rate for that year were increased or reduced in accordance with the resolution of the Scottish Parliament.

(3) In subsection (2) the reference to the income of Scottish taxpayers does not include a reference to any income of Scottish taxpayers which, had it been income for the year 1998–99, would have been income to which section 1A of the Income and Corporation Taxes Act 1988 (income from savings and distributions) applied for that year.

(4) In this section—

(a) a reference, in relation to any year of assessment, to income tax being charged for that year includes a reference to the passing of a PCTA resolution that provides for the charging of that tax for that year, and

(b) a reference, in relation to a year of assessment, to the determination by the Parliament of the United Kingdom of a rate to be the basic rate for that year includes a reference to the passing of a PCTA resolution specifying a percentage to be the basic rate for that year.

(5) In this section "a PCTA resolution" means a resolution of the House of Commons containing such a declaration as is mentioned in section 1(2)(b) of the Provisional Collection of Taxes Act 1968.

DEFINITIONS
"the Parliament": s.126(1).
"a PCTA resolution": subs. (5).
"Scottish taxpayers": s.75(1).

GENERAL NOTE
Probably the best starting point is s.73(2), which provides that the Income Tax Acts shall have effect in relation to the income of Scottish taxpayers as if the rate determined by the U.K. Parliament as the basic rate were increased or reduced in accordance with a resolution of the

Scottish Parliament. The term "Scottish taxpayers" is defined in s.75 but it is subs. (3) of this section which narrows the meaning of the "income of Scottish taxpayers" to exclude income currently identified as income from savings and (dividend) distributions by s.1A of the Income and Corporation Taxes Act 1988 (c.1). This was an exclusion heralded in the White Paper to ensure consistent treatment across the United Kingdom and to avoid economic distortion (para. 7.15).

The section takes account of the machinery adopted in the Westminster Parliament by which the House of Commons passes a resolution ("a PCTA resolution") which authorises the collection of taxes at a specified rate, pending the passing of the Finance Act which gives final authority for the levying of the tax at that rate. In terms of subss. (4), (5) references to the charging of income tax at a particular rate include the passing of a PCTA resolution and references to the "determination" of a rate also include a reference to the passing of a PCTA resolution. This is important because the fixing of the adjusted rate of tax for Scottish taxpayers has to be specified by reference to the rate determined at Westminster and in accordance with a timetable set by reference to that determination (see subs. (1) and s.74).

Finally, one returns to subs. (1) which, subject to the (primarily timetabling) provisions of s.74, specifies the conditions under which the other rules in the section apply. The section applies in any tax year (year of assessment) in respect of which a "tax-varying resolution" (see s.74(1)) has been passed and not been cancelled. The resolution must specify the number by which the percentage determined as the U.K. basic rate is to be increased or reduced for Scottish taxpayers (subs. (1)(a)). That number has to be a "number not exceeding three" and "either a whole number of half of a whole number" (*i.e.* 0.5, 1, 1.5, 2, 2.5, 3) (subs. (1)(b)).

Supplemental provision with respect to resolutions

74.—(1) This section applies to any resolution of the Parliament ("a tax-varying resolution") which—

(a) provides, in accordance with section 73, for an increase or reduction for Scottish taxpayers of the basic rate for any year of assessment, or

(b) cancels a previous resolution of the Parliament providing for such an increase or reduction.

(2) Subject to subsection (3), a tax-varying resolution—

(a) must be expressed so as to relate to no more than a single year of assessment beginning after, but no more than twelve months after, the passing of the resolution, but

(b) shall have effect in relation to a determination by the Parliament of the United Kingdom of the rate to be the basic rate for that year irrespective of whether that determination had been made at the time of the passing of the resolution.

(3) Subsection (2) shall not prevent a tax-varying resolution relating to any year of assessment from being passed and having effect where—

(a) a determination by the Parliament of the United Kingdom of the rate to be the basic rate for that year is made after, or less than a month before, the beginning of that year,

(b) that determination is not confined to the passing of the enactment by which a determination of the same rate by a PCTA resolution is ratified, and

(c) the tax-varying resolution is passed within the period of one month beginning with the day of the making by the Parliament of the United Kingdom of its determination.

(4) Where, in a case to which subsection (3) applies, a tax-varying resolution is passed after the beginning of the year of assessment to which it relates—

(a) the resolution shall have effect as from the beginning of that year, and

(b) all such payments, repayments, deductions and other adjustments shall be made as are required to restore the position to what it would have been if the resolution had been passed before the beginning of that year.

(5) Standing orders shall ensure that only a member of the Scottish Executive may move a motion for a tax-varying resolution.

(6) A tax-varying resolution shall not be passed so as to have effect in relation to any year of assessment before the year 2000–01.

(7) Subsections (4) and (5) of section 73 apply for the purposes of this section as they apply for the purposes of that section.

DEFINITIONS
"enactment": ss.113(6), 126(1).
"member of the Scottish Executive": s.44(1).
"the Parliament": s.126(1).
"a PCTA resolution": subs. (7) and s.73(5).
"Scottish taxpayers": s.75(1).
"standing orders": s.126(1).
"a tax-varying resolution": subs. (1).

GENERAL NOTE

As explained in relation to s.73, the procedure by which the Scottish Parliament may vary the level of income tax for a particular year of assessment is the passing of a resolution to that effect. Section 74 now makes important further provision in relation to such resolutions.

A "tax-varying resolution" is defined to include a resolution which, in accordance with s.73, provides for an increase or reduction of the basic rate and also a resolution which cancels a previous such resolution of the Parliament (subs. (1)). In accordance with the practice established in the Westminster Parliament, standing orders must ensure that a tax-varying resolution is moved only by a member of the Scottish Executive (subs. (5)). It is also provided that no tax-varying resolution may be passed in relation to a year prior to 2000–01 (subs. (6)).

Also with reference to the timing of a resolution, the principal contribution of the section is then to provide that, subject to a number of qualifications, a tax-varying resolution must be expressed to relate to a single year of assessment and that that year of assessment must begin after the passing of the resolution but not more than twelve months after its passing (subs. (2) (a)). As explained in relation to s.73, a resolution has to relate to a rate of the basic rate of tax determined by the U.K. Parliament but it is provided that this can be done irrespective of whether the determination has actually been made at the time of the resolution (subs. (2)(b)), *i.e.* a resolution to increase the rate of tax for Scottish taxpayers by 3 pence could be passed before the general U.K. rate is known—at which point, for example, the Scottish Parliament might be in recess.

However, the general rule that a tax-varying resolution must be passed before the beginning of the tax year to which it relates does not have to apply in circumstances where the U.K. Parliament itself leaves the determination of the U.K. rate until after the beginning of the tax year or indeed until sometime in the final month of the preceding tax year, *i.e.* after March 6, (subs. (3)(a)). If that is the case, the Scottish Parliament is given a full month within which to pass its own tax-varying resolution (subs. (3)(c)). It should be noted that, for the purposes of this rule, the definition of "determination" is incorporated from s.73 (4), (5). See subs. (7).

A further gloss is that, whenever a tax-varying resolution is passed after the beginning of the tax year to which it relates, the resolution nevertheless has effect from the beginning of the year and financial adjustments must, if necessary, be made to restore the position to what it would have been if the resolution had been passed before the beginning of the year (subs. (4)). See also s.110(2).

Provision for motions for tax-varying resolutions has been made by Rule 8.10 of the Parliament's Standing Orders. The remit of the Finance Committee includes consideration of proposals to make a tax-varying resolution (Rule 6.6).

Scottish taxpayers

75.—(1) For the purposes of this Part a person is a Scottish taxpayer in relation to any year of assessment if—

(a) he is an individual who, for income tax purposes, is treated as resident in the United Kingdom in that year, and

(b) Scotland is the part of the United Kingdom with which he has the closest connection during that year.

(2) For the purposes of this section an individual who is treated for income tax purposes as resident in the United Kingdom in any year of assessment has his closest connection with Scotland during that year if, but only if, one or more of the following paragraphs applies in his case—

(a) he is an individual to whom subsection (3) applies for that year,

(b) the number of days which he spends in Scotland in that year is equal to or exceeds the number of days in that year which he spends elsewhere in the United Kingdom,

(c) he is an individual who, for the whole or any part of that year, is a member of Parliament for a constituency in Scotland, a member of the European Parliament for Scotland or a member of the Scottish Parliament.

(3) This subsection applies to an individual for a year of assessment if—

(a) he spends at least a part of that year in Scotland,

(b) for at least a part of the time that he spends in Scotland in that year, his principal UK home is located in Scotland and he makes use of it as a place of residence, and

(c) the times in that year when Scotland is where his principal UK home is located comprise (in aggregate) at least as much of that year as the times (if any) in that year when the location of his principal UK home is not in Scotland.

(4) For the purposes of this section—

(a) an individual spends a day in Scotland if, but only if, he is in Scotland at the end of that day, and

(b) an individual spends a day elsewhere in the United Kingdom if, but only if, he is in the United Kingdom at the end of that day and it is not a day that he spends in Scotland.

(5) For the purposes of this section an individual's principal UK home at any time is located in Scotland if at that time—

(a) he is an individual with a place of residence in Scotland, and

(b) in the case of an individual with two or more places of residence in the United Kingdom, Scotland is the location of such one of those places as at that time is his main place of residence in the United Kingdom.

(6) In this section "place" includes a place on board a vessel or other means of transport.

DEFINITIONS
"place,": subs. (6).
"Scotland": s.126(1), (2).

GENERAL NOTE
Crucial to the scheme for incorporating a tax-varying power is the identification of those taxpayers to be affected by the increase or reduction in tax resulting from a tax-varying resolution. The White Paper did not say much about this, beyond confirming that the "test of liability will be residence—a well established concept in tax law" (para. 7.16).

Section 73(1) applies the effect of a tax-varying resolution to "Scottish taxpayers" and now s.75 defines what is meant by that term. (It should also be noted that, for certain purposes in relation to social security, s.110 enables a different meaning to be given to the term.)

A person is defined as a "Scottish taxpayer" if, in relation to any year of assessment, he or she is (a) an individual who, for income tax purposes, is treated as resident in the U.K. in that year and (b) Scotland is the part of the U.K. with which he or she has the closest connection during that year (subs. (1)). The concept of "residence" for income tax purposes is one which, as the White Paper said, is reasonably well settled in its meaning and is unlikely to be unduly problematic in its application to the tax-varying power, but the idea of a person's having a "closest connection" with Scotland rather than some other part of the U.K. is new and may cause more difficulties. There is, however, further assistance. Subsection (2) states that a person has his or her closest connection with Scotland in a particular year of assessment only if one or more of three specified conditions applies:

1. He or she is a person who

(a) spends at least a part of that year in Scotland;

(b) for at least a part of that time, his or her principal U.K. home is located in Scotland and he or she makes use of it as a place of residence; and

(c) the times in the year when Scotland is where his or her principal U.K. home is located comprise (in aggregate) at least as much of that year as the times (if any) in that year when the location of his or her principal U.K. home is not in Scotland (subss. (2), (3)).

This is the "principal home" test of closest connection and will doubtless be the test which will come to define the vast majority of "Scottish taxpayers" as such. It requires that a part of the year be spent in Scotland and then that for a part of that part the person's principal U.K. home is in Scotland and is made use of as a place of residence. But, in addition, the person's principal U.K. home must be located for at least as long in Scotland as elsewhere.

Some further assistance is provided by the Act this Act on both the "spending" of time and on the location of a principal home. As to the spending of time, it is provided that (a) an individual spends a day in Scotland if, but only if, he or she is in Scotland at the end of that day and similarly that (b) an individual spends a day elsewhere in the United Kingdom, if, but only if, he or she is in the U.K. at the end of that day and it is not a day that he or she spends in Scotland (subs. (4)).

Secondly, it is provided that an individual's principal U.K. home at any time is located in Scotland if at that time (a) he or she is an individual with a place (which may include a place on board a vessel or other means of transport (subs. (6)) of residence in Scotland and (b) in the case of an individual with two or more places of residence in the United Kingdom, Scotland is the location of such one of those places as at that time is his or her main place of residence in the United Kingdom (subs. (5)).

2. The number of days which he or spends in Scotland in the year of assessment is equal to or exceeds the number of days in that year which he or she spends elsewhere in the United Kingdom.

This may be termed the "days spent" test and, as with the rules of the "principal home" test, must be read together with the further rules on the spending of time in subs. (4). It ensures that some of those who do not qualify as "Scottish taxpayers" by virtue of the location of (and residence in) their principal home will nevertheless qualify on grounds of days spent in Scotland. Perhaps the people most obviously qualifying on this ground will be U.K. taxpayers whose work brings them to Scotland but who return to their principal home for weekends or, for example, for a week in each month. Subsection (4) was amended at report stage in the House of Lords (*Hansard*, H.L. Vol. 593, cols. 2056–59) to delete the words "beginning or" before "the end of that day" in para. (a) and to make a related amendment to para. (b). At an earlier state, the case had been identified of the "famous lorry driver" who, if in Scotland at midnight, would have chalked up both the day before and the day after as days in Scotland. This could have led the lorry driver to qualify as a Scottish taxpayer on the basis of spending a mere 92 non-consecutive nights in Scotland. With the deletion of "beginning or" and the end of double-counting, the number of such nights would rise to 183. If the change had not been made and regional government with tax-varying powers were introduced across the United Kingdom, individuals might have had the misfortune to qualify as a variable rate taxpayer in three different areas!

3. The person is an individual who, for the whole or part of the year of assessment, is an MP, MEP or MSP.

Just in case they do not establish a "closest connection" with Scotland on either of the other two grounds, this "MP test" brings into the fold of "Scottish taxpayers" all types of Scotland-based parliamentarian. No doubt this is felt to be constitutionally appropriate. It also avoids the politically embarrassing possibility that the people's own representatives might otherwise escape liability to pay any higher level of taxation imposed on Scottish taxpayers.

Changes to income tax structure

76.—(1) This section applies where—
- (a) there has been a proposal for the modification of any provision made by or under the Income Tax Acts,
- (b) that proposal is one made and published by the Treasury or the Board, or (without having been so made and published) appears to the Treasury to be a proposal to which effect is likely to be given by Act of Parliament, and
- (c) it appears to the Treasury that the proposed modification would have a significant effect on the practical extent for any year of assessment of the Parliament's tax-varying powers.

(2) It shall be the duty of the Treasury, as soon as reasonably practicable after the publication of the proposal, or (as the case may be) as soon as reasonably practicable after it first appears to the Treasury that the proposal is likely to be enacted, to lay before the House of Commons—
- (a) a statement of whether, in the Treasury's opinion, an amendment of the Parliament's tax-varying powers is required as a consequence of the proposal, and
- (b) if in their opinion an amendment of those powers is required, the Treasury's proposals for amending those powers.

(3) Any proposals for amending the Parliament's tax-varying powers that are laid before the House of Commons by the Treasury under this section—
- (a) must be confined to income tax,
- (b) must appear to the Treasury to satisfy the conditions set out in subsections (4) and (5), and
- (c) must not contain any proposal for the Parliament's tax-varying powers to be exercisable in relation to the taxation of income from savings or distributions.

(4) The first condition mentioned in subsection (3)(b) is that the proposals would secure—
- (a) so far as possible, and
- (b) after making due allowance for annual changes in the retail prices index,

that the practical extent of the Parliament's tax-varying powers would remain broadly the same from year to year as it would be if (apart from any resolution of the Parliament) the law relating to income tax were the same from year to year as it was in relation to the year 1997–98.

(5) The second condition so mentioned is that the proposals would not enable the Parliament's tax-varying powers to be exercised for any year of assessment so as to have an effect on the levels of the after-tax income of Scottish taxpayers generally that would be significantly different from the effect their exercise could have had in any previous year of assessment.

(6) References in this section to the practical extent of the Parliament's tax-varying powers are references to the amounts of income tax for any year of assessment which appear to be or (as the case may be) to have been the maximum amounts capable of being raised and foregone in that year in pursuance of a resolution of the Parliament.

(7) In this section "income from savings or distributions" means income which, had it been income for the year 1998–99, would have been income to which section 1A of the Income and Corporation Taxes Act 1988 applied for that year.

DEFINITIONS
"income from savings or distributions": subs. (7).
"modification": s.126(1).
"the Parliament": s.126(1).
"practical extent of the Parliament's tax-raising powers": subs. (6).
"Scottish taxpayers": s.75(1).

GENERAL NOTE
When the proposals for a tax-varying power were made in the White Paper, it was acknowledged that some mechanism would be required to take account of future changes in the U.K. income tax structure (paras. 7.12–7.14). The power to be conferred by this Act would produce the possibility of the Scottish Parliament's increasing or reducing its revenue by about £450m. That amount was, however, contingent upon the general tax structure for the time being. If that structure were to be changed for quite unrelated reasons but the provisions of Pt. IV of this Act left entirely the same, this might have the undesirable effect of varying the impact of the tax-varying power. The figure of £450m might move sharply upwards or downwards. To avoid this, it would be necessary for the Parliament's powers to be preserved at the initial level. The sum of £450m would be index-linked to maintain its real value and a mechanism for protecting the Scottish tax take would be built in.

This section contains the mechanism for the handling of future changes to the income tax structure. At the core of the section is an obligation on the Treasury, presumably (but this is not made explicit) after consultation with the Scottish Ministers, to make proposals for the amendment of the present tax-varying powers in the light of some other future proposal to modify the Income Tax Acts in a way that "would have a significant effect on the practical extent for any year of assessment of the Parliament's tax-varying powers" (subs. (1)(c)). The Treasury would merely make proposals for amendments. These must be laid before the House of Commons. However, it would require an Act of Parliament to give effect to any changes. The Treasury does have some defined powers to amend existing enactments (see s.79) but not the terms of Pt. IV of this Act.

Other conditions attach to the Treasury's powers to review and to propose changes:
1. The Treasury can act only if there is a proposal (for the modification of a provision made by or under the Income Tax Acts) as defined in subs. (1) and where it appears that it would have the "significant effect" mentioned above.
2. The Treasury must, "as soon as reasonably practicable after the publication of the proposal" (or, if not published, "as soon as reasonably practicable after it first appears to the Treasury that the proposal is likely to be enacted"), lay before the Commons its statement of whether an amendment of the tax-varying power is required and, if so, its amendment proposals (subs. (2)).
3. Additional conditions are:
   (a) The proposals must be confined to income tax (subs. (3)(a)). There is no power to propose a tax-varying power related to some quite different aspect of the tax system.
   (b) The proposals must appear to satisfy other conditions laid down (subs. (3)(b)). These are that
   (i) so far as possible and allowing for changes in the R.P.I., the proposals would secure that "the practical extent of the Parliament's tax-varying powers would remain broadly the same from year to year" as it would if income tax law were the same as in relation to 1997–98 (subss. (4), (6)) (This condition is designed, as the White Paper promised, to preserve the tax take.); and
   (ii) the proposals would not enable the tax-varying powers to be exercised "so as to have an effect on the levels of the after-tax income of Scottish taxpayers generally that would be significantly different from the effect their exercise could have had in any previous year of assessment" (subs. (5)). (Although the terminology builds in quite a lot of flexibility, this condition is designed to ensure that the proposals, as well as preserving the overall tax take, will not have an unfairly abrupt effect on the income of Scottish taxpayers.)

(c) The Treasury's proposals must not contain any proposal to make the Parliament's tax-varying powers exercisable in relation to the taxation of income from savings or distributions (subss. (3)(c), (7)). For the exclusion of such income from the existing scheme, see s.73(3).

Although they have not led to proposals for amendment, Treasury statements under the section have been made on the occasion of the 1999 and 2000 Budgets. In the 1999 Budget Statement it was acknowledged that the Budget changes would make a one penny change in the Scottish variable rate worth £230m rather than £180m but, in the Treasury's view this did not require amendment of the tax-varying powers. In March, 2000 that figure was stated to have risen to £240m. (See Financial Statement and Budget Report.)

Accounting for additional Scottish tax

77.—(1) Where the basic rate for any year of assessment is increased for Scottish taxpayers by a resolution of the Parliament, it shall be the duty of the Board to pay amounts into the Scottish Consolidated Fund in accordance with this section.

(2) The amounts of the payments to be made by the Board under this section, and the times at which they are to be made, shall be determined by the Board and notified to the Scottish Ministers as soon as reasonably practicable after the passing of the resolution providing for the increase to which they relate.

(3) Any determination made by the Board under subsection (2) for any year of assessment shall be such as appears to the Board to be necessary for securing that, in the course of that year, amounts are paid into the Scottish Consolidated Fund which are equal in total to the amount estimated by the Board to represent the proportion of the income tax receipts for that year that is properly attributable to a resolution of the Parliament.

(4) For the purposes of this section the Board shall make and maintain arrangements as to—

(a) the manner of estimating the proportion of the income tax receipts for a year of assessment that is properly attributable to a resolution of the Parliament,

(b) the circumstances and manner in which an estimate of that proportion or of those receipts may be revised before or in the course of the year of assessment to which it relates,

(c) the manner of determining the amount of each payment to be made in respect of any such estimate, and

(d) the times at which, and manner in which, those amounts are to be paid by the Board into the Scottish Consolidated Fund.

(5) Arrangements under subsection (4) may include provision for the making of adjustments to the amounts paid by the Board where any estimate made for the purposes of this section in respect of any year of assessment (whether the current year or a previous year) turns out to have been inaccurate.

(6) Before making or modifying any arrangements under subsection (4) or (5), the Board shall consult with the Scottish Ministers.

(7) In this section "income tax receipts", in relation to any year of assessment, means so much as is referable to income tax charged for that year of any sums which, disregarding both—

(a) subsection (8), and

(b) any regulations or direction made or given by the Treasury,

are sums that have to be paid into the Consolidated Fund under section 10 of the Exchequer and Audit Departments Act 1866 (gross revenues of Board's department to be paid into that Fund after the making of specified deductions).

(8) Sums required by the Board for making payments under this section shall be paid out of the gross revenues of the Board's department; and, accordingly, those sums shall be treated as included in the amounts to be deducted from those revenues before they are paid into the Consolidated Fund under section 10 of the Exchequer and Audit Departments Act 1866.

DEFINITIONS
"income tax receipts": subs. (7).
"the Parliament": s.126(1).
"Scottish Ministers": s.44(2).

GENERAL NOTE
This section (together with s.78 which complements it) makes provision consequential upon the power conferred by s.73 on the Scottish Parliament to pass a tax-varying resolution. The machinery for the collection of the additional tax revenues will be by way of the Inland Revenue. The White Paper made the necessary further proposal that, when the Parliament does exercise its tax-varying powers, the resources available to it will be adjusted upwards or downwards by the appropriate amount (para. 7.20). Section 78 deals with the effect of a reduction of tax. This section deals with the effect of a tax increase and, most importantly, makes provision in subs. (1) for the payment by the Board to the Scottish Consolidated Fund of the appropriate amounts due. Such amounts will not, as a consequence, be paid by the Board into the U.K. Consolidated Fund (subs. (8)).

The other provisions make the necessary administrative arrangements. Note the requirement in subs. (6) to consult the Scottish Ministers.

Effect of tax reduction for Scottish taxpayers

78.—(1) Where the basic rate for any year of assessment is reduced for Scottish taxpayers by a resolution of the Parliament, payments to the Board in accordance with this section shall be charged on the Scottish Consolidated Fund.

(2) The amounts of the payments to be made out of the Scottish Consolidated Fund under this section, and the times at which they are to be made, shall be determined by the Board and notified to the Scottish Ministers as soon as reasonably practicable after the passing of the resolution providing for the reduction to which they relate.

(3) Any determination made by the Board under subsection (2) for any year of assessment shall be such as appears to the Board to be necessary for securing that in the course of that year amounts are paid to the Board which are equal in total to the amount estimated by the Board to represent the shortfall in income tax receipts for that year that is properly attributable to a resolution of the Parliament.

(4) For the purposes of this section the Board shall make and maintain arrangements as to—
   (a) the manner of estimating the shortfall in income tax receipts for any year of assessment that is properly attributable to a resolution of the Parliament,
   (b) the circumstances and manner in which an estimate of that shortfall may be revised before or in the course of the year of assessment to which it relates,
   (c) the manner of determining the amount of each payment to be made in respect of any such estimate, and
   (d) the times at which, and manner in which, those amounts are to be paid to the Board.

(5) Arrangements under subsection (4) may include provision for the making of adjustments to the amounts paid to the Board where any estimate made for the purposes of this section in respect of any year of assessment (whether the current year or a previous year) turns out to have been inaccurate.

(6) Before making or modifying any arrangements under subsection (4) or (5), the Board shall consult with the Scottish Ministers.

(7) In this section "income tax receipts" has the same meaning as in section 77.

(8) The sums paid to the Board under this section shall be treated for the purposes of section 10 of the Exchequer and Audit Departments Act 1866 (payment, after the making of the specified deductions, of gross revenues into the Consolidated Fund) as comprised in their department's gross revenues.

DEFINITIONS
"income tax receipts": subs. (7) and s.77.

"modify": s.126(1).
"the Parliament": s.126(1).
"Scottish Ministers": s.44(2).
"Scottish taxpayers": s.75(1).

GENERAL NOTE
This section makes provision which complements s.77, but this time to take account of the consequences of what most will view as the less likely event of a resolution to reduce the tax rate for Scottish taxpayers.

As the White Paper made clear, if the Scottish Parliament exercised the tax-varying powers, the resources available to it would be adjusted upwards or downwards by the appropriate amount (para. 7.20). This section makes provision for the necessary payments to be made out of the Scottish Consolidate Fund to the Board (and, thus, to the U.K. Consolidate Fund) in the event of a resolution to reduce the basic rate. By subs. (1) they are charged on the Scottish Consolidated Fund and payment does not, therefore, require any further authority from the Parliament—see s.65(1).

The technical aspects of this section closely track those made in respect of a tax-increasing resolution by s.77 and reference should be made to that section.

Supplemental powers to modify enactments

79.—(1) The Treasury may by order make such modifications of any enactment as they consider necessary or expedient in consequence of—
   (a) the fact that the Parliament has, or is to have, the power to pass a tax-varying resolution, or
   (b) the fact (where it is the case) that the Parliament has passed such a resolution.

(2) The Treasury may by order make provision—
   (a) excluding the operation of section 73(2) in relation to any enactment, and
   (b) making any such other modifications of any enactment as they consider necessary or expedient in connection with, or for the purposes of, any such exclusion.

(3) Without prejudice to the generality of the powers conferred by the preceding provisions of this section, an order under this section may provide that, where any tax-varying resolution relating to any year of assessment is passed, that resolution does not require any change in the amounts repayable or deductible under section 203 of the Income and Corporation Taxes Act 1988 (PAYE) between—
   (a) the beginning of that year, and
   (b) such day falling after the passing of the resolution as may be specified in the order.

(4) An order under this section may, to the extent that the Treasury consider it to be appropriate, take effect retrospectively from the beginning of the year of assessment in which it is made.

(5) In this section "tax-varying resolution" has the same meaning as in section 74.

DEFINITIONS
"enactment": ss.113(6), 126(1).
"modifications": s.126(1).
"the Parliament": s.126(1).
"tax-varying resolution": subs. (5) and s.74.

GENERAL NOTE
Described as "entirely supplementary" to the provisions of ss.69 and 70 (see Scottish Office Memorandum attached to the 24th Report of the House of Lords Committee on Delegated Powers and Deregulation-see ss.112, 113) this section nevertheless confers important powers on the Treasury. It was included by the House of Lords Committee as one of the "Henry VIII clauses" to which it drew attention.

The section enables the Treasury by order to make supplementary provision, including the modification of enactments, in the light of the other provisions in Pt. IV. An order under the section attracts Type E procedure under Sched. 7, *i.e.* subject to affirmative resolution in the House of Commons. See also the order-making power under s.110.

Subs. (1)
This authorises the modification of enactments. By s.113(6), this does not include the power to amend the Scotland Act itself.

Subs. (2)
This makes more specific provision for excluding the operation of s.73(2) (*i.e.* increasing or reducing the basic rate) in relation to any enactment and making consequential modifications.

Subs. (3)
This enables the Treasury to postpone temporarily the effect of a tax-varying resolution in relation to the operation of PAYE.

Subs. (4)
Any order made under the powers in this section may take effect retrospectively from the beginning of the year of assessment in which it is made.

Reimbursement of expenses

80. The Scottish Ministers may reimburse any Minister of the Crown or government department for administrative expenses incurred by virtue of this Part at any time after the passing of this Act by the Minister or department.

DEFINITIONS
"by virtue of": s.126(11).
"government department": s.126(1).
"Minister of the Crown": s.126(1).
"Scottish Ministers": s.44(2).

GENERAL NOTE
This section was added as a new clause at House of Lords committee stage. It was explained that its purpose was to ensure that all expenses incurred by U.K. departments in connection with the tax-varying power can be reimbursed to those departments out of the Scottish Consolidated Fund (*Hansard*, H.L. Vol. 593, col. 337). Without this section reimbursement might not have been possible in respect of certain expenses which will be incurred *regardless* of whether the tax-varying power is actually used. There will be some "standing charges" involved in having the infrastructure in place.

This section ensures that the necessary sums could become payable out of the Scottish Consolidated Fund under s.65. It does not appear to *require* the Scottish Ministers to make reimbursements sought by U.K. departments. In the financial memorandum on the Scotland Bill, the cost of establishing the administrative machinery was estimated at £10m (with annual running costs of £8m) plus set-up costs of £6m (and running costs of £1m) for the Department of Social Security.

PART V

MISCELLANEOUS AND GENERAL

Remuneration of members of the Parliament and Executive

Remuneration of members of the Parliament and Executive

81.—(1) The Parliament shall make provision for the payment of salaries to members of the Parliament and members of the Scottish Executive.

(2) The Parliament may make provision for the payment of allowances to members of the Parliament or members of the Scottish Executive.

(3) The Parliament may make provision for the payment of pensions, gratuities or allowances to, or in respect of, any person who—
(a) has ceased to be a member of the Parliament or the Scottish Executive, or
(b) has ceased to hold such office, employment or other post in connection with the Parliament or the Scottish Executive as the Parliament may determine but continues to be a member of the Parliament or the Scottish Executive.

(4) Such provision may, in particular, include provision for—
(a) contributions or payments towards provision for such pensions, gratuities or allowances,
(b) the establishment and administration (whether by the Parliamentary corporation or otherwise) of one or more pension schemes.

(5) In this section "provision" includes provision—

(a) by an Act of the Scottish Parliament, or
(b) by a resolution of the Parliament conferring functions on the Parliamentary corporation;

and references to a member of the Scottish Executive include a junior Scottish Minister.

DEFINITIONS
"members of the Scottish Executive": subs. (5) and s.44(1).
"the Parliament": s.126(1).
"the Parliamentary corporation": s.21(1).
"provision": subs. (5).

GENERAL NOTE
This is the first of three consecutive sections dealing with remuneration. This section empowers the Parliament to determine the salaries (subs. (1)) and allowances such as secretarial allowances and travelling allowances (subs. (2)) to be paid to members of the Parliament and members of the Scottish Executive, including junior Scottish Ministers for this purpose (subs. (5)). The Parliament is also enabled to determine the pensions and other payment to or in respect of persons formerly in these categories (subss. (3),(4)) and to make arrangements in this connection, if it chooses, through pension schemes (subs. (4)). The Scottish Parliamentary Corporate Body established by s.21 may be involved in the arrangements and provision may be made, as well as by an Act of the Scottish Parliament, by a resolution conferring functions on it (subss. (4)(5)).

Members of the Parliament may appear under these provisions to be judges in their own cause, but in practice they are not entirely unconstrained, as the Senior Salaries Review Body may be consulted by the United Kingdom Government, which will retain some influence.

Pending action by the Scottish Parliament, there were made transitional provisions for salaries and allowances, pensions and grants in the Scotland Act 1998 (Transitory and Transitional Provisions) (Salaries and Allowances) Order 1999 (S.I. 1999 No. 1097), the Scotland Act 1998 (Transitory and Transitional Provisions) (Grants to Members and Officeholders) Order 1999 (S.I. 1999 No. 1081), the Scotland Act 1998 (Transitory and Transitional Provisions) (Scottish Parliamentary Scheme) Order 1999 (S.I. 1999 No. 1082) and the Scotland Act 1998 (Transitory and Transitional Provisions) (Grants to Members and Officeholders and Scottish Parliamentary Pension Scheme) Amendment Order 1999 (S.I. 1999 No. 1891).

One of the earliest actions of the Scottish Parliament was to debate and agree on a Members' Allowances Scheme, providing for staff allowances, local office costs allowances, travel allowances, Edinburgh accommodation allowances and family travel allowances, amongst others. See SPOR 8 June, 1999, cols. 1215–1259.

By the generality of these provisions and by s. 83(5) below, there is latitude so that, for example, some members of the Scottish Executive may be paid more than others. Members of the Parliament with particular functions, such as the chairmanship of a committee, could also be more highly salaried, if it were thought appropriate.

Limits on salaries of members of the Parliament

82.—(1) The Parliament shall ensure that the amount of salary payable to a member of the Parliament in accordance with section 81 is reduced if any salary is payable to him—

(a) pursuant to a resolution (or combination of resolutions) of either House of Parliament relating to the remuneration of members of that House, or

(b) under section 1 of the European Parliament (Pay and Pensions) Act 1979 (remuneration of United Kingdom MEPs).

(2) The Parliament shall ensure that the amount of salary is reduced—

(a) to a particular proportion of what it would otherwise be or to a particular amount, or

(b) by the amount of any salary payable to the member as mentioned in subsection (1)(a) or (b), by a particular proportion of that amount or by some other particular amount.

DEFINITIONS
"the Parliament": s.126(1).

GENERAL NOTE
This is the second section dealing with remuneration. As has already been noted (General Note to s. 15, above), various forms of dual mandate are not prohibited: The purpose of this section is to preclude double salaries in some such instances. When a member of the Scottish

Parliament is salaried as a member of the Westminster Parliament or as a United Kingdom member of the European Parliament, then the Scottish Parliament is required to ensure that there is a reduction in the salary payable to such a person as Member of the Scottish Parliament, by such proportion or amount as it determines. It may, in its discretion, treat different cases differently (under s.83(5)). Under the Scotland Act 1998 (Transitory and Transitional Provisions) (Salaries and Allowances) Order 1999 (1999 S.I. No. 1097), the Scottish Parliament salary is reduced by two-thirds in these cases.

Remuneration: supplementary

83.—(1) The Parliament shall ensure that information concerning sums paid as salaries, allowances, pensions or gratuities of the kind mentioned in section 81 is published for each financial year.

(2) No payment of salary or allowances of the kind mentioned in section 81(1) or (2) shall be made to a person who is required by section 84 to take an oath unless he has done so.

(3) Subsection (2) does not affect any entitlement to payments in respect of the period before the person concerned took the oath once he has done so.

(4) For the purposes of sections 81 and 82, a person who is a member of the Parliament immediately before the Parliament is dissolved shall be treated—

    (a) if he continues to hold office by virtue of section 19(2) or paragraph 1 of Schedule 2, as if he were such a member until the end of the day on which he ceases to hold such office, and

    (b) if he does not fall within paragraph (a) but is nominated as a candidate at the subsequent general election, as if he were such a member until the end of the day on which the election is held.

(5) Different provision may be made under section 81 or 82 for different cases.

DEFINITIONS
"by virtue of": s.126(11).
"financial year": s.126(1).
"the Parliament": s.126(1).

GENERAL NOTE
This is the third section on remuneration, dealing with some supplementary matters.

Subs. (1)
Publication of information concerning remuneration is required. The provision does not specify how the information must be made available, and the wording might be criticised as too unspecific.

Subss. (2), (3)
The potential bar on payments emphasises the significance of the oaths required under s.84. However, on the requirement being satisfied, a person's entitlement to payments extends to the period from assumption of office to the taking of the oath.

Subs. (4)
This provides for a person who was a member of the Scottish Parliament prior to a dissolution of the Parliament to continue to receive remuneration in one of two circumstances. These are, first, if he or she continues to hold office as a member of the Scottish Parliamentary Corporate Body or the Presiding Officer or deputy Presiding Officer, in which case a person is treated as a member of the Parliament until ceasing to hold office; and secondly, if a person is nominated as a candidate at the subsequent election, he or she is treated as a member for the purpose of remuneration until the end of the day of that election.

Subs. (5)
The generality of the provisions in ss.81 and 82 perhaps renders this otiose, but for the avoidance of doubt the Parliament's discretion to treat cases differently is made explicit. This discretion does, for example, allow the member who holds the office of Presiding Officer to be paid a higher salary than other members.

Other provision about members of the Parliament etc.

Oaths

84.—(1) A person who is returned as a member of the Parliament shall take the oath of allegiance (whether or not he has taken the oath after being returned on a previous occasion or otherwise than as a member of the Parliament).

(2) He shall do so at a meeting of the Parliament and shall not take part in any other proceedings of the Parliament until he has done so.

(3) If he has not done so within the period of two months beginning with the day on which he was returned, or such longer period as the Parliament may have allowed before the end of that period, he shall cease to be a member of the Parliament (so that his seat is vacant).

(4) Each member of the Scottish Executive shall on appointment—

(a) take the official oath in the form provided by the Promissory Oaths Act 1868, and

(b) take the oath of allegiance.

(5) Each junior Scottish Minister shall on appointment take the oath of allegiance.

(6) Subsections (4) and (5) do not require a member of the Parliament to take the oath of allegiance again if he has already done so in compliance with his duty as a member.

(7) In this section, references to taking the oath of allegiance are to taking it in the form provided by the Promissory Oaths Act 1868.

DEFINITIONS
"oath of allegiance": subs. (7).
"the Parliament": s.126(1).
"proceedings": s.126(1).

GENERAL NOTE
This section requires all the members of the Parliament to take the oath of allegiance provided by the Promissory Oaths Act 1868 (c.72) or to make the corresponding affirmation. It also requires the members of the Scottish Executive to take the official oath provided by the 1868 Act, and to take the oath of allegiance unless they have already done so as a member of the Parliament, and requires junior Scottish Minister to take the oath of allegiance unless they have already done so as a member of the Parliament.

These requirements parallel the arrangements in the U.K. Parliament, and are symbolic of the relationship between these bodies and the Crown. Significantly, an elected member may not take part in proceedings of the Parliament until he or she has taken the required oath (subs. (2)), and members and ministers will not be entitled to payment of salary or allowances without having complied with their obligations (s.83(2)). A member's seat is also vacated if an oath has not been taken within two months of the member's being returned, unless the Parliament allows an extension (subs. (3)), which it might presumably in cases of illness or excusable absence.

The customary Scottish manner is to take the oath with open hand uplifted, although some variations were to be seen and were tolerated at the ceremony following the first general election in May 1999 (when some members also chose to add glosses to the words). Following general elections, the procedure should be for the oath to be administered by the Clerk at the start of the first meeting of the Parliament, because otherwise subs. (2) would prevent participation of members in proceedings, such as those to elect a Presiding Officer and deputies under s.19(1). For further provision on the administration of the oath, see the Standing Orders, Rule 1.2. The oath is also referred to in the Code of Conduct for Members.

Subs. (1)
This requires all the members of the Parliament to take the oath of allegiance each time they are returned, irrespective of whether they may have taken it on a previous occasion. The oath of allegiance provided by the Promissory Oaths Act 1868 has the following form: "I, . . ., do swear that I will be faithful and bear true allegiance to Her Majesty Queen Elizabeth, her heirs and successors, according to law. So help me God."

Gradually, in nineteenth century legislation, provision was made for Quakers, Jews and atheists to be able to make an equivalent affirmation consistently with their principles. By the Oaths Act 1978 (c.19), the alternative form is available for anyone "who objects to being sworn". The alternative form is: "I, . . ., do solemnly, sincerely, and truly declare and affirm that I will be faithful and bear true allegiance to Her Majesty Queen Elizabeth, her heirs and successors, according to law."

Subs. (4)
The official oath. The form of this, as set out in s.3 of the Promissory Oaths Act 1868, is as follows: "I do swear that I will well and truly serve Her Majesty Queen Elizabeth in the office of . . ., so help me God." Again, a corresponding form of the affirmation is available, under the Oaths Act 1978. The same oath is sworn by Ministers in the U.K. Government.

Subs. (7)
See note to subs. (1) above.

Exemption from jury service

85.—(1) In Part III of Schedule 1 to the Juries Act 1974 (persons excusable as of right from jury service), after the entries under the heading "Parliament" there is inserted—

"Scottish Parliament and Scottish Executive

Members of the Scottish Parliament.
Members of the Scottish Executive.
Junior Scottish Ministers."

(2) In Part III of Schedule 1 to the Law Reform (Miscellaneous Provisions) (Scotland) Act 1980 (persons excusable as of right from jury service), after the entries in Group A there is inserted—

"GROUP AB

Scottish Parliament and Scottish Executive

(a) members of the Scottish Parliament;
(b) members of the Scottish Executive; and
(c) junior Scottish Ministers."

DEFINITIONS
"members of the Scottish Executive": s.44(1).

GENERAL NOTE
By this section, members of the Scottish Parliament, the Scottish Executive and junior Scottish Ministers are exempted from jury service in England, Wales and Scotland. Separate provision is made for jury service in England and Wales (subs. (1)) and Scotland (subs. (2)). Provision for exemption from jury service in Northern Ireland has also been made, by equivalent amendments to the Juries (Northern Ireland) Order 1996 (S.I. 1996 No. 1141) through paragraph 23 of Sched. 1 to the Scotland Act 1998 (Consequential Modifications) (No.1) Order 1999 (S.I. 1999 No. 1042). The latter instrument also provides exemption from jury service for the Auditor General for Scotland.
Persons who are exempted from jury service are entitled to be excused as of right, but may nevertheless serve if they wish to do so.
The effect of the section is to put members of the Scottish Parliament in the same situation as members of the Houses of Parliament at Westminster. Exemption from jury service is a privilege of the Houses, given statutory form in the enactments referred to in this section, and exemption for the new categories is achieved by their amendment.
Specific mention is made of the different categories because first, the Lord Advocate and the Solicitor General for Scotland are members of the Scottish Executive who need not be members of the Parliament, and secondly, the terms of office of members of the Parliament and of members of the Executive and junior Scottish Ministers need not be coterminous, as the executive offices may continue during a dissolution of the Parliament.

Arrangements at Westminster

Scottish representation at Westminster

86.—(1) Schedule 2 to the Parliamentary Constituencies Act 1986 (rules for redistribution of seats) is amended as follows.
(2) Rule 1(2) (Scotland to have not less than 71 constituencies) is omitted.
(3) After rule 3 there is inserted—
"3A. A constituency which includes the Orkney Islands or the Shetland Islands shall not include the whole or any part of a local government area other than the Orkney Islands and the Shetland Islands."; and in rule 4, for "3" there is substituted "3A".
(4) In applying rule 5 (electoral quotas for each part of the United Kingdom) to Scotland for the purposes of the first report of the Boundary Commission for Scotland to be submitted under section 3(1) of that Act after the commencement of this subsection, "electoral quota" means the number which, on the enumeration date in relation to that report, is the electoral quota for England.

(5) In paragraph 7 (Commissions do not have to give full effect to all rules), after "rules" there is inserted "(except rule 3A)".

DEFINITIONS
"Scotland": s.126(1), (2).

GENERAL NOTE
The people of Scotland are at present represented by 72 MPs in the House of Commons, and the Parliamentary Constituencies Act 1986 (c.56) had provided that the number of constituencies should not be less than 71. It may plausibly be argued that Scotland is over-represented. In 1997, Scotland had an average of 55,339 electors per constituency, Wales 55,563 and England 69,578. If electoral area apportionment in the United Kingdom were carried out on a basis of strict arithmetical equality, as in the United States in constitutionally required, it has been calculated that Scotland would have 58 constituencies instead of 72. The "Celtic preference" evinced by these figures must in part be attributed to political factors.

With the creation of a Scottish Parliament having substantial competence over domestic affairs, there is less need (and perhaps less entitlement) for the same level of Scottish representation at Westminster. There is also a precedent because, when there was devolution of legislative powers to the Northern Ireland Parliament, the number of Northern Ireland seats was reduced to 12, being raised to 17 after the reimposition of direct rule in the 1970s. The Scottish Liberal Democrats have conceded for some years that, in fairness, the establishment of a devolved Parliament and the diminished interest of Scottish MPs in Westminster's business would justify a reduction in the number of Scottish seats in the Commons, at least to the extent of preventing over-representation.

The Government's attitude was previously less certain, but the White Paper (para. 4.5) implied that Westminster representation would be reduced, and this section translates that intention into action quite subtly. The rule which required the Boundary Commission for Scotland to propose that there be not less than 71 constituencies is removed by subs. (2). More significantly, the guidance to the effect that constituency electorates should approximate to equal size (which has previously been expressed to apply not across England, Scotland, Wales and Northern Ireland, but to each of the four separately) is modified so as to apply to Scotland on the same basis as England for the purpose of the next review, by subs. (4). These are amendments to the Parliamentary Constituencies Act 1986.

However, it is noteworthy that other provisions concerning the boundary reviews are untouched. The statutory guidance to the Boundary Commissions allows departure from strict arithmetical equalisation when it is justified by "special geographical considerations, including in particular the size, shape and accessibility of a constituency," a criterion which seems apt to refer to parts of rural Scotland, and in considering alterations, the Commissions are also required to take account of "any local ties which would be broken by such alternations." When discretion is applied to these guidelines, it may be that the resultant reduction in the number of Scottish seats will not be too severe.

The Boundary Commission for Scotland submitted its last report following a general review in December 1994, and so, as mandatory reviews are due at periods of eight to twelve years under the provisions of the 1986 Act as amended, the next report is not due until December 2002 (at the earliest) and December 2006 (at the latest). Notice too that the instruction to the Boundary Commission for Scotland to use the electoral quota for England applies to the next mandatory review only, after which it would revert to using the Scottish quota as it then appears.

A reduction in the number of Scottish seats in the Commons does not provide a solution to the so called "West Lothian question", which points to the anomaly of Scottish MPs at Westminster being able to debate and vote on English affairs, after there is devolution of corresponding Scottish affairs, when MPs will have no say in what happens on health or education in West Lothian, for example. However, while not addressing the question in principle, a reduction in seats does tend to alleviate the effects of the problem, as was observed in the debates when Mr Tam Dalyell MP and others raised it: *Hansard*, H.C. Vol. 311, cols. 734–836.

A reduction in the number of Scottish seats in the Commons will affect the Scottish Parliament's composition too. By Sched. 1, any alteration to the U.K. parliamentary constituencies will automatically involve a corresponding alteration in the constituency seats portion of the Scottish Parliament, and the Boundary Commission's report should make such recommendations as are appropriate for consequential alteration of the regional seats portion to satisfy the principle that, so far as reasonably practicable, the ratio of constituency member seats to regional member seats is to remain constant. So, for example, if after review the number of Scottish constituencies were reduced to 60, the number of regional members should fall to 46 or thereabouts. Schedule 1 is annotated below.

At time of writing, the Political Parties, Elections and Referendums Bill is in passage through the Westminster Parliament. By its terms, the functions of review of distribution of constituencies would fall to the new Electoral Commission, working through Boundary Committees.

Subss. (3), (5)
In recognition of the diversity of Orkney and Shetland and perhaps in hope of allaying some concerns, the Government indicated in the White Paper (para. 8.2) that Orkney and Shetland (which at present form one Westminster constituency) would become two separate constituen-

cies for the Scottish Parliament, and that proposal is effected by Sched. 1. Here the Boundary Commission is subjected to a particular rule to the effect that, when undertaking a review of Westminster constituencies, it cannot, in any constituency containing the Orkney Islands or Shetland Islands, include the whole or any part of a local government area other than those two areas. There were attempts in the Houses of Parliament to amend the Bill so as to put the Western Isles constituency in the same privileged position, but the Government was not persuaded, and they failed.

The Advocate General for Scotland

87.—(1) In Schedule 2 to the House of Commons Disqualification Act 1975 (Ministerial offices) and Part III of Schedule 1 to the Ministerial and other Salaries Act 1975 (salaries of the Law Officers), after the entry for the Solicitor General there is inserted— "Advocate General for Scotland".

(2) The validity of anything done in relation to the Advocate General is not affected by a vacancy in that office.

(3) If that office is vacant or the Advocate General is for any reason unable to act, his functions shall be exercisable by such other Minister of the Crown as the Prime Minister may determine in writing.

DEFINITIONS
"Advocate General": s.32(4).
"functions": s.126(1).
"Minister of the Crown": s.126(1).

GENERAL NOTE
The creation of a new Law Officer post in the United Kingdom Government is effected by this section. The new office is designated Advocate General for Scotland. The familiar Scottish Law Officer posts of Lord Advocate and Solicitor General for Scotland are not abolished, but are effectively transferred: appointed on recommendation of the First Minister with the agreement of the Parliament (s.48), the holders of those offices form part of the Scottish Executive (s.44) and (whether elected members or not) are able to participate in proceedings of the Parliament (s.27). In consequence of that transfer of responsibilities, the Government recognised a need for the provision to the United Kingdom Government of advice on Scots law, whether on reserved subjects or devolved (or indeed on the division between them), and so for the creation of this new office. The appointee may also represent the U.K. Government. Arrangements for the transfer to the Advocate General of some statutory functions previously exercised by the Lord Advocate and some transitional arrangements were made by the Transfer of Functions (Lord Advocate and Advocate General for Scotland) Order 1999 (S.I. 1999 No. 679) and the Scotland Act 1998 (General Transitory, Transitional and Savings Provisions) Order 1999 (S.I. 1999 No. 901).
There is no requirement here that a person appointed to the office need be a member of either House of Parliament, but in this and other respects constitutional conventions may develop concerning the holding and discharge of the office. The first appointee was an MP who was also an advocate. The Government's spokesman accepted that "whoever is appointed to this post should have appropriate standing and qualification in Scots law", but successfully resisted an amendment which would have required qualification as either an advocate or a Scottish solicitor, partly to skirt the issue of the possible appointment of a solicitor, and partly because of recognition of the possibility that there might be a suitable person ("a professor of law" was mentioned) who was not a member of either profession (*Hansard*, H.L. Vol. 593, cols. 371–378).

Subs. (1)
By this, the new office is brought within arrangements for ministerial salaries, contained in the Ministerial and other Salaries Act 1975 (c.27), and for the maximum number of ministerial office holders in the House of Commons under the House of Commons Disqualification Act 1975 (c.24), the latter only being relevant if the appointee is an MP.

Subss. (2), (3)
These provide for occasions of vacancy in the office, by preserving the validity of anything done in relation to the office and by empowering the Prime Minister to appoint another Minister of the Crown to exercise the Advocate General's functions, as may also be done when the Advocate General is for any reason unable to act.

Cross-border public authorities

Cross-border public authorities: initial status

88.—(1) Sections 53 and 118 to 121 shall not apply in relation to any function which is specifically exercisable in relation to a cross-border public authority; and section 118 shall not apply in relation to any function of such an authority.

(2) A Minister of the Crown shall consult the Scottish Ministers before he exercises, in relation to a cross-border public authority, any specific function—

    (a) which relates to any appointment or removal of the cross-border public authority concerned or of any members or office-holders of the cross-border public authority concerned, or

    (b) whose exercise might affect Scotland otherwise than wholly in relation to reserved matters.

(3) Any cross-border public authority or other person which is required by a pre-commencement enactment or a prerogative instrument to lay any report relating to a cross-border public authority before Parliament or either House of Parliament shall also lay the report before the Scottish Parliament.

(4) Subsections (1) to (3) are subject to any Order in Council made under section 89.

(5) In this Act "cross-border public authority" means any body, government department, office or office-holder specified in an Order in Council made by Her Majesty under this section.

(6) Such an Order may only specify a body, government department, office or office-holder which (at the time when the Order is made) has, in addition to other functions, functions which are exercisable in or as regards Scotland and do not relate to reserved matters.

(7) In this section—

    "office-holder" includes employee or other post-holder,

    "report" includes accounts and any statement.

DEFINITIONS
"body": s.126(1).
"cross-border public authority": subs. (5).
"function": s.126(1).
"government department": s.126(1).
"Minister of the Crown": s.126(1).
"office-holder": subs. (7).
"pre-commencement enactment": s.53(3).
"prerogative instrument": s.126(1).
"report": subs. (7).
"reserved matters": Sched. 5.
"Scotland": s.126(1), (2).
"Scottish Minister": s.44(2).

GENERAL NOTE
    This is the first of a group of three sections dealing with what the Act calls "cross-border public authorities". They constitute one of the groups of public bodies to have responsibilities for functions in Scotland that were identified in the White Paper in paras. 2.8–2.11. It would be helpful, therefore, if discussion of cross-border public authorities were prefaced by a note on the treatment by the Act of public bodies in general.

(a) *Public Bodies in the Scotland Act*
    There are, first, those bodies whose responsibilities (a) relate to Scotland only and (b) are confined to devolved matters. A list of such bodies was appended to the White Paper in Annex A and included three nationalised industries:

    • Scottish Transport Group
    • Highlands and Islands Airports Ltd
    • Caledonian MacBrayne Ltd;

a group of tribunals:

    • Children's Panels
    • Horse Race Betting Levy Appeal Tribunal for Scotland
    • Lands Tribunal for Scotland
    • Rent Assessment Panel for Scotland;

the three statutory water authorities; and health bodies:

    • Common Services Agency of the Scottish Health Service
    • Health Boards
    • Health Education Board for Scotland
    • Local Health Councils

- Mental Welfare Commission for Scotland
- National Health Service Trusts
- National Board for Nursing, Midwifery and Health Visiting for Scotland
- National Centre for Training and Education in Prosthetics and Orthotics
- NHS in Scotland Professional Advisory Committees
- Post Qualification Education Board for Health Service Pharmacists in Scotland
- Scottish Council for Postgraduate Medical and Dental Education
- Scottish Health Advisory Service
- Scottish Hospital Trusts
- State Hospitals Board for Scotland:

Annex A also listed a large number of miscellaneous executive bodies:

- The Accounts Commission for Scotland
- Scottish Agricultural and Biological Research Institutes-Governing Bodies
    Hannah Research Institute
    Macaulay Land Use Research Institute
    Moredun Research Institute
    Rowett Research Institute
    Scottish Crop Research Institute
- Crofters' Commission
- Deer Commission for Scotland
- Highlands and Islands Enterprise
- National Galleries of Scotland
- National Library of Scotland
- National Museums of Scotland
- Parole Board for Scotland
- Royal Botanic Garden, Edinburgh
- Royal Commission on the Ancient and Historical Monuments of Scotland
- Scottish Agricultural Wages Board
- Scottish Arts Council
- Scottish Children's Reporter Administration
- Scottish Community Education Council
- Scottish Conveyancing and Executry Services
- Board Scottish Council for Educational Technology
- Scottish Enterprise
- Scottish Environment Protection Agency
- Scottish Further Education Unit
- Scottish Higher Education Funding Council
- Scottish Homes
- Scottish Hospital Endowments Research Trust
- Scottish Legal Aid Board
- Scottish Medical Practices Committee
- Scottish Natural Heritage
- Scottish Qualifications Authority
- Scottish Screen
- Scottish Seed Potato Development Council
- Scottish Sports Council
- Scottish Tourist Board
- Scottish Water and Sewerage Customers Council;

and another long list of advisory bodies:

- Advisory Committee on Dental Establishments
- Advisory Committee on Sites of Special Scientific Interest
- Ancient Monuments Board for Scotland
- Building Standards Advisory Committee
- Central Advisory Committee on Justices of the Peace (Scotland)
- Children's Panel Advisory Committees
- Extra Parliamentary Panel
- General Teaching Council for Scotland
- Health Appointments Advisory Committee
- Hill Farming Advisory Committee for Scotland
- Historic Buildings Council for Scotland
- Justices of the Peace Advisory Committees
- Local Government Boundary Commission for Scotland
- Local Government Property Commission
- Police Advisory Board for Scotland
- Royal Fine Art Commission for Scotland
- Scottish Advisory Committee on Drug Misuse
- Scottish Advisory Committee on the Medical Workforce
- Scottish Agricultural Consultative Panel
- Scottish Consultative Council on the Curriculum
- Scottish Crime Prevention Council
- Scottish Economic Council
- Scottish Industrial Development Advisory Board
- Scottish Law Commission (but see below)

- Scottish Police College Board of Governors
- Scottish Records Advisory Council
- Scottish Standing Committee for the Calculation of Residual Values of Fertilisers and Feeding Stuffs
- Scottish Studentship Selection Committee
- Scottish Valuation and Rating Council
- Secretary of State for Scotland's Advisory Group on Sustainable Development
- Secretary of State's Advisory Group on Scotland's Travelling People
- Secretary of State's Advisory Panel of Economic Consultants
- Secretary of State's (Electricity) Fisheries Committee

(In addition, it was stated that the Scottish Executive would exercise ministerial functions in relation to appointments to the Rail Users Consultative Committee for Scotland).

All of these bodies would be within the remit of the Scottish Parliament. The Parliament would hold them to account by receiving reports from them and by investigating and monitoring their activities. The Parliament would also be able to legislate for these bodies. It would be able to alter their structure or wind them up and create new ones. In the same way, the Scottish Executive would inherit the powers of U.K. Ministers of the Crown to make appointments to them and to fund and direct their activities.

As far as the Scotland Act itself is concerned, the objectives sought in the White Paper are achieved simply by the Act's definition of the legislative competence of the Scottish Parliament (ss. 29, 30 and Scheds. 4, 5) which ensures that all these bodies are, since they deal only with devolved matters in Scotland, within that competence and the Act's transfer of executive competence for these bodies to the Scottish Minister by s.53. Section 23, which gives the Parliament the power to call for witnesses and documents, also applies to these bodies.

However, one consequence of the incorporation into legislation of the White Paper proposals for "devolved bodies" has been a recognition that they can, for practical purposes, be treated as belonging to a wider category of "Scottish public authorities with mixed functions or no reserved functions". The effects of this categorisation, which merges the wholly devolved bodies (*i.e.* with "no reserved functions") with hybrid bodies which have "mixed functions" are considered below.

At the other end of the scale, the White Paper identified a group of bodies as operating on a U.K. or G.B. basis and solely in relation to reserved areas. Clearly the intention would be that these should remain subject to the supervision and control of the U.K. Government and Parliament. The White Paper recognised, however, that many such bodies would "continue to be significant in the economic or social life of Scotland" and, therefore, of interest also to the Scottish Parliament. The Government's proposal in the White Paper was that the Scottish Parliament would be able to "invite" the submission of reports and the presentation of oral evidence before its committees. There was also an undertaking that, in relation to the BBC (which was one body identified in this group) the Scottish Executive would be consulted on the appointment of the National Governor and the same would apply to corresponding appointments to the Independent Television Commission. Also identified in the White Paper as examples of bodies in this reserved group were the energy regulators; the Office of Passenger Rail Franchising and the Office of the Rail Regulator; the Health and Safety Commission; the Commission for Racial Equality and the Equal Opportunities Commission and the Employment Service and the Benefits Agency.

The arrangements in the Scotland Act for these bodies are set out in para. 3 of Pt. III of Sched. 5 which defines "reserved bodies" as those reserved by name in Pt. II of the Schedule, the Research Councils and the Commission for Racial Equality, the Equal Opportunities Commission and the National Disability Council (now the National Disability Commission). The same paragraph sets out the effect for those bodies of their reservation. (See the General Note to the paragraph). The arrangements made for some of these reserved bodies are, however, affected by the transfer of additional executive functions to the Scottish Ministers by Order in Council under s.63 and the General Note to that section should also be consulted. The power of the Scottish Parliament to invite reports and evidence from reserved bodies is left on a non-statutory basis (see s.23(6) but see also s.26).

This classification of public bodies leaves other groups which have hybrid characteristics. There are the bodies whose responsibilities are in the devolved areas but extend beyond Scotland on a U.K. or G.B. basis. Then there are bodies whose responsibilities relate solely to Scotland but include both devolved and reserved matters. There are also bodies which are hybrid in both these senses, *i.e.* their responsibilities extend both beyond Scotland and to both devolved and reserved matters. Addressing mainly bodies made hybrid by their extension of responsibilities beyond Scotland, the White Paper stated that the Scottish Parliament would be able to decide whether to put in place separate Scottish bodies. In the meantime, however, the Government envisaged that "the Scottish Parliament will want to continue most such U.K. or G.B. arrangements in the light of the advantages of sharing knowledge and expertise on a U.K. or G.B. basis and of the greater efficiency in the use of resources" (para. 2.10). As long as that was the case, the Scottish Parliament would have the power to investigate and debate what they do. There would be a statutory right for the Scottish Executive to be consulted on membership of these bodies and on other matters. There would be provision for the transfer of functions to the Scottish Executive and also for the consequences of a decision to split up a body in this category. White Paper examples of these hybrid bodies were the U.K. Sports Council, the Central Council for Education and Training in Social Work, the Criminal Injuries Compensation Authority and the Meat Hygiene Service. The White Paper also noted that there were many non-statutory bodies with a U.K. or G.B. remit and that, in these cases, arrangements based on the principles outlined would be made under non-statutory agreements.

When it comes to the Scotland Act itself, these hybrid groups of bodies are identified as susceptible to designation as "cross-border public authorities". This is rather odd terminology for a group which has to include bodies which may have no "cross-border" jurisdiction in the sense of operating on a U.K. or G.B. basis. Section 88(5), (6) define a "cross-border public authority" as a body (or government department, office or office-holder) specified by Order in Council with the essential characteristics of having (a) functions "exercisable in or as regards Scotland" which (b) do not relate to reserved matters in addition to (c) other functions (*i.e.* functions which are not Scottish or which do relate to reserved matters or both).

The other key elements of ss.88–90 required to give effect to the White Paper's objectives in this area are (a) the recognition (reflected in s.90(1)) that it is within the power of the Scottish Parliament to legislate afresh in relation to the "devolved" powers of a body so far as they relate to Scotland; (b) the power by Order in Council to specify cross-border authorities and, very importantly, the suspension (by s.88(1)) in relation to them of the operation of s.53 (and also ss.118–121) of the Act, with the effect that executive powers in relation to cross-border authorities are not (despite the devolved nature of some of their functions) transferred from Ministers of the Crown to the Scottish Ministers; (c) the obligations to consult and to report (s.88(2), (3)); (d) the modification of the working of the bodies (s.89), in particular to involve the Scottish Ministers; and (e) the provision for transfer of property and liabilities in the event of the Scottish Parliament's intervention to remove powers from a cross-border authority (s.90).

One consequence of providing that only those bodies "specified" as "cross-border public authorities" will be subject to the other provisions of ss. 88–90 is that some bodies with the qualifying degree of hybridity can be left unspecified. Scottish local authorities are an important instance of "Scottish public authorities with mixed functions" which have not become cross-border bodies. Instead, the consequences of their hybridity are dealt with by Sched. 5, Pt. III, para.1 (see the Note to that paragraph) and, as indicated above, they are, for most purposes, grouped with "Scottish public authorities with no reserved functions", See Sched. 5, Pt. III and ss.119–121. Section 23 (Power of the Parliament to call for witnesses) on the other hand, extends to all Scottish public authorities and cross-border public authorities. See also s.56(4), (5) which enable the Scottish Ministers and Ministers of the Crown jointly to establish, maintain or abolish mixed function bodies.

(b) *Section 88*
As indicated in the introduction in (a) above the most important functions of this section are to:
1. Define a "cross-border public authority" ("CBPA"). This is done is subss. (5), (6) which stipulate that a CBPA is any of the bodies of the types and with the mix of functions referred to and specified in an Order in Council, such Order normally being subject to approval in the Westminster Parliament under the negative procedure (as Type I under Sched. 7). Although other Orders in Council made under this section and ss.89, 90 require prior consultation with the Scottish Ministers or the CBPA concerned, the initial order to specify CBPAs attracts no formal requirement of consultation. In terms of the Scotland Act 1998 (Cross-Border Public Authorities) (Specification) Order 1999 (S.I. 1999 No. 1319) the following bodies have been specified:
   - Administration of Radioactive Substances Advisory Committee
   - Advisory Committee on Hazardous Substances
   - Advisory Committee on Historic Wreck Sites
   - Advisory Committee on Pesticides
   - Advisory Committee on Releases to the Environment
   - Advisory Council on the Misuse of Drugs
   - Advisory Group on Hepatitis
   - Alcohol Education and Research Council
   - British Library Board
   - British Potato Council
   - British Tourist Authority
   - British Waterways Board
   - British Wool Marketing Board
   - Central Bureau for Educational Visits and Exchanges
   - Central Council for Education and Training in Social Work
   - Chief Commissioner and Commissioners
   - Clinical Standards Advisory Group
   - Committee of Investigation for Great Britain
   - Community Development Foundation
   - Construction Industry Training Board
   - Consumers' Committee for Great Britain
   - Controller of Plant Variety Rights
   - Council on Tribunals
   - The Criminal Injuries Compensation Appeals Panel
   - The Criminal Injuries Compensation Authority
   - Criminal Injuries Compensation Board
   - Design Council
   - Disabled Persons Transport Advisory Committee
   - Engineering Construction Industry

- The Fire Services Examinations Board
- Food from Britain
- Forestry Commissioners
- Government Chemist
- Home-Grown Cereals Authority
- Horticultural Development Council
- Inland Waterways Amenity Advisory Council
- Intervention Board for Agricultural Produce
- Joint Committee on General Practitioner Training
- Joint Nature Conservation Committee
- The licensing authority (Activity Centres)
- Meat and Livestock Commission
- Meat and Livestock Commission Consumers' Committee
- Milk Development Council
- Museums and Galleries Commission
- National Consumer Council
- The National Criminal Intelligence Service
- National Radiological Protection Board
- Plant Varieties and Seeds Tribunal
- Plant Varieties Rights Office
- Police Information Technology Organisation
- Police Negotiating Board for the United Kingdom
- Rail Users' Consultative Committee for Scotland
- Royal Commission on Environmental Pollution
- Scottish Association of Citizens Advice Bureaux
- Scottish Committee of the Council on Tribunals
- Scottish Consumer Council
- Sea Fish Industry Authority
- Sea Fish Licence Tribunal
- The Service Authority for the National Criminal Intelligence Service
- The Theatres Trust
- Traffic Commissioner for the Scottish Traffic Area
- The Trustees of the National Heritage Memorial Fund
- United Kingdom Sports Council
- United Kingdom Transplant Support Service Authority
- Unrelated Live Transplant Regulatory Authority

It should also be noted that the Food Standards Agency is to be treated as a cross-border public authority for certain purposes (Food Standards Act 1999 (c.28) s.35).

2. Disapply the key s.53 in relation to CBP As in order to except them from direct transfer to the Scottish Ministers. This is done by subs. (1) which also disapplies ss.118–121. Thus a CBPA, for as long as it retains that status, remains subject to the executive authority of a Minister of the Crown and any arrangements of the type made by ss.118–121 (concerning subordinate legislation, the Scottish Consolidated Fund, reporting etc.) are made under subss. (2), (3) and by Order in Council under s.89.

3. On the other hand, require a Minister of the Crown to consult the Scottish Ministers. Subsection (2) requires such consultation in relation to appointments to (or removals from) office or membership and also in relation to functions which might affect Scotland, otherwise than wholly in relation to reserved matters.

4. Require the laying of reports in relation to CBPAs before the Scottish Parliament as well as the U.K. Parliament (subs. (3)).

It should be noted, however, that those requirements imposed by subss. (2), (3) are themselves subject to variation by an Order made under s.89.

Power to adapt etc. cross-border public authorities

89.—(1) Her Majesty may by Order in Council make such provision in relation to a cross-border public authority as She considers necessary or expedient in consequence of this Act.

(2) Such provision may, in particular, include provision—

(a) modifying any function of a cross-border public authority or of a Minister of the Crown in relation to such an authority,

(b) conferring any function on a cross-border public authority or on a Minister of the Crown or the Scottish Ministers in relation to such an authority,

(c) modifying the constitution of a cross-border public authority,

(d) modifying the application of section 56(4) or 88(1), (2) or (3),

(e) for any function to be exercisable by the Scottish Ministers instead of by a Minister of the Crown, or by the one concurrently with the other, or by both jointly or by either with the agreement of or after consultation with the other,

(f) apportioning any assets or liabilities,
(g) imposing, or enabling the imposition of, any limits or other restrictions in addition to or in substitution for existing limits or restrictions,
(h) providing for sums to be charged on or payable out of, or paid into, the Scottish Consolidated Fund (instead of or in addition to payments into or out of the Consolidated Fund or the National Loans Fund or out of money provided by Parliament),
(i) requiring payments, with or without interest, to a Minister of the Crown or into the Consolidated Fund or National Loans Fund.

(3) No recommendation shall be made to Her Majesty in Council to make an Order under this section unless the cross-border public authority concerned has been consulted.

DEFINITIONS
"cross-border public authority": s.88(5).
"function": s.126(1).
"Minister of the Crown": s.126(1).
"modify": s.126(1).
"Scottish Ministers": s.44(2).

GENERAL NOTE
As explained in para. (b) of the General Note to s.88, one of the purposes of the special statutory regime being created for cross-border public authorities (CBPAs) is to enable their functions and aspects of their operation to be adjusted to take account of the conditions of devolved government in Scotland (and also in Wales). This section requires that to be done by Order in Council subject to Type F procedure under Sched 7, *i.e.* requiring an affirmative resolution of both Houses of Parliament and the Scottish Parliament, subject also to the requirement of prior consultation with the CBPA concerned (subs. (3)).

The provision which may be made is required simply to be "necessary or expedient" and may include provision of the types listed in subs. (2). The principal order made under the section is the Scotland Act 1998 (Cross-Border Public Authorities) (Adaptation of Functions etc.) Order 1999 (S.I. 1999 No.1747). This makes provision in respect of thirty authorities listed in Schedule 1 to the Order. One of the listed authorities was the Forestry Commissioners in respect of whom further modifications have been made by the Scotland Act 1998 (Cross-Border Public Authorities) (Forestry Commissioners) Order 2000 (S.I. 2000 No. 746) and additional modifications were made by the Scotland Act 1998 (Cross-Border Public Authorities) (British Wool Marketing Board) Order 2000 (S.I. 2000 No.1113). An adaptation of functions order has since been made in respect of three more authorities by the Scotland Act 1998 (Cross-Border Public Authorities) (Adaptation of Functions etc) Order 2000 (S.I. 2000 No.1102).

There are some indications in inter-departmental concordats that further adaptations of functions will be made. (See, *e.g.* the DETR Concordat and the Royal Commission on Environmental Pollution).

Power to transfer property of cross-border public authorities

90.—(1) This section applies if an Act of the Scottish Parliament provides for any functions of a cross-border public authority to be no longer exercisable in or as regards Scotland.

(2) Her Majesty may by Order in Council provide—
(a) for the transfer of any property to which this section applies, or
(b) for any person to have such rights or interests in relation to any property to which this section applies as Her Majesty considers appropriate (whether in connection with a transfer or otherwise).

(3) This section applies to property belonging to the cross-border public authority concerned which appears to Her Majesty—
(a) to be held or used wholly or partly for or in connection with the exercise of any of the functions concerned, or
(b) not to be within paragraph (a) but, when last held or used for or in connection with the exercise of any function, to have been so held or used for or in connection with the exercise of any of the functions concerned.

(4) Her Majesty may by Order in Council provide for the transfer of any liabilities—
(a) to which the cross-border public authority concerned is subject, and
(b) which appear to Her Majesty to have been incurred wholly or partly for or in connection with the exercise of any of the functions concerned.

(5) No recommendation shall be made to Her Majesty in Council to make an Order under this section unless the cross-border public authority concerned has been consulted.

DEFINITIONS
"Act of the Scottish Parliament": s.28(1).
"cross-border public authority": s.88(5).
"functions": s.126(1).
"property": s.126(1).
"Scotland": s.126(1), (2).

GENERAL NOTE
   As explained in para. (b) of the General Note to s.88, one of the purposes of the special statutory regime being created for cross-border public authorities (CBPAs) is to enable provision to be made for the property consequences for a CBPA if and when the Scottish Parliament exercises its powers to legislate to remove those functions which fall within the legislative competence of the Parliament, *i.e.* functions exercisable in or as regards Scotland and in relation to devolved matters.
   The procedure, which closely resembles that laid down in ss.60, 62, is in this case by Order in Council made, following consultation with the CBPA concerned, by the type F procedure under Sched. 7, *i.e.* requiring an affirmative resolution of both Houses of Parliament and of the Scottish Parliament. The section is cast in terms intended to be flexible enough to accommodate a very wide range of CBPAs, types of removal of functions and need for consequential property adjustments. The Orders required to handle the break-up (or partial break-up) of a CBPA may be quite complex. It is not completely clear what would be the consequence of a failure by the Scottish Parliament to approve an Order.

Miscellaneous

Maladministration

91.—(1) The Parliament shall make provision for the investigation of relevant complaints made to its members in respect of any action taken by or on behalf of—
   (a) a member of the Scottish Executive in the exercise of functions conferred on the Scottish Ministers, or
   (b) any other office-holder in the Scottish Administration.
   (2) For the purposes of subsection (1), a complaint is a relevant complaint if it is a complaint of a kind which could be investigated under the Parliamentary Commissioner Act 1967 if it were made to a member of the House of Commons in respect of a government department or other authority to which that Act applies.
   (3) The Parliament may make provision for the investigation of complaints in respect of—
   (a) any action taken by or on behalf of an office-holder in the Scottish Administration,
   (b) any action taken by or on behalf of the Parliamentary corporation,
   (c) any action taken by or on behalf of a Scottish public authority with mixed functions or no reserved functions, or
   (d) any action concerning Scotland and not relating to reserved matters which is taken by or on behalf of a cross-border public authority.
   (4) In making provision of the kind required by subsection (1), the Parliament shall have regard (among other things) to the Act of 1967.
   (5) Sections 53 and 117 to 121 shall not apply in relation to functions conferred by or under the Act of 1967.
   (6) In this section—
      "action" includes failure to act (and related expressions shall be read accordingly),
      "provision" means provision by an Act of the Scottish Parliament;
and the references to the Act of 1967 are to that Act as it has effect on the commencement of this section.

DEFINITIONS
"Act of the Scottish Parliament": s.28(1).

"action": subs. (6).
"cross-border public authority": s.88(5).
"functions": s.126(1).
"government department": s.126(1).
"members of the Scottish Executive": s.44(1).
"office-holder in the Scottish Administration": s.126(7).
"the Parliament": s.126(1).
"the Parliamentary corporation": s.21(1).
"provision": subs. (6).
"reserved matters": Sched. 5.
"Scotland": s.126(1), (2).
"Scottish Ministers": s.44(2).
"Scottish public authority with mixed functions or no reserved functions": paras. 1, 2 of Pt. III of Sched. 5.

GENERAL NOTE
    Since the creation of the Parliamentary Ombudsman by the Parliamentary Commissioner Act 1967 (c.13), ombudsmen have become a familiar characteristic of British public administration. They have a responsibility to investigate complaints made by individuals (and others) aggrieved by maladministration or other misbehaviour by public bodies. A number of ombudsmen have also appeared in the private sector, especially in relation to complaints made about financial institutions. Because these are in the private sector and because they operate in relation to "reserved matters", they will not be directly affected by devolution under the Scotland Act.
    Ombudsmen in the public sector are, however, in a different position and the effects of devolution vary from one to another. The local government ombudsman (appointed under Pt. II of the Local Government (Scotland) Act 1975) continues to operate. Because the office falls into the "devolved" sector, it is subject to any legislative change made by the Scottish Parliament and administratively it is subject to the Scottish Ministers. The same applies to the Health Service ombudsman (appointed under the Health Service Commissioners Act 1993). One difference that is, however, likely to emerge is that, whereas at present the same person has in practice been appointed to all three offices of Parliamentary Ombudsman, Health Service Ombudsman for England and Wales and Health Service Ombudsman for Scotland, a different person may be appointed as the Scottish Health Service Ombudsman.
    As far as the Parliamentary Ombudsman is concerned, the office continues to operate on a U.K. basis. In Scotland the scope of the Ombudsman's jurisdiction is restricted to "reserved" areas of government (*e.g.* tax and social security) while most functions exercised by the former Scottish Office but now transferred to the Scottish Ministers have ceased to be subject to the Ombudsman's supervision. The Scottish Ministers are no longer listed in Sched. 2 to the 1967 Act. The same considerations apply to "devolved" quangos and other bodies which have bene deleted from Sched. 2. (The necessary amendments to the Parliamentary Commissioner Act 1967 were made by art.39 of the Scotland Act 1998 (Consequential Modifications) (No.2) Order 1999 (S.I. 1999 No. 1820).)
    Cross-border public authorities on the other hand, remain subject to the Parliamentary Ombudsman in so far as their functions *do not* concern Scotland or *do* relate to reserved matters (see subs. (3)(d)). As part of the "reservation" of matters affecting the Parliamentary Ombudsman, s.91(5) ensures that functions of Ministers of the Crown under the 1967 Act are *not* transferred (under s.53) to the Scottish Ministers. (One aspect of these arrangements which seems not completely clear is the legislative competence of the Scottish Parliament in relation to the Parliamentary Ombudsman. The need for subs. (5) implies that the subject matter of the 1967 Act is not, or not entirely, reserved. That Act is not directly protected by Pt. I of Sched. 4— and see para. 10 of that Schedule. Could the Scottish Parliament amend the rules of access to the Parliamentary Ombudsman?)
    The White Paper proposed that an ombudsman similar to the Parliamentary Ombudsman should be established in relation to the Scottish Executive (para. 4.11) but the Scotland Act did not itself make direct provision for this. It is one of those areas where the UK Government thought it appropriate for provision to be made by the Scottish Parliament and s.91 requires that such provision be made.
    No doubt the Scottish Executive will bring forward proposals for legislation shortly. In the meantime, however, transitional arrangements introduced with effect from July 1, 1999 continue to operate. The Scotland Act 1998 (Transitory and Transitional Provisions) (Complaints of Maladministration) Order 1999 (S.I. 1999 No. 1351) (as amended by S.I. 1999 No. 1595) created the Scottish Parliamentary Commissioner for Administration, an office held so far by the (UK) Parliamentary Ombudsman, for the period until new provision is made by an Act of the Scottish Parliament. The Scottish Commissioner enjoys the same status, tenure of office and general powers of investigation as the UK Ombudsman. Access is by way of written complaint to an MSP and the persons, bodies and authorities subject to investigation are any member of the Scottish Executive; any other office-holder in the Scottish Administration; the Parliamentary corporation; and certain listed public authorities (including certain cross-border public authorities).

Subss. (1), (2), (4), (6)
    These subsections require that, having regard (among other things) to the 1967 Act (as at the commencement of this section), the Scottish Parliament must establish a system for the

investigation of complaints such as could be investigated by the Parliamentary Ombudsman under that Act (*i.e.* complaints of "injustice in consequence of maladministration"). The Parliament is not confined to the adoption of all the rules of access, investigation or of remedies prescribed in the 1967 Act but provision must extend to the Ministers and officials stipulated in subs. (1)(a), (b). For transitional arrangements, see the General Note above.

Subss. (3), (6)
Subsection (3) extends, on a permissive rather than mandatory basis, the scope of the provision which may be made, *i.e.* to include the Parliamentary corporation and public bodies.

Queen's Printer for Scotland

92.—(1) There shall be a Queen's Printer for Scotland who shall—

(a) exercise the Queen's Printer functions in relation to Acts of the Scottish Parliament and subordinate legislation to which this section applies, and

(b) exercise any other functions conferred on her by this Act or any other enactment.

(2) In subsection (1), "the Queen's Printer functions" means the printing functions in relation to Acts of Parliament and subordinate legislation of the Queen's Printer of Acts of Parliament.

(3) The Queen's Printer for Scotland shall also on behalf of Her Majesty exercise Her rights and privileges in connection with—

(a) Crown copyright in Acts of the Scottish Parliament,

(b) Crown copyright in subordinate legislation to which this section applies,

(c) Crown copyright in any existing or future works (other than subordinate legislation) made in the exercise of a function which is exercisable by any office-holder in, or member of the staff of, the Scottish Administration (or would be so exercisable if the function had not ceased to exist),

(d) other copyright assigned to Her Majesty in works made in connection with the exercise of functions by any such office-holder or member.

(4) This section applies to subordinate legislation made, confirmed or approved—

(a) by a member of the Scottish Executive,

(b) by a Scottish public authority with mixed functions or no reserved functions, or

(c) within devolved competence by a person other than a Minister of the Crown or such a member or authority.

(5) The Queen's Printer of Acts of Parliament shall hold the office of Queen's Printer for Scotland.

(6) References in this Act to a Scottish public authority include the Queen's Printer for Scotland.

DEFINITIONS
"Act of the Scottish Parliament": s.28(1).
"devolved competence": s.54.
"enactment": ss.113(6), 126(1).
"function": s.126(1).
"member of the Scottish Executive": s.44(1).
"member of the staff of the Scottish Administration": s.126(7).
"Minister of the Crown": s.44(1).
"office-holder in the Scottish Administration": s.126(7).
"Scottish public authority": s.126(1).
"Scottish public authority with mixed functions or no reserved functions": paras 1, 2 of Pt. III of Sched. 5.
"subordinate legislation": s.126(1).

GENERAL NOTE
This section was added to the Scotland Bill as a new clause at report stage in the House of Lords (*Hansard*, H.L. Vol. 594, cols. 11–15). It establishes the new office of Queen's Printer for Scotland to carry out the printing functions in relation to Acts of the Scottish Parliament and the subordinate legislation defined by subs. (4). The Printer enjoys the Crown rights and privileges in

respect of those documents as well as the others mentioned in subs. (3)(c), (d). See also Sched. 8, para. 25.

The Minister explained that the present holder of the office of Queen's Printer of Acts of Parliament is Mrs. Carol Tullo—the reason why in subs. (1)(b) the reference is to "her" rather than "him" (a novelty in drafting practice?)—and that, "to facilitate consistency and coherency of approach" the holder of the new office would be the holder of the office of Queen's Printer (see subs. (5)) who also holds the office of Government Printer for Northern Ireland (cols. 12, 15).

In response to questions, the Minister further explained that the appointment of the Queen's Printer is by Her Majesty by Letters Patent, on the recommendation of the head of the Home Civil Service and that, in the appointment of any future Queen's Printer, it was expected that administrative arrangements would be made to consult the Scottish Administration (col. 15).

In response to concerns on other matters, the Minister assured peers that nothing in this Act would preclude contracting out the printing of Scottish Acts to the private sector, if that were desired; the Scottish Parliament would be fully able to subsidise publication if it wished; and the creation of a computerised database for Acts of the Scottish Parliament was being explored.

Since then, the website of the Stationery Office has indeed been expanded to incorporate special provision for "Scotland Legislation", including Acts of the Scottish Parliament, Scottish Statutory Instruments and other Scotland-related material. There is also a Guidance Note (on copyright) issued by the Queen's Printer for Scotland.

Agency arrangements

93.—(1) A Minister of the Crown may make arrangements for any of his specified functions to be exercised on his behalf by the Scottish Ministers; and the Scottish Ministers may make arrangements for any of their specified functions to be exercised on their behalf by a Minister of the Crown.

(2) An arrangement under this section does not affect a person's responsibility for the exercise of his functions.

(3) In this section—

"functions" does not include a function of making, confirming or approving subordinate legislation,

"Minister of the Crown" includes government department,

"specified" means specified in an Order in Council made by Her Majesty under this subsection;

and this section applies to the Lord Advocate as it applies to the Scottish Ministers.

DEFINITIONS
"functions": subs. (3) and s.126(1).
"government department": s.126(1).
"Minister of the Crown": subs. (3) and s.126(1).
"Scottish Ministers": s.44(2).
"specified": subs. (3).
"subordinate legislation": s.126(1).

GENERAL NOTE
This version of the section was substituted at report stage in the House of Lords (*Hansard*, H.L. Vol. 594, cols. 15–17), replacing a version which would have permitted arrangements to be made by the Scottish Ministers or the Lord Advocate with defined "relevant authorities" for the provision of "administrative, professional or technical services" by one for the other.

It was explained (col. 16) that the power to arrange for the provision of services by the Scottish Ministers is available under the ordinary law and that, if necessary, consequential amendments to other legislation would be made to enable public bodies to reciprocate.

However, the power to make arrangements for specified functions to be exercised (in either direction between the Scottish Ministers—or the Lord Advocate—and a Minister of the Crown) is retained.

Subsection (2) makes the interesting proviso that such an arrangement does not affect "a person's responsibility for the exercise of his functions". The Minister referred to this as "ministerial responsibility" (col. 16) and the subsection does indeed appear to give some statutory recognition to the conventional rule on responsibility.

The Minister gave "an unqualified, clear and irrevocable answer no" in response to a question whether the arrangements under the section would extend to the "retained functions" of the Lord Advocate (col. 17).

The procedure for the "specification" of functions is by Order in Council and is Type H for the purposes of Sched. 7, *i.e.* subject to annulment by resolution of either House of the UK Parliament or a resolution of the Scottish Parliament. Two Orders have been made. The first (the Scotland Act 1998 (Agency Arrangements) (Specification) Order 1999 (S.I. 1999 No. 1512)) provided *inter alia* for the specification of certain of the Secretary of State's functions under election law and of some of the Scottish Ministers' environmental functions. The second (the Scotland Act 1998 (Agency Arrangements) (Specification) Order 2000 (S.I. 2000 No. 745)) specified certain of the Scottish Ministers' functions under the Medicines Act 1968, under the Wildlife and Countryside (Registration and Ringing of Certain Captive Birds Regulations 1982 (S.I. 1982 No. 1221)) and in respect of Creutzfeld-Jakob Disease surveillance.

Private legislation

94.—(1) This section applies where a pre-commencement enactment makes provision which has the effect of—

(a) requiring any order to be confirmed by Act of Parliament, or

(b) requiring any order (within the meaning of the Statutory Orders (Special Procedure) Act 1945) to be subject to special parliamentary procedure,

and power to make, confirm or approve the order in question is exercisable by the Scottish Ministers by virtue of section 53.

(2) The provision shall have effect, so far as it relates to the exercise of the power to make, confirm or approve the order by virtue of section 53, as if it required the order—

(a) to be confirmed by an Act of the Scottish Parliament, or

(b) (as the case may be) to be subject to such special procedure as may be provided by or under such an Act.

DEFINITIONS
"Act of the Scottish Parliament": s.28(1).
"by virtue of": s.126(11).
"enactment": ss.113(6), 126(1).
"pre-commencement enactment": s.53(3).
"Scottish Ministers": s.44(2).

GENERAL NOTE
It has been mentioned elsewhere (see s.36) that the possibility that the Scottish Parliament will want to pass measures equivalent to the private legislation of the Westminster Parliament has been provided for in outline. The Parliament has adopted standing orders to enable this to happen—at least on a temporary basis. See the note on s.36(3).
Despite its rather misleading heading, s.94 deals with the operation of existing statutory powers (to make provisional orders or to make orders subject to special procedure) in relation to devolved matters and it simply transfers the procedures which are otherwise initiated and promoted by Ministers of the Crown at Westminster to equivalent procedures at Holyrood by the Scottish Ministers to whom executive authority has been transferred by s.53. It substitutes references to Holyrood procedures for Westminster procedures and performs a similar function to that in s.118 (in relation to subordinate instruments generally).
Section 94(2)(b) anticipates that the Scottish Parliament will, in due course, pass an Act making provision equivalent to that made by the Statutory Orders (Special Procedure) Act 1945. In the meantime, the Scotland Act 1998 (Transitory and Transitional Provisions) (Orders subject to Special Parliamentary Procedure) Order 1999 (S.I. 1999 No. 1593) has made temporary provision and is to be treated as if provided by or under an Act of the Scottish Parliament (art.3). The Order includes a requirement for confirmation (by confusion) of a special procedure order by an Act of the Scottish Parliament in circumstances where an objection is made (art.6).

Appointment and removal of judges

95.—(1) It shall continue to be for the Prime Minister to recommend to Her Majesty the appointment of a person as Lord President of the Court of Session or Lord Justice Clerk.

(2) The Prime Minister shall not recommend to Her Majesty the appointment of any person who has not been nominated by the First Minister for such appointment.

(3) Before nominating persons for such appointment the First Minister shall consult the Lord President and the Lord Justice Clerk (unless, in either case, the office is vacant).

(4) It is for the First Minister, after consulting the Lord President, to recommend to Her Majesty the appointment of a person as—

(a) a judge of the Court of Session (other than the Lord President or the Lord Justice Clerk), or

(b) a sheriff principal or a sheriff.

(5) The First Minister shall comply with any requirement in relation to—
(a) a nomination under subsection (2), or
(b) a recommendation under subsection (4),
imposed by virtue of any enactment.

(6) A judge of the Court of Session and the Chairman of the Scottish Land Court may be removed from office only by Her Majesty; and any recommendation to Her Majesty for such removal shall be made by the First Minister.

(7) The First Minister shall make such a recommendation if (and only if) the Parliament, on a motion made by the First Minister, resolves that such a recommendation should be made.

(8) Provision shall be made for a tribunal constituted by the First Minister to investigate and report on whether a judge of the Court of Session or the Chairman of the Scottish Land Court is unfit for office by reason of inability, neglect of duty or misbehaviour and for the report to be laid before the Parliament.

(9) Such provision shall include provision—
(a) for the constitution of the tribunal by the First Minister when requested by the Lord President to do so and in such other circumstances as the First Minister thinks fit, and
(b) for the appointment to chair the tribunal of a member of the Judicial Committee who holds or has held any of the offices referred to in section 103(2),
and may include provision for suspension from office.

(10) The First Minister may make a motion under subsection (7) only if—
(a) he has received from a tribunal constituted in pursuance of subsection (8) a written report concluding that the person in question is unfit for office by reason of inability, neglect of duty or misbehaviour and giving reasons for that conclusion,
(b) where the person in question is the Lord President or the Lord Justice Clerk, he has consulted the Prime Minister, and
(c) he has complied with any other requirement imposed by virtue of any enactment.

(11) In subsections (8) to (10)—
"provision" means provision by or under an Act of the Scottish Parliament,
"tribunal" means a tribunal of at least three persons.

DEFINITIONS
"by virtue of": s.126(11).
"enactment": ss.113(6) and 126(1).
"Judicial Committee": s.32(4).
"the Parliament": s.126(1).
"provision": subs. (11).
"tribunal": subs. (11) and s.126(1).

GENERAL NOTE
The White Paper (para. 2.4) envisaged that Scottish judicial appointments would be devolved, subject to the appointments of the Lord President of the Court of Session and the Lord Justice Clerk being made by Her Majesty on the advice of the Prime Minister, on the basis of nominations from the Scottish Executive. This section develops that proposal, but continues to reflect a duality of devolved decision-making alongside the symbolic retention of roles for the Crown and the U.K. Prime Minister in regard to the two senior judicial offices. There are other provisions touching on judicial independence in the exemption of judges from the Parliament's power of summons (s.23) and the allocation to reserved matters of the determination of judicial salaries and pensions (Sched. 5, also Sched. 4, para. 5 and Sched. 8, para. 9).

For further discussion, see C.M.G. Himsworth, "Securing the Tenure of Scottish Judges—A Somewhat Academic Exercise", [1999] P.L. 14.

Subss. (1), (2), (3), (4), (5)
Appointment to the two senior judicial posts of Lord President of the Court of Session and Lord Justice Clerk will continue to be by Her Majesty on the recommendation of the Prime Minister, as it is at present—and in this respect a constitutional convention becomes instead a

rule of law—but with the difference that the Prime Minister may only put forward candidates who have been nominated by the First Minister. The First Minister must, before making nominations, consult the Lord President and the Lord Justice Clerk (unless in either case the office is vacant), so that in many cases, presumably, holders of these offices will be consulted about their successors. The wording of subs. (3) ensures that "the First Minister should be able to nominate more than one person for the appointment of Lord President or Lord Justice Clerk for the Prime Minister to consider" (*Hansard*, H.L., Vol. 593, col. 403): it is believed to be current practice for two or three names to be put forward. The First Minister also has to comply with any requirement imposed by legislation, so that it is open to the Scottish Parliament to impose further requirements or constraints in relation to such nominations.

Other judges of the Court of Session and sheriffs principal and sheriffs will be appointed by Her Majesty on the recommendation of the First Minister, who must consult the Lord President and must also comply with any requirement which may be imposed by legislation (so it would be open to the Parliament to establish a judicial appointments committee which would have to be consulted, for example). The Government resisted amendments which would have added a requirement to consult the Lord Advocate on appointments as being unnecessary and undesirable to incorporate in the Act. (*Hansard*, H.L., Vol. 594, cols. 17–27). In fact, the pivotal role of the Lord Advocate in practice has become, if it was not already, somewhat problematic in view of human rights law considerations (*cf. Starrs v. Ruxton*, 2000 S.L.T. 42). That being so, there are some signs of practice altering, even in advance of the introduction of new arrangements which, at time of writing, seem likely to be brought forward by the Scottish Executive in due course.

Subss. (6), (7), (8), (9), (10), (11)

Up to the passing of this Act, there was no instance of the removal of a Court of Session judge, although resignations were not unknown. Under the Claim of Right (1689), their tenure was *ad vitam aut culpam*, except as qualified by statutory provision for retirements. It was arguably within the powers of the Crown to dismiss Court of Session judges from office in cases of *culpa*, but there was an absence of authority on the requisite procedure and it was uncertain whether, for example, the approval of the Houses of Parliament would have been necessary or material. These provisions create a procedure for the removal of Court of Session judges, and to that extent may be claimed to rectify an anomaly.

Powers already existed for the removal of sheriffs principal and sheriffs, under s.12 of the Sheriff Courts (Scotland) Act 1971 (c. 58), where unfitness for judicial office such as may justify removal is constituted by "inability, neglect of duty or misbehaviour, "In *Stewart v. Secretary of State for Scotland* 1998 S.C. (H.L.) 81, a narrower construction of "inability" which the appellant (who had been removed from office on that ground) argued for was rejected by the House of Lords.

The provisions here apply to judges of the Court of Session and also the Chairman of the Scottish Land Court (Sched. 8, incidentally, amends the Scottish Land Court Act 1993 (c.45) in connection with the appointment of members of the Scottish Land Court), and provide a procedure for removal. As originally drafted, the Bill would have allowed removal by Her Majesty on the recommendation of the First Minister, conditional upon the approval of a qualified majority in the Parliament, but the original proposal was the object of an effective onslaught, in the House of Lords especially, on the ground that it gave insufficient protection for judicial tenure to leave it prey to party politicians, at a time when, Lord McCluskey suggested, "the obligation of judges to step into what has hitherto been the political field is greatly increased (*Hansard*, H.L., Vol. 590, col. 1659). Lord McCluskey, a former Solicitor General for Scotland (in 1974–79) and then a Senator of the College of Justice himself, led the onslaught, aided by influential interventions from Lord Hope of Craighead and Lord Clyde amongst others. When an amendment tabled by Lord McCluskey was carried at Report stage in the House of Lords (*Hansard*, H.L., Vol. 594, cols. 41–71), the Government bowed to pressure and introduced instead its own amendments to roughly similar effect.

In the result, the role of the First Minister is reduced and the role of the Parliament is made more formal while, in an adaptation of the procedure applicable to removal of sheriffs, an independent tribunal investigates and reports on fitness for office when cases arise. Provision for establishing the tribunal must be made by or under an Act of the Scottish Parliament and may enable the suspension from office of a judge who is under investigation. The procedure may be invoked at the request of the Lord President to the First Minister, or otherwise at the First Minister's discretion. The tribunal has to be chaired by a person eligible to sit as a member of the Judicial Committee of the Privy Council for the purpose of adjudication under s.103. However, the other members of the tribunal (which must be composed of at least three persons) are not expressly required to hold or to have held judicial offices. Only if the tribunal reports in writing and with reasons to the effect that a judge is "unfit for office by reason of inability, neglect of duty or misbehaviour", may the First Minister make a motion in the Scottish Parliament for the judge's removal and he or she must additionally have complied with any other requirements in legislation (and, if the judge in question is the Lord President or Lord Justice Clerk, have consulted the Prime Minister). Then, but only if the Scottish Parliament so resolves, the First Minister may recommend to Her Majesty the judge's removal from office.

Until the Parliament makes its own provision for the investigative tribunal, provision has been made for the constitution of such a tribunal and associated matters by the Scotland Act (Transitory and Transitional Provisions) (Removal of Judges) Order 1999 (S.I.1999 No.1017).

Provision of information to the Treasury

96.—(1) The Treasury may require the Scottish Ministers to provide, within such period as the Treasury may reasonably specify, such information, in such form and prepared in such manner, as the Treasury may reasonably specify.

(2) If the information is not in their possession or under their control, their duty under subsection (1) is to take all reasonable steps to comply with the requirement.

DEFINITIONS
"Scottish Ministers": s.44(2).

GENERAL NOTE
  This section enables the Treasury to obtain from the Scottish Ministers such information as it may "reasonably specify". It permits the Treasury to continue to obtain information necessary to monitor expenditure or to compile macroeconomic data on a U.K. basis.

Assistance for opposition parties

97.—(1) Her Majesty may by Order in Council provide for the Parliamentary corporation to make payments to registered political parties for the purpose of assisting members of the Parliament who are connected with such parties to perform their Parliamentary duties.

(2) The corporation shall not make any payment to a party in pursuance of such an Order if any of the members of the Parliament who are connected with the party are also members of the Scottish Executive or junior Scottish Ministers.

(3) But such an Order may, in any circumstances specified in the Order, require the fact that any members who are connected with a party are also members of the Scottish Executive or junior Scottish Ministers to be disregarded.

(4) Such an Order may determine the circumstances in which a member of the Parliament and a registered political party are to be regarded for the purposes of this section as connected.

DEFINITIONS
"members of the Scottish Executive": s.44(1).
"the Parliament": s.126(1).
"the Parliamentary corporation": s.21(1).
"registered political party": s.5(9).

GENERAL NOTE
  By these provisions, an Order may enable the Parliamentary corporation to make payments to registered political parties represented in the Scottish Parliament for the purpose of aiding them in their parliamentary duties, for example through the provision of research and support facilities and staff. The money comes out of the Scottish Consolidated Fund.
  Corresponding arrangements are made at Westminster to support opposition parties in their parliamentary roles, with payments of so called "Short money" for those parties in the Commons and so called "Cranborne money" in the Lords. The amounts are relatively modest, but the aim is to help to compensate for the enormous advantages in support, facilities and information which are enjoyed by the party in government. The intention here is similar.
  For the Order in Council procedure, see s.115 and Sched. 7 and the notes hereto. However, modification of this section by the Parliament became possible with the making of the Scotland Act 1998 (Modifications of Schedules 4 and 5) Order 1999 (S.I. 1999 No. 1749), which removed a bar in this respect.
  Subsections (2) and (3) may at first sight seem rather contradictory. A party which forms part of the executive might be expected to be excluded from receiving assistance under provisions designed to help parties in opposition. However, some flexibility in this regard is retained because of possible circumstances where total exclusion might not be justified, as for example where only one of a party's members has a ministerial office.
  The Scottish Parliament (Assistance for Registered Political Parties) Order 1999 (S.I. 1999 No. 1745) was made under this section to enable qualifying political parties to receive assistance, the amounts being based on an appropriate multiplier of a figure fixed for the initial period and then increasing annually in line with increases in the retail prices index. The Order provided that the fact that any MSPs connected with a qualifying party were also members of the Scottish Executive or junior Scottish Ministers should be disregarded if they did not number more than

one fifth of the total number of such ministerial officeholders; however, such MSPs were also to be disregarded in calculating the total amount to be paid to their party.

Under these terms the Scottish Liberal Democrats were enabled to receive some financial assistance, even although four of their MSPs accepted ministerial posts (two of them in the Executive) when, following the general election in May 1999, a coalition administration was formed.

Juridical

Devolution issues

98. Schedule 6 (which makes provision in relation to devolution issues) shall have effect.

GENERAL NOTE

This section simply gives effect to Sched. 6 which deals with "devolution issues". See the notes on the Schedule for discussion of the definition of devolution issues, the powers of the law officers and courts, and the procedural rules which have been made.

Rights and liabilities of the Crown in different capacities

99.—(1) Rights and liabilities may arise between the Crown in right of Her Majesty's Government in the United Kingdom and the Crown in right of the Scottish Administration by virtue of a contract, by operation of law or by virtue of an enactment as they may arise between subjects.

(2) Property and liabilities may be transferred between the Crown in one of those capacities and the Crown in the other capacity as they may be transferred between subjects; and they may together create, vary or extinguish any property or liability as subjects may.

(3) Proceedings in respect of—

(a) any property or liabilities to which the Crown in one of those capacities is entitled or subject under subsection (1) or (2), or

(b) the exercise of, or failure to exercise, any function exercisable by an office-holder of the Crown in one of those capacities,

may be instituted by the Crown in either capacity; and the Crown in the other capacity may be a separate party in the proceedings.

(4) This section applies to a unilateral obligation as it applies to a contract.

(5) In this section—

"office-holder", in relation to the Crown in right of Her Majesty's Government in the United Kingdom, means any Minister of the Crown or other office-holder under the Crown in that capacity and, in relation to the Crown in right of the Scottish Administration, means any office-holder in the Scottish Administration,

"subject" means a person not acting on behalf of the Crown.

DEFINITIONS

"by virtue of": s.126(11).
"enactment": ss.113(6), 126(1).
"function": s.126(1).
"Minister of the Crown": s.126(1).
"office-holder": subs. (5).
"office-holder in the Scottish Administration": s.126(7).
"property": s.126(1).
"the Scottish Administration": s.126(6).
"subject": subs. (5).

GENERAL NOTE

This section was inserted into the Scotland Bill as a new clause at report stage in the House of Lords (*Hansard*, H.L. Vol. 594, cols. 74–77).

As explained by the Lord Advocate, the purpose of s.99 is to make clear that legal relations may be entered into between the Crown in right of the U.K. Government and the Crown in right of the Scottish Administration (col. 75).

In the amendments made by Sched. 8 to the Crown Suits (Scotland) Act 1857 (c.44) and the Crown Proceedings Act 1947 (c.44), there is already an acknowledgement of a distinction drawn between the two capacities in which the Crown may sue and be sued. (See also Sched. 8, para.

18.) The Lord Advocate went on, however, to explain that, in addition, it was intended (a) that legal relations should be capable of being entered into between the U.K. Government and the Scottish Administration so as to transfer rights, liabilities and other property between them; and (b) that, when a U.K. Minister of the Crown makes an order under s.58 requiring some action to be taken by the Scottish Ministers, it should be possible for the Scottish Ministers to seek judicial review of the order and, on the other hand, for the U.K. Minister to enforce the order against the Scottish Ministers, subject to the 1947 Act. "It was thought", Lord Hardie continued, "that without an express provision in the Bill, the view may be taken that the doctrine of Crown indivisibility would prevent this" (col. 75).

This section is, therefore, intended to clarify that position. When the Crown in right of the U.K. Government and the Crown in right of the Scottish Administration enter into legal relations, they are placed in the same relationship as that between "subjects". This rule is applied to "rights and liabilities" which arise by contract (including a unilateral obligation) or otherwise; to the transfer of "property and liabilities"; and to the institution of legal proceedings.

The revival of the unfashionable concept of the "subject" in this context is interesting (*c.f.* the "private person of full age and capacity" in s.2 of the Crown Proceedings Act 1947).

Human rights

100.—(1) This Act does not enable a person—

(a) to bring any proceedings in a court or tribunal on the ground that an act is incompatible with the Convention rights, or

(b) to rely on any of the Convention rights in any such proceedings,

unless he would be a victim for the purposes of Article 34 of the Convention (within the meaning of the Human Rights Act 1998) if proceedings in respect of the act were brought in the European Court of Human Rights.

(2) Subsection (1) does not apply to the Lord Advocate, the Advocate General, the Attorney General or the Attorney General for Northern Ireland.

(3) This Act does not enable a court or tribunal to award any damages in respect of an act which is incompatible with any of the Convention rights which it could not award if section 8(3) and (4) of the Human Rights Act 1998 applied.

(4) In this section "act" means—

(a) making any legislation,

(b) any other act or failure to act, if it is the act or failure of a member of the Scottish Executive.

DEFINITIONS
"act": subs. (4).
"Advocate General": s.32(4).
"the Convention rights": s.126(1).
"member of the Scottish Executive": s.44(1).
"proceedings": s.126(1).
"tribunal": s.126(1).

GENERAL NOTE
This section was added as a new clause at House of Lords committee stage. It was explained that its purpose was to ensure that approaches to the protection of human rights under the Scotland Act would be consistent, so far as possible, with those taken under the Human Rights Act 1998 (c.42) (*Hansard*, H.L. Vol. 593, cols. 417–428).

Obligations not to act in breach of the ECHR, as imported under the terms of the Human Rights Act, are imposed upon the Scottish Parliament and members of the Scottish Executive by ss.29(2)(d), 54, 57. By Sched. 4, para. 1, the Human Rights Act 1998 is made unamendable (subject to certain exceptions) by the Scottish Parliament and Sched. 6, para. 1 provides that (either directly or as an aspect of legislative or devolved competence) alleged breaches of the Convention become "devolution issues" for the purposes of that Schedule. Section 129 (2) (which includes specific reference to this section) was designed to ensure that provisions of this Act which were brought into force before the date of implementation of the Human Rights Act itself would nevertheless have the same effect before and after that date, October 2, 2000.

What this section does is to ensure that, in proceedings brought under the Scotland Act rather than the Human Rights Act, the same restrictions requiring a litigant to be a "victim" and limiting the award of damages will apply. (See also s.57(3).)

Subs. (1), (2)
Section 7(1) of the Human Rights Act 1998 restricts the bringing of proceedings or reliance on Convention rights in any proceedings to a person who is (or would be) a "victim" of the alleged unlawful act. Subsection (1), therefore, makes equivalent provision in relation to proceedings

under this Act. Article 34 of the Convention requires that applications to the Human Rights Court be from "any person, non-governmental organisation or groups of individuals claiming to be a victim of a violation" of a Convention right. However, proceedings brought by the law officers named in subs.(2) are an exception, which means that proceedings initiated by a law officer by reference to the Judicial Committee under s.33 or for the determination of a devolution issue under Sched. 6 could raise a question of compatibility with a Convention right, even though no "victim" is involved.

Subs. (3)
Section 8(3) of the Human Rights Act 1998 provides: "No award of damages is to be made unless, taking account of all the circumstances of the case, including-(a) any other relief or remedy granted, or order made, in relation to the act in question (by that or any other court) and (b) the consequences of any decision (of that or any other court) in respect of that act, the court is satisfied that the award is necessary to afford just satisfaction to the person in whose favour it is made".
Section 8(4) then provides:
"in determining-
(a) whether to award damages, or
(b) the amount of the award,
the court must take into account the principles applied by the European Court of Human Rights in relation to the award of compensation under Article 41 of the Convention".
Article 41 of the Convention requires that, where the Human Rights Court has held that a violation of a Convention right has occurred and if the internal law of the state concerned allows only partial reparation to be made, the Court shall, if necessary, afford just satisfaction to the injured party.

Interpretation of Acts of the Scottish Parliament etc

101.—(1) This section applies to—
(a) any provision of an Act of the Scottish Parliament, or of a Bill for such an Act, and
(b) any provision of subordinate legislation made, confirmed or approved, or purporting to be made, confirmed or approved, by a member of the Scottish Executive,
which could be read in such a way as to be outside competence.

(2) Such a provision is to be read as narrowly as is required for it to be within competence, if such a reading is possible, and is to have effect accordingly.

(3) In this section "competence"—
(a) in relation to an Act of the Scottish Parliament, or a Bill for such an Act, means the legislative competence of the Parliament, and
(b) in relation to subordinate legislation, means the powers conferred by virtue of this Act.

DEFINITIONS
"Act of the Scottish Parliament": s.28(1).
"by virtue of": s.126(11).
"competence": subs. (3).
"legislative competence": s.29.
"member of the Scottish Executive": s.44(1).
"the Parliament": s.126(1).
"subordinate legislation": s.126(1).

GENERAL NOTE
This section was inserted into the Bill as a new clause at report stage in the House of Lords (*Hansard*, H.L. Vol. 594, col. 98) but serves a purpose formerly achieved by provisions separately contained in clauses which became ss.29 and 54. The section is intended to give interpretative guidance to courts at points where they are required to apply or to consider provisions in Acts (or Bills) of the Scottish Parliament or in the subordinate legislation of members of the Scottish Executive. It has to be read with those other provisions in the Act which define the legislative competence of the Scottish Parliament (ss.29, 30 and Scheds. 4, 5) and, subject to points raised below, the competence of members of the Scottish Executive (ss.53, 54, 63).
As explained by the Lord Advocate (*Hansard*, H.L. Vol. 593, cols. 1952–56) the point of s.101 is to enable courts to give effect to legislation, wherever possible, rather then invalidate it. He took the example of an Act of the Scottish Parliament which enabled the Scottish Ministers to hold a referendum on any matters. Such an Act could be read as permitting a referendum on reserved matters such as independence (for Scotland) or the monarchy. The Act would, he suggested, be in danger of being held *ultra vires* to that extent but, to preserve its validity, this

section requires the courts to read it as narrowly as is required for it to be *intra vires*, so far as that is possible. In this case they could read the Act as enabling only the holding of referendums on matters within the Parliament's competence and the Act would, therefore, not be rendered *ultra vires* to any extent.

Four specific features of the formula adopted in s. 101 to achieve these purposes warrant further comment:

1. In the earlier versions of this section in the Scotland Bill, the wording used was that any provision of an Act (or, as the case may be, subordinate legislation) was to be read, so far as possible, in such a way as to be within the legislative competence of the Scottish Parliament (or within the powers conferred by virtue of this Act) and was to have effect accordingly. This was similar to the formula used in s.3(1) of the Human Rights Act 1998 which provides: "So far as it is possible to do so, primary legislation and subordinate legislation must be read and given effect in a way which is compatible with the Convention rights."

   Section 101, however, adjusts that formula (a) explicitly to apply the interpretative test only in circumstances where a provision "could be read in such a way as to be outside competence"; and (b) to incorporate the instruction not simply that a provision be "read, so far as possible, in such a way as to be within competence" but that it be "read as narrowly as is required for it to be within competence, if such a reading is possible".

   It may be that the specific obligations imposed by (a)—*i.e.* that the ambiguity of meaning of the provision concerned must first be recognised—will make little difference in practice. An issue pointed up, but perhaps not resolved, by the use of the formula required by (b), is that of whether any interpretative formula of this sort is intended to assist a court towards a positive conclusion as to the validity of the provision under review by the more "generous" interpretation of both the rules defining competence (whether in the Scotland Act or elsewhere) and the rules actually contained in the provision under review or simply those rules in that provision itself. The formulation of the instruction to require the courts to "read narrowly" the provision under review appears to direct attention to the flexibility of meaning available in that provision alone—even though the original uncertainty as to competence may arise as much from ambiguity in the interpretation of the Scotland Act (*e.g.* Sched. 4 or 5) or other rules which the Act incorporates as part of the definition of the scope of legislative competence (*e.g.* Community law or Convention rights).

2. This serves to remind that the legislative competence of the Scottish Parliament (and then, by virtue of s.54, the devolved competence of members of the Scottish Executive) is defined by reference to a number of distinct parameters. The question may be asked, however, whether it is appropriate to have the rule of interpretation laid down in this section applied to them all. The main purpose of the provision must be to urge a court to tend towards a construction of the Scotland Act which places a particular matter outside the scope of the reserved matters in Sched. 5 and, therefore, within the competence of the Parliament. Thus, a generous view should be taken of the extent of devolved matters, as opposed to those reserved.

   The tests of legislative competence, however, extend more broadly—to include the restrictions imposed by the "entrenchment" of enactments by Sched. 4, the limits of the territory of Scotland, incompatibility with Convention rights or Community law and preservation of the powers of the Lord Advocate.

   With specific reference to human rights, this means that a differently drafted rule of interpretation applies to issues taken under the Scotland Act from that applicable under the Human Rights Act. Some care has been taken to keep the provisions in the two Acts running in parallel but this appears not to have been achieved completely. (See *Hansard*, H.L. Vol. 593, cols. 1954–56) Another question about competence based on compatibility with the Convention is what the effect of a "narrower" reading of a Scottish measure would be. The point has been taken that, from the perspective of human rights protection, it is not necessarily an advantage to have a measure survive, because narrowly construed rather than struck down as invalid under a more natural interpretation of the measure. (See G. Marshall "Interpreting interpretation in the Human Rights Bill" [1998] P.L. 167.) Whether or not harmonised with the rest of the United Kingdom, is there merit in requiring a court to give a "narrow" reading to Acts of the Scottish Parliament (or subordinate instruments) which are arguably incompatible with the Convention?

   Then, in relation to compatibility with Community law, one is bound to ask whether the rule of interpretation laid down in this section is intended to achieve (or will in practice achieve) a different approach to the construction of an Act of the Scottish Parliament (or subordinate legislation of the Scottish Ministers) as opposed to an Act of the Westminster Parliament (or subordinate legislation of Ministers of the Crown) in the light of Community law with which it is thought to be incompatible? The Scottish measure must be read "as narrowly as is required for it to be within competence" whereas the non-Scottish measure (which might be identical) need not.

   Perhaps the restriction on competence based on preserving the powers of the Lord Advocate is less generally significant but it may be interesting to see how a "narrow reading" rule applies. If an Act of the Scottish Parliament purported to confer on designated statutory bodies a power to prosecute, that might well be read as outside legislative competence. But might a "narrow" reading be possible and, therefore, save it? Was such a saving intended?

3. The limits of the scope of this interpretation provision should be noted. It extends to Acts, Bills or subordinate legislation. It does not, therefore, extend to other actions of the Scottish Parliament (*e.g.* tax-varying resolutions under s.73). Nor does it apply to action taken by members of the Scottish Executive where that action is not the making (or confirmation or approval) of subordinate legislation. This last restriction may be the cause of some difficulty because the distinction between, on the one hand, those things required to be done by order and thus by subordinate legislation and those things to be done merely by executive decision is sometimes no more than formal. When the competence of a regulation and the competence of a "mere" decision are raised as "devolution issues", there may be no particularly good reason why the regulation but not the decision should be given the benefit of a "narrow" construction in order to save its validity?

4. It should, on the other hand, be noted that, in so far as the benefits of this interpretation section do extend to subordinate legislation of members of the Scottish Executive, they do so in relation to questions of "competence" deriving "from powers conferred by virtue of this Act". This is interesting in that the definition of "competence" is not-tied to the definition of "devolved competence" set out in s.54. There "devolved competence" is in turn tied to the "legislative competence" of the Scottish Parliament. Here, however, "competence" is defined by reference to the powers conferred by the Scotland Act— which is, of course, a test which incorporates the limitations imposed by s.54 but may also be capable of reaching other limitations of the powers conferred on the Scottish Ministers by ss.53, 63. Those sections confer powers to make subordinate legislation on Scottish Ministers which were previously vested in (and, in some cases, remain shared by) Ministers of the Crown. When those powers are exercised, a question of "competence" might relate to an aspect of legislative competence of the Scottish Parliament but it might not. It might be a question of whether the member of the Scottish Executive is acting *ultra vires*, with reference instead to the powers originally conferred by the Westminster Parliament or, indeed, the Scottish Parliament. One wonders why, in either of these cases, the subordinate legislation should benefit from the "narrow reading" and not be subject instead to ordinary rules of construction? In relation to those powers to be exercised under the same Westminster Act by Ministers of the Crown in respect of the other parts of the United Kingdom but, by virtue of the Scotland Act 1998, by the Scottish Ministers in respect of Scotland, different interpretative rules are to apply to what may be identical subordinate legislation.

Powers of courts or tribunals to vary retrospective decisions

102.—(1) This section applies where any court or tribunal decides that—

(a) an Act of the Scottish Parliament or any provision of such an Act is not within the legislative competence of the Parliament, or

(b) a member of the Scottish Executive does not have the power to make, confirm or approve a provision of subordinate legislation that he has purported to make, confirm or approve.

(2) The court or tribunal may make an order—

(a) removing or limiting any retrospective effect of the decision, or

(b) suspending the effect of the decision for any period and on any conditions to allow the defect to be corrected.

(3) In deciding whether to make an order under this section, the court or tribunal shall (among other things) have regard to the extent to which persons who are not parties to the proceedings would otherwise be adversely affected.

(4) Where a court or tribunal is considering whether to make an order under this section, it shall order intimation of that fact to be given to—

(a) the Lord Advocate, and

(b) the appropriate law officer, where the decision mentioned in subsection (1) relates to a devolution issue (within the meaning of Schedule 6),

unless the person to whom the intimation would be given is a party to the proceedings.

(5) A person to whom intimation is given under subsection (4) may take part as a party in the proceedings so far as they relate to the making of the order.

(6) Paragraphs 36 and 37 of Schedule 6 apply with necessary modifications for the purposes of subsections (4) and (5) as they apply for the purposes of that Schedule.

(7) In this section—

"intimation" includes notice,
"the appropriate law officer" means—(a) in relation to proceedings in Scotland, the Advocate General,

(b) in relation to proceedings in England and Wales, the Attorney General,

(c) in relation to proceedings in Northern Ireland, the Attorney General for Northern Ireland.

DEFINITIONS
"Act of the Scottish Parliament": s.28(1).
"Advocate General": s.32(4).
"the appropriate law officer": subs. (7).
"intimation": subs. (7).
"legislative competence": s.29.
"member of the Scottish Executive": s.44(1).
"the Parliament": s.126(1).
"Scotland": s.126(1), (2).
"subordinate legislation": s.126(1).
"tribunal": s.126(1).

GENERAL NOTE
Certain consequences flow from the creation of a Scottish Parliament (and Executive) with defined competence. One such consequence is that a court or tribunal may hold that a provision of an Act of the Parliament or subordinate legislation purportedly made by a member of the Scottish Executive is invalid, because *ultra vires*.

Such a decision could well be a cause of difficulty for those who have, for instance, relied on the validity of an Act or order and now find that it is not valid, especially since the decision would, in the absence of provision such as is made in s.102, be fully retrospective in effect. Persons affected in this way might well not be parties to the proceedings from which the decision results. The purpose of this section is to permit courts and tribunals to vary the effect of retrospective decisions. A parallel provision appears in s.172(1) of the Constitution of South Africa 1996.

The procedural rules which have been made for the handling of devolution issues (see Note on Sched. 6 para. 37) include provision to regulate the giving of notice to those entitled to intervene where a court is considering making an order under s.102. See S.I. 1999 No. 1345 (Rule of Court 25A .12); S.I. 1999 No. 1346 (Rule 40.12); and S.I. 1999 No. 1347 (Rules 8, 9).

Subss. (1)–(3)
These provisions identify the circumstances to which the section applies (subs. (1)); confer the power either to remove or limit any retrospective effect of the court's decision or to suspend the effect of the decision to allow the defect (presumably the defect which gave rise to the invalidity of the Act or order) to be "corrected". It was acknowledged at House of Lords committee stage (*Hansard*, H.L. Vol.593, col. 610) that the defect might well not be of a type to raise a "devolution issue" under Sched. 6.

Under subs. (3), the court or tribunal must have regard to the adverse effect that would "otherwise" befall non-parties. Presumably some of the "other things" the court should also take into account are the benefits that might otherwise accrue to parties or non-parties if no order is made?

Subss. (4), (5), (7)
These subsections require intimation of consideration of the making of an order under the section to be given to the Lord Advocate and, if the decision to be made by the court does relate to a devolution issue, to another "appropriate law officer" as defined.

Subs. (6)
Paragraphs 36 and 37 of Sched. 6 relate to special provision for expenses and for court procedures respectively.

The Judicial Committee

103.—(1) Any decision of the Judicial Committee in proceedings under this Act shall be stated in open court and shall be binding in all legal proceedings (other than proceedings before the Committee).

(2) No member of the Judicial Committee shall sit and act as a member of the Committee in proceedings under this Act unless he holds or has held—

(a) the office of a Lord of Appeal in Ordinary, or

(b) high judicial office as defined in section 25 of the Appellate Jurisdiction Act 1876 (ignoring for this purpose section 5 of the Appellate Jurisdiction Act 1887).

(3) Her Majesty may by Order in Council—
  (a) confer on the Judicial Committee in relation to proceedings under this Act such powers as Her Majesty considers necessary or expedient,
  (b) apply the Judicial Committee Act 1833 in relation to proceedings under this Act with exceptions or modifications,
  (c) make rules for regulating the procedure in relation to proceedings under this Act before the Judicial Committee.

(4) In this section "proceedings under this Act" means proceedings on a question referred to the Judicial Committee under section 33 or proceedings under Schedule 6.

DEFINITIONS
"Judicial Committee": s.32(4).
"modifications": s.126(1).
"proceedings under this Act": subs. (4).

GENERAL NOTE
  This Act gives important functions to the Judicial Committee of the Privy Council. Under s.33 a question about whether a Bill (or a provision in a Bill) is within the legislative competence of the Scottish Parliament may be referred to the Judicial Committee. Under Sched. 6, a "devolution issue" may be referred to the Judicial Committee or reach it on appeal. As proposed in Chapter 4 of the White Paper, the Judicial Committee thereby becomes the important court of last resort in matters of the legal competence of the Scottish Parliament and Executive. The Government preferred the Judicial Committee to the House of Lords for this purpose.
  In the course of the parliamentary debates on the Scotland Bill, a radical alternative was proposed in the shape of a new Constitutional Court which would have performed the new tasks in relation to "devolution issues" resulting from the Scotland Act as well as the Government of Wales Act 1998 and the Northern Ireland Act 1998. (See *Hansard*, H.L. Vol. 593, cols. 1963–1986).
  See also Lord Hope of Craighead "The SCPC: Its Practice and Procedure" (1999) 4 S.L.P.Q. 1.

Subs. (1)
  This makes formal provision for decisions of the Judicial Committee to be binding in all legal proceedings in all other courts. It is necessary to establish the Judicial Committee's new place in the hierarchy of courts, not only in Scotland but also in the other jurisdictions in the United Kingdom.
  It must also be desirable in principle that, in the context of the Scotland Act's own arrangements, the decisions of the Judicial Committee made at the pre-Assent stage of a Bill under s.33 will subsequently bind other courts before which the same question of legislative competence may be raised. Depending, however, on the terms in which such "decisions" come to be expressed, there may be room for questions to be raised at a later stage about exactly what was "decided" at the pre-Assent stage of a Bill which is permitted to pass into law. Nor will it always be obvious that a "decision" at that stage, made on the basis of what may be arguments presented on limited grounds by the Law Officers, should prevail when a more focused challenge to the *vires* of a provision is subsequently made. A "decision" that an entire Bill was *intra vires* may be difficult to uphold in the light of a later challenge to a specific section in the Act once on the statute book.

Subs. (2)
  This subsection makes important provision for the membership of the Judicial Committee for the purposes of proceedings under the Act. As far as other business in concerned, the membership of the court includes the Lords of Appeal in Ordinary, the Lord Chancellor, the Lord Justices of Appeal and the members of the Privy Council who have been judges in the higher courts of Commonwealth states.
  In the Government's proposals, as presented in the White Paper, the intention was that the membership, for Scotland Act purposes, should be confined to Lords of Appeal in Ordinary and that at least five Law Lords should sit (para. 4.17). This proposal was, however, amended before the Scotland Bill was published and membership of the Judicial Committee was expanded, as now provided in this section, to include both serving and retired Law Lords and also those members of the Judicial Committee who hold or have held "high judicial office" as defined by s.25 of the Appellate Jurisdiction Act 1876. This extends membership, for Scotland Act purposes, to include the Lord Chancellor, judges of the Court of Session and judges of the English (or Northern Irish) High Court or Court of Appeal. (The disapplication by subs.(2)(b) of s.5 of the Appellate Jurisdiction Act 1887 is necessary because that would negate the intended restriction of membership.)
  However, the extension of membership—especially the extension to include the Lord Chancellor—was the cause of much dispute and was, indeed, an important element in the case for establishing instead a Constitutional Court with a clearer independence from the influence of

Government. See, *e.g.* Lord Lester of Herne Hill, *Hansard*, H.L. Vol.593, cols. 1968–1972. The wish was also expressed to draw on the Commonwealth membership of the Judicial Committee. See Lord Hope of Craighead, *Hansard*, H.L. Vol. 594, cols. 594–5.

Subs. (3)

This subsection enables provision to be made by Order in Council to confer powers on the Judicial Committee; to apply the Judicial Committee Act 1833 with exceptions or modifications; and to make procedural rules.

Under the terms of Sched. 7, Orders in Council under (3)(a) and (3)(b) are of Type I and subject to annulment by either House of Parliament.

Orders have been made under the subsection as follows:

1. The Judicial Committee (Powers in Devolution Cases) Order 1999 (S.I. 1999 No. 1320)(a) confers on the JCPC all the powers and authority of "the appropriate superior court", whether the House of Lords or, in cases from Scotland, the Court of Session or the High Court of Justiciary; and (b) confers the same powers of enforcement of decisions (art.4). Additional powers are conferred in relation to appeals and references from courts other than the appropriate superior court (art.5); and in respect of the Registrar of the Privy Council (art.6).
2. The Judicial Committee (Devolution Issues) Rules Order 1999 (S.I. 1999 No.665) regulates the procedure for the conduct of proceedings before the JCPC under both s.33 and Sched. 6.

Subs. (4)

As explained above, this subsection applies the section to proceedings under s.33 and Sched. 6.

Supplementary powers

Power to make provision consequential on legislation of, or scrutinised by, the Parliament

104.—(1) Subordinate legislation may make such provision as the person making the legislation considers necessary or expedient in consequence of any provision made by or under any Act of the Scottish Parliament or made by legislation mentioned in subsection (2).

(2) The legislation is subordinate legislation under an Act of Parliament made by—

(a) a member of the Scottish Executive,

(b) a Scottish public authority with mixed functions or no reserved functions, or

(c) any other person (not being a Minister of the Crown) if the function of making the legislation is exercisable within devolved competence.

DEFINITIONS
"Act of the Scottish Parliament": s.28(1).
"devolved competence": s.54.
"member of the Scottish Executive": s.44(1).
"Minister of the Crown": s.126(1).
"Scottish public authority with mixed functions or no reserved functions": Sched. 5., Pt. III, paras 1 and 2.
"subordinate legislation": s.126(1).

GENERAL NOTE

This section confers what is defined by s.112 as an "open power" (in that it is exercisable either by Order in Council or by a Minister of the Crown by order). The power is to be read subject to the "extensions" conferred by s.113 (including the power to modify other enactments under s.113(5)); it may be used to amend the Scotland Act itself (s.114(1)) and to make provision with retrospective effect (s.114(3)). In terms of Sched. 7, the use of s.104 is made subject to Type G (negative procedure at Westminster—but Type B or C (affirmative) if used to modify an Act of Parliament).

In its own terms, s.104 clearly confers a potentially very—even extraordinarily—broad power. It has been explained that it could enable English law or the law of Northern Ireland to be altered-or indeed the law of Scotland where the Scottish Parliament lacks legislative competence-in consequence of an Act of the Scottish Parliament or provision made under it. The section could, for instance, be used to provide a coherent scheme of enforcement across the U.K. where this is considered necessary or desirable, *e.g.* by making Scottish fishing licences enforceable elsewhere.

Subsection (2) extends the categories of legislation in response to which the subordinate legislation may be made to include not only Acts of the Scottish Parliament but also subordinate legislation by the persons and bodies named.

The powers conferred by the section were used to make the Public Finance and Accountability (Scotland) Act 2000 (Transfer of NAO Staff etc.) Order 2000 (S.I. 2000 No. 935). With effect from April 1, 2000, this transferred to Audit Scotland those staff of the National Audit Office whose principal place of employment was in the City of Edinburgh. It also made ancillary provision for the application of the Superannuation Act 1972 (c.11) to such staff and for the transfer of property, rights and liabilities.

Power to make provision consequential on this Act

105. Subordinate legislation may make such modifications in any pre-commencement enactment or prerogative instrument or any other instrument or document as appear to the person making the legislation necessary or expedient in consequence of this Act.

DEFINITIONS
"document": s.126(1).
"enactment": s.126(1).
"modifications": s.126(1).
"pre-commencement enactment": s.53(3).
"prerogative instrument": s.126(1).
"subordinate legislation": s.126(1).

GENERAL NOTE
This section confers what is defined by s.112 as an "open power" (in that it is exercisable either by Order in Council or by a Minister of the Crown by order). The power is to be read subject to the "extensions" conferred by s.113 (including the power to modify other enactments under s.113(5)). In terms of Sched. 7, the use of s.105 is made subject to Type G (negative) procedure at Westminster—but Type B or C (affirmative), if used to modify an Act of Parliament.
The terms of the power conferred by s.105 are very broad-the justification being that it would have been impractical to make provision in the Scotland Act itself for every modification of an existing enactment which may be necessary. For the modifications which *are* made by the Act itself, see s. 125 and Scheds. 8, 9. (See also ss.117–123.).
Three substantial orders have been made under the section: the Scotland Act 1998 (Consequential Modifications) (No.1) Order 1999 (S.I. 1999 No. 1042); the Scotland Act 1998 (Consequential Modifications) (No. 2) Order 1999 (S.I. 1999 No. 1820) and the Scotland Act 1998 (Consequential Modifications) Order 2000 (S.I. 2000 No. 2040).

Power to adapt functions

106.—(1) Subordinate legislation may make such provision (including, in particular, provision modifying a function exercisable by a Minister of the Crown) as the person making the legislation considers appropriate for the purpose of enabling or otherwise facilitating the transfer of a function to the Scottish Ministers by virtue of section 53 or 63.

(2) Subordinate legislation under subsection (1) may, in particular, provide for any function which—

(a) is not exercisable separately in or as regards Scotland to be so exercisable, or

(b) is not otherwise exercisable separately within devolved competence to be so exercisable.

(3) The reference in subsection (1) to the transfer of a function to the Scottish Ministers shall be read as including the sharing of a function with the Scottish Ministers or its other adaptation.

(4) No recommendation shall be made to Her Majesty in Council to make, and no Minister of the Crown shall make, subordinate legislation under this section which modifies a function of observing or implementing an obligation mentioned in subsection (5) unless the Scottish Ministers have been consulted about the modification.

(5) The obligation is an international obligation, or an obligation under Community law, to achieve a result defined by reference to a quantity (whether expressed as an amount, proportion or ratio or otherwise), where the quantity relates to the United Kingdom (or to an area including the United Kingdom or to an area consisting of a part of the United Kingdom which includes the whole or part of Scotland).

(6) If subordinate legislation under this section modifies a function of observing or implementing such an international obligation so that the function to be transferred to the Scottish Ministers relates only to achieving so much of the result to be achieved under the obligation as is specified in the legislation, references in section 58 to the international obligation are to be read as references to the requirement to achieve that much of the result.

(7) If subordinate legislation under this section modifies a function of observing or implementing such an obligation under Community law so that the function to be transferred to the Scottish Ministers relates only to achieving so much of the result to be achieved under the obligation as is specified in the legislation, references in sections 29(2)(d) and 57(2) and paragraph 1 of Schedule 6 to Community law are to be read as including references to the requirement to achieve that much of the result.

DEFINITIONS
"Community law": s.126(9).
"devolved competence": s.54.
"function": s.126(1).
"international obligation": s.126(10).
"Minister of the Crown": s.126(1).
"modify": s.126(1).
"Scotland": s.126(1), (2).
"Scottish Ministers": s.44(2).
"subordinate legislation": s.126(1).

GENERAL NOTE
This section confers what is defined by s.112 as an "open power" (in that it is exercisable either by Order in Council or by a Minister of the Crown by order). The power is to be read subject to the "extensions" conferred by s.113 (including the power to modify enactments under s.113(5)). In terms of Sched. 7, the use of s.106 is made subject to Type G (negative) procedure at Westminster—but Type B or C (affirmative) if used to modify an Act of Parliament.
   This section and s.107 make further provision consequential upon that already made in ss.53 and 63. Those sections provide for the initial transfer of functions from Ministers of the Crown to the Scottish Ministers and for the transfer of additional functions respectively.

Subss. (1)—(3)
   Subsection (1) recognises that the achievement of the transfer of such functions is a process complicated by the fact that existing patterns of statutory provision did not readily lend themselves to the sort of division of functions which would be necessary. In particular, functions which were organised on a G.B. or U.K. basis had to be made divisible into functions exercisable "in or as regards Scotland", which could then be transferred to the Scottish Ministers, and, on the other hand, functions exercisable elsewhere, which could remain with Ministers of the Crown. The other situation is where functions involved an intermingling of devolved and reserved matters and needed to be made divisible between the two when ss.53 and 63 were applied to them. There is something of a parallel here between the measures needed to deal with "cross-border public authorities" whose powers also contain the same sort of overlaps (see ss.88–90). In the case of s.106 the principal targets were powers in relation to agriculture, fisheries and forestry. All are (substantially) devolved matters but much existing legislation involves the joint exercise of powers. Many fisheries functions, for instance, were exercisable by four ministers acting jointly.
   Thus subss. (1)(2) authorise the subordinate legislation required to facilitate the transfer of functions by the separation (and, if necessary, modification) of existing functions, although the actual language of subs. (1) would enable the use of subordinate legislation to make rather wider "appropriate" provision as well.
   The extension by subs. (3) of the transfer of a function to include the sharing of the function or its other adaptation is to take account, in particular, of the variety of such arrangements to be made under s.56(2) or s.63.
   The Scotland Act 1998 (Modification of Functions) Order 1999 (S.I. 1999 No. 1756) was made, with effect from the principal appointed day (July 1, 1999). Article 2 and the Schedule modify 22 listed enactments for the purpose of enabling the division and transfer of functions under ss.53, 56. Articles 3–7 provide for the modification of functions (including functions under Community Law) for the same purpose and in respect of sea fisheries, aquaculture and agriculture. The Order should be read in conjunction with the Scotland Act 1998 (Functions Exercisable in or as Regards Scotland) Order 1999 (S.I. 1999 No. 1748). The transfer of functions orders mentioned in the General Note s.55 may also be referred to.
   See also the Scotland Act 1998 (Modification of Functions) Order 2000 (S.I. 2000 No. 1458) which modified the Disability Rights Commission Act 1999.

Subss. (4)—(7)

These subsections were added at House of Lords committee stage (*Hansard*, H.L. Vol. 593 cols. 626–631). They deal with the situation in which the powers in this section are used to divide between different parts of the U.K. responsibilities imposed by the European Community or other international agreements and which are expressed in quantitative terms (subs. (5)). Examples mentioned in debate were EC quotas for livestock subsidies, the United Kingdom's obligations under the Kyoto Protocol on climate change and related Community measures to achieve targets for the reduction of greenhouse gas emissions. In circumstances such as these, the Government's view was that all parts of the U.K. should be required to meet a fair proportion of the obligations concerned, "not least to ensure that unfair burdens are not placed on business in one area compared to another" (col. 627). Similar provision has been made in s.10 of the Government of Wales Act 1998 (c.38) and s.27 of the Northern Ireland Act 1998 (c.47).

The U.K. Government will make final decisions but a requirement to consult the Scottish Ministers prior to the making of an order is imposed by subs. (4).

Subsection (6) then refers back to the enforcement mechanism in s.58 to provide that the powers in that section may be used only to the extent of the international obligation imposed by an order under this section. The Scottish Ministers could not be compelled to achieve more than the proportion required under this section. Subsection (7) makes a similar adjustment to the interpretation of ss.29 (with consequential effect upon the interpretation of s.54) and 57, intended to ensure also that any failure of the Scottish Ministers to act in a manner compatible with Community Law will be read subject to the provisions of orders under this section.

Legislative power to remedy ultra vires acts

107. Subordinate legislation may make such provision as the person making the legislation considers necessary or expedient in consequence of—

(a) an Act of the Scottish Parliament or any provision of an Act of the Scottish Parliament which is not, or may not be, within the legislative competence of the Parliament, or

(b) any purported exercise by a member of the Scottish Executive of his functions which is not, or may not be, an exercise or a proper exercise of those functions.

DEFINITIONS

"Act of the Scottish Parliament": s.28(1).
"functions": s.126(1).
"legislative competence": s.29.
"member of the Scottish Executive": s.44(1).
"the Parliament": s.126(1).
"subordinate legislation": s.126(1).

GENERAL NOTE

The creation of the Scottish Parliament as a legislative body of defined competence (see especially ss.29, 30 and Scheds. 4, 5) and the existence, whether by virtue of this Act (especially s.98 and Sched. 6) or otherwise, of mechanisms for holding a provision in an Act of the Scottish Parliament to be *ultra vires* provide the rationale for this section. There may be consequences which flow from the purported (but unlawful) exercise of power by the Parliament which need to be rectified. The section provides a procedure by means of subordinate legislation to make such consequential provision as is considered "necessary or expedient". Defined as an "open power" by s.112, the power to make subordinate legislation may be exercised either by Her Majesty by Order in Council or by a Minister of the Crown by order. The power is to be read subject to the extensions provided by s.113 (including the power under s.113(5) to modify enactments) and, by s.114(1), may be used to modify provisions in the Scotland Act (except Scheds. 4 and 5). Section 114(3) provides that it may also make provision having retrospective effect. By Sched. 7, a statutory instrument containing subordinate legislation under this section is of Type G and is subject to annulment by resolution of either House of Parliament or, if it amends an Act of Parliament, of Type B or C and subject to affirmative procedure.

Cast in very broad terms, s.107 the section confers considerable power on the U.K. Government. The grounds on which the power may be exercised (*i.e.* where it is considered necessary or expedient) and the remedial measures available (*i.e.* by way of amendment of enactments and retrospectivity) are very wide.

The Government explained (*Hansard*, H.L. Vol. 593, cols. 592–594) that the power might be used in a situation where, after judicial deliberation, it was discovered that a provision of an Act of the Scottish Parliament was *ultra vires*. The power would allow the Act to be amended and enable provision to be made to remedy any consequential problems, for example, concerning rights purportedly accrued or liabilities purportedly incurred by virtue of this Act. Such provision could be given retrospective effect, thus putting third parties in the position they thought they were in before the flaw was discovered. (See also (1997–98) H.L. 124). There might be a need to act quickly and, therefore, to avoid primary legislation.

It has also been explained that, in that sense, the power is complementary to that given to the courts in s.102 *inter alia* to limit the retrospectively or suspend the effect of a decision that something done by the Scottish Parliament or the Scottish Executive is *ultra vires*.

It has further been acknowledged, however, that it is not a prerequisite for the use of s.107 to have the decision of a court. The power under the section could be used to remedy a defect or suspected defect before judicial proceedings were commenced. It should also be noted that the scope of the section extends not only to circumstances where a provision is purportedly made by an Act of the Scottish Parliament but "is not, or may not be, within the legislative competence of the Parliament" but also to "any purported exercise" of functions by a member of the Scottish Executive which is not, or may not be, "an exercise or a proper exercise of those functions".

What, in this context, is a "proper exercise" of functions? It is a very broad formula and confines the power neither to an issue of "devolved competence" nor indeed to an issue of legality at all. Doubts were expressed in debate about how this section might be used in the case of deliberate, rather than unintentional, misuse (or threatened misuse) of power by the Scottish Parliament or the Scottish Executive.

Agreed redistribution of functions exercisable by the Scottish Ministers etc

108.—(1) Her Majesty may by Order in Council provide for any functions exercisable by a member of the Scottish Executive to be exercisable—

(a) by a Minister of the Crown instead of by the member of the Scottish Executive,

(b) by a Minister of the Crown concurrently with the member of the Scottish Executive, or

(c) by the member of the Scottish Executive only with the agreement of, or after consultation with, a Minister of the Crown.

(2) Where an Order is made under subsection (1)(a) or (b) in relation to a function of the Scottish Ministers, the First Minister or the Lord Advocate which is exercisable only with the agreement of, or after consultation with, any other of those persons, the function shall, unless the Order provides otherwise, be exercisable by the Minister of the Crown free from any such requirement.

(3) An Order under this section may, in particular, provide for any function exercisable by a Minister of the Crown by virtue of an Order under subsection (1)(a) or (b) to be exercisable subject to a requirement for the function to be exercised with the agreement of, or after consultation with, another person.

(4) This section does not apply to any retained functions of the Lord Advocate which fall within section 52(6)(a).

DEFINITIONS
"by virtue of": s.126(11).
"function": s.126(1).
"member of the Scottish Executive": s.44(1).
"Minister of the Crown": s.126(1).
"retained functions": s.52(6).
"Scottish Ministers": s.44(2).

GENERAL NOTE
This section was added as a new clause at House of Commons report stage (see *Hansard*, H.C. Vol. 312, col. 244 *et seq.*) and it joins s.106 in making provision for the use of subordinate legislation (in this case, Orders in Council) to deal with important matters consequential upon the allocation of powers to the Scottish Ministers. Such powers may be conferred directly (notably by the Scottish Parliament) under s.52; others are transferred by this Act from Ministers of the Crown under s.53; and further powers may be transferred under s.63.

It was, however, thought necessary to have the power to transfer functions in the opposite direction, *i.e.* from a member of the Scottish Executive to a Minister of the Crown. The U.K. Government might simply wish to vary the executive devolution settlement. Alternatively, it might wish to transfer functions conferred on the Scottish Ministers by an Act of the Scottish Parliament when matters covered by that Act have been added to matters reserved under Sched. 5 by virtue of an Order in Council under s.30. The provision could also be used to enable U.K. Ministers to exercise particular functions on a U.K. wide basis, for example in relation to the collection of certain statistics.

It should be noted that, as reflected in the reference in the marginal note to an "*Agreed redistribution of functions*", any Order in Council used to effect such a redistribution is one which is an affirmative instrument in both the Westminster and Scottish Parliaments (*i.e.* Type A procedure under Sched. 7). The power under this section is to be read subject to the "extensions" authorised by s.113 and, by virtue of s.114(1), may be used to modify the Scotland Act itself.

Agreed redistribution of property and liabilities

109.—(1) Her Majesty may by Order in Council provide—

(a) for the transfer to a Minister of the Crown or government department of any property belonging to the Scottish Ministers or the Lord Advocate, or

(b) for a Minister of the Crown or government department to have such rights or interests in relation to any property belonging to the Scottish Ministers or the Lord Advocate as Her Majesty considers appropriate (whether in connection with a transfer or otherwise).

(2) Her Majesty may by Order in Council provide for the transfer to a Minister of the Crown or government department of any liabilities to which the Scottish Ministers or the Lord Advocate are subject.

(3) An Order in Council under this section may only be made in connection with any transfer or sharing of functions of a member of the Scottish Executive by virtue of section 108 or in any other circumstances in which Her Majesty considers it appropriate to do so for the purposes of this Act.

DEFINITIONS
"by virtue of": s.126(11).
"function": s.126(1).
"government department": s.126(1).
"member of the Scottish Executive": s.44(1).
"Minister of the Crown": s.126(1).
"property": s.126(1).
"Scottish Ministers": s.44(2).

GENERAL NOTE
    This section was added as a new clause at House of Lords committee stage (*Hansard*, H.L. Vol. 593, cols. 633—634). As subs: (3) makes clear, the power to make an Order in Council transferring property and liabilities from the Scottish Ministers or the Lord Advocate to a Minister of the Crown or government department, is exercisable only in connection with an Order to redistribute functions in the same direction under s.108. Thus, the section reflects the equivalent provision made in ss.60, 62 in respect of the transfer of functions in the other direction.

Scottish taxpayers for social security purposes

110.—(1) The Secretary of State may by order provide for individuals of any description specified in the order to be treated for the purposes of any of the matters that are reserved matters by virtue of Head F of Part II of Schedule 5 as if they were, or were not, Scottish taxpayers.

(2) The Secretary of State may by order provide in relation to any year of assessment that, for those purposes, the basic rate in relation to the income of Scottish taxpayers shall be treated as being such rate as is specified in the order (instead of the rate increased or reduced for that year by virtue of any resolution of the Parliament in pursuance of section 73 passed after the beginning of the year).

(3) An order under this section may apply in respect of any individuals whether Scotland is the part of the United Kingdom with which they have the closest connection or not.

(4) In this section "Scottish taxpayer" has the same meaning as in Part IV.

DEFINITIONS
"by virtue of": s.126(11).
"the Parliament": s.126(1).
"reserved matters": Sched. 5.
"Scotland": s.126(1), (2).
"Scottish taxpayer": subs. (4) and s.75.

GENERAL NOTE
    This is a section consequential upon (a) the reservation to the Westminster Parliament of "Social Security" under Head F of Pt. II of Sched. 5 and (b) the provisions in Pt. IV of the Act which enable the Scottish Parliament to vary the basic rate of income tax for Scottish taxpayers and, in particular, the power to do so after the start of the tax year. The purpose of this section is to prevent any consequential disruption to the social security, child support and pension systems.
    The entitlement to many social security benefits, including the principal income-related benefits of jobseeker's allowance, income support, family credit and housing and council tax

benefit, is assessed by reference to income net of tax (and national insurance contributions). Thus, if the Scottish Parliament exercises its power to vary the basic rate of tax, it will be necessary to determine whether a benefit claimant should be treated as a Scottish taxpayer, so that the correct amount of benefit can be paid.

Section 75 does already set out criteria for deciding whether or not someone is a Scottish taxpayer but those are designed to apply over a full year. To make a clear decision for benefit purposes, it is necessary to know whether a person is a Scottish taxpayer or not at the point of claim.

Section 75 also provides, in certain circumstances, for changes in the Scottish rate of tax at short notice and after the start of the tax year. This could present operational difficulties for the social security system to reflect changes at very short notice and could mean that large numbers of benefit claims decided before a tax change might need to be re-examined.

This section, therefore, provides powers to put the benefit position beyond doubt by specifying who is to be regarded as a Scottish taxpayer and what the relevant rate of tax should be. This should enable benefit decisions to be made promptly and without uncertainty about the appropriate tax rate to apply. It has been stated that, in the great majority of cases, there will be no effect on benefit entitlement. There will be a reduction of administrative costs and of inconvenience to claimants both in Scotland and the rest of the United Kingdom.

Subs. (1)
As explained, the purpose of this section is to reduce uncertainty and delay in the assessment process in relation to social security entitlement, including, in particular, child support. The power to be given by order to treat a person as a Scottish taxpayer, or not, is designed to achieve this and will, in particular, remove the need to ask all benefit claimants, including claimants in England, about connections with Scotland. The intention is to exercise the power so that, for benefit and child support purposes, a person's address at the time of assessment will normally be the determining factor in deciding whether or not the Scottish tax rate should apply.

An order under this subsection is to be made under the Type C procedure in Sched. 7, *i.e.* affirmative procedure at Westminster.

See also s.113(3).

Subs. (2)
Here the Secretary of State is empowered to specify the rate of income tax to be treated as the rate for benefit assessment purposes. Because this is stated to operate instead of the rate eventually specified by the Scottish Parliament after the beginning of the tax year, it is expected to remove uncertainty, particularly in the early part of the year.

An order under this subsection is subject to the Type I procedure in Sched. 7, *i.e.* negative procedure at Westminster.

Subs. (3)
This enables the prescription of a person's address as the determining factor without recourse to the more complicated rules in s.75.

Regulation of Tweed and Esk fisheries

111.—(1) Her Majesty may by Order in Council make provision for or in connection with the conservation, management and exploitation of salmon, trout, eels and freshwater fish in the Border rivers.

(2) An Order under subsection (1) may—

(a) exclude the application of section 53 in relation to any Border rivers function,

(b) confer power to make subordinate legislation.

(3) In particular, provision may be made by such an Order—

(a) conferring any function on a Minister of the Crown, the Scottish Ministers or a public body in relation to the Border rivers,

(b) for any Border rivers function exercisable by any person to be exercisable instead by a person (or another person) mentioned in paragraph (a),

(c) for any Border rivers function exercisable by any person to be exercisable concurrently or jointly with, or with the agreement of or after consultation with, a person (or another person) mentioned in paragraph (a).

(4) In this section—

"the Border rivers" means the Rivers Tweed and Esk,

"Border rivers function" means a function conferred by any enactment, so far as exercisable in relation to the Border rivers,

"conservation", in relation to salmon, trout, eels and freshwater fish, includes the protection of their environment, "eels", "freshwater fish", "salmon" and "trout" have the same meanings as in the Salmon and Freshwater Fisheries Act 1975,

"the River Tweed" has the same meaning as in section 39 of the Salmon and Freshwater Fisheries Act 1975,

"the River Esk" means the river of that name which, for part of its length, constitutes the border between England and Scotland including—

(a) its tributary streams (which for this purpose include the River Sark and its tributary streams), and

(b) such waters on the landward side of its estuary limits as are determined by an Order under subsection (1),

together with its banks;

and references to the Border rivers include any part of the Border rivers.

(5) An Order under subsection (1) may modify the definitions in subsection (4) of the River Tweed and the River Esk.

DEFINITIONS
"the Border rivers": subs. (4).
"Border river function": subs. (4).
"conservation": subs. (4).
"eels": subs. (4).
"freshwater fish": subs. (4).
"function": s.126(1).
"Minister of the Crown": s.126(1).
"modify": s.126(1).
"the River Esk": subs. (4).
"the River Tweed": subs. (4).
"salmon": subs. (4).
"Scotland": s.126(1), (2).
"Scottish Ministers": s.44(2).
"subordinate legislation": s.126(1).
"trout": subs. (4).

GENERAL NOTE
It is generally the case that the regulation of fishing, as a devolved matter, is within the competence of the Scottish Parliament. Fishing does, however, raise special problems because some aspects of fishing extend beyond Scotland itself and *prima facie*, therefore, beyond the competence of the Parliament for that reason. One response to this difficulty is the special provision made in s. 30(3).

A more specific problem arises in relation to the Border rivers—the Tweed and the Esk—where the Government has taken the view that policies of "whole river fisheries management" should be sustained. At present, salmon and freshwater fisheries management on the Tweed is governed by the Tweed Fisheries Acts 1857–1969, which provided for a River Tweed Council, drawn from the Tweed Commissioners, with special rules governing fishing throughout the whole Tweed river system, including the area of inshore sea at the mouth of the Tweed known as the "Tweed Box". In addition, some provisions of general Scottish public legislation apply on the Tweed, including in England where English legislation is disapplied.

On the Esk, fisheries management is regulated under English legislation, with Scottish legislation generally disapplied—the exception being s.21 of the Salmon and Freshwater Fisheries (Protection) (Scotland) Act 1951 which creates an offence in Scots law of taking salmon illegally from the Esk in Scotland. Management of the Esk fisheries is a function of the Environment Agency.

The device used to achieve a continuation of joint regulation of the two rivers is an Order in Council which, by virtue of Sched. 7, requires (affirmative) approval in both the Westminster and Scottish Parliaments. By virtue of s.113(5) an Order in Council may amend existing legislation (other than the Scotland Act itself).

The Scotland Act 1998 (Border Rivers) Order 1999 (S.I. 1999 No. 1746) was made with effect from July 1, 1999.

Subss. (1), (2), (3)
These provide for the making of an Order in Council. S.I. 1999 No.1746 makes separate provisions for the River Esk (Part II) and the River Tweed (Part III). In relation to the Esk, the Order

Disapplies s.53 of the Scotland Act (art.3)
- Modifies the Water Resources Act 1991 and the Environment Act 1995 (arts. 4,5)
- Creates new forms of control, offences and powers of enforcement in relation to the Lower Esk (arts. 6, 7, 8)
- Requires the Environment Agency to send copies of reports it submits to the Minister of Agriculture, Fisheries and Food to the Scottish Ministers and requires that they be laid before the Scottish Parliament (art.10).

In relation to the River Tweed, the Order
- Confers new powers on the Scottish Ministers in respect of the Tweed outside Scotland (art.11)
- Modifies the Salmon and Freshwater Fisheries (Protection) (Scotland) Act 1951 so far as it relates to the Tweed outside Scotland (art.12).

Subss. (4), (5)

By virtue of the Salmon and Freshwater Fisheries Act 1975:

"eels" includes elvers and the fry of eels.

"freshwater fish" means any fish living in fresh water exclusive of salmon and trout and of any kinds of fish which migrate to and from tidal waters and of eels.

"salmon" means all fish of the salmon species and includes part of a salmon.

"trout" means any fish of the salmon family commonly known as trout, including migratory trout and char and also includes part of a trout.

"the River Tweed" is defined by reference to section 39 of the Salmon and Freshwater Fisheries Act 1975, which in turn refers to the definition contained in the Tweed Fisheries (Amendment) Act 1859, as itself amended by any bylaws amending that definition. Section II of the 1859 Act defines the Tweed to include "every river, brook or stream which flows into the said river and also the mouth or entrance of the said river, as described and defined in the Act". Section IV of that Act (as amended) defines the mouth or entrance of the Tweed (commonly known as the Tweed Box) to include an area extending 5 miles out to sea and from the Scottish border to a point 7 miles south of the Queen Elizabeth pier in Berwick.

"the River Esk" is not otherwise defined in statute and is, therefore, newly defined for the purposes of this section in subs. (4). Subsection (5) provides for the modification of the definitions of both rivers.

Article 9 of S.I. 1999 No. 1746 determines the limits of the waters on the landward side of the estuary limits of the River Esk.

PART VI

SUPPLEMENTARY

Subordinate legislation

Subordinate legislation: general

112.—(1) Any power to make subordinate legislation conferred by this Act shall, if no other provision is made as to the person by whom the power is exercisable, be exercisable by Her Majesty by Order in Council or by a Minister of the Crown by order.

(2) But the power to make subordinate legislation under section 129(1) providing—

(a) for the appropriation of sums forming part of the Scottish Consolidated Fund, or

(b) for sums received by any person to be appropriated in aid of sums appropriated as mentioned in paragraph (a),

shall be exercisable only by Her Majesty by Order in Council.

(3) References in this Act to an open power are to a power to which subsection (1) applies (and include a power to make subordinate legislation under section 129(1) whether or not the legislation makes provision as mentioned in subsection (2)).

(4) An Order in Council under an open power may revoke, amend or re-enact an order, as well as an Order in Council, under the power; and an order under an open power may revoke, amend or re-enact an Order in Council, as well as an order, under the power.

(5) Any power to make subordinate legislation conferred by this Act shall, in relation to its exercise by a Minister of the Crown or a member of the Scottish Executive, be exercisable by statutory instrument.

DEFINITIONS
"conferred": s.126(1).
"member of the Scottish Executive": s.44(1).
"Minister of the Crown": s.126(1).
"open power": subs. (3).

"subordinate legislation": s.126(1).

GENERAL NOTE

Many provisions in this Act contain powers to make subordinate legislation. Overall these present a complex picture, reflecting the very wide range of constitutional provision made by the Act as a whole. Powers are made exercisable by Ministers of the U.K. and Scottish Governments. Powers have to be made subject to scrutiny by the Westminster or Scottish Parliament or both. In some instances, powers are being created which have a special constitutional importance in that they may be used with retrospective effect or to amend existing legislation or the Scotland Act itself.

In accordance with normal practice, the Scotland Bill, on transfer into the House of Lords, was scrutinised by the Delegated Powers and Deregulation Committee of that House in the light of a memorandum prepared by the Scottish Office. The Committee issued a Report (24th Report (1997–98) H.L. 124 to which the Scottish Office memorandum was appended) and later a further Report (32nd Report (1997–98) H.L. 146). To this Report was appended a letter from Lord Sewel, responding to some of the concerns expressed by the Committee in their earlier Report and containing proposals for amending the Bill at House of Lords Committee and Report stages. Those amendments produced a very substantially remodelled version of what is now contained in ss.112–115 (and Sched. 7) of the Act.

This note forms an introduction to those four sections and Sched. 7, all of which make general provision in relation to the powers to make subordinate legislation by Order in Council or by order made by a Minister of the Crown; the scope of those powers; the modification of other legislation or making subordinate legislation having retrospective effect; and the procedures for the scrutiny of such legislation, whether by the Westminster Parliament, the Scottish Parliament or both.

It should, however, be noted that related provision is made elsewhere in this Act:

1. Section 30 contains special provision (in earlier versions of the Bill contained in the clause which is now s.114) for the modification of Scheds. 4, 5 and "functions which are exercisable in or as regards Scotland".

2. Section 118 provides for the making of subordinate legislation by members of the Scottish Executive and especially for the adaptation of procedures in the Westminster Parliament to procedures in the Scottish Parliament. That section relates to powers formerly exercised by Ministers of the Crown but now transferred to the Scottish Ministers. The Act does confer one new power on the Scottish Ministers to make subordinate legislation by order (s.18(5)). Because that power *is* new, procedural provision is made for it in Sched. 7.

As to the provision made in ss.112–115 and Sched. 7, the aim is to draw together some general provisions applicable to order-making powers, whether by Order in Council or other form of order, of the U.K. Government. The main purpose of s.112 is to introduce the concept of the "open power". Section 113 then provides for a general extension of the scope of order-making powers, including *inter alia* the power to modify enactments. Section 114 provides that powers contained in certain enumerated sections may be used to modify the Scotland Act itself (with the exception of Scheds. 4, 5, for which see instead s.30) and to make retrospective provision. The main purpose of s.115 is to give effect to Sched. 7 which allocates to each order-making power a parliamentary procedure deemed to be appropriate to it.

Subss. (1)—(3)

Many order-making powers in this Act are conferred simply as a power to make "subordinate legislation" without specifying whether the power should be exercised by Order in Council (in the more important cases) or by other ministerial orders (in the more routine cases). Subsection (1) confirms that, where powers are conferred in this general way, they may indeed be exercised in either style. The Government explained that the inclusion of such powers was intended to provide the flexibility to deal in appropriate ways with the subordinate legislation which will be needed. Different uses of the powers may be very different in terms of scale and importance. Conferring powers in this way was compared with the provisions in the European Communities Act 1972 which deal with the incorporation into U.K. law of Community rights and obligations (See (1997—98) H.L. 124; Scottish Office memorandum, para. 11.2).

Subsection (3) identifies such a power as an "open power" and that term is used in subs. (4), s.113 and Sched. 7 to attach specific rules to "open powers". One qualification of this general position is in relation to s.129(1) under which transitional provision may be made. Section 129(1) is defined as one of the group of "open powers" but s.112(2) requires that where, in the course of making such transitional provision, the order is used to appropriate sums from the Scottish Consolidated Fund (or the related appropriation in subs.(2)(b)), the procedure by way of Order in Council must be used. It will be noted that Sched. 7, para. 4 requires that, where s.129(1) is used to make provision as in s.112(2), then the Type D procedure (involving approval of a draft by the Scottish Parliament rather than by Westminster parliamentary procedure under Type G) must be deployed. (See also s.115(3)).

Subs. (4)

This extends the flexibility in an open power to enable the use of the power in the one order to "revoke, amend or re-enact" a provision earlier made in another. See also Sched. 7, para. 5.

Subs. (5)

By s.1 of the Statutory Instruments Act 1946 an Order in Council is always to be made by statutory instrument. This subsection makes general provision that where a power to make subordinate legislation, conferred by the Scotland Act, is exercisable by either a Minister of the Crown or by a member of the Scottish Executive, it is exercisable by statutory instrument and the terms of the 1946 Act will, therefore, apply.

Subordinate legislation: scope of powers

113.—(1) References in this section to a power are to an open power and to any other power to make subordinate legislation conferred by this Act which is exercisable by Her Majesty in Council or by a Minister of the Crown, and include a power as extended by this section.

(2) A power may be exercised so as to make different provision for different purposes.

(3) A power (as well as being exercisable in relation to all cases to which it extends) may be exercised in relation to—

(a) those cases subject to specified exceptions, or

(b) any particular case or class of case.

(4) A power includes power to make—

(a) any supplementary, incidental or consequential provision, and

(b) any transitory, transitional or saving provision,

which the person making the legislation considers necessary or expedient.

(5) A power may be exercised by modifying—

(a) any enactment or prerogative instrument,

(b) any other instrument or document,

if the subordinate legislation (or a statutory instrument containing it) would be subject to any of the types of procedure referred to in Schedule 7.

(6) But a power to modify enactments does not (unless otherwise stated) extend to making modifications of this Act or subordinate legislation under it.

(7) A power may be exercised so as to make provision for the delegation of functions.

(8) A power includes power to make provision for sums to be payable out of the Scottish Consolidated Fund or charged on the Fund.

(9) A power includes power to make provision for the payment of sums out of money provided by Parliament or for sums to be charged on and paid out of the Consolidated Fund.

(10) A power may not be exercised so as to create any criminal offence punishable—

(a) on summary conviction, with imprisonment for a period exceeding three months or with a fine exceeding the amount specified as level 5 on the standard scale,

(b) on conviction on indictment, with a period of imprisonment exceeding two years.

(11) The fact that a power is conferred does not prejudice the extent of any other power.

DEFINITIONS
"document": s.126(1).
"enactment": ss.113(6), 126(1).
"functions": s.126(1).
"Minister of the Crown": s.126(1).
"modify": s.126(1).
"open power": s.112(3).
"prerogative instrument": s.126(1).
"subordinate legislation": s.126(1).

GENERAL NOTE
As mentioned in the General Note on s.112, this is one of the group of sections, dealing with the making of subordinate legislation under the Act, which were substantially remodelled at committee and report stages in the House of Lords.
This section serves to extend the scope of all the powers in the Act to make subordinate legislation to which it applies, *i.e.* all those defined as an "open power" by s. 112 and then all others exercisable by Order in Council or by a Minister of the Crown. The intention is that the extensions conferred should provide a desirable flexibility in the use of order-making powers.

Subss. (1), (2)
See above.

Subs. (3)
In the ministerial letter attached to the 32nd Report of the Delegated Powers and Deregulation Committee (see the General Note to s.112), it was suggested that the power in this subsection would have particular relevance to the exercise of the order-making power in s.110 (Scottish taxpayers for social security purposes).

Subs. (4)
This enables supplementary provisions to be made, but see subss. (5), (6).

Subss. (5), (6)
These subsections confer a general power to modify enactments (and other instruments), including the "Henry VIII" power to amend Acts of Parliament. However, subs. (6) prohibits amendment of the Scotland Act itself (or subordinate legislation under it), a power confined to the provisions listed in s.114(1), or, in the case of the power to amend Scheds. 4, 5, s.30. A power to be extended to the modification of enactments or other documents must be one already subject to a parliamentary procedure under Sched. 7. Para. 3 of that Schedule "upgrades" the degree of scrutiny required where the delegated legislation concerned "contains provisions which add to, replace or omit any part of the text of an Act".
It should be noted that the restriction imposed by subs. (6) has had the wider effect of requiring an expanded entry for "enactment" in the index of defined expressions in s.127.

Subss. (8), (9)
For the Scottish Consolidated Fund see ss.64, 65 and, for statutory modifications from the Consolidated Fund to the Scottish Consolidated Fund, see s.119.

Subs. (10)
This enables the creation of criminal offences.

Subs. (11)
This is inserted as an interpretative aid.

Subordinate legislation: particular provisions

114.—(1) A power to make subordinate legislation conferred by any of the following provisions of this Act may be exercised by modifying any enactment comprised in or made under this Act (except Schedules 4 and 5): sections 89, 104, 107, 108 and 129(1).

(2) The reference in subsection (1) to a power to make subordinate legislation includes a power as extended by section 113.

(3) A power to make subordinate legislation conferred by any of the following provisions of this Act may be exercised so as to make provision having retrospective effect: sections 30, 58(4), 104 and 107.

DEFINITIONS
"conferred": s.126(1).
"enactment": ss.113(6), 126(1).
"modify": s.126(1).
"subordinate legislation": s.126(1).

GENERAL NOTE
For an introduction to ss.112–115 and Sched. 7, see the General Note to s.112. See also s.113 which makes general provision to "extend" the scope of the powers to make subordinate legislation conferred by this Act. Now s.114 identifies two groups of provisions to provide that the powers conferred by the first group may be used to modify the Scotland Act itself (or enactments made under it) and that those in the second may be used to retrospective effect. Both types of provision (especially the "Henry VIII clauses" in the first group) attracted the attention of the Delegated Powers and Deregulation Committee of the House of Lords (see the General Note to s.112).

Subss. (1), (2)
Subsection (1) lists the powers to make subordinate legislation which may be used to modify an "enactment comprised in or made under" the Scotland Act itself, with the exception of Scheds. 4, 5. In the Government's response (appended to H.L. 146) to the Delegated Powers Committee's first report (H.L. 124), they referred to the special protection to be afforded to Scheds. 4 and 5 which went to the "heart of the devolution settlement". Section 30 provided a

"bespoke mechanism" for their amendment, with the agreement of both Parliaments and it would be inappropriate to permit other subordinate legislation to amend them.

At the same time the Government shortened the list of powers under which other provisions of this Act can be modified (whilst the scope of s.113(5) was widened) to those now listed in subs. (1):

Section 89	(Power to make provision consequential on Acts of the Scottish Parliament)
Section 107	(Power to remedy *ultra vires* acts)
Section 108	(Power to redistribute functions by agreement)
Section 129(1)	(Power to make provision for transitional purposes)

It should be noted that subs. (2) confirms that the power to modify the Scotland Act under any of the listed provisions may relate to that provision as "extended" by the terms of s.113 (see Note on that section).

Also important to the exercise of these powers by modification of the Scotland Act (as also to the exercise of the broader powers to modify other enactments under s.113(5)) are the terms of para. 3 of Sched. 7. That paragraph provides that, where the relevant subordinate legislation "contains provisions which add to, replace or omit any part of the text of an Act (including this Act)", the level of parliamentary control is upgraded from the use of negative procedure to the use of affirmative procedure.

Thus the procedure for s.89 (normally Type F) moves to Type A; for ss.104, 107 (normally Type G) to Type B or C; and for s.129(1) (normally Type G) to Type B or C. Section 108 is always Type A.

Subs. (3)

The other specially identified group of powers to make subordinate legislation contains those which may have retrospective effect:

Section 30	(Legislative competence—especially the power to amend Scheds 4, 5)
Section 58(4)	(Power to revoke subordinate legislation)
Section 104	(Power to make provision consequential on Acts of the Scottish Parliament)
Section 107	(Power to remedy *ultra vires* acts)

Subordinate legislation: procedure

115.—(1) Schedule 7 (which determines the procedure which is to apply to subordinate legislation under this Act in relation to each House of Parliament and the Scottish Parliament) shall have effect.

(2) In spite of the fact that that Schedule provides for subordinate legislation under a particular provision of this Act (or the statutory instrument containing it) to be subject to any type of procedure in relation to the Parliament, the provision conferring the power to make that legislation may be brought into force at any time after the passing of this Act.

(3) Accordingly, any subordinate legislation (or the statutory instrument containing it) made in the exercise of the power in the period beginning with that time and ending immediately before the principal appointed day is to be subject to such other type of procedure (if any) as may be specified in subordinate legislation made under section 129(1).

DEFINITIONS
"conferring": s.126(1).
"the Parliament": s.126(1).
"principal appointed day": s.126(1).
"subordinate legislation": s.126(1).

GENERAL NOTE
For a general introduction to the organisation of the powers and procedures used in the Act for the making of subordinate legislation, see the General Note to s.112.

The procedures to be used by the Scottish Ministers (and the Scottish Parliament) in the making of Scottish Statutory Instruments—established on a transitional basis by the Scotland Act 1998 (Transitory and Transitional Provisions) (Statutory Instruments) Order 1999 (S.I. 1999 No.1096) are discussed in the note on s.52.

Subs. (1)
The main purpose of s.115 is to give effect to Sched. 7 which specifies the procedures (labelled Types A—K) which apply to the making of subordinate legislation under each relevant provision in the Act. A Note is attached to that Schedule.

Subss. (2), (3)
These made transitional provision to deal with order-making procedures in the period between the passing of this Act and the time when the Scottish Parliament acquired its powers

(including the power to approve relevant subordinate legislation) on the principal appointed day. Subsection (2) (adopting the curious opening language of "In spite of the fact that", instead of, *e.g.* "Notwithstanding") established that it would be permissible to have in force an order-making section which, when read with Sched. 7, required the participation of the Scottish Parliament before the Parliament acquired its powers.

The solution to the apparent anomaly is then found in subs. (3) which provides that s.129(1), which contains the general power to make transitional provision, could be used to specify a modified procedure to be used during the period up to the time the Scottish Parliament was established.

The power was used to make the Scotland Act 1998 (Transitional and Transitory Provisions) (Subordinate Legislation under the Act) Order 1998 (S.I. 1998 No. 3216) which adjusted procedures for a transitional period.

Transfer of property: supplementary

116.—(1) This section applies in relation to subordinate legislation under section 60, 62, 90 or 109 or paragraph 2 of Schedule 2.

(2) Any such subordinate legislation may, in particular—

(a) provide for the creation of rights or interests, or the imposition of liabilities or conditions, in relation to property transferred, or rights or interests acquired, by virtue of such legislation,

(b) provide for any property, liabilities or conditions to be determined under such legislation,

(c) make provision (other than provision imposing a charge to tax) as to the tax treatment of anything done by virtue of such legislation.

(3) No order shall be made by a Minister of the Crown by virtue of subsection (2)(c), and no recommendation shall be made to Her Majesty in Council to make an Order in Council by virtue of subsection (2)(c), without the agreement of the Treasury.

(4) Subordinate legislation to which this section applies shall have effect in relation to any property or liabilities to which it applies despite any provision (of whatever nature) which would otherwise prevent, penalise or restrict the transfer of the property or liabilities.

(5) A right of pre-emption, right of irritancy, right of return or other similar right shall not operate or become exercisable as a result of any transfer of property by virtue of any subordinate legislation to which this section applies.

(6) Any such right shall have effect in the case of any such transfer as if the transferee were the same person in law as the transferor and as if no transfer of the property had taken place.

(7) Such compensation as is just shall be paid to any person in respect of any such right which would, apart from subsection (5), have operated in favour of, or become exercisable by, that person but which, in consequence of the operation of that subsection, cannot subsequently operate in his favour or (as the case may be) become exercisable by him.

(8) Any compensation payable by virtue of subsection (7) shall be paid by the transferor or by the transferee or by both.

(9) Subordinate legislation under this subsection may provide for the determination of any disputes as to whether and, if so, how much, compensation is payable by virtue of subsection (7) and as to the person to whom or by whom it shall be paid.

(10) Subsections (4) to (9) apply in relation to the creation of rights or interests, or the doing of anything else, in relation to property as they apply in relation to a transfer of property; and references to the transferor and transferee shall be read accordingly.

(11) A certificate issued by the Secretary of State that any property or liability has, or has not, been transferred by virtue of subordinate legislation under section 60 or 62 or paragraph 2 of Schedule 2 shall be conclusive evidence of the transfer or (as the case may be) the fact that there has not been a transfer.

(12) A certificate issued by the Secretary of State and the Scottish Ministers that any property or liability has, or has not, been transferred by

virtue of an Order in Council under section 90 or 109 shall be conclusive evidence of the transfer or (as the case may be) the fact that there has not been a transfer.

(13) In this section "right of return" means any right under a provision for the return or reversion of property in specified circumstances.

DEFINITIONS
"by virtue of": s.126(11).
"Minister of the Crown": s.126(1).
"property": s.126(1).
"right of return": subs. (13).
"subordinate legislation": s.126(1).

GENERAL NOTE
This section makes provision supplementary to ss.60, 62, 90 and 109 and para. 2 of Sched. 2, which deal with the transfer of property to the Scottish Ministers, the Lord Advocate, successors to cross-border public authorities, Ministers of the Crown and the Parliamentary corporation respectively.
All of these provisions authorise the making of subordinate legislation to give effect to the transfer of property and are to be read subject to the extensions of their scope authorised by s.113 and to the parliamentary procedures prescribed under s.115 and Sched. 7. Now this section authorises additional provision to be made in the relevant subordinate legislation.
The notes on ss.60, 62 and para. 2 of Sched. 2 contain references to the transfer of property orders made so far. It may, in particular, be observed that art.12 of S.I. 1999 No. 1104, art. 6 of S.I. 1999 No. 1105, and art. 4 of S.I. 1999 No. 1106 all make provision as to the determination of questions as to whether and to what extent property and liabilities are transferred and of disputes concerning compensation which may be payable under s.116(7).

Subss. (2), (3)
Subsection (2), read subject to Treasury approval in respect of (2)(c), makes the main substantive provision. The subordinate legislation under the property transfer sections may provide for the "creation of rights or interests", etc.; provide for the property, etc., to be "determined" (rather than specified in the legislation itself); and provide for tax treatment, *e.g.* exemption from stamp duty in respect of the transfer of property from (former) cross-border public authorities.

Subs. (4)
This ensures that the relevant subordinate legislation overrides "any provision (of whatever nature)" which might otherwise prevent, penalise or restrict the transfer. See also subs. (10).

Subss. (5)—(10) and (13)
These subsections make more specific provision to ensure that rights of pre-emption, etc., cannot become exercisable as a result of a relevant transfer; but also for "such compensation as is just" to be payable (whether by transferor or transferee or both); and for the determination of disputes. Subsection (10) extends the scope of all of subss. (4)–(9) to "the creation of rights or interests, or the doing of anything else".

Subss. (11), (12)
These subsections make provision for certificates issued by the Secretary of State (in the case of transfer to the Scottish Ministers, the Lord Advocate and the Parliamentary Corporation) and by the Secretary of State and the Scottish Ministers (in the case of transfers to successors to cross-border public authorities and Ministers of the Crown) to be "conclusive evidence" of a transfer (or a non-transfer).

General modification of enactments

Ministers of the Crown

117. So far as may be necessary for the purpose or in consequence of the exercise of a function by a member of the Scottish Executive within devolved competence, any pre-commencement enactment or prerogative instrument, and any other instrument or document, shall be read as if references to a Minister of the Crown (however described) were or included references to the Scottish Ministers.

DEFINITIONS
"devolved competence": s.54.
"document": s.126(1).

"enactment": ss.113(6), 126(1).
"function": s.126(1).
"member of the Scottish Executive": s.44(1).
"Minister of the Crown": s.126(1).
"pre-commencement enactment": s.53(3).
"prerogative instrument": s.126(1).
"Scottish Ministers": s.44(2).

GENERAL NOTE

The first of a series, this section makes provision for the modification of all types of enactment and document referred to in order to accommodate the transfer of powers (principally by ss.53, 54 and read subject to s.106) from Ministers of the Crown to the Scottish Ministers.

This section (along with ss.118–121) has been modified for extended application by subordinate legislation under s.124. That power has been used to apply this group of sections to functions transferred to the Scottish Ministers under s.63.

It should also be noted that many of the statutory modifications made by Sched. 8 to the Act and also by the Scotland Act 1998 (Consequential Modifications) (No.1) Order 1999 (S.I. 1999 No. 1042) and the Scotland Act 1998 (Consequential Modifications) (No.2) Order 1999 (S.I. 1999 No. 1820) make specific provision to similar effect.

Subordinate instruments

118.—(1) Subsection (2) applies in relation to the exercise by a member of the Scottish Executive within devolved competence of a function to make, confirm or approve subordinate legislation.

(2) If a pre-commencement enactment makes provision—

(a) for any instrument or the draft of any instrument made in the exercise of such a function to be laid before Parliament or either House of Parliament,

(b) for the annulment or approval of any such instrument or draft by or in pursuance of a resolution of either or both Houses of Parliament, or

(c) prohibiting the making of such an instrument without that approval,

the provision shall have effect, so far as it relates to the exercise of the function by a member of the Scottish Executive within devolved competence, as if any reference in it to Parliament or either House of Parliament were a reference to the Scottish Parliament.

(3) Where—

(a) a function of making, confirming or approving subordinate legislation conferred by a pre-commencement enactment is exercisable by a Scottish public authority with mixed functions or no reserved functions, and

(b) a pre-commencement enactment makes such provision in relation to the exercise of the function as is mentioned in subsection (2),

the provision shall have effect, so far as it relates to the exercise of the function by that authority, as if any reference in it to Parliament or either House of Parliament were a reference to the Scottish Parliament.

(4) Where—

(a) a function of making, confirming or approving subordinate legislation conferred by a pre-commencement enactment is exercisable within devolved competence by a person other than a Minister of the Crown, a member of the Scottish Executive or a Scottish public authority with mixed functions or no reserved functions, and

(b) a pre-commencement enactment makes such provision in relation to the exercise of the function as is mentioned in subsection (2),

the provision shall have effect, so far as it relates to the exercise of the function by that person within devolved competence, as if any reference in it to Parliament or either House of Parliament were a reference to the Scottish Parliament.

(5) If a pre-commencement enactment applies the Statutory Instruments Act 1946 as if a function of the kind mentioned in subsection (3) or (4) were exercisable by a Minister of the Crown, that Act shall apply, so far as the function is exercisable as mentioned in paragraph (a) of subsection (3) or (as the case may be) (4), as if the function were exercisable by the Scottish Ministers.

DEFINITIONS
"conferred": s.126(1).
"devolved competence": s.54.
"enactment": ss.113(6), 126(1).
"function": s.126(1).
"member of the Scottish Executive": s.44(1).
"Minister of the Crown": s.126(1).
"pre-commencement enactment": s.53(3).
"Scottish Ministers": s.44(2).
"Scottish public authority with mixed functions or no reserved functions": paras 1, 2 of Pt III of Sched. 5.
"subordinate legislation": s.126(1).

GENERAL NOTE
This section is one of a group of provisions making general modifications of existing legislation consequential upon the transfer of powers to the Scottish Parliament, the Scottish Executive and other bodies. In the case of this section, the purpose is to make an appropriate adaptation of provisions relating to the parliamentary procedures applicable to subordinate legislation. The section adapts existing provisions in "pre-commencement enactments" which require the Westminster procedure referred to in subs. (2) to require instead procedures in the Scottish Parliament. It is (along with ss.119–121) disapplied in relation to cross-border public authorities by s.88(1).
The section has itself been modified by subordinate legislation made under s.124 for application to functions allocated to the Scottish Ministers under s.63.
See also Sched. 4 para. 11.
The general provision made for the procedures to be used by the Scottish Ministers (and the Scottish Parliament) in the making of Scottish Statutory Instruments—established on a transitional basis by the Scotland Act 1998 (Transitory and Transitional Provisions) (Statutory Instruments) Order 1999 (S.I. 1999 No. 1096)—is discussed in the note on s.52.

Subss. (1), (2)
The principal case is that of the powers to make subordinate legislation which are transferred to members of the Scottish Executive by s.53 and defined as within "devolved competence" by s.54.
Subsection (2) requires that the Westminster references, *i.e.* to Parliament or to either House of Parliament stipulated for the scrutiny and control of subordinate legislation become equivalent references to the Scottish Parliament.

Subs. (3)
This does the same in respect of a "Scottish public authority with mixed functions or no reserved functions"—except that s.88(1) disapplies this section in relation to cross-border public authorities for which separate provision is made by ss.88, 89.

Subs. (4)
This extends the same modification to the powers, exercisable within devolved competence by some other "person". This could include the Registrar General for Births, Deaths and Marriages or Her Majesty in Council.

Subs. (5)
Some statutes apply the Statutory Instruments Act 1946 to situations in which subordinate legislation is made by persons other than Ministers. This subsection applies these statutory provisions, as so extended, to the Scottish Ministers.

Consolidated Fund etc

119.—(1) In this section "Scottish functions" means—
(a) functions of the Scottish Ministers, the First Minister or the Lord Advocate which are exercisable within devolved competence,
(b) functions of any Scottish public authority with mixed functions or no reserved functions.
(2) Subject to subsections (3) and (5), a provision of a pre-commencement enactment which—
(a) requires or authorises the payment of any sum out of the Consolidated Fund or money provided by Parliament, or
(b) requires or authorises the payment of any sum into the Consolidated Fund,
shall cease to have effect in relation to any Scottish functions.
(3) A provision of a pre-commencement enactment which—

(a) charges any sum on the Consolidated Fund,
(b) requires the payment of any sum out of the Consolidated Fund without further appropriation, or
(c) requires or authorises the payment of any sum into the Consolidated Fund by a person other than a Minister of the Crown,

shall have effect in relation to any Scottish functions as if it provided for the sum to be charged on the Scottish Consolidated Fund or required it to be paid out of that Fund without further approval or required or authorised it to be paid into that Fund (as the case may be).

(4) Subsections (2) and (3) do not apply to the words from the beginning of section 2(3) of the European Communities Act 1972 (general implementation of Treaties) to "such Community obligation".

(5) A provision of a pre-commencement enactment which authorises any sums to be applied as money provided by Parliament instead of being paid into the Consolidated Fund shall have effect in relation to any Scottish functions as if it authorised those sums to be applied as if they had been paid out of the Scottish Consolidated Fund in accordance with rules under section 65(1)(c) instead of being paid into that Fund.

(6) Where a power to lend money under a pre-commencement enactment is exercisable by the Scottish Ministers, subsection (7) applies to any sums which, for the purpose or as the result of the exercise of the power, would be required (apart from that subsection)—
(a) to be issued by the Treasury out of the National Loans Fund, or
(b) to be paid into that Fund.
(7) Those sums shall instead—
(a) be paid out of the Scottish Consolidated Fund without further approval, or
(b) be paid into that Fund,
(as the case may be).

DEFINITIONS
"devolved competence": s.54.
"enactment": ss.113(6), 126(1).
"functions": s.126(1).
"member of the Scottish Executive": s.44(1).
"Minister of the Crown": s.126(1).
"pre-commencement enactment": s.53(3).
"Scottish functions": subs. (1).
"Scottish Ministers": s.44(2).
"Scottish public authority with mixed functions or no reserved functions": paras 1, 2 of Pt III of Sched. 5.

GENERAL NOTE
This section is one of a group of provisions making general modifications of existing legislation consequential upon the transfer of powers to the Scottish Parliament and the Scottish Executive. Section 64 establishes the Scottish Consolidated Fund and s.65 provides for payments out of the fund. The purpose of this section is to translate, as necessary, the existing statutory references to the (U.K.) Consolidated Fund into references to the Scottish Consolidated Fund. In relation to the "Scottish functions" defined in subs. (1), references to the Scottish Consolidated Fund are to be substituted, subject to the special provision made under s.124 to modify the effect of this section for its extension to functions allocated to the Scottish Ministers under s.63.

Subs. (1)
The translation of terms made by the later subsections is done by reference to "Scottish functions", a term defined by this subsection. The same term is adopted into the provision made by ss. 120, 121.
"Scottish Functions" include functions both of members of the Scottish Executive and of a "Scottish public authority with mixed functions or no reserved functions".
In relation to the Ministers in para. (a), the definition of "Scottish functions" depends, in turn, upon the definition of "devolved competence" in s.54. That section defines the term primarily for the purposes of s.53 which provides for the general transfer of ministerial functions from Ministers of the Crown to the Scottish Ministers. Functions are transferred if they are exercisable within devolved competence. The terminology of "devolved competence" is also adopted into ss.117, 118.
The Scottish public authorities in para. (b), are those defined by paras 1, 2 of Pt III of Sched. 5 (see the notes on those paragraphs). By virtue of s.88(1), s.119 does not apply to cross-border public authorities, for which separate provision is made by ss.88, 89.

Subs. (2)

Subject to subs. (3), (5) (and see also subs. (4)), this subsection disapplies, in relation to Scottish functions, provisions requiring payment out of or into the Consolidated Fund.

Subs. (3)

This makes the necessary 'translations' in respect of charges, requirements of payment without appropriation and payments into the two funds. See Sched. 4, paras. 4(3), 5(a) which prevent modification by the Scottish Parliament of s.119 and "the effect of section 119(3) in relation to any provision of an Act of Parliament relating to judicial salaries" on which, see also Sched. 5, section L1 and Sched. 8, para. 9(b).

Subs. (4)

This subsection ensures that the changes introduced by subss. (2), (3) do not apply to the first part of s.2(3) of the European Communities Act 1972 which relates to charges required to meet payments to the European institutions and payments in respect of the European Investment Bank. Such charges and payments are not to be met from the Scottish Consolidated Fund.

Subs. (5)

Section 65(1) specifies the circumstances under which sums may be paid out of the Scottish Consolidated Fund. Paragraph (c) provides for such payments for certain purposes "in accordance with rules made by or under an Act of the Scottish Parliament". This subsection extends that authority to sums authorised by a pre-commencement enactment to be applied as money provided by Parliament, instead of their being paid into the Consolidated Fund.

Subss. (6), (7)

These subsections provide a modification in relation to payments in and out of the National Loans Fund similar to the modifications effected by subss. (2), (3).

See also para. 4(4) of Sched. 4 which enables the creation of a new loans fund.

Accounts and audit

120. A provision of a pre-commencement enactment which—

(a) requires any account to be examined, certified and reported on by, or to be open to the inspection of, the Comptroller and Auditor General, or

(b) requires him to have access to any other document for carrying out any such examination,

shall have effect in relation to any Scottish functions (within the meaning of section 119) as if the references to the Comptroller and Auditor General were to the Auditor General for Scotland.

DEFINITIONS

"Auditor General for Scotland": s.69.
"document": s.126(1).
"pre-commencement enactment": s.53(3).
"Scottish functions": s.119(1).

GENERAL NOTE

In earlier versions of the Bill, this section had been included within what is now s.119. At House of Lords Committee stage the original clause was divided into two parts (see *Hansard*, H.L. Vol. 593, col. 646).

The section joins the others in this group of provisions which modify enactments in ways consequential upon transfer of powers to the Scottish Parliament and the Scottish Executive. With the important exception of functions exercisable in relation to cross-border public authorities (for which separate provision is made by ss. 88, 89 and s. 70(6)), a requirement to have an account examined by the Comptroller and Auditor General (or for him to have access to documents) becomes, in relation to "Scottish functions" as defined in s.119(1), a requirement instead in relation to the Auditor General for Scotland appointed under s.69. See also s.70.

This is one of the group of sections which may be modified by s.124, *e.g.* for extension to functions conferred by s.63.

Requirements to lay reports etc. before Parliament

121.—(1) This section applies where—

(a) a pre-commencement enactment makes provision for any report to be laid before Parliament or either House of Parliament, and

(b) the report concerns Scottish functions.

(2) If the report only concerns Scottish functions, it shall be laid instead before the Scottish Parliament.

(3) In any other case, it shall be laid before the Scottish Parliament as well as before Parliament or (as the case may be) either House of Parliament.

(4) In this section—

"report" includes accounts and any statement,

"Scottish functions" has the same meaning as in section 119.

DEFINITIONS

"enactment": ss.113(6), 126(1).
"pre-commencement enactment": s.53(3).
"report": subs. (4).
"Scottish functions": subs. (4) and s.119(1).

GENERAL NOTE

This section is one of a group making provision for the modification of enactments consequential upon the transfer of power to the Scottish Parliament and the Scottish Executive. With the important exception of functions exercisable in relation to cross-border public authorities (for which separate provision is made by ss.88–89) an obligation to lay a report before Parliament (or either House of Parliament) becomes, in relation to "Scottish functions" defined in s.119(1), an obligation either to lay the report before the Scottish Parliament alone or, where the report extends beyond "Scottish functions", the Scottish Parliament as well as the Westminster Parliament.

See s.124, which may be used to modify the effect of this section, *e.g.* for its extension to apply to functions conferred on the Scottish Ministers by s.63. The Scotland Act 1998 (Transitory and Transitional Provisions) (Laying of Reports) Order 1999 (S.I. 1999 No. 1594) made supplementary provision—including provision for "pre-Scottish functions", as defined in the order. It revoked art.24 of the Scotland Act 1998 (Transitory and Transitional Provisions) (Finance) Order 1999 (S.I. 1999 No. 441.).

Crown land

122.—(1) In any provision about the application of any pre-commencement enactment to Crown land—

(a) references to a Minister of the Crown or government department shall be read as including the Scottish Ministers and the Lord Advocate, and

(b) references to a Minister of the Crown or government department having the management of the land shall be read as including any member of the Scottish Executive having the management of the land.

(2) In this section, "Crown land" has the meaning given by section 242 of the Town and Country Planning (Scotland) Act 1997.

DEFINITIONS

"Crown land": subs.(2).
"enactment": ss.113(6), 126(1).
"government department": s.126(1).
"member of the Scottish Executive": s.44(1).
"Minister of the Crown": s.126(1).
"pre-commencement enactment": s.53(3).
"Scottish Ministers": s.44(2).

GENERAL NOTE

Section 242 of the Town and Country Planning (Scotland) Act 1997 (c.8) defines "Crown Land" as "land in which there is Crown interest", *i.e.* "an interest belonging to Her Majesty in right of the Crown or belonging to a government department or held in trust for Her Majesty for the purposes of a government department".

This section extends the meaning of "Crown land" to include also land held or managed by the Scottish Ministers (or member of the Scottish Executive) and the Lord Advocate. For provisions dealing with the holding and transfer of property, see ss.59–62, 116. Although para. 1 of Pt. I of Sched. 5 provides that reserved matters include the Crown, para. 3(1) also provides that para. 1 "does not reserve property belonging to Her Majesty in right of the Crown or belonging to any person acting on behalf of the Crown or held in trust for Her Majesty for the purpose of any person acting on behalf of the Crown".

Section 124 may be used to modify the effect of this section.

Stamp duty

123. In section 55 of the Finance Act 1987 (Crown exemption from stamp duty) references to a Minister of the Crown shall be read as including the Scottish Ministers, the Lord Advocate and the Parliamentary corporation.

DEFINITIONS

"Minister of the Crown": s.126(1).

"the Parliamentary corporation": s.21(1).
"Scottish Ministers": s.44(2).

GENERAL NOTE

Section 55 of the Finance Act 1987 (c.16) provides for exemption from stamp duty (chargeable by virtue of Sched. 1 to the Stamp Act 1891 (c.39)) in respect of any "Conveyance or Transfer on Sale", "Conveyance or Transfer of any kind not herein before described", or "Lease or Tack" made or agreed to be made to a Minister of the Crown or the Treasury Solicitor. This section extends the exemption to the Scottish Ministers, the Lord Advocate and the Parliamentary corporation. Taxes are reserved matters under Sched. 5, although amendments to property law, which would, in principle, be within the competence of the Scottish Parliament, might affect the incidence of Stamp Duty.

Modification of sections 94 and 117 to 122

124.—(1) Subordinate legislation may provide for any provision of sections 94 and 117 to 122 not to apply, or to apply with modifications, in such cases as the person making the legislation considers appropriate.

(2) Subordinate legislation made by Her Majesty in Council or a Minister of the Crown under this Act may, in connection with any other provision made by the legislation, also provide for any provision of sections 94 and 117 to 122 not to apply, or to apply with modifications.

DEFINITIONS

"Minister of the Crown": s.126(1).
"modification": s.126(1).
"subordinate legislation": s.126(1).

GENERAL NOTE

This section was added as a new clause at House of Lords committee stage (*Hansard*, H.L. Vol. 593, col. 647). For a comment on amendments made to the Bill at this stage, in large measure to accommodate the concerns of the Delegated Powers and Deregulation Committee, see the General Notes to ss.112, 113, 114, 115.

This section can be used to adjust the application of ss.94, 117—122 and has been used, in particular, to extend some of those provisions, with appropriate modifications, to the "additional" powers conferred on the Scottish Ministers by s.63. The provisions need to apply beyond "devolved competence" and to statutes other than "pre-commencement enactments", as initially defined.

Amendments and repeals

Amendments and repeals

125.—(1) Schedule 8 (which makes modifications of enactments) shall have effect.

(2) The enactments mentioned in Schedule 9 are repealed to the extent specified in that Schedule.

GENERAL NOTE

See Scheds 8, 9.

Section 105 of the Act confers the power to make further consequential modifications. For the three orders so far made, see the General Note on that section.

Final provisions

Interpretation

126.—(1) In this Act—

"body" includes unincorporated association,

"constituencies" and "regions", in relation to the Parliament, mean the constituencies and regions provided for by Schedule 1,

"constituency member" means a member of the Parliament for a constituency,

"the Convention rights" has the same meaning as in the Human Rights Act 1998,

"document" means anything in which information is recorded in any form (and references to producing a document are to be read accordingly), "enactment" includes an Act of the Scottish Parliament, Northern Ireland legislation (within the meaning of the Northern Ireland Act 1998) and an enactment comprised in subordinate legislation, and includes an enactment comprised in, or in subordinate legislation under, an Act of Parliament, whenever passed or made,

"financial year" means a year ending with 31st March,

"functions" includes powers and duties, and "confer", in relation to functions, includes impose,

"government department" means any department of the Government of the United Kingdom,

"the Human Rights Convention" means—
    (a) the Convention for the Protection of Human Rights and Fundamental Freedoms, agreed by the Council of Europe at Rome on 4th November 1950, and
    (b) the Protocols to the Convention,
as they have effect for the time being in relation to the United Kingdom,

"Minister of the Crown" includes the Treasury,

"modify" includes amend or repeal,

"occupational pension scheme", "personal pension scheme" and "public service pension scheme" have the meanings given by section 1 of the Pension Schemes Act 1993, but as if the reference to employed earners in the definition of personal pension scheme were to any earners,

"the Parliament" means the Scottish Parliament,

"parliamentary", in relation to constituencies, elections and electors, is to be taken to refer to the Parliament of the United Kingdom,

"prerogative instrument" means an Order in Council, warrant, charter or other instrument made under the prerogative,

"the principal appointed day" means the day appointed by an order under section 130 which is designated by the order as the principal appointed day,

"proceedings", in relation to the Parliament, includes proceedings of any committee or sub-committee,

"property" includes rights and interests of any description,

"regional member" means a member of the Parliament for a region,

"Scotland" includes so much of the internal waters and territorial sea of the United Kingdom as are adjacent to Scotland,

"Scottish public authority" means any public body (except the Parliamentary corporation), public office or holder of such an office whose functions (in each case) are exercisable only in or as regards Scotland,

"the Scottish zone" means the sea within British fishery limits (that is, the limits set by or under section 1 of the Fishery Limits Act 1976) which is adjacent to Scotland,

"standing orders" means standing orders of the Parliament,

"subordinate legislation" has the same meaning as in the Interpretation Act 1978 and also includes an instrument made under an Act of the Scottish Parliament,

"tribunal" means any tribunal in which legal proceedings may be brought.

(2) Her Majesty may by Order in Council determine, or make provision for determining, for the purposes of this Act any boundary between waters which are to be treated as internal waters or territorial sea of the United Kingdom, or sea within British fishery limits, adjacent to Scotland and those which are not.

(3) For the purposes of this Act—

(a) the question whether any function of a body, government department, office or office-holder relates to reserved matters is to be determined by reference to the purpose for which the function is exercisable, having regard (among other things) to the likely effects in all the circumstances of any exercise of the function, but

(b) bodies to which paragraph 3 of Part III of Schedule 5 applies are to be treated as if all their functions were functions which relate to reserved matters.

(4) References in this Act to Scots private law are to the following areas of the civil law of Scotland—

(a) the general principles of private law (including private international law),

(b) the law of persons (including natural persons, legal persons and unincorporated bodies),

(c) the law of obligations (including obligations arising from contract, unilateral promise, delict, unjustified enrichment and *negotiorum gestio*),

(d) the law of property (including heritable and moveable property, trusts and succession), and

(e) the law of actions (including jurisdiction, remedies, evidence, procedure, diligence, recognition and enforcement of court orders, limitation of actions and arbitration),

and include references to judicial review of administrative action.

(5) References in this Act to Scots criminal law include criminal offences, jurisdiction, evidence, procedure and penalties and the treatment of offenders.

(6) References in this Act and in any other enactment to the Scottish Administration are to the office-holders in the Scottish Administration and the members of the staff of the Scottish Administration.

(7) For the purposes of this Act—

(a) references to office-holders in the Scottish Administration are to—

(i) members of the Scottish Executive and junior Scottish Ministers, and

(ii) the holders of offices in the Scottish Administration which are not ministerial offices, and

(b) references to members of the staff of the Scottish Administration are to the staff of the persons referred to in paragraph (a).

(8) For the purposes of this Act, the offices in the Scottish Administration which are not ministerial offices are—

(a) the Registrar General of Births, Deaths and Marriages for Scotland, the Keeper of the Registers of Scotland and the Keeper of the Records of Scotland, and

(b) any other office of a description specified in an Order in Council made by Her Majesty under this subsection.

(9) In this Act—

(a) all those rights, powers, liabilities, obligations and restrictions from time to time created or arising by or under the Community Treaties, and

(b) all those remedies and procedures from time to time provided for by or under the Community Treaties,

are referred to as "Community law".

(10) In this Act, "international obligations" means any international obligations of the United Kingdom other than obligations to observe and implement Community law or the Convention rights.

(11) In this Act, "by virtue of" includes "by" and "under".

GENERAL NOTE

For the most part, this interpretation section does not require additional comment. Notes are, however, added selectively. For an index of defined expressions, see s.127.

Subs. (1)

"*the Convention rights*". Section 1(1) of the Human Rights Act 1998 (c.42) defines "the Convention rights" as "the rights and fundamental freedoms" set out in:

1. Arts. 2–12 and 14 of the Convention—*i.e.* the "Convention for the Protection of Human Rights and Fundamental Freedoms, agreed by the Council of Europe at Rome on November 4, 1950 as it has effect for the time being in relation to the United Kingdom" (Human Rights Act 1998, s.21(1));

2. Arts. 1–3 of the First Protocol—*i.e.* the protocol agreed at Paris on March 20, 1952 (which deals with the protection of property, the right to education and the right to free elections); and

3. Arts. 1, 2 of the Sixth Protocol—*i.e.* the protocol agreed at Strasbourg on April 28, 1983 (which deals with the death penalty). All those provisions are required to be read to be with Arts. 16–18 of the Convention.

It should be noted that the Convention rights are derived from the Convention *"as it has effect for the time being in relation to the United Kingdom"* (Human Rights Act 1998, s.21(1). See also "the Human Rights Convention" as also separately defined in this subsection.) For the purposes of the Human Rights Act 1998, the Articles of the Convention have effect "subject to any designated derogation or reservation" (Human Rights Act 1998, s.1(2))-defined to include the 1988/9 derogation from Art. 5(3) of the Convention (detention in relation to terrorism) (s.14 and Sched. 3); and the 1952 reservation in relation to Art. 2 of the First Protocol (application of education rights to be "only so far as is compatible with the provision of efficient instruction and training and the avoidance of unreasonable public expenditure".) (s.15 and Sched. 3.)

The relevant Articles (and Protocols) of the ECHR are set out in Sched. 1 to the Human Rights Act 1998 and are: Art. 2 (Right to life), Art. 3 (Prohibition of torture), Art. 4 (Prohibition of slavery and forced labour), Art. 5 (Right to liberty and security), Art. 6 (Right to a fair trial), Art. 7 (No punishment without law), Art. 8 (Right to respect for private and family life), Art. 9 (Freedom of thought, conscience and religion), Art. 10 (Freedom of expression), Art. 11 (Freedom of assembly and association), Art. 12 (Right to marry), Art 14 (Prohibition of discrimination), Art. 16 (Restriction on political activity of aliens), Art. 17 (Prohibition of abuse of rights), Art. 18 (limitation on use of restrictions on rights), First Protocol (Prohibition of property, Right, to education and Right to free elections) and Sixth Protocol (Abolition of the death penalty).

For provisions of the Scotland Act where "the Convention rights" and/or the Human Rights Act 1998 are referred to see s.29; s.57; s.100; s.129; Sched.4 paras. 1(2)(f), 13(1)(b), Sched.5, Pt I, para. 7(2); and Sched. 6 para. 1(d), (e).

"enactment". See "subordinate legislation" below. See also the amendment made to the Interpretation Act 1978 (c.30) by Sched. 8, para. 16.

"the Human Rights Convention". See "the Convention rights".

"occupational pension scheme", etc.. The three types of pension scheme are defined by s.1 of the Pension Schemes Act 1993 (c. 48) as follows:

1. *"occupational pension scheme"* means any scheme or arrangement which is comprised in one or more instruments or agreements and which has, or is capable of having, effect in relation to one or more descriptions or categories of employments so as to provide benefits, in the form of pensions or otherwise, payable on termination of service, or on death or retirement, to or in respect of earners with qualifying service in an employment of any such description or category;

2. *"personal pension scheme"* means any scheme or arrangement which is comprised in one or more instruments or agreements and which has, or is capable of having, effect so as to provide benefits, in the form of pensions or otherwise, payable on death or retirement to or in respect of employed earners who have made arrangements with the trustees or managers of the scheme for them to become members of it;

3. *"public service pension scheme"* means an occupational pension scheme established by or under an enactment or the Royal prerogative or a Royal charter, being a scheme:

   (a) all the particulars of which are set out in, or in a legislative instrument made under, an enactment, Royal warrant or charter, or

   (b) which cannot come into force, or be amended, without the scheme or amendment being approved by a Minister of the Crown or government department,

   and includes any occupational pension scheme established, with the concurrence of the Treasury, by or with the approval of any Minister of the Crown and any occupational pension scheme prescribed by regulations made by the Secretary of State and the Treasury jointly as being a scheme which ought in their opinion to be treated as a public service pension scheme for the purposes of this Act.

The terms occur in Sched. 4 para. 2(3)(b) and Sched. 5, Section F3.

"Internal waters" are those on the landward side of the territorial sea baselines. Territorial seas extend from these baselines to a distance of 12 miles (Territorial Seas Act 1987). On being "adjacent" to Scotland, see s.126(2). Scotland includes Rockall (Island of Rockall Act 1972 (c.2)).

"Scottish public authority" is the terminology used in ss.118, 119; (and, by way of "Scottish functions", in ss.120 and 121) and Sched. 5, Pt III. For a general commentary on "public authorities", see the General Note to s.88.

"the Scottish Zone". Subject to its adjustment by Order in Council, s.1 of the Fishery Limits Act 1976 (c.86) provides that "British fishery limits extend to 200 miles from the baselines from which the breadth of the territorial sea adjacent to the United Kingdom, the Channel Islands and the Isle of Man is measured". But see also s.126(2). This is terminology used in Sched. 5, Section C6. See also subs. (2) and the General Note to s.30(3).

"subordinate legislation". Section 21 of the Interpretation Act 1978 (c.30) defines "subordinate legislation" as "Orders in Council, orders, rules, regulations, schemes, warrants, byelaws and other instruments made or to be made under any Act". Here, that definition is extended to include "an instrument made under an Act of the Scottish Parliament".

Subs.(2)
Orders in Council under this subsection are to be made as a Type B instrument under Sched. 7, *i.e.* only after a draft of the instrument has been approved by resolution in both Houses of Parliament. See the General Note to s.30(3).

The Scottish Adjacent Waters Boundaries Order 1999 (S.I. 1999 No. 1126) was made, with effect from July 1, 1999. Article 3 of the Order defines the boundaries between waters which are to be treated as internal waters or territorial sea adjacent to Scotland and those which are not. Article 4 defines the boundaries of sea within British fishing limits adjacent to Scotland. For the (sometimes acrimonious) debate on the content of the Order in the Scottish Parliament, see SPOR 3 June 1999.

Subs. (3)
For a general commentary on "public authorities" see the General Note to s.88. For bodies whose functions do or do not "relate to reserved matters", see Sched. 5, Pt III where, in relation to "Scottish public authorities" (which are not also "cross-border public authorities"), special rules are applies to such authorities with mixed functions (paras. 1,2); and, in relation to certain "reserved bodies", other rules are applied (para. 3). See the General Note on that Part.

This subsection is an aid to the interpretation of those provisions. In relation to the identification of public authorities with mixed functions, para. (a) provides, in a manner very similar to that adopted in s.29(3), a test for whether a function "relates to reserved matters" expressed in terms of the purpose for which the function is exercisable, having regard (among other things) to the likely effects in all the circumstances of any exercise of the function. It is of interest to note the inclusion in this formula of the word "likely", which does not appear in the version used in s.29(3).

Paragraph (b) is presumably intended to reinforce the reserved character of the bodies identified and regulated by para. 3 of Sched. 5, Pt III. Even functions which, if the test in para. (a) were applied, might be construed as not relating to reserved matters will be treated as doing so. They could never, therefore, be treated as, *e.g.* "Scottish public authorities with mixed functions".

Subss. (4), (5)
This Act makes reference to "Scots private law" and "Scots criminal law" in s.29(4) and para. 2(3) of Sched. 4. At both points, the references relate to the definition of the legislative competence of the Scottish Parliament and the use of the terms is explained in the General Note to s.29. The point is to confer a competence on the Parliament enabling it to legislate in areas of "Scots private law" and "Scots criminal law", even though that might take the Parliament into what are prima facie "reserved matters". This extension of competence is not unproblematic, as explained in the note referred to, but essential to its operation at all are Definitions of the two fields of Scots law. These are provided in these subsections which, however, are themselves not without difficulty.

"Scots private law" and "Scots criminal law" are not the subject of statutory definition, although an earlier attempt was made in the Scotland Act 1978—the famous "Table of Contents of Professor D.M. Walker's *Principles of Scottish Private Law*" (W.A. Wilson 1988 JR 207 at 232).

One specific point of interest is the inclusion within the definition of "Scots private law" of "judicial review of administrative action". It may seem a curiosity that an area of law which most commentators, if forced to draw a line between "public" and "private" law, would place on the "public" side of the line, is categorised here as an aspect of "Scots private law". Appearing first (as an early amendment to the Bill) as "administrative law", "judicial review of administrative action" (presumably the only appearance of the phrase in the statute book) was adopted at third reading in the House of Lords (*Hansard*, H.L. Vol. 594, col. 602). The explanation for including it must be the wish to include all aspects of the "law of actions" (para. (e)) and, therefore, all aspects of procedural law. These areas of the law do not recognise easy boundaries between private and public but there might well have been doubt about whether, without express reference, judicial review would have been included. Its inclusion may not, however, be the end of difficulties. "Judicial review of administrative action" is not an expression formally defined else-where despite its appearance in the title of a distinguished text book (see de Smith, Jowell, Woolf (eds.) *Judicial Review of Administrative Action* (5th ed., 1995))—and may turn out to be ambiguous in its interpretation. Does it, for instance, include both "common law" and statutory review?

Furthermore, its inclusion points to the possibility of other difficulties at the margins of "public" and "private" law in relation to procedure and evidence. Is, for instance, the law of "Crown privilege" or "public interest immunity" to be treated as part of "Scots private law"?

Subs. (6)

In this Act and in other Acts amended by this Act, the expression "the Scottish Administration" is to be found in ss.51, 65, 70, 91, 99 of this Act and, by virtue of their amendment by Sched. 8, the Crown Suits (Scotland) Act 1857, the Crown Proceedings Act 1947, the European Communities Act 1972, the Civil Jurisdiction and Judgements Act 1982, the National Audit Act 1983, the Copyright, Designs and Patents Act 1988, the Official Secrets Act 1989, the Value Added Tax Act 1994.

The term also appears as the heading to Pt. II of the Act. Until this definition was added, it was unclear what exactly "the Scottish Administration" referred to, but the term is now to be understood as a reference to its office-holders and staff. See also the General Note to subss. (7), (8).

Subss. (7),(8)

These serve, first, to define the two types of "office-holder in the Scottish Administration" a term used in ss.51, 91, 99 and the Official Secrets Act 1989 as well as in subs. (6)—to distinguish between the ministerial (political) office-holders and the holders of the non-ministerial offices listed in subs. (8), *i.e.* the Registrar General of Births, Deaths and Marriages and the Keepers of the Registers and the Records, together with any others specified by Order in Council (under Sched. 7, and instrument subject to Type H procedure; *i.e.* subject to annulment by resolution of either House of Parliament or by the Scottish Parliament). The Scottish Administration (Offices) Order 1999 (S.I. 1999 No. 1127) has specified certain non-ministerial offices. These include the offices of procurator fiscal (and deputes), Her Majesty's Chief Inspector (and Inspectors) of Constabulary, Prisons, Fire Services and Schools.

On a transitional basis only (*i.e.* until the principal appointment day), the Scotland Act 1998 (General Transitory, Transitional and Savings Provisions) Order 1999 (S.I. 1999 No. 901) modified references to the Scottish Administration in the Crown Suits (Scotland) Act 1857 (c.44) and the Crown Proceedings Act 1947 (c.44) (as amended in both cases by Sched. 8 to this Act).

"Members of the staff of the Scottish Administration" are then defined as the staff of both categories of officer-holder. Those staff, together with the non-ministerial office-holders, are all civil servants. See s.51(2).

Subs. (9)

The term "Community Law" is used in the following sections/Schedules: s.29, s.57, s.106, Sched. 5 para. 7, Sched. 6 para. 1. See also s.34, Sched. 4 paras. 1, 13, Sched. 8 para. 15.

For a General Note on "Community law" and its significance in the Act, see s.57.

Subs. (10)

The term "international obligations" is used in the following sections/Schedules: s.35, s.58, s.106, Sched.5, para. 7.

Index of defined expressions

127. In this Act, the expressions listed in the left-hand column have the meaning given by, or are to be interpreted in accordance with, the provisions listed in the right-hand column.

Expression	*Provision of this Act*
Act of the Scottish Parliament	Section 28(1)
Advocate General	Section 32(4)
Auditor General for Scotland	Section 69
Body Section	126(1)
By virtue of	Section 126(11)
Clerk, and Assistant Clerk	Section 20 and paragraph 3 of Schedule 2
Community law	Section 126(9)

Expression	Provision of this Act
Constituencies and constituency member	Section 126(1)
The Convention rights	Section 126(1)
Cross-border public authority	Section 88(5)
Devolved competence (in relation to the exercise of functions)	Section 54
Document	Section 126(1)
Enactment	Sections 113(6) and 126(1)
Financial year	Section 126(1)
Functions	Section 126(1)
Government department	Section 126(1)
The Human Rights Convention	Section 126(1)
International obligations	Section 126(10)
Judicial Committee	Section 32(4)
Legislative competence	Section 29
Member of the Scottish Executive	Section 44(1)
Members of the staff of the Scottish Administration	Section 126(7)
Minister of the Crown	Section 126(1)
Modify	Section 126(1)
Occupational pension scheme, personal pension scheme and public service pension scheme	Section 126(1)
Office-holders in the Scottish Administration	Section 126(7)
Offices in the Scottish Administration which are not ministerial offices	Section 126(8)
Open power	Section 112(3)
The Parliament	Section 126(1)
"parliamentary" (in relation to constituencies, elections and electors)	Section 126(1)
The Parliamentary corporation	Section 21(1)
Pre-commencement enactment	Section 53(3)
Prerogative instrument	Section 126(1)
Presiding Officer	Section 19
Principal appointed day	Section 126(1)
Proceedings	Section 126(1)
Property	Section 126(1)
Regional list (in relation to a party)	Section 5(4)
Regional returning officer	Section 12(6)
Regional vote	Section 6(2)
Regions and regional member	Section 126(1)
Registered political party	Section 5(9)
Reserved matters	Schedule 5
Retained functions (in relation to the Lord Advocate)	Section 52(6)
Scotland	Section 126(1) and (2)
Scots criminal law	Section 126(5)
Scots private law	Section 126(4)
Scottish Administration	Section 126(6)
Scottish Ministers	Section 44(2)
Scottish public authority	Section 126(1)
Scottish public authority with mixed functions or no reserved functions	Paragraphs 1 and 2 of Part III of Schedule 5

Expression	Provision of this Act
Scottish Seal	Section 2(6)
The Scottish zone	Section 126(1)
Staff of the Parliament	Paragraph 3 of Schedule 2
Standing orders	Section 126(1)
Subordinate legislation	Section 126(1)
Tribunal	Section 126(1)

Expenses

128.—(1) There shall be paid out of money provided by Parliament—

(a) any expenditure incurred by a Minister of the Crown by virtue of this Act, and

(b) any increase attributable to this Act in the sums payable out of money so provided under any other enactment.

(2) There shall be paid into the Consolidated Fund any sums received by a Minister of the Crown by virtue of this Act which are not payable into the National Loans Fund.

DEFINITIONS
"by virtue of": s.126(11).
"enactment": s.126(1).
"Minister of the Crown": s.126(1).

GENERAL NOTE

Subs.(1)
As a standard "expenses" provision, this section authorises the payment of expenditure under the Act. In the financial memorandum on the Scotland Bill as originally published, it was stated that it would "not lead to any increase in overall public expenditure funded by U.K. tax-payers as a whole". Estimated annual running costs for the Scottish Parliament were between £20m and £30m; for the administration of the tax-varying power about £9m (plus start-up costs) (see s.80); and for each general election about £6m.

Transitional provisions etc

129.—(1) Subordinate legislation may make such provision as the person making the legislation considers necessary or expedient for transitory or transitional purposes in connection with the coming into force of any provision of this Act.

(2) If any of the following provisions come into force before the Human Rights Act 1998 has come into force (or come fully into force), the provision shall have effect until the time when that Act is fully in force as it will have effect after that time: sections 29(2)(d), 57(2) and (3), 100 and 126(1) and Schedule 6.

GENERAL NOTE
This section was created in this form at House of Lords committee stage (*Hansard*, H.L. Vol. 593, cols. 658–659).

Subs. (1).
This subsection recognises the need for provision to be made by subordinate legislation for "transitory or transitional" purposes.
The following orders have been made:
- The Scotland Act 1998 (Transitional and Transitory Provisions) (Subordinate Legislation under the Act) Order 1998 (S.I. 1998 No. 3216)
- The Scotland Act 1998 (Transitory and Transitional Provisions) (Finance) Order 1999 (S.I. 1999 No. 441)
- The Scotland Act 1998 (Transitory and Transitional Provisions) (Appropriations) Order 1999 (S.I. 1999 No. 674)

- The Scotland Act 1998 (General Transitory, Transitional and Savings Provisions) Order 1999 (S.I. 1999 No. 901)
- The Scotland Act 1998 (Transitory and Transitional Provisions) (Removal of Judges) Order 1999 (S.I. 1999 No.1017)
- The Scotland Act 1998 (Transitory and Transitional Provisions) (Grants to Members and Officeholders) Order 1999 (S.I. 1999 No.1081)
- The Scotland Act 1998 (Transitory and Transitional Provisions) (Scottish Parliamentary Pension Scheme) Order 1999 (S.I. 1999 No. 1082)
- The Scotland Act 1998 (Transitory and Transitional Provisions) (Standing Orders and Parliamentary Publications) Order 1999 (S.I. 1999 No. 1095)
- The Scotland Act 1998 (Transitory and Transitional Provisions) (Statutory Instruments) Order 1999 (S.I. 1999 No. 1096)
- The Scotland Act 1998 (Transitory and Transitional Provisions) (Salaries and Allowances) Order 1999 (S.I. 1999 No. 1097)
- The Scotland Act 1998 (Transitory and Transitional Provisions) (Administration of the Parliament) Order 1999 (S.I. 1999 No. 1098)
- The Scotland Act 1998 (General Transitory, Transitional and Savings Provisions) (Amendment) Order 1999 (S.I. 1999 No. 1334)
- The Scotland Act 1998 (Transitory and Transitional Provisions) (Members' Interests) Order 1999 (S.I. 1999 No. 1350)
- The Scotland Act 1998 (Transitory and Transitional Provisions) (Complaints of Maladministration) Order 1999 (S.I. 1999 No. 1351)
- The Scotland Act 1998 (Transitory and Transitional Provisions) (Publication and Interpretation etc. of Acts of the Scottish Parliament) Order 1999 (S.I. 1999 No. 1379)
- The Scotland Act 1998 (Transitory and Transitional Provisions) (Orders subject to Special Parliamentary Procedure) Order 1999 (S.I. 1999 No. 1593)
- The Scotland Act 1998 (Transitory and Transitional Provisions) (Laying of Reports) Order 1999 (S.I. 1999 No. 1594)
- The Scotland Act 1998 (Transitory and Transitional Provisions) (Complaints of Maladministration) (Amendment) Order 1999 (S.I. 1999 No. 1595)
- The Scotland Act 1998 (Transitory and Transitional Provisions) (Grants to Members and Officeholders and Scottish Parliamentary Pension Scheme) (Amendment) Order 1999 (S.I. 1999 No.1891)
- The Scotland Act 1998 (Transitory and Transitional Provisions) (Finance) (Amendment) Order 1999 (S.I. 1999 No. 3273)

Subs. (2)

This subsection makes important provision to take account of the fact that, although this Act and the Human Rights Act 1998 (c.42) reached the statute book at just about the same time, (most provisions of) the Human Rights Act would not be brought into force until some date in 2000, subsequently confirmed as 2 October. Since this Act (and in particular the provisions designed to protect Convention rights specified in the subsection) were to be brought into force before that time, it was considered necessary to make this special transitional provision.

The transitional impact of the imposition of obligations under the ECHR upon the Scottish Parliament (with effect from July 1, 1999) and the Scottish Executive (Law Officers from May 20 1999, Scottish Ministers in general from July 1, 1999) has been significant. See the note on s.57.

The interpretation to be given to "shall have effect until the time when that Act is fully in force as it will have effect after that time" was considered in *Clancy v. Caird* 2000 S.L.T. 546 (Lord Penrose at para.9).

Commencement

130.—(1) Sections 19 to 43, Parts II to V, sections 117 to 124 and section 125 (except so far as relating to paragraphs 10, 11, 19 and 23(1) and (6) of Schedule 8) shall come into force on such day as the Secretary of State may by order appoint.

(2) Different days may be appointed under this section for different purposes.

GENERAL NOTE

Only a limited number of provisions in the Act came into force on November 19, 1998, the date of Royal Assent. These are ss. 1–18 and Sched. 1 (establishing and defining the membership of the Scottish Parliament); ss. 112–116 and Sched. 7 (subordinate legislation); paras 10, 11, 19 and 23(1) and (6) of Sched. 8, making amendments to the Defamation Act 1952, the Defamation (Northern Ireland) Act 1955, The Mental Health Act 1983 and certain of the amendments to the Insolvency Act 1986 respectively: ss. 126–132.

All other provisions were brought into force on days appointed by order by the Secretary of State. The "principal appointed day" (s.126(1)) was July 1, 1999.

SEE COMMENCEMENT.

Extent

131. Section 25 extends only to Scotland.

DEFINITIONS
"Scotland": s.126(1), (2).

GENERAL NOTE

The extent clause may at first sight seem slightly paradoxical, since many of the provisions in this Act only take effect within Scotland in any substantial way. However, since there are provisions affecting the U.K. Parliament and Government, provisions dealing with the interface between legal systems and provisions concerning the resolution of "devolution issues", perhaps arising in England, Wales or Northern Ireland, it is necessary for the Act generally to extend to the other jurisdictions as well. In fact, the Scotland Act 1978 (c.51) did not have an extent clause and neither does the Government of Wales Act 1998 (c.38) or the Northern Ireland Act 1998 (c.47) so in those instances the presumption of application throughout the U.K. was left silent and untouched, whereas here it emerges by implication, subject to the single exception.

Section 25 is the only provision in this Act which creates a new criminal offence of general application. The Scottish Parliament's powers of compulsion over witnesses are designedly limited (see the annotations to ss.23–26 above) and the circumscription of jurisdiction here is perhaps symbolic.

Short title

132. This Act may be cited as the Scotland Act 1998.

SCHEDULES

Section 1   SCHEDULE 1

CONSTITUENCIES, REGIONS AND REGIONAL MEMBERS

General

1. The constituencies for the purposes of this Act are—
   (a) the Orkney Islands,
   (b) the Shetland Islands, and
   (c) the parliamentary constituencies in Scotland, except a parliamentary constituency including either of those islands.

2.—(1) There shall be eight regions for the purposes of this Act.

(2) Those regions shall be the eight European Parliamentary constituencies which were provided for by the European Parliamentary Constituencies (Scotland) Order 1996.

(3) Seven regional members shall be returned for each region.

(4) Sub-paragraphs (2) and (3) are subject to any Order in Council under the Parliamentary Constituencies Act 1986 (referred to in this Schedule as the 1986 Act), as that Act is extended by this Schedule.

Reports of Boundary Commission

3.—(1) This paragraph applies where the Boundary Commission for Scotland (referred to in this Schedule as the Commission) submit a report to the Secretary of State under section 3(1) or (3) of the 1986 Act recommending any alteration in any parliamentary constituencies.

(2) In the report the Commission shall recommend any alteration—
   (a) in any of the regions, or
   (b) in the number of regional members to be returned for any of the regions,
which, in their opinion, is required to be made in order to give effect to the rules in paragraph 7.

(3) If in the case of a report under section 3(1) or (3) of that Act the Commission do not make any recommendation within sub-paragraph (2), they shall in the report state that, in their opinion, no such alteration is required.

(4) A report making a recommendation for an alteration in any region shall state—
(a) the name by which the Commission recommend that the region should be known, and
(b) the number of regional members to be returned for the region.

(5) The Commission shall lay any report recommending any alteration in parliamentary constituencies before the Parliament.

4.—(1) An Order in Council under section 4 of the 1986 Act which has the effect of making any alteration in any constituency of the Parliament, or makes any alteration within paragraph 3(2), may come into force for the purposes of any election for membership of the Parliament on a different day from the day on which it comes into force for the purposes of any parliamentary election; and paragraph 1(c) shall be read accordingly.

(2) The coming into force of such an Order, so far as it has the effect of making any alteration in any constituency of the Parliament or makes any alteration within paragraph 3(2), shall not affect the return of any member of the Parliament, or its constitution, until the Parliament is dissolved.

Notices

5.—(1) Where the Commission have provisionally determined to make recommendations affecting any region, they shall publish in at least one newspaper circulating in the region a notice stating—
(a) the effect of the proposed recommendations and (except in a case where they propose to recommend that no alteration within paragraph 3(2) be made) that a copy of the recommendations is open to inspection at a specified place or places within the region, and
(b) that representations with respect to the proposed recommendations may be made to the Commission within one month after the publication of the notice;
and the Commission shall take into consideration any representations duly made in accordance with any such notice.

(2) Where the Commission revise any proposed recommendations after publishing notice of them under sub-paragraph (1), the Commission shall comply again with that sub-paragraph in relation to the revised recommendations, as if no earlier notice had been published.

Local inquiries

6.—(1) The Commission may, if they think fit, cause a local inquiry to be held in respect of any region.

(2) If, on the publication of a notice under paragraph 5(1) of a recommendation for any alteration within paragraph 3(2), the Commission receive any representation objecting to the proposed recommendation—
(a) from an interested authority, or
(b) from a body of electors numbering 500 or more,
the Commission shall not make the recommendation unless a local inquiry has been held in respect of the region since the publication of the notice.

(3) If a local inquiry was held in respect of the region before the publication of the notice under paragraph 5(1), sub-paragraph (2) shall not apply if the Commission, after considering the matters discussed at the local inquiry, the nature of the representations received on the publication of the notice and any other relevant circumstances, are of the opinion that a further local inquiry would not be justified.

(4) In this paragraph, in relation to any recommendation—
"interested authority" means the council for an area which is wholly or partly included in the region affected by the recommendation, and
"elector" means an elector for the purposes of an election for membership of the Parliament in any constituency included in the region.

(5) Sections 210(4) and (5) of the Local Government (Scotland) Act 1973 (attendance of witnesses at inquiries) shall apply in relation to any local inquiry held under this paragraph.

The rules

7.—(1) The rules referred to in paragraph 3 are:
1. A constituency shall fall wholly within a region.
2. The regional electorate of any region shall be as near the regional electorate of each of the other regions as is reasonably practicable having regard, where appropriate, to special geographical considerations.

3. So far as reasonably practicable, the ratio which the number of regional member seats bears to the number of constituency member seats shall be 56 to 73.

4. The number of regional member seats for a region shall be—

(a) one eighth of the total number of regional member seats, or

(b) (if that total number is not exactly divisible by eight) either one eighth of the highest number which is less than that total number and exactly divisible by eight or the number produced by adding one to one eighth of that highest number (as provided by sub-paragraphs (2) to (4)).

(2) If the total number of regional member seats is not exactly divisible by eight, the Commission shall calculate the difference between—

(a) the total number of regional member seats, and

(b) the highest number which is less than that total number and exactly divisible by eight, and that is the number of residual seats to be allocated by the Commission.

(3) The Commission shall not allocate more than one residual seat for a region.

(4) The Commission shall divide the regional electorate for each region by the aggregate of—

(a) the number of constituencies in the region, and

(b) one eighth of the highest number which is less than the total number of regional member seats and exactly divisible by eight,

and, in allocating the residual seat or seats for a region or regions, shall have regard to the desirability of allocating the residual seat or seats to the region or regions for which that calculation produces the highest number or numbers.

8.—(1) For the purposes of any report of the Commission in relation to a region, the regional electorate is the number of persons—

(a) whose names appear on the enumeration date on the registers of local government electors, and

(b) who are registered at addresses within a constituency included in the region.

(2) In sub-paragraph (1), "the enumeration date" means the date on which the notice about the report is published in accordance with section 5(1) of the 1986 Act.

DEFINITIONS
"constituencies": s.126(1).
"elector": para. 6(4).
"enumeration date": para. 8(2).
"interested authority": para. 6(4).
"the Parliament": s.126(1).
"parliamentary": s.126(1).
"regional electorate": para. 8(1).
"regional member": s.126(1).
"regions": s.126(1).

GENERAL NOTE
This Schedule is linked to the set of sections on elections (ss.1–12) and to the section concerning Scottish representation in the House of Commons (s.86). It makes provision for the electoral areas for the purpose of elections to the Scottish Parliament, and for review of the numbers and distribution of such areas with a view to possible redistributions in future.

Para. 1
The term "constituency" is employed for the areas which return a single member each to the Parliament, under the simple majority system, as provided by s.1(2). The Orkney Islands and the Shetland Islands each form a constituency for Scottish Parliament purposes. Otherwise, the Scottish Parliament constituencies correspond to the Scottish constituencies as they are defined for House of Commons purposes for the time being. Currently there are 72 Commons seats in Scotland, but the alteration of the rules for the next periodic review which is made by s.86 should result in a reduction of that number. Alterations of that number will automatically involve corresponding alterations to the constituency element of the Scottish Parliament, and an alteration in the number of the constituency element will in turn affect the number of regional member seats by the operation of para. 7 below.

The reduction in the number of seats in the Parliament, which may be foreseen under this and associated provisions, proved to be one of the most controversial issues during the passage of the Bill. The Liberal Democrats were opposed to the reduction. Lord Steel of Aikwood suggested that it involved "a major breach of the agreement reached in the Constitutional Convention" and besides was "simply not sensible", since the membership figure of 129 had been conceived "as the right number of members . . . to carry out the functions bestowed on them." (*Hansard*, H.L. Vol.591, cols. 1332–1334.) However, the Government took its stand on the White Paper, which had contained the proposition that "the integrity of the U.K. will be strengthened by common U.K. and Scottish Parliament boundaries" and had acknowledged that there might accordingly be "consequential adjustments to the size of the Scottish Parliament so as to maintain the present balance between constituency and additional member seats" (para. 8.7.) An amendment in the Lords on the matter was therefore reversed in the Commons (*Hansard*, H.C. Vol. 319, cols. 377–405).

Para. 2

In conjunction with s.1(3) and (5), this provides for the return of members for regional seats under the electoral system set out in ss.5–7. There are seven regional members for each of eight regions, which are defined as the regions which were to be used as electoral areas in Scotland for the return of representatives to the European Parliament under the European Parliamentary Constituencies (Scotland) Order 1996 (S.I. 1996 No. 1926), although they were not in fact used for the original purpose since the law was altered by the European Parliamentary Elections Act 1999 (c.1). The regions as there defined (each of which comprises not fewer than seven nor greater than ten parliamentary constituencies) and the numbers of members for each are alterable for Scottish Parliament purposes by Order in Council under the Parliamentary Constituencies Act 1986 (c.56).

Para. 3

This effectively provides that when the Boundary Commission for Scotland makes recommendations for the alteration of the U.K. parliamentary constituencies, it must also give consideration to whether or not changes are also needed to the boundaries of regions and the numbers of seats for each, under the rules set out in para. 7 below. Under the Parliamentary Constituencies Act 1986, reports must be laid before the Houses of Parliament and here it is provided that they must be laid before the Scottish Parliament.

Para. 7

This provides rules for the Boundary Commission for Scotland to follow, when it is considering regional representation, as required under para. 3, along with its consideration of the constituencies. Rules and guidelines for consideration of the constituencies are found in the Parliamentary Constituencies Act 1986, as modified by s.86. The rules here for review of regional representation are designed to ensure: (i) that no constituency falls within more than one region; (ii) that the electorates of regions approximate to numerical equality, except in so far as special geographical considerations justify some departure; (iii) that the ratio of regional seats to constituency seats remains constant; and (iv) that regions will each have the same number of seats or at least approximately so, with those with the larger electorates possibly having one more in number.

Section 21   SCHEDULE 2

SCOTTISH PARLIAMENTARY CORPORATE BODY

Membership

1. A person appointed under section 21(2)(b) shall hold office until another member of the Parliament is appointed in his place unless he previously resigns, ceases to be a member of the Parliament otherwise than by virtue of a dissolution or is removed from office by resolution of the Parliament.

Property

2.—(1) The corporation may hold property.

(2) Subordinate legislation may provide—

   (a) for the transfer to the corporation of any property belonging to a Minister of the Crown or government department, or

   (b) for the corporation to have such rights or interests in relation to any property belonging to a Minister of the Crown or government department as the person making the legislation considers appropriate (whether in connection with a transfer or otherwise).

(3) Subordinate legislation under sub-paragraph (2) in relation to any property may provide for the transfer to the corporation of any liabilities relating to the property to which a Minister of the Crown or government department is subject and which subsist immediately before the subordinate legislation comes into force.

(4) Subordinate legislation under sub-paragraph (2) may only be made if the person making the legislation considers it appropriate to do so to enable the corporation to exercise its functions or to facilitate their exercise or in connection with their exercise or proposed exercise.

Staff

3.—(1) The corporation shall appoint Assistant Clerks and may appoint other staff.

(2) The Clerk and other persons appointed by the corporation are referred to in this Act as the staff of the Parliament.

(3) It is for the corporation to determine the terms and conditions of appointment of the staff of the Parliament, including arrangements for the payment of pensions, gratuities or allowances to, or in respect of, any person who has ceased to be a member of the staff of the Parliament.

(4) In particular, the corporation may—
 (a) make contributions or payments towards provision for such pensions, gratuities or allowances,
 (b) establish and administer one or more pension schemes.

Powers

4.—(1) Subject to sub-paragraph (4), the corporation may do anything which appears to it to be necessary or expedient for the purpose of or in connection with the discharge of its functions.

(2) That includes, in particular—
 (a) entering into contracts,
 (b) charging for goods or services,
 (c) investing sums not immediately required in relation to the discharge of its functions, and
 (d) accepting gifts.

(3) The corporation may sell goods or provide services, and may make arrangements for the sale of goods or provision of services, to the public.

(4) The corporation may borrow sums in sterling by way of overdraft or otherwise for the purpose of meeting a temporary excess of expenditure over sums otherwise available to meet that expenditure.

(5) The corporation may borrow money only under sub-paragraph (4) and may borrow under that sub-paragraph only in accordance with the special or general approval of the Parliament.

Delegation

5. The corporation may delegate any of its functions to the Presiding Officer or the Clerk.

Proceedings and business

6.—(1) The validity of any act of the corporation shall not be affected by any vacancy among the members, or by any defect in the appointment, or qualification for membership, of any member.

(2) The corporation may determine its own procedure.

(3) The Presiding Officer shall preside at meetings of the corporation, but the corporation may appoint another of its members to preside if the office of Presiding Officer is vacant or the Presiding Officer is for any reason unable to act.

Crown status

7.—(1) Her Majesty may by Order in Council provide for the corporation to be treated to any extent as a Crown body for the purposes of any enactment.

(2) In particular, the Order may for the purposes of any enactment provide—
 (a) for employment under the corporation to be treated as employment under the corporation as a Crown body,
 (b) for land held, used or managed by the corporation, or operations carried out by or on behalf of the corporation, to be treated (as the case may be) as land held, used or managed, or operations carried out by or on behalf of, the corporation as a Crown body.

(3) For the purposes of this paragraph, "Crown body" means a body which is the servant or agent of the Crown, and includes a government department.

GENERAL NOTE
This Schedule makes further provision for the Scottish Parliamentary Corporate Body which is established by s.21. In particular it defines the members' term of office (para. 1); confers powers and imposes functions on the body (paras. 2, 3 and 4); empowers the body to delegate (para. 5) and makes provision for its procedures (para. 6). The Scottish Parliamentary Corporate Body is not a Crown body, but there is provision for it to be treated for certain purposes as if it was (para. 7), as there is similarly for the parliamentary corporate bodies of the House of Commons and the House of Lords, and the provision was implemented by the Scottish Parliamentary Corporate Body (Crown Status) Order 1999 (S.I. 1999 No. 677). The transfer of certain property and liabilities of Ministers of the Crown and government departments to the Scottish Parliamentary Corporate Body was effected by the Transfer of Property etc. (Scottish Parliamentary Corporate Body) Order 1999 (S.I. 1999 No. 1106). The Scottish Parliamentary Corporate Body was given title to copyright in certain works by the Parliamentary Copyright (Scottish Parliament) Order 1999 (S.I. 1999 No. 676).

Section 22 SCHEDULE 3

STANDING ORDERS—FURTHER PROVISION

Preservation of order

1.—(1) The standing orders shall include provision for preserving order in the proceedings of the Parliament, including provision for—
  (a) preventing conduct which would constitute a criminal offence or contempt of court, and
  (b) a sub judice rule.
(2) Such provision may provide for excluding a member of the Parliament from proceedings.

Withdrawal of rights and privileges

2. The standing orders may include provision for withdrawing from a member of the Parliament his rights and privileges as a member.

Proceedings to be in public

3.—(1) The standing orders shall include provision requiring the proceedings of the Parliament to be held in public, except in such circumstances as the standing orders may provide.
(2) The standing orders may include provision as to the conditions to be complied with by any member of the public attending the proceedings, including provision for excluding from the proceedings any member of the public who does not comply with those conditions.

Reporting and publishing proceedings

4. The standing orders shall include provision for reporting the proceedings of the Parliament and for publishing the reports.

The Presiding Officer and deputies

5. The standing orders shall include provision for ensuring that the Presiding Officer and deputies do not all represent the same political party.

Committees

6.—(1) Standing orders which provide for the appointment of committees may include provision for those committees to have power to appoint sub-committees.
(2) The standing orders shall include provision for ensuring that, in appointing members to committees and sub-committees, regard is had to the balance of political parties in the Parliament.
(3) The standing orders may include provision for excluding from the proceedings of a committee or sub-committee a member of the Parliament who is not a member of the committee or sub-committee.

Crown interests

7. The standing orders shall include provision for ensuring that a Bill containing provisions which would, if the Bill were a Bill for an Act of Parliament, require the consent of Her

Majesty, the Prince and Steward of Scotland or the Duke of Cornwall shall not pass unless such consent has been signified to the Parliament.

GENERAL NOTE
See the General Note to s.22, above. Some, but not all, of the matters which must, or may, be dealt with in standing orders are detailed here. For the provision actually made currently on these and other matters, see the Standing Orders.

Para. 1
It was thought prudent to require that provision should be made for a *sub judice* rule, even when it was already required that there should be provision to prevent conduct which would constitute contempt of court.

Para. 2
The general power here to provide for withdrawal of rights and privileges would extend to loss of salary (*Hansard*, H.C. Vol. 305, col. 557).

Para. 3
It should be noted that the requirement is not absolute, but subject to discretionary exceptions. In October 1999, when the Standards Committee of the Parliament was possibly proposing to meet in private on a matter, a petition for judicial review was initiated by *The Scotsman* newspaper, but was subsequently withdrawn.

Para. 5
The Government tabled an amendment to provide that the three posts should be held by representatives of at least two parties and considered that "it would be a breach of the spirit of the amendment if the two coalition parties took the whole lot" (*Hansard*, H.L. Vol. 593, col. 1674).

Para. 6
These provisions leave considerable discretion. The requirement that "regard is had to the balance of political parties in the Parliament," according to the Government's spokesman, "does not preclude the Parliament taking account of other factors" (*Hansard*, H.L. Vol. 592, col. 448).

Sections 29 and 53(4)   SCHEDULE 4

ENACTMENTS ETC. PROTECTED FROM MODIFICATION

PART I

THE PROTECTED PROVISIONS

Particular enactments

1.—(1) An Act of the Scottish Parliament cannot modify, or confer power by subordinate legislation to modify, any of the following provisions.
(2) The provisions are—
  (a) Articles 4 and 6 of the Union with Scotland Act 1706 and of the Union with England Act 1707 so far as they relate to freedom of trade,
  (b) the Private Legislation Procedure (Scotland) Act 1936,
  (c) the following provisions of the European Communities Act 1972— Section 1 and Schedule 1, Section 2, other than subsection (2), the words following "such Community obligation" in subsection (3) and the words "subject to Schedule 2 to this Act" in subsection (4), Section 3(1) and (2), Section 11(2),
  (d) paragraphs 5(3)(b) and 15(4)(b) of Schedule 32 to the Local Government, Planning and Land Act 1980 (designation of enterprise zones),
  (e) sections 140A to 140G of the Social Security Administration Act 1992 (rent rebate and rent allowance subsidy and council tax benefit),
  (f) the Human Rights Act 1998.

The law on reserved matters

2.—(1) An Act of the Scottish Parliament cannot modify, or confer power by subordinate legislation to modify, the law on reserved matters.

164

(2) In this paragraph, "the law on reserved matters" means—
  (a) any enactment the subject-matter of which is a reserved matter and which is comprised in an Act of Parliament or subordinate legislation under an Act of Parliament, and
  (b) any rule of law which is not contained in an enactment and the subject-matter of which is a reserved matter,
and in this sub-paragraph "Act of Parliament" does not include this Act.

(3) Sub-paragraph (1) applies in relation to a rule of Scots private law or Scots criminal law (whether or not contained in an enactment) only to the extent that the rule in question is special to a reserved matter or the subject-matter of the rule is—
  (a) interest on sums due in respect of taxes or excise duties and refunds of such taxes or duties, or
  (b) the obligations, in relation to occupational or personal pension schemes, of the trustees or managers.
  (c) the obligations under an order made by virtue of section 12A(2) or (3) of the Family Law (Scotland) Act 1985 (orders relating to pensions lump sums) of the person responsible for a pension arrangement other than an occupational or personal pension scheme; or
  (d) the obligations under Chapter I of Part IV of the Welfare Reform and Pensions Act 1999 (sharing of rights under pension arrangements) of the person responsible for such a pension arrangement; or
  (e) the effect of Chapter II of Part IV of that Act of 1999 (sharing of rights in state pension schemes) as read with Part II of the Social Security Contributions and Benefits Act 1992 (contributory benefits).

(4) In sub paragraph (3)(c) "pension arrangement" and "person responsible for a pension arrangement" have the same meaning as in section 27(1) of the Family Law (Scotland) Act 1985.

3.—(1) Paragraph 2 does not apply to modifications which—
  (a) are incidental to, or consequential on, provision made (whether by virtue of the Act in question or another enactment) which does not relate to reserved matters, and
  (b) do not have a greater effect on reserved matters than is necessary to give effect to the purpose of the provision.

(2) In determining for the purposes of sub-paragraph (1)(b) what is necessary to give effect to the purpose of a provision, any power to make laws other than the power of the Parliament is to be disregarded.

This Act

4.—(1) An Act of the Scottish Parliament cannot modify, or confer power by subordinate legislation to modify, this Act.

[1](2) This paragraph does not apply to modifying sections 1(4), 17(5), 19(7), 21(5), 24(2), 28(5), 39(7), 40 to 43, 50, 69(3), 85, 93 and 97 and paragraphs 4(1) to (3) and 6(1) of Schedule 2.

(3) This paragraph does not apply to modifying any provision of this Act (other than sections 64(7), 66(2), 71(7), 77, 78 and 119) which—
  (a) charges any sum on the Scottish Consolidated Fund,
  (b) requires any sum to be paid out of that Fund without further approval, or
  (c) requires any sum to be payable out of that Fund, or
  (d) requires or authorises the payment of any sum into that Fund.

(4) This paragraph does not apply to any modifications of Part III which are necessary or expedient for the purpose or in consequence of the establishment of a new fund, in addition to the Scottish Consolidated Fund, out of which loans may be made by the Scottish Ministers.

(5) This paragraph does not apply to—
  (a) modifying so much of any enactment as is modified by this Act,
  (b) repealing so much of any provision of this Act as amends any enactment, if the provision ceases to have effect in consequence of any enactment comprised in or made under an Act of the Scottish Parliament.

NOTE
[1] As amended by S.I. 1999 No. 1749. Effective July 1, 1999.

Enactments modified by this Act

5. An Act of the Scottish Parliament cannot modify, or confer power by subordinate legislation to modify—

(a) the effect of section 119(3) in relation to any provision of an Act of Parliament relating to judicial salaries,
(b) so much of any enactment as—
  (i) is amended by paragraph 2, 7 or 32 of Schedule 8, and
  (ii) relates to the Advocate General,
(c) so much of any enactment as is amended by paragraph 9(b) or 29 of Schedule 8.

Shared powers

6. An Act of the Scottish Parliament cannot modify, or confer power by subordinate legislation to modify, any enactment so far as the enactment relates to powers exercisable by a Minister of the Crown by virtue of section 56.

PART II

GENERAL EXCEPTIONS

Restatement, etc.

7.—(1) Part I of this Schedule does not prevent an Act of the Scottish Parliament—
  (a) restating the law (or restating it with such modifications as are not prevented by that Part), or
  (b) repealing any spent enactment,
or conferring power by subordinate legislation to do so.
(2) For the purposes of paragraph 2, the law on reserved matters includes any restatement in an Act of the Scottish Parliament, or subordinate legislation under such an Act, of the law on reserved matters if the subject-matter of the restatement is a reserved matter.

Effect of Interpretation Act 1978

8. Part I of this Schedule does not prevent the operation of any provision of the Interpretation Act 1978.

Change of title etc.

9.—(1) Part I of this Schedule does not prevent an Act of the Scottish Parliament amending, or conferring power by subordinate legislation to amend, any enactment by changing—
  (a) any of the titles referred to in sub-paragraph (2), or
  (b) any reference to a declarator,
in consequence of any provision made by or under an Act of the Scottish Parliament.
(2) The titles are those of—
  (a) any court or tribunal or any judge, chairman or officer of a court or tribunal,
  (b) any holder of an office in the Scottish Administration which is not a ministerial office or any member of the staff of the Scottish Administration,
  (c) any register.

Accounts and audit and maladministration

10. Part I of this Schedule does not prevent an Act of the Scottish Parliament modifying, or conferring power by subordinate legislation to modify, any enactment for or in connection with the purposes of section 70 or 91.

Subordinate legislation

11.—(1) Part I of this Schedule does not prevent an Act of the Scottish Parliament modifying, or conferring power by subordinate legislation to modify, any enactment for or in connection with any of the following purposes.
(2) Those purposes are—
  (a) making different provision in respect of the document by which a power to make subordinate legislation within sub-paragraph (3) is to be exercised,
  (b) making different provision (or no provision) for the procedure, in relation to the Parliament, to which legislation made in the exercise of such a power (or the instrument or other document in which it is contained) is to be subject,
  (c) applying any enactment comprised in or made under an Act of the Scottish Parliament relating to the documents by which such powers may be exercised.
(3) The power to make the subordinate legislation, or a power to confirm or approve the legislation, must be exercisable by—

(a) a member of the Scottish Executive,
(b) any Scottish public authority with mixed functions or no reserved functions,
(c) any other person (not being a Minister of the Crown) within devolved competence.

PART III

CONSEQUENTIAL MODIFICATION OF SECTIONS 53 AND 54

12.—(1) This paragraph applies to a function which (apart from this Schedule) would be transferred to the Scottish Ministers by virtue of section 53(2)(c).

(2) If, because of anything in Part I of this Schedule, a provision of an Act of the Scottish Parliament modifying an enactment so as to provide for the function to be exercisable by a different person would be outside the legislative competence of the Parliament, the function is not so transferred.

13.—(1) Paragraph 12 does not apply to any function conferred by any provision of—
(a) the European Communities Act 1972,
(b) the Human Rights Act 1998, except sections 1, 5, 14 to 17 and 22 of that Act,
(c) the law on reserved matters (for the purposes of paragraph 2) so far as contained in an enactment.

(2) For the purpose of determining—
(a) whether any function under any of the provisions referred to in sub-paragraph (1) is transferred to the Scottish Ministers by virtue of section 53, and
(b) the extent to which any such function (other than a function of making, confirming or approving subordinate legislation) is exercisable by them,
the references in section 54 to the legislative competence of the Parliament are to be read as if section 29(2)(c) were omitted.

(3) Part I of this Schedule does not prevent an Act of the Scottish Parliament modifying, or conferring power by subordinate legislation to modify, any of the provisions mentioned in sub-paragraph (1) so as to provide for a function transferred to the Scottish Ministers by virtue of section 53 to be exercisable by a different person.

14. If any pre-commencement enactment or prerogative instrument is modified by subordinate legislation under section 105, a function under that enactment or instrument (whether as it has effect before or after the modification) is not transferred by virtue of section 53 if the subordinate legislation provides that it is not to be so transferred.

DEFINITIONS
"Act of the Scottish Parliament": s.28(1).
"Advocate General": s.32(4).
"by virtue of": s.126(11).
"confer": s.126(1).
"devolved competence": s.54.
"document": s.126(1).
"enactment": s.126(1).
"function": s.126(1).
"legislative competence": s.126(1).
"member of the Scottish Executive": s.44(1).
"member of the staff of the Scottish Administration": s.126(7).
"Minister of the Crown": s.126(1).
"modify": s.126(1).
"office in the Scottish Administration which is not in a ministerial office": s.126(8).
"the Parliament": s.112(1).
"pre-commencement enactment": s.53(3).
"prerogative instrument": s.126(1).
"reserved matters": Sched.5.
"Scots criminal law": s.126(5).
"Scots private law": s.126(4).
"Scottish Ministers": s.44(2).
"Scottish public authority with mixed functions or no reserved functions": Paras. 1, 2 of Pt. III of Sched. 5.
"subordinate legislation": s.126(1).
"tribunal": s.126(1).

GENERAL NOTE
This Schedule was substantially amended during the passage of the Bill through Parliament to reflect an important shift in the function assigned to it within the Bill's overall design. In

the original version of the Bill, Sched. 4 served the very limited purpose of providing a list of exceptions to a general rule then contained in what is now s.29 that the terms of the Scotland Act itself could not be modified by the Scottish Parliament. That purpose is still served by paras. 4–6 of the Schedule as now enacted. Read with s.29(2)(c), they impose a general ban (with specified exceptions) on the modification of the Scotland Act. It remains an important element in the general devolution scheme that the Scottish Parliament should not be free to adjust the terms of the scheme itself.

However, other provisions now contained in Sched. 4 reach far beyond this. Section 29(2)(c) provides that any provision in an Act of the Scottish Parliament will be outside the legislative competence of the Parliament if "it modifies the law in breach of the restrictions in Schedule 4". This has enabled a list of specific U.K. Acts (and, in the case of the Acts of Union in para. 1, Acts of the old Scottish and English Parliaments) to be protected from modification in whole or in part. In addition, the Schedule provides that, subject to important qualifications, "the law on reserved matters" cannot be modified. There follows Pt. II (paras. 7–11) which contains "Exceptions" to the preceding restrictions and Pt. III which contains "modifications" of ss.53, 54.

Further commentary is to be found in the notes on individual paragraphs. One additional general comment should, however, be added at this stage. This is that Sched. 4 now occupies a curious (some might say ambiguous) role in the Act's overall scheme for defining the legislative competence of the Scottish Parliament. Especially in paras. 2, 3, 7 on "the law on reserved matters", the Schedule provides a very important series of qualifications to the rules otherwise contained in ss.29, 30 and Sched. 5. Working out the distinction between the matters reserved directly under Sched. 5 and the provisions of Sched. 4 will become one of the most interesting aspects of the interpretative life of the scheme of legislative competence. The same may apply in relation to paras. 1(2)(f), 13(1)(b) on human rights. Human rights are not reserved but some human rights legislation is unamendable. Along with two specified provisions of the Acts of Union and of the European Communities Act 1972, they are preserved against future amendment as part of the new "Constitution" of Scotland.

PART I

Para. 1

Subject to Pts II, III of the Schedule, this paragraph prohibits the modification of the statutory provisions it identifies:

(a) *Articles 4, 6 of the Union with Scotland Act 1706/Union with England Act 1707, so far as they relate to freedom of trade.*

The Union itself is a reserved matter under Sched. 5, Pt.I, para. 1(b).

See also s.37 of this Act but also Head C of Pt. II of Sched. 5 (reservation of trade and industry).

(b) *Private Legislation Procedure (Scotland) Act 1936 (c.52).*

See also s.36(3) of this Act and para. 5 of Sched. 8.

(c) *European Communities Act 1972 (c.36).*

This entrenches the "institutional" aspects of the 1972 Act. Section 1 defines terms; s.2 provides for the "General implementation of Treaties"; s.3 for "Decisions on and proof of, Treaties and Community instruments"; and s.11(2) for an offence of unauthorised disclosure of information. However, s.106; para. 7(2) of Sched. 5, Pt. I; and the amendments made to the European Communities Act 1972 by para. 15 of Sched. 8 make clear that aspects of observing and implementing obligations under Community law are for the Scottish Parliament and Executive and the flexibility given in this subparagraph (e.g. reprovision for incorporating EC law) reflects this. Much of s.2 of the 1972 Act (together with Sched.2) is not protected from modification. See also the notes on Pt. III of the Schedule.

(d) *Local Government, Planning and Land Act 1980.*

These provisions (in relation to enterprise zones) are unamendable. See also s.55(2); and Sections C13, C14 of Pt. II of Sched. 5.

(e) *Social Security Administration Act 1992.*

These sections, inserted into the 1992 Act by the Housing Act 1996 (c.52), s.121, Sched. 12, make provision for the Secretary of State to pay subsidy to relevant local (and other public) authorities in respect of the costs of providing rent rebate, rent allowance and council tax benefit. Prohibiting their modification by the Scottish Parliament reinforces the reservation by Sched. 3, Section F1 of the administration and funding of housing benefit and council tax benefit.

The related question of levels of council tax and house rents (which are not reserved) and their impact on levels of council tax and housing benefits was mentioned in the White Paper (para. 7.25). There it was suggested that resources for those payments would be made available in "the Block" (see note on Pt. III of the Act) but that any extra costs would have to be found by the Scottish Parliament—a position subsequently adjusted in the Treasury Statement of Funding Policy of 31 March 1999 (para. 5.3) (See note on s.64(2).)

(f) *Human Rights Act 1998.*

This becomes unamendable although, with the exception of, *e.g.* "equal opportunities" the subject matter of human rights is not reserved by Sched. 5. See also ss.57,100 as well as ss.29, 54.

See also the notes on Pt. III of the Schedule.

Paras. 2, 3

These paragraphs (which should be read with para. 7) deal with the "law on reserved matters". For general comment on the Act's treatment of "reserved matters" and the "law on reserved matters", see the General Note to s.29(2)(b).

See also the notes on Pt. III of the Schedule.

Para. 4

Subpara. (1). In the first published version of Sched. 4 to the Scotland Bill, it provided a series of limited exceptions to a general rule that the Scotland Act would not itself be amendable by the Scottish Parliament. The Act would be "entrenched" against such change. That original purpose of Sched. 4 is now fulfilled in paras. 4–6.

This sub-paragraph states the basic rule against modification of the Scotland Act—whether directly or by conferring power to modify by subordinate legislation.

Subpara. (2). This subparagraph is the first of four containing exceptions to the general rule. It permits modification of a number of specified provisions. They include a group of provisions which prevent legal challenge to certain types of act or decision on grounds of some formal defect (ss.1(4), 17(5), 19(7), 28(5), 50, 69(3)); certain provisions concerning the Parliamentary corporation (s.21(5) and the paragraphs of Sched. 2); certain provisions of a (minor) procedural nature fixing a penalty level (s.24(2), 39(7); provisions concerning actions against the Scottish Parliament or affecting rights of its members (ss.40—43, 85); and agency arrangements (s.93). The exception of s.97 (assistance for opposition parties) was added by the Scotland Act 1998 (Modifications of Schedules 4 and 5) Order 1999 (S.I. 1999 No.1749), art.2.

Subpara. (3). This permits the modification of provisions which charge sums, etc., on the Scottish Consolidated Fund (for which general provision is made by ss.64, 65) with the exception of those listed as remaining "entrenched". All of those are protective of the interests of the U.K. Government.

Subpara. (4). Part III of the Act is concerned with financial provision but there is, at present, no provision for the establishment of a Loans Fund for purposes similar to these for which the U.K. National Loans Fund is established. Such provision is permitted under this subparagraph.

Subpara. (5). This makes clear that the rule against modifying the Scotland Act itself does not extend to the modification of the amendments which this Act makes to other enactments or, indeed, the repeal of a provision which amends the other enactments—subject, of course, to any other limitations on the legislative competence of the Scottish Parliament. See para. 5 below.

Para. 5

This paragraph supplements the general rule in para. 4 by specifically "entrenching" the effect of certain provisions modified by this Act:-

(a) The arrangement by which judicial salaries are transferred by s.119(3) from being a charge on the Consolidated Fund to being a charge on the Scottish Consolidated Fund.

(b) The provisions of the Crown Suits (Scotland) Act 1857, the Crown Proceedings Act 1947 and the Criminal Procedure (Scotland) Act 1995 which are amended by Sched. 8 and relate to the Advocate General for Scotland—the U.K. Law Officer for Scotland established by s.87.

(c) The provisions of the Lands Tribunal Act 1949 and the Scottish Land Court Act 1993 which are amended by Sched. 8 and provide for the remuneration of members of the Lands Tribunal for Scotland to be charged on the Scottish Consolidated Fund and for the appointment of the Chairman of the Land Court respectively.

Para. 6

This entrenchment of the enactments conferring the powers shared by the Scottish Ministers and a Minister of the Crown under the terms of s.56 is necessary to preserve their shared character. None of the powers is within the compass of reserved matters but, if they were amended, the role of the U.K. Minister might be extinguished.

PART II

Para. 7

This paragraph achieves two purposes. Subparagraph (1) frees the Scottish Parliament to "restate" the law or repeal "spent" law without infringing the prohibitions on the modifications of enactments imposed by Pt. I.

Secondly, subpara. (2) extends the prohibition on modification of the law on reserved matters imposed by para. 2 to restatements of the law on reserved matters.

For a note on this and other aspects of reserved matters, see s.29(2)(b).

Para. 8

One effect of this paragraph is to preserve that effect of s.17(2)(a) of the Interpretation Act 1978. That provides that where an Act repeals and re-enacts a previous enactment, unless a contrary intention appears, any reference in another enactment to the repealed enactment is construed as a reference to the new provision. It also preserves the effect of subordinate legislation.

For other references to the Interpretation Act, see Sched. 7, para. 5 and Sched. 8 para. 16. Note, in particular, the new s.23A added by the latter paragraph.

Para. 9

The main purpose of this paragraph is to free the Scottish Parliament to amend the "title" (but not, of course, substantive rules as to status or function) of the offices (and registers) listed in subpara. (2). It should be noted that deliberate exceptions from the list are ministerial positions including the title "First Minister" which, therefore, remain entrenched.

Secondly, flexibility is also given to amend "any reference to a declarator" in any enactment. See s.18 (judicial proceedings as to disqualification) in this Act.

Para. 10

Sections 70 (Financial control, accounts and audit) and 91 (Maladministration) lay down only framework requirements in the areas they deal with and leave the Scottish Parliament some freedom as to how the purposes of the section are to be achieved. This paragraph reinforces that flexibility.

Para. 11

Other sections in this Act make provision for conferring powers to make subordinate legislation and the procedures according to which it is to be made. In particular, s.53 (with s.54) provides for the general transfer of functions to the Scottish Ministers; s.117 modifies existing references to a Minister of the Crown to references to the Scottish Ministers; and s.118 converts parliamentary procedures applicable to the making of subordinate legislation by members of the Scottish Executive, Scottish public authorities and others from procedures at Westminster to procedures in the Scottish Parliament.

This paragraph gives freedom to the Scottish Parliament to adjust the existing rules to make arrangements for the purposes set out in subpara. (2).

PART III

The purpose of this Part of the Schedule is to add some necessary qualifications to the rules in Pt. I (restricting the Parliament's powers to modify enactments) in so far as they have consequences for the transfer of functions to the Scottish Ministers under s.53.

Probably the best starting point is para. 13(3) which makes, in some circumstances, an exception to the rules in Pt. I where the purpose of the Act of the Scottish Parliament is confined to providing for a power transferred by the Scotland Act 1998 to the Scottish Ministers to be exercisable by a different person. Such flexibility is permitted.

It is, however, a flexibility restricted to the functions listed in para. 13(1) and that restriction is reinforced by para. 12 which provides that, except for the specific concessions made by para. 13, the effect of an Act of the Scottish Parliament, purporting to make a function exercisable by a different person, would be to render the function not transferred i.e. retained by a Minister of the Crown.

One knock-on consequence of the concession permitted by para. 13 might be to place a function *prima facie* outwith "devolved competence" (consequential upon being outwith legislative competence) because, in turn, s.29(2)(c) (imposing the restrictions in Sched. 4) would have been breached by the making of an amendment prohibited by paras. 1, 2. Para. 13(2) overcomes that difficulty by requiring s.29(2)(c) to be ignored for this purpose.

As to the functions excluded from the operation of para. 12 by para. 13(1) (and thereby serving the main purpose of Pt. III of the Schedule), these are identified by reference to two of the Acts which are, in large part, unamendable by the Scottish Parliament by virtue of para. 1 of the Schedule and other legislation made unamendable by the operation of para. 2 of the Schedule (law on reserved matters). Despite the operation of paras. 1, 2 the Parliament is free to provide for functions under the specified legislation to be "exercisable by a different person" without loss of transfer of the function by s.53. But *excepted from* that flexibility are the provisions of the Human Rights Act 1998 (c.42) containing most ministerial powers under the Act, *e.g.* including s.1 enabling 'incorporation' of a new protocol. Section 5 of the Human Rights Act 1998 (Right of Crown to intervene), however, gives express power to "a member of the Scottish Executive" and the powers of ministers to take remedial action (s.10 and Sched. 2) will be available to the Scottish Ministers. Another target is s.12(1) of the Official Secrets Act 1989, by which a minister prescribes who are to be Crown servants for the purposes of the Act. As a part of "the law on reserved matters", the Act could not be modified by the Scottish Parliament. However, para. 13(1)(c) permits the Scottish Ministers to exercise the function for a devolved purpose.

<table>
<tr><td>Section 30</td><td style="text-align:center">SCHEDULE 5</td></tr>
</table>

Section 30

SCHEDULE 5

RESERVED MATTERS

PART I

GENERAL RESERVATIONS

The Constitution

1. The following aspects of the constitution are reserved matters, that is—
   (a) the Crown, including succession to the Crown and a regency,
   (b) the Union of the Kingdoms of Scotland and England,
   (c) the Parliament of the United Kingdom,
   (d) the continued existence of the High Court of Justiciary as a criminal court of first instance and of appeal,
   (e) the continued existence of the Court of Session as a civil court of first instance and of appeal.

2.—(1) Paragraph 1 does not reserve—
   (a) Her Majesty's prerogative and other executive functions,
   (b) functions exercisable by any person acting on behalf of the Crown, or
   (c) any office in the Scottish Administration.

(2) Sub-paragraph (1) does not affect the reservation by paragraph 1 of honours and dignities or the functions of the Lord Lyon King of Arms so far as relating to the granting of arms; but this sub-paragraph does not apply to the Lord Lyon King of Arms in his judicial capacity.

(3) Sub-paragraph (1) does not affect the reservation by paragraph 1 of the management (in accordance with any enactment regulating the use of land) of the Crown Estate.

(4) Sub-paragraph (1) does not affect the reservation by paragraph 1 of the functions of the Security Service, the Secret Intelligence Service and the Government Communications Headquarters.

[1](5) Sub-paragraph (1) does not affect the reservation by paragraph 1 of the functions exercisable though the Export Credits Guarantee Department.

NOTE
[1] Inserted by S.I. 1999 No. 1749. Effective July 1, 1999.

3.—(1) Paragraph 1 does not reserve property belonging to Her Majesty in right of the Crown or belonging to any person acting on behalf of the Crown or held in trust for Her Majesty for the purposes of any person acting on behalf of the Crown.

(2) Paragraph 1 does not reserve the ultimate superiority of the Crown or the superiority of the Prince and Steward of Scotland.

(3) Sub-paragraph (1) does not affect the reservation by paragraph 1 of—
   (a) the hereditary revenues of the Crown, other than revenues from bona vacantia, ultimus haeres and treasure trove,
   (b) the royal arms and standard,
   (c) the compulsory acquisition of property held or used by a Minister of the Crown or government department.

4.—(1) Paragraph 1 does not reserve property held by Her Majesty in Her private capacity.

(2) Sub-paragraph (1) does not affect the reservation by paragraph 1 of the subject-matter of the Crown Private Estates Acts 1800 to 1873.

5. Paragraph 1 does not reserve the use of the Scottish Seal.

Political parties

[1]6. The registration and funding of political parties is a reserved matter but this paragraph does not reserve making payments to any political party for the purpose of assisting members of the Parliament who are connected with the party to perform their Parliamentary duties.

NOTE
[1] As amended by S.I. 1999 No. 1749. Effective July 1, 1999.

Foreign affairs etc.

7.—(1) International relations, including relations with territories outside the United Kingdom, the European Communities (and their institutions) and other international organisations, regulation of international trade, and international development assistance and co-operation are reserved matters.

(2) Sub-paragraph (1) does not reserve—
  (a) observing and implementing international obligations, obligations under the Human Rights Convention and obligations under Community law,
  (b) assisting Ministers of the Crown in relation to any matter to which that sub-paragraph applies.

Public service

8.—(1) The Civil Service of the State is a reserved matter.
(2) Sub-paragraph (1) does not reserve the subject-matter of—
  (a) Part I of the Sheriff Courts and Legal Officers (Scotland) Act 1927 (appointment of sheriff clerks and procurators fiscal etc.),
  (b) Part III of the Administration of Justice (Scotland) Act 1933 (officers of the High Court of Justiciary and of the Court of Session).

Defence

9.—(1) The following are reserved matters—
  (a) the defence of the realm,
  (b) the naval, military or air forces of the Crown, including reserve forces,
  (c) visiting forces,
  (d) international headquarters and defence organisations,
  (e) trading with the enemy and enemy property.
(2) Sub-paragraph (1) does not reserve—
  (a) the exercise of civil defence functions by any person otherwise than as a member of any force or organisation referred to in sub-paragraph (1)(b) to (d) or any other force or organisation reserved by virtue of sub-paragraph (1)(a),
  (b) the conferral of enforcement powers in relation to sea fishing.

Treason

10. Treason (including constructive treason), treason felony and misprision of treason are reserved matters.

PART II

SPECIFIC RESERVATIONS

Preliminary

1. The matters to which any of the Sections in this Part apply are reserved matters for the purposes of this Act.
2. A Section applies to any matter described or referred to in it when read with any illustrations, exceptions or interpretation provisions in that Section.
3. Any illustrations, exceptions or interpretation provisions in a Section relate only to that Section (so that an entry under the heading "exceptions" does not affect any other Section).

Reservations

Head A—Financial and Economic Matters

A1. Fiscal, economic and monetary policy
Fiscal, economic and monetary policy, including the issue and circulation of money, taxes and excise duties, government borrowing and lending, control over United Kingdom public expenditure, the exchange rate and the Bank of England.

Exception
Local taxes to fund local authority expenditure (for example, council tax and non-domestic rates).

A2. The currency

Coinage, legal tender and bank notes.

A3. Financial services

Financial services, including investment business, banking and deposit—taking, collective investment schemes and insurance.

Exception

The subject-matter of section 1 of the Banking and Financial Dealings Act 1971 (bank holidays).

A4. Financial markets

Financial markets, including listing and public offers of securities and investments, transfer of securities and insider dealing.

A5. Money laundering

The subject-matter of the Money Laundering Regulations 1993, but in relation to any type of business.

Head B—Home Affairs

B1. Misuse of drug

The subject-matter of—
    (a) the Misuse of Drugs Act 1971,
    (b) sections 12 to 14 of the Criminal Justice (International Co-operation) Act 1990 (substances useful for manufacture of controlled drugs), and
    (c) Part V of the Criminal Law (Consolidation) (Scotland) Act 1995 (drug trafficking) and, so far as relating to drug trafficking, the Proceeds of Crime (Scotland) Act 1995.

B2. Data protection

The subject-matter of—
    (a) the Data Protection Act 1998, and
    (b) Council Directive 95/46/EC (protection of individuals with regard to the processing of personal data and on the free movement of such data).

Interpretation

If any provision of the Data Protection Act 1998 is not in force on the principal appointed day, it is to be treated for the purposes of this reservation as if it were.

B3. Elections

Elections for membership of the House of Commons, the European Parliament and the Parliament, including the subject-matter of—
    (a) the European Parliamentary Elections Act 1978,
    (b) the Representation of the People Act 1983 and the Representation of the People Act 1985, and
    (c) the Parliamentary Constituencies Act 1986,
so far as those enactments apply, or may be applied, in respect of such membership.
The franchise at local government elections.

B4. Firearms

The subject-matter of the Firearms Acts 1968 to 1997.

B5. Entertainment

The subject-matter of—
    (a) the Video Recordings Act 1984, and
    (b) sections 1 to 3 and 5 to 16 of the Cinemas Act 1985 (control of exhibitions).
The classification of films for public exhibition by reference to their suitability for viewing by persons generally or above a particular age, with or without any advice as to the desirability of parental guidance.

B6. Immigration and nationality

Nationality; immigration, including asylum and the status and capacity of persons in the United Kingdom who are not British citizens; free movement of persons within the European Economic Area; issue of travel documents.

173

B7. Scientific procedures on live animals

The subject-matter of the Animals (Scientific Procedures) Act 1986.

[1]B8. National security, interception of communications, official secrets and terrorism

National security.

The interception of communications; but not
  (a) the interception of any communication made to or by a person detained at a place of detention, if the communication—
  (i) is a written communication and is intercepted there, or
  (ii) is intercepted in the course of its transmission by means of a private telecommunication system running there,
  (b) the subject-matter of Part III of the Police Act 1997 (authorisation to interfere with property etc.) or surveillance not involving interference with property.

The subject-matter of—
  (a) the Official Secrets Acts 1911 and 1920, and
  (b) the Official Secrets Act 1989, except so far as relating to any information, document or other article protected against disclosure by section 4(2) (crime) and not by any other provision of sections 1 to 4.

Special powers, and other special provisions, for dealing with terrorism.

[1]Interpretation

"Place of detention" means a prison, young offenders institution, remand centre or legalised police cell (as those expressions are defined for the purposes of the Prisons (Scotland) Act 1989 or a hospital (within the meaning of the Mental Health (Scotland) Act 1984; and "person detained", in relation to a hospital, means a person detained there within the meaning given by section 6(1) of the Sex Offenders Act 1997 as it extends to Scotland.

"Private telecommunication system" means a telecommunication system which is not a public telecommunication system (as those expressions are defined for the purposes of the Telecommunications Act 1984).

NOTE
[1] As amended by S.I. 1999 No. 1749, art. 4(2). Effective July 1, 1999.

B9. Betting, gaming and lotteries

Betting, gaming and lotteries.

B10. Emergency powers

Emergency powers.

B11. Extradition

Extradition.

B12. Lieutenancies

The subject-matter of the Lieutenancies Act 1997.

[1]B13. Access to information

Public access to information held by public bodies or holders of public offices (including government departments and persons acting on behalf of the Crown).

Exception

Information held by—
  (a) the Parliament,
  (b) any part of the Scottish Administration,
  (c) the Parliamentary corporation,
  (d) any Scottish public authority with mixed functions or no reserved functions,
unless supplied by a Minister of the Crown or government department and held in confidence.

NOTE
[1] Inserted by S.I. 1999 No. 1749, art. 5. Effective July 1, 1999.

Head C—Trade and Industry

C1. Business associations

The creation, operation, regulation and dissolution of types of business association.

Exceptions

The creation, operation, regulation and dissolution of—
  (a) particular public bodies, or public bodies of a particular type, established by or under any enactment, and
  (b) charities.

Interpretation

"Business association" means any person (other than an individual) established for the purpose of carrying on any kind of business, whether or not for profit; and "business" includes the provision of benefits to the members of an association.

C2. Insolvency

In relation to business associations—
  (a) the modes of, the grounds for and the general legal effect of winding up, and the persons who may initiate winding up,
  (b) liability to contribute to assets on winding up,
  (c) powers of courts in relation to proceedings for winding up, other than the power to sist proceedings,
  (d) arrangements with creditors, and
  (e) procedures giving protection from creditors.
Preferred or preferential debts for the purposes of the Bankruptcy (Scotland) Act 1985, the Insolvency Act 1986, and any other enactment relating to the sequestration of the estate of any person or to the winding up of business associations, the preference of such debts against other such debts and the extent of their preference over other types of debt.
Regulation of insolvency practitioners.
Co-operation of insolvency courts.

Exceptions

In relation to business associations—
  (a) the process of winding up, including the person having responsibility for the conduct of a winding up or any part of it, and his conduct of it or of that part,
  (b) the effect of winding up on diligence, and
  (c) avoidance and adjustment of prior transactions on winding up.
Floating charges and receivers, except in relation to preferential debts, regulation of insolvency practitioners and co-operation of insolvency courts.

Interpretation

"Business association" has the meaning given in Section C1 of this Part of this Schedule, but does not include any person whose estate may be sequestrated under the Bankruptcy (Scotland) Act 1985 or any public body established by or under an enactment.
"Winding up", in relation to business associations, includes winding up of solvent, as well as insolvent, business associations.

C3. Competition

Regulation of anti—competitive practices and agreements; abuse of dominant position; monopolies and mergers.

Exception

Regulation of particular practices in the legal profession for the purpose of regulating that profession or the provision of legal services.

Interpretation

"The legal profession" means advocates, solicitors and qualified conveyancers and executry practitioners within the meaning of Part II of the Law Reform (Miscellaneous Provisions) (Scotland) Act 1990.

C4. Intellectual property

Intellectual property.

Exception

The subject-matter of Parts I and II of the Plant Varieties Act 1997 (plant varieties and the Plant Varieties and Seeds Tribunal).

C5. Import and export control

The subject-matter of the Import, Export and Customs Powers (Defence) Act 1939.
Prohibition and regulation of the import and export of endangered species of animals and plants.

Exceptions
Prohibition and regulation of movement into and out of Scotland of—
(a) food, animals, animal products, plants and plant products for the purposes of protecting human, animal or plant health, animal welfare or the environment or observing or implementing obligations under the Common Agricultural Policy, and
(b) animal feeding stuffs, fertilisers and pesticides for the purposes of protecting human, animal or plant health or the environment.

C6. Sea fishing

Regulation of sea fishing outside the Scottish zone (except in relation to Scottish fishing boats).

Interpretation
"Scottish fishing boat" means a fishing vessel which is registered in the register maintained under section 8 of the Merchant Shipping Act 1995 and whose entry in the register specifies a port in Scotland as the port to which the vessel is to be treated as belonging.

C7. Consumer protection

Regulation of—
(a) the sale and supply of goods and services to consumers,
(b) guarantees in relation to such goods and services,
(c) hire—purchase, including the subject-matter of Part III of the Hire—Purchase Act 1964,
(d) trade descriptions, except in relation to food,
(e) misleading and comparative advertising, except regulation specifically in relation to food, tobacco and tobacco products,
(f) price indications,
(g) trading stamps,
(h) auctions and mock auctions of goods and services, and
(i) hallmarking and gun barrel proofing.
Safety of, and liability for, services supplied to consumers.
The subject-matter of—
(a) the Hearing Aid Council Act 1968,
(b) the Unsolicited Goods and Services Acts 1971 and 1975,
(c) Parts I to III and XI of the Fair Trading Act 1973,
(d) the Consumer Credit Act 1974,
(e) the Estate Agents Act 1979,
(f) the Timeshare Act 1992,
(g) the Package Travel, Package Holidays and Package Tours Regulations 1992, and
(h) the Commercial Agents (Council Directive) Regulations 1993.

Exception
The subject-matter of section 16 of the Food Safety Act 1990 (food safety and consumer protection).

C8. Product standards, safety and liability

Technical standards and requirements in relation to products in pursuance of an obligation under Community law.
Product safety and liability.
Product labelling.

Exceptions
Food, agricultural and horticultural produce, fish and fish products, seeds, animal feeding stuffs, fertilisers and pesticides.
In relation to food safety, materials which come into contact with food.

C9. Weights and measures

Units and standards of weight and measurement.

Regulation of trade so far as involving weighing, measuring and quantities.

C10. Telecommunications and wireless telegraphy

Telecommunications and wireless telegraphy.
Internet services.
Electronic encryption.
The subject-matter of Part II of the Wireless Telegraphy Act 1949 (electromagnetic disturbance).

Exception
The subject-matter of Part III of the Police Act 1997 (authorisation to interfere with property etc.).

C11. Post Office, posts and postal services

The Post Office, posts (including postage stamps, postal orders and postal packets) and regulation of postal services.

C12. Research Councils

Research Councils within the meaning of the Science and Technology Act 1965.
The subject-matter of section 5 of that Act (funding of scientific research) so far as relating to Research Councils.

C13. Designation of assisted areas

The subject-matter of section 1 of the Industrial Development Act 1982.

C14. Industrial Development Advisory Board

The Industrial Development Advisory Board.

C15. Protection of trading and economic interests

The subject-matter of—
(a) section 2 of the Emergency Laws (Re—enactments and Repeals) Act 1964 (Treasury power in relation to action damaging to economic position of United Kingdom),
(b) Part II of the Industry Act 1975 (powers in relation to transfer of control of important manufacturing undertakings), and
(c) the Protection of Trading Interests Act 1980.

Head D—Energy

D1. Electricity Generation, transmission, distribution and supply of electricity

The subject-matter of Part II of the Electricity Act 1989.

Exception
The subject-matter of Part I of the Environmental Protection Act 1990.

D2. Oil and gas

Oil and gas, including—
(a) the ownership of, exploration for and exploitation of deposits of oil and natural gas,
(b) the subject-matter of section 1 of the Mineral Exploration and Investment Grants Act 1972 (contributions in connection with mineral exploration) so far as relating to exploration for oil and gas,
(c) offshore installations and pipelines,
(d) the subject-matter of the Pipe—lines Act 1962 (including section 5 (deemed planning permission)) so far as relating to pipelines within the meaning of section 65 of that Act,
(e) the application of Scots law and the jurisdiction of the Scottish courts in relation to offshore activities,
(f) pollution relating to oil and gas exploration and exploitation, but only outside controlled waters (within the meaning of section 30A(1) of the Control of Pollution Act 1974),
(g) the subject-matter of Part II of the Food and Environment Protection Act 1985 so far as relating to oil and gas exploration and exploitation, but only in relation to activities outside such controlled waters,

(h) restrictions on navigation, fishing and other activities in connection with offshore activities,

(i) liquefaction of natural gas, and

(j) the conveyance, shipping and supply of gas through pipes.

Exceptions

The subject-matter of—

(a) sections 10 to 12 of the Industry Act 1972 (credits and grants for construction of ships and offshore installations),

(b) the Offshore Petroleum Development (Scotland) Act 1975, other than sections 3 to 7, and

(c) Part I of the Environmental Protection Act 1990.

The manufacture of gas.

The conveyance, shipping and supply of gas other than through pipes.

D3. Coal

Coal, including its ownership and exploitation, deep and opencast coal mining and coal mining subsidence.

Exceptions

The subject-matter of—

(a) Part I of the Environmental Protection Act 1990, and

(b) sections 53 (environmental duties in connection with planning) and 54 (obligation to restore land affected by coal—mining operations) of the Coal Industry Act 1994.

D4. Nuclear energy

Nuclear energy and nuclear installations, including—

(a) nuclear safety, security and safeguards, and

(b) liability for nuclear occurrences.

Exceptions

The subject-matter of—

(a) Part I of the Environmental Protection Act 1990, and

(b) the Radioactive Substances Act 1993.

D5. Energy conservation

The subject-matter of the Energy Act 1976, other than section 9.

Exception

The encouragement of energy efficiency other than by prohibition or regulation.

Head E—Transport

E1. Road transport

The subject-matter of—

(a) the Motor Vehicles (International Circulation) Act 1952,

(b) the Public Passenger Vehicles Act 1981 and the Transport Act 1985, so far as relating to public service vehicle operator licensing,

(c) section 17 (traffic regulation on special roads), section 25 (pedestrian crossings), Part V (traffic signs) and Part VI (speed limits) of the Road Traffic Regulation Act 1984,

(d) the Road Traffic Act 1988 and the Road Traffic Offenders Act 1988,

(e) the Vehicle Excise and Registration Act 1994,

(f) the Road Traffic (New Drivers) Act 1995, and

(g) the Goods Vehicles (Licensing of Operators) Act 1995.

Regulation of proper hours or periods of work by persons engaged in the carriage of passengers or goods by road.

The conditions under which international road transport services for passengers or goods may be undertaken.

Regulation of the instruction of drivers of motor vehicles.

Exceptions

The subject-matter of sections 39 and 40 (road safety information and training) and 157 to 159 (payments for treatment of traffic casualties) of the Road Traffic Act 1988.

E2. Rail transport

Provision and regulation of railway services.
Rail transport security.
The subject-matter of the Channel Tunnel Act 1987.
The subject-matter of the Railway Heritage Act 1996.

Exceptions

Grants so far as relating to railway services; but this exception does not apply in relation to—
   (a) the subject-matter of section 63 of the Railways Act 1993 (government financial assistance where railway administration orders made),
   (b) "railway services" as defined in section 82(1)(b) of the Railways Act 1993 (carriage of goods by railway), or
   (c) the subject-matter of section 136 of the Railways Act 1993 (grants and subsidies).

Interpretation

"Railway services" has the meaning given by section 82 of the Railways Act 1993 (excluding the wider meaning of "railway" given by section 81(2) of that Act).

E3. Marine transport

The subject-matter of—
   (a) the Coastguard Act 1925,
   (b) the Hovercraft Act 1968, except so far as relating to the regulation of noise and vibration caused by hovercraft,
   (c) the Carriage of Goods by Sea Act 1971,
   (d) section 2 of the Protection of Wrecks Act 1973 (prohibition on approaching dangerous wrecks),
   (e) the Merchant Shipping (Liner Conferences) Act 1982,
   (f) the Dangerous Vessels Act 1985,
   (g) the Aviation and Maritime Security Act 1990, other than Part I (aviation security),
   (h) the Carriage of Goods by Sea Act 1992,
   (i) the Merchant Shipping Act 1995,
   (j) the Shipping and Trading Interests (Protection) Act 1995, and
   (k) sections 24 (implementation of international agreements relating to protection of wrecks), 26 (piracy) and 27 and 28 (international bodies concerned with maritime matters) of the Merchant Shipping and Maritime Security Act 1997.
Navigational rights and freedoms.
Financial assistance for shipping services which start or finish or both outside Scotland.

Exceptions

Ports, harbours, piers and boatslips, except in relation to the matters reserved by virtue of paragraph (d), (f), (g) or (i).
Regulation of works which may obstruct or endanger navigation.
The subject-matter of the Highlands and Islands Shipping Services Act 1960 in relation to financial assistance for bulk freight services.

E4. Air transport

Regulation of aviation and air transport, including the subject matter of-
   (a) the Carriage by Air Act 1961
   (b) the Carriage by Air (Supplementary Provisions) Act 1962,
   (c) the Carriage by Air and Road Act 1979 so far as relating to carriage by air,
   (d) the Civil Aviation Act 1982,
   (e) the Aviation Security Act 1982,
   (f) the Airports Act 1986, and
   (g) sections 1 (endangering safety at aerodromes) and 48 (powers in relation to certain aircraft) of the Aviation and Maritime Security Act 1990,
and arrangements to compensate or repatriate passenger in the events of an air transport operator's insolvency.

Exceptions

The subject-matter of the following sections of the Civil Aviation Act 1982—
   (a) section 25 (Secretary of State's power to provide aerodromes),
   (b) section 30 (provision of aerodromes and facilities at aerodromes by local authorities),

(c) section 31 (Power to carry on ancillary business in connection with local authority aerodromes).

(d) section 34 (financial assistance for certain aerodromes),

(e) section 35 (facilities for consultation at certain aerodromes),

(f) section 36 (health control at Secretary of State's aerodromes and aerodromes of Civil Aviation Authority), and

(g) Section 41 to 43 and 50 (powers in relation to land exercisable in connection with civil aviation) where land is to be or was acquired for the purpose of airport development or expansion.

The subject-matter of Part II (transfer of airport undertakings of local authorities), sections 63 and 64 (airport byelaws) and 66 (functions of operators of designated airports as respects abandoned vehicles) of the Airports Act 1986.

The subject-matter of sections 59 (acquisition of land and rights over land) and 60 (disposal of compulsorily acquired land)of the Airports Act 1986 where land is to be or was acquired for the purpose of airport development of expansion.

E5. Other matters

Transport of radioactive material,

Technical specifications for public passenger transport for disabled persons, including the subject-matter of—

(a) section 125(7) and (8) of the Transport Act 1985 (Secretary of States guidance and con- sultation with the Disabled Persons Transport Advisory Committee), and

(b) Part V of the Disability Discrimination Act 1995 (public transport).

Regulation of the carriage of dangerous goods.

Interpretation

"Radioactive material" has the same meaning as in section 1(1) of the Radioactive Material (Road Transport)Act 1991.

Head F—Social Security

F1. Social Security Schemes

Schemes supported from central or local funds which provide assistance for social security purposes to or in respect of individuals by way of benefits.

Requiring persons to—

(a) establish and administer schemes providing assistance for social security purposes to or in respect of individuals, or

(b) make payments to or in respect of such schemes and to keep records and supply information in connection with such schemes.

The circumstances in which a person is liable to maintain himself or another for the purposes of the enactments relating to social security and the Child Support Acts 1991 and 1995.

The subject-matter of the Vaccine Damage Payment Scheme.

Illustrations

National Insurance: Social Fund: administration and funding of housing benefit and council tax benefit; recovery of benefits for accident, injury of disease from persons paying damages; deductions from benefits for the purpose of meeting an individual's debts; sharing information between government departments for the purposes of the enactments relating to social security; making decisions for the purposes of schemes mentioned in the reservation and appeals against such decisions.

Exceptions

The subject-matter of Part II of the Social Work (Scotland)Act 1968 (social welfare services), section 2 of the Chronically Sick and Disabled Persons Act 1970 (provision of welfare services), section 50 of the Children Art 1975 (payments towards maintenance of children), section 15 of the Enterprise and New Towns (Scotland)Act 1990 (industrial injuries benefit), and section 22 (promotion of welfare of children in need), 29 and 30 (advice and assistance for young persons formerly looked after by local authorities) of the Children (Scotland) Act 1995.

Interpretation

"Benefit" includes pensions, allowances, grants, loans and any other form of financial assistance. Providing assistance for social security purposes to or in respect of individuals includes (among other things) providing assistance to or in respect of individuals—

(a) who qualify by reason of old age, survivorship, disability, sickness, incapacity, injury, unemployment, maternity or the care of children or others needing care,

(b) who qualify by reason of low income, or

(c) in relation to their housing costs or liabilities for local taxes.

F2. Child support

The subject-matter of the Child Support Acts 1991 and 1995.

Exception

The subject-matter of section 1 to 7 of the Family Law (Scotland) Act 1985 (aliment)

Interpretation

In section 30(2) of the Child Support Act 1991 (collection of payments other than child support maintenance)is not in force on the principal appointed day, it is to be treated for the purposes of this reservation as if it were.

F3. Occupational and personal pensions

The regulation of occupational pension schemes and personal pension schemes, including the obligations of the trustees or managers of such schemes.

Provision about pensions payable to, or in respect of, any persons, except—

(a) the persons referred to in section 81(3),

(b) in relation to a Scottish public authority with mixed functions or no reserved functions, persons who are or have been a member of the public body, the holder of the public officer, or a member of the staff of the body, holder or office.

The subject-matter of the Pensions (Increase) Act 1971.

Schemes for the payment of pensions which are listed in Schedule 2 to the Act, except those mentioned in Paragraph graphs 38A and 38AB.

Where pension payable to or in respect of any class of persons under a public service pension scheme is covered by this reservation, so is making provision in their case—

(a) for compensation for loss of office or employment, for their office or employment being] affected by constitutional changes, or circumstances arising from such changes, in any territory or territories or for loss or diminution of emoluments, or

(b) for benefits in respect of death or incapacity resulting from injury or disease.

"Pension" includes; gratuities and allowance.

F4. War pensions

Schemes for the payment of pensions for or in respect of persons who have a disablement or have died in consequence of service as member of the armed forces of the Crown.

The subject-matter of any scheme under the Personal Injuries (Emergency Provisions) Act 1939, section 3 to 5 and 7 of the Pensions (Navy, Army, Air Force and Mercantile Marine)Act 1939 or section 1 of the Polish Resettlement Act 1947.

Illustration

The provision of pensions under the Naval, Military and Air Forces Etc. (Disablement and Death) Service Pensions Order 1983.

Interpretation

"Pension" includes grants, allowances, supplements and gratuities.

Head G—Regulation of the Professions

G1. Architects

Regulation of the profession of architect.

G2. Health Professions

Exceptions

The subject-matter of—

(a) section 21 of the National Health Service (Scotland)Act 1978(requirement of suitable experience for medical practitioners), and

(b) section 25 of that Act (arrangements for the provisions of general dental services), so far as it relates to vocational training and disciplinary proceedings.

Interpretation
"The health professions" means the professions regulated by-
(a) the Pharmacy Act 1954,
(b) the Professions Supplementary to Medicine Act 1960,
(c) the Veterinary Surgeons Act 1996.
(d) the Medical Act 1983,
(e) the Dentists Act 1984,
(f) the Opticians Act 1989,
(g) the Osteopaths Act 1993,
(h) the Chiropractors Act 1994,and
(i) the Nurses, Midwives and Health Visitors Act 1997.

G3. Auditors
Regulation of the profession of auditor.

Head H—Employment

H1. Employment and industrial relations
Employment rights and duties and industrial relations, including the subject-matter of—
(a) the Employers' Liability(Compulsory Insurance) Act 1969.
(b) the Employment Agencies Act 1973,
(c) the Pneumoconiosis etc.(Worker's Compensation) Act 1979,
(d) the Transfer of Undertakings (Protection of Employment) Regulations 1981,
(e) the Trade Union and Labour Relations (Consolidation) Act 1992,
(f) the Industrial Tribunals Act 1996
(g) the Employment Rights Act 1996, and
(h) the National Minimum Wages Act 1998.

Exception
The subject-matter of the Agricultural Wages (Scotland) Act 1949.

[1]H2. Health and safety
The subject-matter of Part I of the Health and Safety at Work etc. Act 1974.
The Health and Safety Commission, the Health and Safety Executive and the Employment Medical Advisory Service.

Interpretation
For the purposes of the reservation of the subject-matter of Part I of the Health and Safety at Work etc. Act 1974—
(a) "work" and "at work" in that Part are to be taken to have the meaning they have on the principal appointed day;
(b) that subject-matter includes—
process fire precautions;
(i) fire precautions in relation to petroleum and petroleum spirit;
(i) fire safety on construction sites, ships and hovercraft, in mines and on offshore installations; and
(ii) fire safety on any other premises which, on the principal appointed day, are of a description specified in Part I of Schedule 1 to the Fire Certificates (Special Premises) Regulations 1976 but does not include any other aspect of fire safety.

NOTE
As amended by S.I. 1999 No. 1749, art. 6. Effective July 1, 1999.

H3. Job search and support
The subject-matter of—
(a) the Disabled Persons (Employment) Act 1944,and
(b) the Employment and Training Act 1973, except so far as relating to training for employment.

Exception
The subject-matter of-

(a) section 8 to 10A of the Employment and Training Act 1973 (career services), and
(b) the following section of Part I of the Enterprise and New Towns (Scotland) Act 1990 (Scottish Enterprise and Highlands and Islands Enterprises)-
    (i) section 2(3)(c)(arrangements for the purpose of assisting persons to establish themselves as self-employed persons), and
    (ii) section 12 (disclosure of information).

Head J—Health and Medicines

J1. Abortion

Abortion.

J2. Xenotransplantation

Xenotransplantation.

J3. Embryology, surrogacy and genetics

Surrogacy arrangements, within the meaning of the Surrogacy Arrangements Act 1985, including the subject-matter of that Act.
The subject-matter of the Human Fertilisation and Embryology Act 1990.
Human genetics.

J4. Medicines, medical supplies and poisons

The subject-matter of—
    (a) the Medicines Act 1968, the Marketing Authorisations for Veterinary Medicinal Products Regulations 1994 and the Medicines for Human Use (Marketing Authorisations Etc.) Regulations 1994,
    (b) the Poisons Act 1972,and
    (c) the Biological Standards Act 1975.
Regulation of prices charged for medical supplies or medicinal products which (in either case) are supplied for the purposes of the health service established under section 1 of the National Health Services (Scotland) Act 1978.

Interpretation

"Medical supplies" has the same meaning as in section 49(3) of the National Health Service (Scotland)Act 1978. "Medicinal products" has the same meaning as in section 130(1) of the Medicines Act 1968.

J5. Welfare foods

Schemes made by regulations under section 13 of the Social Security Act 1988 (schemes for distribution of welfare foods).

Head K—Media and Culture

K1. Broadcasting

The subject-matter of the Broadcasting Act 1990 and the Broadcasting Act 1996.
The British Broadcasting Corporation.

K2. Public lending right

The subject-matter of the Public Lending Right Act 1979.

K3. Government indemnity Scheme

The subject-matter of section 16 and 16A of the National Heritage Act 1980 (public indemnities for objects on loan to museums, art galleries etc).

K4. Property accepted in satisfaction of tax

The subject-matter of sections 8 and 9 of the National Heritage Act 1980 (payments to Inland Revenue in respect of property accepted in satisfaction of tax, and disposal of such property).

Head L—Miscellaneous

L1. Judicial remuneration

Determination of the remuneration of-

(a) judge of the Court of Session,
(b) sheriffs principal and sheriffs,
(c) members of the Lands Tribunal for Scotland, and
(d) the Chairman of the Scottish Land Court.

L2. Equal opportunities

Equal opportunities, including the subject-matter of-
(a) the Equal Pay Act 1970,
(b) the Sex Discrimination Act 1975,
(c) the Race Relations Act 1976,and
(d) the Disability Discrimination Act 1995.

Exceptions
The encouragement (other than by prohibition or regulation) of equal opportunities, and in particular of the observance of the equal opportunity requirements.
Imposing duties on—
(a) any office-holder in the Scottish Administration, or any Scottish public authority with mixed functions or no reserved functions, to make arrangements with a view to securing that the functions of the office-holder or authority are carried out with due regard to the need to meet the equal opportunity requirements, or
(b) any cross-border public authority to make arrangements with a view to securing that its Scottish functions are carried out with due regard to the need to meet the equal opportunity requirements.

Interpretation
"Equal opportunities" means the prevention, elimination or regulation of discrimination between persons on grounds of sex or marital status, on racial grounds, or on grounds of disability, age, sexual orientation, language or social origin, or of other personal attributes, including beliefs or opinions, such as religious beliefs or political opinions. "Equal opportunity requirements" means the requirements of the law for the time being relating to equal opportunities. "Scottish functions" means functions which are exercisable in or as regards Scotland and which do not relate to reserved matters.

L3. Control of weapons

Control of nuclear, biological land chemical weapons and other weapons of mass destruction.

L4. Ordnance survey

The subject-matter of the Ordnance Survey Act 1841.

L5. Time

Timescales, time zones and the subject-matter of the Summer Time Act 1972.
The calendar, units of time; the date of Easter.

Exceptions
The computation of periods of time
The subject-matter of—
(a) section 1 of the Banking and Financial Dealings Act 1971 (bank holidays), and
(b) the Term and Quarter Days (Scotland) Act 1990.

L6. Outer space

Regulation of activities in outer space.

PART III

GENERAL PROVISIONS

Scottish public authorities

1.—(1) This Schedule does not reserve any Scottish public authority if some of its functions relate to reserved matters and some do not, unless it is a cross-border public authority.

(2) Sub-paragraph (1) has effect as regards—

(a) the constitution of the authority, including its establishment and dissolution, its assets and liabilities and its funding and receipts,

(b) conferring or removing any functions specifically exercisable in relation to the authority.

(3) Sub-paragraph (2)(b) does not apply to any function which is specifically exercisable in relation to a particular function of the authority if the particular function relates to reserved matters.

(4) An authority to which this paragraph applies is referred to in this Act as a Scottish public authority with mixed functions.

2. Paragraph 1 of Part I of this Schedule does not reserve any Scottish public authority with functions none of which relate to reserved matters (referred to in this Act as a Scottish public authority with no reserved functions).

Reserved bodies

3.—(1) The reservation of any body to which this paragraph applies has effect to reserve—

(a) its constitution, including its establishment and dissolution, its assets and liabilities and its funding and receipts,

(b) conferring functions on it or removing functions from it,

(c) conferring or removing any functions specifically exercisable in relation to it.

(2) This paragraph applies to—

(a) a body reserved by name by Part II of this Schedule,

(b) each of the councils reserved by Section C12 of that Part,

(c) the Commission for Racial Equality, the Equal Opportunities Commission and the Disability Rights Commission.

Financial assistance to industry

4.—(1) This Schedule does not reserve giving financial assistance to commercial activities for the purpose of promoting or sustaining economic development or employment.

(2) Sub-paragraph (1)—

(a) does not apply to giving financial assistance to any activities in pursuance of a power exercisable only in relation to activities which are reserved,

(b) does not apply to Part I of this Schedule, except paragraph 9, or to a body to which paragraph 3 of this Part of this Schedule applies,

(c) is without prejudice to the exceptions from the reservations in Sections E2 and E3 of Part II of this Schedule.

(3) Sub-paragraph (1) does not affect the question whether any matter other than financial assistance to which that sub-paragraph applies is reserved.

Interpretation

5.—(1) References in this Schedule to the subject-matter of any enactment are to be read as references to the subject-matter of that enactment as it has effect on the principal appointed day or, if it ceased to have effect at any time within the period ending with that day and beginning with the day on which this Act is passed, as it had effect immediately before that time.

(2) Subordinate legislation under section 129(1) may, in relation to the operation of this Schedule at any time before the principal appointed day, modify the references to that day in sub-paragraph (1).

DEFINITIONS
"body": s.126(1).
"Community law": s.126(9).
"confer": s.126(1).
"the Convention rights": s.126(1).
"cross-border public authority": s.88(5).

"enactment": ss.113(6), 126(1).
"functions": s.126(1).
"government department": s.126(1).
"the Human Rights Convention": s.126(1).
"international obligations": s.126(10).
"legislative competence": s.29.
"Minister of the Crown": s.126(1).
"occupational pension scheme": s.126(1).
"office-holder in the Scottish Administration": s.126(7).
"the Parliament": s.126(1).
"personal pension scheme": s.126(1).
"principal appointed day": s.126(1).
"property": s.126(1).
"Scotland": s.126(1), (2).
"Scottish public authority with mixed functions or no reserved functions": paras. 1, 2 of Pt. III.
"Scottish seal": s.2(6).
"staff of the Parliament": para. 3 of Sched. 2.

GENERAL NOTE

This Schedule, which is given effect by s.30, is an important element in the scheme adopted in the Scotland Act for the definition of the legislative competence of the Scottish Parliament and (in large measure) the competence too of the Scottish Executive. The other rules are contained in s.29, s.30 itself and Sched. 4 in relation to the Parliament and ss.52–54, 63 in relation to the Scottish Executive.

For a general introduction to the rules of legislative competence, see the General Note to s.29. For the power to amend Sched. 5 and thus the extent of the "reserved matters" which it defines, see the General Note to s.30.

Schedule 5 consists of three parts. Part I sets out some "General Reservations"; Pt. II the "Specific Reservations"; and Pt. III what are called "General Provisions". Part III is important because of the assistance it gives for the interpretation of Parts I and II but also because of its contributions to the definition of the position of public authorities in Scotland.

The annotations on the paragraphs in Pts. I and II provide a brief description of the reservation made by each paragraph, together with the stipulated exceptions from reservation where applicable. In addition, the annotations contain a note on "Executive devolution" where, in relation to the paragraphs concerned, powers have been executively devolved by Order in Council under s.63. At the time of writing, this is a reference to the arrangements made by the Scotland Act 1998 (Transfer of Functions to the Scottish Ministers etc.) Order 1999 (S.I. 1999 No. 1750) under which specified functions of a Minister of the Crown became exercisable instead by the Scottish Ministers; or concurrently exercisable by the Scottish Ministers; or exercisable subject to the arrangement of or consultation with the Scottish Minister. The extent of such executive devolution is noted in relation to each relevant paragraph.

PART I

Paras. 1–5

Para. 2(5) was added by the Scotland Act 1998 (Modifications of Schedules 4 and 5) Order 1999 (S.I. 1999 No.1749)).

These paragraphs reserve certain "aspects of the constitution", subject to the exceptions set out in paras. 2–5 (see also Pt.III para.2). Thus the reservation of the Crown by para. 1(a) does not reserve the exercise of prerogative or other executive functions (transferred by s.53); or offices in the Scottish Administration. Honours and dignities (and the functions of the Lord Lyon so far as relating to the granting of arms *are* reserved, but not the judicial functions of the Lord Lyon. The management of the Crown Estate *is* reserved (see the Crown Estate Act 1961) but Crown property (property held in right of the Crown, etc.), including the foreshore, is *not* reserved (para. 3(1)). Equally the ultimate superiority of the Crown has not been reserved (para.3(2)), enabling the passing of the Abolition of Feudal Tenure etc. (Scotland) Act 2000.

On the other hand hereditary revenues, the royal arms and standard, and the compulsory acquisition of property held or used by a Minister of the Crown or government department *are* reserved (para. 3(3)). Property held by Her Majesty in Her private capacity (e.g. the Balmoral estate) is *not* reserved (para. 4(1)) but Crown consent is required (by virtue of para. 4(2)) where the Scottish Parliament proposes to legislate (see Standing Orders, Rule 9.11). The use of the Scottish Seal is not reserved (para. 5 and see s.38).

Para. 6

This paragraph was amended by the Scotland Act 1998 (Modifications of Schedule 4 and 5) Order 1999 (S.I. 1999 No.1749) to enable the Scottish Parliament to legislate for making payments to political parties to assist MSPs. See also s.97 of the Act and the modification made to Sched.4 para. 4(2).

Para 7

This reserves international relations etc. but, importantly, not the observing and implementation of international, ECHR or EC obligations. The non-reservation of assisting Ministers of the Crown enables, *inter alia* the participation of members of the Scottish Executive in meetings of the EC Council of Ministers.

Para 8

This reserves the civil service (see also s.51), with the exception of the matters relating to the court officials and procurators fiscal referred to.

EXECUTIVE DEVOLUTION

TRANSFERRED FUNCTIONS

1. The function of the Secretary of State to provide for procedures for the determination of rates of pay and other conditions of employment for prison officers in Scotland, under the Criminal Justice and Public Order Act 1994, s.128.

Para 9

This reserves the defence of the realm, as extended by subpara. (1)(b)-(e) but subject to the exceptions in respect of civil defence and sea fishing.

EXECUTIVE DEVOLUTION

TRANSFERRED FUNCTIONS

1. The Secretary of State's functions to give directions in connection with the charitable property of reserve forces units, under the Reserve Forces Act 1996, Sched. 5 (paras. 10, 12).

CONSULTATIVE FUNCTIONS

1. The functions of the Secretary of State and the Lord Chancellor to appoint the chairmen and ordinary members of reserve forces appeal tribunals, and determine their terms of appointment, under the Reserve Forces Act 1996, ss.90(1), (3) and 91(1), (3).

PART II

This Part of the Schedule lists the "specific reservations" and does so under Heads A to L, with provision made under each Head in numbered Sections. The statutory preliminary notes on Pt. II are important and especially note 3 which explains that any illustrations, exceptions or interpretation provisions in a Section relate only to that Section.

SECTION A1

This reservation does not, of course, affect the Scottish Parliament's (limited) tax-varying powers, expressly provided for in Part IV of the Act. The Scottish Parliament is also responsible for allocating resources for Scotland, either raised through its tax-varying powers or from its assigned budget.

EXECUTIVE DEVOLUTION

TRANSFERRED FUNCTIONS

1. The Secretary of State's functions under the Taxes Management Act 1970, ss.2(3), 2(6), 3(4), 4(1), (4), 4A(1) and 56B(1): the functions, *inter alia*, to appoint Scottish General Commissioners, to vary tax area boundaries, and to consent to regulations made by the Lord Chancellor concerning jurisdiction in tax appeals.

2. The Secretary of State's functions under the Income and Corporation Taxes Act 1988, ss.79(4) and 79(8): the function, *inter alia*, of approving a body as an "approved local enterprise agency".

3. The Secretary of State's function to consent to regulations by the Lord Chancellor providing for Commissioners to hold office by a different name, under s.75(1) of the Finance (No.2) Act 1992.

4. The Secretary of State's functions under the Value Added Tax Act 1994, Sched. 12 (paras. 2, 3(2), (4), (5), 7(8), 9): the functions, *inter alia*, of being consulted by the Lord Chancellor on the appointment of the President of VAT tribunals and on procedural rules for VAT tribunals.

5. The function of providing premises for the purposes of carrying out the functions of VAT and duties tribunals (established under the Value Added Tax Act 1994, Sched. 12 (para. 1)) (non-statutory function).

SECTION A2
The reservation includes matters relating to the determination of currency denominations, legal tender and the issue of coins/ notes.

SECTION A3
This reservation, along with Section A4, is intended to preserve common markets in the finance and investment sectors. Section A3 reserves all matters relating to financial services: including the regulation of financial advisers, banks, building societies, friendly societies, collective investment vehicles (such as unit trusts and open-ended investment companies) and insurers.

Exception
The determination of bank holidays, under s.1 of the Banking and Financial Dealings Act 1971, is devolved (see also Section L5).

EXECUTIVE DEVOLUTION

TRANSFERRED FUNCTIONS
1. The Secretary of State's function to make rules in connection with the functions of assessors, under the Insurance Brokers (Registration) Act 1977, s.20.
2. The Secretary of State's function to appoint chairmen to building society appeal tribunals, under the Building Societies Act 1986, s.47(2)(a).
3. The Secretary of State's function of being consulted by the Lord Chancellor on the appointment of legally qualified members to the Financial Services Tribunal, under the Financial Services Act 1986, s.96(2)(a).
4. The Secretary of State's function to be consulted by the Lord Chancellor on the appointment of chairmen to appeal tribunals and to make certain procedural rules, under the Banking Act 1987, ss.28(2)(a), 30(4).
5. The Secretary of State's function to make certain provisions in connection with the conduct of certain arbitration proceedings, under the Multilateral Investment Guarantee Agency Act 1988, s.6.
6. The Secretary of State's function to be consulted by the Lord Chancellor on the appointment of certain appeal tribunal chairmen and to make certain regulations in connection with appeals procedure, under the Friendly Societies Act 1992, ss.59(2)(a), 60(4).
7. The Secretary of State's functions under the following subordinate legislation: Building Societies Appeal Tribunal (Scottish Appeals) Regulations 1987 (S.I. 1987 No. 891), reg. 6; the Banking Appeal Tribunal (Scottish Appeals) Regulations 1987 (S.I. 1987 No. 1336), reg. 6.

SECTION A4
This reservation includes all forms of dealing in securities and other financial instruments, as well as foreign exchange and all matters relating to insider dealing. This Section complements the reservation of financial services in Section A3.

SECTION A5
The Money Laundering Regulations 1993 (S.I.1993, No.1933) regulate certain types of business with a view to preventing money laundering: the illegitimate use and control of the proceeds of criminal conduct. The reservation applies to the regulation of business in general, and not merely of the financial sector. Criminal law matters in relation to money laundering are *not* in general reserved. (Certain statutory offences involving the money laundering of the proceeds of drug trafficking are reserved, however, under Section B1).

SECTION B1
This Section reserves the criminal law insofar as it applies to the possession, cultivation, production, supply, import and export of drugs, as well as to matters relating to drug trafficking. The subject-matter of the following enactments is reserved:

(i) The Misuse of Drugs Act 1971: makes provision in relation to the control of dangerous/ harmful drugs, and related matters. It also provides for the establishment of the Advisory Council on the Misuse of Drugs.

(ii) The Criminal Justice (International Co-operation) Act 1990, ss.12–14: makes provision, *inter alia*, in relation to the manufacture/supply of certain substances while knowing/ suspecting that the substance is to be used in the unlawful production of a controlled drug.

(iii) The Criminal Law (Consolidation) (Scotland) Act 1995, Part V: creates certain offences, and confers powers of search/investigation, in relation to drug trafficking.

(iv) The Proceeds of Crime (Scotland) Act 1995 (insofar as relating to drug trafficking): makes provision for the forfeiture of things used in the commission of crime, and the confiscation of the proceeds of crime.

Other drug-related matters are devolved: including education, health, social work and the police.

EXECUTIVE DEVOLUTION

TRANSFERRED FUNCTIONS

1. The Secretary of State's functions under the Misuse of Drugs Act 1971, Sched. 3 (paras. 1(1)(b),4,13(1)(b), 17): the function, *inter alia*, to appoint members to Scottish tribunals and to make procedural rules for Scottish tribunals.

SECTION B2

This Section reserves matters relating to the obtaining, holding, processing, disclosure and free movement of personal information. The subject-matter of the following enactments is reserved:

(i) The Data Protection Act 1998: broadened the provisions of the Data Protection Act 1994, which was repealed. In particular, the 1998 Act extended data protection legislation to include manually held as well as electronic records, and also "accessible records": certain records in the social work, housing, health and education sectors. The 1998 Act also made provision in connection with the office of Data Protection Registrar.

Note: Those sections of the 1998 Act not already in force came into force on March 31, 2000, under the Data Protection Act 1998 (Commencement) Order 2000 (S.I. 2000 No.183), with the exception of s.56 (prohibition of requirement as to production of certain records). *All* provisions of the Act are affected by this reservation, however, whether or not they were in force on the principal appointed day (July 1, 1999).

(ii) Council Directive 95/46/EC: requires provision to be made for the protection of individuals with regard to the use of personal data, and on the free movement of such data. The Directive, largely implemented by the Data Protection Act 1998, requires, *inter alia*, that specific conditions are imposed on the processing of certain data.

EXECUTIVE DEVOLUTION

TRANSFERRED FUNCTIONS

1. The Secretary of State's function to be consulted by the Lord Chancellor on the appointment of chairmen and deputy chairmen to the Data Protection Tribunal, under the Data Protection Act 1984, ss.3(3)(a)-(b).

2. The Secretary of State's function to be consulted by the Lord Chancellor on appointments of chairmen and deputy chairmen to the Data Protection Tribunal, under the Data Protection Act 1998, s.6(4)(a), (b).

SECTION B3

This reservation covers electoral law in relation to elections of the UK and Scottish Parliaments, and European Parliamentary elections. This includes provisions on the franchise, system of voting, delimitation of electoral boundaries and rules of candidature for these elections. In particular, this Section reserves the subject-matter of the following enactments:

(i) the European Parliamentary Elections Act 1978: provides for the election of UK MEPs, including the delimitation of electoral boundaries with respect to European Parliamentary elections.

(ii) the Representation of the People Acts 1983 and 1985: make provision for UK Parliamentary elections, including the franchise and the conduct of elections. (See also the Representation of the People Act 2000.)

(iii) the Parliamentary Constituencies Act 1986: makes provision for Boundary Commissions to review the distribution of UK Parliamentary seats, and related matters.

It will be noticed that this Section also reserves the subject-matter of electoral provisions in the Scotland Act 1998, such as those contained in ss.2–14, although these matters will also be outwith the legislative competence of the Scottish Parliament under s.29(2)(c) and Sched. 4 (para. 4) of the Act.

Electoral law in relation to local authority elections is not reserved, except insofar as concerning the franchise.

EXECUTIVE DEVOLUTION

Functions in relation to elections were not devolved by S.I. 1999 No.1750. Extensive provision has, however, been made for the transfer of responsibilities by the Scotland Act 1998 (Agency Arrangements) (Specification) Order 1999 (S.I. 1999 No.1512). See s.93 of the Act.

SECTION B4

This Section reserves matters relating to the manufacture, possession, handling, purchase or acquisition, sale, distribution and transfer of firearms. In particular, the subject-matter of the following enactments is reserved:

(i) the Firearms Act 1968.

(ii) the Firearms Act 1982.

(iii) the Firearms (Amendment) Act 1988.

(iv) the Firearms (Amendment) Act 1992.

(v) the Firearms (Amendment) Act 1997.

These enactments provide, *inter alia*, for certain criminal offences in relation to the handling/ purchase/ distribution of certain firearms and imitation firearms; for the issue of firearms certificates; for the regulation of firearms dealers; and for the licensing and regulation of pistol clubs.

The Section also covers subordinate legislation made under these enactments, such as the Firearms (Scotland) Rules 1989 (S.I.1989 No.889.)

EXECUTIVE DEVOLUTION

TRANSFERRED FUNCTIONS

1. The Secretary of State's function to grant/revoke/vary authority permitting the possession of prohibited weapons and ammunition, under the Firearms Act 1968, ss.5, 12(2).

2. The Secretary of State's functions to approve certain rifle and pistol clubs and to grant museums firearms licenses, and related powers, under the Firearms (Amendment) Act 1988, ss.15, 19, and the Schedule (except para. 3(1)(a)).

3. The Secretary of State's function to designate a place at which a firearm is to be kept and used in accordance with a condition in a firearms certificate, under the Firearms (Amendment) Act 1997, s.7(3).

SECTION B5

This reservation covers certain matters relating to entertainment, including the licensing of premises for film exhibition, the classification of films for public exhibition and the classification of video recordings. (Broadcasting is covered separately, under Section K1). In particular, Section B5 covers the subject-matter of the following enactments:

(i) the Video Recordings Act 1984: provides for the classification and labelling of video recordings and the supply/ possession of non-classified recordings.

(ii) the Cinemas Act 1985, ss.1–3, 5, 16: provides for the licensing of premises for film exhibition.

The reservation also covers the classification of films for public exhibition, as currently carried out by the non-statutory body, the British Board of Film Classification.

EXECUTIVE DEVOLUTION

TRANSFERRED FUNCTIONS

1. The Secretary of State's function to issue/revoke certificates for non-profit organisations, under the Cinemas Act 1985, ss.6(6), (7).

SECTION B6

This reservation covers, *inter alia*, the law (largely statutory) in relation to entry to the UK, the granting of all forms of asylum, the status/ legal capacity of non-British citizens in the UK, the granting of work permits and the free movement of persons within the EEA. This Section includes the subject-matter of the following enactments:

(i) the Immigration Act 1971 (as amended).
(ii) the British Nationality Act 1981.
(iii) the Immigration (Carriers' Liability) Act 1987.
The granting of passports and other travel documents, a prerogative power, is also covered.

EXECUTIVE DEVOLUTION

TRANSFERRED FUNCTIONS
The Secretary of State's function to appoint and to give instructions to medical inspectors, under the Immigration Act 1971, Sched. 2 (para. 1(2), (3)).

SECTION B7
Scientific Procedures on Live Animals:
The reservation covers the subject-matter of the Animals (Scientific Procedures) Act 1986. This enactment provides for the granting of licences to persons/programmes with respect to the carrying out of certain procedures on live animals. The 1986 Act makes it an offence to carry out a procedure, without the required licenses, which may cause an animal pain, distress or lasting harm. The Act regulates the premises where such work can be carried out, and provides for the breeding of animals for scientific purposes. There is also provision for the appointment of inspectors and for the Animal Procedures Committee.
Note that the use of viable animal tissues/ organs for transplantation into humans is dealt with separately, under Section J2 (Xenotransplantation). General matters of animal health/ welfare are addressed in the Animal Health Act 1981, the subject-matter of which is *not* reserved.

SECTION B8
This reservation covers national security, official secrets and special powers and provisions for dealing with terrorism. The Section also reserves the interception of communications, but not the subject-matter of Part III of the Police Act 1997 (provisions for the authorisation of interference with property) or surveillance not involving interference with property. In particular, the reservation covers the subject-matter of the following enactments:
(i) the Interception of Communications Act 1985: provides, *inter alia*, for the interception of communications, and the issue of warrants for this purpose.
(ii) the Official Secrets Act 1911: makes provisions on spying, defining certain locations, such as military establishments, as "prohibited places".
(iii) the Official Secrets Act 1920: makes further provision for the protection of "prohibited places".
(iv) the Official Secrets Act 1989: makes provision in relation to the disclosure of certain official information. The reservation does *not* cover, however, provisions in s.4(2) of the 1989 Act concerning the protection of information/documents, the disclosure of which would result in the commission of a crime, facilitate an escape, or otherwise prejudice the safekeeping of persons in legal custody, or impede the prevention/ detection of offences or the apprehension/ prosecution of suspected offenders.
The subject-matter of special statutory provisions on terrorism, such as the Suppression of Terrorism Act 1978, the Prevention of Terrorism (Temporary Provisions) Act 1989 and the Prevention of Terrorism (Additional Powers) Act 1996, is also reserved.
Note that the functions of the Security Service, the Secret Intelligence Service and the Government Communications Headquarters are reserved separately, in Part I (para 2(4)).

EXECUTIVE DEVOLUTION

TRANSFERRED FUNCTIONS
1. The Secretary of State's function to authorise the use of wireless telegraphy apparatus in order to disclose information for the purpose of preventing/detecting serious crime, under the Wireless Telegraphy Act 1949, s.5(b).
2. The Secretary of State's function to issue/renew/modify/cancel warrants requiring the interception of certain communications for the purpose of preventing/detecting serious crime, and to provide certain related safeguards, under the Interception of Communications Act 1985, ss.2, 4(3), (4), 5(1)(a), (2) and 6(1).
3. The Secretary of State's function to prescribe certain bodies, office-holders and others, for the purposes of the Official Secrets Act 1989, ss.7(5), 8(9), 12.
4. The Secretary of State's function to issue/renew/cancel certain warrants for the prevention/detection of serious crime, under the Intelligence Services Act 1994, ss5, 6(3), (4).

SHARED FUNCTIONS:
1. The Secretary of State's function to make grants in respect of expenses incurred by a police authority/ joint police board in connection with safeguarding national security, under the Police (Scotland) Act 1967, s.32A.
2. The Secretary of State's function to specify information to be excluded, on the grounds of national security, from a sewerage authority register, and to certify that certain powers of entry should not apply to specified Crown premises, under the Sewerage (Scotland) Act 1968, ss.37B, 55(4).
3. The Secretary of State's functions under the Control of Pollution Act 1974, ss.36(2B), 42A(1), 42A(2), 42A(4), 105(3C): the function, *inter alia*, to certify that, in the interests of national security, details of a discharge consent application should not be advertised, and to certify that certain powers of entry should not apply to specified Crown premises.
4. The Secretary of State's function to certify that, in the interests of national security, certain powers of entry should not apply to specified Crown premises, under the Water (Scotland) Act 1980, s.110A(4).
5. The Secretary of State's function to issue directions concerning the exclusion, in the interests of national security, of information from SEPA registers, and to certify that certain powers of entry should not apply to specified Crown premises, under the Environmental Protection Act 1990, ss.21(1),(2), (4), 65(1),(2), (4), 159(4).
6. The Secretary of State's function to direct that, on the grounds of national security, knowledge of a particular application, registration or authorisation should be restricted, under the Radioactive Substances Act 1993, ss.25(1), (2), 39(1).
7. The Secretary of State's function to give directions to a water/sewerage authority in the interests of national security, and to notify a person that certain actings should not be revealed, under the Local Government etc (Scotland) Act 1994, s.117(1),(2), (5).
8. The Secretary of State's function to express an opinion that disclosure of certain information would be contrary to the interests of national security, and to certify that certain powers of entry should not apply to specified Crown premises, under the Environment Act 1995, ss.113(2), (3), 115(5).

SECTION B9
This reservation covers the (largely statutory) regulation of betting, gaming and lotteries (including the National Lottery), along with the taxation of the proceeds of such activities. The Section includes, in particular, the subject-matter of the following enactments:
   (i) the Betting, Gaming & Lotteries Act 1963: provides, *inter alia*, for the granting of betting office licences and betting agency permits, as well as for the Horserace Totalisator Board (the "Tote").
   (ii) the Gaming Act 1986: provides, *inter alia*, for the establishment of the Gaming Board for Great Britain.
   (iii) the Lotteries and Amusements Act 1976: provides for the regulation of lotteries.
   (iv) the National Lottery etc. Act 1993: provides, *inter alia*, for the licensing of a body to run the National Lottery. The 1993 Act also makes provision for the distribution of lottery proceeds, in Scotland by bodies including the Scottish Arts Council and the Scottish Sports Council.
   (v) the National Lottery Act 1998: provides, *inter alia*, for the establishment of the New Opportunities Fund.

EXECUTIVE DEVOLUTION

TRANSFERRED FUNCTIONS:
1. The Secretary of State's functions to appoint members of the Horserace Betting Levy Appeal Tribunal for Scotland, and to vary licensing provisions for bookmakers/ betting offices etc, under s.29(2)(b), (4) and Sched. 1 (para. 20(1A)) of the Betting, Gaming and Lotteries Act 1963.
2. The Secretary of State's function to vary certain fees in connection with track betting licences and the registration of pool promoters, under s.42(2) of the Local Government (Scotland) Act 1966.
3. The Secretary of State's functions to impose and vary licensing regulations, under ss.22(3), (4), 48(5)(b) of the Gaming Act 1968.
4. The Secretary of State's functions to approve alternative uses for local lottery revenue, and to vary certain registration/ permit fees, under ss.7(4), 18(1)(d), (f) of the Lotteries and Amusements Act 1976.
5. Certain functions of the Secretary of State under the National Lottery etc Act 1993, ss. 26(1)-(2), as read with s.26A(2)(b); ss.26(3)-(4), as read with s.26A(1)(a); ss.29(1),(3),(4) &

(5), as read with s.29(6)(c)-(d); ss.35(3), s.43B(1) & 43C(1), as read with s.43CC(2)(b); ss.25C(1), 26(1), as read with s.26A(1)(a); ss.26(5), 27(1), (8), 43C(2),(4), (5); and Sched. 3A (para. 2(1)-(2)), as read with Sched. 3A (para. 2(6)(a)): including, *inter alia*, the function to give directions to the National Lotteries Charities Board, the New Opportunities Fund, or to the Trustees of the National Heritage Memorial Fund, in connection with the distribution of lottery money.

SHARED FUNCTIONS:
1. Certain functions of the Secretary of State under the National Lottery etc. Act 1993, ss.14, 25(5)(c),(d), (6), 34, 35(4), 39(3), 43(D)(3), including, *inter alia*, the function to receive annual reports/strategic plans/annual statements of accounts from the National Lottery Commission, distributing bodies, the National Lotteries Charities Board, the New Opportunities Fund etc.

CONSULTATIVE FUNCTIONS:
1. Certain functions of the Secretary of State under the National Lottery etc. Act 1993, ss.26(1) & (2), as read with s.26A(2)(a); s.26(3A), as read with s.26A(1)(b); ss.28, 43C(1), as read with s.43CC(2)(a); Sched. 3A (para 2(1)-(2)), as read with Sched. 3A (2(6)(b)); ss.29(1),(3),(4), (5), as read with, s.29(6)(a), (b); and Sched. 6A (1)-(2): including, *inter alia*, the function to give certain directions to the National Lottery Charities Board, the New Opportunities Fund, or to the Trustees of the National Heritage Memorial Fund, and to appoint certain members of the New Opportunities Fund.

SECTION B10
The reservation covers all matters relating to the exercise of emergency powers. This includes the subject-matter of the Emergency Powers Act 1920, which grants power to Her Majesty to declare a state of emergency and to make provisions to secure the essentials of life to the community: for securing food/ water/ fuel supplies, etc., and for the preservation of peace. The prerogative power to employ servicemen in extraordinary circumstances is also reserved.

EXECUTIVE DEVOLUTION

CONSULTATIVE FUNCTIONS:
1. Powers of the Secretary of State under s.117 of the Local Government etc (Scotland) Act 1994 (c.39) to give directions to water authorities for the mitigation of the effects of a civil emergency.

SECTION B11
The reservation covers all matters relating to extradition. In particular, this Section covers the subject-matter of the following enactments:
  (i) the Extradition Act 1989: consolidates and amends the Extradition Acts 1870–1935, and makes procedural provision for the extradition of persons to countries other than the Republic of Ireland.
  (ii) the Backing of Warrants Act 1965: provides for extradition to the Republic of Ireland.
UK provisions on extradition to the UK are also reserved.

EXECUTIVE DEVOLUTION

TRANSFERRED FUNCTIONS:
1. The Secretary of State's functions under the the Extradition Act 1989, ss.6(1)-(4), (6), (7), 7(1), (4), 8(4), 9(5), 11(1), 12, 13(1) & (4), 16(5), 20(2): the function, *inter alia*, of deciding whether a person should be returned to another country, of issuing an order for the surrender of a person, and related powers.

SECTION B12
This Section reserves the regulation of lieutenancies. Lord Lieutenants' functions are now largely ceremonial and include representing the Crown in a number of capacities: attending upon visiting Heads of State, presenting medals and colours, etc. The reservation covers the subject-matter of the Lieutenancies Act 1997, which provides, *inter alia*, for the division of Scotland for lieutenancy purposes, for the appointment/ removal of Lieutenants and for the functions/ privileges of the office.

EXECUTIVE DEVOLUTION

TRANSFERRED POWERS:
1. The Secretary of State's function to inform a Lord Lieutenant that Her Majesty does not approve of a proposed appointment to the position of Deputy Lieutenant, under the Lieutenancies Act 1997, s.2(4).

SECTION B13
This Section was added by the Scotland Act 1998 (Modifications of Schedules 4 and 5) Order 1999 (S.I. 1999 No.1749). It clarifies legislative competence in relation to pubic access to information by reserving it in general but then by excepting from the reservation information held by the Scottish Parliament, the Scottish Administration, the Parliamentary Corporation and public authorities with mixed or no reserved functions. That exception is, in turn, subject to a further exception in respect of information supplied by a Minister of the Crown or government department and held in confidence. Subject to that exception, the Scottish Parliament is free to legislate on access to information held by the Scottish bodies.

SECTION C1
This Section reserves all matters relating to the regulation of companies and business organisations, defined broadly to include any person (other than an individual) established for the purpose of carrying on any kind of business, whether or not for profit. Matters relating to, *inter alia*, companies (whether or not registered under the companies legislation), partnerships, building societies, friendly societies and European economic interest groupings (under Council Regulation No. 2137/85, Art.1) are therefore reserved. (The regulation of sole traders is not covered by the reservation). The reservation includes the creation, operation, regulation and dissolution of such 'business associations', and covers the subject matter of relevant statutory provisions, such as those contained in the Companies Act 1985.

Exception:
The creation, operation, regulation and dissolution of:
   (i) particular statutory public bodies, or statutory public bodies of a particular type: this exception permits the Scottish Parliament to establish public bodies *for devolved purposes*.
  (ii) charities: the regulation of matters relating to charities is devolved.

SECTION C2
This Section reserves most matters in relation to the insolvency and winding up of business associations. 'Business association' is defined as in Section C1, except that it does not include for these purposes any person whose estate may be sequestrated under the Bankruptcy (Scotland) Act 1985, such as a partnership, nor does it include statutory public bodies. Reserved matters include, *inter alia*, the circumstances in which a business association may be wound up voluntarily or by the courts, the grounds on which a petition for winding up may be presented, the persons who may initiate a winding up, the powers of the courts on hearing a petition for winding up and the liability of, for example, shareholders to contribute to the assets on a winding up.
The Section also reserves a number of matters in relation to all persons (not just business associations):
a. preferred/ preferential debts for the purposes of certain enactments and the preference of such debts over other debts in bankruptcy/ sequestration/ winding up.
b. the regulation of insolvency practitioners: including, in particular, provisions contained in Part XIII of the Insolvency Act 1986.
c. matters relating to the co-operation of insolvency courts.

Exceptions:
The following are excepted from the reservation, in relation to business associations:
i. matters relating to the actual process of winding up.
ii. the effect of winding up on diligence. In Scots law, diligences done within a certain time of the commencement of winding up are equalised so that all creditors are treated equally in the ranking of their claims.
iii. the avoidance and adjustment of prior transactions on winding up. It will thus be open to the Scottish Parliament to legislate in respect of transactions concluded before the winding up of a business association, to provide for them to be rendered void, or for some other appropriate remedy.

Matters relating to floating charges and receivers are not reserved, except in relation to preferential debts, the regulation of insolvency practitioners and the co-operation of insolvency courts. This exception includes the circumstances and effect of receivers' appointments.

SECTION C3
This section reserves all matters in relation to the regulation of anti-competitive practices and agreements, the abuse of a dominant position, and monopolies and mergers. Responsibility for competition policy thus remains with the President of the Board of Trade. The reservation covers the subject-matter of the Competition Act 1998 and includes the function of investigating any body/ person for the purposes of enforcing competition law.

Exception:
The regulation of particular practices in the Scottish legal profession, as defined. This includes regulation of the rules and organisations of the legal profession, where the regulation may affect competition in the provision of legal services.

SECTION C4
The reservation covers all matters relating to existing and future intellectual property and ancillary matters, including, *inter alia*, patents, design right, trade marks and copyright.

Exception:
The subject-matter of the Plant Varieties Act 1997, Pts. I, II: dealing with the proprietary rights of plant breeders, the licensing of certain plant use, the establishment of an appeals tribunal, and related matters.

EXECUTIVE DEVOLUTION

TRANSFERRED POWERS:
1. The Secretary of State's function to be consulted by the Lord Chancellor on the appointment of a chairman and 2 deputy chairmen to the Copyright Tribunal, and to be consulted by the Lord Chancellor on procedural rules for the Copyright Tribunal, under the Copyright, Designs and Patents Act 1988, ss.145(2), 150(1).
2. The Secretary of State's function to be consulted by the Lord Chancellor on the appointment (and removal from office) of persons to hear appeals, under the Trade Marks Act 1994, s.77(4).

SECTION C5
The reservation covers the control of movement of food, animals, plants and other items into and out of Scotland. In particular, this Section covers the subject-matter of the Import, Export and Customs Powers (Defence) Act 1939. The 1939 Act empowers the Secretary of State, *inter alia*, to prohibit/regulate the movement of goods to/from the UK/specified parts of the UK and to make provision to enforce such regulations. The reservation also covers the subject-matter of the Convention on International Trade in Endangered Species (CITES), and its associated enactments.

Exceptions:
The prohibition and regulation of the import/ export of:
  (i) food, animals, animal products, plants and plant products, but only for the purposes of protecting human, animal or plant health, animal welfare or the environment or observing or implementing obligations under the Common Agricultural Policy; and
  (ii) animal feed stuffs, fertilisers and pesticides, but only for the purposes of protecting human, animal or plant health or the environment.
These exceptions are in line with the general devolution of agriculture, fisheries, food and related matters.

SECTION C6
This reserves the regulation of sea fishing outside the Scottish zone (except by Scottish fishing bodies). See also the note on s.30(3).

SECTION C7
The reservation covers:
I. The regulation of the following matters:
  (a) the sale and supply of goods and services to consumers: including certain provisions of the Sale of Goods Act 1979, the Supply of Goods and Services Act 1982, the Unfair Contract Terms Act 1977 and the Unfair Terms in Consumer Contracts Regulations 1994.

(b) guarantees in relation to such goods and services.
(c) hire-purchase, including the subject-matter of Pt. III of the Hire Purchase Act 1964: including provisions contained in the Supply of Goods (Implied Terms) Act 1973. Part III of the 1964 Act deals with title to motor vehicles disposed of while subject to hire purchase agreements.
(d) trade descriptions, except in relation to food: covers all matters relating to false trade descriptions, including the subject-matter of the Trade Descriptions Act 1968.
(e) misleading and comparative advertising, except regulation specifically in relation to food, tobacco and tobacco products: includes the subject-matter of the Control of Misleading Advertisements Regulations 1988, and of the Comparative Advertising Directive 1997.
(f) price indications: includes provisions contained in the Consumer Protection Act 1987 and the EC Directive on Price Indications.
(g) trading stamps: includes the subject-matter of the Trading Stamps Act 1964.
(h) auctions and mock auctions of goods and services: includes the subject-matter of the Auctioneers Act 1845, the Auctioneers (Bidding Agreements) Act 1969 and the Mock Auctions Act 1961.
(i) hall-marking and gun barrel proofing.

II. Matters relating to the safety of, and liability for, services to consumers. This complements the reservation of matters relating to product safety and liability, under C8.

III. The subject-matter of the following enactments:
(a) the Hearing Aid Council Act 1968: provide, *inter alia*, for the establishment of the Hearing Aid Council.
(b) the Unsolicited Goods and Services Acts 1971 and 1975: provides, *inter alia*, for the protection of persons in receipt of unsolicited goods.
(c) the Fair Trading Act 1973, Pts. I-III and XI: makes provision, *inter alia*, in relation to the role, functions and powers of the Director General of Fair Trading and the establishment of a Consumer Protection Advisory Committee.
(d.) the Consumer Credit Act 1974: provides, *inter alia*, for the advertising and provision of credit and hire arrangements to individuals.
(e) the Estate Agents Act 1979: regulates the activities of solicitors.
(f) the Timeshare Act 1992: regulates timeshare contracts, as amended by the Timeshare Regulations 1997.
(g) the Package Travel, Package Holiday and Package Tours Regulations 1992: makes provision, *inter alia*, on brochures, traders' obligations, and the content and form of contracts.
(h) the Commercial Agents (Council Directive) Regulation 1993: makes provision in relation to the rights/ duties of agents and principals. The regulations do not deal with consumers, but the matter is dealt with under this Section because of the frequent imbalance of power in the agent-principal relationship.

Exception:
The subject-matter of the Food Safety Act 1990, s.16: providing for regulations to be made in relation to food hygiene, composition, labelling and advertising.

SECTION C8
This Section covers regulations in relation to the technical standard and requirements of products put on the market in pursuance of obligations under EC law, and in particular under the European Single Market Harmonisation Directives. The reservation also includes product safety and liability and product labelling.

Exceptions:
(a) food (which includes drink) and, in relation to food safety, materials which come into contact with food (for example, packaging).
(b) agricultural and horticultural produce.
(c) fish products.
(d) seeds, animal feeding stuffs, fertilisers and pesticides.
These exceptions relate to the general devolution of agriculture and fisheries.

SECTION C9
The reservation covers units and standards of weight and measurement, and the registration of trade so far as involving weighing, measuring and quantities.

SECTION C10
The reservation covers all matters relating to telecommunications and wireless telegraphy, including the subject-matter of the following enactments:—
  (a) the Telecommunications Act 1984: provides for the regulatory and licensing regime for telecommunications systems.
  (b) the Wireless Telegraphy Act 1949, the Wireless Telegraphy Act 1967 and the Marine etc Broadcasting (Offences) Act 1967: provide, *inter alia*, for the regulatory and licensing regime for wireless telegraphy.
The reservation also covers internet services and electronic encryption.

Exception:
  Part III of the Police Act 1997: makes provision in relation to police interference in property for the purpose of surveillance etc.
  The same statutory provisions are excepted under Section B8.

EXECUTIVE DEVOLUTION

TRANSFERRED FUNCTIONS:
  1. The Secretary of State's function to assign radio frequencies in relation to certain activities undertaken by the Crown, the police, fire services, or local government, except in connection with activities reserved under Sched. 5, Pt. I, para. 9 of this Act.

SECTION C11
  This Section covers all matters relating to the Post Office and its subsidiaries, including Post Office Counters Ltd, Subscription Services Ltd and the Post Office Users Council for Scotland. The reservation includes subject-matter contained in the following enactments:
  (a) the Post Office Act 1969
  (b) the Telecommunications Act 1981, Pt. II
  (c) the Post Office Act 1953.

SECTION C12
  The reservation covers matters relating to Research Councils within the meaning of the Science and Technology Act 1965, including their establishment, functions, powers and duties. The function of funding scientific research through Research Councils is also reserved, under s.5 of the 1965 Act.
  The Scottish Parliament does have legislative competence with respect to research funding in general. The functions of the Scottish Higher Education Funding Council, for example, are not a reserved matter.

SECTION C13
  This Section reserves the function of the Secretary of State to designate assisted areas for the purposes of s.1 of the Industrial Development Act 1982, and related powers. The designation of such areas applies also in relation to other enactments, such as the Derelict Land Act 1982.

SECTION C14
  This Section reserves all matters relating to the Industrial Development Advisory Board (IDAB). IDAB is a statutory body appointed under s.10 of the Industrial Development Act 1982 to advise the Secretary of State for Trade and Industry on the use of powers to provide financial assistance to industry. A separate body, the Scottish Industrial Development Board serves this function for Scotland.

SECTION C15
  The reservation covers the subject-matter of the following enactments:
  (a) the Emergency Laws (Re-enactments and Repeals) Act 1964, s.2: empowers the Treasury to block the transfer of funds, gold or securities where that transfer will be made by a person/government outside the UK to the detriment of the UK economy.
  (b) the Industry Act 1975, Pt. II: empowers the Secretary of State for Trade and Industry to prohibit/restrict the transfer of control of certain important manufacturing undertakings.
  (c) the Protection of Trading Interests Act 1980: makes provision in relation to the protection of UK trading/business interests from requirements/ prohibitions imposed under the laws of other states.

EXECUTIVE DEVOLUTION

TRANSFERRED POWERS:
1. The Secretary of State's function to make rules in connection with Scottish tribunal proceedings, under the Industry Act 1975, Sched. 3 (para. 24).

SECTION D1
This Section covers matters relating to the regulation of the electricity supply industry. In particular, the reservation includes the subject-matter of the following enactments:-
  (a) Part I of the Electricity Act 1989: empowers the Secretary of State and the Director General of Electricity Supply to regulate the industry through a system of licensing of generation, transmission and supply; sets out the duties of public electricity suppliers; and imposes controls on the protection of the public interest and the protection of consumers.
  (b) Part II of the 1989 Act: makes provision in relation to the reorganisation of the industry by privatisation.

Exception:
The subject-matter of Part I of the Environmental Protection Act 1990, which makes certain provisions in relation to the control of pollution. But see now the Pollution Prevention and Control Act 1999 (c.24).

EXECUTIVE DEVOLUTION

TRANSFERRED FUNCTIONS:
1. The Secretary of State's functions under the Electricity Act 1989, ss.2(2)(b), (3)(a), 3, 32(1), (9), 33–37, 39(1)(a), 58, 60, 61, Sched. 3 (part I), Sched. 3 (Pt. III, paras. 15–17, 20 including Sched. I (para. 11) to the Acquisition of Land (Authorisation Procedure) (Scotland) Act 1947, as applied by those provisions), Sched. 4 (paras. 6,8,9, 10(4)(b)), Sched. 5, Sched. 8, Sched. 9 (paras. 3, 5): the function, *inter alia*, to require public electricity suppliers to demonstrate arrangements for supplies from non-fossil fuel sources, to impose a fossil fuel levy on suppliers, to consent to construction/ extension/ operation of generating stations and to approve the installation of certain electric lines.
2. The Secretary of State's functions under the following subordinate legislation:
   (i) The Environmental Assessment (Scotland) Regulations 1988 (S.I. 1988, No. 1221), Pt. III.
   (ii) The Electricity and Pipe-Line Works (Assessment of Environmental Effects) Regulations 1990 (S.I. 1990 No. 442.)
   (iii) The Electricity (Applications for Consent) Regulations 1990 (S.I. 1990 No. 455.)
   (iv) The Overhead Lines (Exemption) Regulations 1990 (S.I. 1990 No. 2035.)

SHARED FUNCTIONS:
1. The function of the Minister of Agriculture, Fisheries and Food/the Treasury/the Secretary of State to make certain provisions in relation to the requirement for environmental impact assessments, under the European Communities Act 1972, s.2(2), and the European Communities (Designation) Order 1988 (S.I. 1988 No. 785.)
2. The Secretary of State's function to serve a notice on a licence holder/ exempted person requiring the supply of statistical information, under the Electricity Act 1989, s.98(1), (2).

CONSULTATIVE FUNCTIONS:
1. The Secretary of State's functions under the Electricity Act 1989, ss.5(1), 6(1), (2): the function, *inter alia*, to grant a license authorising electricity generation/transmission/supply, and to grant exemption from certain licensing requirements.

SECTION D2
This Section covers matters in relation to the oil and gas industries, including:
  (a) the ownership of, exploration for and exploitation of deposits of oil and natural gas: this covers the subject-matter of the Petroleum (Production) Act 1934, and related legislation, which vests ownership of oil and gas deposits in the Crown and provides for the licensing of deposit exploration/ exploitation.
  (b) the subject-matter of s.1 of the Mineral Exploration and Investment Grants Act 1972, so far as relating to exploration for oil and gas: makes provision in relation to the provision of financial assistance for oil/gas exploration.
      The granting of financial assistance in respect of other types of mineral exploration is not reserved, and is a 'shared power' for the purposes of s.56(1)(e) of the Scotland Act 1998.

(c) offshore installations and pipelines: covers the regulation of such installations and pipelines, including the construction/ laying/ dismantling of them.

(d) the subject-matter of the Pipelines Act 1962 (including s.5 (deemed planning permission)) so far as relating to pipelines within the meaning of s.65 of that Act: provides for the authorisation of the laying of pipelines on land. Deemed planning permission for other types of development, granted under planning legislation, is not reserved.

(e) the application of Scots law and the jurisdiction of the Scottish courts in relation to offshore activities: includes the subject-matter of Pt. IV of the Oil and Gas (Enterprise) Act 1982.

(f) pollution relating to oil and gas exploration and exploitation, but only outside controlled waters (within the meaning of the Control of Pollution Act 1974): includes the subject-matter of the Prevention of Oil Pollution Act 1971. Pollution in controlled waters—relevant territorial, coastal and inland and ground waters—is not reserved. Pollution from ships (as opposed to pipelines/installations), including provisions of the Merchant Shipping Act 1995, is reserved separately, under Section E3.

(g) the subject-matter of Pt. II of the Food and Environment Protection Act 1985, so far as relating to oil and gas exploration and exploitation, but only in relation to activities outside such controlled waters: covers the regulation of activities at sea, such as the deposit of substances/articles and the incineration/flaring of gas, so far as relating to oil and gas exploitation/exploration. Matters relating to other types of 'marine dumping' are not reserved.

(h) restrictions on navigation, fishing and other activities in connection with offshore activities: includes the subject-matter of ss.3–7 of the Offshore Petroleum Development (Scotland) Act 1975 and provisions contained in Pt. III of the Petroleum Act 1987.

(i) liquefaction of natural gas: covers the subject-matter of s.9 of the Energy Act 1976.

(j) the conveyance, shipping and supply of gas through pipes: covers the subject-matter of the Gas Acts 1986 and 1995.

Exceptions:

(i) the subject-matter of ss.10–12 of the Industry Act 1972: provides for the granting of financial assistance for the construction of ships and offshore installations. The granting of financial assistance to industry in general is not reserved, unless it relates to a reserved commercial activity, such as oil and gas exploration. Certain powers to grant financial assistance to industry, including the one covered by this exception, are 'shared' for the purposes of s.56 of the 1998 Act.

(ii) the subject-matter of the Offshore Petroleum Development (Scotland) Act 1975, other than ss.3–7: provides for the granting of financial assistance for onshore activities in support of offshore activities.

(iii) the subject-matter of Pt. I of the Environmental Protection Act 1990: provides for the control of pollution. See now the Pollution Prevention and Control Act 1999 (c.24).

(iv) the manufacture of gas: the production of combustible gas other than natural gas is not reserved.

(v) the conveyance, shipping and supply of gas other than through pipes.

EXECUTIVE DEVOLUTION

TRANSFERRED FUNCTIONS:
1. The Secretary of State's functions under the Pipe-Lines Act 1962, ss.1,4,5,9,9A,10–12,13 (except subs. (7)), 15,26A,35,36,38,39(2),43,44, Sched. 1, Sched. 2 (except para. 8): the function, *inter alia*, to control the construction of Scottish pipe-lines, direct the compulsory acquisition of land for the purposes of pipe-line construction, determine certain disputes, and related functions.

CONSULTATIVE FUNCTIONS:
1. The Secretary of State's function to declare a part of Scottish waters to be a designated area for the purposes of the Offshore Petroleum Development (Scotland) Act 1975, s.3.
2. The Secretary of State's functions under the Petroleum Act 1998, ss.32(1), 33(1), 34(7), 35(1), 37(1), 39(1): the function, *inter alia*, to approve an abandonment programme, to require remedial action to be taken in connection with an abandonment programme, and to make regulations relating to the abandonment of offshore installations and submarine pipe-lines.

SECTION D3

The reservation covers all matters relating to coal, including ownership and exploitation, deep and opencast mining and subsidence. Operational matters in relation to coal reserves and the issue of mining licences are dealt with by the Coal Authority, a UK body.

Exceptions:
The subject-matter of:
(a) Pt. I of the Environmental Protection Act 1990: provides for the control of pollution.
(b) the Coal Industry Act 1994, ss.53–54: provide for environmental duties in respect of planning approval and obligations to restore land affected by coal-mining operations.

SECTION D4

This Section covers all matters relating to nuclear energy and nuclear installations, including the development, production and use of nuclear energy, nuclear site licensing, nuclear safety, nuclear security and safeguards, liability for nuclear occurrences, and the UK Atomic Energy Authority.

Exceptions:
The subject-matter of:
(a) Pt. I of the Environmental Protection Act 1990. See now the Pollution Prevention and Control Act 1999 (c.24).
(b) The Radioactive Substances Act 1993.
These enactments deal with the duties of the Scottish Environment Protection Agency and the Secretary of State for Scotland in relation to the keeping and use of radioactive material other than at licensed nuclear sites, the disposal of radioactive waste and the regulation of non-nuclear activities at nuclear installations.

EXECUTIVE DEVOLUTION

TRANSFERRED FUNCTIONS:

1. The Secretary of State's functions under the Nuclear Installations Act 1965, ss.2,6,17(1), (4), 19(1),(3), (4), 20, 23: the function, *inter alia*, to grant permits, maintain a list of licensed sites and certify certain matters relating to jurisdiction, shared liability and foreign judgements.

SHARED FUNCTIONS:

CONSULTATIVE FUNCTIONS:

1. The Secretary of State's functions under the Nuclear Installations Act 1965, ss.1(1)(b), (2), 16(1), (1A), 18(1B), 21(1A), (3), 22(1), (2), and, in 26(1), the definitions of "excepted matter" and "nuclear matter": the function, *inter alia*, to prescribe a class/description of installation/occurrence and to increase prescribed compensation limits.

SECTION D5

The reservation covers the subject-matter of the Energy Act 1976, other than s.9. The 1976 Act provides for the regulation/ prohibition of the use of certain fuels and electricity for the purpose of energy conservation, and related matters. The subject-matter of s.9, concerning the use/ liquidation of offshore natural gas, is reserved separately, under Section D2.

Exception:
The encouragement of energy efficiency other than by prohibition or regulation: including encouragement by advice, publicity, grants and loans, or other positive incentives.

SECTION E1

The reservation includes the subject-matter of the following enactments:
(a) the Motor Vehicles (International Circulation) Act 1952: provides for the issue of international driving permits and the recognition of foreign permits.
(b) the Public Passenger Vehicles Act 1981 and the Transport Act 1985, so far as relating to public service vehicle operator licensing: the licensing system administered by the Traffic Commissioner for the Scottish Traffic Area constituted under the 1981 Act.
(c) the Road Traffic Regulation Act 1984, ss.17 & 25, and Pts. V-VI: provide for the use of 'special roads', as defined in s.151 of the Roads (Scotland) Act 1984, the design, layout and operation of pedestrian crossings, the regulation of traffic signs, and for speed limits.

(d) the Road Traffic Act 1988 and the Road Traffic Offenders Act 1988. The Road Traffic Offenders Act 1988 provides for matters relating to the prosecution and punishment of road traffic offenders. The Road Traffic Act 1988 makes provision, *inter alia*, in respect of road safety, vehicle use and construction, motor car driving instruction and motor insurance.

(e) the Vehicle Excise and Registration Act 1994: provides for the licensing and registration of vehicles.

(f) the Road Traffic (New Drivers) Act 1995: provides for the revocation of driving licences during a licence-holder's probationary period.

(g) the Goods Vehicle (Licensing of Operators) Act 1995: provides for the licensing of goods vehicle operators.

This Section also reserves:

(i) the regulation of the working hours of persons engaged in the carriage of passengers/ goods by road.

(i) the conditions applying to international road transport services.

(ii) the regulation of motor vehicle driving instruction: includes the paid instruction of drivers of *all* types of motor vehicle.

Exceptions:

The subject-matter of:

(i) The Road Road Traffic Act 1988, ss.39, 40: provide for the promotion of road safety by local authorities or other bodies, and related matters. This is a 'shared power' for the purposes of s.56(1)(i).

(ii) The Road Traffic Act 1988, ss.157–159: make provisions in relation to payments for hospital treatment of road traffic accident casualties. The National Health Service in Scotland currently recovers the costs incurred in treating road accident casualties from insurers.

EXECUTIVE DEVOLUTION

TRANSFERRED FUNCTIONS:

1. The Secretary of State's functions under the Road Traffic Regulation Act 1984, ss.14(1),(2),(3), (5), 15(2),(3),(5),(6), (7), 16(2), (2A), 17(2), (5), 28(4)(a), 64(1)(b), (2), 65(1),(2), (3A)(b)(ii), 69(1),(2), (3), 70(1), 71(1), 79(1), 82(1)(b), (2), (3), 83(1), 84(1),(1A), (1B), 85(1), (3), 85(2), Sched. 9, Pt. I (paras. 1,3(1),4,7,8,9), Pt. II (paras. 13,15,16(1), (2), 17), Pt. III (paras. 21,24, 26(1), (2)): the function, *inter alia*, to impose temporary restrictions on road use, to make regulations with respect to the use of specific roads, to issue directions with respect to the use/specification of certain traffic signs, and related powers.

2. The Secretary of State's function to make certain provisions in connection with the granting of small bus permits to educational and other bodies, and to be consulted by the Lord Chancellor in relation to the appointment of judicial members to the tribunal, and related powers, under the Transport Act 1985, s.19(7), Sched. 4 (para. 15).

3. The Secretary of State's functions under the Road Traffic Act 1988, ss.13(2), 13A(1), 27(6), 31(2): the function, *inter alia*, to make regulations authorising the holding of certain competitions or trials on a public way, to authorise a motoring event in a public place, to make regulations in connection with the control of dogs on roads, and related powers.

4. The Secretary of State's functions under the following subordinate legislation:-

(i) The Road Traffic (Temporary Retrictions) (Procedure) Regulations 1992 (S.I. 1992 No. 1215).

(ii) The Traffic Signs Regulations and General Directions 1994 (S.I. 1994 No. 1519).

(iii) The Roads (Traffic Calming) (Scotland) Regulations 1994 (S.I. 1994 No. 2488).

(iv) The Zebra, Pelican and Puffin Pedestrian Crossings Regulations and General Directions 1997 (S.I. 1997 No. 2400).

v. The Road Humps (Scotland) Regulations 1998 (S.I. 1998 No. 1448).

CONSULTATIVE FUNCTIONS:

1. The Secretary of State's functions under the Road Traffic Regulation Act 1984, ss.17(2), 25(1),64(1)(a),65(1),81(2),85(2)(a),86(2), 88(1), (4): the function, *inter alia*, to make regulations with respect to the use of special roads and the movement of traffic, to permit the use of traffic signs, and to vary the speed limit on restricted roads, and for specified classes of traffic.

2. The function of the Secretary of State for Scotland, acting with the Secretary of State for Transport and the Secretary of State for Wales, to nominate road signs enforceable by discretionary disqualification, under the Road Traffic Act 1988, s.36(5).

SECTION E2

This Section reserves the provision and regulation of railway services, as defined, including rail safety and security. The reservation does not include matters relating to tramways and guided transport systems. In particular, the subject-matter of the following enactments is reserved:
    (a) the Channel Tunnel Act 1987.
    (b) the Railway Heritage Act 1996: makes provision for a railway heritage scheme.

Exceptions:

Grants in relation to railway services, including powers in relation to special grants to local authorities under s.108A of the Local Government Finance Act 1992 and grants for public passenger transport services under s.56 of the Transport Act 1968, where the grants relate to railway services.

The following matters are, however, excluded from this exception:
    (i) the subject-matter of s.63 of the Railways Act 1993: provides for government financial assistance where railway administration orders are made.
    (ii) grants in relation to railway services as defined in s.82(1)(b) of the Railways Act 1993.
    (iii) the subject-matter of s.136 of the Railways Act 1993: makes provision in relation to compensation payable to a passenger service operator who is required to run a passenger service which would not be commercially viable, in accordance with a public service obligation under Council Regulation (EEC) 1191/69, as amended.

EXECUTIVE DEVOLUTION

SHARED POWERS:

1. The Secretary of State's functions under the Railways Act 1993, ss.74(1), (3), 75(1),(2), 76(6)(a), 79(1), 137, 139(1),(2),(3),(5), (6): the function, *inter alia*, to receive certain reports from the Rail Regulator, the Director of Passenger Rail Franchising and the Central Rail Users' Consultative Committee, to enter into certain agreements with goods service operators, and to make grants towards the provision of certain railway facilities.

SECTION E3

The reservation covers matters in relation to marine transport, including the subject-matter of the following enactments:
    (a) the Coastguard Act 1925: defines the activities and powers of HM Coastguard.
    (b) The Hovercraft Act 1968, except so far as relating to the regulation of noise pollution and vibration caused by hovercraft: provides, *inter alia*, for marine safety matters in relation to hovercraft.
    (c) the Carriage of Goods by Sea Act 1971: incorporates into UK law international agreements (the Hague-Visby rules) setting out the circumstances in which the carrier/ cargo owner are liable for loss/ damage of goods at sea.
    (d) the Protection of Wrecks Act 1973: provides for the designation of protected areas around wrecks.
    (e) the Merchant Shipping (Liner Conferences) Act 1982: provides for the exemption from normal competition regulations of 'liner conferences': certain cartels of deep sea container shipping operators. The 1982 Act also incorporates into UK law the United Nations Convention on a Code of Conduct for Liner Conferences.
    (f) the Dangerous Vessels Act 1985: deals with the powers of harbour masters and the Secretary of State in relation to dangerous vessels.
    (g) the Aviation and Maritime Security Act 1990, other than Pt. I (aviation security).
    (h) the Carriage of Goods by Sea Act 1992: makes provision in relation to bills of lading and shipping contract rights/liabilities.
    (i) the Merchant Shipping Act 1995: makes provision, *inter alia*, in relation to the registration of ships, marine safety, fishing vessels, marine pollution and salvage.
    (j) the Shipping and Trading Interests (Protection) Act 1995: makes provision in relation to foreign conduct prejudicial to UK shipping and trade interests.
    (k) the Merchant Shipping and Maritime Security Act 1997, ss.24, 26–28: make provision in relation to wrecks, piracy and international bodies.

The reservation also includes:-
    (i) navigational rights and freedoms: the UK's international obligations not to impose certain requirements on passing shipping traffic.
    (ii) financial assistance for shipping services which start/finish outside Scotland. The Scottish Parliament can, however, legislate with respect to financial assistance for shipping services operating wholly within Scotland.

Exceptions:

I. Ports, harbours, piers and boatslips, except in relation to the matters reserved by paragraphs d, f, g or i of this Section: the Scottish Parliament does have legislative competence over ports, harbours, piers and boatslips in Scotland. The exception does not include the reserved matters of maritime security and safety.

II. Regulation of works which may obstruct or endanger navigation. The authorisation of works relating to oil and gas and telecommunications is reserved, however, under Sections D2 and C10 respectively.

III. The subject-matter of the Highlands and Islands Shipping Services Act 1960 in relation to financial assistance for bulk freight services. The 1960 Act provides for financial assistance to shipping services serving the Highlands and Islands from any port of embarkation.

EXECUTIVE DEVOLUTION

TRANSFERRED FUNCTIONS:
1. The Secretary of State's functions under the following subordinate legislation:
  (i) The Merchant Shipping (Section 52 Inquiries) Rules 1982 (S.I. 1982 No. 1752), rule 5(1).
  (ii) The Merchant Shipping (Formal Investigations) Rules 1985 (S.I. 1985 No. 1001), rule 4(1).
  (iii) The Merchant Shipping (Section 63 Inquiries) Rules 1997 (S.I. 1997 No. 347), rule 5(1).

CONSULTATIVE FUNCTIONS:
1. The Secretary of State's functions as licensing authority in relation to deposits of substances/ articles in the sea/ under the sea bed, and related functions, under the Food and Environment Protection Act 1985, ss.5,6,7,10(1), Sched. 3.
2. The Secretary of State's function to provide for the registration of a fishing vessel as a British ship, and related powers, under the Merchant Shipping Act 1995, s.10(2)(f).

SECTION E4
The reservation includes the subject-matter of the following enactments:
(a–c) the Carriage by Air Act 1961, the Carriage by Air (Supplementary Provisions) Act 1962 and the Carriage by Air and Road Act 1979, so far as relating to carriage by air: implement the provisions of the Warsaw Convention (as amended), which applies to all international carriage by aircraft of persons, baggage or cargo for reward.
  (d) the Civil Aviation Act 1982: makes provision, *inter alia*, in relation to the constitution and functions of the Civil Aviation Authority, aerodromes, the regulation of civil aviation, aircraft and related matters.
  (e) the Aviation Security Act 1982: makes provision in relation to offences against the safety of aircraft and the protection of aircraft, aerodromes and air navigation installations.
  (f) the Airports Act 1986: makes provision, *inter alia*, for the regulation of the use of airports, the status of airport operators, and related matters.
  (g) the Aviation and Maritime Security Act 1990, ss.1, 48: make provision in relation to aerodrome safety and provide for powers in relation to certain aircraft.
This Section also includes matters relating to the compensation and repatriation of passengers in the event of an air transport operator becoming insolvent.

Exceptions:
The subject-matter of the following enactments is excepted from the reservation:
  (I) The following sections of the Civil Aviation Act 1982:
    (i) s.25 (the power of the Secretary of State to provide aerodromes).
    (ii) s.30 (the provision of aerodromes and aerodrome facilities by local authorities).
    (iii) s.31 (power to carry on ancillary business in connection with local authority aerodromes).
    (iv) s.34 (financial assistance for certain aerodromes).
    (v) s.35 (facilities for consultation at certain aerodromes).
    (vi) s.36 (health controls at certain aerodromes).
    (vii) ss.41–43, 50 (powers in relation to land) where land is to be or was acquired for airport development or expansion.

(II) The Airports Act 1986, Pt. II & ss.63, 64, 66: provide for the transfer of local authority airport undertakings, airport bylaws, and the functions of certain airport operators in respect of abandoned vehicles.

(III) The Airports Act 1986, ss.59, 60 (acquisition and disposal of land) where land is to be or was acquired for the purpose of airport development or expansion.

EXECUTIVE DEVOLUTION

TRANSFERRED FUNCTIONS:

1. The Secretary of State's functions under the Civil Aviation Act 1982, ss.38(2), 42(1), 50(2), 78,79(1),80, 88(10), (11): the function, *inter alia*, to require aerodrome authorities to fix certain charges for aerodrome use, to authorise compulsory land acquisition, to impose noise pollution regulations, and related powers.

2. The Secretary of State's functions under the Airports Act 1986, ss,37(5), 65(2), (6), 68(1): the function, *inter alia*, to determine that an airport should cease to be subject to economic regulation under Pt. IV, to apply certain road traffic enactments to airports and to require airport operators to provide and operate equipment for monitoring aircraft movement.

SECTION E5

The reservation covers:

(i) The transport of radioactive material. Radioactive material is defined by reference to s.1(1) of the Radioactive Material (Road Transport) Act 1991 as material having a specific activity in excess of 70 kilobecquerels/ kilogram, or any lesser specific activity specified in an order made by the Secretary of State.

(ii) Technical specifications for public passenger transport for disabled persons, including the subject-matter of:

    (a) the Transport Act 1985, ss.125(7), (8): provide for consultation with the Disabled Persons Transport Advisory Committee in relation to the function of the Secretary of State to issue guidance on the public transport needs of disabled people.

    (b) the Disability Discrimination Act 1995, Part V: makes provision in relation to the accessibility of certain forms of transport for disabled people, and related matters.

(iii) Regulation of the carriage of dangerous goods.

EXECUTIVE DEVOLUTION

TRANSFERRED FUNCTIONS:

1. The Secretary of State's functions under the Civic Government (Scotland) Act 1982, s.20: the function, *inter alia*, to make regulations in connection with the granting of taxi and private hire car licenses, insofar as necessary to implement in Scotland the Disability Discrimination Act 1995, Pt. 5.

2. The Secretary of State's function, *inter alia*, to make certain taxi vehicle/driver provisions, and to designate certain transport facilities, for the purposes of the Disability Discrimination Act 1995, s.33.

SECTION F1

The reservation of social security schemes by this Section is the principal example in the Schedule of a reservation cast in broad terms but supported by a list of "illustrations"—the other being Section F4 below. The generality of the references to schemes (supplemented by more specific reference to child support—see also Section F2—and vaccine damage) and their administration provides scope for broad initial coverage and developments over time. The exceptions from reservation mainly relate to local authority welfare functions.

EXECUTIVE DEVOLUTION

TRANSFERRED FUNCTIONS:

1. The Secretary of State's functions of being consulted by the Lord Chancellor on certain appointments and regulations, and on the removal from office of Social Security Commissioners or the President/chairman of tribunals, under the Social Security Administration Act 1992, ss.51(1), 52(3), 189(10), Sched. 2 (para. 1(5)).

2. The Secretary of State's functions under the Social Security Act 1998, ss.5(1), 79(2), Sched. 1 (para. 1(4)), Sched. 4 (para. 8)): the function, *inter alia*, of being consulted by the Lord Chancellor regarding (a) the appointment/ removal of appeal tribunal Presidents, (b) regulations in connection with proceedings before the Commissioners.

3. The Secretary of State's function of concurring in Board regulations in connection with appeals to the tax appeal Commissioners, under the Social Security Contributions (Transfer of Functions, etc) Act 1999, s.13(1).

4. The Secretary of State's function to provide premises and staff for the purposes of carrying out the functions of Social Security Commissioners (appointed under the Social Security Administration Act 1992, s.52, or the Social Security Act 1998, Sched. 4(1)). (Non-statutory function).

SHARED FUNCTIONS:

1. The Secretary of State's function to pay allowances for attendance at proceedings, under the Social Security Administration Act 1992, Sched. 2 (para. 7(1)(b)).

SECTION F2

With the exception of aliment (as an aspect of Scots private law for which the Scottish Parliament may make broader provision (s.29)), the subject matter of the Child Support Acts 1991 and 1995 is reserved.

EXECUTIVE DEVOLUTION

TRANSFERRED FUNCTIONS:

1. The Secretary of State's functions under the Child Support Act 1991, ss.22(3), 24(9), 25(6),45(1), (6), Sched. 4 (paras. 2A, 7): the function, *inter alia*, of being consulted by the Lord Chancellor on regulations in connection with proceedings before Child Support Commissioners, of sending certain appeals to courts, rather than appeal tribunals, and of paying allowances to persons attending proceedings.

2. The Secretary of State's function to provide premises and staff for the purposes of carrying out the functions of Child Support Commissioners (appointed under the Child Support Act 1991, s.22). (Non-statutory function).

SECTION F3

With the exception of pensions under s.81(3) (pensions for MSPs and members of the Scottish Executive) and provision for the Scottish public authorities referred, the regulation of occupational and personal pension schemes is reserved. For definitions of the categories of pensions referred to, see s.126(1). The law on pensions produces difficult overlaps between those aspects of regulation reserved by this Section and the unreserved rules of Scots private law on trusts and family law. This has, for instance, produced the separate treatment of devolved aspects of the Welfare Reform and Pensions Act 1999. See the Divorce etc. (Pensions) (Scotland) Regulations 2000 (S.S.I. 2000 No.112).

EXECUTIVE DEVOLUTION

TRANSFERRED FUNCTIONS:

1. The Secretary of State's function to provide for pensions under s.4 of the Small Landholders (Scotland) Act 1911 (promotion of Scottish rural industries).

2. The Lord Chancellor's function to remunerate Pensions Appeal Tribunal members, and the Treasury's function to decide the level of that remuneration, under the Pensions Appeal Tribunals Act 1943 (Sched, para. 2).

3. The Secretary of State's functions in relation to the Firemen's Pension Scheme, under ss.26, 27A(a) of the Fire Services Act 1947.

4. The Secretary of State's functions under s.7 of the Superannuation (Miscellaneous Provisions) Act 1967.

5. The Secretary of State's functions to make police pension provisions under ss.26, 27 of the Police (Scotland) Act 1967.

6. The Secretary of State's functions to make provision for pensions/allowances/gratuities for local government employees, teachers, NHS employees, fire-fighters, police officers etc, and related powers, under ss.7–10,11(2),12,15(5),16, 24 of the Superannuation Act 1972.

7. The Secretary of State's functions to make police retirement and pension provisions, and related powers, under ss.1–8A of the Police Pensions Act 1976.

8. The Secretary of State's functions to make provision for tribunals/inquiries held in Scotland, under ss.9, 10(7)-(8), 13 & 16(2) of the Tribunals and Inquiries Act 1992.

9. The Secretary of State's functions to make police pensions provisions under s.60 of the Police Act 1996.

10. The Secretary of State's functions under the following subordinate legislation:-

   (i) The National Health Service (Transfer of Officers and Compensation) (Scotland) Regulations 1948 (S.I. 1948 No. 1465.)

   (ii) The National Health Service (Superannuation) (England and Scotland) Regulations 1948 (S.I. 1948 No. 1483.)

  (iii) The Police Pensions Regulations 1971 (S.I. 1971 No. 232.).

  (iv) The Special Constables (Pensions) (Scotland) Regulations 1971 (S.I. 1971 No. 234.)

   (v) The Police Cadets (Pensions) (Scotland) Regulations 1971 (S.I. 1971 No. 246.)

  (vi) The Special Constables (Pensions) (Scotland) (Lump Sum Payments to Widows etc.) Regulations 1972 (S.I. 1972 No. 1847.)

  (vii) The Special Constables (Pensions) (Scotland) Regulations 1973 (S.I. 1973 No. 433.)

 (viii) The Police Cadets (Pensions) (Scotland) Regulations 1973 (S.I. 1973 No. 434.)

  (ix) The Special Constables (Pensions) (Scotland) (Lump Sum Payments to Widows) Regulations 1973 (S.I. 1973 No. 1835.)

   (x) The National Health Service Reorganisation (Retirement of Senior Officers) (Scotland) Regulations 1974 (S.I. 1974 No. 182.)

  (xi) The National Health Service (Compensation) (Scotland) Regulations 1974 (S.I. 1974 No. 1902.)

  (xii) The Special Constables (Pensions) (Scotland) (Lump Sum Payments to Widows) Regulations 1974 (S.I. 1974 No. 1902.)

 (xiii) The Local Government (Compensation) (Scotland) Regulations 1975 (S.I. 1975 No. 734.)

 (xiv) The Fire Services (Compensation) (Scotland) Regulations 1975 (S.I. 1975 No.1800.)

  (xv) The Scottish Development Agency (Compensation) Regulations 1976 (S.I. 1976 No. 2182.)

 (xvi) The Grant-Aided Colleges (Compensation) (Scotland) Regulations 1977 (S.I. 1977 No. 1777.)

 (xvii) The National Health Service (Compensation for Premature Retirement) (Scotland) Regulations 1981 (S.I. 1981 No. 1752.)

(xviii) The National Health Service (Superannuation- Special Provisions) (Scotland) Regulations 1984 (S.I. 1984 No. 1970.)

 (xix) The Police (Injury Benefit) Regulations 1987 (S.I. 1987 No. 156.)

  (xx) The Police Pensions Regulations 1987 (S.I. 1987 No. 257.)

 (xxi) The Special Constables (Injury Benefit) (Scotland) Regulations 1987 (S.I. 1987 No. 1698.)

 (xxii) The Police Cadets (Injury Benefit) (Scotland) Regulations 1987 (S.I. 1987 No. 1700.)

(xxiii) The Local Government Superannuation (Scotland) Regulations 1987 (S.I. 1987 No. 1850.)

(xxiv) The Police Pensions (Purchase of Increased Benefits) Regulations 1987 (S.I. 1987 No. 2215.)

 (xxv) The Police Pensions (Additional Voluntary Contributions) Regulations 1991 (S.I. 1991 No. 1304.)

 (xxvi) The Firemen's Pension Scheme Order 1992 (S.I. 1992 No. 129.)

(xxvii) The Teachers' Superannuation (Scotland) Regulations 1992 (S.I. 1992 No. 280.)

(xxviii) The National Health Service Superannuation Scheme (Scotland) Regulations 1995 (S.I. 1995 No. 365.)

 (xxix) The Teachers' Superannuation (Additional Voluntary Contributions) (Scotland) Regulations 1995 (S.I. 1995 No. 2814.)

 (xxx) The Teachers (Compensation for Premature Retirement and Redundancy) (Scotland) Regulations 1996 (S.I. 1996 No. 2317.)

 (xxxi) The Local Government Superannuation (Scotland) Amendment (No.3) Regulations 1997 (S.I. 1997 No. 1435.)

(xxxii) The Local Government (Discretionary Payments and Injury Benefits) (Scotland) Regulations 1998 (S.I. 1998 No. 192.)

(xxxiii) The Local Government Pension Scheme (Transitional Provisions) (Scotland) Regulations 1998 (S.I. 1998 No. 364.)

(xxxiv) The Local Government Pension Scheme (Scotland) Regulations 1998 (S.I. 1998 No. 366.)

 (xxxv) The National Health Service Superannuation Scheme (Scotland) (Additional Voluntary Contributions) Regulations 1998 (S.I. 1998 No. 1451.)

(xxxvi) The National Health Service (Scotland) (Injury Benefits) Regulations 1998, (S.I. 1998 No. 1594.)

11. The function of providing premises and staff for the purposes of carrying out the functions of a Pensions Appeal Tribunal (constituted under the Schedule to the Pensions Appeal Tribunals Act 1943). (Non-Statutory function).

12. The function to fund payments made by a Pensions Appeal Tribunal under rules 26–28 of the Pensions Appeal Tribunals (Scotland) Rules 1981. (Non-Statutory function).

SECTION F4

War pensions, for which provision is made across a wide range of statute law and prerogative orders, are reserved.

SECTION G1

Reserving the regulation of the profession of architect, this Section is the first of three which regulate certain professions.

EXECUTIVE DEVOLUTION

TRANSFERRED FUNCTIONS:

1. The Secretary of State's functions under the following Subordinate legislation:
   (i) The National Health Service (Superannuation) (War Service, etc) (Scotland) Regulations 1977, (S.I. 1977 No. 2138).
   (ii) The Police Pensions (War Service) Regulations 1979, (S.I. 1979 No. 1259).
   (iii) The Police Pensions (War Service) (Transferees) Regulations 1985, (S.I. 1985 No. 2029).

SECTION G2

This reserves the regulation of the listed health professions. It would include professional qualifications and standards but not matters of pay or management. The specific exceptions relate to certain matters to be treated as devolved as part of the general devolution of the National Health Service.

EXECUTIVE DEVOLUTION

TRANSFERRED FUNCTIONS:

1. The Secretary of State's function to approve the appointment of chairmen/ deputy chairmen to appeal tribunals, under the Pharmacy Act 1954, Sched. 1C (para. 3(4)(b)).

2. The Secretary of State's function to make rules on the functions of assessors appointed to advise the Professional Conduct Committee, the Health Committee and the Preliminary Proceedings Committee, under the Medical Act 1983, Sched. 4 (para. 7).

3. The function of the Secretary of State and the Lord Chancellor to approve certain rules in connection with Scottish proceedings, and to make certain provisions relating to the function of assessors, under the Nurses, Midwives and Health Visitors Act 1997, s.19(5) and Sched. 2 (para. 4).

SECTION G3

The regulation of the profession of audition is reserved.

SECTION H1

This section makes general provision for the reservation of employment rights and duties and industrial relations. It includes the subject matter of the listed Acts:
   (a) The Employer's Liability (Compulsory Insurance) Act 1969 requires employers to insure against liability for injury or disease sustained by employees.
   (b) The Employment Agencies Act 1973 regulates employment agencies and employment businesses.
   (c) The Pneumoconiosis etc. (Workers' Compensation) Act 1979 makes provision for lump sum payments to be paid in respect of persons disabled by industrial lung diseases.
   (d) The Transfer of Undertaking (Protection of Employment) Regulations 1981 provide for the protection of employees' rights to the transfer of an undertaking.
   (e) The Trade Union and Labour Relations (Consolidation) Act 1992 provides for a wide range of matters to do with trade unions and labour relations including such matters as employees' associations and collective bargaining.
   (f) The Industrial Tribunals Act 1996 provides for industrial tribunals and the Employment Appeal Tribunal.
   (g) The Employment Rights Act 1996 consolidates earlier enactments about employment rights such as protection of wages, suspension from work, etc.
   (h) The National Minimum Wage Act 1998 provides for the setting of minimum wages.

Section H2

The text of this Section was substituted by the Scotland Act 1998 (Modifications of Schedules 4 and 5) Order 1999 (S.I. 1999 No. 1749).

Importantly the interpretation provision specifies the subject-matter of Part 1 of the Health and Safety at Work etc. Act 1974 and fixes the definition of "work" and "at work" as they were on July 1, 1999.

Executive Devolution

Transferred Functions:

1. The Secretary of State's function to provide that certain proceedings may be brought before an employment tribunal, under the Employment Tribunals Act 1996, s.3.

2. The Secretary of State's function to prescribe a standard of achievement and specify qualification awarding bodies for Scottish employees, under the Employment Rights Act 1996, s.63A(1)(c), (2).

3. The Secretary of State's functions under the New Town (Stonehouse) (Revocation of Designation) (Compensation) Regulations 1979 (S.I. 1979 No. 98).

Section H3

With exception of the specified matters relating to careers services and training, job search and support (defined by reference to the subject-matter of the Disabled Persons (Employment) Act 1944 and the Employment and Training Act 1973) are reserved.

Executive Devolution

Transferred Functions:

1. The Secretary of State's function to authorise/direct Scottish Enterprise/Highlands and Islands Enterprise to act on his behalf in making certain arrangements, under the Employment and Training Act 1973, s.2(3A).

2. The functions of a Minister of the Crown to confer powers/impose duties on Scottish Enterprise and Highlands and Islands Enterprise to act in connection with unemployment/ training, under the Enterprise and New Towns (Scotland) Act 1990, s.14A.

Section J1

One of the more controversial reservations debated during proceedings on the Scotland Bill (see Introduction), abortion is a reserved matter. The Scottish Parliament cannot, for instance, modify the provisions of the Abortion Act 1967 (as already amended), although related aspects of Scots private law might be modified.

Executive Devolution

Transferred Functions:

1. The Secretary of State's function, *inter alia*, to approve places where a termination of pregnancy may be carried out, to prescribe the arrangements for the certifying of medical opinions and to notify terminations to the Chief Medical Officer in Scotland, under the Abortion Act 1967, ss.1(3) & 2.

Section J2

Zenotransplantation (transplantation from animals to humans) is reserved. There is no reservation of the regulation of other forms of (human) transplantation.

Section J3

This Section makes extensive provision for the reservation of surrogacy; human fertilisation (including the regulation of the creation and keeping of embryos, etc); and human genetics.

Executive Devolution

Transferred Functions:

1. The Secretary of State's function, *inter alia*, to provide that adoption provisions are to have effect in relation to certain adoption orders, under the Human Fertilisation and Embryology Act 1990, s.30(9).

Section J4

This Section reserves the regulation and control of medicines (for human and animals) poisons, biological substances and the prices of medicines and products supplied to the National Health Service, by reference to the subject-matter of the specified Acts and regulations.

EXECUTIVE DEVOLUTION

TRANSFERRED FUNCTIONS:
1. The Secretary of State's function, *inter alia*, to enforce the provisions of the Medicines Act 1968, s.109.

CONSULTATIVE FUNCTIONS:
1. The Secretary of State's function to appoint Medicines Commission members and chairman and to appoint committee members, under the Medicines Act 1968, ss.2(2), (4), 4(5).

SECTION J5
This Section reserves the welfare foods provision which is, or may be, made under s.13 of the Social Security Act 1988. Existing provision includes nutritional supplements for expectant and breast-feeding mothers.

EXECUTIVE DEVOLUTION

TRANSFERRED FUNCTIONS:
1. The Secretary of State's functions under the Welfare Food Regulations 1996 (S.I. 1996 No. 1434), reg. 12(2), 15(2), 16, 20.
2. The Secretary of State's function to reimburse an NHS Trust/ a Health Board for tokens exchanged for dried milk and for dried milk sold to family credit beneficiaries at a reduced price in connection with the Welfare Foods Regulations 1996, or to pay suppliers' invoices for the supply of vitamins to such a Trust or Health Board in connection with the 1996 Regulations. (Non-Statutory functions).

SECTION K1
This general reservation of broadcasting was one of the most contested reservations during parliamentary debates on the Scotland Bill (see Introduction). It covers all regulatory aspects of television and radio broadcasting.

EXECUTIVE DEVOLUTION

TRANSFERRED FUNCTIONS:
1. The Secretary of State's function to make annual payments to the Independent Television Commission for the financing of programmes in Gaelic, under the Broadcasting Act 1990, s.183.

SHARED FUNCTIONS:
1. The Secretary of State's functions under the Broadcasting Act 1990, Sched. 1 (para. 15(1)), Sched. 8 (para. 15(1)), Sched. 9 (para. 12(3)): the functions, *inter alia*, of receiving reports from the Independent Television Commission, the Radio Authority and the Gaelic Television Committee.
2. The Secretary of State's function, *inter alia*, to receive annual reports from the Broadcasting Standards Commission, under the Broadcasting Act 1996, s.125(1).

CONSULTATIVE FUNCTIONS:
1. The Secretary of State's functions under the Broadcasting Act 1990, ss.1(2)(b), as read with Sched. 1 (para. 2(3)), 83(2)(b), as read with Sched. 8 (para. 2(1A)): the function of appointing certain members of the Independent Television Commission and the Radio Authority.
2. The Secretary of State's function of appointing certain members of the Broadcasting Standards Commission, under the Broadcasting Act 1996, s.106(2)(c), as read with Sched. 3 (para. 3(1A)).

SECTION K2
This reserves the public lending right established by the Act of 1979.

SECTION K3
The indemnity scheme reserved by this Section is established to indemnify libraries, museums and art galleries in the event of loss or damage when works of art are lent to other institutions.

SECTION K4
The general power of the Inland Revenue to accept property in satisfaction of liability to inheritance tax is reserved by virtue of Section A1 above. This additional reservation relates to legislative competence in respect of the power of ministers (currently contained in the two sections referred to) to direct how such property should be disposed of.

EXECUTIVE DEVOLUTION

A: TRANSFERRED FUNCTIONS:
1. The Secretary of State's functions under the National Heritage Act 1980, ss.9(1)–(6), as read with 9(8), (9)(a),(b), (c); 16, 16A: the function, *inter alia*, to direct the disposal of certain property accepted in satisfaction of tax and to undertake to indemnify any party for the loss of/ damage to an object while on loan to another party in Scotland.
2. The Secretary of State's functions to approve the acceptance of certain property in satisfaction of tax or interest payable, under the Inheritance Tax Act 1984, s.230.

CONSULTATIVE FUNCTIONS:
1. The Secretary of State's function to direct the disposal of certain property accepted in satisfaction of tax, under the National Heritage Act 1980, ss.9(1)-(5), as read with ss.9(8), (9)(d).

SECTION L1
The determination of the amount remuneration of the enumerated judges is reserved, although the responsibility for making the payments themselves falls to the Scottish Ministers and are charged to the Scottish Consolidated Fund. (See also s.119(3) and Sched. 4 para. 5(a).) Responsibility for judicial *pensions* is reserved by Section F3 above. For the appointment and dismissal of judges of the Court of Session, see s.95.
It may be observed that, whilst the determination of the remuneration of all members of the Lands Tribunal for Scotland (see also Sched. 7 para. 8) is reserved, it is only the Chairman of the Scottish Land Court whose salary is covered by the reservation.

SECTION L2
Legislative competence in respect of equal opportunities is reserved. This is stated to *include* the subject-matter of the four enumerated statutes but extends more broadly to include discrimination on grounds such as sexual orientation (not addressed by the Sex Discrimination Act 1975), language, religious beliefs, political opinions or age. All are reserved. The Disability Discrimination Act 1995 has since been supplemented by the Disability Rights Commission Act 1999 (c.17), which inter alia substitutes the Disability Rights Commission for the National Disability Council.
Despite the general reservation, the exceptions ensure that the Scottish Parliament (which currently has an Equal Opportunities Committee by virtue of Rule 6.9 of the Standing Orders) may competently legislate to encourage equal opportunities and the *observance* of equal opportunities requirements by the Scottish Administration, Scottish public authorities and cross-border public authorities.

EXECUTIVE DEVOLUTION

TRANSFERRED FUNCTIONS:
1. The Secretary of State's function to cause a local inquiry to be held in relation to certain matters and to give notice to claimants in relation to certain discrimination claims, under the Race Relations Act 1976, ss.19(5), 57(5).
2. The Secretary of State's function to enforce certain duties, under the Education (Scotland) Act 1980, s.70, as applied by the Race Relations Act 1976, s.19(3).

CONSULTATIVE FUNCTIONS:
1. The Secretary of State's function to appoint certain commissioners to the Equal Opportunities Commission, under the Sex Discrimination Act 1975, s.53(1), as read with s.53(1A).
2. The Secretary of State's function to appoint certain commissioners to the Commission for Racial Equality, under the Race Relations Act 1976, s.43(1), as read with s.43(1A).
3. The Secretary of State's function to appoint certain members of the National Disability Council, under the Disability Discrimination Act 1995, Sched. 5 (para. 3(3)), as read with Sched. 5 (para. 3(3A)).

SECTION L3
This reserves the control of weapons of mass destruction. Existing legislation includes the Biological Weapons Act 1974 and the Chemical Weapons Act 1996. See also Section B4 (Firearms).

SECTION L4
This reserves the functions of the Ordnance Survey, the national mapping organisation, currently defined by the Ordnance Survey Act 1841.

SECTION L5
This reserves timescales, time zones and the Summer Time Act 1972, as well as the calendar, units of time and the date of Easter (see the Easter Act 1928).
On the other hand, the computation of periods of time (*e.g.*. in relation to limitations) and the designation of bank holidays (and public and local holidays) and of term and quarter days—Whitsunday (28 May), Martinmas (28 November), Candlemas (28 February) and Lammas (28 August)—are excepted from the reservation.

SECTION L6
The regulation of activities in outer space (see the Outer Space Act 1986) is reserved. For the general reservation of international relations, see Sched. 5 Pt. 1 para.7.

PART III
The General Notes on ss.88–89, 90 explain some of the difficulties raised by the devolution settlement as it relates to public bodies whose functions concern a mixture of matters within the competence of the Scottish Parliament and matters outside that competence, either because the functions are exercisable outside Scotland or because they relate to reserved matters. Many such bodies have been "specified" as cross-border public authorities under s.88.
At many points in the Act, the two types of authority in paras. 1, 2 (*i.e.* with mixed functions or with no reserved functions) are treated in combination. See ss.91, 92, 118, 119 (and ss.120, 121), Sched. 5 Section L2.
It should be noted that s.126(3) is an interpretative aid in the identification of whether a function of a body "relates to reserved matters". This is to be determined "by reference to the purpose for which the function is exercisable, having regard (among other things) to the likely effects in all the circumstances of any exercise of the function". (cf. s.29(3).)

Para. 1
This paragraph targets Scottish public authorities (as defined in s. 126(1)) with mixed functions but not specified as cross-border authorities. A good example is that of a Scottish local authority which has predominantly "devolved" functions but also some which relate to reserved matters such as weights and measures. The purpose of this paragraph is to ensure that those authorities do not thereby become reserved and that the matters referred to in subpara. (2) are properly within the competence of the Parliament, although subpara. (3) is intended to ensure that functions of an authority which do relate to reserved matters are indeed reserved and conferring or removing those functions is not within the Parliament's competence.

Para. 2
This paragraph is intended to ensure that the reservation of the Crown by para. 1 of Pt. I of the Schedule does not, of itself, operate to reserve a Scottish public authority none of whose functions relate to reserved matters.

Para. 3
Complementing the provision made in paras. 1, 2, this paragraph determines the position of "reserved bodies".
In the case of such bodies, the Scottish Parliament does not have the freedom it enjoys in relation to the bodies with mixed functions. All aspects of the body identified in para. 3(1) are reserved.
The reserved bodies themselves are defined in para. 3(2). Those "reserved by name by Pt II" of the Schedule are (subject to future amendment of the Schedule under s.30(2)):
Post Office (C11).
Industrial Development Advisory Board (C14).
Disabled Persons Transport Advisory Committee (E5).
Employment Medical Advisory Service (H2).
BBC (K1).
The Councils in Section C12 are the Research Councils.
Section 126(3)(b) provides that bodies to which para. 3 applies "are to be treated as if all their functions were functions which relate to reserved matters".
It may be observed that, although this paragraph provides specific guidance in relation to the reserved bodies referred to, there are many other bodies constituted in the reserved areas. In relation to those, the extent of the powers of the Scottish Parliament, if used for a devolved purpose, is less clear.

Para. 4

This paragraph relates to a difficult interface between reserved and non-reserved matters. With the principal exception of the content of para. 4(2)(a), the giving of financial assistance for the purpose of promoting or sustaining economic activity is not reserved.

Para. 5

Many reservations (or exceptions from reservation) in Sched. 5 are expressed by reference to the subject matter of specific Acts of Parliament. This paragraph applies a rule of interpretation requiring these Acts to be read as they have effect on the principal appointed day (*i.e.* as appointed by s.130(1)), unless repealed prior to that day, in which case as at the date of repeal.

Section 129(1) provides for the making of transitional provision and enables the date fixed under para. 5(1) to be varied.

Section 98   SCHEDULE 6

DEVOLUTION ISSUES

PART I

PRELIMINARY

1. In this Schedule "devolution issue" means—
   (a) a question whether an Act of the Scottish Parliament or any provision of an Act of the Scottish Parliament is within the legislative competence of the Parliament,
   (b) a question whether any function (being a function which any person has purported, or is proposing, to exercise) is a function of the Scottish Ministers, the First Minister or the Lord Advocate,
   (c) a question whether the purported or proposed exercise of a function by a member of the Scottish Executive is, or would be, within devolved competence,
   (d) a question whether a purported or proposed exercise of a function by a member of the Scottish Executive is, or would be, incompatible with any of the Convention rights or with Community law,
   (e) a question whether a failure to act by a member of the Scottish Executive is incompatible with any of the Convention rights or with Community law,
   (f) any other question about whether a function is exercisable within devolved competence or in or as regards Scotland and any other question arising by virtue of this Act about reserved matters.

2. A devolution issue shall not be taken to arise in any proceedings merely because of any contention of a party to the proceedings which appears to the court or tribunal before which the proceedings take place to be frivolous or vexatious.

PART II

PROCEEDINGS IN SCOTLAND

Application of Part II

3. This Part of this Schedule applies in relation to devolution issues in proceedings in Scotland.

Institution of proceedings

4.—(1) Proceedings for the determination of a devolution issue may be instituted by the Advocate General or the Lord Advocate.

(2) The Lord Advocate may defend any such proceedings instituted by the Advocate General.

(3) This paragraph is without prejudice to any power to institute or defend proceedings exercisable apart from this paragraph by any person.

Intimation of devolution issue

5. Intimation of any devolution issue which arises in any proceedings before a court or tribunal shall be given to the Advocate General and the Lord Advocate (unless the person to whom the intimation would be given is a party to the proceedings).

6. A person to whom intimation is given in pursuance of paragraph 5 may take part as a party in the proceedings, so far as they relate to a devolution issue.

Reference of devolution issue to higher court

7. A court, other than the House of Lords or any court consisting of three or more judges of the Court of Session, may refer any devolution issue which arises in proceedings (other than criminal proceedings) before it to the Inner House of the Court of Session.

8. A tribunal from which there is no appeal shall refer any devolution issue which arises in proceedings before it to the Inner House of the Court of Session; and any other tribunal may make such a reference.

9. A court, other than any court consisting of two or more judges of the High Court of Justiciary, may refer any devolution issue which arises in criminal proceedings before it to the High Court of Justiciary.

References from superior courts to Judicial Committee

10. Any court consisting of three or more judges of the Court of Session may refer any devolution issue which arises in proceedings before it (otherwise than on a reference under paragraph 7 or 8) to the Judicial Committee.

11. Any court consisting of two or more judges of the High Court of Justiciary may refer any devolution issue which arises in proceedings before it (otherwise than on a reference under paragraph 9) to the Judicial Committee.

Appeals from superior courts to Judicial Committee

12. An appeal against a determination of a devolution issue by the Inner House of the Court of Session on a reference under paragraph 7 or 8 shall lie to the Judicial Committee.

13. An appeal against a determination of a devolution issue by—
   (a) a court of two or more judges of the High Court of Justiciary (whether in the ordinary course of proceedings or on a reference under paragraph 9), or
   (b) a court of three or more judges of the Court of Session from which there is no appeal to the House of Lords,
shall lie to the Judicial Committee, but only with leave of the court concerned or, failing such leave, with special leave of the Judicial Committee.

PART III

PROCEEDINGS IN ENGLAND AND WALES

Application of Part III

14. This Part of this Schedule applies in relation to devolution issues in proceedings in England and Wales.

Institution of proceedings

15.—(1) Proceedings for the determination of a devolution issue may be instituted by the Attorney General.

(2) The Lord Advocate may defend any such proceedings.

(3) This paragraph is without prejudice to any power to institute or defend proceedings exercisable apart from this paragraph by any person.

Notice of devolution issue

16. A court or tribunal shall order notice of any devolution issue which arises in any proceedings before it to be given to the Attorney General and the Lord Advocate (unless the person to whom the notice would be given is a party to the proceedings).

17. A person to whom notice is given in pursuance of paragraph 16 may take part as a party in the proceedings, so far as they relate to a devolution issue.

Reference of devolution issue to High Court or Court of Appeal

18. A magistrates' court may refer any devolution issue which arises in proceedings (other than criminal proceedings) before it to the High Court.

19.—(1) A court may refer any devolution issue which arises in proceedings (other than criminal proceedings) before it to the Court of Appeal.

(2) Sub-paragraph (1) does not apply to—
   (a) a magistrates' court, the Court of Appeal or the House of Lords, or
   (b) the High Court if the devolution issue arises in proceedings on a reference under paragraph 18.

20. A tribunal from which there is no appeal shall refer any devolution issue which arises in proceedings before it to the Court of Appeal; and any other tribunal may make such a reference.

21. A court, other than the House of Lords or the Court of Appeal, may refer any devolution issue which arises in criminal proceedings before it to—

(a) the High Court (if the proceedings are summary proceedings), or

(b) the Court of Appeal (if the proceedings are proceedings on indictment).

References from Court of Appeal to Judicial Committee

22. The Court of Appeal may refer any devolution issue which arises in proceedings before it (otherwise than on a reference under paragraph 19, 20 or 21) to the Judicial Committee.

Appeals from superior courts to Judicial Committee

23. An appeal against a determination of a devolution issue by the High Court or the Court of Appeal on a reference under paragraph 18, 19, 20 or 21 shall lie to the Judicial Committee, but only with leave of the High Court or (as the case may be) the Court of Appeal or, failing such leave, with special leave of the Judicial Committee.

PART IV

PROCEEDINGS IN NORTHERN IRELAND

Application of Part IV

24. This Part of this Schedule applies in relation to devolution issues in proceedings in Northern Ireland.

Institution of proceedings

25.—(1) Proceedings for the determination of a devolution issue may be instituted by the Attorney General for Northern Ireland.

(2) The Lord Advocate may defend any such proceedings.

(3) This paragraph is without prejudice to any power to institute or defend proceedings exercisable apart from this paragraph by any person.

Notice of devolution issue

26. A court or tribunal shall order notice of any devolution issue which arises in any proceedings before it to be given to the Attorney General for Northern Ireland and the Lord Advocate (unless the person to whom the notice would be given is a party to the proceedings).

27. A person to whom notice is given in pursuance of paragraph 26 may take part as a party in the proceedings, so far as they relate to a devolution issue.

Reference of devolution issue to Court of Appeal

28. A court, other than the House of Lords or the Court of Appeal in Northern Ireland, may refer any devolution issue which arises in any proceedings before it to the Court of Appeal in Northern Ireland.

29. A tribunal from which there is no appeal shall refer any devolution issue which arises in any proceedings before it to the Court of Appeal in Northern Ireland; and any other tribunal may make such a reference.

References from Court of Appeal to Judicial Committee

30. The Court of Appeal in Northern Ireland may refer any devolution issue which arises in proceedings before it (otherwise than on a reference under paragraph 28 or 29) to the Judicial Committee.

Appeals from Court of Appeal to Judicial Committee

31. An appeal against a determination of a devolution issue by the Court of Appeal in Northern Ireland on a reference under paragraph 28 or 29 shall lie to the Judicial Committee, but only with leave of the Court of Appeal in Northern Ireland or, failing such leave, with special leave of the Judicial Committee.

PART V

GENERAL

Proceedings in the House of Lords

32. Any devolution issue which arises in judicial proceedings in the House of Lords shall be referred to the Judicial Committee unless the House considers it more appropriate, having regard to all the circumstances, that it should determine the issue.

Direct references to Judicial Committee

33. The Lord Advocate, the Advocate General, the Attorney General or the Attorney General for Northern Ireland may require any court or tribunal to refer to the Judicial Committee any devolution issue which has arisen in proceedings before it to which he is a party.

34. The Lord Advocate, the Attorney General, the Advocate General or the Attorney General for Northern Ireland may refer to the Judicial Committee any devolution issue which is not the subject of proceedings.

35.—(1) This paragraph applies where a reference is made under paragraph 34 in relation to a devolution issue which relates to the proposed exercise of a function by a member of the Scottish Executive.

(2) The person making the reference shall notify a member of the Scottish Executive of that fact.

(3) No member of the Scottish Executive shall exercise the function in the manner proposed during the period beginning with the receipt of the notification under sub-paragraph (2) and ending with the reference being decided or otherwise disposed of.

(4) Proceedings relating to any possible failure by a member of the Scottish Executive to comply with sub-paragraph (3) may be instituted by the Advocate General.

(5) Sub-paragraph (4) is without prejudice to any power to institute proceedings exercisable apart from that sub-paragraph by any person.

Expenses

36.—(1) A court or tribunal before which any proceedings take place may take account of any additional expense of the kind mentioned in sub-paragraph (3) in deciding any question as to costs or expenses.

(2) In deciding any such question, the court or tribunal may award the whole or part of the additional expense as costs or (as the case may be) expenses to the party who incurred it (whatever the decision on the devolution issue).

(3) The additional expense is any additional expense which the court or tribunal considers that any party to the proceedings has incurred as a result of the participation of any person in pursuance of paragraph 6, 17 or 27.

Procedure of courts and tribunals

37. Any power to make provision for regulating the procedure before any court or tribunal shall include power to make provision for the purposes of this Schedule including, in particular, provision—

(a) for prescribing the stage in the proceedings at which a devolution issue is to be raised or referred,

(b) for the sisting or staying of proceedings for the purpose of any proceedings under this Schedule, and

(c) for determining the manner in which and the time within which any intimation or notice is to be given.

Interpretation

38. Any duty or power conferred by this Schedule to refer a devolution issue to a court shall be construed as a duty or (as the case may be) power to refer the issue to the court for decision.

DEFINITIONS

"Act of the Scottish Parliament": s.28(1).

"Advocate General": s.32(4).

"Community law": s.126(9).

"the Convention rights": s.126(1).

"devolution issue": para. 1.

"function": s.126(1).

"Judicial Committee": s.32(4).

"legislative competence": s.29.

"Minister of the Crown": s.126(1).

"the Parliament": s.126(1).

"reserved matter": Sched. 5.

"tribunal": s.126(1).

GENERAL NOTE

It will be recalled (see the General Note to s.29) that one of the Government's hopes expressed in the White Paper was that the method adopted for the allocation of powers to the Scottish Parliament, by way of reservation of certain classes of function to Westminster whilst devolving the rest, would bring clarity and stability (para. 43). It would produce fewer disputes in the courts than the method adopted in the Scotland Act 1978. Equally, however, the Government recognised that questions about the extent of the Parliament's powers would still arise and mechanisms have been included in the Scotland Act 1998 to deal with such questions. Some of these are to be invoked during the enactment of a Bill by the Parliament. There is provision for the scrutiny of Bills by the relevant members of the Scottish Executive and by the Presiding Officer (s.31); and for the reference of Bills at the pre-Assent stage to the Judicial Committee of the Privy Council (ss.32–36). There is also the related power of the Secretary of State to intervene in certain cases (s.35).

The general scheme of the Act also acknowledges, however, that questions about the legislative competence of the Parliament may also arise in relation to an Act which has reached the statute book. As s.29(1) states, "(a)n Act of the Scottish Parliament is not law so far as any provision of the Act is outside the legislative competence of the Parliament". It has, therefore, to be within the power of the courts in appropriate proceedings to decide whether or not a particular provision of an Act is within or outside legislative competence.

In each case that will be a question of interpretation, a question of matching the meaning of the provision of an Act which is challenged against the meaning of the relevant provisions in the Scotland Act itself to establish their compatibility. That process of interpretation and the assistance given by the terms of ss.29, 30 and Scheds. 4, 5 have been discussed in the notes on those provisions.

The court in which a question about the competence of a Scottish Act may be initially raised is not something determined by the Scotland Act itself. Nor, of course, does the Act attempt to prejudge who will be the probable parties to proceedings in which these questions of competence will be raised. It may be that the proceedings will be raised by the U.K. Government to challenge the validity of an Act of the Parliament-producing a case between the Government and a devolved institution. Equally, however, it might be a citizen or group of citizens who wish to make the challenge—usually producing, therefore, a case between individuals and a devolved institution. In either of these circumstances the most likely but not inevitable form of proceedings would be judicial review in the Court of Session. Other possibilities, however, are that a questions of the validity of a provision in a Scottish Act might arise in proceedings between two individuals in a civil case; or in the course of a criminal prosecution.

The Scotland Act 1998 leaves open all these possibilities. It does, however, superimpose upon them the special procedures laid down in Sched. 6, under the authority of s.98. The Schedule applies to what are defined as "devolution issues", which include not only questions of legislative competence of the Scottish Parliament but also questions about the lawfulness (in various respects) of actions of members of the Scottish Executive and, by implication, of Ministers of the Crown. The detailed definitions of the "devolution issues" are discussed in the General Note to para.1.

The Schedule then provides a special regime governing "devolution issues" which includes mechanisms which in summary:
  (a) enable a devolution issue which arises in civil proceedings below the level of the Inner House of the Court of Session to be separated from other issues in the case and referred for decision by the Inner House, with an appeal available to the Judicial Committee of the Privy Council (paras. 7, 12, 13);
  (b) make similar provision in relation to criminal proceedings (but 'with special leave' on appeal) (paras. 9, 13). (See also Sched.8, para.32);
  (c) enable a devolution issue arising in the Inner House to be referred to the Judicial Committee (para.10);
  (d) provide similarly for criminal proceedings (para.11);
  (e) require the House of Lords to refer a devolution issue to the Judicial Committee unless the House considers it more appropriate to determine the issue itself (para.32);
  (f) require courts to order intimation of a devolution issue which arises before them to the Advocate General and the Lord Advocate and enable those law officers to take part in proceedings so far as they relate to a devolution issues (paras. 5, 6);
  (g) enable a law officer to institute proceedings for the determination of a devolution issue (para.4); and
  (h) enable a law officer to require any court to refer to a devolution issue directly to the Judicial Committee and to refer to the Judicial Committee a devolution issue which is not the subject of proceedings (paras.33,34).

The Schedule makes further provision for the award of expenses and for the regulation of procedures (paras. 36, 37). It also extends the mechanism for dealing with devolution issues to tribunals (para.8). Parallel provision is also made for devolution issues which may arise in proceedings in England and Wales (Part III) and in Northern Ireland (Part IV).

This Act also makes provision for certain situations consequential upon legal proceedings taken to challenge the validity of legislation made by the Scottish Parliament or action taken by members of the Scottish Executive. Section 107 authorises the making of such subordinate legislation by a U.K. Minister as is necessary or expedient in consequence of ultra vires and other acts by either the Scottish Parliament or members of the Scottish Executive. Section 102 permits a court or tribunal which has made a finding of invalidity to temper the impact of the decision by varying any retrospective effect or by suspending its effect. The Lord Advocate must be given intimation of the possibility of such an order and the opportunity to be a party to the proceedings.

PART I

Para. 1

This list of "devolution issues" was amended in important ways at committee stage in the House of Lords (Hansard, H.L. Vol. 593, cols. 578—581). It was explained that the devolution issues are, as far as possible, "confined to issues which raise vires questions which arise from the devolution settlement". Amendments made were stated to be partly in consequence of other changes affecting the description of the legislative competence of the Parliament (col. 579). However, one interesting omission from the amended list was a question "Whether a matter in relation to which a Minister of the Crown has purported to exercise or proposes to exercise a function is a devolved matter.". An amendment was necessary because the terminology "devolved matter" was being dropped from the Bill but the further result is the omission from the list of any express reference to action taken by a Minister of the Crown-although relevant questions could presumably be taken under subparas (b), (f).

In any particular case arising before the courts, it may be a matter of dispute whether an issue raised does indeed fall within one or other of the definitions of "devolution issue" and, therefore, become subject to the special procedures in the Schedule. In *Clancy v. Caird,* 2000, S.L.T. 546 this question arose in relation to a *failure* to act which produced an alleged incompatibility with the ECHR and whether this, therefore, raised a devolution issue under s.57(2). The question was answered affirmatively in that case (see especially Lord Penrose, paras. 3–14) but the case leaves open the issue of how such matters should be finally decided. In deciding that a question arose under s.57(2), the court held this to be based on the obligation of the state (hence of the Scottish Executive) to ensure the means of affording the public a hearing before an independent and impartial tribunal within a reasonable time.

Subpara. (a)

This must be the archetypal form of devolution issue-one which goes to the legislative competence of the Scottish Parliament, as defined by ss.29, 30 and Scheds. 4, 5. There might have been the opportunity for a challenge to the validity of a provision by reference to the Judicial Committee under s.33, but the question of competence could again arise as a devolution issue.

Subpara. (b)

Under the terms of this Act, certain functions are conferred on the First Minister; on the Lord Advocate; and also the Scottish Ministers, as such. This subparagraph identifies a question whether a particular functions is one of those functions as a "devolution issue". This might arise where the function challenged is being exercised (or proposed) by one of the three named persons or, presumably, where the function is purportedly being exercised by some "other" person, *e.g.* a Minister of the Crown where the function has been transferred by s.53 (and not shared by s.56) or s.63.

Slightly oddly, it seems to raise the possibility that the question whether a function has been conferred on e.g. the Scottish Ministers by the Scottish Parliament is also a "devolution issue", And does the "purported exercise" of a function by (a) a civil servant or (b) a local authority or other public authority also become a "devolution issue"?

Subpara. (c)

Clearly related to (b), this defines as a "devolution issue" the question of whether the exercise (or purported exercise) of a function (by a member of the Scottish Executive) is within "devolved competence". Powers transferred by s.53 are exercisable within "devolved competence", which is defined by reference to the legislative competence of the Scottish Parliament by s.54.

Functions conferred by s.63 must be exercisable "in or as regards Scotland" but are "outside devolved competence" in that they relate to reserved matters. Therefore, to resolve the question of whether the exercise of a function by a member of the Scottish Executive is "within devolved competence" will not necessarily decide its legality.

Subparas. (d), (e)

The obligation on members of the Scottish Executive not to do anything incompatible with any of the Convention rights or with Community law is imposed by s.57(2) and in relation to powers transferred by s.53, by s.54.

See *Clancy v. Caird* above.

Subpara. (f)

This subparagraph has the character of a catch-all provision, in particular "any other question arising by virtue of this Act about reserved matters." Presumably, it would, as earlier mentioned, enable some forms of challenge to acts or decisions of Ministers of the Crown to be treated as "devolution issues".

Para. 2

This is intended to prevent abuse of procedures provided by the Schedule. It may be thought unlikely that litigants will be tempted to present contentions which might be considered "frivolous or vexatious". It has, however, been stated that, as of February 2000, there had already been some 337 human rights questions raised as devolution issues (SPOR, 17 February 2000, col. 1233).

PART II

For the provision made for the institution of proceedings, the intimation to law officers of devolution issues, the reference of issues to higher courts and reference or appeal to the Judicial Committee, see the note above. It should be borne in mind that, in addition to the special procedures provided, devolution issues may be taken on appeal by the use of normal appellate procedures. It is for this reason that new powers have been given to the Advocate General for use in criminal proceedings. See Sched. 8, para. 32.

PARTS III, IV

These make parallel provision for England and Wales and Northern Ireland.

PART V

In addition to making provision for referring devolution issues from the House of Lords to the Judicial Committee (para. 32), this Part provides for the procedure for direct reference to the Judicial Committee on the initiative of a law officer (paras. 33, 34). para35 makes interesting supplementary provision for a Judicial Committee reference under para. 34 (*i.e.* of a devolution issue which is not the subject of legal proceedings) by a law officer when this "relates to the proposed exercise of a function by a member of the Scottish Executive". The function must not be exercised before the reference is resolved. No equivalent provision is made for the stalling of proposed decision-making by a Minister of the Crown which might equally raise a devolution issue.

The procedural rules made in relation to devolution issues arising in Scottish Courts are: the Judicial Committee (Devolution Issues) Rules Order 1999 (S.I. 1999 No. 665); the Act of Sederunt (Devolution Issues Rules) 1999 (S.I. 1999 No. 1345); the Act of Adjournal (Devolution Issues Rules) 1999 (S.I. 1999 No. 1346); and the Act of Sederunt (Proceedings for Determination of Devolution Issues Rules) 1999 (S.I. 1999 No. 1347).

Section 115   SCHEDULE 7

PROCEDURE FOR SUBORDINATE LEGISLATION

General provision

1.—(1) Subordinate legislation (or a statutory instrument containing it) under a provision listed in the left—hand column is subject to the type of procedure in the right-hand column.

(2) This paragraph is subject to paragraphs 3 and 4.

Provision of the Act	Type of procedure
Section 2(1)	Type C
Section 12(1)	Type C
Section 15	Type D
Section 18(5)	Type J
Section 30	Type A
Section 35	Type I
Section 38	Type J
Section 56(2)	Type G
Section 58	Type I
Section 60	Type G
Section 62	Type G
Section 63	Type A
Section 64(5)	Type K
Section 67(3)	Type E
Section 71(6)	Type K
Section 79	Type E
Section 88	Type I
Section 89	Type F
Section 90	Type F
Section 93	Type H
Section 97	Type A
Section 103(3)(a) and (b)	Type I
Section 104	Type G
Section 105	Type G
Section 106	Type G
Section 107	Type G
Section 108	Type A
Section 109	Type H
Section 110(1)	Type C
Section 110(2)	Type I
Section 111	Type A
Section 116(9)	Type G
Section 124(1)	Type G
Section 126(2)	Type B
Section 126(8)	Type H
Section 129(1)	Type G
Schedule 2, paragraph 2	Type G
Schedule 2, paragraph 7	Type H

Notes

The entry for section 58 does not apply to an instrument containing an order merely revoking an order under subsection (1) of that section.

The entry for section 79, in relation to an instrument containing an order which makes only such provision as is mentioned in section 79(3), is to be read as referring to type K instead of type E.

Types of procedure

2. The types of procedure referred to in this Schedule are—
    Type A: No recommendation to make the legislation is to be made to Her Majesty in Council unless a draft of the instrument—
        (a) has been laid before, and approved by resolution of, each House of Parliament, and
        (b) has been laid before, and approved by resolution of, the Parliament.
    Type B: No recommendation to make the legislation is to be made to Her Majesty in Council unless a draft of the instrument has been laid before, and approved by resolution of, each House of Parliament.
    Type C: No Minister of the Crown is to make the legislation unless a draft of the instrument has been laid before, and approved by resolution of, each House of Parliament.
    Type D: No recommendation to make the legislation is to be made to Her Majesty in Council unless a draft of the instrument has been laid before, and approved by resolution of, the Parliament.

219

Type E: No Minister of the Crown is to make the legislation unless a draft of the instrument has been laid before, and approved by resolution of, the House of Commons.

Type F: The instrument containing the legislation, if made without a draft having been approved by resolution of each House of Parliament and of the Parliament, shall be subject to annulment in pursuance of—
    (a) a resolution of either House, or
    (b) a resolution of the Parliament.

Type G: The instrument containing the legislation, if made without a draft having been approved by resolution of each House of Parliament, shall be subject to annulment in pursuance of a resolution of either House.

Type H: The instrument containing the legislation shall be subject to annulment in pursuance of—
    (a) a resolution of either House of Parliament, or
    (b) a resolution of the Parliament.

Type I: The instrument containing the legislation shall be subject to annulment in pursuance of a resolution of either House of Parliament.

Type J: The instrument containing the legislation shall be subject to annulment in pursuance of a resolution of the Parliament.

Type K: The instrument containing the legislation shall be subject to annulment in pursuance of a resolution of the House of Commons.

Special cases

3.—(1) This paragraph applies if—
(a) the instrument containing the legislation would, apart from this paragraph, be subject to the type F, G, H, I or K procedure, and
(b) the legislation contains provisions which add to, replace or omit any part of the text of an Act.
(2) Where this paragraph applies—
(a) instead of the type F procedure, the type A procedure shall apply,
(b) instead of the type G procedure, the type B or (as the case may be) C procedure shall apply,
(c) instead of the type H procedure, the type A procedure shall apply,
(d) instead of the type I procedure, the type B or (as the case may be) C procedure shall apply,
(e) instead of the type K procedure, the type E procedure shall apply.
4. If legislation under section 129(1) makes provision as mentioned in section 112(2) then, instead of the type G procedure, the type D procedure shall apply.
5.—(1) An instrument containing an Order in Council or order under an open power which revokes, amends or re—enacts subordinate legislation under an open power may (in spite of section 14 of the Interpretation Act 1978) be subject to a different procedure under this Schedule from the procedure to which the instrument containing the original legislation was subject.
(2) An instrument containing an Order in Council under section 89 or 90 which revokes, amends or re—enacts an Order under either section may (in spite of section 14 of the Interpretation Act 1978) be subject to a different procedure under this Schedule from the procedure to which the instrument containing the original Order was subject.

DEFINITIONS
"Minister of the Crown": s.126(1).
"open power": s.112(3).
"the Parliament": s.126(1).
"subordinate legislation": s.126(1).

GENERAL NOTE
This Schedule is given effect by s.115. For a general introduction to the powers and procedures used in this Act for the making of subordinate legislation, see the General Note to s.112. The Schedule, which was added as part of the general restructuring of the order-making provisions at House of Lords committee stage (see Hansard, H.L. Vol. 593, cols. 624—626, 641—642, 647—649), plays a very important part in the overall scheme. By reference to 11 types (A—K) of parliamentary procedure in the Westminster or Scottish Parliament or both, it specifies the procedure applicable to each order-making power in the Act.

Para. 1

This paragraph provides an index of the powers in the order in which they appear in the Act.

It may be useful to have a reverse index (*i.e.* regrouping the powers under the type of procedure) and this would be as follows:

Type A

Section 30	(Legislative competence of the Scottish Parliament)
Section 60	(Transfer of functions)
Section 97	(Assistance for opposition parties)
Section 108	(Agreed redistribution of functions)
Section 111	(Regulation of Tweed and Esk fisheries)

Type B

Section 126(2)	(Boundaries between waters)

Type C

Section 2(1)	(First ordinary general election meeting)
Section 12(1)	(Conduct of elections, etc.)
Section 110(1)	(Scottish taxpayers for social security purposes)

Type D

Section 15	(Disqualification from membership of the Scottish Parliament)

Type E

Section 67(3)	(Increased lending by Secretary of State)
*Section 79	(Supplemental powers to modify enactments in relation to tax-varying power)

Type F

Section 89	(Power to adapt, etc., cross-border public authorities)
Section 90	(Transfer of property of cross-border public authorities)

Type G

Section 56(2)	(Shared powers)
Section 60	(Transfer of property and liabilities to Scottish Ministers)
Section 62	(Transfers to Lord Advocate)
Section 104	(Provision consequential on Acts of the Scottish Parliament)
Section 105	(Provision consequential on this Act)
Section 106	(Power to adapt functions)
Section 107	(Power to remedy *ultra vires* acts)
Section 116(9)	(Determination of disputes re transfer of property)
Section 124(1)	(Modification of ss94, 117–122)
Section 129(1)	(Transitional provision)
Schedule 2, para. 3	(Transfers to Parliamentary corporation)

Type H

Section 93	(Agency arrangements)
Section 109	(Transfers to Ministers of the Crown, etc.)
Section 126(8)	(Offices in the Scottish Administration)
Schedule 2, para. 7	(Crown status of Parliamentary corporation)

Type I

Section 35	(Secretary of State's power to intervene)
**Section 58	(Power to prevent or require action)
Section 88	(Specification to cross-border authorities)
Section 103(3) (a) and (b)	(Powers of Judicial Committee)
Section 110(2)	(Scottish taxpayers for social security purposes)

Type J

Section 18(5)	(Caution in respect of disqualification proceedings)
Section 38	(Letters Patent and Proclamations)

Type K
> Section 64(5)   (Designation of receipts payable in Scottish Consolidated Fund)
>
> Section 71(6)   (Existing debt)

* An order confined to provision under s.79(3) (PAYE) is subject to Type K procedure, rather than Type E.

** As noted in the table in the Schedule, the Type I procedure does not apply to an order "merely revoking" an order under s.54(1).

Para.2

This specifies the 11 different types of procedure by reference to formulations of
1. the type of subordinate legislation
   i.e. exclusively by Order in Council (Types A, B, D)
   or any form of legislation (Types C, E, F, G, H, I, J, K)
2. which Parliament is involved
   i.e. both (Types A, F, H)
   or Scottish Parliament only (Types D, J)
   or Westminster only (Types B, C, E, G, I, K) and, in that case, divided between procedure in both Houses (Types B, C, G, I) or the Commons alone (Types E and K)
3. whether affirmative or negative procedure
   i.e. affirmative (Types A, B, C, D, E)
   or negative (Types F, G, H, I, J, K).

Para. 3

At a number of points in this Act, provision is made for the amendment of Acts of Parliament by subordinate legislation. Specifically conferred powers include those in ss.79, 105, 106, 111(5). A general power to amend enactments (other than the Scotland Act itself) is, however, conferred by s.113(5), (6) and s.114(1) contains a list of provisions under which the Scotland Act (except Scheds. 4,5) may be amended. Section 30(2) authorises the amendment of Scheds. 4, 5.

This paragraph "upgrades" the parliamentary procedure required if a power is used for the purpose of amending (*i.e.* "add to, replace or omit any part of the text of") an Act.

Para. 4

This identifies the special case of the use of s.129(1) to make transitional provision for appropriation from the Scottish Consolidated Fund by Order in Council and makes the change from use of the Westminster procedure to procedure in the Scottish Parliament. (See s.112(2).)

Para. 5

Section 14 of the Interpretation Act 1978 (c.30) provides that a power to make various categories of subordinate legislation "implies, unless the contrary intention appears, a power exercisable in the same manner and subject to the same conditions or limitations, to revoke, amend or re-enact any instrument made under the power". Because the powers under the Scotland Act include the "open power" exercisable in two different ways (and also the specific case of ss.89,90), these provisions disapplying s.14 are included.

Section 125   SCHEDULE 8

MODIFICATIONS OF ENACTMENTS

Public Revenue (Scotland) Act 1833 (c.13)

1. In section 2 of the Public Revenue (Scotland) Act 1833 (regulation of Queen's and Lord Treasurer's Remembrancer), for "Treasury" in both places there is substituted "Scottish Ministers".

Crown Suits (Scotland) Act 1857 (c.44)

2.—(1) The Crown Suits (Scotland) Act 1857 is amended as follows.
(2) In section 1 (Crown suits may be brought by or against Lord Advocate)—
   (a) after "Crown" there is inserted "(including the Scottish Administration)", and
   (b) for "Her Majesty's Advocate for the time being" there is substituted "the appropriate Law Officer".

(3) In section 2 (authority of Crown required)—
 (a) for "Her Majesty's Advocate" there is substituted "the appropriate Law Officer", and
 (b) after "Majesty" there is inserted "of the part of the Scottish Administration".
(4) In section 3 (absence of authority cannot be founded upon), for "Her Majesty's Advocate" there is substituted "the appropriate Law Officer".
(5) After section 4 there is inserted—
 "Meaning of "the appropriate Law Officer"
 4A. In this Act "the appropriate Law Officer" means—
  (a) the Lord Advocate, where the action, suit or proceeding is on behalf of or against any part of the Scottish Administration, and
  (b) the Advocate General for Scotland, in any other case."
(6) In section 5 (change of Lord Advocate not to affect proceedings)—
 (a) for "Her Majesty's Advocate" there is substituted "the Lord Advocate or the Advocate General for Scotland", and
 (b) for "the office of Her Majesty's Advocate" there is substituted "that office".

Sheriff Courts and Legal Officers (Scotland) Act 1927 (c.35)

3.—(1) The Sheriff Courts and Legal Officers (Scotland) Act 1927 is amended as follows.
(2) In section 1(2) (appointment etc. of procurator fiscal), "with the consent of the Treasury" is omitted.
(3) In section 2 (appointment of sheriff clerk and procurator fiscal deputes), "with the consent of the Treasury as to numbers and salaries" is omitted.
(4) In section 3 (whole-time sheriff clerks and procurators fiscal and deputes), "and in either case with the consent of the Treasury" is omitted.
(5) In section 5 (whole-time clerks), "with the consent of the Treasury as to numbers and salaries" is omitted.
(6) In section 12 (prosecutions at instance of procurator fiscal), "after consultation with the Treasury" is omitted.

Administration of Justice (Scotland) Act 1933 (c.41)

4. In the Administration of Justice (Scotland) Act 1933, in sections 24(7) and 25 (officers of Court of Session etc.), "and shall be exercised on nomination by the Lord Advocate" is omitted.

Private Legislation Procedure (Scotland) Act 1936 (c.52)

5. In section 1 of the Private Legislation Procedure (Scotland) Act 1936 (application for provisional order: notices), after subsection (4) there is added—
 "(5) This section shall not apply where any public authority or any persons desire to obtain parliamentary powers the conferring of which is wholly within the legislative competence of the Scottish Parliament."

United Nations Act 1946 (c.45)

6. In section 1 of the United Nations Act 1946 (measures to give effect to decisions of Security Council), in subsection (4), for the words following "shall" there is substituted "forthwith after it is made be laid—
 (a) before Parliament; and
 (b) if any provision made by the Order would, if it were included in an Act of the Scottish Parliament, be within the legislative competence of that Parliament, before that Parliament."

Crown Proceedings Act 1947 (c.44)

7.—(1) The Crown Proceedings Act 1947 is amended as follows.
(2) In section 38(2) (interpretation)—
 (a) in the definition of "His Majesty's aircraft", after "Kingdom" there is inserted "or the Scottish Administration",
 (b) in the definition of "His Majesty's ships", after "Kingdom" there is inserted "or the Scottish Administration" and after "said Government" there is inserted "or Administration", and
 (c) in the definition of "officer", after "Minister of the Crown" there is inserted "and a member of the Scottish Executive".
(3) In section 40 (savings)—
 (a) in subsection (2), after "in the United Kingdom", in each place where those words appear, there is inserted "or the Scottish Administration", and

(b) after subsection (3) there is inserted—

"(3A) A certificate of the Scottish Ministers to the effect that—

(a) any alleged liability of the Crown arises otherwise than in respect of the Scottish Administration,

(b) any proceedings by the Crown are proceedings otherwise than in right of the Scottish Administration,

shall, for the purposes of this Act, be conclusive as to that matter."

(4) In the proviso to section 44 (remit from sheriff court to Court of Session on Lord Advocate's certificate)—

(a) for "Lord Advocate" there is substituted "appropriate Law Officer", and

(b) at the end there is inserted—

"In this proviso, "the appropriate Law Officer" means—(a) the Lord Advocate, where the proceedings are against any part of the Scottish Administration, and

(b) the Advocate General for Scotland, in any other case."

(5) In section 50 (application to Scotland of section 35), subsection (2) of section 35 as substituted for Scotland is amended as follows—

(a) in paragraph (d)—(i) after "Crown" there is inserted "in right of Her Majesty's Government in the United Kingdom",

(ii) for "Lord Advocate" there is substituted "Advocate General for Scotland", and

(iii) after "department", in the second place where it appears, there is inserted—

"(i) shall not be entitled to avail itself of any set—off or counterclaim if the subject matter thereof relates to the Scottish Administration, and

(ii) ", and

(b) after that paragraph there is inserted—

"(e) a part of the Scottish Administration, in any proceedings against that part or against the Lord Advocate on its behalf, shall not be entitled to avail itself of any set—off or counterclaim if the subject matter thereof relates to another part of the Scottish Administration or to the Crown in right of Her Majesty's Government in the United Kingdom."

(6) In section 51(2) (application to Scotland of section 38), in paragraph (ii), after "Lord Advocate" there is inserted "or the Advocate General for Scotland".

Public Registers and Records (Scotland) Act 1948 (c.57)

8. In section 1(1) of the Public Registers and Records (Scotland) Act 1948 (appointment etc. of Keeper of the Registers and Keeper of the Records), for "Secretary of State" there is substituted "Scottish Ministers".

Lands Tribunal Act 1949 (c.42)

9. In section 2 of the Lands Tribunal Act 1949 (members etc. of Lands Tribunal for Scotland)—

(a) in subsection (9)—

(i) after "effect" there is inserted "with the omission of subsection (8) and", and

(ii) in paragraph (a), for "(8)" there is substituted "(7)", and

(b) after that subsection there is inserted— "(10) The remuneration of members of the Lands Tribunal for Scotland shall be charged on the Scottish Consolidated Fund."

Defamation Act 1952 (c.66)

10. In section 10 of the Defamation Act 1952 (limitation on privilege at elections), after "local government authority" there is inserted "to the Scottish Parliament".

Defamation Act (Northern Ireland) 1955 (c.11 (N.I.))

11. In section 10(2) of the Defamation Act (Northern Ireland) 1955 (limitation on privilege at elections), after "Parliament of the United Kingdom" there is inserted "or to the Scottish Parliament".

Registration of Births, Deaths and Marriages (Scotland) Act 1965 (c.49)

12. In section 1(1) of the Registration of Births, Deaths and Marriages (Scotland) Act 1965 (power of Secretary of State to appoint Registrar General), for "Secretary of State" there is substituted "Scottish Ministers".

Pensions (Increase) Act 1971 (c.56)

13. In Part II of Schedule 2 to the Pensions (Increase) Act 1971 (official pensions out of local funds), before paragraph 39 there is inserted—

"Scottish Parliament and Scottish Executive

38AB. A pension payable under a scheme established by virtue of section 81(4)(b) of, or paragraph 3(4)(b) of Schedule 2 to, the Scotland Act 1998."

Superannuation Act 1972 (c.11)

14. In section 1(6) of the Superannuation Act 1972 (superannuation as respects civil servants etc.), for "or the Consolidated Fund" there is substituted "the Consolidated Fund or the Scottish Consolidated Fund".

European Communities Act 1972 (c.68)

15.—(1) The European Communities Act 1972 is amended as follows.

(2) In section 2 (general implementation of Treaties)—
  (a) references to a statutory power or duty include a power or duty conferred by an Act of the Scottish Parliament or an instrument made under such an Act, and
  (b) references to an enactment include an enactment within the meaning of this Act.

(3) In relation to regulations made by the Scottish Ministers, or an Order in Council made on the recommendation of the First Minister, under section 2—
  (a) in subsection (2), "designated" in the first sentence, and the second sentence, shall be disregarded,
  (b) references to an Act of Parliament shall be read as references to an Act of the Scottish Parliament, and
  (c) paragraph 2(2) of Schedule 2 shall have effect as if the references to each, or either, House of Parliament were to the Scottish Parliament.

(4) In section 3(4) (evidence), references to a government department include any part of the Scottish Administration.

Interpretation Act 1978 (c.30)

16.—(1) The Interpretation Act 1978 is amended as follows.

(2) After section 23 there is inserted—

"Acts of the Scottish Parliament etc.

23A.—(1) This Act applies in relation to an Act of the Scottish Parliament and an instrument made under such an Act only to the extent provided in this section.

(2) Except as provided in subsection (3) below, sections 15 to 18 apply to—
  (a) an Act of the Scottish Parliament as they apply to an Act,
  (b) an instrument made under an Act of the Scottish Parliament as they apply to subordinate legislation.

(3) In the application of those sections to an Act and to subordinate legislation—
  (a) references to an enactment include an enactment comprised in, or in an instrument made under, an Act of the Scottish Parliament, and
  (b) the reference in section 17(2)(b) to subordinate legislation includes an instrument made under an Act of the Scottish Parliament.

(4) In the application of section 20 to an Act and to subordinate legislation, references to an enactment include an enactment comprised in, or in an instrument made under, an Act of the Scottish Parliament."

(3) In Schedule 1 (words and expressions defined), the following Definitions are inserted in the appropriate places—

"Act" means an Act of Parliament."

"Enactment" does not include an enactment comprised in, or in an instrument made under, an Act of the Scottish Parliament."

Education (Scotland) Act 1980 (c.44)

17. In section 135(1) of the Education (Scotland) Act 1980 (interpretation), in the definition of "Her Majesty's inspectors", "on the recommendation of the Secretary of State" is omitted.

Civil Jurisdiction and Judgments Act 1982 (c.27)

18.—(1) Section 46 of the Civil Jurisdiction and Judgments Act 1982 (domicile and seat of the Crown) is amended as follows.

(2) In subsection (3), after paragraph (a) there is inserted—

"(aa) the Crown in right of the Scottish Administration has its seat in, and in every place in, Scotland,".

(3) In subsection (7), after "Kingdom" there is inserted ", the Scottish Administration".

Mental Health Act 1983 (c.20)

19. In section 141 of the Mental Health Act 1983 (members of the House of Commons suffering from mental illness), after subsection (7), there is added—
"(8) This section also has effect in relation to members of the Scottish Parliament but as if—
   (a) any references to the House of Commons or the Speaker were references to the Scottish Parliament or (as the case may be) the Presiding Officer, and
   (b) subsection (7) were omitted."

National Audit Act 1983 (c.44)

20. Sections 6 and 7 of the National Audit Act 1983 (value for money studies) shall not apply in relation to—
   (a) the Scottish Administration or any part of it, or
   (b) any Scottish public authority with mixed functions or no reserved functions.

Tourism (Overseas Promotion) (Scotland) Act 1984 (c.4)

21. In section 1 of the Tourism (Overseas Promotion) (Scotland) Act 1984 (power of Scottish Tourist Board to promote tourism in Scotland outside UK), subsection (2) is omitted.

Bankruptcy (Scotland) Act 1985 (c.66)

22. For section 1 of the Bankruptcy (Scotland) Act 1985 there is substituted—
"Accountant in Bankruptcy
   1.—(1) The Accountant in Bankruptcy shall be appointed by the Scottish Ministers.
   (2) The Scottish Ministers may appoint a member of the staff of the Accountant in Bankruptcy to be Depute Accountant in Bankruptcy to exercise all of the functions of the Accountant in Bankruptcy at any time when the Accountant in Bankruptcy is unable to do so."

Insolvency Act 1986 (c.45)

23.—(1) The Insolvency Act 1986 is amended as follows.
(2) Anything directed to be done, or which may be done, to or by—
   (a) the registrar of companies in Scotland by virtue of any of the provisions mentioned in sub-paragraph (3), or
   (b) the assistant registrar of friendly societies for Scotland by virtue of any of those provisions as applied (with or without modification) in relation to friendly societies, industrial and provident societies or building societies,
shall, or (as the case may be) may, also be done to or by the Accountant in Bankruptcy.
(3) Those provisions are: sections 53(1), 54(3), 61(6), 62(5) (so far as relating to the giving of notice), 67(1), 69(2), 84(3), 94(3), 106(3) and (5), 112(3), 130(1), 147(3), 170(2) and 172(8).
(4) Anything directed to be done to or by—
   (a) the registrar of companies in Scotland by virtue of any of the provisions mentioned in sub-paragraph (5), or
   (b) the assistant registrar of friendly societies for Scotland by virtue of any of those provisions as applied (with or without modification) in relation to friendly societies, industrial and provident societies or building societies,
shall instead be done to or by the Accountant in Bankruptcy.
(5) Those provisions are: sections 89(3), 109(1), 171(5) and (6), 173(2)(a) and 192(1).
(6) In section 427 (members of the House of Commons whose estates are sequestrated etc.), after subsection (6) there is inserted—
   "(6A) Subsections (4) to (6) have effect in relation to a member of the Scottish Parliament but as if—
   (a) references to the House of Commons were to the Parliament and references to the Speaker were to the Presiding Officer, and
   (b) in subsection (4), for "under this section" there were substituted "under section 15(1)(b) of the Scotland Act 1998 by virtue of this section"."

Public Order Act 1986 (c.64)

24. In section 26(1) of the Public Order Act 1986 (savings for reports of parliamentary proceedings), after "Parliament" there is inserted "or in the Scottish Parliament".

Copyright, Designs and Patents Act 1988 (c.48)

25.—(1) The Copyright, Designs and Patents Act 1988 is amended as follows.

(2) In section 12(9) (duration of copyright in literary, dramatic, musical or artistic works), for "166" there is substituted "166A".

(3) In section 153(2) (qualification for copyright protection), for "166" there is substituted "166A".

(4) In section 163(6) (Crown copyright), for "and 166" there is substituted "to 166A".

(5) In section 164(1) (Crown copyright in Acts of Parliament etc.), after "Parliament" there is inserted "Act of the Scottish Parliament".

(6) After section 166 there is inserted—

"Copyright in Bills of the Scottish Parliament.

166A.—(1) Copyright in every Bill introduced into the Scottish Parliament belongs to the Scottish Parliamentary Corporate Body.

(2) Copyright under this section subsists from the time when the text of the Bill is handed in to the Parliament for introduction—

(a) until the Bill receives Royal Assent, or

(b) if the Bill does not receive Royal Assent, until it is withdrawn or rejected or no further parliamentary proceedings may be taken in respect of it.

(3) References in this Part to Parliamentary copyright (except in section 165) include copyright under this section; and, except as mentioned above, the provisions of this Part apply in relation to copyright under this section as to other Parliamentary copyright.

(4) No other copyright, or right in the nature of copyright, subsists in a Bill after copyright has once subsisted under this section; but without prejudice to the subsequent operation of this section in relation to a Bill which, not having received Royal Assent, is later reintroduced into the Parliament."

(7) In section 178 (minor Definitions)—

(a) in the definition of "the Crown", after "of" there is inserted "the Scottish Administration or of", and

(b) in the definition of "parliamentary proceedings", after "Assembly" there is inserted "of the Scottish Parliament".

(8) In section 179 (index of defined expressions), in column 2 of the entry for "Parliamentary copyright", for "and 166(6)" there is substituted "166(6) and 166A(3)".

Official Secrets Act 1989 (c.6)

26.—(1) Section 12 of the Official Secrets Act 1989 (meaning of "Crown servant" and "government contractor" for the purposes of that Act) is amended as follows.

(2) In subsection (1), after paragraph (a) there is inserted—

"(aa) a member of the Scottish Executive or a junior Scottish Minister;".

(3) In subsection (2)(a), after "above," there is inserted "of any office-holder in the Scottish Administration,".

(4) After subsection (3) there is inserted—

"(4) In this section "office-holder in the Scottish Administration" has the same meaning as in section 126(7)(a) of the Scotland Act 1998.".

Prisons (Scotland) Act 1989 (c.45)

27.—(1) The Prisons (Scotland) Act 1989 is amended as follows.

(2) Section 2 of that Act (appointment of officers etc.) is omitted.

(3) In section 3(1) (prison officers), for the words following "Secretary of State" there is substituted—

"(1A) Every prison shall have a governor and such other officers as may be necessary."

(4) In section 3A (medical services)—

(a) in subsection (2), for "appointing" there is substituted "providing" and for "appointment" there is substituted "provision", and

(b) in subsection (4), for "appointed" there is substituted "provided".

European Communities (Amendment) Act 1993 (c.32)

28. In section 6 of the European Communities (Amendment) Act 1993 (persons who may be proposed for membership of the Committee of the Regions), after "he is" there is inserted "a member of the Scottish Parliament".

Scottish Land Court Act 1993 (c.45)

29. In section 1 of the Scottish Land Court Act 1993 (the Scottish Land Court)—

(a) in subsection (2), for "Secretary of State" there is substituted "First Minister", and

(b) after subsection (2) there is inserted— "(2A) Before recommending the appointment of a person as Chairman, the First Minister shall consult the Lord President of the Court of Session."

Scotland Act 1998

Value Added Tax Act 1994 (c.23)

30. In section 41 of the Value Added Tax Act 1994 (application to the Crown), in subsection (6), after "includes" there is inserted "the Scottish Administration".

Requirements of Writing (Scotland) Act 1995 (c.7)

31. In section 12(1) of the Requirements of Writing (Scotland) Act 1995 (interpretation)—
   (a) in the definition of "Minister", after "1975" there is inserted "and also includes a member of the Scottish Executive", and
   (b) in paragraph (a) of the definition of "officer", after "Department" there is inserted "or, as the case may be, as a member of the staff of the Scottish Ministers or the Lord Advocate".

Criminal Procedure (Scotland) Act 1995 (c.46)

32.—(1) The Criminal Procedure (Scotland) Act 1995 is amended as follows.
(2) After section 288 there is inserted—

"Devolution issues
Rights of appeal for Advocate General: devolution issues
288A.—(1) This section applies where—
(a) a person is acquitted or convicted of a charge (whether on indictment or in summary proceedings), and
(b) the Advocate General for Scotland was a party to the proceedings in pursuance of paragraph 6 of Schedule 6 to the Scotland Act 1998 (devolution issues).
(2) The Advocate General for Scotland may refer any devolution issue which has arisen in the proceedings to the High Court for their opinion; and the Clerk of Justiciary shall send to the person acquitted or convicted and to any solicitor who acted for that person at the trial, a copy of the reference and intimation of the date fixed by the Court for a hearing.
(3) The person may, not later than seven days before the date so fixed, intimate in writing to the Clerk of Justiciary and to the Advocate General for Scotland either—
(a) that he elects to appear personally at the hearing, or
(b) that he elects to be represented by counsel at the hearing,
but, except by leave of the Court on cause shown, and without prejudice to his right to attend, he shall not appear or be represented at the hearing other than by and in conformity with an election under this subsection.
(4) Where there is no intimation under subsection (3)(b), the High Court shall appoint counsel to act at the hearing as amicus curiae.
(5) The costs of representation elected under subsection (3)(b) or of an appointment under subsection (4) shall, after being taxed by the Auditor of the Court of Session, be paid by the Advocate General for Scotland out of money provided by Parliament.
(6) The opinion on the point referred under subsection (2) shall not affect the acquittal or (as the case may be) conviction in the trial.
Appeals to Judicial Committee of the Privy Council
288B.—(1) This section applies where the Judicial Committee of the Privy Council determines an appeal under paragraph 13(a) of Schedule 6 to the Scotland Act 1998 against a determination of a devolution issue by the High Court in the ordinary course of proceedings.
(2) The determination of the appeal shall not affect any earlier acquittal or earlier quashing of any conviction in the proceedings.
(3) Subject to subsection (2) above, the High Court shall have the same powers in relation to the proceedings when remitted to it by the Judicial Committee as it would have if it were considering the proceedings otherwise than as a trial court."
(3) In section 307(1) (interpretation), after the definition of "crime" there is inserted—
"'devolution issue' has the same meaning as in Schedule 6 to the Scotland Act 1998;".

Defamation Act 1996 (c.31)

33.—(1) The Defamation Act 1996 is amended as follows.
(2) In section 17(1) (interpretation), in the definition of "statutory provision", after "1978" there is inserted—
"(aa) a provision contained in an Act of the Scottish Parliament or in an instrument made under such an Act,".
(3) In paragraph 11(1)(c) of Schedule 1 (qualified privilege), after "Minister of the Crown" there is inserted "a member of the Scottish Executive".

Damages Act 1996 (c.48)

34. In section 6 of the Damages Act 1996 (guarantees for public sector settlements), after subsection (8) there is inserted—
"(8A) In the application of subsection (3) above to Scotland, for the words from "guidelines" to the end there shall be substituted "the Minister"."

GENERAL NOTE

This Schedule is given effect by s.125(1) and makes a number of amendments/modifications to existing enactments for purposes including the need to reflect the transfer of functions to the Scottish Ministers; to make amendments consequential upon the redistribution of law officer functions; and to make other amendments consequential upon provisions in the Act.

See also ss.117–124 which provide for the "general modification" of enactments to achieve similar purposes and s.105 which enables further modifications to be made to "pre-commencement enactments" by subordinate legislation.

Para. 1

The Queen's and Lord Treasurer's Remembrancer is responsible for the collection of certain hereditary revenues of the Crown—*bona vacantia, ultimus haeres* and treasure trove—which are to be excepted from the general reservation of the Crown. See Sched. 5, Pt. I, paras. 1(a) and 3(3)(a).

The 1833 Act provides for the regulation of and the power to issue directions in respect of the performance of these duties in Scotland. The modification provides for these powers to be exercised by the Scottish Ministers.

Para 2

The Crown Suits (Scotland) Act 1857 (c. 44) regulates the institution of suits at the instance of and against, the Crown and public departments in the courts of Scotland. It provides that "(e)very action, suit, or proceeding to be instituted in Scotland on the behalf of or against Her Majesty, or in the interest of the Crown, or on the behalf of or against any public department, may be lawfully raised in the name and at the instance of or directed against Her Majesty's Advocate for the time being".

The modifications add the Scottish Administration to the references to the Crown and public departments as appropriate, to extend the application of the Crown Suits (Scotland) Act 1857 to every action, suit or proceeding to be instituted in Scotland on behalf of or against the Scottish Administration. They also amend references to "Her Majesty's Advocate" to refer instead to "the appropriate Law Officer" and insert a definition of "appropriate Law Officer" to mean
   (a) the Lord Advocate, where the action, suit or proceedings is on behalf of or against any part of the Scottish Administration; and
   (b) the Advocate General for Scotland, in any other case.
For the distribution of the functions of law officers, see ss.48, 87. See also s.99; para. 7 below; and repeals in Sched. 9.

Para. 3

Part I of the Sheriff Courts and Legal Officers (Scotland) Act 1927 (c.35) provides for the appointment of sheriff clerks, procurators fiscal and their deputes. The provisions of Pt. I of Sheriff Courts and Legal Officers (Scotland) Act 1927 are, by virtue of para. 8(2) of Pt. I of Sched. 5, not reserved and some ministerial functions conferred by Pt. I of that Act will transfer to the Scottish Ministers under s.53. Section 55(1) will provide for Treasury consent requirements no longer to apply to the exercise of those functions by the Scottish Ministers. However, this will not apply in relation to the functions conferred by Pt. I of the 1927 Act on the Lord Advocate in relation to the appointment of procurators fiscal and their deputes. These will remain part of the retained functions of the Lord Advocate. This paragraph removes the need for consultation with the Treasury on decisions about the appointment, numbers and salary levels of procurators fiscal and their deputes. The amendments will as a consequence also repeal the Treasury consent requirements in relation to the appointment, numbers and salary levels of sheriff clerks and their deputes.

Para. 4

The powers of the Secretary of State to appoint macers and other officials of the High Court of Justiciary under the 1933 Act are at present stated to be exercisable "on nomination by the Lord Advocate".

Para. 5

The 1936 Act provides the procedure by way of provisional order by which any public authority or person may obtain parliamentary powers in relation to certain matters in Scotland. This paragraph amends s.1 of that Act so as to ensure that it does not apply where the powers sought are wholly within the competence of the Scottish Parliament. Such powers would have to be sought from the Scottish Parliament under its private legislation procedures. (See s.36(3)(c)).

The 1936 Act procedure can still be used where the powers sought relate to reserved matters or to a combination of devolved and reserved matters. In the Scotland Act 1998 (General Transitory, Transitional and Savings Provisions) Amendment Order 1999 (S.I. 1999 No. 1334) art.4 it was provided that the amendment made by para.5 was not to affect a petition for a Provisional Order presented before July 1, 1999.

See also Sched. 4, para. 1(2)(b).

Para. 6

This amends the 1946 Act to add the need for laying before the Scottish Parliament. See also s.56(1)(b) and Sched. 5, Part Pt. I, para. 7(2).

Para. 7

These amendments should be read with the amendments made in para. 2 to the Crown Suits (Scotland) Act 1857.

The Crown Proceedings Act 1947 makes provision for the civil liabilities and rights of the Crown and for civil proceedings by and against the Crown and related matters. Part V of that Act provides for the application of the Act in Scotland.

The modifications listed in para. 7 add the Scottish Administration to the references to the Crown and public departments as appropriate. They further amend references to "the Lord Advocate" to refer instead to the Advocate General for Scotland or to "the appropriate Law Officer" as appropriate and insert a definition of "appropriate Law Officer" to mean

   (a) the Lord Advocate, where the proceedings are on behalf or against the Scottish Administration; and

   (b) the Advocate General for Scotland, in any other case.

See also s.99.

Para. 8

Section 1(1) of the Public Registers and Records (Scotland) Act 1948 provides the Secretary of State with the power to appoint the Keeper of the Registers and the Keeper of the Records. Para. 8 substitutes "Scottish Ministers" for Secretary of State.

Para. 9

This paragraph amends the Lands Tribunal Act 1949 (c.42) so that the remuneration of members of the Lands Tribunal for Scotland is a charge on the Scottish Consolidated Fund.

It is related to other provisions concerning the remuneration of the senior judiciary. Under Sched. 5 (Part II, Section L1) the determination of the remuneration of judges of the Court of Session, sheriffs etc. is a reserved matter. Payment of the remuneration will be funded from the assigned budget of the Scottish Parliament. Most judicial salaries were a direct charge on the Consolidated Fund and under s.119 they became a direct charge on the Scottish Consolidated Fund. (See also Sched. 4, para. 5.)

The present amendment removes the anomaly that the remuneration of members of the Lands Tribunal was not a direct charge on the Consolidated Fund. That too becomes a charge on the Scottish Consolidated Fund.

Para. 10

Section 10 of the Defamation Act 1952 (c.66) provides that a defamatory statement published by a candidate at a local government or parliamentary election is not entitled to privilege for the purposes of the law of defamation on the grounds that it is material to an election issue. This amendment applies the same provision to elections to the Scottish Parliament and complements s.41 (Defamatory Statements) and the amendments to the Defamation Act 1996 at para. 33 of this Schedule. Para. 11 makes the same modification for the purposes of the law of defamation in Northern Ireland.

Para. 11

Section 10(2) of the Defamation Act (Northern Ireland) 1955 makes the same provision in the law of Northern Ireland as s.10 of the Defamation Act 1952, relating to the limitation on privilege at elections. As with the amendment to s.10 of the 1952 Act in para. 10, this provision ensures that the same limitation on privilege applies to elections to the Scottish Parliament.

Para. 12

Section 1(1) of the Registration of Births, Deaths and Marriages (Scotland) Act 1965 (c.49) provides the Secretary of State with the power to appoint the Registrar General for Births, Deaths and Marriages for Scotland. "Scottish Ministers" is substituted.

Para. 13

This amends the Pensions (Increase) Act 1971 (c.56) so as to ensure that any pensions payable to or in respect of Members of the Scottish Parliament, members of the Scottish Executive and the staff of the Scottish Parliamentary Corporate Body under pension schemes established in accordance with s.81 and para. 3 of Sched. 2 are increased in accordance with the provision made in the 1971 Act. The effect of this is that the levels of pensions payable under such schemes would, like other official pensions, have to be increased annually in line with the Retail Price Index figure set out in an order by the Treasury.

Para. 14

Section 1(6) of the 1972 Act provides that no additions may be made to the scheduled list of employments and offices "unless the remuneration of persons serving in that employment or office is paid out of moneys provided by Parliament or the Consolidated Fund".

See also s.51(5)–(7).

Para. 15

This provision is one of a number dealing with the relations between the Scottish Parliament and Executive and the European Union. Schedule 5 provides that international relations including those with the European Communities (and their institutions) are to be reserved but the Scottish Parliament and Executive will be responsible for observing and implementing obligations under Community law in relation to devolved matters.

Section 29 provides that it will be ultra vires for the Scottish Parliament to legislate in a way that is incompatible with Community law. Section 53 transfers to the Scottish Ministers any functions of Ministers of the Crown of observing and implementing Community law in relation to devolved matters in or as regards Scotland. Section 57(1) provides, however, that Ministers of the Crown shall continue to be able to exercise those functions as regards Scotland for the purposes specified in s.2(2) of the European Communities Act 1972. Section 57(2) provides that it is *ultra vires* for the Scottish Executive to make subordinate legislation or otherwise to act in any way which is incompatible with Community law.

The European Communities Act 1972 is not itself reserved but certain sections of the Act this Act are "entrenched" by para. 1 of Sched. 4. The effect of s.53 is that Scottish Ministers are able to exercise the powers under s.2(2) of the 1972 Act to make regulations for the purpose of implementing any Community obligation in relation to devolved matters and as regards Scotland. This paragraph makes certain consequential amendments to the Act. It should be noted, in particular, that para. 15(3)(a) provides that the Scottish Ministers do not require to be "designated" for the purposes of s.2 of the European Communities Act 1972.

Para. 16

The Interpretation Act 1978 (c.30) is not expressly protected from modification by para. 1 of Sched. 4 (see also para. 8 of that Schedule) and it could presumably be amended or replaced, in relation to matters which are not reserved, by the Scottish Parliament.

These amendments to the 1978 Act clarify its application to Acts of the Parliament and instruments made under them. The amendments to Sched. 1 restrict the scope of the Act to exclude such Scottish Acts and instruments but the new s.23A extends the coverage of certain sections to include them. The sections are s.15 (Repeal of repeal), s.16 (General savings), s.17 (Repeal and re-enactment) and s.18 (Duplicated offences).

Para. 17

Section 135(1) of the Education (Scotland) Act 1980 (c.44) defines "Her Majesty's inspectors" as the inspectors of schools appointed by Her Majesty on the recommendation of the Secretary of State. This paragraph removes the reference to the recommendation to the Secretary of State. (These recommendations would be expected to be made by the First Minister.)

Para. 18

Section 46(3) of the 1982 Act provides that "the Crown in right of Her Majesty's government in the United Kingdom has its seat in every part of and every place, in the United Kingdom" and equivalent provision is made in respect of Northern Ireland.

Such provision is now made in respect of Scotland. See also s.99.

Para. 19

Section 141 of the Mental Health Act 1983 makes provision for the Speaker to be informed if a member of the House of Commons is authorised to be detained on grounds of mental illness. When the Speaker receives such a notification, or is notified by two MPs that they are credibly informed that such an authorisation has been made, the Speaker can have the member examined by two registered medical practitioners appointed by the Royal College of Psychiatrists. If they report that the MP is suffering from mental illness and is authorised to be detained, the Speaker is to have the MP examined again after six months. If after the second examination the position has not changed, the Speaker must lay both medical reports before the House of Commons and the member's seat then becomes vacant. This amendment provides for the same procedures to apply to members of the Scottish Parliament.

Section 17(4) of the Scotland Act makes further provision in relation to a MSP to whom s.141 as amended applies. In particular it provides that he or she may not take part in the proceedings of the Scottish Parliament while disqualified, even though the seat is not yet vacated.

Para. 20

This paragraph amends ss.6, 7 of the National Audit Act 1983 so as to ensure that the current powers of the U.K. Comptroller and Auditor General do not apply in relation to the Scottish Administration or any Scottish public authority to which para. 1 or 2 of Pt. III of Sched. 5 applies i.e. any Scottish public authority (as defined in s.126(1)) with mixed functions, which is not a cross-border public authority; or any Scottish public authority with no reserved functions.

Para. 21

This amendment deletes a provision which requires that the consent of the Secretary of State be obtained before the Scottish Tourist Board promotes tourism in Scotland outside the U.K.

Para. 22

This paragraph provides that the Accountant in Bankruptcy with powers under the Bankruptcy (Scotland) Act 1985 (amended by the Bankruptcy (Scotland) Act 1993) will be appointed by the Scottish Ministers. It further provides that the Scottish Ministers may appoint a member of staff to be Depute Accountant and to exercise all statutory functions when the Accountant is unable to do so. It replaces existing provisions for the Secretary of State to appoint the Accountant in Bankruptcy on such terms and conditions and to pay such remuneration and allowances as he determines, with the approval of the Treasury. The existing provision also provides for the Secretary of State to appoint a member of staff to be Depute Accountant in Bankruptcy.

Para. 23

The provision made by subparas. (1)–(5) revises the enumerated sections of the 1986 Act to enable functions currently discharged by the registrar of companies in Scotland and the assistant registrar of friendly societies for Scotland to be discharged as well, or instead, by the Accountant in Bankruptcy (see also para. 22).

The provision made by subpara. (6) applies the requirements of s.427(4)–(6) of the 1986 Act (which require a court to notify a bankruptcy adjudication or award of sequestration of a Member of Parliament to the Speaker) to members of the Scottish Parliament.

Section 427(1) of the 1986 Act provides that where a bankruptcy adjudication or award of sequestration is made against any person, he or she is disqualified from sitting and voting in the House of Commons. Section 427(4) provides that where a member of the House of Commons continues to be disqualified until the end of the 6 month period beginning with the day of adjudication or award, then the seat shall be vacated at the end of that period. By virtue of s.15(1)(b) of this Act, he or she would also become disqualified for membership of the Scottish Parliament. It is therefore appropriate that notification should also be given to the Presiding Officer of the Parliament in respect of the bankruptcy or sequestration of any MSP.

Para. 24

Part III of the Public Order Act 1986 creates certain offences in relation to the stirring up of racial hatred. Section 26(1) of this Act provides that nothing in Pt. III applies to a fair and accurate report of proceedings in Parliament. This paragraph amends s.26(1) so that Pt. III equally does not apply to such a report of proceedings in the Scottish Parliament.

Para. 25

This paragraph has the effect that the Crown will be entitled to copyright in every Act of the Scottish Parliament and that copyright in every Bill introduced into the Scottish Parliament will belong to the Scottish Parliamentary Corporate Body. The provisions of s.45 of the Copyright, Designs and Patents Act 1988, which provides that copyright is not infringed by anything done for the purposes of parliamentary proceedings, will apply to the Scottish Parliament. See also s.92 of this Act (Queen's Printer for Scotland).

Para. 26

This makes amendments to s.12 of the 1989 Act to insert references to members of the Scottish Executive and junior Scottish Ministers into the definition of "Crown servant" and adds office-holders in the Scottish Administration as persons to whom "government contractors" provide goods or services.

Para. 27

This paragraph amends the Prisons (Scotland) Act 1989 to remove or adjust specific provision for appointment of staff in relation to prisons. These powers of appointment are required as a consequence of the general provision in s.51 for the Scottish Ministers to appoint persons to be members of the staff of the Scottish Administration.

Para. 28

This paragraph amends s.6 of the European Communities (Amendment) Act 1993 to provide that a person may be proposed as a member (for the United Kingdom) of the Committee of the Regions if he or she is a member of the Scottish Parliament.

Para. 29

This paragraph amends the Scottish Land Court Act 1993 to provide that it is for the First Minister to make recommendations to the Queen for the appointment of members of the Scottish Land Court and adds a new subsection requiring the First Minister to consult the Lord President of the Court of Session before recommending a person as Chairman of the Court.

Para. 30

Rules under s.41 of the Value Added Tax Act 1994 apply to the treatment of supplies of goods and services by and to government departments for VAT purposes. In particular the section allows the Treasury to direct that VAT should be charged on any goods or services provided by a government department even though the supply of those goods or services does not amount to the carrying on of a business. This paragraph applies these rules to the Scottish Administration.

Para. 31

The Requirements of Writing (Scotland) Act 1995 makes provision with regard to the execution and formal validity of documents.

This paragraph amends s.12(1) of the 1995 Act (interpretation) to extend the definition of "Minister" to include a member of the Scottish Executive and the definition of "officer" to include a member of staff of the Scottish Ministers or the Lord Advocate.

Section 59(4) provides that a document is validly executed by the Scottish Ministers if it is executed by any member of the Scottish Executive.

Para. 32

This paragraph is an important addition to the rules in Sched. 6 on devolution issues.

The two sections added to the Criminal Procedure (Scotland) Act 1995 make the following extra provision:

The new s.288A fills a gap in the general arrangements made by Sched. 6 in that it provides the Advocate General with the right to appeal against the determination of a devolution issue by a trial judge. The accused person has such a right of appeal under s.106 or s.175 of the 1995 Act. Sections 123, 175(3), 191 provide the Lord Advocate with a right to refer and right of appeal, as appropriate. Cast in terms similar to s.123, the new s.288A provides the Advocate General with the right to refer a devolution issue to the High Court, where a person has been acquitted or convicted of a charge and the Advocate General was a party to the proceedings.

The new s.288B, which was added at committee stage in the House of Lords (see *Hansard*, H.L. Vol. 593, cols. 653–655), is intended to ensure that the High Court has appropriate powers to give effect to a decision by the Judicial Committee on an appeal from the High Court. Any earlier acquittal or quashing of a conviction will not be affected but the Court will otherwise have wide powers to uphold or quash a conviction; to authorise a new prosecution; or to review a sentence.

Further amendments to the 1995 Act were made by the Scotland Act 1998 (Consequential Modifications) (No.2) Order 1999 (S.I. 1999 No.1820), Sched. 2, para. 122.

Para. 33

This paragraph makes amendments to the Defamation Act 1996 which are consequential upon the establishment of the Parliament and the Scottish Parliament and the Scottish Executive to ensure that relevant provisions made by or under Acts of the Parliament the Scottish Parliament and appointments made by members of the Scottish Executive are covered by the 1996 Act in the same way that equivalent provisions made by or under U.K. Acts or appointments by U.K. Ministers are covered.

The Defamation Act 1996 makes provision amending the law of defamation in each part of the United Kingdom. In particulars ss.14 and 15 make provision as to the circumstances in which certain reports enjoy absolute privilege and qualified privilege. These amendments ensure that the Act will apply taking account of provisions that may be made by or under Acts of the Scottish Parliament and appointments made by the Scottish Executive. It complements s.41 (Defamatory Statements), and paras. 10, 11 of this Schedule.

Para. 34

This removes, in relation to Scotland, the need for the rules on guarantees for public sector settlements to be subject to "guidelines" agreed with the Treasury. For the general removal of the need for functions to be exercised with the agreement of other Ministers (including the Treasury) see s.55.

Section 125 SCHEDULE 9

REPEALS

Chapter	Short title	Extent of repeal
1927 c. 35.	The Sheriff Courts and Legal Officers (Scotland) Act 1927.	In section 1(2), "with the consent of the Treasury". In section 2, "with the consent of the Treasury as to numbers and salaries". In section 3, "and in either case with the consent of the Treasury". In section 5, "with the consent of the Treasury as to numbers and salaries". In section 12, "after consultation with the Treasury".
1933 c. 41.	The Administration of Justice (Scotland) Act 1933.	In sections 24(7) and 25, "and shall be exercised on nomination by the Lord Advocate".
1975 c. 24.	The House of Commons Disqualification Act 1975.	In Schedule 2, the entries for the Lord Advocate and the Solicitor General for Scotland.
1975 c. 27.	The Ministerial and other Salaries Act 1975.	In Part III of Schedule 1, the entries for the Lord Advocate and the Solicitor General for Scotland.
1980 c. 44.	The Education (Scotland) Act 1980.	In section 135(1), in the definition of "Her Majesty's inspectors", "on the recommendation of the Secretary of State".
1984 c. 4.	The Tourism (Overseas Promotion) (Scotland) Act 1984.	Section 1(2).
1986 c. 56.	The Parliamentary Constituencies Act 1986.	In Schedule 2, rule 1(2).
1989 c. 45.	The Prisons (Scotland) Act 1989.	Section 2.

Scotland Act 1998

STANDING ORDERS OF THE SCOTTISH PARLIAMENT

EDITION 2

[JANUARY 20, 2000]

Introduction

Contents

CHAPTER 1

Members

CHAPTER 2

Meetings of the Parliament

CHAPTER 3

Officers of the Parliament

CHAPTER 4

The Scottish Executive

Scotland Act 1998

Chapter 5

The Parliamentary Bureau and Management of Business

5.1 Parliamentary Bureau
5.2 Members of the Parliamentary Bureau
5.3 Procedure of Parliamentary Bureau
5.4 Business programme
5.5 Daily business list
5.6 Special cases of Parliamentary business
5.7 Programme of the Scottish Executive
5.8 Financial business
5.9 Business Bulletin

Chapter 6

Committees

6.1 Establishment of committees
6.2 Functions of all committees
6.3 Membership of committees
6.4 Procedures Committee
6.5 Standards Committee
6.6 Finance Committee
6.7 Audit Committee
6.8 European Committee
6.9 Equal Opportunities Committee
6.10 Public Petitions Committee
6.11 Subordinate Legislation Committee
6.12 Duration of committees
6.13 Questions regarding competence
6.14 Joint consideration by committees

Chapter 7

Conduct of Meetings

7.1 Languages
7.2 Calling speakers and contents of speeches
7.3 Order in the chamber
7.4 Suspension and closure of meetings by Presiding Officer
7.5 Sub judice
7.6 Forms of address
7.7 Calculating the length of debates or the number of speakers
7.8 Committee proceedings

Chapter 8

Motions and Points of Order

8.1 Motions
8.2 Notice of Motions
8.3 Motions taken by the Parliament
8.4 Amendments to motions
8.5 Notice of amendments
8.6 Amendments taken by the Parliament
8.7 Amendments to amendments
8.8 Application to committees
8.9 Motions of First Minister
8.10 Tax-varying resolutions
8.11 Business motions
8.12 Motions of no confidence
8.13 Procedural motions
8.14 Closure of a debate
8.15 Motions for adjournment of a debate

CHAPTER 13

Statements of Parliamentary Questions

CHAPTER 14

Laying and Publication of Documents

CHAPTER 15

Openness and Accessibility

CHAPTER 16

Reporting of Proceedings

CHAPTER 17

Miscellaneous

Scotland Act 1998

CHAPTER 18

Glossary

18.1 Interpretation
18.2 Index of defined expressions
18.3 Other references

The following Rules are the Standing Orders of the Scottish Parliament made in accordance with section 22 of and Schedule 3 to the Scotland Act 1998 (c.46). They were made by resolution of the Parliament of 9 December 1999 and came into force on 17 December 1999.

CHAPTER 1

Members

Rule 1.1 The Scottish Parliament

1. The Scottish Parliament is established by the Scotland Act 1998 (1998 c.46).

2. The members of the Parliament returned for each constituency or region shall be known as members of the Scottish Parliament (MSPs) and are referred to in these Rules as members.

Rule 1.2 Oath of allegiance

1. Every person who is returned as a member shall take the oath of allegiance or shall make his or her solemn affirmation at a meeting of the Parliament before the Clerk. A member shall not take part in any other proceedings of the Parliament until he or she has done so.

2. A member may, immediately after taking the oath or making his or her solemn affirmation, repeat the oath or affirmation in a language other than English.

3. The member shall then sign a register kept by the Clerk for the purpose indicating that he or she has taken the oath or, as the case may be, made a solemn affirmation.

4. The Parliament's power under section 84(3) (where a member fails to take the oath of allegiance) to decide, before the end of the period of two months within which a member must take the oath or make a solemn affirmation, to allow him or her a longer period to do so is exercisable on a motion of any member. The motion is valid only if it is seconded by another member.

5. In these Rules, "oath of allegiance" means the oath in the form provided in section 2 of the Promissory Oaths Act 1868 and "solemn affirmation" means the affirmation in the form provided in section 6(1) of the Oaths Act 1978.

Rule 1.3 Term of office

1. The term of office of a member begins on the day on which the member is declared to be returned and ends with the dissolution of the Parliament or, if earlier, that member's death or resignation.

2. A member may at any time resign his or her seat by giving notice in writing to the Presiding Officer.

3. A member may also cease to be a member in accordance with section 17(1) or (2) (where a member is or becomes disqualified) or section 84(3) (where a member fails to take the oath of allegiance).

Rule 1.4 Disqualification

1. The Presiding Officer shall notify the Parliament where a person is, or is alleged to be, disqualified from being a member (either generally or for a particular constituency or region) on any ground other than one falling within section 15(1)(b) (disqualification otherwise than under House of Commons Disqualification Act 1975).

2. Any member may, within 3 sitting days of such notification, by motion propose that the Parliament disregard the disqualification because it is considered that the ground has been removed and that it is proper to disregard the disqualification. The motion is valid only if it is seconded by another member.

Rule 1.5 Vacancies

1. For the purposes of section 9 (constituency vacancies), the date on which a vacancy in the seat of a constituency member is to be treated as occurring shall be determined in accordance with paragraph 2. The Presiding Officer shall notify the Parliament of that date.

2. The date on which a constituency vacancy is to be treated as occurring is—

(a) in the case of a vacancy arising on the death of a member, the date of death;

(b) in the case of a vacancy arising on the resignation of a member, the date on which written notice of the resignation is given to the Presiding Officer;

(c) in the case of a vacancy arising under section 17(1) (effect of disqualification where a disqualified person is returned), the date on which the person concerned was returned as a member;

(d) in the case of a vacancy arising under section 17(2) (effect of disqualification where a member becomes disqualified), the date on which the member became disqualified;

(e) in the case of a vacancy arising under section 84(3) (failure of member to take the oath of allegiance), the expiry of the period of 2 months beginning with the day on which he or she was returned or such longer period as the Parliament may have allowed; or

(f) in any other case, such date as the Presiding Officer may determine.

3. If, in any of the cases mentioned in paragraph 2(a) and (c) to (e), the vacancy does not come to the notice of the Presiding Officer within the period of one month beginning with its occurrence, the Presiding Officer shall notify the Parliament of the date when the vacancy did come to his or her notice.

4. For the purposes of section 10 (regional vacancies), the date on which a vacancy in the seat of a regional member is to be treated as occurring shall be determined by the Presiding Officer. The Presiding Officer shall notify the Parliament of that date.

Rule 1.6 Code of Conduct

1. The Parliament may, on a motion of the Standards Committee, lay down a Code of Conduct for members. The Parliamentary corporation shall arrange for the Code of Conduct to be printed and published.

Rule 1.7 Withdrawal of rights and privileges

1. The Parliament may, on a motion of the Standards Committee, withdraw from a member his or her rights and privileges as a member to such extent and for such period as are specified in the motion.

CHAPTER 2

Meetings of the Parliament

Rule 2.1 Session of the Parliament

1. A session of the Parliament shall be the period from the date of the first meeting of the Parliament following a general election until the Parliament is dissolved.

2. Each session shall be divided into Parliamentary years. The first Parliamentary year shall be the year beginning with the date of the first meeting of the Parliament following a general election. Subsequent Parliamentary years shall begin on each succeeding anniversary of that date in that session.

3. A sitting day is any day when the office of the Clerk is open but not when the Parliament is in recess or dissolved. The Parliament shall decide, on a motion of the Parliamentary Bureau, the days on which the office of the Clerk is to be open. Until the Parliament has so decided, the Presiding Officer shall appoint those days. The days on which the office of the Clerk is to be open shall be notified to members by the Presiding Officer.

Rule 2.2 Meetings of the Parliament

1. The Parliament shall meet on the day appointed or determined for its first meeting following a general election.

2. The Parliament shall decide, on a motion of the Parliamentary Bureau, the date and time for any other meeting of the Parliament, or, until the Parliament has so determined, the Presiding Officer shall appoint such dates and times. This is subject to the following paragraphs.

3. The Parliament may, except as mentioned in paragraph 4 or 5 or in an emergency, meet on any sitting day during the normal Parliamentary week. The normal Parliamentary week is between the hours of 14:30 and 17:30 on Monday, 09:30 and 17:30 on Tuesday, Wednesday and Thursday and 09:30 and 12:30 on Friday.

4. A meeting of the Parliament may continue to 19:00 on Wednesday if the Parliament so decides on a motion of the Parliamentary Bureau.

5. A meeting of the Parliament may continue beyond—
17:30 on Monday, Tuesday or Thursday;
> 17:30 on Wednesday where the Parliament has not taken a decision under paragraph 4;
> 19:00 on Wednesday where the Parliament has taken a decision under paragraph 4; or 12:30 on Friday,
in any of the circumstances specified in paragraph 6.

6. The circumstances in which a meeting of the Parliament may continue beyond any of the times specified in paragraph 5 are—
(a) if it is necessary in order to complete any voting which is not adjourned to a later meeting under Rule 11.2.5;
(b) if it is necessary in order to complete the election of the Presiding Officer or a deputy Presiding Officer under Rule 11.9 or the election of a member or members of the Parliamentary corporation or selection of a nominee for appointment as First Minister under Rule 11.10;
(c) if the Parliament so decides, on a motion of the Parliamentary Bureau, in order to consider Members' Business; or
(d) in other cases, if the Parliament so decides on a motion of a member of the Scottish Executive or of the member who moved the business under consideration at that time.

7. Any motion mentioned in paragraph 6(d) may be moved without notice. It may be debated for up to 10 minutes. Each speaker may speak for no more than 3 minutes. The motion may be amended but only by proposing that the time specified in it is increased or decreased.

8. A meeting of the Parliament shall normally begin and end on the same day and normally not more than one meeting of the Parliament may take place on the same day.

9. A meeting of the Parliament begins when the Presiding Officer or other person chairing the meeting takes the chair.

10. The Presiding Officer may convene the Parliament on other dates or at other times in an emergency.

11. In these Rules "Members' Business" means any item of business, other than a Member's Bill, proposed by a member who is neither a member of the Scottish Executive nor a junior Scottish Minister.

Rule 2.3 Parliamentary recess

1. The Parliament shall decide, on a motion of the Parliamentary Bureau, the dates of any Parliamentary recess.

2. In considering dates of any Parliamentary recess, the Parliamentary Bureau shall have regard to the dates when schools in any part of Scotland are to be on holiday.

3. The dates on which a Parliamentary recess is to begin and end shall be notified by the Clerk to members.

Rule 2.4 First meeting following general election

1. The first meeting of the Parliament following the first ordinary general election shall be chaired—
  - (a) by the Clerk but only for the purpose of presiding over the proceedings to enable the oldest qualified member to take the oath of allegiance or make a solemn affirmation; and
  - (b) thereafter, by the oldest qualified member but only for the purpose of presiding over the proceedings when members are taking the oath of allegiance or making a solemn affirmation and for the election of the Presiding Officer; and
  - (c) thereafter, by the elected Presiding Officer.

2. The first meeting of the Parliament following any subsequent general election shall be held on the day and at the time determined by the Presiding Officer. The Presiding Officer shall notify members of the date and time of that meeting.

3. Subject to paragraphs 4 and 5, that meeting shall be chaired—
  - (a) by the Clerk but only for the purpose of presiding over the proceedings to enable the former Officer to take the oath of allegiance or make a solemn affirmation; and
  - (b) thereafter, by the former Officer but only for the purpose of presiding over the proceedings when members are taking the oath of allegiance or making a solemn affirmation and for the election of the new Presiding Officer; and
  - (c) thereafter, by the elected Presiding Officer.

4. If the person holding the office of Presiding Officer as mentioned in section 19(2) is not a member of the Parliament, that meeting shall be chaired by that person but only until a new Presiding Officer is elected. Thereafter it shall be chaired by the elected Presiding Officer.

5. If neither that person nor the former Officer is present at that meeting or able to chair that meeting, that meeting shall be chaired as mentioned in paragraph 1.

6. The chair may be taken by a member only if that member has taken the oath of allegiance or made a solemn affirmation.

7. Any reference to "the oldest qualified member" means the oldest member—
  - (a) who is present at the meeting;
  - (b) who has indicated to the Clerk that he or she does not intend to stand as a candidate for the office of Presiding Officer or First Minister; and
  - (c) who is not a leader within the Parliament of a political party represented by 5 or more members of the Parliament.

8. When the Clerk or the oldest qualified member is in the chair, he or she shall, so far as necessary for the purposes of concluding the business over which he or she is presiding, have similar functions as the Presiding

Officer has for the purposes of conducting meetings under Rules 7.1 to 7.7 and 8.17.

9. Any reference to "the former Officer" means—

(a) the member holding the office of Presiding Officer as mentioned in section 19(2); or

(b) if that office is vacant or that member is unable to chair the meeting, a member holding the office of deputy Presiding Officer as mentioned in that section, but only if, in either case, that member has indicated to the Clerk that he or she does not intend to stand as a candidate for election as Presiding Officer.

Rule 2.5 Chairing of meetings

1. Except as provided in Rule 2.4, meetings of the Parliament shall be chaired by the Presiding Officer or by a deputy Presiding Officer.

2. Where the offices of Presiding Officer and of both deputy Presiding Officers are vacant, a meeting of the Parliament shall be chaired by the oldest qualified member but only for the purpose of presiding over the proceedings for the election of the Presiding Officer.

3. Where the Presiding Officer and both deputy Presiding Officers are unable to act, a meeting of the Parliament shall be chaired by the oldest member who is present at the meeting but only during such period as all of those officers are unable to act. When the oldest member is in the chair, he or she shall, so far as necessary for the purposes of concluding the business over which he or she is presiding, have similar functions to those of the Presiding Officer for the purpose of conducting meetings under Rules 7.1 to 7.7 and 8.17.

4. Paragraphs 2 and 3 are subject to the special provisions applying to the first meeting of the Parliament following a general election mentioned in Rule 2.4.

Rule 2.6 Witnesses and documents

1. The Parliament may in connection with any matter invite any person—

(a) to attend its proceedings for the purpose of giving evidence; or

(b) to produce documents in that person's custody or under that person's control, but this is in addition to its power under section 23 (power to call for witnesses and documents) to require any person to do so but subject to and in accordance with the terms of that section and section 24 (notice provisions in relation to witnesses and documents).

2. The Parliament shall arrange for the Parliamentary corporation to pay to persons whom it requires, and may arrange for the Parliamentary corporation to pay to persons whom it invites to attend its proceedings to give evidence or to produce any documents, such allowances and expenses as may be determined by the Parliament.

Rule 2.7 Location

1. Meetings of the Parliament shall be held in the Church of Scotland Assembly Hall, The Mound, Edinburgh, subject to the following provisions.

2. The Parliament may decide, on a motion of the Parliamentary Bureau, that a meeting of the Parliament shall be held in another place in Scotland.

3. Where it is not practicable for the Parliament to meet to decide the matter, the Presiding Officer may decide that a meeting of the Parliament shall be held in another place in Scotland and members shall be notified of that place.

CHAPTER 3

Officers of the Parliament

Rule 3.1 Presiding Officer and deputy Presiding Officers

1. The Presiding Officer shall—
(a) preside over any meeting of the Parliament except as provided in Rule 2.4 and 2.5 and, except where Rule 11.9 or 11.10 applies, exercise a casting vote in the event of a tie;
(b) convene and chair any meeting of the Parliamentary Bureau and exercise a casting vote in the event of a tie;
(c) determine any question as to the interpretation or application of these Rules and give a ruling on any such question; and
(d) represent the Parliament in discussions and exchanges with any parliamentary, governmental, administrative or other body, whether within or outwith the United Kingdom.

2. The Presiding Officer shall have such other functions as may be conferred upon him or her by the Act, by the Parliament or by these Rules.

3. In exercising any functions, the Presiding Officer and deputy Presiding Officers shall act impartially, taking account of the interests of all members equally.

4. The Presiding Officer's functions may be exercised by a deputy Presiding Officer if the office of Presiding Officer is vacant or if the Presiding Officer is for any reason unable to act.

5. The Presiding Officer may authorise a deputy Presiding Officer to exercise any of his or her functions on his or her behalf but shall not authorise him or her to sit in place of the Presiding Officer as a member of the Parliamentary corporation under section 21(2)(a).

Rule 3.2 Election of Presiding Officer

1. The Parliament shall, at its first meeting following a general election, elect from among its members a Presiding Officer.

2. If the Presiding Officer ceases to hold office before the Parliament is dissolved, the Parliament shall elect another from among its members.

3. In the case of the election of the Presiding Officer under paragraph 1, the voting period at the election ("the voting period") shall take place at such time during the first meeting as may be notified in the Business Bulletin or as may be appointed by the person chairing the meeting.

4. In the case of the election of a Presiding Officer under paragraph 2, the voting period shall take place on the day and at the time appointed by the Parliament on a motion of the Parliamentary Bureau. That date shall not be later than fourteen days after the date on which the Presiding Officer ceased to hold office. If this is not possible because the Parliament is in recess at that time, the voting period shall take place on the day and at the time notified in the Business Bulletin.

5. For the purposes of paragraph 4, the date on which the Presiding Officer ceased to hold office shall be—
(a) in the case where he or she resigns, the date on which the resignation takes effect;
(b) in the case where he or she is removed from office by resolution of the Parliament, the date on which he or she is so removed; or
(c) in the case where he or she ceases to be a member of the Parliament, the date on which a vacancy is to be treated as occurring for the purposes of section 9 (constituency vacancies) or 10 (regional vacancies) in accordance with Rule 1.5.

6. A member may, at any time during the period which is not earlier than 2 hours and not later than 15 minutes before the time appointed for the beginning of the voting period, nominate a candidate for appointment as the Presiding Officer by submitting a written nomination to the Clerk. A nomination shall be valid only if it is seconded by another member.

7. Where there are 2 elected deputy Presiding Officers who represent the same political party, a member representing that party is not eligible for nomination as a candidate for appointment as Presiding Officer. The person chairing the meeting shall reject any such nomination as being invalid.

8. A person nominated as a candidate must take the oath of allegiance or make a solemn affirmation before for the beginning of the voting period. If he or she has not done so, the person chairing the meeting shall reject his or her nomination.

9. At the beginning of the voting period, the person chairing the meeting shall announce the name or names of the candidate or candidates validly nominated and an election shall be held in accordance with Rule 11.9.

10. After the person chairing the meeting has declared the result of the election of the Presiding Officer, the elected Presiding Officer shall take the chair.

Rule 3.3 Election of deputy Presiding Officers

1. The Parliament shall, at its first meeting following a general election, elect from among its members two deputy Presiding Officers.

2. If a deputy Presiding Officer ceases to hold office before the Parliament is dissolved, the Parliament shall elect another deputy Presiding Officer from among its members.

3. Where there is a vacancy in the office of Presiding Officer and in the office of a deputy Presiding Officer, the election of the Presiding Officer shall precede the election of the deputy Presiding Officer.

4. Where there are vacancies in the offices of both deputy Presiding Officers, consecutive elections shall be held for the offices.

5. In the case of the election of deputy Presiding Officers under paragraph 1, the voting period for the election of the first deputy Presiding Officer ("the first voting period") shall take place at such time during the first meeting as may be appointed by the Presiding Officer, which shall be not earlier than 30 minutes after the Presiding Officer informed the Parliament as to when the first voting period is to take place. The voting period for the election of the second deputy Presiding Officer shall take place immediately after the completion of the first voting period.

6. Paragraph 5 shall also apply in any other case where there are vacancies in the offices of both deputy Presiding Officers except that, where the Parliament is not dissolved or is not in recess, the date and time for the first voting period shall be appointed by the Parliament on a motion of the Parliamentary Bureau. That date shall not be later than 14 days after the date on which both those offices became vacant. If this is not possible because the Parliament is in recess at that time, the date and time for the first voting period shall be appointed by the Presiding Officer.

7. In the case of an election under paragraph 5 or 6, the candidates in the election for the second deputy Presiding Officer shall be the candidates not elected in the election for the first deputy Presiding Officer, except that, where the Presiding Officer and the first deputy Presiding Officer represent the same political party, any candidate representing that party shall not be a candidate for election as the second deputy Presiding Officer.

8. In the case where there is a vacancy in only one of the offices of deputy Presiding Officer, the voting period for the election of the deputy Presiding Officer shall take place on the date and at the time appointed by the Parliament on a motion of the Parliamentary Bureau. That date shall not be later than 14 days after the date on which the office became vacant. If this is not possible because the Parliament is in recess at that time, the

date and time for the voting period shall be appointed by the Presiding Officer.

9. In the case of an election under paragraph 8, where the elected Presiding Officer and a deputy Presiding Officer represent the same political party and there is a vacancy in the office of the other deputy Presiding Officer, a member representing that party is not eligible for nomination as a candidate for election as that other deputy Presiding Officer.

10. For the purposes of paragraphs 6 and 8, the date on which the deputy Presiding Officer ceased to hold office shall be—

(a) in the case where he or she resigns, the date on which the resignation takes effect;

(b) in the case where he or she is removed from office by resolution of the Parliament, the date on which he or she is so removed; or

(c) in the case where he or she ceases to be a member of the Parliament, the date on which a vacancy is to be treated as occurring for the purposes of section 9 (constituency vacancies) or 10 (regional vacancies) in accordance with Rule 1.5.

11. The following paragraphs apply to an election in any of the cases mentioned in paragraphs 5, 6 and 8.

12. A member may at any time during the period which is not earlier than 30 minutes before and not later than 15 minutes before the beginning of the first voting period in the cases mentioned in paragraphs 5 and 6 and the voting period in the case mentioned in paragraph 8, nominate a candidate for appointment as deputy Presiding Officer by submitting a written nomination to the Clerk. A nomination shall be valid only if it is seconded by another member.

13. A person nominated as a candidate must take the oath of allegiance or make a solemn affirmation before the time appointed for a voting period. If he or she has not done so, the Presiding Officer shall reject his or her nomination.

12. At the beginning of a voting period, the Presiding Officer shall announce the name or names of the candidate or candidates validly nominated and an election shall be held in accordance with Rule 11.9.

Rule 3.4 Resignation of Presiding Officer and deputy Presiding Officers

1. The Presiding Officer or a deputy Presiding Officer may resign office by giving notice in writing to the Clerk.

2. The Clerk shall notify the Parliament of any such resignation.

Rule 3.5 Removal of Presiding Officer and deputy Presiding Officers

1. A member may by motion propose that the Presiding Officer or a deputy Presiding Officer be removed from office. The motion is valid only if it is seconded by another member.

2. The Presiding Officer or deputy Presiding Officer is removed from office if the Parliament so decides by an absolute majority.

Rule 3.6 Members of the Parliamentary corporation

1. The four members of the Scottish Parliamentary Corporate Body ("the Parliamentary corporation") referred to in section 21(2)(b) shall be appointed by the Presiding Officer either after an election in accordance with Rule 3.7 or in accordance with Rule 3.8. Those members are referred to as "appointed members".

Rule 3.7 Election of members of the Parliamentary corporation

1. Not later than 10 sitting days after a general election, the Parliament shall hold consecutive elections to elect the four appointed members of the Parliamentary corporation.

2. An election shall also be held to fill any vacancy which arises when an appointed member—

(a) resigns;

(b) ceases to be a member of the Parliament otherwise than by virtue of a dissolution; or

(c) is removed from office by resolution of the Parliament.

3. In the case of an election under paragraph 1, the voting period for the election of the first appointed member ("the first voting period") shall take place on such date and at such time as may be appointed by the Presiding Officer. The voting period for the election of the second and other appointed members under paragraph 1 shall take place immediately after the completion of the first voting period.

4. Paragraph 3 shall also apply in any other case where there are vacancies in the offices of more than one appointed member except that, where the Parliament is not dissolved or is not in recess, the date and time for the first voting period shall be appointed by the Parliament on a motion of the Parliamentary Bureau.

5. In the case of an election under paragraph 3 or 4, the candidates in the election for the second and other appointed members shall be the candidates not elected in the election for the first appointed member.

6. In the case where there is a vacancy in only one of the offices of an appointed member, the voting period for the election shall take place on the date and at the time appointed by the Parliament on a motion of the Parliamentary Bureau.

7. Any member may, not later than 30 minutes before the beginning of the first voting period in the cases mentioned in paragraphs 3 and 4 and the voting period in the case mentioned in paragraph 6, nominate a candidate for election by submitting a written nomination to the Clerk.

8. A nomination of a candidate shall be valid only if it is seconded by another member.

9. At the beginning of a voting period, the Presiding Officer shall announce the name or names of the candidate or candidates validly nominated and an election shall then be held in accordance with Rule 11.10.

10. The Presiding Officer shall appoint as a member of the Parliamentary corporation a member elected in accordance with this Rule.

Rule 3.8 Appointment of members of the Parliamentary corporation

1. If any office of an appointed member is not filled in accordance with Rule 3.7, the Presiding Officer may appoint a member to that office and shall do so if the office remains vacant for more than 28 days. In calculating the period of 28 days for this purpose, no account shall be taken of any time when the Parliament is dissolved.

2. The Presiding Officer shall notify the Parliament of any appointment under paragraph 1.

Rule 3.9 Resignation of members of the Parliamentary corporation

1. An appointed member may at any time resign office by giving notice in writing to the Presiding Officer.

2. The Presiding Officer shall notify the Parliament of the resignation.

Rule 3.10 Removal of members of the Parliamentary corporation

1. A member may by motion propose that an appointed member be removed from office. The motion is valid only if it is seconded by another member.

2. An appointed member is removed from office as a member of the Parliamentary corporation if the Parliament so decides on such a motion.

Rule 3.11 Auditor General for Scotland

1. If the office of Auditor General for Scotland is, or is expected to become, vacant, a panel (referred to as the "Selection Panel") shall be established for the purpose of recommending a person for nomination by the Parliament to Her Majesty for appointment as Auditor General for Scotland.

2. The members of the Selection Panel shall be the Presiding Officer, the Convener of the Audit Committee and at least 4 but not more than 7 other members appointed by the Presiding Officer. In appointing members of the Selection Panel the Presiding Officer shall have regard to the balance of political parties in the Parliament.

3. The Selection Panel shall recommend to a meeting of the Parliament one person for nomination by the Parliament.

4. Any member of the Selection Panel may by motion propose that the Parliament nominates the person recommended by the Selection Panel.

5. Any debate on such a motion shall be restricted to 30 minutes. Each speaker may speak for no more than 5 minutes.

6. If there is a division on such a motion, the result is valid only if the number of members who voted is more than one quarter of the total number of seats for members. In calculating the number of members who have voted for this purpose, account shall be taken not only of those voting for or against the motion but also of those voting to abstain.

Rule 3.12 Removal of Auditor General for Scotland

1. Any member may by motion propose that the Parliament resolve that a recommendation be made to Her Majesty for the removal from office of the Auditor General for Scotland.

2. If there is a division on such a motion, the motion shall be taken to be agreed to only if the number of members voting in favour is not less than two-thirds of the total number of seats for members of the Parliament.

CHAPTER 4

The Scottish Executive

Rule 4.1 Nomination of First Minister

1. The nomination of a member for appointment as First Minister under section 46(1) shall be conducted in accordance with the following provisions.

2. The date and time for the voting period to select a nominee shall be determined—

(a) in the case of a selection following a general election when the Parliamentary Bureau has not been established, by the Presiding Officer, provided that the date of the first such voting period shall not be later than 14 days after the date of the general election; and

(b) in any other case, by the Parliament on a motion of the Parliamentary Bureau, and the date and time of the voting period shall be notified to members.

3. Any member may, not later than 30 minutes before the time appointed for the voting period for selection of a nominee, nominate a candidate for appointment as First Minister by submitting a written nomination to the Clerk.

4. A nomination shall be valid only if it is seconded by another member.

5. A member nominated as a candidate must take the oath of allegiance or make a solemn affirmation before the time appointed for the voting period to select a nominee. If he or she has not done so, the Presiding Officer shall reject his or her nomination.

6. At the time appointed for the voting period to select a nominee, the Presiding Officer shall announce the name or names of the candidate or candidates and the nominee shall then be selected in accordance with Rule 11.10.

Rule 4.2 Designation of person to exercise functions of First

Minister

1. The Presiding Officer shall notify the Parliament of the name of any person whom he or she has designated to exercise the functions of the First Minister under section 45(4).

Rule 4.3 Appointment of Scottish Law Officers

1. The agreement of the Parliament to the First Minister's recommendation to Her Majesty for the appointment of a person as Lord Advocate or Solicitor General for Scotland under section 48(1) shall be sought on a motion of the First Minister that a person specified in the motion be so recommended. The provisions of Rules 8.2.5 and 8.2.6 shall not apply to such a motion.

2. Such a motion may relate to one or both of the appointments to be recommended.

3. Before the Presiding Officer puts to the Parliament the question on a motion relating to both appointments, the motion may be amended without notice but only to delete that part of the motion relating to one of the appointments.

4. If there is a division on such a motion, the result is valid only if the number of members who voted is more than one quarter of the total number of seats for members. In calculating the number of members who have voted for this purpose, account shall be taken not only of those voting for or against the motion but also of those voting to abstain.

Rule 4.4 Removal of Scottish Law Officers

1. The provisions of Rule 4.3 shall apply, with such modifications as are appropriate, in relation to a recommendation for the removal of a person as Lord Advocate or Solicitor General for Scotland as they apply in relation to a recommendation for an appointment.

Rule 4.5 Participation of Scottish Law Officers in proceedings

1. This Rule applies where the Lord Advocate or Solicitor General for Scotland ("the Scottish Law Officer") is not a member of the Parliament.

2. The Scottish Law Officer may (subject always to the provision in section 27(1)(a) preventing him or her from voting) participate in any of the proceedings of the Parliament as fully as any member but he or she may not be appointed as a member of the Parliamentary corporation or the Parliamentary Bureau.

3. These Rules shall apply to the Scottish Law Officer, when he or she is participating in any proceedings of the Parliament, as if he or she were a member of the Parliament.

4. Paragraphs 2 and 3 are without prejudice to section 27(2) (application of rules regarding members' interests) and section 27(3) (questions and documents relating to operation of system of criminal prosecution).

Rule 4.6 Appointment of other Scottish Ministers

1. Where the First Minister proposes to appoint any Minister or Ministers under section 47(1), he or she shall, before seeking Her Majesty's approval for any appointment, seek the agreement of the Parliament to his or her proposal in accordance with the following provisions.

2. He or she shall by motion seek the agreement of the Parliament to the appointment of either—
  (a) an individual member to be a Minister; or
  (b) a group of 2 or more members to be Ministers.
      The provisions of Rules 8.2.5 and 8.2.6 shall not apply to such a motion.
3. Before the Presiding Officer puts to the Parliament the question on a motion relating to a group of members, the motion may be amended but only to delete that part of the motion relating to a particular member or members.
4. If there is a division on such a motion, the result is valid only if the number of members who voted is more than one quarter of the total number of seats for members. In calculating the number of members who have voted for this purpose, account shall be taken not only of those voting for or against the motion but also of those voting to abstain.

Rule 4.7 Appointment of junior Scottish Ministers

1. The provisions of Rule 4.6 shall apply, with such modifications as are appropriate, where the First Minister proposes to appoint one or more junior Scottish Ministers under section 49(1).

Rule 4.8 Resignation of Ministers

1. If the First Minister tenders his or her resignation to Her Majesty under section 45(2), the Presiding Officer shall, if the resignation is accepted by Her Majesty, notify the Parliament.
2. Where any other member of the Scottish Executive or a junior Scottish Minister resigns, the Presiding Officer shall notify the resignation to the Parliament.

CHAPTER 5

The Parliamentary Bureau and Management of Business

Rule 5.1 Parliamentary Bureau

1. The Parliament shall establish the Parliamentary Bureau in accordance with these Rules.
2. The main functions of the Parliamentary Bureau shall be—
  (a) to propose the business programme as mentioned in Rule 5.4;
  (b) to propose alterations to the daily business list;
  (c) to propose the establishment, remit, membership, and duration of any committee or sub-committee; and
  (d) to determine any question regarding the competence of a committee to deal with a matter and, if two or more committees are competent to deal with a matter, to determine which of those committees is to be the lead committee responsible for that matter.
3. The Parliamentary Bureau shall have such other functions relating to the business of the Parliament or of any committee or sub-committee as may be conferred upon it by these Rules or by the Parliament.
4. The Parliamentary Bureau shall not be regarded as a committee for the purpose of these Rules.

Rule 5.2 Members of the Parliamentary Bureau

1. The Parliamentary Bureau shall consist of—
  (a) the Presiding Officer; and
  (b) a representative of each political party represented by 5 or more members of the Parliament ("a party representative") who is nominated by the leader within the Parliament of that party; and

(c) a representative of any group formed under paragraph 2 ("a group representative") who is nominated by that group.

2. Members who represent a political party with fewer than 5 representatives in the Parliament and members who do not represent a political party may join together to form a group for the purposes of nominating a group representative under paragraph 1(c). The number of members in any such group shall be at least 5.

3. A nomination of a party or group representative may be made to the Presiding Officer at any time during a Parliamentary session but must be made in writing and, in the case of the nomination of a group representative, must be signed by each member of the group.

4. If a member wishes to join a group or no longer wishes to form part of that group, he or she shall notify the Presiding Officer and the group representative that the group representative represents or, as the case may be, no longer represents him or her.

5. If, at any time and for whatever reason, a party or group representative no longer represents 5 or more members (including himself or herself), he or she shall cease to hold office as a member of the Parliamentary Bureau and the Presiding Officer shall notify the Parliament accordingly.

6. Where a party or group representative ceases to hold office as a member of the Parliamentary Bureau in any circumstances other than those mentioned in paragraph 5, the leader of the party or the group which nominated that representative shall nominate another representative to it in place of him or her.

7. A party or group representative may arrange for another member to take his or her place at a meeting of the Parliamentary Bureau if the Presiding Officer has been notified in writing in advance of that meeting.

Rule 5.3 Procedure of Parliamentary Bureau

1. The Presiding Officer shall convene and chair meetings of the Parliamentary Bureau. He or she shall have a casting vote but shall not otherwise vote in the proceedings.

2. The Parliamentary Bureau shall meet in private.

3. The Parliamentary Bureau shall not consider any business if the number of members of the Bureau who are present is fewer than half of the total number of members of the Bureau.

4. Matters to be decided by the Parliamentary Bureau shall, in the event of any disagreement, be decided by a vote. The vote shall be conducted in such a manner as the Presiding Officer may determine.

5. A party or group representative shall carry one vote for each member of the party or group which he or she represents (including himself or herself). The representative shall notify the Presiding Officer and other members of the Parliamentary Bureau of the number of votes which he or she carries and of any changes to that number.

6. A deputy Presiding Officer may attend any meeting of the Parliamentary Bureau and may participate in the proceedings but may not vote unless he or she is chairing the meeting in place of the Presiding Officer when he or she shall have a casting vote.

7. The Parliamentary Bureau may invite members who are not members of the Parliamentary Bureau to attend a meeting of the Parliamentary Bureau and those persons may participate in the meeting but may not vote.

Rule 5.4 Business programme

1. The Parliament shall decide, on a business motion of the Parliamentary Bureau, a programme of business (referred to as "the business programme") for such period as may be specified in that motion.

2. The business programme shall include an agenda of business for any meeting of the Parliament which is due to be held during that period and

may include the timetable for consideration by the Parliament, any committee or sub-committee of—
  (a) any Bill or any provision of a Bill;
  (b) any legislation or draft legislation of the European Communities or any provision of such legislation; or
  (c) any subordinate legislation or draft subordinate legislation.
  3. The business programme shall be notified to members in the Business Bulletin.

Rule 5.5 Daily business list

1. On the basis of the business programme and other decisions of the Parliament and the Presiding Officer, the Clerk shall publish a daily business list containing details of business to be considered by the Parliament and by each committee or sub-committee on each day when the Parliament or a committee or sub-committee meets. The daily business list shall also contain details of the times at which particular items of business are to be taken at any meeting if such times have been allocated in the business programme or in the decisions of the Parliament or the Presiding Officer.

2. The daily business list shall be notified to members in the Business Bulletin.

3. The Parliament may, on a motion of the Parliamentary Bureau, make alterations to the daily business list. Any such alterations shall be notified to members in the Business Bulletin.

4. If any emergency business arises, the Presiding Officer may allow that business to be taken at an appropriate point during a meeting of the Parliament and shall make any necessary alteration to the daily business list. Members shall be notified that the emergency business is to be taken and of any subsequent alteration to the daily business list.

Rule 5.6 Special cases of Parliamentary business

1. In proposing the business programme, the Parliamentary Bureau shall ensure that—
  (a) on 12 half sitting days in each Parliamentary year, the business of committees is given priority over the business of the Scottish Executive at meetings of the Parliament;
  (b) on 16 half sitting days in each Parliamentary year, meetings of the Parliament consider business chosen by political parties which are not represented in the Scottish Executive or by any group formed under Rule 5.2.2; and
  (c) at each meeting of the Parliament there is a period of up to 30 minutes for any Members' Business at the end of the meeting following Decision Time.

2. For the purposes of this Rule, a half sitting day is the period between 09:30 and 12:30 or between 14:30 and 17:00 on a sitting day from Monday to Thursday and the period between 09:30 to 12:00 on a sitting day on Friday.

Rule 5.7 Programme of the Scottish Executive

1. When the First Minister wishes to make a statement to a meeting of the Parliament setting out the proposed policy objectives and legislative programme of the Scottish Executive for any Parliamentary year, he or she shall give notice of his or her proposal to the Presiding Officer. The Presiding Officer shall then notify the Parliamentary Bureau.

2. The Parliamentary Bureau shall ensure that sufficient time is set aside in the business programme for the statement to be made and debated.

Rule 5.8 Financial business

1. In proposing the business programme, the Parliamentary Bureau shall ensure that sufficient time is set aside—

(a) between the beginning of May and the end of June each year for the consideration of financial proposals;
(b) between the beginning of October and the end of November each year for consideration of draft budgets; and
(c) between the beginning of January and the end of February each year for the Stages of the main Budget Bill.

2. "Consideration of financial proposals" means consideration by committees of documents laid before the Parliament setting out outline proposals for public expenditure in the forthcoming financial year and consideration by the Parliament of any report and recommendations of the Finance Committee concerning such documents.

3. "Consideration of draft budgets" means consideration by committees of documents laid before the Parliament setting out preliminary draft budgets of public expenditure in the forthcoming financial year.

4. "Financial year" means the year beginning on 1st April.

Rule 5.9 Business Bulletin

1. The Clerk shall produce the Business Bulletin.
2. The Business Bulletin shall include—
(a) the business programme;
(b) the daily business list;
(c) agendas for committee meetings;
(d) notices of oral questions for answer at Question Time or First Minister's Question Time;
(e) written questions;
(f) notices of motions and amendments to motions;
(g) notices of Bills introduced into the Parliament and amendments to Bills;
(h) notices of any subordinate legislation or draft subordinate legislation or any other document which is laid before the Parliament; and
(i) any other item which requires to be notified to members,
and the Business Bulletin may include any other information which the Clerk considers appropriate.

3. The Business Bulletin shall be issued to members by whatever means the Presiding Officer considers appropriate and shall be made public.

4. The Clerk shall keep the Business Bulletin under review and if necessary shall issue to members an amended version of any part of it.

CHAPTER 6

Committees

Rule 6.1 Establishment of committees

1. The Parliament may, on a motion of the Parliamentary Bureau, establish such committees as it thinks fit.

2. Any member may by motion propose the establishment of a committee.

3. The Parliamentary Bureau may, whether in response to such a proposal or otherwise, by motion propose the establishment, membership, remit and duration of a committee.

4. A committee established by the Parliament to deal with a particular subject, other than a mandatory committee, is referred to as a subject committee.

5. In addition, the Parliament shall, on a motion of the Parliamentary Bureau, establish the following mandatory committees—
(a) the Procedures Committee;
(b) the Standards Committee;

(c) the Finance Committee;
(d) the Audit Committee;
(e) the European Committee;
(f) the Equal Opportunities Committee;
(g) the Public Petitions Committee;
(h) the Subordinate Legislation Committee.

6. The Parliamentary Bureau shall by motion propose the establishment of—

(a) the Procedures, Standards and Finance Committees within 21 sitting days of a general election; and
(b) the other mandatory committees mentioned in paragraph 5 within 42 sitting days of a general election.

Rule 6.2 Functions of all committees

1. A committee shall examine such matters within its remit (referred to as "competent matters") as it may determine appropriate or as may be referred to it by the Parliament or another committee and shall report to the Parliament on any such matter.

2. In particular, each committee shall conduct such inquiries into such competent matters as it may consider appropriate or as the Parliament or another committee may require, and may—

(a) consider the policy and administration of the Scottish Administration upon any competent matter;
(b) consider any proposals for legislation which relate to or affect any competent matter, including proposals for primary or secondary legislation, whether before the Scottish Parliament or the United Kingdom Parliament;
(c) consider any European Communities legislation or any international conventions or agreements or any drafts which relate to or affect any competent matter;
(d) consider the need for the reform of the law which relates to or affects any competent matter;
(e) initiate Bills on any competent matter; and
(f) consider the financial proposals and financial administration of the Scottish Administration (including variation of taxes, estimates, budgets, audit and performance) which relate to or affect any competent matter.

Rule 6.3 Membership of committees

1. The membership of each committee shall be approved by the Parliament on a motion of the Parliamentary Bureau.

2. Each committee shall have at least 5 but not more than 15 members.

3. A member may indicate to the Parliamentary Bureau his or her interest in serving on a particular committee.

4. In proposing a member to be a committee member, the Parliamentary Bureau shall have regard to the balance of political parties in the Parliament and, where that member has expressed an interest in serving on that committee, to his or her qualifications and experience as indicated by him or her.

5. A committee member shall serve as a member of a committee for the duration of that committee unless—

(a) he or she resigns from that office by intimating his or her resignation to the Parliamentary Bureau;
(b) he or she is removed from that office by the Parliament on a motion of the committee; or
(c) he or she ceases to be a member of the Parliament otherwise than by virtue of a dissolution.

6. A committee member may not be represented at a meeting of the committee by a substitute.

Rule 6.4 Procedures Committee

1. The remit of the Procedures Committee is to consider and report on the practice and procedures of the Parliament in relation to its business.

Rule 6.5 Standards Committee

1. The remit of the Standards Committee is to consider and report on—

(a) whether a member's conduct is in accordance with these Rules and any Code of Conduct for members, matters relating to members' interests, and any other matters relating to the conduct of members in carrying out their Parliamentary duties; and

(b) the adoption, amendment and application of any Code of Conduct for members.

2. Where the Committee considers it appropriate, it may by motion recommend that a member's rights and privileges be withdrawn to such extent and for such period as are specified in the motion.

Rule 6.6 Finance Committee

1. The remit of the Finance Committee is to consider and report on—

(a) any report or other document laid before the Parliament by members of the Scottish Executive containing proposals for, or budgets of, public expenditure or proposals for the making of a tax-varying resolution, taking into account any report or recommendations concerning such documents made to them by any other committee with power to consider such documents or any part of them;

(b) any report made by a committee setting out proposals concerning public expenditure;

(c) Budget Bills; and

(d) any other matter relating to or affecting the expenditure of the Scottish Administration or other expenditure payable out of the Scottish Consolidated Fund.

2. The Committee may also consider and, where it sees fit, report to the Parliament on the timetable for the Stages of Budget Bills and on the handling of financial business.

3. In these Rules, "public expenditure" means expenditure of the Scottish Administration, other expenditure payable out of the Scottish Consolidated Fund and any other expenditure met out of taxes, charges and other public revenue.

Rule 6.7 Audit Committee

1. The remit of the Audit Committee is to consider and report on—

(a) any accounts laid before the Parliament;

(b) any report laid before the Parliament by the Auditor General for Scotland; and

(c) any other document laid before the Parliament concerning financial control, accounting and auditing in relation to public expenditure.

2. No member of the Scottish Executive or junior Scottish Minister may be a member of the Committee and no member who represents a political party which is represented in the Scottish Executive may be convener of the Committee.

Rule 6.8 European Committee

1. The remit of the European Committee is to consider and report on—

(a) proposals for European Communities legislation;

(b) the implementation of European Communities legislation; and

(c) any European Communities or European Union issue.

2. The Committee may refer matters to the Parliamentary Bureau or other committees where it considers it appropriate to do so.

3. The convener of the Committee shall not be the convener of any other committee whose remit is, in the opinion of the Parliamentary Bureau, relevant to that of the Committee.

4. The Parliamentary Bureau shall normally propose a person to be a member of the Committee only if he or she is a member of another committee whose remit is, in the opinion of the Parliamentary Bureau, relevant to that of the Committee.

Rule 6.9 Equal Opportunities Committee

1. The remit of the Equal Opportunities Committee is to consider and report on matters relating to equal opportunities and upon the observance of equal opportunities within the Parliament.

2. In these Rules, "equal opportunities" includes the prevention, elimination or regulation of discrimination between persons on grounds of sex or marital status, on racial grounds, or on grounds of disability, age, sexual orientation, language or social origin, or of other personal attributes, including beliefs or opinions, such as religious beliefs or political opinions.

Rule 6.10 Public Petitions Committee

1. The remit of the Public Petitions Committee is to consider and report on—

(a) whether a public petition is admissible; and

(b) what action should be taken upon the petition,

in accordance with the Rules in Chapter 15.

Rule 6.11 Subordinate Legislation Committee

1. The remit of the Subordinate Legislation Committee is to consider and report on—

(i) subordinate legislation which is laid before the Parliament;

(ii) any Scottish Statutory Instrument not laid before the Parliament but classified as general according to its subject matter,

and, in particular, to determine whether the attention of the Parliament should be drawn to any of the matters mentioned in Rule 10.3.1;

(b) proposed powers to make subordinate legislation in particular Bills or other proposed legislation; and

(c) general questions relating to powers to make subordinate legislation.

Rule 6.12 Duration of committees

1. The mandatory committees referred to in Rule 6.1.5 shall be established for the whole session of the Parliament.

2. The Parliament shall, on a motion of the Parliamentary Bureau, determine the duration of any other committee.

3. The Parliament may decide, on a motion of the Parliamentary Bureau, that any other committee be disbanded.

Rule 6.13 Questions regarding competence

1. Any question whether a matter is within the remit of a committee shall be determined by the Parliamentary Bureau.

2. If a matter falls within the remit of more than one committee the Parliament may, on a motion of the Parliamentary Bureau, name one of the committees as the lead committee responsible for that matter. The other committee or committees shall be asked to give their opinion to the lead committee. This is without prejudice to Rule 6.14.

Rule 6.14 Joint consideration by committees

1. Where a matter falls within the remit of more than one committee, the committees concerned may, with the agreement of the Parliamentary Bureau, decide to consider that matter jointly.

2. Where a matter is to be considered jointly under paragraph 1, any meeting to consider that matter shall be held jointly by the committees concerned. Such a meeting may be convened by the convener of any of those committees. At such a meeting the convener of any of those committees may take the chair.

3. Any report on the joint consideration of a matter shall be produced jointly by those committees.

4. Any of those committees may establish a sub-committee to consider the matter jointly with a sub-committee of another of those committees.

CHAPTER 7

Conduct of Meetings

Rule 7.1 Languages

1. The Parliament shall normally conduct its business in English but members may speak in Scots Gaelic or in any other language with the agreement of the Presiding Officer.

2. Any person addressing the Parliament on the invitation of the Parliament in accordance with Rule 15.3.5, may do so in any language other than English with the agreement of the Presiding Officer.

Rule 7.2 Calling speakers and content of speeches

1. No member except the Presiding Officer may speak unless called upon to do so by the Presiding Officer. In deciding who should be called, the Presiding Officer shall have regard to the nature of the business under consideration. Normally, members shall speak standing at their places and shall address the Presiding Officer.

2. The Presiding Officer may allocate speaking time, whether for proceedings in relation to a particular item of business or for a particular speaker in any proceedings, and may do so whether or not the proceedings have started or the speaker has started to speak. The Presiding Officer may not allocate speaking time in a manner which would disrupt any timetable of business set out in the daily business list.

3. The Presiding Officer may order a member to stop speaking if that member continues to speak beyond any time allocated to him or her or to that item of business (whether by the Presiding Officer or in the daily business list or under these Rules) or if, in the opinion of the Presiding Officer, the member departs from the subject or repeats himself or herself.

4. A speaker may not be interrupted except by the Presiding Officer. The speaker may, however, give way to allow another member to intervene.

Rule 7.3 Order in the chamber

1. Members shall at all times conduct themselves in a courteous and respectful manner and shall respect the authority of the Presiding Officer. In particular, members shall not speak or stand when the Presiding Officer is speaking.

2. Members shall at all times conduct themselves in an orderly manner and, in particular, shall not conduct themselves in a manner which would constitute a criminal offence or contempt of court.

3. Any member who is in breach of paragraph 2 may be ordered by the Presiding Officer to leave the chamber and may be excluded from the chamber—

(a) on the order of the Presiding Officer for such period as the Presiding Officer thinks fit but not beyond the end of the next sitting day; and

(b) for such further period as the Parliament may decide, on a motion of the Parliamentary Bureau.

4. A motion under paragraph 3(b) may not be amended. If the motion is debated only the following may speak, namely—

(a) the member concerned; and

(b) one member for the motion and one member against the motion.

Rule 7.4 Suspension and closure of meetings by Presiding Officer

1. The Presiding Officer may, if he or she considers it appropriate, suspend a meeting of the Parliament—

if an emergency occurs which would place members attending the meeting at risk; if a disturbance interferes with the conduct of business; where the electronic voting system or any other electronic equipment which is required for the purposes of the meeting cannot be used for any reason; where debate on a particular item of business has concluded before the time set out in the daily business list for commencement of the next item of business; or for a meal break.

2. In the case of a suspension under paragraph 1(b) a meeting is suspended if the Presiding Officer leaves the chair after ordering the person or persons causing the disturbance to stop the disturbance.

3. The Presiding Officer may reconvene a meeting suspended under paragraph 1(a), (b) or (c) only at a time later in the same day. The Presiding Officer may suspend a meeting under paragraph 1(d) or (e) only until a specified time later in the same day when it shall be reconvened. A suspended meeting which is not reconvened at a time later in the same day is deemed to have been closed at the time it was suspended.

4. The Presiding Officer shall make any necessary alteration to the daily business list as a result of the suspension of a meeting. Members shall be notified of any such alteration.

5. The Presiding Officer may, if he or she considers it appropriate, at any time close a meeting of the Parliament.

Rule 7.5 Sub judice

1. A member may not in the proceedings of the Parliament refer to any matter in relation to which legal proceedings are active except to the extent permitted by the Presiding Officer.

2. For the purposes of paragraph 1, legal proceedings are active in relation to a matter if they are active for the purposes of section 2 of the Contempt of Court Act 1981.

3. Where any member refers to a matter in relation to which legal proceedings are active the Presiding Officer may order that member not to do so.

4. Nothing in this Rule shall prevent the Parliament from legislating about any matter.

Rule 7.6 Forms of address

1. Each member shall be referred to in any proceedings of the Parliament by name and, if he or she wishes, by his or her title, if any, except—

(a) the Presiding Officer, who may, in addition or as an alternative, be referred to by that title;

(b) a deputy Presiding Officer, who may, in addition or as an alternative, be referred to by that title; and

(c) any member of the Scottish Executive or junior Scottish Minister, who may, in addition or as an alternative, be referred to by such titles as the First Minister may notify to the Presiding Officer.

Rule 7.7 Calculating the length of debates or the number of speakers

1. For the purposes of any Rule limiting the length of a debate or the number of speakers—

(a) if the member moving the motion speaks in support of it, he or she shall be treated as a speaker for that motion and the time for which he or she speaks shall be treated as part of the debate; and

(b) any debate on an amendment shall form part of the debate on the motion.

Rule 7.8 Committee proceedings

1. Rules 7.1 to 7.3, 7.4.1(b), 7.4.2, 7.4.3 and 7.5 to 7.7 shall apply to proceedings at meetings of committees and sub-committees as they apply to proceedings at meetings of the Parliament, with such modifications as are appropriate. However, only the Presiding Officer may grant the permission referred to in Rule 7.5.1.

CHAPTER 8

Motions and Points of Order

Rule 8.1 Motions

1. Any member may, except where these Rules provide otherwise, give notice of a motion or move a motion about any matter.

2. A motion may be moved without notice being given only as permitted by these Rules or, exceptionally, as permitted by the Presiding Officer.

3. Where these Rules provide for a motion of a committee or of the Parliamentary Bureau, notice of the motion (if required) may be given, and the motion may be moved, only by a member of that committee or, as the case may be, of the Parliamentary Bureau.

Rule 8.2 Notice of motions

1. Notice of a motion shall be given by being lodged by a member with the Clerk. Notice of a motion shall contain the text of the motion and the name of the member giving notice of it.

2. A motion shall—

(a) be in English;

(b) not contain offensive language;

(c) not breach any enactment or rule of law or be contrary to the public interest; and

(d) not contravene Rule 7.5.1.

3. The Clerk may refuse to accept notice of a motion only if the motion is not permitted under these Rules or if, in the opinion of the Clerk, it is not in accordance with paragraph 2.

4. Any member may indicate his or her support for a motion by notifying the Clerk.

5. The text of a motion and the name of the member who gave notice of it and of any member supporting it shall be printed in the Business Bulletin.

6. Normally, a motion shall not be taken before the sitting day after the day on which notice of it is given under paragraph 1. A motion may be taken on shorter notice if the Parliament so decides on a motion without notice. Such a motion may be taken only with the agreement of the Presiding Officer.

7. Where time has been allocated for a debate on a particular subject, the Presiding Officer shall consider all motions on that subject of which notice has been given and shall decide which of those motions are to be taken by the Parliament. In all other cases, the Parliamentary Bureau shall consider motions of which notice has been given and shall by motion propose which of those motions are to be taken by the Parliament. A business motion shall always be taken by the Parliament.

Rule 8.3 Motions taken by the Parliament

1. A motion is taken by the Parliament when it is called at a meeting of the Parliament by the Presiding Officer.

2. When a motion is taken by the Parliament the motion may be moved by the member who gave notice of it or, except in the cases referred to in Rule 8.9, Rules 8.10 and Rule 8.11, if that member does not move the motion, by any other member who has indicated his or her support for it before the end of the previous sitting day.

3. Before the member moves the motion, he or she may speak in support of it.

4. Immediately after the motion is moved, the Presiding Officer may call on any other member to speak.

5. All motions may be debated, except as provided in these Rules.

6. After a motion is moved, it may be withdrawn by the member who moved it at any time before the question is put unless any member objects to it being withdrawn.

7. After the debate has been closed or, where there is no debate, after the motion has been moved, the question on the motion shall be put at the time when it requires to be put in accordance with Rules 11.2 to 11.4.

Rule 8.4 Amendments to motions

1. A motion may be amended except as provided in these Rules.

2. A motion without notice may be amended without notice.

Rule 8.5 Notice of amendments

1. Notice of an amendment to a motion of which notice has been given shall be given by being lodged by a member with the Clerk at any time after notice of the motion has been given. Notice of an amendment shall contain the text of the amendment and the name of the member giving notice of it.

2. An amendment shall—
(a) be in English;
(b) not contain offensive language;
(c) not breach any enactment or rule of law or be contrary to the public interest; and
(d) not contravene Rule 7.5.1.

3. The Clerk may refuse to accept notice of an amendment only if the amendment is not permitted under these Rules or if, in the opinion of the Clerk, it is not in accordance with paragraph 2.

4. Any member may indicate his or her support for an amendment by notifying the Clerk.

5. The text of an amendment and the name of the member who gave notice of it and of any member supporting it shall be printed in the Business Bulletin.

6. The Presiding Officer shall examine all amendments of which notice has been given and shall decide which amendments are to be taken by the Parliament.

Rule 8.6 Amendments taken by the Parliament

1. If an amendment to a motion is to be taken by the Parliament, it shall be taken immediately after the motion is moved.

2. When an amendment is taken, it may be moved by the member who gave notice of it or by any member who has indicated his or her support for it.

3. Before the member moves the amendment, he or she may speak in support of it.

4. An amendment may be debated only if the motion may be debated.

5. The question on an amendment shall be put in accordance with Rules 11.2 to 11.4.

Rule 8.7 Amendments to amendments

1. The provisions of Rules 8.4 to 8.6 shall apply to amendments to amendments as they apply to amendments to motions with such modifications as are appropriate.

Rule 8.8 Application to committees

1. The provisions of Rules 8.1 to 8.7 shall apply to proceedings at meetings of committees and sub-committees as they apply to proceedings at meetings of the Parliament, with such modifications as are appropriate.

Rule 8.9 Motions of First Minister

1. The following motions may be moved, and notice of any such motion may be given, only by the First Minister, namely—

(a) a motion seeking the agreement of the Parliament under section 48(1) that a recommendation be made to Her Majesty for the appointment or removal of a person as Lord Advocate or Solicitor General for Scotland;

(b) a motion seeking the agreement of the Parliament under section 47(2) or 49(3) that a member be appointed a Minister or a junior Scottish Minister respectively;

(c) a motion under section 95(7) that a recommendation be made to Her Majesty for the removal of a judge.

Rule 8.10 Tax-varying resolutions

1. A motion for a tax-varying resolution under section 74 may be moved, and notice of such a motion may be given, only by a member of the Scottish Executive. Such a motion may not be amended.

2. Subject to paragraph 3, a motion for a tax-varying resolution may be moved no earlier than 12 months before the beginning of the year of assessment to which it relates.

3. A motion for a tax-varying resolution may be moved after the beginning of the year of assessment to which it relates only at Stage 3 of a Budget Bill, or a Bill to amend a Budget Act, relating to that year.

Rule 8.11 Business motions

1. A motion seeking the approval of the Parliament to the Parliamentary Bureau's proposals on the business programme shall be known as a business motion.

2. A business motion may be moved, and notice of such a motion may be given, only by a member of the Parliamentary Bureau.

3. Any debate on a business motion shall be restricted to 30 minutes. There shall be no more than one speaker for and one speaker against the motion and any amendment to it and each speaker may speak for no more than 5 minutes.

4. Members may propose amendments to a business motion. If, when notice of an amendment is given, it is supported by at least 10 members, that amendment shall be taken by the Parliament.

Rule 8.12 Motions of no confidence

1. Any member may give notice of a motion that the Scottish Executive or a member of the Scottish Executive or a junior Scottish Minister no longer enjoys the confidence of the Parliament ("a motion of no confidence").

2. If notice of a motion of no confidence is supported by at least 25 members, it shall be included in a proposed business programme.

3. Members shall normally be given at least 2 sitting days' notice of a motion of no confidence. Exceptionally, members may be given a shorter period of notice if in the opinion of the Parliamentary Bureau a shorter period is appropriate.

Rule 8.13 Procedural motions

1. Only the member moving the motion and one speaker against may speak on a motion mentioned in Rules 8.14 to 8.16. Each such person may speak for no more than 3 minutes.

2. A motion referred to in paragraph 1 shall take precedence over the business under consideration, the debate on which shall be suspended while the motion is being considered.

Rule 8.14 Closure of a debate

1. Where time has been allocated for a debate (whether by the Presiding Officer or in the daily business list) the debate shall, subject to paragraphs 2 and 3, be closed when the time allocated has been exhausted.

2. A member may, by motion without notice, propose that a debate be closed earlier than the end of the period of time allocated for that debate. Such a motion may be taken only with the agreement of the Presiding Officer. If the motion is agreed to, the debate shall be closed. If the motion is not agreed to, the same or a similar motion may not be moved again during that debate.

3. Any member may, by motion without notice, propose that a debate be extended for up to 30 minutes beyond the end of the period of time allocated for that debate. Such a motion may be taken only with the agreement of the Presiding Officer. If the motion is agreed to, the debate shall be extended. If the motion is not agreed to, the same or a similar motion may not be moved again during that debate.

4. If a debate is closed or extended under this Rule the Presiding Officer shall make any necessary alteration to the daily business list. Members shall be notified of any such alteration.

Rule 8.15 Motions for adjournment of a debate

1. At any time during a debate a member may, by motion without notice, propose that the debate be adjourned. Such a motion may be taken only with the agreement of the Presiding Officer.

2. If the motion is agreed to, the Parliament shall proceed to the next business. If a debate is adjourned under this Rule the Presiding Officer shall make any necessary alteration to the daily business list. Members shall be notified of any such alteration.

3. If the motion is not agreed to, the same or a similar motion may not be moved again during that debate.

Rule 8.16 Motions for adjournment and closure of meetings

1. Any member may, by motion without notice, propose that a meeting of the Parliament be adjourned or closed. Such a motion may be taken only with the agreement of the Presiding Officer. A meeting may be adjourned only to a time later in the same day. If a meeting is so adjourned, the

Presiding Officer shall make any necessary alteration to the daily business list. Members shall be notified of any such alteration.

Rule 8.17 Points of order

1. A member may in any proceedings question whether proper procedures have been or are being followed by making a point of order.

2. In making a point of order, a member may not speak for more than 3 minutes and may not speak on the question under consideration. Points of order shall take precedence over the question under consideration, the discussion of which shall be suspended while they are being considered.

3. The Presiding Officer shall normally take an immediate decision on any point of order in accordance with these Rules but may exceptionally defer taking a decision. He or she shall announce his or her ruling.

CHAPTER 9

Bill Procedures

Rule 9.1 General Rules and Special Rules

1. The General Rules set out in Rules 9.2 to 9.13 shall apply in relation to every Bill introduced in the Parliament but, where any of the Special Rules set out in Rules 9.14 to 9.21 (special provision about Member's Bills, Committee Bills, Budget Bills, Private Bills, Consolidation Bills, Codification Bills, Statute Law Repeals Bills, Statute Law Revision Bills and Emergency Bills) applies in relation to the Bill, then the Special Rule shall supersede the General Rules to the extent that they are inconsistent.

Rule 9.2 Form and introduction of Bills

1. A Bill may be introduced by any member on a sitting day. The member introducing a Bill or any other member nominated by him or her for the purpose is referred to as "the member in charge of the Bill".

2. A Bill shall be introduced by being lodged with the Clerk.

3. A Bill may not be introduced unless it is in proper form. The Presiding Officer shall determine the proper form of Bills and the Clerk shall arrange for the determinations of the Presiding Officer to be notified to the Parliament.

4. A Bill must, before introduction, be signed by the member introducing it and may also be signed by any other member or members who support the Bill.

5. The Clerk shall ensure that notice of the introduction of a Bill in the Parliament is published in the Business Bulletin. Such notice shall set out the short and long titles of the Bill, the name of the member who has introduced it and the name of any member supporting the Bill and shall indicate what type of Bill it is.

6. No Bill, other than a Budget Bill, may be introduced in the Parliament if it contains any provision which would have the effect of authorising sums to be paid out of the Scottish Consolidated Fund (as opposed to a provision which charges expenditure on that Fund).

Rule 9.3 Accompanying documents

1. A Bill shall on introduction be accompanied by a written statement signed by the Presiding Officer which shall—

    (a) indicate whether or not in his or her view the provisions of the Bill would be within the legislative competence of the Parliament; and

    (b) if in his or her view any of the provisions would not be within legislative competence, indicate which those provisions are and the reasons for that view.

2. A Bill shall on introduction be accompanied by a Financial Memorandum which shall set out the best estimates of the administrative, compliance and other costs to which the provisions of the Bill would give rise, best estimates of the timescales over which such costs would be expected to arise, and an indication of the margins of uncertainty in such estimates. The Financial Memorandum must distinguish separately such costs as would fall upon—

    (a) the Scottish Administration;

    (b) local authorities; and

    (c) other bodies, individuals and businesses.

3. A Bill introduced by a member of the Scottish Executive (referred to as "an Executive Bill") shall also be accompanied by—

    (a) a written statement signed by the member of the Scottish Executive in charge of the Bill which states that in his or her view the provisions of the Bill would be within the legislative competence of the Parliament;

    (b) Explanatory Notes which summarise objectively what each of the provisions of the Bill does and give other information necessary or expedient to explain the effect of the Bill; and

    (c) a Policy Memorandum which sets out—

    (i) the policy objectives of the Bill;

    (ii) whether alternative ways of meeting those objectives were considered and, if so, why the approach taken in the Bill was adopted;

    (iii) the consultation, if any, which was undertaken on those objectives and the ways of meeting them or on the detail of the Bill and a summary of the outcome of that consultation; and

    (iv) an assessment of the effects, if any, of the Bill on equal opportunities, human rights, island communities, local government, sustainable development and any other matter which the Scottish Ministers consider relevant.

4. A Bill which contains any provision charging expenditure on the Scottish Consolidated Fund shall be accompanied by a report signed by the Auditor General for Scotland (referred to as "an Auditor General's Report") setting out his or her views on whether the charge is appropriate.

5. The documents which must accompany a Bill under this Rule are referred to as its "accompanying documents".

6. A Bill may be introduced without one or more of its accompanying documents only with the agreement of the Parliament.

Rule 9.4 Printing and publishing of Bills and accompanying documents

1. As soon as a Bill has been introduced the Clerk shall arrange for the Bill, together with its accompanying documents, to be printed and published.

Rule 9.5 Stages of Bills

1. The procedure for a Bill introduced in the Parliament shall be—

    (a) consideration of the Bill's general principles and a decision on whether they are agreed to (Stage 1);

    (b) consideration of the details of the Bill (Stage 2); and

    (c) final consideration of the Bill and a decision whether it is passed or rejected (Stage 3).

2. A Bill which has been passed by the Parliament may additionally be subject to reconsideration at a further stage in the circumstances described in Rule 9.9.

3. The business programme shall set out the time or times at which each Stage, or any part of any Stage, of a Bill is to be taken but there must be at least 2 weeks between completion of Stage 1 and the start of Stage 2 and, if the Bill is amended at Stage 2, between completion of that Stage and the start of Stage 3.

4. If at any Stage a Bill falls or is rejected by the Parliament, no further proceedings shall be taken on the Bill and a Bill in the same or similar terms may not be introduced within the period of 6 months from the date on which the Bill fell or was rejected.

5. A Bill introduced in any session of the Parliament falls if it has not been passed by the Parliament before the end of that session but a Bill in the same or similar terms may be introduced in any subsequent session.

Rule 9.6 Stage 1

1. Once a Bill has been printed, the Parliamentary Bureau shall refer it to the committee within whose remit the subject matter of the Bill falls. That committee (referred to as "the lead committee") shall consider and report on the general principles of the Bill. Where the subject matter of the Bill falls within the remit of more than one committee the Parliament may, on a motion of the Parliamentary Bureau, designate one of those committees as the lead committee and the other committee or committees may also consider the general principles of the Bill and report its or their views to the lead committee.

2. The Parliamentary Bureau shall also refer any provision in the Bill conferring powers to make subordinate legislation to the Subordinate Legislation Committee, which shall consider and report on those provisions to the lead committee.

3. In considering the general principles of the Bill and preparing its report on them, the lead committee shall take into account any views submitted by any other committee, and shall incorporate in its report any report submitted by the Subordinate Legislation Committee. If the Bill is an Executive Bill, the lead committee shall also consider and report on its Policy Memorandum.

4. Once the lead committee has reported on the Bill, the Parliament shall consider the general principles of the Bill in the light of the lead committee's report and decide the question whether those general principles are agreed to.

5. Any member may by motion propose that the Bill be referred back to the lead committee for a further report on the general principles of the Bill, or any specified part of the Bill, before the Parliament decides whether to agree to them.

6. If the motion is agreed to, consideration of the Bill's general principles is adjourned to a time to be determined by the Parliamentary Bureau. The Parliamentary Bureau shall refer the Bill back to the lead committee which shall prepare a further report in accordance with the Parliament's decision.

7. If the Parliament agrees to the Bill's general principles the Bill proceeds to Stage 2. If the Parliament does not agree to the Bill's general principles the Bill falls.

Rule 9.7 Stage 2

1. If the Parliament has agreed to the Bill's general principles, the Parliamentary Bureau shall—
   (a) refer the Bill back to the lead committee which shall consider the details of the Bill in accordance with this Rule; or
   (b) by motion propose that Stage 2 of the Bill be taken, in whole or in part, by a Committee of the Whole Parliament or a committee or committees other than the lead committee.

2. The Presiding Officer shall be the convener of a Committee of the Whole Parliament and shall chair its proceedings and the provisions of these Rules about committees shall apply with such modifications as are appropriate.

3. At Stage 2, each section and schedule and the long title of the Bill shall be considered separately and the committee shall decide whether they are agreed to. The question whether a section or schedule or the long title is agreed to shall be put by the convener without the need for any member to move a motion to that effect. Sections or schedules to which no amendments are proposed and which fall to be considered consecutively may be taken and agreed to together.

4. Unless the Parliament has decided, on a motion of the Parliamentary Bureau, the order in which the sections and schedules of the Bill are to be considered at Stage 2, the committee may decide the order. Normally, a schedule shall be taken immediately after the section which introduces it. The long title shall be taken last.

5. A Bill may be amended at Stage 2. Notice of an amendment may be given by any member after the completion of Stage 1.

6. At Stage 2, amendments to any section or schedule or to the long title shall be disposed of before the committee considers whether to agree to the provision in question. Where no amendments are proposed to a section, a schedule or the long title, the committee shall proceed immediately to decide the question whether that provision is agreed to. If an amendment to leave out a section or schedule is not agreed to, that section or schedule shall be treated as agreed to.

7. In addition to the provisions of Rule 12.2.2—

(a) a member who is not a member of a committee taking Stage 2 of a Bill, or part of it, is entitled to participate in the proceedings for the purpose of moving, debating or seeking agreement to withdraw an amendment in his or her name but he or she shall not vote;

(b) the member in charge of the Bill, if not a member of the committee, is entitled to attend the committee and participate in the proceedings but he or she shall not vote; and

(c) in the case of a Bill which is not an Executive Bill, the member of the Scottish Executive with general responsibility for the subject matter of the Bill, if not a member of the committee, is entitled to attend the committee and participate in the proceedings but he or she shall not vote.

8. At the end of Stage 2, the Clerk shall, if the Bill has been amended, arrange for the Bill as amended to be printed and published.

9. If the Bill has been amended at Stage 2 so as to insert or substantially alter provisions conferring powers to make subordinate legislation, the Bill as amended shall be referred to the Subordinate Legislation Committee to consider and report to the Parliament on those amendments.

Rule 9.8 Stage 3

1. Stage 3 of a Bill shall be taken at a meeting of the Parliament.

2. At Stage 3, the Parliament shall decide the question whether the Bill is passed.

3. A Bill may be amended at Stage 3. Notice of an amendment may be given by any member after completion of Stage 2.

4. The Presiding Officer may select, as he or she sees fit, those amendments which are to be taken at Stage 3 from amongst the amendments of which notice has been given.

5. Unless the Parliament has decided, on a motion of the Parliamentary Bureau, the order in which amendments are to be disposed of, they shall be disposed of in the order in which the provisions to which they relate arise in the Bill, before the Parliament debates the question whether the Bill is passed. If the Bill is amended, the member in charge of the Bill may, immediately after the last amendment is disposed of, by motion without notice propose that the remaining proceedings at Stage 3 be adjourned to a later day. Such a motion may not be debated or amended. If the motion is agreed to, the member in charge of the Bill may give notice of amendments to the Bill to be moved at the adjourned proceedings. Such amendments may only be for the purpose of clarifying uncertainties or giving effect to commitments given at the earlier proceedings at Stage 3. If the motion is not agreed to, the Parliament shall proceed immediately to debate the question whether the Bill is passed.

6. At the beginning of the debate on the question whether the Bill is passed, the member in charge of the Bill may by motion propose that such part of the Bill as may be specified in the motion, amounting to no more than half of the total number of sections of the Bill, be referred back to committee for further Stage 2 consideration. If the motion is agreed to, the proceedings are adjourned to a time to be determined by the Parliamentary Bureau which shall refer the Bill to a committee in accordance with the Parliament's decision. When the Stage 3 proceedings resume, amendments may be made to the Bill but only to the provisions which were referred back to committee or if they are necessary in consequence of any amendment made at the further Stage 2 proceedings.

7. This Rule, apart from paragraph 6, shall apply to the resumed Stage 3 proceedings as it applies to the initial Stage 3 proceedings.

8. At Stage 3 a Bill may be referred back to committee for further Stage 2 consideration only once.

9. If there is a division at Stage 3 on the question whether the Bill is passed, the result is valid only if the number of members who voted is more than one quarter of the total number of seats for members of the Parliament. In calculating the number of members who voted for this purpose, account shall be taken not only of those voting for and against the motion but also of those voting to abstain.

10. If the result of such a division is not valid the Bill shall be treated as rejected.

Rule 9.9 Reconsideration of Bills passed

1. The member in charge of a Bill may, after the Bill is passed, by motion propose that the Parliament resolve that it wishes to reconsider the Bill if—

(a) a question in relation to the Bill has been referred to the Judicial Committee of the Privy Council under section 33;

(b) a reference for a preliminary ruling (within the meaning of section 34(3)) has been made by the Judicial Committee in connection with that reference; and

(c) neither of those references has been decided or otherwise disposed of.

2. The member in charge of a Bill may by motion propose that the Parliament resolve to reconsider the Bill if—

(a) the Judicial Committee of the Privy Council decides that the Bill or any provision of it would not be within the legislative competence of the Parliament; or

(b) an order is made in relation to the Bill under section 35 (order prohibiting Presiding Officer from submitting Bill for Royal Assent).

3. Proceedings on reconsideration shall be taken at a meeting of the Parliament.

4. A Bill may be amended on reconsideration of the Bill but only for the purpose of resolving the problem which is the subject of the reference for a preliminary ruling or which is the subject of the decision of the Judicial Committee or the order under section 35.

5. After amendments have been disposed of, the Parliament shall consider and decide the question whether to approve the Bill.

Rule 9.10 Amendments to Bills

1. Amendments to a Bill shall be in such form as the Presiding Officer may determine. The Clerk shall ensure that any such determinations of the Presiding Officer are notified to the Parliament.

2. Subject to paragraph 6, where a member intends to move an amendment to a Bill at any Stage, he or she shall give notice of the amendment by lodging it with the Clerk no later than 2 sitting days before the day on which that Stage is due to start. Where the Stage is being taken over more than one day, notice of amendments may be given by no later than 2 sitting days before each day of proceedings at that Stage.

3. Notice of an amendment shall set out the text of the amendment, together with the name of the member proposing it. The member in charge of the Bill (if not the member proposing the amendment) and up to 4 other members may indicate their support for an amendment by notifying the Clerk.

4. The convener or, as the case may be, the Presiding Officer shall determine whether an amendment of which notice has been given is admissible and, if it is, the notice shall be printed in the Business Bulletin.

5. An amendment is admissible unless—

(a) it is not in proper form;

(b) it is not relevant to the Bill or the provisions of the Bill which it would amend;

(c) it is inconsistent with the general principles of the Bill as agreed by the Parliament;

(d) it is inconsistent with a decision already taken at the Stage at which the amendment is proposed; or

(e) it would have the effect of taking the Bill or any of its provisions outwith the terms of any Financial Resolution of the Parliament in relation to the Bill or the amendment.

6. An amendment may be moved at Stage 2 with notice of less than 2 sitting days having been given but only with the agreement of the convener. The convener shall give his or her agreement to such an amendment (referred to as "a manuscript amendment") being moved only if he or she considers that the merits of the amendment outweigh the disadvantages of lack of proper notice. A manuscript amendment may not be moved at Stage 3.

7. An amendment may be made to an amendment and this Rule shall apply accordingly.

8. Where, at any Stage, notice of amendments to a Bill has been given, the Clerk shall prepare, for each day of proceedings on the Bill at which amendments are to be considered, a marshalled list of the amendments proposed. The list shall set out the amendments so far as not disposed of in the order in which they are to be disposed of as determined by the Clerk.

9. An amendment to insert a new section or schedule shall normally specify where it is to be inserted and shall be disposed of accordingly.

10. An amendment to an amendment shall be disposed of before the amendment which it would amend.

11. An amendment at any Stage which would be inconsistent with a decision already taken at the same Stage shall not be taken.

12. The convener or, as the case may be, the Presiding Officer may group amendments for the purposes of debate as he or she sees fit. An amendment debated as part of a group may not be debated again when it comes to be disposed of.

13. The member moving an amendment may speak in support of it. The member in charge of the Bill and any member of the Scottish Executive or junior Scottish Minister present at the proceedings may also speak on the amendment. Other members may speak on an amendment at the discretion of the convener or, as the case may be, the Presiding Officer.

14. If a member who has given notice of an amendment does not move the amendment when that amendment comes to be disposed of, the amendment may be moved by any other member present at those proceedings.

15. An amendment may be withdrawn by the member who moved it, but only with the unanimous agreement of the committee or the Parliament, as the case may be.

Rule 9.11 Crown consent

1. Where a Bill contains provisions, or is amended so as to include provisions, which would, if the Bill were a Bill for an Act of the United Kingdom Parliament, require the consent of Her Majesty, the Prince and Steward of Scotland or the Duke of Cornwall, the Parliament shall not debate any question whether the Bill is passed or approved unless such consent to those provisions has been signified by a member of the Scottish Executive during proceedings on the Bill at a meeting of the Parliament.

Rule 9.12 Financial Resolutions

1. A resolution under this Rule is referred to as "a Financial Resolution".

2. Where a Bill, or an amendment to a Bill, contains provisions which introduce new, or increase existing, expenditure charged on or payable out of the Scottish Consolidated Fund, no proceedings may be taken on the Bill or the amendment at any Stage after Stage 1 unless the Parliament has by resolution agreed to the expenditure.

3. Where a Bill, or an amendment to a Bill, contains provisions which impose or increase, or confer a power to impose or increase, any tax or charge, or otherwise requires any payment to be made, no proceedings may be taken on the Bill or the amendment at any Stage after Stage 1 unless the Parliament has by resolution agreed to the charge or tax or payment.

4. A motion for a resolution under this Rule may be moved, and notice of such a motion may be given, only by a member of the Scottish Executive or a junior Scottish Minister.

5. Any Bill which contains any provisions such as are mentioned in paragraph 2 or 3 shall be referred on introduction to the Finance Committee who shall prepare a report on the provisions.

6. Unless the Parliament passes a resolution required in relation to the provisions of a Bill (as opposed to an amendment to a Bill) by this Rule within 90 days of the Bill's introduction, the Bill falls.

7. In calculating for the purpose of this Rule the period of 90 days, no account shall be taken of any time during which the Parliament is in recess for more than 4 days.

Rule 9.13 Withdrawal of Bills

1. A Bill may be withdrawn at any time by the member in charge but shall not be withdrawn after completion of Stage 1 except with the agreement of the Parliament.

Rule 9.14 Member's Bills

1. "Member's Bill" means a Public Bill, other than a Committee Bill, which is introduced by a member who is not a member of the Scottish Executive and the purpose of which is to give effect to a proposal for a Bill made by that member in accordance with this Rule.

2. Each member may introduce no more than 2 Member's Bills in the same session. For the purposes of this paragraph only, a draft proposal for a Bill submitted by a member to the Parliamentary Bureau in pursuance of

Rule 9.15.4 and subsequently introduced as a Committee Bill shall be treated as if it were a Member's Bill introduced by that member.

3. A member who is not a member of the Scottish Executive may give notice of a proposal for a Bill by lodging it with the Clerk. The notice shall set out the name of the member making the proposal, the proposed short title of the Bill and a brief explanation of the purposes of the proposed Bill. The notice shall be printed in the Business Bulletin for a period of one month from the date on which it is lodged.

4. Any other member may notify the Clerk of his or her support for the proposal and the name of any member supporting the proposal shall be printed in the Business Bulletin along with the notice of the proposal.

5. A Member's Bill may be introduced by a member only if at least 11 other members have notified their support for the proposal within one month of the notice of the proposal having been given.

6. If the proposal has not by the end of that period received support from a sufficient number of members to allow a Member's Bill to be introduced, the proposal falls and a proposal in the same or similar terms may not be made by any member within 6 months of that proposal falling.

Rule 9.15 Committee Bills

1. A Bill introduced in pursuance of this Rule is referred to as " a Committee Bill".

2. A committee may make a proposal for a Bill in relation to competent matters within that committee's remit in accordance with this Rule.

3. For the purposes of deciding whether to make a proposal for a Bill, or what such a proposal should contain, a committee may hold an inquiry into the need for a Bill.

4. Any member may submit to the Parliamentary Bureau a draft proposal for a Bill. The Parliamentary Bureau shall refer the draft proposal to a committee within whose remit the draft proposal falls. The committee shall consider whether it should make the proposal in accordance with this Rule.

5. A proposal for a Bill under this Rule shall be made in the form of a report setting out the committee's recommendations as to the provisions to be contained in the Bill, together with an explanation of the need for the Bill. The proposal may also contain a draft of a Bill to give effect to the proposal.

6. A time shall be appointed in the business programme for consideration of the proposal by the Parliament.

7. If the Parliament agrees to the proposal, the convener of the committee which made the proposal may, no earlier than the fifth sitting day after the date on which the Parliament agrees the proposal—

(a) if necessary, instruct the drafting of a Bill to give effect to the proposal; and

(b) introduce the Bill, unless any member of the Scottish Executive or junior Scottish Minister has indicated before that day that an Executive Bill will be introduced to give effect to the proposal.

8. At Stage 1 of a Committee Bill, the Bill shall be referred immediately to the Parliament for consideration of its general principles and a decision on whether they are agreed to. A report on the Bill's general principles by a committee shall not be required.

Rule 9.16 Budget Bills

1. A Budget Bill is an Executive Bill for a Budget Act within the meaning of section 29(3) of the Public Finance and Accountability (Scotland) Act 2000.

2. A Budget Bill may be introduced only by a member of the Scottish Executive and shall not require to be accompanied by a Financial Memorandum, Explanatory Notes or a Policy Memorandum.

3. At Stage 1 of a Budget Bill, the Bill shall be referred immediately to the Parliament for consideration of its general principles and a decision on whether they are agreed to. A report on the Bill's general principles from a committee shall not be required. Stage 2 shall be taken by the Finance Committee.

4. The requirement in Rule 9.5.3 that there be at least 2 weeks between Stages 1 and 2 and, if the Bill is amended at Stage 2, between Stages 2 and 3 shall not apply.

5. Stage 3 shall begin no earlier than 20 days after introduction of the Bill. If Stage 3 is not completed before the expiry of 30 days after introduction of the Bill, the Bill falls.

6. Amendments to a Budget Bill may be moved, and notice of amendments to such a Bill may be given, only by a member of the Scottish Executive.

7. If a Budget Bill is dependent upon the Parliament passing a tax-varying resolution which provides, in accordance with section 73, for an increase for Scottish taxpayers of the basic rate and the Parliament rejects the motion for such a resolution, the Bill falls.

8. If a Budget Bill falls or is rejected at any Stage by the Parliament, a Budget Bill in the same or similar terms may be introduced at any time thereafter.

Rule 9.17 Private Bills

1. A Private Bill is a Bill introduced by an individual person, a body corporate or an unincorporated association of persons (referred to as "the promoter") for the purpose of obtaining for the promoter particular powers or benefits in excess of or in conflict with the general law, and includes a Bill relating to the estate, property, status or style, or otherwise relating to the personal affairs, of the promoter. A Bill which is not a Private Bill is referred to as "a Public Bill".

2. A Private Bill may be introduced in the Parliament only on 27th March and 27th November in each year or, if either of those days is not a sitting day, the next sitting day after it.

3. A Private Bill introduced in the Parliament shall be signed by or on behalf of the promoter.

4. At Stage 1 of a Private Bill, the lead committee shall also consider and prepare a report to the Parliament on the need for the provision sought in the Bill and the extent to which there is opposition to the provision sought. For those purposes the committee may require the promoter, at the promoter's own expense, to—

(a) deposit such further documents concerning the Bill as the committee sees fit;

(b) give such notice by advertisement of the provision sought as the committee considers necessary;

(c) make the Bill and any documents deposited available for public inspection within such areas and for such period as the committee considers appropriate;

(d) give notice of the provision sought to each of any owners, lessees and occupiers of any property affected by the provision;

(e) invite objections to the Bill or any of its provisions to be deposited with the Clerk by such date or dates as the Parliamentary Bureau may determine.

5. If any requirement imposed by the committee is not complied with then, unless the committee agrees to dispense with the requirement, it shall report the matter to the Parliament which may decide that the Bill should be rejected.

6. For the purposes of determining whether any of the provisions of a Private Bill are necessary or for disposing of any objections to the Bill or

271

any of its provisions, a committee conducting Stage 2 may hold, or may arrange for a reporter appointed under Rule 12.6 or a person appointed for the purpose under Rule 12.7 to hold, an inquiry into the Bill or any of its provisions or any of the objections.

Rule 9.18 Consolidation Bills

1. A Consolidation Bill is a Bill the purpose of which is to restate the existing law, whether or not with amendments to give effect to recommendations of the Scottish Law Commission or of the Scottish Law Commission and the Law Commission jointly. Where appropriate, such a Bill may be referred to as a Codification Bill.

2. A Consolidation Bill shall not require to be accompanied by any accompanying documents but shall, where appropriate, be accompanied by tables of derivations and destinations.

3. Where a Consolidation Bill has been introduced in the Parliament, the Parliamentary Bureau shall by motion propose, in accordance with Rule 6.1, the establishment of a committee (referred to as "a Consolidation Committee") to consider the Bill in accordance with this Rule.

4. In proposing the membership of a Consolidation Committee under Rule 6.3, the Parliamentary Bureau shall have regard to the subject matter of the Bill and shall, where possible, ensure that at least one member of the Committee is drawn from amongst the members of a committee within whose remit the subject matter of the Bill falls.

5. At Stage 1 of a Consolidation Bill, the Consolidation Committee for that Bill, instead of the lead committee, shall consider and report on the question whether the law which is restated in the Bill should be restated. Once the Consolidation Committee has reported, the Parliament shall decide that question. There shall be no debate on that question.

6. Stage 2 of a Consolidation Bill shall be taken by the Consolidation Committee for that Bill. No amendment may be made to the Bill which would cause it to cease to be a Consolidation Bill.

7. At Stage 3 of a Consolidation Bill, the Parliament shall, without any debate on that question, decide whether the Bill is passed. Amendments may be made to the Bill at Stage 3 only if they are necessary to ensure that the Bill, if passed, is an accurate restatement of the law or are necessary to give effect to any recommendations of the Scottish Law Commission or of the Scottish Law Commission and the Law Commission jointly.

Rule 9.19 Statute Law Repeals Bills

1. A Statute Law Repeals Bill is a Bill the purpose of which is to repeal, in accordance with recommendations of the Scottish Law Commission, spent enactments.

2. Rule 9.18 shall apply to a Statute Law Repeals Bill with such modifications as are appropriate. In particular, the committee referred to in that Rule shall be known as "a Statute Law Repeals Committee".

Rule 9.20 Statute Law Revision Bills

1. A Statute Law Revision Bill is a Bill the purpose of which is to revise the statute law by repealing enactments which are no longer in force or have become unnecessary and re-enacting provisions of Acts (whether of the United Kingdom Parliament or the Scottish Parliament) which are otherwise spent.

2. Rule 9.18 shall apply to a Statute Law Revision Bill with such modifications as are appropriate. In particular, the committee referred to in that Rule shall be known as "a Statute Law Revision Committee".

Rule 9.21 Emergency Bills

1. Any member of the Scottish Executive or a junior Scottish Minister may by motion propose that an Executive Bill introduced in the Parliament be treated as an Emergency Bill. If the Parliament agrees to such a motion, the provisions of this Rule shall apply to such a Bill.

2. At Stage 1, an Emergency Bill shall be referred immediately to the Parliament for consideration of its general principles and a decision on whether they are agreed to. A report on the Bill's general principles from a committee shall not be required.

3. Stage 2 of an Emergency Bill shall be taken by a Committee of the Whole Parliament.

4. The requirement in Rule 9.5.3 that there be at least 2 weeks between Stages 1 and 2 and, if the Bill is amended at Stage 2, between Stages 2 and 3, shall not apply to an Emergency Bill.

5. Unless the Parliament decides otherwise on a motion of the Parliamentary Bureau, all of the Stages of an Emergency Bill shall be taken on the day on which the Parliament decides that the Bill is to be treated as an Emergency Bill. The time available for each of the Stages of an Emergency Bill, and for debates at each of those Stages, shall be decided by the Parliament on a motion of the Parliamentary Bureau. A motion under this paragraph may not be debated or amended.

CHAPTER 10

Subordinate Legislation Procedure

Rule 10.1 Laying of instruments

1. Where, by virtue of any enactment, any instrument or a draft of any instrument made in the exercise of a power to make, confirm or approve subordinate legislation is required to be laid before the Scottish Parliament, the lodging of a copy of the instrument or the draft with the Clerk at any time when the office of the Clerk is open shall be treated for all purposes as being the laying of it before the Parliament.

2. The Clerk may require the person laying the instrument or draft instrument to provide such additional copies as he or she considers necessary.

3. Where any instrument or draft instrument is laid before the Parliament, the Clerk shall give members notice of that fact in accordance with Rule 10.9 and shall refer the instrument or draft instrument to the lead committee and to the Subordinate Legislation Committee for consideration, unless the Parliament, on a motion of the Parliamentary Bureau, decides that the instrument or draft instrument is to be considered by the Parliament.

Rule 10.2 Lead committee

1. The lead committee is the committee within whose remit the subject matter of the instrument falls.

2. Where the subject matter of the instrument falls within the remit of more than one committee, the Parliament may, on a motion of the Parliamentary Bureau designate one committee to be the lead committee. Copies of the instrument or draft instrument shall be sent to the other committees which may also consider the instrument or draft instrument and make any recommendations they consider necessary to the lead committee by a date specified in the business programme.

Rule 10.3 Subordinate Legislation Committee

1. In considering the instrument or draft instrument, the Subordinate Legislation Committee shall determine whether the attention of the Parliament should be drawn to the instrument on the grounds—
  (a) that it imposes a charge on the Scottish Consolidated Fund or contains provisions requiring payments to be made to that Fund or

any part of the Scottish Administration or to any local or public authority in consideration of any licence or consent or of any services to be rendered, or prescribes the amount of any such charge or payment;

(b) that it is made in pursuance of any enactment containing specific provisions excluding it from challenge in the courts, on all or certain grounds, either at all times or after the expiration of a specific period or that it contains such provisions;

(c) that it purports to have retrospective effect where the parent statute confers no express authority so to provide;

(d) that there appears to have been unjustifiable delay in the publication or in the laying of it before the Parliament;

(e) that there appears to be a doubt whether it is *intra vires*;

(f) that it raises a devolution issue;

(g) that it has been made by what appears to be an unusual or unexpected use of the powers conferred by the parent statute;

(h) that for any special reason its form or meaning could be clearer;

(i) that its drafting appears to be defective;

or on any other ground which does not impinge on its substance or on the policy behind it.

2. The Committee shall report its decision with its reasons in any particular case to the Parliament and to the lead committee. It shall do so no later than 20 days after the instrument or draft instrument is laid.

Rule 10.4 Motion for annulment

1. In the case of any instrument which is subject to annulment in pursuance of a resolution of the Parliament, any member (whether or not a member of the lead committee) may, not later than 40 days after the instrument is laid, by motion propose to the lead committee that the committee recommend that nothing further is to be done under the instrument.

2. In addition to the provisions of Rule 12.2.2, that member and the member of the Scottish Executive or junior Scottish Minister in charge of the instrument, if not members of the lead committee, are entitled to attend the committee and participate in the proceedings for the purpose of debating the motion but may not vote. The debate on the motion shall last no more than 90 minutes.

3. The lead committee shall report to the Parliament on the instrument setting out its recommendations, taking into account any recommendations made by any other committee. It shall do so no later than 40 days after the instrument is laid.

4. If the lead committee makes a recommendation as mentioned in paragraph 1, the Parliamentary Bureau shall, no later than 40 days after the instrument is laid, by motion propose that nothing further is to be done under the instrument. Only the member moving the motion and the member of the Scottish Executive or junior Scottish Minister in charge of the instrument may speak in any debate on such a motion. Each such person may speak for no more than 3 minutes.

Rule 10.5 Motion that draft instrument be not made or submitted

1. In the case of any draft instrument laid before the Parliament where the instrument may be made without the approval of the Parliament, any member (whether or not a member of the lead committee) may, no later than 40 days after the draft instrument is laid, by motion propose to the lead committee that the committee recommend that the instrument be not made (or, in the case of a draft Order in Council, be not submitted to Her Majesty in Council).

2. In addition to the provisions of Rule 12.2.2, that member and the member of the Scottish Executive or junior Scottish Minister in charge of the draft instrument, if not members of the lead committee, are entitled to attend the committee and participate in the proceedings for the purpose of debating the motion but may not vote. The debate on the motion shall last no more than 90 minutes.

3. The lead committee shall report to the Parliament on the draft instrument setting out its recommendations, taking into account any recommendations made by any other committee. It shall do so no later than 40 days after the instrument is laid.

4. If the lead committee recommends that the instrument be not made or, as the case may be, be not submitted to Her Majesty in Council, the Parliamentary Bureau shall, no later than 40 days after the draft instrument is laid, by motion propose that the instrument be not made or, as the case may be, be not submitted to Her Majesty in Council. Only the member moving the motion and the member of the Scottish Executive or junior Scottish Minister in charge of the draft instrument may speak in any debate on such a motion. Each such person may speak for no more than 3 minutes.

Rule 10.6 Motion for approval

1. In the case of any instrument or draft instrument laid before the Parliament where the instrument or draft instrument—
  (a) cannot be made;
  (b) cannot come into force; or
  (c) cannot remain in force beyond a stated period,
    unless the Parliament by resolution approves the instrument or draft, the lead committee shall decide whether to recommend that the instrument or draft instrument be approved.

2. Any member of the Scottish Executive or junior Scottish Minister (whether or not a member of the lead committee) may by motion propose to the lead committee that the committee recommend that the instrument or draft instrument be approved.

3. In addition to the provisions of Rule 12.2.2, that member and the member of the Scottish Executive in charge of the instrument or draft instrument, if not members of the lead committee, are entitled to attend the committee and participate in the proceedings for the purposes of debating any such motion but may not vote. The debate on the motion shall last no more than 90 minutes.

4. The lead committee shall report to the Parliament on the draft instrument setting out its recommendations, taking into account any recommendations made by any other committee. It shall do so no later than 40 days after the instrument is laid or, in the case of an instrument falling within paragraph 1(c), by the end of the stated period.

5. If the lead committee recommends that the draft instrument be approved, the Parliamentary Bureau shall by motion propose that the Parliament approve the instrument. Only the member moving the motion, the member of the Scottish Executive or junior Scottish Minister in charge of the draft instrument (if he or she is not the member moving the motion) and one speaker against the motion may speak in any debate on the motion. Each such person may speak for no more than 3 minutes.

Rule 10.7 Instruments considered by the Parliament

1. Where the Parliament has decided that an instrument or draft instrument laid before the Parliament be considered by the Parliament, any member may give notice of and move the relevant motion in relation to that instrument or draft instrument, as provided for in Rule 10.4.4, 10.5.4 or 10.6.5, within any relevant time limit set by that Rule. The debate on the motion shall last no more than 90 minutes.

Rule 10.8 Withdrawal of instruments

1. An instrument or draft instrument laid before the Parliament may be withdrawn at any time by the member of the Scottish Executive or junior Scottish Minister in charge of it.

Rule 10.9 Notice of instruments and draft instruments

1. The Clerk shall ensure that notice of any instrument or draft instrument laid before the Parliament is published in the Business Bulletin. The notice shall give the title of the instrument or draft instrument.

Rule 10.10 Application to other documents

1. The Rules in this Chapter shall also apply, with such modifications as are appropriate, to any report, guidance, code of practice or other document laid before the Parliament which is subject to any form of Parliamentary control having the same or equivalent effect to those mentioned in Rules 10.4.1, 10.5.1 or 10.6.1.

Rule 10.11 Calculation of days

1. In calculating for the purposes of this Chapter any period of 20 days or 40 days, no account shall be taken of any time during which the Parliament is dissolved or is in recess for more than 4 days.

CHAPTER 11

Decisions and Voting

Rule 11.1 Decisions of the Parliament

1. All decisions of the Parliament shall be taken by resolution.

2. A matter requiring a decision of the Parliament shall be decided by a question being put to a meeting of the Parliament by the Presiding Officer on the motion of a member. The question shall be that the motion is agreed to.

3. Where any question requires to be put to the Parliament, it shall be put in accordance with Rules 11.2 to 11.4.

Rule 11.2 Decision Time

1. Except as provided in Rule 11.3, the Presiding Officer shall put any question in relation to a motion during Decision Time on the day on which the motion is moved.

2. Decision Time is the period which normally begins at 17:00 where a meeting of the Parliament is held on Monday, Tuesday, Wednesday or Thursday and at 12:00 where a meeting of the Parliament is held on Friday and which ends when every decision which is to be taken during Decision Time has been taken.

3. Normally, Decision Time shall end not later than 30 minutes after it begins but, in accordance with Rule 2.2.6(a), it may continue, in order to complete any voting which is not adjourned to a later meeting under paragraph 5.

4. The Parliament may, on a motion of the Parliamentary Bureau, decide that Decision Time on a particular day or days shall begin at a time other than that mentioned in paragraph 2.

5. The Parliament may, on a motion of any member moved without notice not more than 30 minutes after the beginning of Decision Time, decide that decisions which have not been taken by the time the motion is moved are to be taken at a later meeting of the Parliament. Members shall be notified of the day and time when such decisions are to be taken.

6. Where—
(a) a motion is listed on the daily business list for consideration before Decision Time; but
(b) that motion has not been moved before Decision Time begins,
the Presiding Officer may allow the motion, and any amendment to it, to be moved at the beginning of Decision Time.

Rule 11.3 Decisions at times other than Decision Time

1. In the following cases the Presiding Officer shall, subject to paragraph 3, put the question immediately after he or she has closed the debate on the motion in relation to that question or, if there is no debate on the motion, immediately after the motion is moved—
(a) a motion seeking the agreement of the Parliament to the First Minister's recommendation for the appointment of a person as Lord Advocate or Solicitor General for Scotland under Rule 4.3 or for the removal of a person as Lord Advocate or Solicitor General for Scotland under Rule 4.4;
(b) a motion seeking the agreement of the Parliament that a person be appointed a Minister under Rule 4.6 or a junior Scottish Minister under Rule 4.7;
(c) a business motion;
(d) a motion for the closure of a debate;
(e) a motion for the adjournment of a debate;
(f) a motion under Rule 9.6.5;
(g) a motion under Rule 9.8.5 or 9.8.6;
(h) a motion in relation to an Emergency Bill;
(i) a motion for the exclusion of a member;
(j) a motion for the adjournment or closure of a meeting of the Parliament;
(k) a motion on Members' Business; and
(l) a motion taken after 17:30 at a meeting of the Parliament in respect of which the Parliament has taken a decision under Rule 2.2.4.

2. The Presiding Officer shall put the question on an amendment to a Bill immediately after the debate on that amendment or, if there is no debate, immediately after the amendment is moved.

3. Decisions may, at the discretion of the Presiding Officer, be taken at a time other than Decision Time or the times mentioned in paragraphs 1 and 2. Members shall be notified of any such time.

Rule 11.4 Order in which questions are put

1. At Decision Time or any alternative time mentioned in Rule 11.3, questions on motions shall be put in the order in which the motions were moved.

2. Questions on amendments to a motion shall be put in the order in which those amendments were moved. The Presiding Officer shall, before putting the question under paragraph 1, put, in turn, each question that an amendment to the motion be agreed to.

3. If any member disagrees with the question put under paragraph 1 or 2, Rule 11.3.2 or if the Presiding Officer asks members to cast their votes again under Rule 11.7.3, there shall immediately be a division.

4. The provisions of this Rule shall apply to amendments to amendments with such modifications as are appropriate.

Rule 11.5 Right to vote

1. Only members have a right to vote at a meeting of the Parliament. A member is not obliged to vote.

2. A member shall vote only in person and shall not vote on behalf of any other member.

3. A member may vote although he or she did not hear the question put.

4. A member shall vote only once on any question except where the Presiding Officer asks members to cast their votes again under Rule 11.7.3.

5. Except in the case of a vote of an election or a selection process under Rule 11.9 or 11.10 the Presiding Officer shall exercise a casting vote in the event of a tie in any vote at a meeting of the Parliament, but he or she shall not otherwise vote in the Parliament.

Rule 11.6 Divisions

1. A division shall be held where it is required by Rule 11.4.3 or 11.8.2 and shall be conducted in accordance with the following provisions.

2. The Presiding Officer shall repeat the question. The Presiding Officer shall then ask members to vote within a specified period of time.

3. Once the Presiding Officer has repeated the question, no-one except the Presiding Officer may speak until the Presiding Officer has declared that the specified period of time has ended.

4. Points of order concerning the validity of the division may be raised only after the Presiding Officer has declared that the specified period of time has ended.

5. The Presiding Officer shall establish the numerical result of the division and shall announce the numbers of votes for and against and the number of votes to abstain.

6. In the event of a tie, the Presiding Officer shall exercise his or her casting vote.

Rule 11.7 Manner of voting

1. Normally members shall vote at a meeting of the Parliament using the electronic voting system.

2. If it appears to the Presiding Officer that the electronic voting system cannot be used for any reason a roll call vote, or a vote in accordance with such other manner of voting as the Presiding Officer may decide shall be held.

3. If it appears to the Presiding Officer that the electronic voting system has produced an unreliable result, he shall ask members to cast their votes again in accordance with any manner of voting the Presiding Officer considers appropriate.

4. In a roll call vote, the roll shall be called in alphabetical order. Voting shall be by word of mouth and shall be expressed by "Yes", "No" or "Abstain".

Rule 11.8 Committees

1. Subject to paragraph 2, the convener of a committee or sub-committee shall determine the time at which members shall take a decision on any item of business.

2. The convener shall put the question on an amendment to a Bill immediately after the debate on that amendment or, if there is no debate, immediately after the amendment is moved. If any member disagrees with the question put under this paragraph, there shall immediately be a division.

3. Except as provided in any direction given to a committee by the Parliament, members of a committee or sub-committee shall vote by show of hands unless, before they do so, a member of the committee or sub-committee requests a roll call vote, as described in Rule 11.7.4, and the convener agrees to that request.

4. Rule 11.5 applies where members vote in a committee or sub-committee except that—

    (a) only members of the committee or sub-committee may vote in that committee or sub-committee, as the case may be; and

(b) the convener of a committee or sub-committee may vote and shall also exercise a casting vote in the event of a tie.

5. Rules 11.4, 11.6 and 11.11 shall apply to the taking of decisions at meetings of committees and sub-committees as they apply to the taking of decisions at meetings of the Parliament, with such modifications as are appropriate.

Rule 11.9 Election of Presiding Officer and deputy Presiding Officers

1. This Rule applies to any election of the Presiding Officer or any deputy Presiding Officer to be held by virtue of Rule 3.2 or 3.3.

2. The vote at an election shall be by secret ballot and shall be held during the voting period appointed under Rule 3.2 or 3.3. Where there is more than one candidate, there may be more than one round of voting in accordance with paragraphs 7 to 12.

3. The result of any vote under this Rule is valid only if the number of members who voted is more than one quarter of the total number of seats for members. For this purpose, in calculating the number of members who voted—

(a) account shall be taken not only of those voting for or against a candidate, but also of those voting to abstain; and

(b) where there is more than one round of voting the result of each round of voting shall be treated as a separate result and the number of members who voted shall be taken to be the total number who voted in that round.

If the result of any vote at an election is invalid under this Rule, no candidate shall be elected at that election.

4. Each candidate may appoint a member to act as a scrutineer on his or her behalf. Each scrutineer may monitor the counting of votes by the Clerk and may request the Clerk to perform a count again. The Clerk may refuse such a request only if he or she considers it unreasonable.

5. Any member may, at the beginning of a round of voting, obtain a ballot paper from the Clerk. Any member who obtains a ballot paper shall immediately mark his or her vote on that ballot paper and then put the ballot paper in the ballot box provided for that purpose by the Clerk. That member may not thereafter obtain another ballot paper or vote during that round of voting.

6. Where there is only one candidate in a round of voting, a member may vote for or against that candidate or to abstain. At the completion of that round of voting the Clerk shall count the votes and inform the person chairing the meeting of the number of votes for the candidate, against the candidate or to abstain. The candidate shall be elected if he or she obtains a simple majority of votes in his or her favour.

7. Where there is more than one candidate in a round of voting, a member may vote for one of those candidates or to abstain. At the completion of each round of voting in which there is more than one candidate, the Clerk shall count the votes and inform the person chairing the meeting of the number of votes for each candidate and the number of votes to abstain.

8. Where there are two candidates in a round of voting, a candidate shall be elected if he or she obtains a simple majority of votes in his or her favour.

9. Where there are more than 2 candidates in a round of voting and the number of votes for one candidate exceeds the total number of votes for all the other candidates, that candidate shall be elected.

10. Where there are more than 2 candidates in a round of voting but no candidate is elected under paragraph 9, the candidate or candidates with the smallest number of votes shall be eliminated and there shall then be a further round or rounds of voting until—

(a) a candidate is elected in accordance with paragraphs 6, 8 or 9;
(b) paragraph 11 applies; or
(c) the result of any vote is invalid under this Rule.

11. Where in any round of voting the candidates all receive the same number of votes no candidate shall be elected at that election.

12. A candidate may withdraw his or her candidature at any stage between the rounds of voting mentioned in paragraphs 7 to 10.

13. In counting the votes, the Clerk may disregard any ballot paper if, in his or her opinion, it does not clearly indicate the voter's choice.

14. When a candidate has been elected in accordance with this Rule the person chairing the meeting shall announce the name of the candidate who has been elected. He or she shall also announce—

(a) after the count in a case where the provisions of paragraph 6 apply, the number of votes for and against the candidate and the number of votes to abstain; and

(b) after the count in any other case, the number of votes for each candidate, the number of votes to abstain and the name of any candidate who has been eliminated at that round.

15. Where no candidate is elected at an election held in accordance with this Rule, the person chairing the meeting shall announce that fact and arrange for another election to be held as soon as possible. The Clerk shall notify members of the day and time appointed for the voting period at that election.

16. Following a declaration that a candidate has been elected or that no candidate has been elected, the Clerk shall destroy all the ballot papers.

Rule 11.10 Election of members of Parliamentary corporation and selection of First Minister

1. This Rule applies to—
(a) the election of members of the Parliamentary corporation to be held by virtue of Rule 3.7; and
(b) the selection of a nominee for appointment as First Minister to be held by virtue of Rule 4.1 ("the selection process").

Where this Rule applies, the procedure for the election or selection process shall be as follows.

2. Voting under this Rule shall be held using the electronic voting system and shall be held during the voting period appointed under Rule 3.7 or 4.1. If it appears to the Presiding Officer that the electronic voting system cannot be used for any reason or that it has produced an unreliable result, he or she shall ask members to cast their votes again in a paper ballot of members, a roll call vote, or in accordance with any manner of voting as the Presiding Officer may consider appropriate. Where there is more than one candidate, there may be more than one round of voting in accordance with paragraphs 6 to 11.

3. A member may only vote once in a round of voting except where the Presiding Officer asks members to cast their votes again under paragraph 2.

4. The result of any vote under this Rule is valid only if the number of members who voted is more than one quarter of the total number of seats for members. For this purpose, in calculating the number of members who voted—

(a) account shall be taken not only of those voting for or against a candidate, but also of those voting to abstain; and

(b) where there is more than one round of voting the result of each round of voting shall be treated as a separate result and the number of members who voted shall be taken to be the total number who voted in that round.

If the result of any vote at an election or selection process is invalid under this Rule, no candidate shall be elected at that election or selected at that selection process.

5. Where there is only one candidate in a round of voting, a member may vote for or against that candidate or to abstain. At the completion of that round of voting, the Presiding Officer shall establish the number of votes for the candidate, against the candidate or to abstain. The candidate shall be elected or selected if he or she obtains a simple majority of votes in his or her favour.

6. Where there is more than one candidate in a round of voting, a member may vote in accordance with the following procedure—

(a) the Presiding Officer shall read out the names of all the candidates;
(b) he or she shall then read out the name of each candidate in turn, in alphabetical order;
(c) after each name is read out, those members who wish to vote for that candidate shall cast their votes;
(d) when the votes for the last candidate have been cast, members shall be given an opportunity to vote to abstain.
   At the completion of each round of voting in which there is more than one candidate, the Presiding Officer shall establish the number of votes for each candidate and the number of votes to abstain.

7. Where there are 2 candidates in a round of voting, a candidate shall be elected or selected if he or she obtains a simple majority of votes in his or her favour.

8. Where there are more than 2 candidates in a round of voting and the number of votes for one candidate exceeds the total number of votes for all the other candidates, that candidate shall be elected or selected.

9. Where there are more than 2 candidates in any round of voting but no candidate is elected under paragraph 8, the candidate or candidates with the smallest number of votes shall be eliminated and there shall then be a further round or rounds of voting until—

(a) a candidate is elected or selected in accordance with paragraphs 5, 7 or 8;
(b) paragraph 10 applies; or
(c) the result of any vote is invalid under this Rule.

10. Where in any round of voting the candidates all receive the same number of votes no candidate shall be elected at that election or selected at that selection process.

11. A candidate may withdraw his or her candidature at any stage between the rounds of voting mentioned in paragraphs 6 to 10.

12. When a candidate has been elected or selected in accordance with this Rule the person chairing the meeting shall announce the name of the candidate who has been elected or selected. He or she shall also announce—

(a) in a case where the provisions of paragraph 5 apply, the number of votes for and against the candidate and the number of votes to abstain; and
(b) in any other case, the number of votes for each candidate and the name of any candidate who has been eliminated at that round.

13. Where no candidate is elected at an election or selected at a selection process held in accordance with this Rule, the Presiding Officer shall announce that fact and arrange for another election or selection process to be held as soon as possible. The Clerk shall notify members of the day and time appointed for the voting period at that election or selection process.

Rule 11.11 Simple and absolute majority

1. Any decision of the Parliament shall be taken by a simple majority unless otherwise expressly stated in any enactment or in these Rules.

2. A simple majority means that the number of members voting for a proposition is more than the number of members voting against that proposition. No account shall be taken of any members who vote to abstain.

3. An absolute majority means that the number of members voting for a proposition is more than half of the total number of seats for members of the Parliament or, in the case of a committee or sub-committee, more than half of the number of members of that committee or sub-committee.

CHAPTER 12

Committee Procedures

Rule 12.1 Conveners of committees

1. Each committee shall have a convener who shall convene and chair the meetings of the committee.

2. The Parliament shall decide, for each committee, on a motion of the Parliamentary Bureau—

    (a) the political party whose members shall be eligible to be convener of the committee; or

    (b) that the convener shall be chosen from the members not representing any political party.

3. The Parliament may, on a motion of the Parliamentary Bureau, decide that all committees shall have a deputy convener.

4. If the Parliament decides that all committees shall have a deputy convener, the Parliament shall decide, for each committee, on a motion of the Parliamentary Bureau—

    (a) the political party whose members shall be eligible to be deputy convener of the committee; or

    (b) that the deputy convener shall be chosen from the members not representing any political party.

5. In making a proposal under paragraph 2 or 4, the Parliamentary Bureau shall have regard to the balance of political parties in the Parliament.

6. At the first meeting of a committee after it is established by the Parliament, members of the committee shall choose a convener. That meeting shall be chaired by the Oldest Committee Member until a convener is chosen . Once a convener is chosen, he or she shall take the chair.

7. The convener of a committee shall be a member of that committee who shall be chosen in accordance with the decision of the Parliament under paragraph 2.

8. The convener of a committee shall hold office for the duration of the committee unless—

    (a) he or she resigns from that office by intimating his or her resignation to the Clerk;

    (b) he or she is removed from that office by a decision taken by an absolute majority of the committee; or

    (c) he or she ceases to be a member of the Parliament or of that committee otherwise than by virtue of a dissolution.

9. Where the convener of a committee ceases to hold office, the committee shall choose another member of the committee to be the convener in accordance with the decision of the Parliament under paragraph 2. If it is not possible for the committee to choose a convener in accordance with that decision, the Parliament shall, on a motion of the Parliamentary Bureau, make a further decision under paragraph 2 in relation to the committee, and the choice of a convener in accordance with paragraph 7 shall proceed accordingly.

10. Where, in accordance with a decision of the Parliament under paragraph 3, a committee is to have a deputy convener, that person shall be a member of that committee who is chosen by the members of that committee in accordance with the decision of the Parliament under

282

paragraph 4. Paragraphs 8 and 9 shall apply to the deputy convener of a committee as they apply to the convener of a committee with such modifications as are appropriate. Where a deputy convener carries out the functions of a convener he or she shall have all the functions of a convener under these Rules for that purpose.

11. Where a committee does not have a deputy convener, the functions of deputy convener shall, so far as required by this Rule, be carried out by a Temporary Convener chosen under paragraph 15. When a Temporary Convener carries out the functions of a deputy convener he or she shall have all the functions of a convener under these Rules for that purpose.

12. Where the convener is not available for any meeting of the committee, or leaves the chair for part of any meeting, that meeting, or that part of the meeting, shall be chaired by the deputy convener. Where at any time other than during a meeting of a committee a convener is unable to act as convener, the deputy convener shall carry out the functions of the convener.

13. Where the office of convener is vacant, a meeting of the committee shall be convened by the deputy convener and that meeting shall be chaired by the deputy convener for the purpose of choosing a convener.

14. When the deputy convener or the Oldest Committee Member chairs a meeting or part of a meeting of a committee, he or she shall have all the functions of a convener under these Rules for the purposes of conducting the business of that meeting or that part of a meeting.

15. Any reference to a Temporary Convener is to a member of a committee chosen under this paragraph. Where a committee does not have a deputy convener, a Temporary Convener shall be chosen by a committee at a meeting of the committee—

where the convener is not available for any meeting or leaves the chair for part of any meeting; or

where at any time other than at a meeting of a committee a convener is unable to act as convener and the oldest member of the committee considers it necessary that a Temporary Convener is appointed.

16. For the purpose of choosing a Temporary Convener under—

paragraph 15(a), the meeting shall be chaired by the convener or Oldest Committee Member; or

paragraph 15(b), the meeting shall be convened by the oldest member of the committee and shall be chaired by the Oldest Committee Member.

17. When a Temporary Convener is chosen by a committee, he or she shall take the chair and shall exercise all functions of the convener of that committee until the convener is again able to act as convener.

18. When the oldest member of a committee convenes a meeting of a committee, he or she shall have all the functions of a convener under these Rules for that purpose.

19. Any reference to the Oldest Committee Member means the oldest member of the committee —

who is present at any meeting; and who has indicated to the Clerk that he or she agrees to chair the meeting.

20. This Rule is subject to any other Rule making express provision about conveners of committees.

Rule 12.2 Procedure in committee

1. A committee shall not commence consideration of any business or vote if the number of committee members present (including the convener, or deputy convener if he or she is in the chair) is fewer than 3.

2. Any member of the Parliament may attend any meeting, or part of a meeting, of any committee of which he or she is not a member which is held in public but he or she may participate in the proceedings of the committee only if invited to do so by the convener and may not vote.

3. Where a committee is considering any of the business mentioned in Rule 6.2.2(b), (c) or (d), the following persons (if not members of the committee) shall be entitled to participate in the proceedings of the committee but may not vote, namely—

(a) the member of the Scottish Executive or junior Scottish Minister who has general responsibility for the matter with which the business is concerned; and

(b) in the case of a Member's Bill, the member in charge of the Bill.

Rule 12.3 Committee meetings

1. A committee shall meet to consider such business on such days and at such times as it may from time to time decide, subject to any timetable specified in the business programme. The convener shall notify the Clerk and the Clerk shall notify members in the Business Bulletin of the agenda for each meeting.

2. A committee shall meet in Scotland at such place as it may decide, with the approval of the Parliamentary Bureau.

3. A committee meeting shall not be held at the same time as a meeting of the Parliament but may be held on any day whether a sitting day or not and whether within or outwith the normal Parliamentary week. Committee meetings shall not normally be held when the Parliament is in recess.

4. Committee meetings shall be held in public except as mentioned in paragraph 5.

5. All or part of a meeting of a committee may be held in private if the committee so decides. Any meeting at which a committee is considering any of the business mentioned in Rule 6.2.2(b), (c) or

(d) shall be held in public except where, for the purpose of taking evidence, the committee decides that it is appropriate that the meeting, or part of the meeting, should be held in private.

Rule 12.4 Witnesses and documents

1. A committee may, in connection with any competent matter, invite any person—

(a) to attend its proceedings for the purpose of giving evidence; or

(b) to produce documents in that person's custody or under that person's control,

and may exercise the power conferred upon the Parliament by section 23 (power to call for witnesses and documents) to require any person to do so but subject to and in accordance with the terms of sections 23 and 24 (notice provisions in relation to witnesses and documents).

2. For the purposes of section 26(1), the convener of a committee may administer an oath or solemn affirmation to any person giving evidence in its proceedings and require that person to take an oath or make a solemn affirmation.

3. The committee shall arrange for the Parliamentary corporation to pay to persons whom it requires, and may arrange for the Parliamentary corporation to pay to persons whom it invites to attend its proceedings to give evidence or to produce any documents, such allowances and expenses as may be determined by the Parliament.

Rule 12.5 Sub-committees

1. A committee may establish one or more sub-committees with the approval of the Parliament on a motion of the Parliamentary Bureau.

2. The remit of any sub-committee of a committee shall be such as is approved by the Parliament, on a motion of the Parliamentary Bureau, but shall not include any matter outwith the remit of that committee.

3. The membership of any sub-committee shall be determined by the Parliament on a motion of the Parliamentary Bureau. The membership of a sub-committee of a committee shall be proposed by that committee to the Parliamentary Bureau. Normally only members of the committee may be members of a sub-committee of that committee but, if the committee so decides, members of other committees may be appointed as members of a sub-committee.

4. In considering the membership of a sub-committee, the committee shall have regard to the balance of political parties in the Parliament.

5. The convener of a sub-committee shall be a member of that sub-committee who shall be chosen by the members of the sub-committee.

6. The duration of a sub-committee shall be determined by the Parliament on a motion of the Parliamentary Bureau.

7. A sub-committee shall report to the committee which established it.

8. Rules 6.3.5, 6.3.6, 12.1.9 to 12.1.19, 12.2 to 12.4 and 12.6 shall apply in relation to the establishment, procedure and meetings of a sub-committee as they apply in relation to committees with such modifications as are appropriate.

Rule 12.6 Reporters

1. Any committee may appoint a committee member (referred to as "a reporter") to report to it upon any competent matter within such time limit as the committee may determine. A committee may appoint different reporters to report to it upon different competent matters.

Rule 12.7 Advisers

1. A committee may, with the approval of the Parliamentary Bureau, issue directions to the Parliamentary corporation in connection with the appointment by the Parliamentary corporation of any person to inquire into and advise the committee or any sub-committee upon any competent matter. Different advisers may be appointed for different competent matters.

Rule 12.8 Reports of committees

1. Where a committee is to report any matter to the Parliament or another committee, it shall do so by lodging the report with the Clerk.

2. Where the report is addressed to the Parliament, the Clerk shall notify members that the report has been lodged. Where the report is addressed to another committee, the Clerk shall notify that committee that the report has been lodged.

3. Any committee report lodged with the Clerk shall be published by the Clerk.

Rule 12.9 Annual reports

1. Each committee shall, as soon as practicable after the end of each Parliamentary year, submit a report to the Parliament containing details of its activities during that Parliamentary year, including details of its meetings and the number of times the committee has met in private. In the case of the Parliamentary year ending on the dissolution of the Parliament before an ordinary general election, each committee shall submit such a report before the Parliament is dissolved.

Rule 12.10 Travelling outwith the United Kingdom

1. A member of a committee who wishes to travel outwith the United Kingdom in connection with any competent matter which is before that committee shall require the prior approval of the Parliamentary Bureau.

CHAPTER 13

Statements and Parliamentary Questions

Rule 13.1 Personal statements

1. Any member may, at the discretion of the Presiding Officer, make a personal statement to a meeting of the Parliament.

2. A member wishing to make a personal statement shall notify the Presiding Officer that he or she wishes to do so.

3. If the Presiding Officer decides that a personal statement may be made, he or she shall notify the Parliamentary Bureau who shall include notice of that statement in a business programme.

4. Where a personal statement is made, it may not be debated.

Rule 13.2 Ministerial statements

1. Where a member of the Scottish Executive or junior Scottish Minister wishes to make a statement to a meeting of the Parliament ("a ministerial statement"), notice shall be given to the Presiding Officer. The Presiding Officer shall then notify the Parliamentary Bureau who shall include notice of the ministerial statement in a business programme. A ministerial statement may be debated.

2. Where a ministerial statement is of an urgent nature, the member of the Scottish Executive or junior Scottish Minister wishing to make the statement may, on giving notice of the statement to the Presiding Officer, request that it be made on that day. If the statement is, in the opinion of the Presiding Officer, sufficiently urgent, he or she shall allow the statement to be made and debated and shall make any necessary alteration to the daily business list. Members shall be notified that any such statement is to be made and of any subsequent alteration to the daily business list.

Rule 13.3 Questions to the Scottish Executive

1. Any member may put a question to the Scottish Executive for answer in the Parliament.

2. Questions shall be in writing and lodged with the Clerk.

3. A question shall—
(a) be brief, clearly worded, and address specific points;
(b) relate to a matter for which the First Minister, the Scottish Ministers or the Scottish Law Officers have general responsibility;
(c) be in English;
(d) be prefaced by the name of the member asking it;
(e) not contain offensive language;
(f) not express a point of view;
(g) not breach any enactment or rule of law or be contrary to the public interest; and
(h) not contravene Rule 7.5.1.

4. A question shall specify whether it is for oral answer ("an oral question") or for written answer ("a written question").

5. A member may withdraw a question lodged by him or her at any time before it is answered by notifying the Clerk. A question which is withdrawn shall not receive an answer.

Rule 13.4 Admissibility of questions

1. A question is admissible unless—
(a) it does not comply with the requirements of Rule 13.3.3; or
(b) the information sought has been provided in response to a similar question in the 6 months before the member seeks to lodge the question.

2. Any dispute as to whether a question is admissible shall be determined by the Presiding Officer.

Rule 13.5 Written questions

1. A written question concerning a matter for which the First Minister is alone responsible may be answered only by the First Minister. A written question concerning the operation of the systems of criminal prosecution and investigation of deaths in Scotland may be answered only by the Lord Advocate or the Solicitor General for Scotland. Other written questions may be answered by any member of the Scottish Executive.

2. The answer to a written question shall be lodged with the Clerk. An answer shall be lodged normally within 14 days of the question being lodged. In the case of a question lodged during a period when the Parliament is in recess for more than 4 days, an answer shall be lodged normally within 21 days of the question being lodged.

3. The Clerk shall publish all written questions in the Business Bulletin. An answer to a written question shall be published along with the question in the Official Report.

Rule 13.6 Oral questions

1. Oral questions may be answered at Question Time or First Minister's Question Time.

2. Question Time shall be a period of up to 40 minutes each week (normally on Thursdays) at a meeting of the Parliament during which questions selected under paragraph 7 may be put to and answered by members of the Scottish Executive or junior Scottish Ministers.

3. First Minister's Question Time shall be a period of up to 20 minutes each week immediately following Question Time during which questions selected under paragraph 5 may, subject to Rule 13.7.1, be put to and answered by the First Minister.

4. Subject to paragraphs 9 and 10, a member may lodge an oral question for answer at Question Time during the period commencing with the completion of the Question Time before the Preceding Question Time and ending at 14:00 on the eighth day before the Question Time at which he or she wishes the question to be answered. The "Preceding Question Time" means the Question Time before the Question Time at which the member wishes his or her question to be answered. A member may lodge only one question for answer at any Question Time.

5. Subject to paragraph 11, a member may lodge an oral question for answer at First Minister's Question Time during the period commencing with the completion of the Preceding First Minister's Question Time and ending at 14:00 on the third day before the First Minister's Question Time at which he or she wishes the question to be answered. The "Preceding First Minister's Question Time" means the First Minister's Question Time before the First Minister's Question Time at which the member wishes the question to be answered. A member may lodge only one question for answer at any First Minister's Question Time.

6. At the end of the third day before First Minister's Question Time the Presiding Officer may select, from all admissible oral questions lodged for answer at First Minister's Question Time, up to 6 questions ("First Minister's Questions") for answer at First Minister's Question Time.

7. At the end of the eighth day before Question Time, the Clerk shall select, from all admissible oral questions lodged for answer at Question Time, questions for answer at Question Time. These questions shall be selected on a random basis.

8. Notice of questions selected under paragraphs 6 and 7 shall be given to members in the Business Bulletin.

9. For the purpose of the first Question Time after these Rules come into force, the period during which members may lodge questions for answer at that Question Time shall commence at 09:30 on the date on which these Rules come into force and shall end at 14:00 on the eighth day before that Question Time.

10. For the purpose of the second Question Time after these Rules come into force, the period during which members may lodge questions for answer at that Question Time shall commence at 14:00 on the fourteenth day before that Question Time and shall end at 14:00 on the eighth day before that Question Time.

11. For the purpose of the first First Minister's Question Time after these Rules come into force, the period during which members may lodge questions for answer at that First Minister's Question Time shall commence at 09:30 on the date on which these Rules come into force and shall end at 14:00 on the third day before that First Minister's Question Time.

Rule 13.7 Question Time and First Minister's Question Time

1. An oral question concerning a matter for which the First Minister is alone responsible shall normally be answered by the First Minister but may exceptionally be answered by any other member of the Scottish Executive. An oral question concerning the operation of the systems of criminal prosecution and investigation of deaths in Scotland shall normally be answered by the Lord Advocate or the Solicitor General for Scotland but may exceptionally be answered by another member of the Scottish Executive. Other oral questions may be answered by any member of the Scottish Executive or a junior Scottish Minister. An oral question selected for answer at First Minister's Question Time shall normally be answered by the First Minister but may, if the First Minister is unable to attend First Minister's Question Time or any part of it, be answered by another member of the Scottish Executive.

2. A question is taken at Question Time or First Minister's Question Time when it is called by the Presiding Officer.

3. Questions shall be taken in the order in which they are printed in the Business Bulletin except where the Presiding Officer decides not to call a question under paragraph 11.

4. When a question is taken at Question Time or First Minister's Question Time, it may be asked only by the member who lodged it.

5. At Question Time, after a question is answered, the member who asked it may ask one supplementary question and any member may, at the discretion of the Presiding Officer, ask further supplementary questions. If the member who asked the question does not ask the first supplementary question, any member may, at the discretion of the Presiding Officer, ask a supplementary question or questions.

6. At First Minister's Question Time, after a question is answered, any member may, at the discretion of the Presiding Officer, ask a supplementary question or questions.

7. A member asking a question shall, in asking the question, not depart from the terms of the question.

8. A member may ask a supplementary question only on the same subject matter as the original question and shall, in asking the question, do so briefly.

9. A question selected for answer at Question Time or First Minister's Question Time but which is not taken shall be treated as a written question and an answer shall normally be lodged on the next day when the office of the Clerk is open following the Question Time or First Minister's Question Time at which the question was due to have been asked.

10. A question which is taken at Question Time or First Minister's Question Time but which is not asked and has not been withdrawn, shall be treated as a written question and an answer shall normally be lodged on the next day when the office of the Clerk is open following the Question Time or First Minister's Question Time at which the question was due to have been asked.

11. Where a member is not in the Chamber to ask a question which is selected for answer at Question Time or First Minister's Question Time, the Presiding Officer may decide not to call the question. Such a question shall be treated as a written question and an answer shall normally be lodged on the next day when the office of the Clerk is open following the Question Time or First Minister's Question Time at which the question was due to have been asked.

Rule 13.8 Emergency Questions

1. Where an oral question is of an urgent nature the member lodging it may, if it is lodged by 10:00 on a day on which there is a meeting of the Parliament, request that it is answered that day, whether or not there is a period set aside for Question Time that day. The Clerk shall notify the Presiding Officer of the lodging of such a question as soon as possible after it is lodged. Such a question is referred to as "an emergency question".

2. If an emergency question is, in the opinion of the Presiding Officer, sufficiently urgent, he or she shall allow the question to be put and answered at an appropriate point during the meeting of the Parliament and shall make any necessary alteration to the daily business list. Members shall be notified that any such question is to be put and of any subsequent alteration to the daily business list.

3. An emergency question concerning a matter for which the First Minister is alone responsible shall normally be answered by the First Minister but may exceptionally be answered by any other member of the Scottish Executive. An emergency question concerning the operation of the systems of criminal prosecution and investigation of deaths in Scotland shall normally be answered by the Lord Advocate or the Solicitor General for Scotland but may exceptionally be answered by another member of the Scottish Executive. Other emergency questions may be answered by any member of the Scottish Executive or a junior Scottish Minister.

4. When an emergency question is taken it may be asked only by the member who lodged it.

5. After an emergency question is answered the member who asked it may ask one supplementary question and any member may, at the discretion of the Presiding Officer, ask further supplementary questions. If the member who asked the question does not ask the first supplementary question, any member may, at the discretion of the Presiding Officer, ask a supplementary question or questions.

6. A member asking an emergency question shall, in asking the question, not depart from the terms of the question. A member asking a supplementary question shall, in asking the question, do so briefly.

7. A member may ask a supplementary question only on the same subject matter as the original question and shall, in asking the question, do so briefly.

Rule 13.9 Questions to Presiding Officer

1. Any member may address a question on a matter concerning the Parliamentary corporation or the staff of the Parliament to the Presiding Officer. Such a question may be answered by any member of the Parliamentary corporation.

2. A question addressed to the Presiding Officer under paragraph 1 shall normally be for written answer but may, exceptionally, be for oral answer.

3. Rules 13.3 to 13.7 shall apply to questions to the Presiding Officer under paragraph 1 as they apply to questions to the Scottish Executive with such modifications as are appropriate.

CHAPTER 14

Laying and Publication of Documents

Rule 14.1 Laying of reports and other documents

1. Where, under an enactment or otherwise, a report or other document is required or authorised to be laid before the Scottish Parliament, the lodging of a copy of that report or document with the Clerk shall be treated for all purposes as being the laying of it before the Parliament.
2. The Clerk may require the person laying the report or document to provide such additional copies as he or she considers necessary.
3. A report or other document may be laid before the Parliament at any time when the office of the Clerk is open.
4. No report or other document shall be laid before the Parliament unless it is required or authorised to be laid under an enactment or otherwise or it is laid by a member of the Scottish Executive.
5. The Clerk shall ensure that notice of any report or other document laid before the Parliament is published in the Business Bulletin. The notice shall give the title of the report or document.

Rule 14.2 Laying of financial reports and documents

1. Any documents laid before the Parliament containing outline proposals for public expenditure in any financial year other than the financial year beginning 1 April 2000 shall not be considered, except with the agreement of the Parliament, unless they are laid before the Parliament no later than the preceding 20 April.
2. Any document laid before the Parliament setting out preliminary draft budgets of public expenditure in any financial year other than the financial year beginning on 1 April 2000 shall not be considered, except with the agreement of the Parliament, unless they are laid before the Parliament no later than the preceding 20 September.

Rule 14.3 Publication of documents

1. Where, under these Rules, the Clerk is required to publish any document, he or she shall arrange for publication through the Parliamentary corporation.
2. If the Parliament so decides, the Clerk shall publish any report or other document laid before the Parliament.
3. In these Rules, "document" means anything in which information is recorded in any form.

Rule 14.4 Publication under the authority of the Parliament

1. Any statement which is required or authorised to be published in pursuance of these Rules is published under the authority of the Parliament.
2. In these Rules, "statement" has the same meaning as in the Defamation Act 1996 (1996 c.31).

Openness and Accessibility

Rule 15.1 Meetings in public

1. The meetings of the Parliament and, subject to Rule 12.3.5, of any committee or sub-committee shall be held in public.

2. Paragraph 1 is subject to the conditions which require to be complied with by any member of the public attending the proceedings of the Parliament as mentioned in Rule 15.2.

Rule 15.2 Public access

1. Members of the public shall be admitted to the public gallery during any meeting of the Parliament.

2. Members of the public admitted to the public gallery during any meeting of the Parliament shall comply with such reasonable conditions as the Presiding Officer may determine and notify to them.

3. The Presiding Officer may order that any member of the public who does not, in the opinion of the Presiding Officer, comply with any of those conditions shall leave the public gallery and may order that any such person be excluded from the proceedings of the Parliament for such period as the Presiding Officer considers appropriate.

4. This Rule shall apply to meetings of committees as it applies to meetings of the Parliament with such modifications as are appropriate.

Rule 15.3 Access to chamber

1. Subject to paragraph 2, no person other than a member may enter the chamber during a meeting of the Parliament except—
   (a) the Lord Advocate or Solicitor General for Scotland (if not a member);
   (b) a person authorised to do so by the Presiding Officer;
   (c) a person addressing the Parliament in accordance with paragraph 5;
   (d) any other person required, invited or permitted by the Parliament to attend a meeting of the Parliament; and
   (e) the Clerk or any person authorised by him or her.

2. If the person holding the office of Presiding Officer or deputy Presiding Officer as mentioned in section 19(2) is not a member of the Parliament, he or she may enter the chamber during a meeting of the Parliament but only for the purpose of chairing proceedings for the election of a new Presiding Officer.

3. Any person mentioned in paragraph 1(b), (d) or (e) may be required to leave the chamber or prevented from entering the chamber by order of the Presiding Officer.

4. Only a member, or the Lord Advocate or Solicitor General for Scotland (if not a member), may sit in any seat in the chamber which is reserved for members.

5. Any person may, on the invitation of the Parliament, address the Parliament.

Rule 15.4 Bringing a petition

1. The Parliament shall consider, in accordance with the provisions of this Rule and Rules 15.5 and 15.6, any petition addressed to it. A petition may be brought by an individual person, a body corporate or an unincorporated association of persons.

2. A petition shall clearly indicate—
   (a) the name of the petitioner;

(b) an address of the petitioner to which all communications concerning the petition should be sent; and

(c) the name and address of any person supporting the petition.

3. All petitions shall be in English.

4. The Public Petitions Committee shall determine the proper form of petitions and shall publish its determinations in such manner as it considers appropriate.

5. A petition may be lodged with the Clerk, or sent to the Clerk by e-mail, at any time when the office of the Clerk is open and the Parliament is not dissolved. Petitions may be lodged or sent by the petitioner or by a member on behalf of the petitioner. When the Clerk receives a petition he or she shall send it as soon as practicable to the Committee.

Rule 15.5 Admissibility of petitions

1. The Public Petitions Committee shall decide whether a petition is admissible.

2. A petition is admissible unless—

(a) it does not comply with Rule 15.4.2 or 3, or is otherwise not in proper form;

(b) it contains language which, in the opinion of the Committee, is offensive; or

(c) it requests the Parliament to do anything which, in the opinion of the Committee, the Parliament clearly has no power to do.

3. If a petition is inadmissible it shall be rejected by the Committee without further consideration. If the Committee decides that a petition is inadmissible it shall, as soon as practicable, notify the petitioner of its decision and of the reasons for that decision.

Rule 15.6 Action on a petition

1. If a petition is admissible, the Public Petitions Committee shall consider the petition.

2. When the Committee has considered the petition it may—

(a) refer the petition to the Scottish Ministers, any other committee of the Parliament or any other person or body for them to take such action as they consider appropriate;

(b) report to the Parliamentary Bureau or to the Parliament; or

(c) take any other action which the Committee considers appropriate.

3. The petitioner shall be notified of the action taken by the Committee under paragraph 2.

CHAPTER 16

Reporting of Proceedings

Rule 16.1 Minutes of proceedings

1. Minutes of the proceedings at each meeting of the Parliament shall be drawn up by the Clerk.

2. The minutes shall record all the items of business taken by the Parliament at that meeting and the results of any decisions taken and of any divisions and elections which took place.

3. The Clerk shall arrange for the minutes of proceedings to be printed and published as soon as possible by whatever means is considered appropriate.

Rule 16.2 Scottish Parliament Official Report

1. The Parliamentary corporation shall ensure that a substantially verbatim report of the proceedings at each meeting of the Parliament is

prepared. It shall be known as the Scottish Parliament Official Report and in these Rules is referred to as the Official Report.

2. The Official Report shall also contain all written questions, together with the answers, in accordance with Rule 13.5.3.

3. The Clerk shall ensure that the Official Report is printed and published for each sitting day during a Parliamentary session.

Rule 16.3 Journal of the Scottish Parliament

1. The Parliamentary corporation shall ensure that a Journal of the Scottish Parliament (referred to as "the Journal") is printed and published at such intervals as the Parliament may, on a motion of the Parliamentary Bureau, determine.

2. The Journal shall contain—

(a) minutes of proceedings;

(b) notice of any instrument or draft instrument or any other document laid before the Parliament in accordance with Chapter 10, which notice shall give the title of the instrument, draft instrument or other document and the date on which it was laid before Parliament;

(c) notice of any report of a committee, which notice shall give the title of the report and the date on which it was lodged with the Clerk; and

(d) any other matter which the Parliament, on a motion of the Parliamentary Bureau, considers should be included in the Journal.

Rule 16.4 Broadcast of proceedings

1. The Parliamentary corporation shall arrange for proceedings at meetings of the Parliament to be broadcast in such manner and subject to such conditions as the Parliament may determine in a Code of Conduct relating to broadcasting of proceedings of the Parliament.

2. Until such a Code of Conduct has been made by the Parliament, the Parliamentary corporation may make such arrangements for the broadcast of proceedings at meetings of the Parliament as it sees fit.

Rule 16.5 Committee proceedings

1. Subject to paragraph 2, Rules 16.1 to 16.4 shall apply to proceedings at meetings of committees and sub-committees as they apply to proceedings at meetings of the Parliament with such modifications as are appropriate.

2. Unless the Parliament decides otherwise, no substantially verbatim report of any proceedings at a meeting of a committee or sub-committee held in private shall be prepared. No such proceedings shall be broadcast.

CHAPTER 17

Miscellaneous

Rule 17.1 Amending standing orders

1. The Parliament may, on a motion of the Procedures Committee, amend these standing orders. Any decision of the Parliament to amend the standing orders shall require an absolute majority. Any amendment to the standing orders must be consistent with the requirements of the Act.

Rule 17.2 Suspension of standing orders

1. The Parliament may, on the motion of any member or of the Parliamentary Bureau, suspend any of these Rules for the purpose of a meeting of the Parliament or of a committee or sub-committee except any Rule which makes provision which the Act requires to be made by standing orders or which reflects a provision of the Act. Such a suspension shall apply only for the purposes of that meeting or of part of that meeting.

2. The Parliament may, on a motion of the Parliamentary Bureau, suspend any of these Rules for the purpose of any item of business except any Rule which makes provision which the Act requires to be made by standing orders or which reflects a provision of the Act. Such a suspension shall apply only for the purpose of the item of business as shall be specified in the motion.

Rule 17.3 Notice to members

1. Where these Rules impose a requirement to notify the Parliament or members of any matter, notification shall normally be given in the Business Bulletin.

2. Where the Parliament is in recess, notice shall be given in whatever form is considered by the person giving that notice to be sufficient.

3. Where notice is given in accordance with paragraph 1 or 2, that notice shall also be made public.

Rule 17.4 Lodging of documents

1. Where these Rules provide for anything, other than a Bill and any instrument or other document to which Chapter 10 or 14 applies, to be lodged with, or notified to, the Clerk by a member, this may be done by its—

(a) being lodged with, or notified in writing to, the Clerk by the member;
(b) being lodged with, or notified in writing to, the Clerk by any other person on behalf of the member, but only if that person has been authorised to do so by the member and the Clerk has been notified of that authorisation in writing; or
(c) being sent by e-mail to the Clerk from the member's e-mail address, but only if the member has notified the Clerk in writing that he or she intends lodging documents by e-mail.

2. In addition, anything to be lodged with, or notified to, the Clerk by a member of the Scottish Executive or a junior Scottish Minister may be sent by e-mail to the Clerk from the e-mail address of a member of the staff of the Scottish Administration but only if that member of staff has been authorised to do so by any member of the Scottish Executive or a junior Scottish Minister and the Clerk has been notified of that authorisation in writing.

CHAPTER 18

Glossary

Rule 18.1 Interpretation

1. Any expression used in these Rules shall have the same meaning as in the Act, unless expressly provided otherwise. The Interpretation Act 1978 (1978 c.30) applies to these Rules.

2. In these Rules—
"the Act" means the Scotland Act 1998 (1998 c.46);
"court" includes tribunal; and
"legal proceedings" means any legal proceedings (whether civil or criminal) in any court in the United Kingdom.

Rule 18.2 Index of defined expressions

1. In these Rules, the expressions listed in the left hand column have the meaning given by, or are to be interpreted in accordance with, the Rules listed in the right-hand column.

Expression	Rule
absolute majority	11.11.3
accompanying documents	9.3.5
Act	18.1.2
Adviser	12.7
appointed members	3.6.1
Auditor General's Report	9.3.4
Budget Bill	9.16
Business Bulletin	5.9
business motions	8.11.1
business programme	5.4
Committee Bill	9.15.1
competent matters	6.2
Consolidation Bill	9.18.1
court	18.1.2
daily business list	5.5.1
Decision Time	11.2.2
division	11.6
document	14.3.3
Emergency Bill	9.21.1
emergency question	13.8.1
equal opportunities	6.9.2
Executive Bill	9.3.3
Explanatory Notes	9.3.3
Financial Memorandum	9.3.2
Financial Resolution	9.12.1
financial year	5.8.4
First Minister's Questions	13.6.6
First Minister's Question Time	13.6.3
former Officer	2.4.9
group representative	5.2.1(c)
Journal of the Scottish Parliament	16.3
legal proceedings	18.1.2
manuscript amendment	9.10.6
meeting of the Parliament	2.2.8

Expression	*Rule*
member in charge of a Bill	9.2.1
members	1.1.2
Member's Bill	9.14.1
Members' Business	2.2.11
ministerial statement	13.2
minutes of proceedings	16.1
motion of no confidence	8.12.1
normal Parliamentary week	2.2.3
oath of allegiance	1.2.5
Oldest Committee Member	12.1.19
oldest qualified member	2.4.7
oral question	13.3.4
Parliamentary Bureau	5.1
parliamentary recess	2.3
parliamentary year	2.1.2
party representative	5.2.1(b)
Policy Memorandum	9.3.3
Preceding First Minister's Question Time	13.6.5
Preceding Question Time	13.6.4
Private Bill	9.17.1
Public Bill	9.17.1
public expenditure	6.6.3
Question Time	13.6.2
reporter	12.6
roll call vote	11.7.4
Scottish Law Officer	4.5.1
Selection Panel	3.11.1
simple majority	11.11.2
sitting day	2.1.3
solemn affirmation	1.2.5
Scottish Parliament Official Report	16.2
statement	14.4.2
Statute Law Repeals Bill	9.19.1
Statute Law Revision Bill	9.20.1

Expression	Rule
subject committee	6.1.4
Temporary Convener	12.1.15
written question	13.3.4

Rule 18.3 Other references

1. Unless otherwise expressly provided, any reference in these Rules to—
(a) a numbered section is to the section having that number in the Act;
(b) a numbered Rule (eg Rule 7.2) is to the Rule having that number in these Rules and, where a Rule number is followed by another number (eg Rule 7.2.1) it refers to the paragraph having that number in that Rule; and
(c) a numbered paragraph in a Rule is to the paragraph having that number in that Rule.

INDEX

References to the Act are to sections and Schedules
References to the Standing Orders are to rules (in bold)